THE TOUCH

THE TOUCH

A novel by

M.C. Bennett

The Touch

ISBN
978-1-956161-07-6 (Paperback)
978-1-956161-06-9 (eBook)

For Shannon, Owen and Nate

Because I will always love you

FORWARD

A few years ago, a friend of mine asked me if I ever felt weird or uncomfortable while my hands were on a client. She referred to it as the "He bee gee bees". Did anyone ever make me feel strange or bizarre things (about them or myself) simply by connecting with them through the power of touch? I could only respond that on several occasions throughout my career, the energy or feelings I had received, be them solicited or not, were at times quite unsettling. Some were good, silly or even playful reasons mind you, but others were not. Some were downright scary.

I am quite sure that I am not the only therapist who has ever felt this way. It might be interesting someday to blog my experiences and review the impending comments. I will point out however that I could just be completely mad from working for so many years in this small, dark room with nothing but fragrant scents and candles to light my way. That of course, seems far more reasonable. So I offer this to you, the reader as food for thought: if we subscribe to the theory that hind sight is twenty/twenty, then what, I propose, would be the consequences of being hands-on?

M. C. Bennett
January 1, 2012
12:01 a.m. PST

In the blackest night, shine the brightest stars,
In the darkest fear, beats the bravest heart,
In the cry of a child, is the power of us all,
Who will answer when you hear them call?

Steve Halliwell, Walter Wray
(King Swamp 1989)

Walk with me, through the long black night,
We keep the unholy out of sight,
I get the sacrament from your lips,
I get redemption at your finger tips.

Steve Halliwell, Walter Wray
(King Swamp 1989)

March 1972.... Just outside of Savannah Georgia

It was getting late and there was still no sign of Casper. The rain was beginning to fall, but the weatherman said they were going to be in for at least a three day storm. Blake and his mother had searched the house but they had come up empty. His biggest fear now was that Casper was going to get caught out in the rain. Actually, that was a lie. Ever since little Jenny Peterson had come by the other day with her mother, Casper was nowhere to be found. She had spent the better part of their hour visit fondling over the cat.

"Nice kitty, pretty kitty," the little bitch said, over and over again. "Boy, I wish I had a kitty like this," she added. All the while Casper just lay there, soaking the whole thing in.

Blake was angry; no, hurt, no, angry. How could Casper betray him like this? He was good to his cat, fed her every day, and not the cheap dry food mind you, but the really cool canned wet stuff. He made sure she had lots of water and even gave her the leftover milk when he was done with his cereal in the morning. How could Casper make him worry like this? The rain was beginning to pick up so Blake made a decision. He went back in the house to talk to his mother.

"I'll drive you over," she offered. "It's raining too hard now for you to walk. Besides it's going to be dark soon," she insisted.

It was only a couple of blocks over so Blake decided it was better to stay dry. When Jenny answered the door, Blake's heart exploded. There was Casper, snuggled safely in her arms.

“I guess I should have called you,” she said “but I was having such a good time.”

Blake scowled. Casper had this smug, arrogant look on her face displaying a total lack of interest. She didn’t even try to break free of Jenny’s grasp when she saw him. When Jenny tried to hand her over, Casper put up a fight. Blake’s mother eventually grabbed her and carried her back to the car herself. Blake mumbled something but was quiet until they got to their own front door. Mom handed her to him and went inside.

“You little sneaky bitch,” he said. “What, it’s not good enough for you around here?” He grabbed Casper by the neck and headed out to the garage. It wasn’t long before the thunder would drown out the screams.

* * * * *

CHAPTER I

August 2011 Anaheim Hills, California

It was late in the day when Grey Thomas sat down in his favorite chair and stared cautiously into the fireplace. The orange and red embers burned bright, each flame erupting into brilliant shades of yellow and blue, illuminating the room with each sudden crackle and pop. He watched in awe as each tendril of fire fondled one another tangling themselves together in an erotic dance as they rose higher and higher climbing into the blackness of the chimney. Hypnotized by their ever changing rhythm, his thoughts began to slip away. A kaleidoscope of colors swirled inside his head. Grey looked down at his empty glass and considered his options. He needed more scotch. Definitely more scotch.

It had been a long day. Hell, for that matter it had been a long summer. Days that should have slowly passed with feelings of leisure and serenity were few and far between. Instead he found that most had left in their wake, an overwhelming level of anxiety and discontent. Now a fire, alive in the hearth on an already warm autumn night somehow didn't seem to be that outside of the ordinary. As the fire roared on, Grey reached for a bottle on the end table and poured himself another drink. The cold glass felt good in his hand so he took a long hard swallow. The ice tumbled across his tongue as his old friend "Mr. Blue" worked its way down to ease his spirit and calm his trembling hands.

It had been three, long months since his last good night's sleep, and just the thought of being able to close his eyes and escape from the world for more than a few minutes was very inviting. He knew that in time his body would recover from the trauma of the past twelve weeks, but he wasn't as sure about his ability to regain a grip on the reality of everything that was still going on inside his head. The demons, however quiet, were still there.

He had to acknowledge the fact that even in his present frame of mind he was still second guessing himself on a regular basis. The possibility that his faculties might not be completely intact weighed heavy in the air. It was hard for him to accept that everything that had transpired over the past summer was not just some terrible dream. He brought the glass to his lips again and took another swallow. Ah.... twenty year old scotch, the great equalizer. Grey turned his attention back to the fire. The flames were waiting.

Maybe now, if he was lucky, things would finally have a chance to get back to normal. If there really was such a thing, would he recognize it anyway? He lifted his glass again. With the explosion of each flaming ember, he was reminded of just how fragile his nerves were and how short his inner fuse had become. As he watched the flames dance violently before him, his mind wandered, turning back in time to the events that began this past June.

* * * * *

Summer had come early to Southern California. For most of the day it had been sunny, eighty-five degrees and not a cloud in the sky. Schools had let out a few weeks earlier and since then thousands of young people had made the pilgrimage to the place of sand and sea. Now it was late afternoon, and the crowds were thinning out. All around him, a relative sense of quiet hung heavy in the air. It was almost eerie, like the lull before a storm. For those who would remain, shirts and shorts would soon be going back on and the fire pits would be slowly springing to life. To the west, the deep blue water of the Pacific Ocean stretched off in the distance as far as the eye could see. At the shoreline, the waves embraced the sand like a hug from an old friend. Now, there were just scattered groups of young people: girls on display in their bikinis covered with oil and an assorted variety of guys who, shy or not, were eye-balling the eye candy every step of the way. It was like a typical vacation postcard, the type of scene people dream about while trapped behind the walls of their tiny office cubicles.

Grey stood on the beach in front of the hotel and watched the surfers as they repeatedly set out into the water to catch the "perfect" wave. All the weekend warriors had come out to play. This was the time of year that his massage business really picked up. This was a perfect place to be. Always looking for a new connection, he had obtained an open ended agreement with the hotel management at the beginning of the year that allowed him to work not only on hotel guests but even the occasional curious beach patron. The place could be a virtual gold mine on a crowded summer's day. He had discovered this spot by accident about six months earlier while out in search of a beer and had since managed to make both the hotel guests and beach front patron's part of his clientele.

Back in January, after having a few drinks with some friends, the manager had seen him 'rubbing' one of the hotel's beach bar waitresses shoulders and well, the rest as they say was history. His eyes scanned the beach looking for a familiar face.

Now, leaning against a low retaining wall that separated the bar area from the beach, he wondered who would come wandering in first. Corey, the hotel's athletic director and local volleyball princess with her burned out shoulders and legs; Ronnie, the surf pro who gave too many lessons and generally abused himself by conquering one too many waves; or Tony, the bartender at the hotel's poolside bar "Wind" who had the reputation of spending as much 'off duty' time with the ladies as he did serving behind the bar. They were quite a diverse group. Each individual came with a different set of problems, most of which he could address with the right touch, a little stretching, and a kind word. When he thought about it, his job was really a lot of fun. He didn't just have a lot of clients; he had a lot of friends.

The past few years had gone well. Being a therapist had many perks. More often than not, you get to make people feel better, make a good living doing it, and generally be in constant demand. Wherever you go, someone would always say, "I have this pain right here." Then of course, came the all but innocent "point" to the area in question. Truth be told, he had a great wife, Rachel, an eighteen month old son named Dylan, (after the Welsh poet Dylan Thomas) who was just beginning to talk, and he had a really great job. Yes, in the big scope of things, life was pretty damn good.

As he stood looking out to sea, he saw a bright red surfboard shoot straight up into the air. A body disappeared beneath the waves as the board came crashing back down. Soon a head and shoulders appeared. The young girl swam over to retrieve her board. She climbed back on and paddled out again.

"Another day, another wave" Grey mumbled to himself, but he was jealous at the same time. He'd tried surfing couple of times, but it would always be his thing. It required too much balance and coordination and there was never enough free time to practice. Athletics had been a constant personal interest, but achieving success at them would always be one step away. He'd figured it out years before that even though he could never actually be competitive himself, he could help those who were.

Just as he was starting to lose interest in the surfers, he felt a tap on his shoulder.

He turned around to a smile. He couldn't help but smile back. It was Corey. She had been teaching volleyball to some hotel guests on the beach for most of the afternoon and had spotted him standing there some time earlier. She needed his help. The look in her eyes screamed total exhaustion. He turned and grabbed his portable massage table that was leaning against the wall and plopped it down on the sand. Corey immediately plopped down with a thud. The sound of her sudden collapse made him laugh. She was done. It was going to take a little time to make her feel better. It usually did. As the sun danced on the horizon and slowly slipped toward the sea, Grey's hands went to work.

* * * * *

It had been so easy ten years ago. Fresh out of school and ready to save the world, he'd landed a job at the Ritz Carlton Hotel in Laguna Beach, California. It was a short twenty-minute drive from home and a great place to work. Grey quickly established himself and earned quite a reputation with the hotel's guests. Peddling his craft to the cream of society brought quick recognition as well as quick cash. All he really had to do was have strong but gentle hands and be a good listener.

It did not take long to discover the endless variety of social classes into which his clients were woven. Each person was an adventure in human psychology. No matter how similar people would appear, each one had their own special needs and a different story to tell. Many would come to air their souls as well as heal their bodies. The key was to listen with kindness, and still remain objective. On more than one occasion he had thought to himself.

"Shrinks make more money and all they have to do is sit and listen to someone on a couch. What's wrong with this picture?"

All in all though, he had no real complaints. He had done well enough in the regular corporate hotel environment that he'd eventually been able to break into private practice over the last four years. Over time, he had worked on a lot of people. It was good to know that most felt better because of him. Everything was going as planned.

It was still almost a week until 4th of July weekend and it looked like it would be a summer to remember. He was planning to spend the next week or two working on some friends and then take the holiday weekend off. Rachel's family, all one hundred of them (a slight if not accurate exaggeration) had planned the usual family party. Grey often joked with her telling her "you don't have a family tree honey, you have a family forest". Being around the pool during a party at her parents felt more like a day at Club Med. A few well earned days of rest and relaxation might just be the ticket to slow things down. It would certainly feel good to do nothing for awhile. Over the years, the physical part of the job had taken its toll in many ways. Grey was tired. The hands and shoulders that he counted on everyday were starting to talk to him more frequently at night. He wondered if it was time to start listening.

* * * * *

Her legs were wet with sweat and the fine grains of sand stuck fast as Grey started to wipe them down with a towel. If he didn't start with a brush off, the lotion he used would mix with the sand and his hands would have the same effect as sandpaper.

As he brushed the sand away, he marveled at the sight of her legs, long, tanned, perfectly toned muscle that seemed to flow gracefully out of each opening of her gym shorts. Each leg ended in a well turned ankle and a strong, but pretty foot. Every toe nail had apparently started the day painted and polished to perfection. Now you could see how a day at the beach had taken its toll. For someone who appeared to be so high maintenance, she was actually quite different when you got to know her. She was soft spoken and unassuming. Grey had met her by accident back in early January at Wind. She had come in limping, almost in tears, and ordered a 'screwdriver'. He remembered thinking; orange juice for the athlete in her, vodka for the pain. She took her drink from the bartender and hobbled off to a table.

Grey watched as she tried to get comfortable, but it was not to be. Pretty as she was, it was still obvious to see that her present condition was taking its toll. A few years ago when he was single, he would have sent over another drink and maybe even asked to join her. Times had changed. Rachel and his son Dylan were his world now, so instead he got the attention of the waitress. After a brief discussion, he had her deliver a bag of ice to the girl's table along with a note written on the back of one of his business cards. The simple note offered advice and instructions. When the girl received the delivery she looked puzzled. She glanced over at him and smiled, then laughed and proceeded to follow the instructions. A short while later, the waitress returned to Grey's table with a beer and a reply. The napkin had a simple message printed on it. It read, "Thank you, I'm Corey". She waved his card at him and they had been friends ever since. Six months later she was still taking time out to see him. He knew right where she hurt and how to help.

It was late by the time they were finished. He sent Corey home to ice her shoulder down. The sun had packed it in for the day and now it was his turn to call it quits. He folded up his table and tossed it in the back of his car. Portable tables were great. You could take them almost anywhere. This one had seen a lot of miles over the years.

"A lot of miles, a lot of smiles" Grey laughed to himself, but only a few more miles today.

The freeway was going to be a frenzied mixture of construction and traffic.

"Your tax dollars at work," the sign always read.

"Tax this," he chuckled.

Alone, he didn't even have the luxury of taking the carpool lane. California freeways, what a nightmare!

His family would be waiting at home and if he didn't get side tracked, he'd get there before his son was asleep. He adored Dylan. He loved to watch the way he reacted to every new thing. It was truly amazing to look at the world through the eyes of a child.

The engine fired up on the first try and the radio kicked in. He pulled his Camaro out onto Pacific Coast Highway and headed south. He decided to head down the coast and look for a surface street to take home rather than having to contend with the freeway traffic. He was really tired. The day was almost over and he was ready to pack it in.

It was nearly a head-on. It might have been, had Grey not been so heavy on the gas pedal. As he turned left onto Beach Boulevard and headed toward home, a red blur slid past him as he entered the intersection. His car radio blasting, he never heard the shrieking sound of the truck's breaks grasping for every inch of asphalt. Their attempt was in vain. Rachel always said that he played the radio too damn loud. There was a massive collision and suddenly the world was spinning counter-clockwise to the sound of AC/DC's "Highway to Hell". Go figure. The big rig clipped him on the right, rear side of the car after its driver had chosen to run a red light. It was all over in a matter of seconds. The car spun in circles (three to be exact, as witnesses would report later) and then smashed into the curb. Grey sat stunned in his seat and tried to collect his thoughts.

A quick review of all body parts confirmed everything seemed to be in its proper place. A glance in the rear-view mirror however, revealed a deep cut above his left eye from his head bashing into the driver's door window. He heard a loud ringing in his ears. He tried to shake it off, but it wouldn't go away. He concluded that this was going to soon evolve into one 'mother' of a headache. The ringing continued but the more he tried to ignore it, the louder it seemed to get. It wasn't until he was completely frustrated that he realized the sounds were not in his head. It was his cell phone which was now sitting on the passenger floor next to him! Whoever it was had the world's worst timing.

Fumbling through the debris and broken glass, he found the phone.

He chuckled and thought, *"What the hell"* and answered it.

Thankfully, the voice was a familiar one. It was Rachel, wanting to know where he was. Dinner was getting cold. Grey rolled his eyes and said, "Honey, I think I'm going to be late."

Then the phone dropped softly on the seat. As the sound of sirens approached from the distance, and the night began to fill with the colors of many flashing lights, Grey Thomas closed his eyes and passed out. He was headed for a different place.

* * * * *

At the moment Grey's mind shut down, she woke up screaming. She was three thousand miles away in a house on Lake Tarpon near the gulf coast of Florida. The rain was coming down so hard that you could barely make out the edge of the dock less than fifty feet outside the window. Bolts of lightning split the sky and the wind blew the rain in toward the house in sheets that made the storm glass rattle. Alexandra Matthews sat up violently in bed.

Her body was drenched in sweat, and the sheets clung to her body as though she had just come out of the lake. In her dream she had seen the accident. Red flashes, sparks, the sound of twisting metal and the ominous sight of fresh blood. She felt the hand of her friend Grey. She reached out to grab him. She managed to hold his hand.

Suddenly, without warning, his hand started to pull away. She felt him being pulled deeper and deeper into a dark abyss. An icy fear came over her but there was nothing she could do. She was helpless.

In a final act of desperation, she grabbed him with both hands and started to pull him toward her. Her grip tightened and he followed her lead. Ever so slowly, she drew him closer and closer. Suddenly, he slipped again. It was then she realized that she could not gain an advantage. Still, hanging on by what seemed to be little or nothing, he appeared to be floating in limbo looking up at her staring into her eyes. She watched in horror as her own hands were starting to slip. She was losing him. She panicked and immediately woke to the sound of her own screams.

Alexandra looked around her room and tried to make sense out of what had happened. The dream seemed so real. Outside, the storm was picking up strength. Just then a gust of wind hit the house with gale force, shattering the bedroom windows and sending a shower of broken glass flying across the room. As the rain came blowing in, she peeled away the wet sheets and got out of bed. Her naked body, now wet and cold, shivered in the night air. Speckles of red covered the parts of her not protected by the sheets, and in a few places the color ran. She had to get to the bedroom door so she could go downstairs to get out of the weather.

The house was old and sturdy, but staying in her room tonight would be impossible. Glass was strewn all over the floor. She would need to cover it with something in order to make her escape. The comforter at the end of the bed would have to do. She grabbed it with both hands and without a second thought she shook it sending glass fragments flying everywhere. Then in one big toss, it spread easily covering the area between the bed and the door. The wind blew hard and cold on her wet skin. Then Alexandra made her move. She grabbed her bathrobe from behind the door. A few quick steps and she reached the top of the landing. She closed the bedroom door behind her and headed downstairs to the safety of the den.

The fireplace glowed with the dying embers of an earlier fire. Thankfully, the wood box in the corner was still three-quarters full. She tossed a few logs into action and in no time the fire was returned to its former glory. She poured a brandy from the crystal decanter on the bar and took a few deep breaths. It all seemed so real. Was it a vision or a dream? She didn't know. It felt more like a nightmare. As the brandy started to calm her, her nerves began to steady. After all this time, why him and why tonight? She had a bad feeling and it wasn't coming from the storm. She rummaged through her purse looking for her address book. She found his private number and dialed the phone. The friendly hello that was always there never came on even after a second try. Something was terribly wrong. Even though she was still chilled to the bone from her recent ordeal upstairs, Alexandra started to sweat.

* * * * *

They had met twelve years earlier at school and had taken an instant liking to one another. He had come to Florida with a hunger to learn and they ended up in the same class. She knew from the moment they met that they were connected somehow. School was merely a conduit for something much larger. He was different. He would listen to her ideas and benefit from her teachings. She took such an instant liking to him that she insisted that he call her Alex. They were both students, but what she would teach him he couldn't learn in any school. He had come to Florida to study sports medicine, but would learn much more from her than even he could possibly imagine. She had a gift. A strange gift, mind you, but a gift just the same. Take for instance, if you could believe, or at the very least entertain the thought of someone whose mind has developed over the years a special way of becoming one with certain forces of nature. Some would say it was witchcraft. Others would call it a religion. Believe what you will. The jury is still out.

She was a presence to be enjoyed. Five foot eight, one hundred and thirty-five pounds, deep blue eyes, and a long mane of red hair that swept off her face like the flames of hell. She was very well put together and a pleasure to the eye. Once, long ago, she had even been a temptation to Grey, but that time had passed. In their world, there would always be a force that would bind them together. It had been five years since their last conversation, so it was even more of a surprise when the dream came.

Time is a funny thing. It may create distance, but it never forgets. The voice inside her head was telling her that he was in trouble and she needed to be there for him now. He was in danger and something strange was about to happen. Something only their kind could understand. It would take all of the powers they once shared to see this thing through. She prayed that he could hold his own until she arrived.

It was eight forty-five a.m. EST when Alexandra boarded American Airlines flight 241 for Los Angeles. She was worn out. She had never gone back to sleep. The storm had not let up until first light. She spent the rest of the night in her den in front of the fire. The wood box was empty when she left the house that morning. In her black trench coat, hood over her head and flickers of red hair hanging out, she looked like the grim reaper. It was going to be a long day.

* * * * *

Rachel did not arrive at the hospital for what seemed like a lifetime. She had done her best though, got dressed, thrown the baby in the car and sped off into the night like a bat out of hell. It was then that things came immediately to an abrupt halt. She instantly found herself in bumper to bumper traffic. There had to be an accident. Getting off the freeway and taking side streets might help, but she wasn't in any frame of mind to deal with surface street traffic either. She decided to stay where she was and ride it out. The freeway would have to ease up someplace.

"Why does this always happen when you're in a hurry?" she shouted. Dylan looked up as if he were listening and then went back to his animal cookies. A normal drive to Hoag Hospital would take about twenty-five minutes. At this rate it would take an hour. Damn freeways! Even on a Monday night, everyone was out in full force.

After finally catching a break in the traffic, she arrived in forty-five minutes. Baby in one hand, keys in the other, Rachel ran full steam for the emergency room door.

She made it inside just in time to see a hospital orderly wheeling Grey through a door labeled "X-ray". She caught up to a nurse and begged for information. The nurse proved to be both helpful and kind. It had taken the paramedics sometime to get Grey out of his car and safely onto a back board. He'd been here at the hospital for about twenty minutes. He had sustained no broken bones, but had arrived unconscious due to what she called a "blunt force" trauma to the head. The doctors were not able to wake him up, so he was sent to X-ray for a full skull series. He was in a coma, and that was all anyone could confirm at this point. The X-rays would show if there was any swelling causing internal pressure in his head.

The nurse also explained that it was generally accepted by doctors that a coma was the brain shutting down a person's conscious state so the body has a chance to heal itself. That's why they were running tests. In an hour or so, maybe they would have more answers. For now it was a waiting game. There was nothing else to do. If Grey woke up, it would be when he was ready. Rachel was holding up pretty well under the circumstances. The nurse said she could see him once they moved him into a private room, but for now it would be best if she joined her family in the waiting room. Sitting in traffic, she had called her friend Renee and asked her to contact family and a few friends. Believe it or not, a few people had already started to arrive. She wouldn't have to wait alone.

For the first time in as long as she could remember, Rachel was afraid. Was she going to lose her husband? Would she have to raise Dylan alone? Would Grey wake up soon, and even if he did, would he be the same? Her mind raced back and forth until the tears started to run down her face. She'd been tough until now, but a sudden sea of emotions overwhelmed her. Dylan stared up at her with a puzzled look. Then he started to smile. He put his head down on her shoulder and drifted off to sleep. Guarded by the darkness, he had the first of many strange dreams.

When Dylan closed his eyes, he saw a lake house being battered by a storm. He saw a shadowy figure pacing back and forth inside the house. The soft glow of the fire illuminated her shape which was now in full view through the back window. The water near the dock was bubbling, sending up steam that kissed the raindrops as they fell from the sky. He was in the middle of a hurricane, but somehow he felt safe. He was concerned but he did not cry. He was not afraid. He knew someone or something was protecting him. Then he saw a face in the window. She was beautiful. She smiled. He knew instantly that she was a friend and that he could trust her. Daddy was in good hands.

Rachel had not put him down for hours. He'd been sleeping on her shoulder for the past few. Her dad had tried to take him at some point, but she had refused to let Dylan go. During that time, the doctors had moved Grey into a private room. The X-rays had been clear enough to not warrant any further action. The swelling would go down on its own with time. He would be staying in this room until he woke up. No one was willing to commit to or even guess at how long this might possibly take. This of course was standard procedure but still very frustrating to everyone concerned.

Rachel was a wreck. One look at her and a nurse suggested that she go home and try to get some sleep. Her family agreed, but she couldn't bring herself to leave him. Not now at least. She wanted to be there when he woke up. She sat by the bed holding his hand and talking to him about anything and everything that happened to come to mind. A few hours later she was asleep in the chair, her hand still tucked safely inside of his.

When the graveyard shift nurse made her final rounds that morning, she looked in on Grey at five forty-five. His breathing was normal but there was no new progress to report. She looked for any sign of movement but saw no changes. Grey lay silent and still on the bed. At first glance, he appeared to be just "sleeping one off". Without the distraction of the bandage over his left eyebrow, you would not have thought anything was wrong. The room was so quiet that you could hear the sound of the air being fed to him through a tube. She adjusted the oxygen lines that were running across his face and then tucked in his sheets. The slow, even movement of his breathing indicated that everything was normal. When she was satisfied with her checkup, she took one last look. Staring back at his face, for a brief second, she thought she saw him smile. She had no idea that at that moment flight 241 was adding a new passenger. Alex was now on board.

* * * * *

The sky was black and ominous when she looked out the window. Nothing except the flashing red light and its reflections on the end of the wing were visible. The wing appeared to slice through the air with the efficiency of a surgeon's scalpel. Conditions were lousy. They had barely received permission to leave the airport because of the storm. Although the worst was over, the flooding that remained made the runways very dangerous. There was still a light rain coming down when they took off. Add to that, heading to Los Angeles, they were flying in the tail of the storm as it moved west across the Gulf of Mexico. Even at their present altitude, all that Alex could see out the window was darkness above and a blanket of angry clouds below. In her mind, she replayed the events of the past twelve hours.

They were in the air for some time, but now it seemed like they were never going to land. Time passed very slowly. Minutes were like hours. It was almost noon by her body clock and it had been eighteen hours since her last meal. Airplane food was the last thing she thought she could stomach, but sitting in first class had its advantages. Maybe the food wouldn't be so bad. She told herself she had to eat. She would need to call on all of her strength in order to help Grey. She had to be ready for anything. All of the time that had passed since their last meeting was somehow now forgotten. It was as if they had spoken yesterday. In a strange way they had. Now, finally after all this time, she would be meeting Rachel and Dylan. She was excited but uneasy at the same time. Would they accept her the way he had so many years ago? Looking down at her hand, she realized she was rubbing her ring. The silver dragon was just like the one she had given him that night on the island. The night that he had joined her and her people and become one of them, a member of their sacred order. Sliding back in her seat, she closed her eyes, and remembered in detail the power and rush of that moment.

The heavens shook the plane like a martini as it passed through some turbulence, startling Alex back into the present. A flight attendant approached and asked her what she'd like for lunch. After choosing a seafood platter with steamed vegetables, she thanked the girl and turned back toward the window. She started rubbing her ring again and drifted off into a deep trance. She needed to have a plan of attack before the plane landed. She was certain Grey would still be unconscious when she got there, so she would have to work fast. She had almost lost him once before, and she swore that it would be a cold day in hell before she would ever let that happen again. She would never allow their connection to break as long as she was alive, but she was running out of time.

In her mind, she reached out to him, searching for the answer that would allow him to wake up. She spoke to him in a quiet tone and in a way only he could feel and understand. The entrance into his mind was closed to the outside world and only available to her now. She had to find a way to open the door.

The light was bright and sterile, like a hospital room. There were people, images and shadows moving about. One particular image caught her attention. There was a tiny mass of white light that appeared to be completely innocent of everything around it. The colors that surrounded the light were warm and peaceful. Alex looked deeper. Two tiny hands appeared, each soft and fragile. There was another hand as well. This one was larger and appeared to be resting on a bed. The large hand was cut and bruised, with tape over it and a needle sticking out of it. Slowly and with great care, Alex brought the two hands together. Instantly the little room filled with a light that was nearly a transparent shade of blue. She heard a baby laugh. Alex smiled and opened her eyes. At that moment, Grey opened his eyes as well.

* * * * *

Everything was blue. It was like looking through Corey's sunglasses. He saw an eerie blue tint that her shades gave to the world when he'd tried them on. Something was different though. He didn't think he was outside and he knew he wasn't wearing any sunglasses. He was in a small room. As the minutes passed, the blue faded away, turning slowly into a milky white. There was a large television hanging high on the wall and there were large silver rails on either side of him. His right hand was wired to a machine. Then he spotted his left hand. Attached to it were a long tube and a needle. Under it was someone else's hand. It was

Rachel's. She was asleep in a chair. She was covered with a blanket and looked quiet and uncomfortable. Dylan was asleep in his baby harness that was strapped to her shoulder and his hand had joined theirs as well. Why was she here? What was this all about? He tried to take his hand away from hers, but it would not move. Strange, he spoke to her in what came out as a whisper, but she did not answer. Could she hear him or was the sound of his voice only in his own head? He tried again to get her attention. No response. It was then he realized that maybe he wasn't really awake. Was this all a dream? Nothing made any sense.

Suddenly, he heard something that sent chills down his spine. A voice on some sort of intercom said, "Code blue, room 214". He glanced over at the open door in front of him. A sign read Room 525. The wheels turned quickly in his head. The truth hit him hard like the evening surf pounding the rocks at high tide. He was in a hospital!

Grey took a brief moment to gather his thoughts, and started to look around. He could see all kinds of activity going on nearby. Down the hall, he could see a group of people in "scrubs" talking. A few seconds later, a woman in white strolled by pushing an old man in a wheelchair down the hall. At the end of the hallway, several elevators were helping to maintain a constant flow of human traffic. Another nurse passed his room carrying a tray of test tubes and specimen cups. He was in a hospital, but why? What happened? He looked back to his left and saw Rachel and Dylan again. He cried out in a panic.

"Rachel, help me," but no one heard.

Was he awake but asleep at the same time? Something was incredibly wrong! He had to wake up! He had to talk to Rachel. If he could get her attention, she would explain everything. He could hear the sounds of things going on around him, and he thought he could see everything as well. No one, however, seemed to know he was awake. He made a few more attempts to speak and move but got no results. He decided to back off. Frustration started to set in. Then, in a final act of desperation, he got an idea. He remembered reading somewhere that children can sometimes hear and see things that adults can't.

He called out to his son, "Dylan, hey little dude, it's Daddy. Dylan!"

To his surprise, Dylan started to stir. It was the same way he would act when he heard the sound of his father's voice. Grey recognized the behavior and was overcome with relief. He called out to him again and Dylan's reaction got louder. Grey took a deep breath. As crazy as it might sound, his connection with Dylan might just be his ticket home.

* * * * *

She almost slept through it. Her body had registered the sound as just another ambulance pulling up to the hospital. Had it not been for the squirming contest going on in her lap, she probably would never have been forced to wake up. Once she opened her eyes, the sound of the siren came more into focus. The sound was no ambulance. It was Dylan. He was wide awake. He'd apparently spent the night on her lap. Frankly, Rachel was surprised that no one had taken him from her during the night.

Carefully, she removed him from the baby carrier sling was still wearing and held him up. Their eyes met and he immediately started to relax. Then his attention turned to his father lying on the bed. At first he looked confused but then he started to smile.

Rachel looked down too. Grey's eyes were partially open but they had been that way when he was brought in. Nothing had changed except that now she was tired and stiff. It was time to get out of this chair.

She would check in with the nurse and then give the baby to her mom and dad for awhile. She needed a drink of water and maybe even a Starbuck's run. A shower wouldn't hurt either. It had been a very long night. With Dylan in one arm, she leaned down and kissed Grey on the cheek. His face felt so soft and warm against her lips. It was as inviting as the last time they'd touched.

"I'll be right back baby, don't go away," she said as she turned and walked out of the room.

Behind her, a single tear was running down Grey's face. He had watched the entire exchange between his wife and son and had been powerless to do anything. Rachel's tough shell was slowly beginning to crumble. Dylan however, had seen the light in his father's eyes, but he had no idea what to do about it. Grey just lay there. Dylan appeared to be his only option. It was crazy idea and presented quite a problem. Who on earth could get through into the mind of a little baby boy?

Still, he had nothing to lose. He would have to wait until they returned to try to make contact with his son again. For now, all he could do was wait. In time, he would find a way to let them know he was still here.

* * * * *

The "fasten your seat belt" sign clicked on as the captain announced their descent into Los Angeles. It was ten-forty-five a.m. local time and they would be landing in about ten minutes. The pilot was just finishing his "thank you for flying" speech. Alex had spent the last few hours sleeping. Lunch was pleasantly good. Nothing but the empty shells had survived. After eating, she fell asleep easily in the big, comfortable seat. The previous night had wiped her out, so even the short rest was deep and refreshing. Upon her arrival, the rental car she had reserved would take her from the airport, south for about an hour to Newport Beach. Once there, she could find the hospital and find her friend. If she had been able to get through to him, he would be holding his own and be ready to accept her help. The short sleep had done wonders for her, and she felt both physically and mentally prepared for whatever challenge would be coming her way. As the plane landed and began to taxi toward the terminal, she closed her eyes and reached out to him again. Grey's world turned blue once more.

* * * * *

Back at the hospital, Rachel and Dylan had returned. Grey had been watching them come in when the white faded and the blue returned. Dylan appeared distracted and turned around as if he were listening to something, but this time Grey heard her voice too. It was like it came to him in a dream. He felt a force touch him. He could feel the energy running through him. He saw a face in the shadows and the flames of her red hair. He knew her power. He remembered her touch. It was Alex.

She came out of nowhere. She was like the sunrise of a new day. Her voice echoed through his head like a song echoing through a canyon. Somehow, he knew she'd been talking to Dylan. She was close now, very close. Dylan was laughing and no one understood why, no one except Grey. He had been given a second chance. Help was on its way.

* * * * *

Alex was absolutely amazed when they opened the door of the plane and she stepped out into the bright California sun. There were very few clouds and a nice cool breeze. All the way to the rental counter she kept looking around. Twelve hours ago she'd been soaked to the skin, battered by the wind, and had survived the shower of glass. Standing here in the mid-morning sun she was warm and dry. What a difference a change of scenery makes. She laughed when the girl at the counter gave her a set of keys to a convertible Mustang. It was black, shiny, and very inviting with the top down. It was the perfect car in which to enjoy the weather. It was also very fast. She threw her bags and coat in the back seat and climbed in. A turn of the key and she was off, hair blowing uncontrollably in the wind.

A quick cruise down the 405 freeway and in about an hour she would arrive at the hospital. If things went according to plan, she'd be with him soon and could set up shop. She knew now what she had to do. Everyone at the hospital was in for a big surprise. They would probably write it off as unexplainable. Only she and Grey would know the truth. Before getting on the plane, she had carefully packed everything she needed. Alex was ready. The accelerator crept closer to the floor, and the Mustang ran with the wind.

* * * * *

For a while, Grey thought he was dead. Maybe he had died and everything that was happening was some insane hallucination, an after-life experience. There were so many questions and so few answers. He lay restless on the bed steaming in his own frustration. All he could do was watch the world move on without him. It wasn't until Rachel sat Dylan on the end of the bed next to him, that things started to look better.

Lying at his father's side, Dylan bumped one of the I.V. tubes. Grey felt a tug and the sting of the needle moving in his hand. He felt the pain. Right then, he knew that everything was real. This was no dream, or hallucination. He was alive. He wasn't sure about the how or why, he just knew that he was. For now, that was enough. Where there is life, there is hope.

As his mind put the pieces together, things began to make sense. He really needed to start paying attention. Expect the unexpected. He had missed something. Could Alex be trying to get him a message through Dylan? She was pretty imaginative. He wouldn't put it past her. Even the smallest of signs would have been enough to get his attention, and give him faith. Maybe even something as simple as pain. Alex had chosen her messenger with great care, and Dylan had delivered. Now all Grey needed to do was be patient. She would be here soon and the nightmare would be over. She would find a way to bring him home.

* * * * *

The hospital lobby was in chaos when Alex arrived. The information desk had virtually disappeared, buried in a sea of people. The two staff members, elderly female volunteers, were being overwhelmed by two Hispanic families who apparently spoke no English. They were in desperate need of a translator. Alex figured it would take longer to reach the information desk than it took to drive down here from the airport. She spotted a phone across the room and headed for it. The hospital operator gave her Grey's room number and the visiting hour's schedule. All that was left to do was head upstairs and check things out.

Once she had assessed the situation, she would have to be patient. She needed a chance at a few minutes alone with him in order to do her thing. She consoled herself with the fact that at least she was here and would be close by when the time came. For now, it might be best to just keep a low profile. That way she wouldn't have to answer a lot of questions. She would just be another "body" hanging around the hospital. The odds of being recognized were small.

If any of Grey's family had seen her, it would only have been in an old photograph. She would stick to her plan. First she would check on him and then try to remain unnoticed. Once in position, she would wait for an opportunity to present itself. While time was of the essence, her patience might prove to be an advantage.

Alex laughed as she headed back through the crowd in search of the elevators.

She felt sorry for the two volunteers, and hoped someone would rescue them soon. As it turned out, the elevators were right around the first corner. Her timing was perfect. When the doors closed behind her, the silence was comforting. It vanished when a young girl in red and white stripes spoke up.

"What floor Miss?"

Alex took a deep breath and smiled, "Five please," she replied.

A push of a button and they were on their way. The floor rattled a little as the elevator lifted off. So did Alex's nerves. Her senses told her that waking Grey up was only the beginning. Something strange was happening to him and now she would be part of it.

Though she was grateful for a chance to see him again, she would have preferred it to have been under different circumstances. Time had changed a lot of things for him. He had a family to think about now. Would he remember what she'd taught him? Did he still believe? Could he trust her with his life? She knew that when the bell rang and the doors opened, the answers would come, and a new chapter in both of their lives would begin. Alex looked at her dragon ring, smiled, and kept her faith.

* * * * *

The waiting was driving him crazy. He had been passing time by trying to assess his situation and evaluate his options. He was trapped in a space that existed between the conscious and unconscious mind. The reality of the pain in his hand suggested to him that he was awake. He recognized the ability to think as well, but the door between thought and action was still closed. Grey wondered if his mind was just putting on a show for him. It was like watching the world through the clear side of a two way mirror. He could see out, but no one could see in. His only comfort had been his contact with Dylan, and how much of that did he really believe?

He found himself questioning everything that had happened until now. Contact with Dylan, the colors, his vision of Alex. Maybe it was all a crazy hallucination, but what if it wasn't? If he was in a space between heaven and hell, Grey figured he was stuck but something or someone was preventing him from slipping away. For the moment he was apparently safe in the middle. The hand that held him in place, the force that would not let him go, it had to belong to Alex. No one else could handle the intensity or the energy level of the situation.

They'd joked once that if given a chance, she could hold an angel in one hand and the devil in the other. He remembered them both having a good laugh when she said it. He was sure that given the chance, she'd surely like to try.

Now it would come down to faith. What did he believe? Was Alex here? Was she sending him a sign through Dylan? Did he really hear her voice, or was it all just "make believe?" He had watched the colors change around him earlier, and now he found himself praying that they would change again. He needed answers and he needed them now. He was running out of time and growing more and more impatient. He didn't have to wait long. He heard the noise again. The ringing sound had become familiar in the last few hours, but this time it was a little different. As Grey lay anxious and frustrated in his bed, the sound of the elevator bell echoed down the hall and into his soul. He felt her presence. Alex was here.

* * * * *

CHAPTER 2

When the bell rang signaling their arrival to the fifth floor, her lungs let go. Without realizing it until now, Alex discovered that she had been holding her breath since they left the lobby. Her mind had been somewhere else. When she finally was forced to exhale, the smells in the elevator overwhelmed her. Everything was acidic and stale. There was something nasty about the smell of fresh ammonia. She was quickly overcome by the need for fresh air. When the doors opened, she suddenly remembered why she was there. She had no idea what to expect and hoped for contact with any friendly face. She was not disappointed.

As she stepped out into the hallway, she was met by a set of the biggest blue eyes she had ever seen. They belonged to a little boy. The man holding him had his back to her, so he had no way of seeing their eyes meet. Alex recognized the little face staring at her as if he were an old friend. He greeted her with a smile that conveyed his approval. She could see a white light around him and knew things were going to be all right. She smiled back at him, and winked. Dylan laughed as she passed by. He had made a new friend.

Alex grinned as she headed down the hall in search of Grey's room. She could feel him now, his energy was still there, but it was just a faint glow of what it should be. The closer she got to him, the more of a draw she felt on her own inner strength. At the end of the hall she saw a faint blue light coming from one of the rooms. Her approach was excited but apprehensive. The room had to be Grey's. She peeked in through the window and saw her friend. For the first time in five years, Alex shed a tear. His hair was longer than she remembered, but his face was still young and tanned. He still wore the five o-clock shadow that he always seemed to have. His eyes were partially opened, but she doubted if the gap was wide enough for him to see. There was a bandage on his head over his left eye and both of his hands were attached by wires to machines. He looked well fed and his hands looked strong. She really wanted to take a look at his chart but there were too many people around. This was not the time to arouse suspicion. The next few hours would be the hardest. She would have to be patient and wait for a chance to be alone with him. He knew by now she was there, and he would be trying even harder to hang on. That was all that was important. He had to hang on!

Now, all she had to do was find a place to wait. She needed a spot that was close enough for her to act quickly, yet subtle enough not to attract any unwanted attention. Her eyes scanned the hallway, nurse's station, and surrounding areas. After a few passes, Alex found her haven. At the end of the hall by the elevators, there was a small group of people. The man holding Dylan was facing her now and was engaged in a conversation with two women who were seated to his right. The child rested comfortably in his arms. The man appeared to be in his early forties. He was well built and clean cut. He was dressed in some sort of uniform. It was not military in design, but still one that insinuated authority. He wore a light blue polo shirt and dark polyester slacks. There appeared to be a hat tucked in his back pocket. As she approached them, she remembered where she had seen a similar outfit. The man was dressed like a baseball umpire. The mask and the big chest pad were missing, but the clothing was still a match. Further examination revealed the remains of a reddish clay substance on his black leather shoes. He had obviously come to the hospital in a hurry and had not taken the time to change clothes. The woman closest to him was speaking, and had his undivided attention. Alex stepped closer and listened intensely.

She heard the woman explaining that Rachel had gone home to take a shower and change. When she returned, the plan was, they should all go out and get something to eat. Grey's condition had not changed and the doctor suggested that they might want to take turns sitting with him so that other family members could rest. This sounded like a reasonable idea. This way someone would always be fresh and available if anything happened. From the sounds of it, more family had gathered in the lobby down stairs and there were still more on the way.

Alex found her spot about ten feet before she reached Dylan and his grandparents. She wasn't sure who the other woman sitting with them was yet, but she was sure the man called Frank was Rachel's father. She had confirmed this with a quick look at Dylan. She could see the resemblance in their eyes. Maybe getting to know these people wouldn't be so hard after all. The colors she saw in them were warm and kind. The location she chose was perfect. Her chair was in a place close to his family. She could hear their conversations without letting them know she was listening. Having knowledge of their plans would give her an advantage, and allow her to decide when the time was right to help Grey. Also, from where she was sitting, it would appear that she was visiting someone else. With a little luck, no one would even acknowledge that she was there. If they all decided to leave when Rachel returned, she would have her chance. It was time to settle in and wait. The hospital felt cold so Alex threw her coat over her lap and made herself comfortable. She sat staring at the faint blue light at the end of the hallway and played with her ring. She thought of Rachel as she passed the time.

* * * * *

Across town, in the middle of her hot shower, the water suddenly turned icy cold. Rachel, had been "zoning out" under its calm, soothing pulse, screamed and nearly jumped out of her skin. Frantically, she shut off the water and reached for a towel. How long had she been in here anyway? It felt like just a minute or two, not long enough to run out of hot water. She dried herself off and headed into her bedroom. There was something strange. The clock on the night stand said she'd only been in the shower about seven minutes. That was not nearly enough time to drain the hot water heater.

Cold and annoyed, Rachel figured it was just as well. She needed to get back to the hospital. She'd been gone too long already. No real make-up or frills today, maybe just a ball cap to hide her hair. Then, she'd call her dad, get an update on Grey, and tell him she was on her way. She threw on a T-shirt and jeans and found a hat." *Funny,*" she thought, "*Grey always liked her in hats.*" She was ready. Rachel took one last look around, grabbed her cell phone, and headed out the door.

When Frank's phone started to ring, Alex just smiled. She knew Rachel was headed back, so it was time to start preparing to execute her plan. There was a lot to do, and not a lot of time. If everything fell into its proper place, she would have a chance to try to wake Grey while Rachel and her family were at dinner. If the timing was even close to perfect, the nurses would be having a shift change around the same time. She would have a small window of ten or fifteen minutes to be alone with him.

To Alex, that was a lifetime. She knew there would be no second chances. She would get only one shot at getting inside Grey's head. She prayed she could. Once there, she would have to take him back in time, to a place he'd most likely buried away in the darkest corners of his mind. It was there he would find the strength to bring himself home. All she had to do was get him there and he could do the rest. Then reality set in. It would all come down to whether or not she could get through to him. If his mind was still open, they would have a good chance, but if time had closed that part of him forever, he would never see another sunrise.

As Alex sat thinking in her chair, a storm began brewing inside her. It started with just a trickle of energy that radiated on the outer edges of her body. At first she hardly noticed it at all. She had a lot on her mind. After all the years of practice and training, what good were her gifts if she couldn't use them when she needed them most? She found herself questioning her faith. Were they really gifts at all or a curse in disguise? She had noticed before that if she moved too far away from his room, the blue light would start to flicker and fade. It was as if Grey's life force had diminished to the point where he was feeding off of her in order to stay alive. Her energy was supporting them both.

Her body must have noticed the power drain because suddenly the trickle became a much greater flow. The energy started to build and Alex began to feel like she had been plugged into a wall. The feeling that was barely noticeable moments earlier had now started to work its way inside her. What had initially concentrated itself on her fingers and toes now engulfed her hands and feet. It was slowly working its way toward the center of her body. To Alex, it was like a million fingers touching her all at once. It gave her feelings of warmth and excitement that border lined on being both erotic and sensual.

As the energy moved further through her body, Alex began to understand what was happening. Her energy level had been drained so low because of Grey that her own existence was starting to be put at risk. Her deepest survival instincts were forced to take over, and she was apparently in the middle of some kind of re-charging process.

The power building inside her was so intense that Grey's light became visibly stronger as well. All of her senses were heightened. She swore she could feel the walls behind her breathing. She knew at that moment that she was in touch with everything around her. It was like her powers and sensitivity had been increased tenfold. Whatever it was, it was giving her the most totally complete and satisfying feeling of both power and control she'd ever had. Her body had evidently decided on its own to protect itself and prepare for the journey ahead. With each passing minute, she could feel herself gaining strength. A little while longer and she'd be her old self again. No, strangely enough, she knew she would be better. When she was ready, it would be time to go and get her friend.

The rush disappeared as fast as it had come. It abandoned her as quickly and easily as it had surprised her when it first appeared. All was quiet now as Alex sat in her chair and waited for Rachel to arrive. Down the hall, Grey's light was now a brilliant blue, but there was no guarantee how long it was going to last. Rachel would be arriving at any moment. For Alex, it would be her first look at the woman who had claimed Grey's heart. She wondered what she would be like. Would her disposition be calm and cool or was she really hard and cold behind her playful exterior? Would she be innocent of evil, or wear her sins on her sleeve?

For as long as she could remember, Alex had a problem meeting people. She could always see through them. The secrets they kept were no longer their own. The worst part of it was that often there were things that Alex saw but could never share. She found herself on more than one occasion contemplating the consequences of sharing with others the knowledge of these events.

There were many times that she had been presented with more information about someone than she ever needed to know. Throughout the years, this had put a tremendous strain on her, as far as getting to know people was concerned. At times it was difficult to look someone straight in the face. She found herself hoping that whatever lay behind Rachel's eyes would be warm and kind. It would be a great foundation to build on, if they were ever to become friends.

* * * * *

Sitting where she was, Alex had the luxury of eavesdropping. The woman talking to Frank was Rachel's mother Lyanna. Listening to Frank and Lyanna's conversation provided her with a lot of interesting information. She was able to learn a great deal about the family and some of its members. The woman sitting next to Lyanna was her sister Liz.

Between the two sisters, there was nothing they couldn't do. Everyone in the family had been contacted about the accident and was standing by, waiting to help. Lyanna reminded Frank and Liz that if too many people were hanging around, it might create a problem. So many people had camped out the night Dylan was born that they'd had a confrontation with hospital security. The three of them broke into laughter when Lyanna said, "Oh, screw them all!" The outburst seemed to break some of the tension. They all needed a good laugh.

* * * * *

As she stood to stretch, Alex laughed inside and thought, *"I like these people already."* It was hard for her to believe that while she longed for their acceptance, she feared their judgment. Was her present deception really necessary? These people were Grey's family now and she wondered how they would react to everything that was about to happen. What would they say if they knew what she was up to? The elevator bell rang once again and shifted her attention. Alex turned and looked, curious to see who would be arriving next. In a matter of seconds, she got her answer. Rachel stood less than ten feet away.

Although their eyes met for only a second, Alex was forced to turn her attention elsewhere. The brief stare she received from Rachel had a cold chill behind it. Something was not right. She decided now was not the time to deal with whatever it was; she sensed that Rachel was hiding. Alex found herself wondering what it was, if anything, she'd really expected. Perhaps she had been imagining someone different, and the real image of Rachel had thrown her off balance a little. She did note that she felt Rachel's presence when she first entered the hall. It would be very interesting to see what was going on inside her, but that would have to wait until later. Right now, Rachel was the least of her worries. She had more important things to do.

Alex returned to her seat and went back to her reconnaissance. In the next few minutes, she would find out if they intended to leave or not. Rachel was speaking to her father in a soft but forceful tone. She was attempting to establish their plans for the next few hours. After some heated debate, it was decided that dinner was not only wise but necessary. They would all remain close by and just head out to a local restaurant. This would allow them to return within an hour or so. They had three cell phones between them in case there were any changes or updates on Grey's condition.

Reluctantly, Rachel agreed, but first she wanted to see Grey. She needed some peace of mind. Alex watched with great curiosity as Rachel passed by her and headed down the hall. As she approached Grey's room, the blue mist started to fade. Only Alex knew why.

* * * * *

He could see the change in her as she came into the room. Her face was brighter now, as if she'd taken the time to "freshen up". A light layer of concealer hid the dark circles under her eyes that she had when she left earlier. She was sporting a T-shirt and jeans and wearing a baseball hat. She looked good. He'd always liked her in hats.

Typical Rachel, even in a crisis she always liked to look presentable. He tried to smile at her as she came in but when he talked to his body, nothing happened. Rachel immediately re-established her position. Once again, she returned to the chair by the bed and held his hand. This time she spoke to him for a while as if they were having a conversation. She explained to him that Dylan was doing fine and that she was really getting tired of all this. The game was over and it was time to wake up. No more screwing around.

She told him, "We're all going to get something to eat, and you sure as hell better be awake by the time I get back!"

As she spoke, her eyes filled with tears. Grey could only imagine how hard this was for her. Her tough shell had become more fragile now. He realized it would probably be the same for him if their roles were reversed. The waiting and the frustration were merciless. He heard her say to herself that she had to stay tough. Then she gathered herself together, kissed him on the cheek and headed back out to join her parents.

As she passed Alex on the way out, Rachel just kept looking straight ahead. To her, Alex was a stranger, but when their paths had crossed earlier, Alex's eyes had given her a funny feeling. Rachel felt transparent. It was like Alex's eyes could see right through her. Their previous exchange had left her feeling nervous and unsettled. Maybe it was just nerves. Maybe she needed something to eat. Add to that, she hadn't had any real sleep in the past twenty-four hours, so maybe her mind was just playing tricks on her. Rachel decided she wasn't willing to take that chance. She walked straight past this strange woman, grabbed her father's hand and headed for the elevator. Her mother and aunt followed close behind. A little food and a little distance might provide a new perspective. That could be just what the doctor ordered.

Alex watched as they boarded the elevator and the doors slowly closed. Then she turned and looked back down the hall, staring at the blue light. It was now or never. The moment was hers. Everything in her life had come full circle. She would now be able to put to the test everything she had learned and believed in. All thoughts were on Grey. She remembered the past. She knew what she had to do. The dragon ring smoldered on her finger.

Suddenly, and without warning, her dragon unfolded its wings and all she could do was watch as they spread out gracefully, covering the palm of her hand. Its eyes came alive as it looked up at her, its presence burning deep into her soul. Then, in the blink of an eye, her hand became empty again and her ring appeared as just a piece of carved metal. Alex had been given a sign. The time to act was now. The energy had returned once more. Alex rose to her feet. For an instant, she wasn't sure she could stand up. Calmly, she got herself together, kissed her ring, and headed toward the blue light. In her hand, she could still feel the heat of the creature's breath. In her mind, she began to see things through the eyes of the dragon. Grey's journey home had begun.

* * * * *

Alex watched as the sun slipped quietly below the horizon. Through the windows in the hall, she could see the reds, pinks, oranges, and blues of twilight as she made her way down the hall to Grey's room. Sunset had always been a good time to play with her "gifts". The world seemed to be mellowing out a little as it slowly wound down at the end of a day. She stopped at the door to his room and took a final look around. It was her last chance to make certain that they would not be disturbed. There was very little traffic in the hallway, so she slipped quietly into his room.

When her body broke the threshold of the door, the blue mist went crazy. Flickers of bright lights and colors came and went like the turning colors of a kaleidoscope. The room suddenly got very warm as if someone had turned up the heat. Grey's body began to glow ever so slightly. As she got closer, Alex could sense the torment going on in Grey's mind. He was very confused but somehow he had managed to keep his faith and acknowledge the signs she had sent him. His mind was open and he was willing to let her in. Alex counted her blessings. In her heart, she knew that one of her prayers had been answered. Grey was still along for the ride.

Time had been kind to her in its own special way. She really hadn't changed at all. He had felt her presence earlier, and had been frustrated by the distance she had chosen to keep. It was funny how none of that seemed to matter anymore, once he saw her come through the door. If anyone could solve this puzzle, he knew it would be her.

She looked happy and sad at the same time, and he found this to be a little disconcerting. Once again, he could hear her voice but couldn't respond. He tried to move again but got nowhere. Things were beginning to look hopeless again. Then it hit him.

What if he could still do some of the things that she had taught him? His heart raced. He found himself searching the deepest corners of his mind, looking for an answer. Then it came to him, like a little light bulb in the back of his mind had suddenly turned on. He remembered something that he'd buried away a long time ago. All he had to do was talk to Alex in his mind, and she would help him work his way back through this! She had always said that two heads were better than one. He knew now that he must focus all his remaining energy on trying to communicate. If he could get through to her, she could help him find some answers. Grey started to concentrate and set his sights on the past. It was time to remember. It was time to come home.

* * * * *

Long ago, in a place that he'd all but forgotten, he had learned how to use his mind. Really, use his mind. In the old days, when he concentrated, he could read Alex's thoughts. She had taught him how. At first, when she mentioned being able to do anything like this, it had been in passing one night over one too many drinks. He remembered thinking how full of shit he thought she was that it wasn't even funny. He recalled that he teased her almost to the point of abuse. She understood his apprehension, but he still listened to her, and never sat in judgment. She knew then that he was someone she could trust.

She had been patient, so very patient with him, and thank God she had. He had learned more from her that summer than he had ever learned about anything before. Most of all, he had learned to believe in himself, and how to truly open his mind. This allowed him not only to accept her and her "gifts", but it enabled him to develop some of his own. She had not given him anything he didn't already have inside; he just wasn't aware of it, or how to use it. Alex had opened the door.

For a long time, he lived in her shadow, sometimes in fear, but mostly in total amazement. When his training was over, she'd invited him to be part of a group of others, blessed and nurtured with the same powers and abilities. The night of his initiation was the first true test, and he had shined like the stars in the sky above. The wind and the rain, the earth and the sea, had all become his friends. They needed to travel back there now, back to the beginning, and their minds would have to take them. It was there, on that night so long ago, that his "gifts" were fresh and new. His heart and his mind were one with the world around him. Now, he realized that time and its many changes, had forced him to file all this away in the back of his head. A lot of dust had gathered on the old trunk, but it would have to be opened again if he wanted a chance to fight. Long ago, he had found the answers, and now, lying in his bed, he knew he had to get back to them. He watched anxiously as Alex began to prepare for their next adventure.

* * * * *

"Things need to be subtle but effective," Alex thought as she placed a small candle in each of the four corners of the room. One black taper and one red one were each set diagonally across from each other in opposite corners. A blue and a white sat as opposites in the remaining corners, so each of earth's four elements were represented. The fluorescent light on the ceiling above was harsh and sterile. Alex extinguished it with a glance. She went to the window and opened the blinds, letting the natural light of the heavens re-illuminate the room. The colors she had

seen earlier coming down the hall cast a strange but welcome shade on the room as they filtered in through the window. From her bag, she removed a small glass vial of water she had taken from the lake. There was also a silver chalice carved with dragon wings, a bottle of red wine, and a dragon ring that matched hers perfectly with one exception; its eyes were closed. The pair had been carved by hand years before out of solid silver. Carefully, she arranged everything on a black silk cloth she had placed on the roll-away tray table next to his bed. Everything was ready. Alex took a deep breath and let out a sigh of relief. The entire set-up had taken just a few minutes. There was still a lot of time left.

For a moment, she thought she felt someone coming, but a quick glance down the hall revealed nothing. It was time to get things underway. Alex found a second chair behind the other bed in the room and placed it at the head of Grey's bed. The scenario she had in mind would require the existence of only positive energy in this room for the next ten to fifteen minutes.

The chair that Rachel had been sitting in was tainted, so she placed it in the bathroom and closed the door. Then, she took the dragon ring and placed it on the ring finger of Grey's left hand. It completely covered the tan line that had been left by his wedding band. As soon as the silver touched his skin, the creature formed in the ring started to change. Alex watched in amazement as its wings started shifting in and out, giving it the appearance that it was breathing and alive. Its eyes, however, remained closed.

By now the room was almost unbearably hot. Alex looked out the window. The sun completely disappeared. All that remained of its visit were fading colors that were slowly at work changing day into night. Alex took a look around. Because he was considered stable and in a private room, the only machines connected to Grey were an oxygen level monitor attached to one finger, an I.V. tube set up and a couple of lead wires on his chest. His vital signs were not being monitored at the nurses' station. The monitors for both the oxygen and the heart leads were here in the room.

Alex got lucky. The nurses would not be alerted to any changes his body might experience unless they were here in his room. The hallway was clear. She glanced at the candles she had placed on the floor, and their wicks instantly burst into flames. Then she walked to the window again and quietly said a prayer. Turning back toward the bed, she began to focus.

Carefully, she moved the head of his bed away from the wall and took a seat in a chair behind him. Then she lowered his head of the bed until it was level with her lap. She placed her hands on his temples. The rush was incredible. She could instantly feel his torment, his frustration and his pain. She could feel the cold desperation. Most of all, she could feel their power building. She heard him call her name, and in her mind she answered him. Grey heard her and a smile broke out across his face. Their minds were one again, and together they were strong. After twenty years, it was time to wake the dragons.

* * * * *

They woke up together, on a small island off the Florida coast. It was there in the Gulf of Mexico, in the middle of the night, they had come together years before to receive their sacrament. Each in their own time, had stood on the sacred hill and been brought face to face with their own mortality. Alex and Grey had stood together, teacher and student as one. For Alex, it was like bringing your child to the hospital. Grey was sick and needed to be healed. But she could not do it alone. He would have to help, and he was exhausted and weak. This kind of travel took a lot of energy and because she was helping him, she was growing tired as well.

At first glance, things were not all that different than they were back then. In the middle of the island, there stood a massive grave of shells. For many centuries, the wind and the sea had deposited the casings of millions of dead, sea creatures here, piling up their last remains in a giant monument-like mound that reached toward the heavens. It was flat on the top and made the perfect altar. If she could get him to the summit, and he was still alive, everything would be all right. The top of the hill was a place where nature had decided that the forces of life and death could merge as one. During a storm, lightning would always strike, and on beautiful days the sun would breathe new life into the exotic plants and flowers that grew at the foot of the hill. The life energy of the foliage entangled itself with the energy left behind by the dead creatures, and created a power with a force all its own. The ability to tap into that energy was the basis for learning how to use one's "gifts". It was all about learning to control the energy that existed between life and death.

On that stormy night, many years ago, Alex and Grey had experienced a virtual "energy overload". By some strange twist of fate, lightning had struck the altar while they were standing on it. The massive charge had brought their inner demons to life. The demons presented themselves before them as dragons. The creatures rose viciously out of the graveyard on which they were standing, and tried to take them back down into the dark world. If Grey had not been as strong as he was, and Alex had not prepared him as well as she did, they would never have survived. It took all of their combined skills to turn the creatures away, and return them back into the darkness below.

That power is what they were searching for now. Over the years, they had befriended the creatures and had learned how to co-exist with them. Their rings were symbols of their permanent connection. Ever since that night, Alex had always worn her ring and maintained her connection. Grey however, had lost touch somewhere along the way. Alex figured if they could expose themselves to that same energy again, this time the creatures would not interfere. They might even come forth as allies. The energy that would come would course through their bodies and the electrical overload would re-animate Grey. When his dragon could open its eyes, Grey would wake up.

In the distance, Alex could see a storm was on its way. It was time to start climbing. If she and Grey could make the summit before the storm hit, they would have a chance. They would have to move fast. Time here was very different than time back at the hospital. Minutes here were only seconds there, but that was not much of a comfort. Time was still against them. The ascent up the hill would be dangerous, even if it were under the most ideal conditions. The elements had not been kind to this place. Only the strong would survive.

Each piece of material that made up the hill before them was bleached and worn smooth. Every bone and shell was so white and polished; they seemed to glow in the dark. There were no real paths, just a slippery, steep climb up about hundred and fifty feet at about a forty- five degree angle. They were both tired and unsteady. One wrong step and they would come crashing down together. The wind was gusting in from the east, and light dew was already starting to settle. If they didn't start now, they had no chance at all. Only sheer will power and determination would get them to the top. The wind started to come up and the dragons grew restless on their hands. It was time to go.

Taking Grey by the hand, Alex started up the hill. She hadn't noticed, but because her ring was on her right hand and his was on his left, their rings were brought together when they held hands. Alex could suddenly feel a warm breath on the palm of her hand. It gave her a secure but uneasy feeling. She knew then that they would not be traveling up the slope alone.

The rain started to fall as they took their first steps. It floated down on them in a slow, misty spray. It was just enough to make Alex feel like she was being teased somehow, and that suddenly, the sky was going to open up. Alex took the lead. Feeling her way along, the first few steps were interesting. The surface was slick to begin with, and the rain just added an additional twist. It was like a car tire having more trouble with a road that had been lightly rained on, than it would have during a hard rain. She discovered immediately that they had to take slow, heavy steps and attempt to keep even pressure on their feet as they placed them down. The slight sinking effect this would cause would keep their steps more solid, giving them better balance, and hopefully prevent either one of them from losing their footing. A tumble now would dangerous enough. One closer to the top, might be deadly. They would have to pace themselves.

Alex had decided that a straight up ascent would be fruitless. Their best chance was to traverse the hill like a boat tacking into the wind. It would take longer perhaps, but it would greatly reduce the risk of a fall. She took a step, steadied herself, and pulled Grey up behind her. Much to her surprise, he moved easily with her. This was a relief. She had been worried that she might end up having to drag him up the hill. He didn't seem like he was "all together there" as yet, but this ease of movement was a good sign. He looked at her, his eyes reassuring her that he was with her all the way. Alex took another few steps and Grey slowly climbed with her. She took a few more.

For the next ten minutes, she led and he followed. Slowly and patiently, they crisscrossed their way back and forth up the hill. Each change of direction brought them closer to the top. As they began to close in on the peak, Alex's worst fears became a reality. Without warning, the sky opened up. It was like they were standing in the mouth of an angry river. The water came down hard and fast almost knocking them off their feet. Any small slip would have sent them crashing down into the darkness below. Alex dragged them both down just in the nick of time. They went to their knees in order to keep a lower center of gravity. Her reaction had been so fast that Grey almost lost his balance. Now, they kneeled together for a few seconds, rested, and adjusted themselves to the rain. Their footing from here on would be crucial. They were so close now they could almost crawl up the rest of the way. Just a few more meters, and they would be at the top.

As they gathered themselves together, Alex looked back at her friend. He looked terrible. The wind had blown his hair wild in every direction, and his eyes were sunken back into his head. He was white as a ghost and shivering in the cold, wet air. She knew what little strength he had left was almost gone. He had given her everything over the past few minutes. She had not carried him up the hill. He had walked with her. She stared deep into his eyes and thanked him. Thanked him for everything.

A smile came to his face as he carefully rose to his feet. They weren't beaten yet. He turned and looked up. Then he started to climb. He set out in front and led Alex the rest of the way up. The storm had tried its best to beat them down, but they would not give in. As Grey reached down to pull Alex up over the top, the first bolt of lightning hit the bottom of the hill. The force sent him flying backwards and Alex landed on top of him. Only the dragon rings held them together.

She rolled off of him, and the two of them lay there on top of the hill, fighting for breath. From this place, you could see nothing but ocean for miles around. The sea was angry, and powerful white caps beat against the rocks below. Flat on their backs, they just lay there for a minute, holding hands. The top of the altar was flat. It appeared to be about forty feet across and maybe fifteen feet wide. It had a peculiar shape to it that Grey hadn't noticed on his first visit. It was very strange. He figured that right now, if you looked down on this place from above, the altar would have an eerie eye like shape to it; with his and Alex's bodies making up the pupil. This gave him an uncomfortable feeling. It was like being the bull's eye in the center of a target.

This storm seemed a lot bigger than the one they had experienced years ago, and they were in for a wild ride. They could almost see the lightning collecting in the clouds. Every time one cloud hit another, the thunder clap was deafening. The river of rain continued to get stronger, and Alex began to wonder how long she and Grey would be able to last. Then they saw them, and for the first time in as long as either one of them could remember, they sensed each other's fear.

There were two giant black masses above them. Each cloud appeared to be miles across and ready to explode. They were headed directly for each other and it looked like they would collide directly over head. There was nowhere to run and no available shelter. Up here they were fully exposed to the elements, and totally at the mercy of the forces of nature around them. Things were really starting to heat up. Their rings had become so hot, steam started to rise from their hands. It felt like they would burst into flames at any moment. Then they both looked up at the sky again. Everything they had worked so hard for would happen in a matter of seconds. The key was to survive. Grey squeezed Alex's hand. They smiled at each other and said a silent prayer. The clouds met.

The explosion above was like a bomb going off in the sky. It was so intense that they could feel the mound beneath them shake. The rain that followed was so overpowering, it was as if the ocean had decided to swallow them whole. Grey was sure that the world he once knew was ending. The water hit them with such force, that it was as if they were being driven into the ground. He and Alex managed to hold on to each other, but they were being pushed dangerously near the edge. If the rain didn't let up, they would be washed over the side. They were holding on for their lives. Then the lightning came.

The first strike hit the mound with such a fury that columns of bone and shell fragments flew high into the air. It was like land mines were exploding all around them. The electricity lit up the altar and them along with it. In an eerie display of smoke and light, they could feel the power surging through them at an alarming rate. Alex realized that this was much more than she had bargained for. It was then that they started to pray that they would make it out alive. Grey sensed her fear and looked up at her through the rain. There, through the rain and smoke, Alex could see the change in Grey's eyes. They were bright and alert. The light behind his eyes was bright and blue. Lying next to her was the friend that she once knew. He was back. Grey had returned to his normal self. Alex smiled but it was only for a moment. As she leaned over to speak to him, a wave of water crashed down upon them and washed them both over the edge of the cliff. Together, they fell into the darkness.

The claws clamped deep into his flesh. Grey felt like he was caught in a vice of some kind and lifted away. It was as if a giant gust of wind had blown up out of the darkness and stopped his descent. He could see the ground below, but was no longer falling. He was floating on the wind. Now, all he could smell was the noxious stench of wet leather in the air. The rain had soaked the creature's wings. He looked over and saw Alex in the claws of another, being carried safely away. Grey glanced up and found himself eye to eye with his savior. The dragon was beautiful. Its body was carved out of pure muscle. He was amazed by the detail of its scaled face, the long sharp teeth, and the strength of its mighty wings.

Its eyes were open and stared back at him through the rain. There was no anger or fear. They told him he was safe and that he would soon be home. As he stared off in the distance, he could see Alex being carried off in the opposite direction. He knew they would meet again in another time, in another place.

* * * * *

Grey heard voices, or maybe it was just one voice, he wasn't really sure. All he knew was that he was hearing it ask the same questions over and over again.

"Who are you? What are you doing here? What's going on?"

Whoever was asking the questions was getting more and more frustrated by the minute. There was no response. The voice was somehow familiar, so Grey opened his eyes. He saw her. He saw them both. Standing at the end of the bed were Alex and Rachel. Rachel was interrogating Alex and not getting anywhere. He watched for awhile until he saw Rachel was about to explode. Without even thinking, he spoke.

"Rachel", his voice came out as whisper. "Rachel honey, it's ok. She's a friend. Everything is going to be all right."

No living soul could have moved fast enough to catch Rachel's chin as it headed for the floor. She stood silent and stunned for a moment before it all sunk in. Instantly, she forgot about Alex and moved towards him. She thought she was hearing things. She turned to the stranger.

"Did he just speak? Did you hear that?" she said looking for some kind of confirmation. Alex didn't respond.

As Rachel got near the head of the bed she said, "Grey, is that you?"

A smile came to his face and he answered her in a whispered voice, "Hey your highness? Where can a guy get a drink around here?" Rachel started to cry.

Then Grey said, "I'm ok honey, but you better buy her a drink too," as he motioned to Alex with his eyes. "We've had one hell of a night!"

Rachel was stunned. When she turned around, the woman had vanished. Rachel looked like she was going to faint. "Trust me honey, I'll explain it all later," he said. His reassurance didn't help much. Grey closed his eyes for a minute, and took a deep breath. He was back.

Somehow, somewhere, he had lost his way. He had been taken to the edge of life and survived. The sun would rise again tomorrow, and he would be there to greet it like a long lost friend. He would be there to watch Dylan grow up. Tears came to his eyes. Only he and Alex knew how close to the end they had really come. For now, it was a story he could never tell. In the back of his mind, he could still smell the wet leather. He knew in his heart, that he would never be lost again. Tonight he would sleep without dreams.

* * * * *

CHAPTER 3

Grey was surprisingly strong and alert when he woke up. It was as if the accident never happened. Rachel had noticed the difference in his behavior right away. The first time she handed him a glass of water, he accidentally crushed the glass in his hand. The strange thing was, he hardly seemed to notice.

While he wasn't acting sleepy or tired, other things were unusual too. When he tried to use the television remote, all he could get was static. When she tried to use it, everything worked just fine. For the first few hours when the lights were off in his room, he seemed to give off a sort of a glow. He became restless when the hospital staff touched him, which was totally out of character. He had always been a touchy, feely kind of person.

He noticed that he was wearing the dragon ring. Although he hadn't seen it in years, it gave him a secure feeling. He was surprised that no one had tried to remove it from his hand or question him about it. Not even Rachel. He wasn't wearing it before the accident. She was so excited to have him back, she hadn't even asked about it nor had she mentioned Alex. This was a great relief. In all honesty, he wasn't sure that she, or anybody else for that matter, would believe his explanation. He really couldn't blame them. He had moved the ring to his right hand, just to be safe.

So far, the only thing that appeared out of the ordinary was the severe bruising on the front and back of both shoulders. When the doctors took a second set of x-rays, they discovered a hairline fracture on his left scapula, and compression damage to a few ribs on the back of his right side. This explained the bruises, but did not explain how they got there. This was not something the emergency room would have missed. It looked like two giant hands had gotten a hold of him and squeezed. The doctors were obviously clueless, and while this concerned Rachel and her family, Grey seemed totally uninterested. He knew the truth, but any explanation he could offer would be incomprehensible.

The doctors insisted that he remain in the hospital for a few days so they could check a few things out. At first he was reluctant, but after experiencing a few unexplainable events, he decided to let them test away. Much to his dismay, he'd spent the last twenty-hour hours "back", seeing more of the insides of machines and gadgets than time with any family or friends. So far, everything medical seemed to check out fine. It was something else he was concerned about. Alex had disappeared immediately after he woke up, right after her run in with Rachel. He was disappointed that Alex wasn't here, but was sure that she had her reasons. He could feel her presence and knew she was still close. He really wanted to talk to her about what the hell was really going on. There was a lot of confusion in his head.

Most of all, he wouldn't talk about the coma. A few doctors and nurses had tried to discuss it with him, but he had politely blown them off. Even Frank had tried with little or no success. He figured that Grey just wasn't ready yet. Rachel said it was just his stubborn side showing through. As far as Grey was concerned, he was ready to move on. All he wanted to do was get out of the hospital, and go back to his life. He wanted to play with Dylan. He wanted to see his friends again. Everything was going to be all right. Everything that is, except the flashes.

* * * * *

The flashes had started the morning after he woke up. The floor nurse was taking his pulse. Velma looked tired. She was working a second shift. All of a sudden a face flashed before his eyes. It was a little girl, maybe six or seven, playing on a swing. She was wearing a flower dress and had ribbons in her hair. She was very unhappy. Her name was

Sydney. She was at day care and out in the play area with her friends. She was sad because she saw her mommy and daddy arguing before they took her to school. Daddy had told mommy that she worked too much. Mommy said that nurses had to work hard to help make sick people well. She had told Sydney that someday, when she was older, she would understand. For now, she had to leave her there. She had to get to work. Sydney was still crying when she left. Grey was stunned. What was he seeing? Who was this little girl? How did he know her? He even knew her name. How on earth was this possible?

When Velma let go of his hand, the vision went away. All he could see now was Velma standing at the end of the bed. She was writing something on his chart. The dream was over, but it left him with an eerie feeling inside. He remembered the face of the little girl. He felt her pain. Who was she and where did she come from? Most importantly, why was he seeing her? Once again, there were too many questions and no answers. It had all happened so fast. He decided to just write it off as a mild hallucination. His mind was so fragile right now, that he didn't want to think too much. He found himself getting bored easily, and that just added to his frustration. He wanted to go home.

* * * * *

Her timing could not have been better. Like an answer to a prayer, Rachel came in with Dylan. The little guy was perfect, and as usual, all smiles. She immediately handed him his son. In a few minutes, he had forgotten all about Sydney. It was as if the incident had never occurred. She also brought good news, and a tray of Aunt Geri's brownies. The brownies were the best medicine ever created. Thank God for Lyanna, Liz and Geri. They'd been smuggling in "snacks" for the past two days. The hospital food was bad enough to put him back into the coma. He sat and listened to Rachel while he stuffed a few brownies in his mouth. He was really making a pig of himself.

"Got milk?" he asked with his mouth full. Rachel laughed. She reached into Dylan's diaper bag and produced a quart-sized carton of milk that she had purchased earlier in the hospital cafeteria. Snack time handled, she gave him the good news. The doctor said that he could check out in the morning. He'd only have to stay here one more night. This was great. In the morning he'd be out of this place. He could walk on the beach, go for a drive, and maybe listen to a little jazz. This nightmare would finally be over. Rachel also looked eager to have him home.

It was already Wednesday and Grey wondered what his office had done about his clients all week. Thursdays were especially cool because he got a chance to see one of his favorite people, Clyde. Even if he wasn't up to working, he could still drop by the house for a visit. The odds of Rachel letting him work were highly unlikely. He was sure the doctors would make him take some time off. He wondered if they would even let him drive right away. Still, the thought of a cigar and a glass of Armagnac sounded good, and his friend was always willing to share. Together, they'd crank up a little jazz; a little Charlie Parker maybe. Yeah, if he played his cards right tomorrow was going to be a good day.

Clyde Hobart had been a client for the past ten years. Talk about cool, Clyde was the man. Clyde's passion was money, or rather making and protecting money; his as well as others. If you wanted your future financially secure, Clyde was the guy to see. He knew all the twists and turns. If you wanted your retirement money to be out there working for you, and kicking some ass, there was no safer place to put your eggs than in his basket. He was a kind and caring man. After sixty plus years on the planet, Clyde had been there and done that with quite a few things. He knew his food. He knew his liquor, and he knew how to treat his lady. Every time Grey worked on him, he learned something new about life. Clyde was someone you could talk to; he even told great jokes. He was one of the clients that Grey always looked forward to seeing. It would be nice to have things back to normal.

* * * * *

While she was visiting, Rachel had talked about the 4th of July weekend. Liz was going to be having her annual barbeque-pool party again this year and the entire family would be there. Liz had asked earlier if Rachel thought she and Grey would be up to it. Based on the speed of his recovery, Rachel had assured her they would. Swimming and sitting in the spa would be great for everyone after this long, hard week. They all needed to have a day of fun in the sun. Dylan had taken to the water like a fish, and Grey was anxious to get in the pool with him. Every time Grey saw him, Dylan had this look of relief on his face. He wondered how much the little guy knew about what had happened.

Had Alex left an impression of some kind on him as well? Grey knew the next time he and Alex could talk the conversation would be very interesting. He found himself making a mental list of all the things he wanted to ask her. He knew that sooner or later she'd surface again. He hoped it would be sooner. Things were so boring here in the hospital, Grey thought he'd go crazy. Rachel had turned on the TV earlier. Re- runs of I Love Lucy had filled the room for the last few hours, just so there would be some background noise and not total silence. He and Rachel had played cards, and then talked for awhile. All the cousins had come by to see him. He considered himself lucky. He'd really had an endless flow of visitors. The nursing staff was both patient and kind. Now, as the day started to wind down, he found himself getting restless. The bed was hard, the room was cold, and everything smelled sterile. He needed some fresh air and a little excitement.

When Rachel left after dinner, she said that she would be back first thing in the morning. He had to find something to do between now and then to keep himself occupied. Then he saw it. There, sitting in the corner of the room was a wheelchair. He got out of bed, walked over, and took a seat. It had been a few years since he had last been in one, but he figured it was like riding a bike: you never really forget. It took him a minute to get re-acquainted with the motion, but soon he was ready to venture into the hall. He quickly discovered he was an old pro with the chair. He was mobile now. This was going to be fun!

Over the next thirty minutes, he wheeled his way down most of the hallways on the wing on his own private reconnaissance mission. He ended up having to duck into a few rooms to avoid contact with the nurses. During his travels, Grey discovered that there were two other people on the unit in comas. One was a drunk driver from a car accident. The other was a child; a young girl. She could not have been more than fifteen or sixteen. Grey slipped into her room while trying to avoid an 'orderly'. She looked so fragile lying there in the bed, almost like Snow White in the Disney story. It made him sad.

From the looks of things around her room, she'd been there for awhile. There were fresh flowers and stuffed teddy bears everywhere. There must have been fifty cards taped to the walls. This girl was obviously very popular with her family and friends. Grey wheeled himself up to her bed. He wanted to see her face. He had the strangest urge to touch her. He reached out and took her hand. He told her that she had to hang on. Everything would be all right.

Suddenly, a warm feeling came over him. He knew that she was going to be ok. He wasn't sure how he knew; he was just sure that he did. After watching her for a few minutes, he wheeled himself back into the hallway. His contact with her confused him even more. After his earlier incident, he really needed to think. What he really needed was to talk to Alex. As he started down the hall again, he got a sudden push from behind.

* * * * *

Her name was Lisa. She was a certified nursing assistant or C.N.A. as they're sometimes called. She was a pretty little blonde thing, who had a body that just wouldn't quit. Grey figured she was about nineteen, nineteen going on thirty. She was bright, funny, and always seemed like she was up to something. She'd caught him out of his room and had him dead to rights. Now the big question was would she give him a hard time? Fortunately, she had heard about his condition from another nurse. She'd stopped by his room last night to see what was going on. She'd been working at the hospital for about thirteen months.

Her job had started as community service assignment to please a judge, but when her time was served, she started to look into nursing school. She decided that she really liked helping people. That's why she came back. She'd been on graveyard shift for the last three months.

As they moved down the hall, they saw another nurse. Lisa made a quick turn, and steered them into an empty room.

"What are you doing out here anyway?" she asked.

"I was going crazy being cooped up in my room," he replied. "I needed to find something to do." "Well, let's get you back to your room before we both end up having to explain ourselves," she said. She peered around the corner of the doorway and saw that the hall was clear. Quickly, she pushed him back to his room. When they were safely inside he asked, "What's with the kid in 512?" "Snowboarding accident, no helmet," Lisa replied. It was then that Grey decided to test a theory.

"Give her another day," he said. "She'll be back."

Lisa looked surprised. As she stood there staring into Grey's eyes, she knew he was telling the truth. She didn't know why, but she knew in her heart that he was right.

There was something about this guy she just couldn't explain. In one sense, he was really cool. On the other hand he was kind of scary. He was different than other people. She just wasn't sure why. That was enough for now. She needed to check in at the nurse's station, and told him she'd be back later. Grey climbed back into bed and turned on the TV. There was still nothing but static.

"How strange he thought, but then again not really."

While he waited for Lisa to return, he thought of the girl in 512. He was sure that she would be waking up soon. He could feel her energy building when he touched her hand. He was starting to feel isolated and alone. What had happened to him that was allowing him this insight into people's lives? He noted that earlier, with Velma, he had seen an event from her recent past, probably that very morning. With the girl down the hall, it was more like a premonition of the future. It seemed to be, that whatever he was seeing was the strongest emotional event that was on the person's mind. The fascinating part was that he was apparently viewing these events, past, present, or future, through their eyes. The flashes he saw would continue as long as contact with the person was maintained. He couldn't understand how this was possible.

Also, he had another problem. How could he explain this to anyone? He still wasn't sure if any of this was real or just more hallucinations. Where in the hell was Alex? She would be the one and only person who would listen, and not think he'd gone totally mad.

Twenty minutes had passed and he was still alone. He tried the TV again. This time, he got nothing at all. If Lisa didn't come back, it was going to be a long night.

* * * * *

She returned about an hour later, just as he was giving up hope that she ever would. She was a little irritated, but kind enough to explain the delay. She had been detained by a nurse who sent her downstairs to retrieve some paper work on another patient. Shuffling paper work wasn't something that she was really supposed to be doing. She could have reported the nurse, but why make trouble. When she saw the look of relief on Grey's face, she laughed. "Didn't think I was coming back, did you?" she teased.

"No," he replied. "I was getting ready to start counting the tiles on the ceiling. I've already finished the ones on the wall behind the TV. Can you stay?"

"Well, I'm yours now for as long as you want me," she said. "All the other patients are asleep."

Grey smiled. This night might not be so bad after all. At least he'd have someone fun to talk to.

"Oh, I almost forgot," she said. "Hang on a sec, ok?"

Grey watched as she vanished out into the hall. About a minute later she came in with a large flat box. It smelled great. "It's just a pizza! I missed dinner, so I figured what the hell." Lisa looked at him and smiled. "Do you want a piece? It may be a long night."

Grey nodded and she threw the box on the end of the bed by his feet. Grey reached down next to her and opened the cooler Rachel had brought earlier. He grabbed two cokes. "I think these will do" he said. Lisa took one and smiled.

It was getting close to one a.m. when the last piece of pizza found its way out of the box and into Lisa's hand. They'd been eating and talking for hours. Lisa had left a few times to check in at the nurse's station, but always found her way back. She had quite a life for such a young kid. At twenty, she had been around the block a few times.

When she was twelve, her mom threw her dad out after he tried to molest her. At sixteen she was arrested for shoplifting and put in juvenile hall. Her latest act at nineteen was "tagging" with some friends. The arresting officer caught her with the paint can still in her hand. That cost her five hundred hours of community service and led to her to the hospital. She told him that's what made her think about going back to school to become a nurse.

She had learned a lot in the past few months working here. She had helped a lot of people outside these walls. Her guy friends just wanted her to party all the time. They always tried to get her drunk and take advantage of her. She had discovered that she was worth more than that. She could have anything she wanted out of life, if she worked hard and didn't quit. It had taken her awhile, but she finally had her head on straight. The more she spoke, the more Grey was impressed. Lisa had obviously been doing a lot of thinking. Maybe all of the problems she had faced and overcome were now giving her the strength to take control of her life. He was glad that he had the opportunity to talk with her. It might be interesting to check back in the future, to see how things worked out. It was going on two a.m. when she left again to check in. Grey sat on the bed wondering what he would see if he could get inside her head.

She'd been kind of flirting with him all evening. It was the way she looked at him, the way she smiled. It was the way she put her legs up on the bed and because her candy striper skirt was so short, the hemline hiked way up exposing a lot of leg. He figured out that maybe he could use her to test whatever was going on here. He wondered what would happen if he touched her. Would just simple contact trigger flashes or did something else have to happen? He felt bad using her, but she would be the perfect test subject. She would never even know unless he told her. His mind made up, Grey waited for Lisa to return.

More than an hour had passed when she finally came back. He had almost fallen asleep when he heard her come back into the room. She had small feet and her tennis shoes made a light, distinctive squeak when they hit the floor. She came over to the bed, looked at him, and then headed back for the door. Only his voice stopped her from leaving.

"I'm still awake silly, you want to talk?" he asked.

He saw the smile as she turned around. He knew then that he had to test his theory. While she was gone, he'd devised a plan. He asked her to look at his ring. When he offered her his hand, she took it. She stared at the ring for a moment and was instantly fascinated by the dragon. He could tell by the look in her eyes. He waited for a second, but nothing happened. It was strange, but what had he really expected? Maybe it was all hallucinations. He was so worked up for this and nothing happened. He took a deep breath and relaxed. Then suddenly, out of nowhere, a picture started to come into focus. Once he relaxed, they started to come. The flashes had returned.

This time Grey was ready for them. He fully understood now that he was viewing the world through Lisa's eyes. It was like both of their spirits were inside her head, together at the same time. She was experiencing something, and he was watching as it happened. There was a guy grabbing at her. Not particularly a playful grab, but more of a forceful one. Grey noticed that he felt light-headed. Lisa must have been drinking. Whoever this yo-yo was, he was trying to cop a feel, and Lisa was enjoying every minute of it. Her face was slowly being bombarded with drunk, wet, kisses, as the guy's hands fondled her chest. Her breasts were beautiful. Large, round, and firm. She was getting hotter by the minute, so he frantically started to peel off her blouse. Inch by inch, his hands explored her body.

His mouth slowly moved down from her lips to her chest, each breast and nipple receiving equal attention. At this point, she had moved and was sitting on the guy's lap, her skirt hiked up almost to her waist. His hands found their way down to her inner thighs, and he quickly slid them up under her skirt. Her head slowly arched back and she let out a whimper. Then his fingers found their way home and she let out a deep moan. Her body started to move in a slow, easy rhythm. Her hips moved gracefully back and forth like she was riding a horse, cantering at first, and then breaking into a hard gallop. As her breathing got heavier, she started to scream.

Grey let go. He was so overwhelmed by all of this, that he pulled his hands away and tried to shield his eyes. This broke the contact. For a minute he just sat there on the bed staring at her. She appeared quiet, relaxed, and totally at ease. Then she saw his face and realized something was wrong. He looked winded. He broke out in a cold sweat. He could almost hear her asking the questions in her head. Ever so carefully, he dragged the sheets across his lap to hide a slight problem that arisen while the experiment was taking place. She had a curious look on her face now. It soon became fear. Why had he reacted this way to her holding his hand? Why did he suddenly pull away? Did he know what I was thinking? Oh my God, what if he did?" she thought.

For a while, they both just sat there, staring at each other. Lisa started to blush.

Grey knew then that she knew something had happened, or at least she suspected. She seemed more embarrassed than angry.

"Need a cigarette?" he asked. This caught her completely off guard. For a moment he could see the fear in her eyes. Then the fear just faded away. She was really blushing now, so he decided to let her off the hook. A simple smirk did the trick. She smiled back.

* * * * *

It was one forty-five when they finally said good night. She told him that she would come back and check on him before the shift change at six a.m. Grey knew he would be sleeping, and that was ok. Even if he missed seeing her before he left, it was not as if he was going to forget this evening anytime soon. He had discovered the way to make the flashes come, but not how to control them. He managed to prove to himself that they were real, very real. He was guessing that either the accident or the journey he'd taken with Alex had brought whatever was causing them to the surface. Now, there were things he needed to know. Would the flashes come every time he touched someone or did he have to be in a certain mood or frame of mind? Were they going to be a permanent thing, or just a temporary side effect of the coma? Maybe Alex would know.

There was a bright side. In about eight hours he'd be going home and could start looking for Alex. He was convinced that she would have a better handle on this, or at least know how to find some of the answers to his questions. She was the only one he could talk to. With her, his secret was safe. He had a feeling that once he was rid of this place, she'd probably come looking for him. Maybe all he had to do was wait. As Grey lay on the bed, he closed his eyes, and thought of Rachel and Dylan. He missed them both so much. Hopefully, they'd be here when he woke up, and they could all go home together. The sounds of silence had come and claimed everything around him. There was a welcome calm. A few minutes later, Grey was fast asleep.

When Lisa checked on him at 6:00 a.m., he was off somewhere in a deep sleep.

He looked so peaceful she decided not to wake him. He needed the rest. Ever since they said goodnight, she was consumed with one thought; somehow he had been inside her. Not sexually, but in some other strange and bizarre way. She could not get the incident out of her head. Before she left, she kissed him on the cheek, and wrote her phone number on his hospital I.D. band. Hopefully, no one would notice it except him. Somehow, he had gotten through, and she had to know how and why. Maybe someday he would tell her, but for now, she had to let him go. Quietly, she turned and walked out of his room.

* * * * *

The morning sunrise was magnificent. It was a shame he slept through it. At 7:45 a.m. the phone by the bed rang, waking him up. It was Rachel. She sounded excited and in good spirits. She and Dylan were up, dressed, and on their way to get him. She said they would be there in about half an hour. Grey was ecstatic. He decided he needed a shower. He looked in the mirror and saw dark circles under his eyes.

He was exhausted, but he wasn't going to tell her he was up most of the night talking to Lisa. That would not go over well.

He knew that sooner or later, he was going to have to explain all of this to her. Now just wasn't the time. He wasn't sure there would ever be a right time, but having some answers would definitely make everything easier to swallow. She was going to have a hard time dealing with most of this. That, he expected. The best he could hope for with her was some patience and understanding. For now, that would have to be enough.

The shower felt good. As the warm water began to hit his face, he thought about everything that had happened in the past twenty-four hours. Velma and the young girl had been interesting. Lisa had been downright scary. He realized that he would have to learn more about the flashes before he talked to anyone about them. Until he had some control, he couldn't go back to work. Otherwise, his job would become a nightmare. He decided to keep things to himself at least until he could talk to Alex. Lisa had some idea, but no real explanation. He was certain she would never share any of this with anyone. He stood there in the shower, until his fingers began to prune.

Refreshed, he turned off the water, grabbed a towel, and stepped out of the shower. In the closet was a fresh pair of jeans and a T-shirt. He hurried into them. It felt good to be wearing real clothes again. He figured he even had time to shave, so off he went. When he came out of the bathroom the second time, Rachel was there waiting.

She gave him a big hug. It was so great to see her and Dylan. Then, still lost in the moment, he realized something escaped him. When he and Rachel embraced, nothing had happened. Oh, the usual normal good feelings were there, but nothing out of the ordinary. He waited a few minutes. Even as relaxed as he was, he saw and felt nothing. No flashes or weird feelings of any kind. Now he was really confused. This was real contact with someone, and nothing had happened!

A nurse came in and asked if he was ready to go. She didn't have to ask twice. After she and Rachel made sure they had all of his things together, he climbed into the wheelchair. He had to be wheeled out. Those were the hospital rules. Grey took a look around then said he was ready. They wheeled him down the hall to the elevators. Moving down the hall, he could see the outside world through the hallway windows. It was bright and sunny outside, and the day looked warm and inviting. As they got closer to the elevator, two people ran past them, into a nearby room. In all the excitement, Grey overheard a nurse say that Shelby Conner in 512 just woke up. Grey smiled.

The elevator arrived, and Grey put Dylan on his lap for the ride downstairs. When the doors closed, Grey looked at his son and smiled. Dylan smiled back. They both knew things were different. Somewhere, between the fifth floor and the lobby, Grey said good bye to everything that forced him to forget the past, and prayed for guidance and assistance in everything that was yet to come.

Once outside, he loaded Dylan and himself into the car. Then he got a strange feeling. He found his attention being drawn toward the sky. It was a beautiful summer day. He was listening to Dylan when, off in the distance, he saw it. A shadow crossed in front of the sun. It was shaped like a dragon, wings spread, floating gently on the wind. He blinked and it was gone. Grey looked back at his son. Dylan laughed. He had seen it too.

Grey knew then, that things had changed forever. His life would be different from now on. He strapped Dylan in and climbed in next to Rachel. As she drove away, Grey rested his head against the window and closed his eyes. Rachel was listening to "That Don't Impress Me Much" by Shania Twain on the radio. Rachel liked to sing along. She wasn't that bad either. She always made a car trip more entertaining. Grey's mind however, was on a different station. He was impressed just to be alive. His ears were filled with the sweet sound of dragon's song. He was totally at ease. The world around him was a bright and beautiful place. He counted his blessings. He was finally going home.

* * * * *

CHAPTER 4

She had made her retreat out of there as quickly as she dared. She determined that she wasn't ready to be grilled for information by Rachel or the family. As she sat on the hotel bed sipping a glass of red wine, she missed him. It had been almost two days. It had been exciting to be around him again after all this time. In the past, every time they were together, something wild happened. This reunion was no exception. She wanted to go back to his room in the days following his awakening, but it had been impossible for her to do so and maintain a low profile. He would be out of the hospital soon, and then she could approach him when it was safe. Alex smiled. Another crazy Grey and Alex adventure.

Who would have believed it! Now the only thing she worried about was whether or not he was ok. He had been through a lot, and she was very curious to hear what he remembered about the accident, her visit, and their little side trip. She had been getting some weird feelings like something was going to happen. It would be safer for them both if she stayed close, so she hid in his shadow.

The location of the hotel she had chosen was perfect. From her room, Alex could look out her window across a field and see the houses on Grey's street. The neighborhood kids had come and gone on their bikes and skateboards. It was a very typical family neighborhood. She could go for a walk anytime, and just casually pass by his house without being noticed. This was a nice setup but it wouldn't last forever. The low profile act would have to be scrapped soon, and Alex knew that she might be under fire as soon as she came out in the open. She and Grey would have to explain her presence here, without really telling anyone much of anything. She would have to explain her appearance at the hospital somehow. Whether Rachel would accept any of it or not, was still up in the air. She knew that once she and Grey sat down and had a chance to talk, everything would work itself through.

"Things might be real simple," she mumbled to herself as she poured another drink. Even running into Rachel again might not prove to be so bad. On second thought, it might even be amusing. A sinister grin came to Alex's face. She laughed, and drifted off into the darkness and another glass of wine.

* * * * *

The always reliable Dylan alarm went off at 7:15 a.m. Grey could hear the little guy crying in his room. This usually meant he'd been up for about fifteen minutes, engaged in some form of self entertainment with his toys; waiting for the right moment to announce his arrival into a new day. Grey automatically rolled out of bed. He turned his bedside clock ringer to off before it could engage, and headed for the kitchen to get his son a drink. After that, Dylan would need his cereal. He sure liked to eat. Grey figured that if he timed it right, he could have him changed, fed, bathed, and dressed before Rachel woke up.

His first night home had been rough on her. Three times during the night, he had awakened her with his tossing and turning. His sleep was so restless, that he kept banging into her all night long. He'd been having strange dreams. During a few of them, it was like he was involved as an active, physical participant. Rachel finally passed out about 3:30 in the morning. When Grey woke up, he felt fine, but he was sure she would stay asleep for at least a couple more hours. He felt badly that he'd kept her up most of the night. He thought about Father Richard.

'I do God's work through the church, my son. You lad, do yours with God's hands,' the Father always joked.

Under the circumstances, he couldn't see the good friar wanting a massage today. Still, he might be up for a chat. Richard was a man of God, and here, an opportunity had presented itself. The church might be willing to offer up some advice on how to deal with his newly acquired talent. Grey knew that whatever secrets he shared would be safe within the walls of the church. Richard was a kind and gentle man with a playful attitude and a warm heart. He was always up for a good conversation and a word of prayer. In the past, he and Grey had bantered for hours about every topic you could imagine. They frequently wound up singing a few songs and having a drink or two. God sure loves the Irish!

Grey decided that he would pay his friend a visit after church on Sunday, if that was ok with Rachel. For now he would let her sleep. After everything they'd been through, she not only needed, but deserved the rest. Besides, it gave him a chance to play with Dylan. It seemed like a lifetime since they had rolled around on the floor together. It would be interesting to see what effect, if any, the past week had had on him. Would holding Dylan for awhile instigate more flashes? Nothing had come of his recent contact with him in the hospital, or when he loaded him into the car. In a strange sort of way, some of this was starting to make sense.

So far, the flashes depended on the level of Grey's intensity with the situation. If he was wound up, there were no flashes. It was only when he was relaxed or in his "zone" that anything happened. So far, it only occurred when he was in contact with strangers. To this point, he had not tried it with anyone he really knew, except his wife and son. Unless he was working, it would not become an immediate problem. He knew however, that he felt uncomfortable around Rachel like this. For now, he had to keep his guard up, but sooner or later something had to give. Then it hit him. There would be a lot of family at the party tomorrow exchanging lots of hugs and handshakes. If he was going to get through the day, he'd better start learning to get control fast.

Rachel started to wake up just as he and Dylan were stepping out of the shower. As he began to dry off he noticed he was still wearing his hospital I.D. bracelet. The nurses would not let him leave the hospital without it. As he passed by the vanity, he caught a glimpse of himself in the mirror; he still saw a strange face. He stopped to remove the bandage over his eye. The entire time, Dylan was watching his every move.

"You think it will scar, little buddy?" he asked. Dylan just giggled. "Me too," Grey assured him.

Then he went back to concentrating on the bracelet. When he started to cut it off, he noticed some strange handwriting on one side. He recognized Lisa's name. She had left her phone number. Grey laughed, and instead of throwing it away, tossed it playfully into his sock drawer. It was an interesting souvenir. Rachel was now awake. He heard her ask in a sleepy voice,

"Need any help with Dylan?"

"No honey," he replied. "Just need to dry him off and get him dressed. Sorry if we woke you up."

"You didn't," she said. "How are you feeling anyway? You tossed and turned all night."

"I'm all right I guess, just a little tired," he lied. He wasn't about to start telling her about the strange dreams. Why make her worry?

"I want to go see Father Richard on Sunday if that's ok with you. I can see him after church." Rachel nodded her approval. Although she didn't speak, inside she was relieved. She knew that he had a great love and respect for Richard. Maybe he could get Grey to open up to him, if not as a friend then maybe as a priest. Grey had been silent about the accident and everything that happened at the hospital. She knew that something was bothering him, and maybe Father Richard could help.

Grey took Dylan into the den and played with him for an hour while Rachel got up and dressed. Dylan seemed like his normal self for the most part. Every time their eyes met though, Dylan had a content look about him. When he looked at his daddy, he was very happy. Grey caught himself wondering what the little guy was thinking. Then again, he was sure he already knew. Grey figured that Dylan had somehow picked up on everything that had happened since that day in the hospital when he was under Alex's influence. Grey was positive that Dylan had seen the dragon in the sun as well. More questions. Communication at the moment was difficult. It wasn't as if Dylan could just look up and say something. It was his facial expressions and his body language that were doing the talking for him. To the rest of the world, he was just a happy little boy; to Grey he was much more. He thought for a minute, and then it dawned on him, "He's one of us!" What had Alex done?

Every inch of him wanted to reach out and 'touch' Dylan, but something in his heart told him no. Leave things the way they are. There was a time and place for everything. He would know when the time was right. Dylan would tell him. For now, he needed to concentrate on how to handle himself at the party. If he could keep himself pumped up a little, then maybe he could keep the flashes away. He didn't want to know all of the things that might come up if he started to relax around some of the family. If he could keep to himself for a while and just try to lay low, things would be easier to handle. Truth was, he needed help.

He picked up Dylan and asked, "Where the hell is Alex when we need her, huh?" Dylan smiled and gave his daddy a big hug. Grey was certain that Dylan knew the answer.

* * * * *

From the balcony of her room, Alex stood and watched the sunrise as a new day began. The light of day came on slowly, gently pushing the darkness away. It was as if God was playing with a giant dimmer switch, and was turning the power up a little bit at a time. Sitting in a chair, she warmed her hands by caressing a cup of black tea. It was made from her own special blend of herbs, roots and berries. It was guaranteed to put her in the exact state of mind she desired. Casually, she sipped her tea, and surveyed the surrounding area. To her left, she had a clear view of everything traveling east on the nearby freeway as it headed into the early morning light. The stream of red tail lights had increased steadily as the sun climbed higher into the sky. Anxious travelers were trying to get out of town for the holiday weekend.

From her vantage point, she could see that many of the lanes were packed with vehicles pulling boats or small water craft. She remembered hearing Grey once talk about going to "the river". From the looks of things, it seemed safe to assume that it was a popular destination. Someday, she'd have to check it out. In front of her, there was a large field. It was planted with corn. It stretched out about one hundred yards deep and ran left to right for almost the same distance. Grey's neighborhood started on the other side of the field and ran parallel to the freeway on her left.

She took comfort in knowing that she would not be going out on the road. As a matter of fact, the way things were going, it might be a quite awhile before she could return home. She finished her tea, and headed back into the room to refill her cup. She laughed. If the hotel only knew: what she was really brewing in the 'complimentary' coffee maker. She poured herself another cup and returned to the balcony. Grey's house became the point of surveillance. If something didn't happen soon, she was going to go stir crazy.

Being cooped up in the hotel for the past few days had bored her senseless. Now that Grey was home, things would start to get interesting. She needed to devise a plan that would enable the two of them to get together and talk. Any immediate success however, depended on whether or not Grey was thinking the same thing. If he was, he would find a way to be alone where she could approach him safely. Her mind worked the problem.

What if he just went out for a walk? Would Rachel even let him go out alone? Maybe he would go out to buy fireworks. There was a big fireworks show tonight at the park across the street. She had seen a sign in the lobby announcing it. It was open to the public. If she could meet him there, under the protection of darkness, things would be much easier and safer for both of them. She knew she had to get a message to him. Now all she had to do was figure out how.

If she could let Grey know how close she actually was, maybe he would come up with a similar idea. This of course, was leaving a lot to faith. Then she thought of Dylan. Could she count on the help of a new friend? It was certainly worth a try. Alex closed her eyes, letting her mind slip away to another place. Somewhere close, she could hear laughter. The soft, playful giggles warmed her heart. After tuning into it, she listened for a while, enjoying the innocence of it all. Then she made her move. Reaching out to the child, she made her request. There was a brief pause, followed by a brief silence, and then the laughter continued. The message had been received.

* * * * *

Rachel came in to see what all the noise was about. All she could hear was the two of them laughing. Grey was holding Dylan up in the air, "bench pressing" him up and down. "One, two, three, four', they were doing the "baby workout". They were both laughing hysterically. Then, for a moment, Dylan was quiet. Rachel watched as his little face went blank. It was as if his mind had wandered off somewhere. Then he held up his arms like he was flying. This continued for a moment or two then he appeared to click back in. He started laughing again even harder than before. Grey had been watching this too with great curiosity. Something obviously distracted the little guy and had done so quite effectively.

Grey remembered how he'd been thinking in the hospital, that he needed to start paying very close attention to things. He was getting that same feeling again. There was no time like the present. A single thought floated through his mind; *"What was Alex up to this time?"* It had to be her. She was close. He could feel it. Dylan had acted like he was a bird or a plane trying to fly. All of a sudden, things clicked. He looked like a dragon! Now it made sense. It was Alex! He'd have to talk to her about her not so subtle signals. She was so smooth it was frightening. Once again, she found a way to use Dylan to make contact. Rachel took Dylan back to his room to change his outfit. She didn't think too highly of Grey's choice of clothes.

Grey sat on the couch, shaking his head in total amazement. Alex was unbelievable. For now, using Dylan was ok, but what worried him was why she had not gone directly to him. Was there a problem he wasn't aware of? Now, more than ever, he was sure they needed to talk. He had to find a way to be alone so she could approach him. Rachel wasn't about to let him out by himself. He'd have to give this some thought. There was the party to attend today, the fireworks show tonight, and Sunday he'd be seeing Father Richard. He was very busy for someone who was supposed to be taking it easy. There had to be some way to get free for a few minutes.

The more he thought about it, the more irritated he became. Since the accident, he'd been like a bug under a microscope. Every move he made was being watched. He was about to give up when the idea hit him. The fireworks show! It would be perfect. He could make himself available in the crowd and no one would suspect a thing. The odds of him standing next to Rachel the whole time were minimal. Anyone else in the family would not recognize Alex even in broad daylight, so meeting in the dark was a safe bet. It might work, but even if they could set it up, they wouldn't have a lot of time to talk. Grey decided it was worth the risk. He was tired of dealing with all of this by himself. If Alex was nearby, he needed to find a way to let her know what he was thinking. Leaving a few fireworks on the porch might be a good idea. That hint would have to do. He was glad that he'd planned ahead and bought some early the day of the accident. If he was lucky, she'd get the message.

* * * * *

Rachel reappeared with Dylan. He was dressed in a white jumper with a flag design on the front. He was very adorable. Rachel wore jean shorts and a red and white striped shirt. Grey didn't recognize the outfit. She and Renee must have been to the mall. He told her that she looked great, and headed for the bedroom. He took out a pair of jeans, a white T-shirt, and sat down on the bed. The clothes were perfect. He wanted to be comfortable. It was going to be a long day. When he was ready to go, he picked up Dylan. Rachel said she preferred to drive and he wasn't in the mood to argue. He put Dylan in his car seat, and then climbed in.

As the van backed out of the driveway, he pretended that he had forgotten something and hurried back into the house. Quietly, he sneaked around and placed a few fireworks on the front porch. The shrubs near the driveway protected him from Rachel's view. Then, he went back in the house and came out through the garage.

Rachel asked him, "All set now?"

"Yeah honey, let's go," he replied. Rachel backed out the rest of the way and they headed off down the street. They were headed for her parent's house and would be riding over to the park with them.

Instantly, Grey felt as though he were being watched. He sensed that somewhere in the distance, a pair of eyes was trained directly on him. He was being watched. Oddly enough, it was a good feeling. He knew that everything was all right.

A few minutes later a lady jogged by the house. Her long red hair bounced gently across her face as she ran. She stopped at the end of the front walkway to catch her breath. The fireworks on the front porch were a welcome sight. She smiled. The ring on her finger started to heat up. Alex took a deep breath and grinned. She knew that before the day was over, they would be face to face again, and then the real fireworks could begin.

* * * * *

The ride to Liz's house took all of five minutes. That was one of the advantages of having most of the family living close by. Grey spent every moment of the ride trying to get a handle on his emotions. He was headed into the danger zone. He would have to find a way to keep things under control. He had one thing in his favor. He hoped that after the initial "Hello's", everyone might just let him be. They'd assume he needed the rest.

If he could get through the greetings, then all he had to do was avoid any major contact. As they turned the corner onto Liz's block, he could see cars parked solidly along both sides of the street. In front of the house, someone had left an open spot so Rachel pulled in and parked. Grey looked at Rachel and smiled. In the back of his mind, he heard a voice inside him say, *"Let the games begin."* With that thought in mind, Grey laughed and got out of the car.

Saying hi to everyone proved to be no problem. There were of course a few big hugs and handshakes but nothing long enough to set any strange wheels in motion. About ten minutes later, Grey got settled in a chair over by the fire pit with a cold drink and a few hot dogs. He wasn't in the mood to swim, but from this vantage point he had a view of all the festivities. He sat and looked around for a while. Watching everyone, he was reminded of how lucky he was to be part of such a great family. This was a group of truly remarkable people. As the day moved along, everyone came over to see what was up. Dylan and Rachel had been in the pool most of the afternoon. Around six o'clock, Lyanna announced that everyone was planning to go over to the park to watch the fireworks. The show would start right after dark. Anyone that wanted to go should be ready to leave in about forty-five minutes. Grey played casually with his ring and smiled. This was good news. With little or no effort, the plan was starting to take shape. If everything proceeded on schedule, he would see Alex later that evening.

Traveling back with her before, in the hospital, had been like a dream. Now they would actually be able to talk. Even if it was only for a few minutes, they could talk about what was going on and make future plans. He looked at his watch, and then at the sky. The sun was fading fast. The comfortable brilliant blues of day had turned to exotic pinks, reds, and purples. The darkness from above was slowly driving them down toward the horizon.

Grey felt a little strange. It had been almost two days since he had experienced any flashes. Even though he hadn't really tried to instigate them, he found himself wondering if they would still come. Did he dare attempt drawing them out again, by using someone in the family? How badly did he really want to know?

After a short debate with himself, common sense won out, and he put the idea out of his head. Right now, he had enough on his mind, without throwing anything else into the fire. It was getting dark. It was time to get ready to leave for the park.

Grey looked around for his wife. Rachel and Dylan had gotten out of the pool and were in the house changing. Everyone was getting ready to leave. Grey finished his lemonade and got out of his chair. He discovered that he was getting very anxious about the evening. As he walked toward the house, his mind wandered.

Suddenly, out of the corner of his eye, he saw it. A ball was coming straight at his head. Instinctively, he shifted his weight to get out of the way, but he was too close to the edge of the pool. He lost his balance. Grey started to fall. The dragon on his hand opened its eyes. At what seemed like the last possible moment a big, strong, burly hand came out of nowhere, grabbed him by the back of his shirt collar and pulled him to safety. Uncle Tony had made a game winning Catch. The pool would not entertain another swimmer today. Grey couldn't believe it. It all happened so fast. He was sure he was going in for a swim. Everyone that had been standing around stopped in their tracks, waiting to see what would happen. Tony and Grey just stood together for a second, staring at each other. Then the silence turned to laughter.

Tony asked, "You ok, man?"

Grey nodded with a positive gesture, took a deep breath and relaxed. Then he reached over and gave Tony a big hug.

If he'd had a chance to think about it, he probably wouldn't have done it. For a moment, he let his guard down and completely forgot about everything that was happening. He was just grateful for the rescue. He didn't need any more distractions or delays. He had a lot more to do that day. The hug was merely a thank you. He remembered everything after it was too late. As soon as their bodies made contact, the sideshow began.

* * * * *

The big delivery truck had backed quickly into the loading dock. The immediate vantage point indicated that Tony was behind the wheel. When the truck stopped, the air brakes, setting themselves, gave off a sound that was similar to a tire blowing out on the highway. Immediately, Tony jumped down out of the cab and hurried toward the rear of the trailer. On his signal, several men came out of the shadows, opened the rear doors and began unloading its contents. Televisions, microwaves and other appliances began to appear on the dock. Tony gave the bill of lading to one of the men to sign, and then found a safe place to be out of the way. The workmen moved fast and the truck was completely empty in twenty minutes.

Some of the boxes, however, never saw the inside of the warehouse. They had been carefully loaded into two large dumpsters located near the rear doors of the loading dock. Tony stood off in the distance, head down and turned away. If he looked up, his eyes would tell him the truth about what was going on. He didn't want to see. Deep inside, he already knew. When he heard the trailer doors finally slam shut, he decided it was ok to look up.

Across the way, on the other side of the delivery area, two men in dark suits were talking to the guy that had just signed the paperwork. One of the 'suits' handed one of the workers a large envelope, then he and his associate turned and vanished into the darkness. As the two men walked off into the night, Tony got an uneasy feeling in his stomach. He'd had the same feeling every third Tuesday for the last eight months. It had gotten worse each time. This time, it was so bad, he was sure it would never go away.

Alone on the loading dock, he lit another cigarette. He was trapped. He'd been in this cage for so long, he was beginning to wonder if he'd ever get out. He had been warned to keep silent with a stern word and a pistol. He had been wise to listen.

He had stumbled across the hijacking ring one night completely by accident. He was forced to stay late that night with a bad stomach that gave him the runs. He was stuck in the 'head' when they locked the place up for the night. Everyone thought the building was empty until he walked out of the Men's room. The few men that remained knew him, and trusted him during the day, so it was decided that rather than instantly "taking care of him", they would give him a chance to make some money in exchange for his silence. Tony figured that at this point, he really didn't have much of a choice.

He continued to drive the trucks like he was supposed to, but closed his eyes to everything else. He had a conscience, but he had to protect himself and his family.

Someday, he hoped he could find a way out. Right now he feared for his life, and the lives of everyone around him. The people running the show were not people he wanted to mess around with. Tony kept on working, but more importantly, he kept quiet. He could never tell a soul, and the fear always lived with him.

* * * * *

When Grey finally let go, he was shaking so badly that Tony asked him if he was all right.

"Yeah, I'm fine," Grey replied. "I'm just a little shaken up."

"Hey man, you'd better sit down," Tony responded. "I wasn't about to let you take a dive!"

Grey helped himself into a nearby chair. This was getting more than a little scary now. For a while, when he looked at Tony, it was as if he could see right through him. They had only embraced for a short time, and still all this enlightening information had presented itself. It was incredible. He had seen all of this in just a few seconds. It was then he realized that the flashes ran in high speed mode. The whole scenario he had just witnessed had played itself out in his head in less than half a minute. He had to get control of this thing and fast, but first he had to get a handle on himself.

The doctors had told him to wait a few weeks before having any alcohol. Shaken and uneasy, he figured that going back a few days early wasn't going to hurt anything. Grey went into the house and poured himself a scotch. As always, it was three fingers and two cubes. It felt good going down. He poured himself another.

* * * * *

The darkness of night had settled in by the time Alex woke up from her nap. The only light that came through the window was the dull, artificial glow of the balcony lights. She'd been asleep for the better part of the afternoon. She had been dreaming, and it was part of that dream that woke her up. For a brief moment, she had seen Grey falling again only this time a strange hand prevented his fall. Her dragon was getting restless and so was she. Her impatience was beginning to show. It was time to get up. She glanced over at the clock on the nightstand. It was close to seven p.m. The fireworks show would be starting shortly. She looked over at the dresser and saw the cones and sparklers sitting where she had left them earlier. He had gotten her message. He had responded. He would be at the show. She knew it. It wouldn't be long now until she would able to see her friend.

Alex climbed out of bed, took a quick shower and got dressed. Her ensemble consisted of jeans, a t-shirt, and black leather boots. Everything she wore was black. Her long trench coat completed the look. At first, she thought the coat might make her look a little out of place, but in the dark of night, she hoped no one would notice. She was betting on the fact that all eyes would be on the sky and she could come and go as she pleased.

"Hey," she thought. "This might be easier than I thought."

She poured a fresh cup of tea, let her hair down and shook her head all around, letting her hair wave about. Finally, she picked up her keys. Once last look in the mirror proved to be friendly, so she grabbed her coat and headed downstairs to the parking lot.

One nice thing about this part of town, it was basically safe to be out walking at night. Anaheim Hills was a pretty upscale part of the city. The Mustang was right where she left it, top down but still untouched. Parking over at the show would probably be a nightmare, so she decided to walk the four or five blocks. She started to venture off. There was a night club style restaurant located just across from her, on the other side of the complex. She knew there would be an abundance of drunken people coming out later, so why ask for trouble. She reconsidered the options, and put the top up on the car. Once everything was locked up tight, Alex headed for the park. In her present attire, she looked like a black shadow floating across the parking lot. Her coat flapped gently behind her in the breeze. It beat slowly like a giant wing. Alex was on her way.

* * * * *

They caught a ride over with his in-laws. As they had expected, traffic was a disaster. The last couple of blocks, you could almost walk faster than drive. People were moving in herds down the sidewalks, like the chaos you might see when the crowd lets out after a baseball game. Children and adults of all ages surrounded the baseball diamond at the west end of the park. The pyrotechnic people would be using the dirt infield to launch their rockets. A man with a bullhorn announced the show would be starting in ten minutes, so everyone needed to get situated. Many people brought blankets or lawn chairs. It was going to be like grass seating at a rock concert. Grey found himself a spot on some playground equipment and the rest of the group followed suit. Considering the sea of people, their seats were pretty good.

The show started on time. A loud thundering boom signaled the launch of the first rocket. It exploded a few hundred feet up and erupted into a giant yellow starburst. The crowd went wild. For the next thirty minutes or so, the sky was overtaken with splashes of color and light. Some rockets were shot high up in the air, while others were kept closer to the ground, giving them a different effect. With each shot, there was a short silence, and then a bang, followed by a cheer from the crowd. Thousands of brilliant colors lit up the night sky. The fireworks totally captured the attention of the audience. Everyone was enthralled with the beauty of the night sky. Looking up at the stars, they waited anxiously for the next rocket to go. A hand touched Grey's shoulder. It startled him. He turned around expecting to see her. To his dismay, it was just Tony.

"Enjoying the show?" Tony asked. "You look a little disappointed."

"No man, this is great." Grey answered. It was a white lie. He was a little disappointed.

Tony smiled, "I'm going for a drink, want anything"?

"No thank you, I'm fine, but thanks for checking," Grey replied.

"Ok then, I'll be back," Tony said. He turned, waved, and disappeared into the crowd.

Grey focused his attention back to the action above. The guys doing these fireworks were really good. They'd obviously put in a lot of time planning this. Another loud shot echoed through the air. This latest one went higher than any of the others. It ended its flight by exploding into a massive sea of blues, greens, and reds. A million little sparkles lit up the sky. It was the best one so far. The crowd went ecstatic with its approval. In the midst of the excitement, Grey felt another hand on his shoulder.

"Yeah, Tony, what do you need?" he asked as he started to turn around. He never completed the turn.

* * * * *

When his shoulders started to shift, a hand from behind stopped him.

"Don't turn around my friend, we don't have a lot of time," a friendly voice from behind said. Grey froze. For a moment his heart stopped beating. Even his breath had been taken away. There was no sound. Everything around him went silent. All he could hear was the sound of her voice. She spoke in a whisper that blew in like the wind.

"Nice to see you," she whispered

"Nice to be seen, I think," Grey replied comically. "So what's the plan?"

"I think we need to do lunch," Alex chuckled. "How's your head?"

"Ok, I think, but I need to talk to you. I picked up some weird problem during all of this craziness," Grey said. Alex squeezed his shoulder.

"Yeah, I had a feeling something strange was up when I had trouble getting through to you. That's why I stuck around. Sorry about having to get Dylan involved. Don't worry about anything for now. We'll figure it all out together later," Alex rambled off all at once. "I'm in the hotel at the end of your street. Come see me when you can."

"I will when I can get away," Grey replied. "I promise I won't keep you waiting too long."

He felt the hand let go of his shoulder. When he turned to face her, she was gone.

Tony appeared a few minutes later carrying a box with sodas and beers.

"Thought you might have changed your mind," Tony said.

"Didn't know what you felt like having, so I bought a bunch of different stuff. We can have what we want, then take the rest over to the girls."

Grey laughed. He loved Tony's way of thinking. He decided to stick with soda for now. The two scotches he'd had earlier had served him well. He didn't need any more booze. Even though he had seen Alex, he still wanted a clear head. Dealing with the flashes was confusing enough sober; adding alcohol would make it almost impossible. Grey drank a soda and relaxed a little.

The evening was slowly drawing to a close. Thinking back, it had been a good day. He felt as though he had accomplished a great deal. He was finally making some progress. He'd met with Alex, survived the party, and even after his experience with Tony, discovered that he had not exposed himself to anything he couldn't handle.

Tomorrow was a new day, and a chance to visit Alex might present itself. Knowing that she was near, allowed him to rest easier. Rachel, however, was still a little shaky about how to get close to him again, so at least he had some space. He hated being treated like he was fragile.

The ride home seemed to last forever. It took twenty minutes just to get out of the parking lot. It was quite an evening. The fireworks show was everything that had been promised. After the show, the sea of people turned into a wave of cars, trucks, and mini vans, each trying to weave its way through the remaining groups of pedestrians that chose to walk home.

Sitting in the back seat of Lyannas' Acadia, Grey was mesmerized, watching all the different kinds of people pass by his window. He sat for a moment wondering what it would be like to touch some of them. Ah, but which one: the cheerleader, the old man walking with the cane, or the young girl in a wheelchair. There was a man pushing a stroller with what appeared to be triplets. That would be a wild one! What strange or unusual things would be going on inside these people? What information would they have to share? What secrets would they be trying so desperately to hide? He found himself wanting to roll down the window so he could reach out and touch them all. Something inside him said no. The experience with Tony had been a rush, but it was mind boggling just the same. Did he really want another "episode"?

Dylan between them, the ride home felt safe. Part of him wanted to reach over and take Rachel's hand, but another part of him wasn't sure that he really wanted to chance it. She'd been acting very peculiar lately. Maybe some things were better left unknown. For now, all he wanted to do was get home and get a good night's sleep. Dylan had already beat him to it, and established an early lead. After sitting bug eyed for the duration of the show, he had fallen asleep the minute his little butt hit the car seat. Rachel, Lyanna, and Frank were all talking about what would be going on tomorrow. In Rachel's family, a holiday weekend usually meant that there would be the kind of party that would last on and off all weekend. Tonight had merely been the start of a long, enjoyable affair. Grey just sat, quietly looking out his window and listening to their conversation.

You had to love the way these people did things. A small family get together regularly consisted of thirty to forty people. Lyanna and Rachel would have the entire weekend planned out by the time they got home. As it was, in the short time they'd been together, they had already planned another day around the pool, and a barbecue. This one would be pot luck. A large extended family was a great asset. There was always a reason to party.

Suddenly, Frank stopped the conversation. The radio had been playing in the background and the disc jockey broke in with a news flash. A young girl's body had been discovered. It had washed up on the rocks just south of Corona Del Mar. There were no details yet, but the police suspected that she was another unfortunate victim in a recent string of attacks on young women in the area. Her naked body had been found about an hour ago by a couple of teenagers looking for a place to make out. The police were advising everyone in the area to be extra careful and not to be out alone. They would provide more information to the public as it became available.

"That's just great, another nut case running around!" Rachel exclaimed.

"You kids need to be careful when you're out at night, ok?" Lyanna chimed in.

Frank turned at the next corner and pulled up in front of the Thomas house. As Rachel got out of the car, she grabbed Dylan's diaper bag. Grey got out and grabbed Dylan. They said their good-byes and headed for the house. Rachel had only taken a few steps when Lyanna called out,

"So we're all set for tomorrow then?"

"Sure Mom, we'll call you in the morning. Thanks again," Rachel replied. As she turned toward the house, the Acadia drove away.

Grey was already inside when Rachel headed up the driveway. She had this funny feeling that she was being watched. It gave her the creeps. It was the same eerie feeling that she'd had back at the hospital with that strange woman. It made her feel cold and empty. She looked around but there was no one in sight.

"Maybe I'm just being silly," she thought and walked into the house. Without thinking, she locked the door behind her.

* * * * *

Sitting on the balcony, Alex sipped her wine. The strong oak flavor of the cabernet sat wonderfully on her tongue. She had just started her second glass, when she saw the car pull up in front of the house. Rachel and Grey got out. Grey looked good. Seeing him acting like his old self again was refreshing. There was something about him that always made her smile. Now, as she watched them with a careful eye, she remembered seeing something behind Rachel's eyes that troubled her.

She decided right then and there to make it her business to find out what it was. It would probably prove to be nothing, and truth be told, she really hoped that her suspicions were unfounded. She would like nothing better than to become friends with this woman, but for now, she needed to protect Grey at any cost. Strange things were happening to him, and until they had a chance to resolve them, she would continue to be on guard.

Standing back on her balcony at the hotel, Alex enjoyed the night air. The wind whispered gently through her white satin robes, allowing the silky fabric to tease her exposed skin. She had changed out of her black attire immediately after she arrived back at the hotel.

Today had been a success. It was a small victory, but a triumph just the same. They had a chance to say hello, and everything went well. Now all she could do was sit and wait to see what tomorrow would bring. Grey would have to make the next move.

Alex downed the remainder of her cabernet and went back inside. She set the empty glass on the night stand and climbed into bed. Tonight, she would not dream of fear nor loss, but of the past and the future. Her mind was at ease. She was at peace with the world around her, and for the moment, the world was at peace with her. Alex slept like a baby, her mind floating away into the darkness of the night.

CHAPTER 5

The jury handed down its verdict. They found his client innocent of all charges. Blake Kendall had done it again. Truth was, his victory really came as no surprise to anyone. He was the best criminal defense lawyer that the firm had to offer. That's why the firm had recruited him ten years earlier and moved him and his family out west to Southern California from Georgia. He knew all the angles, and how to exploit the system. There was simply nobody better. As he walked out of the courthouse, he smiled. It was that old Cheshire grin of his. It always let the press know what had happened inside. Once again, the 'Cat' had devoured the canary.

Now, standing outside on the steps of the courthouse, he would take a moment to address the press. It was a beautiful day, hot, a little humid, but without a cloud in the sky. The sun warmed his face like a barber's towel, the kind the old timers used to put on your face after a close shave. It had been much cooler inside until the verdict was read. His victory had impressed some but angered others. He really didn't care, though, what people thought. He had won for himself, as much as for his client. Nothing could compare to the kind of high that winning gave him. He straightened his tie, removed his Ben Franklin style glasses, and fielded some questions. After indulging a few reporters, he headed for the curb and got into his car. He drove away quietly through the crowd. A few miles down the road, he turned south and headed toward the coast.

Cruising south down Pacific Coast Highway, he lit a cigar and cranked up the tunes. The black Mercedes 500 SL was a smooth drive.

Top down, wind in his hair and music blasting; it was the perfect way to ride out the high. Blake figured that he'd make it to Dana Point before turning back. He was good today. No, he was downright brilliant!

These West Coast yuppie lawyers were no match for his superior Southern intellect. He was sharp. Sharp as the blade he had used this morning to remove the shadow from his face before coming to court. The razor was beautiful, an antique that had been handed down through the family for several generations. It was a work of art, six glorious inches of shiny polished steel that flowed gracefully from an ivory handle. It had once belonged to his great grandfather, then his father, and then it had been passed down to him. Like his father before him, Blake could handle the old straight edge with the precision of a surgeon. He controlled a courtroom with the same finesse.

In the world of judges and juries, he was a dangerous man. His clients were his children, and he protected them, like a lioness protects her young. He attacked each case with a vengeance. All day, every day, he would read and write. The research never ended. He did his homework, and it always paid off. He wasn't perfect, but his ability to win cases was as close to perfection as anyone would ever get. The courtroom was his home. His wife, the kid, the house in Laguna Beach; were all just an afterthought. Somehow, they had taken a back seat to his practice the past few years. The law had become his mistress. He was home every night, but at strange hours and seldom for meals. His wife Katie was forced to spend many nights without him.

Financially, he was a great provider, but as a husband and a father he was always one step behind. His daughter hardly knew him, and Katie seemed distant as well. He wasn't concerned about her. In his eyes, she didn't have it all that bad. She had her friends and her country club. She had a great house and a fancy little sports car. She even had a private massage therapist who came to the house. Blake really liked the guy, mostly because he kept Katie from getting too stressed out. He liked him so much in fact, that after the end of each case, he usually scheduled an appointment for himself. Grey had been coming to the house at least once a week for the last year. He helped keep Katie happy, and that on its own was a big responsibility. Blake made sure that he was well paid. Katie could be a nuisance.

* * * * *

The road was his friend. As he approached Dana Point, Blake decided to swing by Walter's place. Walter Greenberg had been Blake's boss for the last seven years. He'd bought a new house, and had been living down here near the Point, for the past six months. His place was about a mile ahead, just off the highway, on the beach side of the street. Walter at fifty-eight, was fifteen years his senior, but the years had been kind. He was six-foot two, 185 lbs, dark hair with gray highlights and a great tan. He had deep blue eyes and a strong jaw. Walter was the senior partner at Greenberg, Weisman, and Davis. Over the past few years, they had offered Blake a partnership on several occasions, but he always turned them down. He told them in his own polite way, that he didn't want to ever have to answer to anyone, or play by anyone else's rules. Blake liked Walter. He had known him for almost twenty years. He had learned a lot from him. Over time, Blake had grown to respect him both as a partner and a friend. Walter was even the honorary "godfather" to his daughter Christine. Walter was a kind and generous man, and in the past, Blake had counted on him for advice and support.

Over the last year however, something had slowly torn them apart. His old friend was getting under his skin and he just couldn't stomach him anymore. As he turned the corner in front of Walter's house, he was reminded why. Parked in the driveway was a little red Porsche. It was Katie's little red Porsche. Funny, she had told him she was playing golf with the girls today. Blake wasn't surprised. He'd suspected something was up, long before he actually discovered the truth. Knowing about it was a comfort, but it still pissed him off. If today was the first time he'd seen the car there, he probably would have blown a gasket.

Sadly, this was not the case. He estimated that Walter had been slipping his wife the old kosher salami for about the last six months. It probably started right after the last company Christmas party. Blame it on the champagne.

Katie was a beautiful woman, and back then, he had really been neglecting her. Still, that was no excuse. Since Christmas, things between he and Walter had started to go downhill. It was around that time he and Katie started to grow further apart. In the beginning he blamed himself, too many cases and too many long hours burning the midnight oil. Then one day, something happened. It caused him to focus the blame and his anger at her. He had seen a woman flirting with every man in the bar. She even tried to hit on him. She reminded him of Katie. All Blake could picture was his wife doing the same thing, so he hired a detective and had Katie followed. When the guy produced pictures of her and Walter, the sparks began to fly. Ever since then, when he looked at Katie, all he could see was a whore. He had done well to keep his feelings to himself for this long. She and Walter didn't have a clue that he knew and he liked it that way.

"Let them play their little games," he thought. *"And I' ll play mine!"*

Blake sat for a minute, looking at her car, trying to remember something good about her. He couldn't. Her betrayal had been festering away inside of him for too long. He had worked too hard to let her infidelity destroy him. After a short while, he found a way to channel his anger. It gave him back his dignity and his sense of control. He could get his revenge. He was angry. Katie had once again spoiled another celebration. Then he remembered something. Tomorrow was the start of the 4th of July weekend. It was a perfect reason to party. He didn't know what Katie had planned but it probably didn't involve him. He decided he needed a drink, but he didn't feel like drinking alone. Excited by the whole idea, he turned his car around and headed back to the highway.

* * * * *

Her car just died. One minute she was sailing along down the road, and the next minute, she could do nothing but watch the steam come pouring out from underneath the hood.

"*Oh shit! Not now,*" was her first thought.

She was forced to pull over, leaving herself in a rather precarious position. She found herself stranded, broken down on a strip of highway between Laguna Beach and Corona Del Mar where the beach front had not yet been developed. There was nothing but dirt and fields on either side of the freeway. Her cell phone kept saying "No Service", so all she could do was sit and wait for help. The day had already gone to hell-in-a hand-basket earlier, so this little mishap was just another inconvenience.

She had just broken up with her boyfriend at school in San Diego. It had been messy. She was heading back up to Santa Barbara to visit her parents. She told them she would come home for the weekend and the fireworks show. At the last minute, she decided to leave a day early. Her parents were out of town and wouldn't even be home, or expecting her until the following evening. Lonely and depressed, she needed the comfort of home. Although the car wouldn't start, the lights were still on so she knew she still had a radio. She put on some music and tried to relax.

When the song ended, the DJ went to a newsbreak. He was giving an update on a local news story. The report gave her the creeps. Now, sitting on the trunk of her car, she watched and waited, hoping that someone would notice her predicament, and come to her rescue. All she really needed was a phone that worked. The sun was almost down, and she didn't want to risk being alone in the dark. She was getting worried. The key pad kept flashing, "No Service". Tired and burned out, all she could do was patient and wait.

Blake caught sight of the red convertible immediately. As he came over the top of the hill, he slowed to take a look. He saw smoke coming from the car, but it was the babe leaning up against the trunk that really got his attention. She was hot, really hot, and the closer he got to her, the better she looked. There was long dark hair; a short skirt, and legs a mile long. She was young, beautiful, and looked to be somewhere in her early twenties. She was the perfect damsel in distress. This was too easy. He had to have her, he had to think fast. In a few seconds he'd be past her.

Lust took over. He turned down the music as his foot went for the brake pedal. The car responded perfectly, sliding slowly in behind her, and came to a stop. After checking her out for a minute or two, he was sure of one thing; a man could easily find his way to heaven, if he followed those legs all the way up to where they began under her skirt.

Just the thought of her made his cigar taste bad. He tossed it out onto the highway. This was going to be fun. Blake knew what he wanted, so he put on his best smile, grabbed his coat, and got out of his car.

* * * * *

She smiled as the headlights pulled up behind her. She was so excited to see someone that the thought of danger never entered her mind. She was just so thankful to be getting some help. A few cars had passed earlier, but everyone had been in too much of a hurry to care. Now, finally, help had arrived. At first, she wasn't the least bit scared. Then suddenly, reality kicked in. She started thinking of what she had heard on the radio. The glare from the headlights prevented her from seeing who was inside the car.

The shiny, black mass just sat there, its lights staring up at her like two big eyes. For a few long minutes, she froze, glued to the side of her car, waiting to see what would happen next. From where she was standing, she left herself at a big disadvantage. She was caught, like a "deer in the headlights", out in the open, and completely vulnerable. She glanced down again at the phone in her hand. It was still flashing "No Service".

When she glanced up, the driver's door of the black car was opening and someone was getting out. Fear took over. Every inch of her body started to tingle. It wasn't until she heard a voice say, "Hey Miss, are you ok?" that she was able to breathe again.

"Mind if I step into the light?" Blake asked. "I'd appreciate that." she answered.

As he came into view, her defenses started to back down a little. He didn't look scary at all. He wore a dark gray suit, conservative tie, jacket over one arm, and shoes that were so well polished they almost glowed in the dark. He was tall, slightly over six feet. He took another step closer.

"Anything I can do to help?" he asked.

"Got a phone?" she inquired.

"Sorry, left mine at my office," Blake lied. "Your car looks dead."

"All I really need is a phone," she said.

"Sorry, best I can do is to offer you a lift. My name is Blake."

Now that she knew his name, he had nothing to lose. He took a chance and slowly approached her.

The closer he got, the more relaxed she became. She could see him clearly now, and it didn't look like he posed much of a threat at all. His actual appearance was very classy and distinguished. He was probably in his late forties, early fifties. The clothes he was wearing were finely tailored and very expensive. When he offered her his hand to say hello, she laughed and even blushed a little. In her mind she was thinking he was one of those sexy, distinguished older men her girlfriends at college were always joking about.

"I'm Blake," he introduced himself again. "At your service," he said with a smile.

"Hi, I'm Casey, thanks for stopping. I was beginning to think I wasn't going to be getting out of here anytime soon."

"The pleasure is mine, I can assure you," Blake responded. "As I indicated previously, I would be more than happy to give you a lift. I'll take you into Corona Del Mar if you wish."

He almost saw a smile. She had started to give him one, but caught herself in the nick of time. She decided that it might not be smart to appear so desperate.

"I'm not too sure about taking a ride from a stranger," she said.

Blake laughed. "Under normal circumstances, I would tend to agree with you Miss, but I'm also not accustomed to leaving a woman stranded and alone in the dark. The city is only a few minutes up the road, and I'm heading that way anyway. Or, if you prefer, I could drive alone into the city and send back help. That however, might take awhile and I would hate to think of you sitting here alone any longer than necessary."

"You've got a point," Casey agreed.

"Well then, I think I've said enough," Blake chuckled. "My offer still stands, but the choice is yours, of course. I'll wait for you if you'd like." Enough said, Blake turned and headed back to his car.

She stood for a moment, trying to decide what to do. If she turned him down, she ran the risk of being stuck out there for God knows how long. It was getting late and colder by the minute. At this point, any way out of there would be a blessing. This guy Blake looked harmless enough, and they would only be traveling a few miles together. She was tired and cold and it didn't take her long to convince herself it was ok. She grabbed her duffel bag off the front seat and casually walked toward his car. When she got to the passenger door, she could see him sitting behind the wheel. He was smoking a cigar and listening to classical music. When she waved at him, he nodded, inviting her to get in.

"Just throw that bag behind the seat and we'll get you out of here," Blake said with a smile.

She threw the bag in the back, and then got in. Her skirt hiked way up as she got in, but he hardly seemed to notice.

Casey thought to herself, *"Maybe this guy is all right after all."*

Blake saw her look up at him but did not respond. No point in tipping his hand. He started the car and pulled onto the highway. The sign ahead read Corona Del Mar- Newport Beach 4 miles. There was just enough time for a friendly hello. She was smart for a kid. He could tell by the way she spoke. No little girl here. This was a young woman with brains and ambition. Of course her great ass, long legs and pretty smile didn't hurt any. She wasn't some college bimbo. She had class, and beauty that needed to be displayed. Blake reminded himself of this as they drove into town.

When they pulled up to the valet at the Five Crowns Restaurant, he laughed and before she could ask, offered an explanation.

"I've been in court all day and haven't eaten since this morning. I was hoping I could talk you into joining me for dinner. I hate to eat alone."

Casey looked puzzled. "Who was this guy anyway?" she thought.

Blake continued, "If you're not comfortable with the idea, the valet can take you to a phone instead. Once again the choice is yours."

Before she could answer, he was out of the car and heading inside the door leaving her at capable hands of the valet. Casey took a moment. She was tired and hungry. It was decision time. He seemed like a nice guy and after all this was a public place. What harm could it do? She could probably get the car towed in, but it would be difficult trying to get it fixed before morning. She had already conceded that finding a hotel for the night was a good idea. She could deal with the car later.

It might not be any easier to find a repair shop in the morning given it was a holiday weekend, but at least it would be daylight. Also, she had to eat. The day had already been such a disaster, why not try to salvage something good out of it. Blake had offered her a meal, so what did she have to lose? Besides, this place looked incredible. Why not give it a try? Her brain gave her the green light. She motioned to the valet.

The young man came over and opened her door.

"Do I look all right for this place?" she asked.

"Yes ma'am," he answered, "you look very nice." His emphasis was on the very. His comment made her blush.

"Thank you," she said, and gave him a wink. She could handle being treated like lady for a few hours. It was rather refreshing. She got out of the car, straightened her skirt, and followed the doorman up the stairs.

* * * * *

Dinner was unbelievable. Casey could not remember a time when she had ever eaten in a place this nice. Everything was perfect. The wine, the seafood, even dessert had been a performance of sorts. A flaming tray of something had been brought to the table simply for her amusement. He even talked her into having an after dinner brandy.

As she sipped the warm liquor from a crystal glass, she felt totally at ease. She forgot the trials and hardships of the past few weeks. The classes she hated, the come-on from one of her professors, her break up with Mike, and now the car, were all slowly fading into the past. Well, maybe not the car. She knew that she'd have to handle that one in the morning. But for now she was being treated like royalty!

The waiter told Blake he had a call. He apologized, excused himself, saying it was his office and he'd better check in. While he was gone she looked around at the restaurant; at the starched white linen, the roaring fire, the beautiful decor.

"I could get used to this," she decided.

He returned shortly and explained that after their brandies, he would have to call her a cab. He was needed back at his office. Blake thanked her for joining him for dinner. He told her that he thought she was both delightful and charming. She was flattered. He really enjoyed her company. She told him that his kindness made her forget all of her troubles for awhile, and for that she would be eternally grateful.

They sat for a little longer, letting the brandy warm their spirits. When they were finished, Blake motioned for the maitre d' and asked him if he would be kind enough to call a cab for the lady. Blake walked her down to the valet station. They chatted for a few minutes until the cab arrived. Casey thanked him again for his help and his kindness, got up on tip-toe, kissed him on the cheek, and got into the cab. He slipped the driver a twenty. It was there they said goodbye.

Blake was sad to see her go. She reminded him of a time when he had been happy with Katie, back when their love was new. He hoped Casey would never turn into what Katie had become. He knew better. He knew he would see Casey again.

During dinner, they had discussed some possible hotels where she could spend the night. He was confident that he had sold her on one in particular. He felt he had been rather persuasive. It was on the beach, and he told her that from any room you could watch the sunrise. You could even walk down to the beach. When she said it was way out of her budget, he handed her three one hundred dollar bills and told her to enjoy herself. After a day like today, she had earned it. She tried to refuse the money but he had insisted. She asked for his card so she could return the money at a later date.

Knowing that he'd never accept it anyway, he'd respected her wishes, and gave her one. She tucked it away in a safe place, next to one of her delicate breasts. Blake knew he would have to get it back. He waved again as the cab turned the corner, and he saw a hand wave back. She was gone, and for a moment, he felt alone again. Then that Cheshire smile returned to his face. He was sure he knew where she was going, and that he'd be able to find her later. It was going to be a long night. He needed another drink. Thoughts of those long, glorious, legs filled his mind as he headed back to the bar. It would soon be time for the 'Cat' to feast again.

* * * * *

The hotel was everything he had said it would be. The view of the ocean was spectacular. The room the night clerk gave her was breathtaking. Everything in the room was decorated in Victorian white, with polished brass accents. Casey walked across the room and opened the French doors that led to the patio. As she did, the smell of the sea air came rushing in, carried by a light breeze. It filled the room with the lightly salted perfume of the many flowers that filled the outside planters. This place was like a dream. Stepping back into the room, she acquainted herself with her new surroundings. The bed was fantastic, a four poster king with an elevated mattress and a lace canopy overhead. There was an ice bucket with champagne on the patio, and the gas fireplace was on. There was even a Jacuzzi tub next to the bedroom. Everything was perfect. For a quiet little inn, this place could not be better.

The beach was nearly close enough to reach out and touch. There were a few stairs leading down to the sand from the patio. She decided that a walk on the beach would be nice, but it would have to wait until later. Right now all she wanted was a hot bath. She turned on the Jacuzzi and opened the champagne. There were fresh strawberries in a bowl next to the bucket, so she popped one into her mouth, and threw another in her glass. While she waited for the tub to fill up, she stood on the patio and watched the waves roll against the shore. What began as one of the worst day of her life, suddenly evolved into one the best times she had ever had. It was ironic. If it wasn't for the kindness of a total stranger, she would probably still be out there on the highway, sitting on the trunk of her car. It was as if her world had suddenly been put on hold, and temporarily replaced with fantasy. She pinched herself, making sure it wasn't a dream.

The champagne tickled her throat as it went down. She finished her glass and headed inside to check on the spa. It was almost ready. Using the dimmer switch on the wall, she turned the lights down low, and carefully peeled off her clothes. The cool air blowing in off the patio gave her goose bumps and excited her flesh. Her naked shadow played on the wall as she slid down slowly into the bubbles.

Contact with the warm water instantly excited her even further, arousing her breasts, and sending shivers up and down her spine. She missed him. He was probably twice her age, but she missed him. She knew it was wrong. Maybe it was the booze. Maybe it was just the heat starting to build in her special place. As the bubbles worked their magic, Casey dove deeper into her champagne.

It was almost midnight when Blake called the bartender over to close out his tab. She'd been gone for hours and he still couldn't get her out of his head. She was so sweet, so innocent, and so very sexy. He had to have her. Funny thing was, he knew right where to look. He figured that a few hundred dollar bills as an investment were a drop in the bucket, when you compared it to the value of what she could do for him. During dinner, he'd found out everything he needed to know about her, and he was not disappointed. Spending time with her was like hanging out with a young Katie.

Katie, the one he had loved so dearly until six months ago, when her evil side had shown through. Katie: the one true love of his life and mother of his child. Not the law, not the clients, just Katie: sweet, sexy, lovable Katie, the woman that shared his bed. That sleazy whore! He had given her everything, and this was how she repaid him!

He was gone for awhile. He was back now. Lost in his world of anger and betrayal, Blake couldn't think straight. He had to get back on track. So he let it go. Deep breath, make that two or three deep breaths. He allowed the anger to go. He focused his mind back on Casey. That smile, those legs. He was hungry for more. If his plan worked, she was just a mile or two down the road, in that little inn, drinking her ass off, and thinking about him. It was almost too much for him to handle. For a moment, he had second thoughts, but then he gave in to the 'Cat'.

* * * * *

The buzz was great. The heat of the Jacuzzi and all that booze had started to catch up with her. If she didn't get out of the tub right now, she never would. This was fun. A lot of fun, but if she didn't get some fresh air soon, she'd pass out and probably drown. Carefully, she climbed out of the spa and put on a robe that was hanging on the bathroom door. She needed some air. It was time for that walk on the beach. It would help clear her head, and keep her from getting sick. She grabbed her phone and the card he'd stuck in her pocket. Maybe she'd make a call.

She stumbled a little on her way to the patio, trying to tie her robe. She walked across the boardwalk and down the stairs. Maybe the beach wasn't such a good idea. She didn't want to end up passing out on the beach somewhere. She sat on the step and let her toes wiggle around in the sand. Ok, now she was ready. She dug her hands into the pockets of the robe and headed out.

There were about ten yards of sand before the wave lines started. When she got to the wet sand, she reminded herself to look back. She wanted to be sure she could find this place again before she wandered off into the darkness. She had to get her bearings. There was a rock formation sticking out into the waves about a couple of hundred yards south of her. That would be a good place to go. She could get there rather quickly, and still make it back ok. Besides if she got tired, she could sit and rest. Her heavy cotton bathrobe was just long enough to cover most of her legs, so she figured she'd be warm enough. She took one more look at the hotel and then started down the beach.

It was much easier for her to walk on the wet sand. It didn't throw her off balance nearly as much as walking in the dry section that ran between the water's edge and the boardwalk. Even the water coming up over her feet felt good. The water was just cold enough to keep her alert. She'd only been walking about ten minutes when she realized that the rocks were further away than she originally thought.

"Oh well, too late now," Casey laughed. "I've come this far," so she kept going.

The smell of the ocean was exhilarating. The breeze had picked up a little, but wasn't really that cold. Her robe was doing a fine job keeping her warm.

She only passed two people before getting to the rocks; a young guy who had been night surfing and his girlfriend. They were packing it in for the night when she passed them. They looked at her kind of funny, but she figured that to them, she probably looked pretty strange, walking down the beach in just a robe. The wind had picked up a little during the last few minutes.

When she arrived at the rocks, her first instinct was to get out of the wind. She climbed up a few yards and found a place to sit. Facing south kept most of the wind at her back. The wind had whipped the waves with such force they were breaking higher than usual against the rocks. It would be hard for her to stay dry. She decided not to stay any longer than it took for her to take a short rest.

It was going to be a long walk home. Casey found herself wishing that she had never left the hotel. She waited a short while, before deciding that it was time to try to make her way back to the hotel. As she came out of the shadows, she saw a dark figure approaching the rocks from about one hundred feet away. Her vision wasn't the best at the moment, so she decided not to take any chances. It was dark where she was sitting, so she climbed down to the beach where there was more light. The dark figure drew closer. Suddenly, she became terribly frightened.

"Casey, is that you?" the voice was familiar.

It sounded like Blake. What the hell was he doing out here?

As they got closer, she realized that it was him. She felt relieved. He looked different somehow. He had on a long black coat, and looked very glamorous.

"You ok?" he asked. "What are you doing out here?"

"Yeah I'm fine, just a little cold and a little drunk," she giggled. "How'd you find me anyway?"

"I thought you might have come down here to the inn after our conversation at dinner. I wanted to make sure you arrived safely. If you want to talk, let's get out of this wind," Blake suggested.

"All right, follow me," she said, as she started to climb back up.

She sat for a minute in the shelter of the rocks. Sitting on what looked like a shelf that protruded out a few feet, she waited for Blake to come the rest of the way up. In front of her, was a drop off of about thirty feet that cascaded down to the darkness until it blended into the water below. At the bottom there was a small inlet carved into the rocks. It was only about fifteen feet across, but looked very deep. The sea would crash in, pounding its way into the cavern, and then pull itself out with the tide. The waves were powerful tonight: beautiful, but ominous. The sea spray had gotten stronger as the tide was coming in. She was out of the wind, but starting to get wet.

He was sure taking his sweet time getting up here. If he wasn't here soon, she'd go down and tell him to forget it. They would need to go back. She was tired now and very cold. The spray had almost completely soaked through her robe. She was starting to feel the cold wetness against her bare skin. Her body longed for the heat of the Jacuzzi. Just thinking about it, she started to become aroused again. She smiled. This time he was here or at least on his way up. Here on the rocks would be both romantic and impulsive. What could possibly be more erotic? She untied her robe.

When Blake came over the top of the last rock, he thought his eyes were playing tricks on him. Standing in front of him, with the moonlight at her back, was Katie, or what he thought was Katie. For a second, Casey was a dead ringer for her. Casey's long dark hair was blowing in the wind, and the reflections of water and light shimmered on her naked body. He was fascinated by her silhouette in the moonlight. He imagined her breasts were round and firm. Her eyes were dark and lustful. Her body was wet and ready. He couldn't speak a word. As he approached her, she turned away, almost inviting him to take her. He moved in slowly from behind and carefully placed his arms around her. He kissed her neck. Her body shuddered. With his right hand, he reached up and took a breast gently into his hand. At the same time, his left hand found its way into the pocket of his coat. Blake continued to kiss her neck and caress her now erect nipple. Lost in the moment, her mind was somewhere else. When his right hand came up searching for her other breast, it didn't stop there. When it finally came to rest, all she could feel was the warm, wet sensation, of liquid running down her chest. The razor had opened her neck from ear to ear. She didn't even have time to scream.

She would never see his face again. He pushed her body over the side, and she fell quietly into the darkness. He heard the sound of bones breaking as she hit the floor of the crevice. The sandy bottom did little to break her fall, as the water was running out of the inlet. The next wave crashed over the top of her, slamming her mutilated body against the rocks. When he looked down again, she had disappeared in a mass of foam and water as the tide drew her body out to sea.

In his mind, he wondered what it would have been like to experience the fall through Katie's eyes, as her body crashed into the rocks below. Blake looked down. All that remained of Casey was the drowned bathrobe, lying empty on the rocks. Carefully, he picked it up, and threw it over the edge. As he did, a small piece of paper landed, wet and crumbled at his feet. He bent down to pick it up. To his relief, it was the business card he had given her earlier. He tore it up, and tossed the pieces into the wind.

Blake was reminded of a quote by Christopher Columbus:

"And the sea will grant each man new hope, as sleep brings dreams of home" he whispered. Then he turned and started to climb back down to the beach. It was a long walk back to the car.

CHAPTER 6

When Blake left the beach, he stopped by Walter's place again. On the way back to his car, he decided that he needed to know where Katie was, in case he needed an alibi. At this point, he felt pretty safe. Casey left the restaurant three hours before he did. There were lots of people around when she got into her cab. She left alone. He went back inside and stayed for awhile. The bartender and his Visa bill were proof of that. When their dinner ended, they went their separate ways. If anyone asked, he was either sitting at the bar when the girl was killed, or at home in bed next to his wife.

His alibi continued to come together. If Katie were home, she'd be asleep by now and he could sneak in. She always went to bed early. He'd accidentally wake her and say hi to establish a time frame that worked to his advantage, and go to bed. She'd never know for sure exactly when he got home. He would be able to prove where he was at the time of the killing.

Explaining having dinner with Casey was easy. He was having dinner with a client. That would give them a reason for arriving together at the restaurant. If Katie was home, that would be an added bonus. As he turned his car onto Walter's street, his prayers were, answered. Walter's driveway was empty. He gave his wife credit. The whore still had enough class not to spend the night.

With a sigh of relief, Blake turned the car around and headed home. Now all he had to do was get home safely. He figured sooner or later, someone might ask a few questions. He scolded himself. Taking Casey to dinner was not one of his better ideas. Still, he managed to work it out. He reminded himself to be more careful next time. He was too smart to be that stupid. Luckily, the cops were even worse. He had to laugh. He'd been doing this for months, and all of their efforts to stop him were futile. He left no trail to follow. He wasn't even worried anymore. His ass was covered.

In the beginning, he had been a little anxious after someone discovered the body of his first victim. She was found floating in Irvine Lake way back at the end of January. He remembered thinking at the time, how he found the young lady quite entertaining. Her only crime was that she reminded him of Katie. That was her downfall. He had to kill her. He was surprised how easy it had been to get away with it. After killing two more girls in the last three months with no repercussions, his confidence level had grown tenfold. The school teacher was missed but the hooker was long forgotten. It was then Blake decided he was invincible.

When he got home, everything was just as he hoped. He woke Katie up by turning on the bathroom light. He added to it by then sitting on the bed. She was half asleep. "You coming to bed?" she asked.

"Yeah honey, sorry I'm late, dinner with a client," he answered, keeping up with his original plan.

"What time is it anyway?" she asked.

"Midnight," he replied. "Sorry I woke you up. Go back to sleep."

Katie rolled over and said, "Good night then," and went back to sleep.

Blake turned off the lights. As he climbed into bed, a glow of green neon stared at him from the nightstand. The clock read two-thirty a.m. The time was set. The valet ticket would say that he'd left the bar around eleven thirty and his house was only twenty minutes away. Katie would tell anyone who asked that he was home in bed at midnight. He'd bought himself two and a half hours. Content and happy, Blake slid between the sheets, pulled up the covers, and closed his eyes. Tomorrow was another day. It was the 4th of July. This meant the usual hotdogs, fireworks, and block parties. Too bad Casey would have to miss it. Blake decided that he could rest now. He congratulated himself on another victory. It had been an exciting day.

* * * * *

When the first ray of sunshine came through the bedroom window, Blake noticed that nothing had changed. In his dream, the police had discovered his alter ego. They had come in the middle of the night and violently dragged him from his bed. They instantly condemned him, and decided that he was to be put to death in the same manner in which he used to kill his victims. The blade in this case however, bore a greater resemblance to a giant guillotine, than it did his straight razor. The cops had turned his execution into a media event. He woke up just as the blade was making its descent.

Dripping in sweat, Blake climbed out of bed and headed for the shower. He'd never had a dream like this before. It took him completely by surprise. On the way to the bathroom, he passed his closet. He peeked back at the bed to see if Katie was still sleeping. She was facing the other direction. Carefully, he fished his razor out of the left front pocket of his coat so he could take it with him into the shower. He needed a shave. The cold steel felt good in his hand. It reminded him of the rush that he felt when he used the instrument on Casey. Once he was safely in the shower, he opened his friend.

When he held the open blade under the shower stream, the water ran red. It was careless of him not to have cleaned it properly last night, but he had been anxious to get home. Blake watched carefully as the last remnants of Casey ran down the drain. As he stared at the red water, his mind wandered back to the beach. He could see Casey's naked body. He could feel her breath on his face. His adrenaline level began to rise. Then he heard a voice.

"Blake, Blake? You ok in there, dear?" It was Katie.

Startled back into reality, Blake dropped the razor. He bent down to pick it up and responded, "Just shaving Katie, I'll be right out. What are we doing today anyway?" he asked.

"I told Mom we would bring Christine down for a barbeque and to see the fireworks," Katie answered. "She said that we can spend the night down there too if we want. It's up to you."

Blake checked his razor thoroughly to make certain it was spotlessly clean. Then he checked the rest of the shower for any signs of blood. Only when he was sure that everything was ok, did he step out and grab a towel.

To his surprise, Katie was staring at him. He was a little worried at first, but then she smiled.

"I'd almost forgotten how cute you look when you're naked," she said.

Blake actually blushed. "So when do you want to leave for San Diego?" he asked. "We can have lunch on the way down if you want. Go downstairs and tell Christine to get ready, ok?" Katie left him where he stood. She always listened to him.

His first instinct was to hide the blade under his towel. After all, it was the murder weapon. The anxiety subsided as Katie left and he came to his senses. He had shaved with this same razor every day for the past ten years. Katie had seen it a million times, so why would it look out of place? Blake felt strange. He'd never been this antsy before. He could feel the gears turning in his head.

"Was there blood in the pocket of his coat?" he thought. Probably not, but why take a chance? He wrapped the towel around himself and walked to the closet to look. When he opened the pocket flap, he was relieved. Everything seemed to be in order, everything except his nerves. Still, first thing Monday morning, the coat was headed for the dry cleaners.

Satisfied, Blake got dressed and went downstairs. Parties at Katie's parents' house were always entertaining. Her folks were good people. Their idea about spending the night down there made sense too. After the fireworks show it would be late. At that hour there would be too many drunks and crazies out on the road. If they waited until Saturday morning, it would be a safer drive home. The decision was made. Within the hour, the girls were packed and ready to go. The Kendall family loaded up their car, and headed south to Grandma's house.

It wasn't until later that night, long after the fireworks had ended, that Blake caught himself thinking about Casey again. Sitting by the pool at his in-laws', he sat quietly reminiscing, with a brandy in hand, staring up at the darkness. Casey would have liked the fireworks, he thought. She would have liked the colors.

* * * * *

It was three a.m., the parties were over, but Grey was still wide awake. The midnight hour had come and gone without him even giving it a thought. Too many things were floating around in his head. It had been quite a day. He turned off the TV at one after the late movie, "Breakfast at Tiffany's", ended. There was something about an old Audrey Hepburn film that just made a person feel better.

Now, sitting on the back patio, Grey sipped at a glass of dark cabernet. In a few hours, the sun would come up, and a new day would begin. Each sunrise was different for him now. Ever since the accident, he seemed to appreciate each one a little more. He wasn't surprised that he couldn't find sleep. There was too much to think about.

After they returned from the fireworks show, Rachel put Dylan to bed. Grey had looked in on him just after midnight, and he was sleeping quietly in his crib. Grey was jealous. He would trade anything for one night of peaceful, uninterrupted sleep. Rachel had dosed off around eleven thirty. The day had worn her out as well. A quiet calm had taken over the house. The silence was as eerie to him as it was soothing.

In a strange way, it added another dimension to the unusual things that were going on around him. The sounds of night always seemed to put things in their proper perspective. If you listened close enough, you could almost hear the earth breathe. A long time ago, Alex had taught him how to really listen. More importantly, she had taken the time to show him what to listen for. Nature was always trying to tell you something. If you could understand any of what it was trying to say, you would always be one step ahead.

Grey sat alone, listening to the darkness, and watching the night sky. It brought him some peace. He thought about his new gift. Once again, he found himself wondering what had really happened to him. What actually caused some part of his brain to click on, enabling him to see these things? The answer to that of course was simple. Everything led back to the accident. But what strange force of nature was at work here? To find the answer, he and Alex would have to work together. They would have to move slowly, and take it one step at a time in order to get control of this thing. First, they would have to understand what it was, and what his abilities and limitations were. That might take some time, and probably a lot of patience.

At the moment, time wasn't a problem, however neither of them was known for their ability to sit and wait for things to happen. They were both very impulsive people. She was the type who would grab the bull by the horns and light the tail on fire. He wasn't far behind. Although this attitude always made for a good time, sometimes joking about it just wasn't practical. Starting today, they would need to look for answers.

There was a lot for them to talk about. He would tell Alex everything. Each experience would have to be described in complete detail. He could leave nothing out. Every little aspect might have significance. So far, it would be easy. He only had to recall the incidents with Lisa and Tony to remember. He knew that she would think he was playing around at first, but whom else could he trust? They could talk about her involvement later. All he needed was time. An hour perhaps if he played it right. It was all he would need to bring her up to speed. Then maybe they could figure out a plan.

The question now was, where and how would he be able to get an hour alone? Getting out of the house was not going to be easy. Rachel would worry if he was gone for more than a short time. He really wasn't up to driving very far either. The doctors had told him to take it easy. They obviously had no clue who they were dealing with. Oh well, why beat himself up over it. He still had a few more hours until dawn. If he just let it go for awhile, an idea was bound to present itself. Grey finished his wine and went inside.

* * * * *

It turned out to be Rachel who gave him the idea. When she discovered he wasn't in bed, she came looking for him. She found him in the family room, about seven-thirty a.m. reading the morning paper. The top story on the front page had big, bold letters reading "RIPPER STRIKES AGAIN!" There was an article about last night's discovery at the beach, with a recent picture of the slain girl. Police said they were checking out a few leads, but that no real clues or motive had been found yet. They were speculating that whoever was doing these killings was no amateur. The police likened him to the old English criminal, "Jack the Ripper." This individual had murdered four young women in the Orange County area in the past six months.

To Grey, it was obvious that the killer was an educated person. Dumping the bodies in water was a well thought out idea. It was more difficult to retrieve forensic evidence from a body that had been in water. Water tended to dissolve or wash away certain kinds of trace evidence, such as fingerprints or body fluids. The police were recommending that, until further notice, young women take extra precautions. Never be out alone at night. Never trust anyone who looks the least bit suspicious, and always be on guard. Sadly enough they also reported that most serial killers appear as normal, everyday people. That's what makes them so hard to catch.

From experience, Grey understood this first hand. People, regardless of their normal appearance, could be quite different underneath. Every now and then, he'd run across someone like that at the office. They always made him feel uneasy. It was uncomfortable to touch them. He wondered what it would be like to touch the person who was responsible for all of this violence. The entire situation was very disturbing. He looked concerned. Rachel had been standing there watching him for a few minutes when he finally looked up.

"Morning, honey, get any sleep?" he asked.

"Yeah, believe it or not, I actually did," she responded. "What are you doing out here so early?" she asked.

"I don't know, couldn't sleep," he answered. Grey set the paper down. "Did you check on Dylan?" he asked.

"Yeah, he's fine, but we're almost out of everything," she said as she opened the refrigerator looking back at him with empty eyes. "Would you mind going to the store?" she asked.

Such a simple question, but it was like lightning had struck. The light bulb turned on in his head! Rachel was brilliant and she didn't even know it! Worst part was, he couldn't even tell her.

"Sure honey, I don't mind," he responded quickly. "I'm tired of feeling so useless around here, anyway. What do we need? Make me a list." His brain was working overtime. It was in high gear.

"I can make you a list, "she said, "but you might be there awhile, are you sure?"

"I don't mind," Grey said. "I could use some fresh air anyway." Things were suddenly coming together.

Rachel had done it. Grocery shopping for her and Dylan would take him an hour or so. It was perfect. He could be gone without raising suspicion. He would be off doing something nice for her, and he could talk to Alex at the same time. She'd just solved his problem. She had handed him the perfect solution. It was too bad he could never tell her what a great help she had been.

"Let me clean up a little and I'm out of here," Grey said.

He got up and headed for the shower. On the way there, he reminded himself to find his cell phone. He hadn't seen it since the accident. He'd have to ask Rachel. Alex was now only a phone call away. In the shower, he decided to take Dylan with him. He was sure Rachel could use the time alone to get herself together. Besides having Dylan with him would only make things more interesting with Alex. She would be totally blown away by the little guy. It would make things fun. As a smile came to his face, Grey laughed. Very soon now, the games would begin.

* * * * *

He made a clean getaway. Rachel even thanked him for offering to take Dylan with him. They were on their way. Grey grabbed the cell phone. The phone rang twice before someone answered.

"Good morning, Hanford Inn. This is David. How may I direct your call?" the voice on the phone inquired.

"Room 323 please," Grey responded. The phone clicked over and then started to ring again. On the third ring, she answered. Grey spoke.

"Morning Alex, I don't have a lot of time so bare with me, ok? I'm in my car headed for the Ralph's grocery store down the street. It's about a half mile east of you. Go out of the hotel parking lot to Canyon Road and turn left. I'll be there for about an hour. Just find me."

Grey paused and waited for a response.

"No problem, see you in a few," she replied. Then the phone went dead.

Rachel had always teased him about being a lousy shopper. He would always run in and run out for just a few things. This time would be different. The list she'd given him would take awhile. This shopping trip was going to be fun. Rachel was going to be very surprised. In the back seat, Dylan was laughing. As they pulled into the parking lot, Grey could swear that that Dylan knew what was happening or could read his mind. Alex was at it again. Maybe she was up to something. There was only one way to find out. Grey and Dylan went inside.

* * * * *

The feeling of being able to get 'back out on his own' again was a welcome relief. Grey was so wrapped up in his train of thought, that he hardly noticed when a voice behind him said,

"If you squeeze them like you would a breast, you'll learn how to find the ripe ones." It took a second for the comment to register in his head. The voice that sounded so strange a moment ago suddenly became music to his ears. Dylan, who was sitting in the shopping cart facing him, was smiling. He was smiling at the person who was standing behind his father. He looked pretty excited. Grey turned to face his friend.

It was like time stood still. Alex was beautiful. She shined with the same soft face that he remembered from long ago. Her eyes were as big and bright as the last time he'd seen her. The years had not changed her one bit. In the hospital, her face and her demeanor had been more serious. She had looked tired and troubled. Now, standing here in front of him she was the answer to a prayer. For a moment, time stood still. They just stood there, staring at each other. Alex spoke first.

"You going to buy those things, or are you just enjoying a free squeeze?" she teased.

She looked so serious. He looked at her, confused. She smiled. It made both of them break up into a hardy laugh. Dylan joined in.

Their meeting was long overdue. Grey leaned over and gave her a hug. It felt good. He had really missed his friend. They chatted as they wandered through the rest of the produce department. Then the conversation began to shift gears. They knew they had to get down to business. Grey had a lot of questions. Alex tried to fill in the blanks. Carefully, she recounted to him all of the events of the past week, including those that lead up to her presence here now: the storm on the lake, her nightmare, her trip out here, and her appearance at the hospital. Grey listened carefully to every word. She explained to him exactly what she had done to bring him out of his deep sleep. It was then she asked him what he remembered.

He told her he could recall every detail of what she was saying, but at the time it had all seemed like a dream. Now he knew better. He knew the truth, and he was grateful. He was grateful to her for giving him back his life, and for having the strength and the courage to risk everything, including herself, in order to bring him out of the darkness. They talked about the hospital and her run in with Rachel. Alex mentioned her concerns. He told her it really wasn't that important. With everything that was going on at the time, they had nothing to worry about. A face in the crowd was nothing, and to Rachel, Alex would have been just another face.

It was at that point, they started to talk about the flashes. He described in detail everything he could remember about his contacts with Lisa and Tony. Alex listened in total amazement as he described each intense moment. Grey noticed that Dylan seemed to be paying very close attention to the conversation. It was as if he were listening to every word. Grey found this a little peculiar. When he finished speaking, he let out a big sigh of relief. He had been carrying this around for days with no one to talk to. It felt so good to let it all go.

Alex said she had heard stories about something like this happening once to someone a long time ago, but had never actually witnessed it for herself. This could end up being a wonderful new thing, or a real pain in the ass. They would probably have to experiment with it for a few days and see what they could come up with. Being close to each other now would really help. Together, they agreed that they would find a way to get a handle on things. Actually, each of them had already given the problem a great deal of thought and had come to the same conclusion. In order to have any chance of figuring this thing out, Alex had to come out in the open. Together, somewhere between the cookies, crackers, and the frozen food aisle, they derived a plan. They prayed it would work.

Alex would return to the hotel and call the Thomas house. Grey would still be out shopping. If she got the machine, she would leave a message for him that she was coming into town for a week or two on business and would like to get together with him and Rachel. If Rachel answered the phone, she would simply give her the same information. It was so simple. Grey reminded her that she would have to make the call from her cell phone, so it would show up as a Florida number on the caller I.D. If she talked to Rachel, she would leave the cell phone number as well so the numbers would match. If they could set it up so that Alex could be around for awhile without arousing suspicion that would give them the time and the freedom to sort this out.

Grey told her he preferred she didn't stay at the hotel much longer, but she assured him that she felt it was the best thing for now. It gave her the privacy she needed to do her thing without an audience, and without explanations. Until they figured out what to do about Grey's problem, things would be more respectable if they maintained a little distance.

They both laughed when they looked down at the shopping cart. Rachel had given him quite a list and he had even added to it. The cart was overflowing with everything from pull-ups to frozen dinners. He bought steaks, fish, chicken and vegetables. Grey looked at Dylan.

"Hope you're hungry little buddy. Who the hell's ever going to eat all this?"

Dylan just smiled. Grey looked at his watch. He'd been gone only forty-five minutes. He and Alex had pretty much covered everything. As he got in the checkout line, he and Dylan said goodbye to Alex. She was headed back to the hotel to make the phone call. Before she left them, she gave Grey a hug, and kissed Dylan on the cheek. She waved goodbye. Grey looked down at his son's face. Dylan was happy. When he looked up again she was gone.

* * * * *

When they got home, Rachel met them in the driveway. When she saw all the grocery bags in the back seat, she was pleasantly surprised.

"Took you two forever, but now I know why," she said.

"Yeah, but we had fun. Didn't we little buddy?" Grey responded as he playfully poked the baby in the tummy. Dylan just laughed.

"You got two calls while you were gone, Grey. Katie Kendall called wanting to know if you would be available Monday for a massage. Her husband wants one too. I told her you'd call."

Grey grabbed some of the bags. "You take Dylan, I'll unload the car." Rachel followed him into the house.

"Oh yeah, I almost forgot, your friend Alex called from Florida. She said she'll be out here on business for a couple of weeks and wanted to know if we could all get together. I told her we'd like that. Her number is on the caller I.D., ok? Isn't she the one you went to school with?"

"Yeah honey, she's a nice lady. You'll like her," Grey answered. "When's she planning on coming?"

"She said very soon. Maybe as soon as the next day or two," Rachel offered. "Call her so we can make plans, ok?"

Grey smiled and headed back out to the car. He'd call when he was finished unloading. Standing in the driveway, he gazed across the field to the hotel. Once again, he knew he was being watched. If she could see him, she'd know that everything had worked perfectly. Within twenty-four hours, she would be entering his world. He had a new life here, a good life, a loving family and a stable environment. He would see to it that she was welcomed with open arms.

It would be interesting to see who would accept her, and who would keep her at a safe distance. It would be fun to watch her around Rachel.

As for Dylan, he didn't even want to think about it. Grey grabbed the rest of the bags and headed into the house.

Tomorrow was Sunday, and he still wanted to see Father Richard. He needed all the help he could get. Besides, if he didn't make the effort to find him, his friend would come looking for him. Alex might tease him a little about talking to the Holy man, but even she had a higher power to answer to. Grey thought he'd invite her to come along. Father Richard was his friend first, Confessor second. With Father Richard, his secrets were safe. Confidentially, he liked the thought of having God on his side.

Since Alex was here to help him, she needed to know all the important players in his life. It would be a great advantage for her to know which ones of his friends could be trusted. They would need to talk about the family as well. Having a little background information on everyone couldn't hurt. It would make things easier as they went along.

Everything would come together now in good time. Sitting on the couch, Grey looked at his wife and his son. He had the perfect family.

In the days to come, this was the picture of them he would carry in his heart, as he and Alex searched for answers.

Grey lifted Dylan up and gave him a hug

"Hang in there buddy, the show's about to begin."

Then suddenly, Grey was silent. What he saw next frightened him. He saw flashes of Rachel feeding him bananas. This time, he knew it wasn't Alex. He was watching Rachel through Dylan's eyes. Whatever it was enabling him to see these things, was becoming stronger and more sensitive with each passing day. It became clear to him then, that the show had already begun. It had started in the hospital, the moment he woke up.

* * * * *

It was seven thirty a.m. when Blake ventured out to get the morning paper. What he saw on the front page caught him completely off guard. Someone had found Casey's body! The paper said she was found washed up on the beach late last night by a couple of kids. Part of him was surprised as hell. The other part was overjoyed. He loved to see his handy work in print. Ever since he'd won his first big case, seeing his achievements in the paper always gave him a high. There was something so thrilling about being recognized. Of course his legal prowess was public knowledge, but the notice of his unidentifiable excursions had become even more stimulating to him. Although the public was unaware of this private, personal victory; he knew, and that was all that really mattered. As he headed back up the driveway, Blake was excited. He wondered if he'd made the morning news.

Last night, he and Katie had decided to stay and spend the night in San Diego. They could return home late in the morning the next day and still avoid some traffic. Most people would be traveling tomorrow afternoon. They could go to the beach or take Christine shopping. It would be a great chance for them to spend time as a family. Blake poured himself some orange juice, and staked out a spot in front of the TV. He was bombarded with nothing but cartoons and cooking shows. He sat for a while and just played "flip". When he finally found a news station, they had already run through the top stories. Blake hoped he could catch the eight o-clock report at the top of the hour.

While channel surfing, he came across CNN. There, he found what he was looking for. The topic of discussion was all the latest information on the discovery of another young girl found slashed to death in Southern California. Blake was impressed. The reporter was not only providing updated information on his most recent victim, she was reviewing the other three killings being credited to the "Ripper" as well. For Blake, it was like a trip down memory lane.

Oddly enough, the news implied that the authorities were making good progress in their investigation. They insinuated there was more information on the case, but that they were unable to release it to the press at this time due to the ongoing investigation. Blake knew they were full of it. The case had become totally political at this point. If they had any evidence that was the least bit credible, they would be kicking down doors by now. The only thing any of the girls had in common was the similarity of their appearance. Blake knew from past experience that somewhere, in some police station, there was a big white board with photos of his victims systematically arranged. Someone of even low intelligence would surely have noticed the resemblance by now.

Last month, local authorities had called in the FBI to assist in the investigation. Together, they had collected a lot of the smaller pieces of the puzzle. The victim's cars had all been found. They had identified the last known whereabouts of each victim. This morning, they had even found the hotel room, full of Casey's personal effects. The problem was, they still had no motive and no evidence that linked anyone to the murders. Whoever was doing this had covered their tracks really well. Blake applauded their ignorance. Unless someone had a crystal ball handy, and knew how to use it, he was home free. In the beginning, he had wondered if he was really that smart. Now he wondered if they were just that stupid.

When the report ended, he went to the kitchen. He was a little concerned that they had found Casey's body so soon. He wanted a drink. On second thought, maybe just a little vodka in his orange juice would do. Katie and Christine would be up soon. His in-laws were already up and out of the house for their morning walk. There were two empty juice glasses, sitting in the sink. By the time they got back from their walk, the rest of the family would be awake. Maybe he'd offer to take everyone out to breakfast.

In the mean time, he enjoyed the peace and quiet. Blake gathered his thoughts. He'd keep an eye on the newspaper and TV for the next week or so just to be safe, but after that he would move on. It was going to be just another long weekend, only this one would have no distractions; phone calls, or case files. He'd left everything at home. His brain craved rest. He was here to relax and that's just what he was going to do. He went to the bar and grabbed the vodka. Katie would have to drive home later. She would all but have to carry him inside.

CHAPTER 7

The bells rang out in the crisp morning air, calling Father Richard Cobrarni's parishioners to God. Having decided to join them for the ten o-clock service, Grey quietly worked his way through the crowd. Once inside, he found a seat near the back of the church. It had been awhile since he was inside these walls. Religion had never really been a force in his life. He was born Jewish, married a Catholic, and was now caught somewhere in the middle. He was not one who was accustomed to the practice of pursuing council or confession through prayer with strangers. It was simply his relationship with the good Father that brought him to church that morning. Later, when the service ended, he would find his friend and seek his advice.

He and Father Richard had spoken briefly, a few days earlier, to set up their meeting. Richard had not merely made time for the visit he had all but demanded it. As the services began, Grey waited patiently, wondering what the topic of today's sermon would be. The choir sang hymns, and the congregation joined them in song. Scriptures were read, and stories were told. When they reached the point in the service where the sermon would be, Father Cobrarni took the pulpit.

As he began to speak, Grey was reminded of a day some time ago, when Richard shared a few personal thoughts about God with him. Grey had been working on him at the time. Even during a massage, Richard was very articulate when he spoke.

"I have found myself directed at times to write my sermon about something different than what we are presently following in the scriptures. In the beginning, I found it quite strange that my subject matter would have no relationship whatsoever to any of the material we were studying. Later, after much thought and deliberation, I came to the following conclusion: it was as if God were saying, I know what the progression of things is supposed to be, but today, someone out there in the congregation really needs to hear this instead."

Grey was certain that today was one of those days. Father Richard's words traveled to him like a long fly ball in baseball. You know, the one that everyone was sure would go out of the park, but was caught on the warning track. Remarkably, the warning track here was the back pew where Grey was sitting. Today's sermon was about new beginnings: about seeing each new day as just that, a new day. A fresh start if you will, knowing that God is giving you another chance. Each sunrise is a rebirth of hope. As always, Father Richard's words dug deep.

When the service ended, Richard motioned to Grey to follow him to his office.

As Grey stood to follow, a hand touched him from behind. Alex had arrived late. He was glad to see her. He nodded his approval to her, and motioned to her to follow. Richard looked confused. As they arrived together at his office door, he gave Grey a look.

"It's ok Father, she's with me," Grey announced.

Richard nodded, opened the door to the office, and the three went inside.

The priest's office was warm and comfortable. Dark oak walls surrounded you on three sides. Set into the fourth wall was a large stained glass window. Strong, carved furniture filled the room. In the office, there was a large bookcase that ran down the north wall. An antique desk sat at the far end of the large chamber. It was placed precisely in front of the window. The window itself was magnificent. The colored glass was hand laid, and formed a scene depicting the creation of man.

As the morning light shined in through the window, it created a soft rainbow of colored lights that flowed gently into the room. Two deep leather chairs sat next to each other at opposing angles facing the desk. Anyone who used them could not help being anything but comfortable. The floor was made of inlaid polished wood. Scattered around on it were small rugs that had been carefully placed to add color and warmth to the room. Father Richard offered Grey and Alex each a seat in one of the grand chairs. He took his place in an equally luxurious chair behind the carved desk.

Grey spoke first. “Nice to see you old friend,” he offered. “Still as subtle with your sermons as always, I see.”

The priest smiled. “Sometimes we get what we ask for,” he chuckled. “You did ask for my thoughts didn’t you, my son?”

“I suppose you’re right,” Grey agreed. “I did ask. I just couldn’t pass up the opportunity to match wits with you again. But enough of these cheerful pleasantries, where are my manners? Father Richard, this is my old friend Alex. While the two of you might not share the same religious beliefs, I think you will find her to be as educated and witty as she is beautiful,”

Alex just laughed.

“She is the one who taught me all of those unusual things that I told you about a few days ago. While I am sure that the two of you might disagree on a few points, I believe that you do share similar interests, especially when it comes to dealing with me.”

Richard looked puzzled.

“I also know, my friend, that one of your greatest attributes is your ability to keep an open mind”, Grey continued. “What we have come here to discuss might initially appear to you as being quite far-fetched. I am, however, quite confident that once you have been presented with all the facts you will be rather intrigued. As I am sure you already know, your opinions and judgments are of great importance to me. You are one of only two people I feel I can trust with this matter. The other one happens to be sitting next to me.”

Grey rested his hand on the arm of Alex’s chair. Richard stood up and offered Alex his hand.

“I see that you come highly recommended,” he chuckled.

“Please consider yourself no longer a guest here, but a member of this Holy family. Whatever circumstances have brought you here today, we will all go through it together. It appears to me that we have all been brought together by a higher power, for a reason that I have yet to learn.

I believe we must all work together to accomplish whatever task has been put before us. So let us say now, for the sake of conversation, that we will do our best not to disappoint who ever that may be."

Alex took Richard's hand in hers and smiled. She liked him already. For a priest he was ok. She could easily understand why Grey had taken a liking to this man and had him as a friend. His hand was warm and gave her a good feeling.

Grey was right. Richard was a man who could be trusted. Alex knew it was safe and took the opportunity to speak.

"You might want to take a seat, Father. What we're about to tell you may test many of your beliefs as well as your faith."

Richard smiled, returned to his chair, and made himself comfortable. There was a brief moment of silence.

"All right, my friends, let's hear what you have to say," he said.

On that cue, Grey took a deep breath, and began to tell their story.

* * * * *

Grey started at the beginning, twelve years ago, when he first met Alex. He gave Richard a complete outline, describing some of the things he learned from her. He walked Richard through everything from the past, to the day before the accident. Then, he explained everything that had happened to him over the past week. He left nothing out. Alex would offer information on occasion to help fill any gaps. While she was speaking, she explained her presence here as well as her decision to remain here to support Grey. Richard listened faithfully, as only a true friend would, until they had completed telling the story. All the while, he remained deep in thought.

When Grey was finished, Richard sat quietly and collected his thoughts. For a moment, he looked completely overwhelmed. A smile slowly came to his face. He addressed them both.

"I'm not certain that I fully understand all of this, but it is apparent to me that if what you say is even close to the truth, then we all have a great deal of work to do. As one who is, as you say, open minded, you can count on my support, both as a friend and a priest, in whatever course of action you may choose."

Alex looked at Richard and knew he was telling the truth. She could see it in his eyes.

"Thank you Father, I know this must be difficult for you," she said. Richard laughed. "The good Lord works in mysterious ways, my child. I've just never seen this approach before. Have either of you intentionally tested this thing out as yet?" he inquired.

"No, not really," Grey answered. "I don't think I'm ready for that. It would be an invasion of someone's privacy. I'm not sure that if it works, I won't find out things that I really don't want to know."

Richard nodded, "I see your point," he said, and then thought about it for a minute. "Do you trust me Grey?" Richard asked.

"You know that I do Father," Grey answered.

"Well then, take my hand and tell me what you see," Richard insisted. "If you wouldn't mind, I'd like to see what happens for myself. I have been thinking about a particular incident from the past for most of the day. I can assure you it's nothing you couldn't handle, or would mind knowing. See what you think. You can use me as an experiment. With your friend here, I think it will be safe. It will be just a simple test to see where we stand with this thing."

Richard offered his hand.

Grey looked over at Alex. She shrugged her shoulders, and then acknowledged her approval with a nod and a smile. Like a leap of faith, Grey stood and took his friend's hand. At first there was nothing. They just stood there together, hand in hand, waiting for something to happen. Richard's hand felt strong and safe in his. Time passed and still nothing. Grey was ready to give up when he started to feel strange. It started slowly. There were just little flashes at first. He saw a kaleidoscope of color images and light. It reminded Grey of how the light came through the office window. Then, all at once, the entire tape ran.

* * * * *

It was a cold wet January day. A light rain was falling gently from the sky. It was one of those days where everything looked like it was painted in black and white instead of color. The only real exception that caught the eye was the green of the cemetery grass. It was like an old Wallace Nutting painting: black and white format on which one color was superimposed somewhere. Grey knew he was seeing the world through Richard's eyes. A large group of mourners had gathered around him. Their open umbrellas created a near tent-like effect around the elaborate white coffin, which lay on a pedestal before him. He was presiding at a funeral service.

He remembered thinking what a waste this was. A young girl, her bright flame extinguished so early in life, and for what? One could only imagine the senseless and tragic reasons. Kelly Richfield had been somebody: a college graduate, a hard worker, a loving daughter, and a member of his former congregation. At the request of her parents, Richard returned to his old church that morning to bury their daughter. It was a task he could not refuse. He was, in fact, burying a friend. He had baptized her as a child. He had seen Kelly grow up in this church. She sang in the choir, was a church volunteer, and had been part of the church youth group until she went off to college. He had presided over her confirmation, and he counseled her in times of need. Now he was committing her body to the ground, and her soul to God.

The end of her life had been tragic. Kelly had simply disappeared one night, coming home from a friend's house. Her body was found a week later, floating in a nearby lake. Her throat was slashed, and she had been stripped of her clothing. Police speculated that the only reason her body was even found, was that whatever the killer used to weigh her down when she was tossed in, had somehow been disengaged. She was found floating near the shore on the east end of Irvine Lake.

To this day, the police had no motive or evidence pertaining to the case. They never found her clothes. All they found was her car. It was parked in front of Cook's Corner, an old biker bar turned restaurant that was located a few miles down the road from where her remains were discovered. It was once a pretty rowdy place, but in recent years it had become much more family friendly. People there remembered Kelly coming in, but no one saw her leave. That was at the end of January, just before Super Bowl weekend. It was July now, and still no one had any clues about Kelly's disappearance. Her death was hard on Richard. It cut him deeply. It also touched his heart. Grey knew he had seen enough. He let go of his friend's hand.

Alex had been curiously watching them both during this entire exchange. It had taken only a couple of minutes, three, perhaps. During the interaction, Grey's expression had changed. His body language was different too. At one point, he put his head down to his chest, as if to concentrate on what was happening. Richard's face changed as well. The Father looked like something had distracted him too. It had.

Grey was overcome with emotion. He returned to his seat. As he sat down, he made eye contact with Alex. At first, Alex thought she saw fear in his eyes, but as time passed, she realized it was more shock than anything else. Richard however, looked very curious. Finally he spoke.

"Well, my friend, what did you see?" he asked.

Grey looked at him with sadness in his eyes. He was hesitant, but then gave Father Richard an answer. His voice was quiet and reserved. "I watched you do what I believe is one of the hardest things you've ever done," he shared. I watched you bury Kelly Richfield. I could feel your pain. It was like on that day, Father, you lost one of your own sheep."

Richard's face went pale. For one brief moment, he swore his heart stopped. It was then Father Richard put his head in his hands. In all his years of counsel and prayer, he'd thought he'd heard everything. That was until today. Desperately, his mind searched for a reason, a logical explanation if you will, that would clarify what he had just heard. His brain was like a computer searching for a lost file. No information found.

When he looked up, Grey could see the confusion in his eyes: desperation and maybe even a little fear. There was a long period of silence, because no one spoke; Grey out of respect for his friend, Alex out of sheer astonishment. She had heard of things like this happening before, but had never actually witnessed it herself. One look at her, and you could tell she was amazed and working on an explanation in her head. She looked rather involved. Richard on the other hand, just sat in his chair, staring at the wall. He had a weird look in his eyes, like he was waiting for the cherries to line up on the old mental slot machine. The cherries called sense, logic, and faith. Grey wondered who would break the silence. He decided to let his friends off the hook.

"Now, Father, I think you may have a better understanding of the situation," Grey said.

There was an eerie quiet, then Richard spoke.

"Just how much of her funeral did you actually see?" Richard asked in a subdued voice.

"All of it, my friend, everything in your memory of that day. It was like a DVD playing in my head. Only it's much faster. The show stopped when I let go of your hand."

The priest looked shocked. Grey's statement gave him the chills.

"And does this happen every time you come in contact with someone?" he continued.

Alex jumped in, "Well, as of right now, we're not exactly sure. I think that's why we came here today, Father, to get a feel for what is going on. I don't think Grey wanted to share this with just anybody," she finished.

"It would be an understatement at this point, to tell you that this whole thing is a little beyond me right now. I am at a loss for words or direction. Any suggestions from either of you, as to what to do next would be helpful," Grey replied.

Richard answered him with a question. "Am I correct in understanding, that for the moment, we three are the only ones who know about this?"

"Yes," Grey and Alex responded in unison.

"Well, I suggest we keep it that way," Richard continued. "Let's keep it in the family for now. Are there any objections?" There was another brief silence.

"Very well then, I trust the two of you will keep me informed of any progress you make with this matter. I want you both to know that I will make myself available at any time, in order to pursue this conversation further. However, the only spiritual advice I can offer at this point is that faith is a very powerful thing. No matter what you encounter, don't lose yours. Please, either one of you."

With that said, Richard turned to look out the window. He needed some time to think.

"God be with you, my friends. You will be in my prayers," he said.

Grey stood and motioned to Alex to do the same. It was time for them to go. As they passed through the door on their way out, Grey stopped and looked back at the window. Richard's back was still facing him.

"I know this will be troubling you for awhile, and for that I am sorry," he said. "Please know that I am grateful for your friendship and support. You do so much for so many. It must be very draining at times, to be able to do all the things that you do."

Grey's words hit home. Richard turned to face his friend, but Grey had quietly slipped away. He had closed the door behind him. Richard turned his attention to the window. Staring out into the court yard, he caught himself thinking out loud.

"We will find a way through this, my son", he whispered to himself. "Somehow, we will find it together."

Then he bowed his head and prayed. He said a prayer for Grey. He said one for Alex. He said one for the congregation. Mostly, he prayed for Kelly Richfield, who never had a chance to grow old.

* * * * *

On the way out of the church, neither one of them said a word. They walked silently past the empty pews, and out the chapel doors. Outside, a few people were still visiting on the front steps. It wasn't until they reached the parking lot that Alex decided it was safe.

"So where do we go from here?" she asked.

Grey leaned up against the side of the Mustang and shook his head.

"I guess we figure out how to bring you out into the open. I'm going to need your help. How about today? We can start right now. We can work much faster if you're actually here. Tell you what, call my house and tell Rachel that you're coming into town today. You'll rent a car, and drive down late this afternoon. We have a family barbeque to go to later this evening, so we'll just invite you along. If we're really going to do this, there's no time like the present."

Alex laughed. She knew he was right. She reached over into the car and grabbed her cell phone. He dialed the number for her. Rachel answered on the third ring.

Alex was surprised by Rachel's attitude. She was very pleasant. Rachel told her that Grey was at church, but she would give him the message when he got back. She also told her that she was more than welcome to stay at their house, rather than looking for a hotel. Alex thanked her, and told her they could work out the details after she arrived. Then she said goodbye. Grey smiled when he heard the news.

Maybe this was going to be easier than he thought. Her staying at the house would sure make things a lot easier. Just then, his cell phone rang. He looked at the caller I.D. It was Rachel. Still sitting on the Mustang, he answered the phone. Rachel called to tell him that Alex was coming into town later that day. She explained everything to him that she had said to Alex. Grey told her he'd be home shortly to help her get ready for company. He got off the phone.

"Guess I'll see you in a few hours," he said.

"It looks that way, doesn't it?" Alex grinned.

Grey looked at her. "Let's make this fun, ok?"

"I was thinking the same thing," Alex replied. "Who knows what will happen if you get too close to Rachel. This could be rather entertaining."

"Great, I'll be trapped somewhere between the two of you," Grey snickered. "That's just what I don't need. Take it easy on her, ok? She is my wife you know."

"I know," Alex shot back. "Don't worry. I'll just hang out with Dylan."

"Somehow, that doesn't make me feel any better," Grey said. "Who knows what kind of trouble the two of you will get into. Listen, I've got to go. I'll see you soon." He winked at her. "Call me if you get lost and need directions."

"Very funny," she said. "See you in a little while."

As Alex drove off, on her way to the hotel, Grey headed home. As he drove, his thoughts were on Father Richard. How difficult it must be at times, to be a man of God. To carry so many burdens and responsibilities must truly be a test of one's faith.

Richard told him that knowing about the Kelly Richfield incident was something he could handle. That part was true. What Richard didn't know, was now that Grey knew about the tragedy, and the consequences it had inflicted on his friend, it gave him an even greater respect for the man. What significance events of that nature must have on a man! To have to deal with issues like that on a regular basis just boggled Grey's mind. He could only hope that over the years, his friend had managed to collect a greater number of happy and joyous outcomes. These would not erase the pain, but they could at least make it bearable. As he pulled into the driveway, the garage door opened. Rachel was waiting. Company was coming and she was going to need help. Grey wondered what was really going on in her head. He told himself that one of these days, he'd make it a point to find out. Right now, he had neither the time nor the patience to open that can of worms. She handed him a dust rag as he came through the door.

"Your friend's going to be here before we know it" she informed him. "We'd better get busy,"

Dylan came crawling by and just giggled. Somewhere in the back of his head, Grey could hear Alex laughing too. He'd settle up with her later. He looked down at Dylan. "Come on little buddy, we've got work to do." he smiled. Dylan smiled and followed his daddy down the hall.

* * * * *

Grey had just finished dusting when the phone rang. Rachel answered it, and told Grey it was for him.

"Mr. Kendall's on the phone," she said.

Grey took the call. "Hi Blake, What's up?" he asked.

"Just confirming tomorrow's appointments for Katie and me," Blake answered. "I'm counting on you to fix her up. She's been better lately, and I'm relying on you to keep her that way. Is noon ok with you?"

"Sure Blake, see you then. Is everything ok?"

Yeah, we're on our way back from San Diego." Blake said. "We spent the fourth with Katie's parents. We'll be home in a couple of hours. Call me if anything changes."

"I'll see you tomorrow at noon then," Grey assured him. "Take care." Then he hung up.

Rachel was surprised. "You sure you're ready to go back yet?" she asked. "The doctor said to take it easy."

"You'll let me dust won't you?" he blurted out. Rachel just rolled her eyes.

"I can't put it off forever", he continued. "Besides, it's easy money with them. And they pay cash".

Grey went to the fridge and grabbed an iced tea. He needed a drink. Rachel had one too.

"You sure you're ok with Alex being here?" he asked.

"Yeah, maybe she can get you to slow down," Rachel replied. "Hope Dylan likes her."

Grey smiled, "I'm sure he will, dear. Alex is great with kids. I think you'll like her too."

Rachel got up. "Come on lazy, we have lots more work to do."

She tugged on Grey's arm. He playfully resisted at first, but then gave in.

"All right already," he said looking over at Dylan. "But I'd still rather be a baby. Have nothing to do all day except eat, sleep, shit, and play."

Rachel smacked him. "You think you're funny don't you?" she teased. Dylan laughed.

"Let's get at it then," Grey conceded. He took Rachel's hand and headed off through the house. Half way down the hall, he started to see colors. It took him by surprise. Before it could go any further, he let go of her hand. Whatever thoughts she had, or secrets she kept, would have to stay that way for awhile. He would deal with her later. This wasn't a game, and he wasn't about to start making it one.

Alex would be knocking on the door in a few hours. Between now and then, he had a lot of planning to do. For now, he'd go scrub a tub or something to stay out of Rachel's way. It would give him some time alone and give him a chance to think. He wasn't concerned about Alex. She was the least of his worries. Everybody would love her. She would fit right in. He was more interested in what would happen at the party.

He had narrowly escaped the last one, having only to deal with Tony. The incident with Tony had bothered him for awhile. He knew Tony was carrying a heavy load. Did he dare mention to Tony, or even insinuate, that he knew what was happening? He wanted to help, but how would he explain that he knew what was going on? For now it was best to keep his mouth shut.

Grey couldn't let it go. What if he got himself into another situation like the one he had with Tony? It could be disastrous! In the past twenty-four hours, Grey's sensitivity with the flashes had reached a new level. Especially after the episode he had with Richard. He was, however, beginning to think that he could see light at the end of the tunnel. He'd been paying attention to the time delay between contact and the feature film. If he could keep the time factor in check, he could at least control whether or not he allowed the flashes to start. By limiting the length of contact time, he could stop things from happening before they got started. It was certainly worth a try. He would try anything to get a handle on the flashes.

There was another thing in his favor. Alex would be there this time to help. If it looked like something was going to happen, she could step in. It would be nice to have back-up. If he started to see colors, all he had to do was let go of whoever he was in contact with. This time, he wasn't going in blind. He had a little more control.

It was frustrating. It was kind of like having a new car, and not being able to drive. There was something else to consider. What if he decided that he really wanted to know what somebody was thinking? That would be a temptation in itself. If so, would he give in to it? And, if he chose that path, would it be possible to maintain contact with the person long enough to get the information he wanted? Once again, there were too many questions. He was thinking so much that he was giving himself a headache.

Grey forced himself to stop speculating. As exciting as it sounded, it just wasn't his way of doing things. The old saying "power corrupts" reared its ugly head. He was not going to use his family to experiment with this thing. He was going to be careful. What was he thinking anyway? The fumes from the bathroom cleaner must have gone to his head. He needed some fresh air.

He rinsed out the tub and went looking for Rachel. Alex would be packing up at the hotel by now. She said she would wait until five-thirty or so before coming over. That would work out great. He could make the introductions, have a quick drink, and then head over to Rachel's folks' house for the party. If Alex agreed, they could get her settled in when they got back. It was only two-twenty, so there was still plenty of time to relax before she got here. He decided to go play with Dylan. He found him in the den.

* * * * *

Rachel was sitting on the couch, talking to her mom on the phone. She was talking to Lyanna about Alex's visit. The rest was just girl talk. Grey got down on the floor to play with Dylan. Dylan liked to wrestle. Grey discovered that wrestling on the floor with him was ok. The contact was so intermittent there was nothing to worry about. Grey thought about practicing the timing thing with him, but then had second thoughts.

Alex would be a more useful test subject. If they worked it right, she could possibly even give him feedback on what, if anything was happening to her. Having her here at the house would really accelerate the learning process. Once they got a handle on this thing, they could decide what to do about it.

Then it hit him! He had a client tomorrow! What on God's earth was he thinking! When he was on the phone earlier with Blake, he must have totally zoned out. How on earth would he be able to do a massage? He thought about it for a minute. If he kept his hands moving, maybe that would that solve the problem, or would it? Would the continuous contact be an issue?

It was three o' clock. Alex would be here in a couple of hours. He started to make a mental list of things they needed to figure out. If they could work out a few details, maybe the appointment tomorrow would work itself out. The longer Grey thought about it, the longer his list grew.

* * * * *

The door bell rang at five fifteen. Alex was right on schedule. When Rachel opened the door, she was shocked. Standing in the doorway was a strikingly good looking woman. Rachel guessed she was in her mid to late thirties. Immediately, she was uneasy. Grey had neglected (probably for his own good) to inform her that Alex was so attractive. Alex was dressed in black jeans, and a white cotton blouse. Her soft red hair was down, and fell gently on her shoulders. She was very pretty.

Rachel opened the screen door and said, "You must be Alex. Hi, I'm Rachel. We've been expecting you. Please come in."

"Thank you. It's so nice to finally meet you," Alex responded. She accepted the invitation, and stepped inside. The house looked nice, and because of that, like with most women, Rachel was in a good mood. At first glance, she wasn't sure what to think of this woman. It was difficult to size her up. She knew that Alex and Grey had a past. Even if it was not a romantic one, Rachel soon discovered that this whole situation made her a little uneasy. There was a face now to go with all the stories. Come to think of it, there was a lot more than a face. The fact that Alex was beautiful just made her more uncomfortable. But she had already told herself that she was going to give this woman a chance. There was something peculiar though. She had the strangest feeling when she answered the door. It was like she had seen Alex somewhere before, but that was impossible. She'd never been back east.

Rachel led Alex into the house. When they reached the end of the front hall, the two of them were greeted by Grey and Dylan. Grey gave his friend a big hug and then, not wanting to appear as one without manners, introduced Rachel again. Then he presented her to Dylan.

Alex asked if she could hold him. Rachel agreed. From the moment Alex took him, Rachel knew everything was going to be all right. Dylan seemed to like this stranger, and that simple fact made things more comfortable. Grey suggested that they all sit and relax. They went into the den, and Grey offered to play bartender. While he worked in the kitchen, the girls had a chance to say hello.

"You must be tired after your long flight," Rachel began.

"Actually, I got a chance to sleep on the plane," Alex replied. "But it's nice to finally be here."

Grey brought out a couple bottles of wine and offered each of them a glass. Rachel chose Chardonnay, while Alex and Grey had a glass of his favorite Cabernet.

"I hope you don't think that we're putting you on the spot Alex, but we thought you might like to join us tonight for a little family get together," Grey offered. "It will give you a chance to meet most of the family."

Sounds good to me," Alex responded. "I could use a little party atmosphere about now."

"Rachel's folks would like us over at their place in about twenty minutes. Will that work for you?" Grey asked.

"Just give me a chance to freshen up, and we're out of here," Alex said.

Rachel pointed her in the right direction as Alex excused herself.

"Hope you brought a bathing suit," Grey yelled after her. "Everyone always ends up in the spa."

When she was out of range, Grey turned to Rachel. "Think she'll fit in?" he asked.

"She seems very pleasant," Rachel replied. "Dylan seems to be fond of her too. If you'd like her to stay here, it's ok by me."

"You should offer that to her when she comes back," Grey suggested, "and thanks, honey, that's a nice thing to do."

A short time later, Alex came around the corner smiling. She looked fresher somehow. A little touch of make-up and a quick run through with a hair brush seemed to do the trick. She announced she was ready to go. Rachel handed her back her wine.

"Let's sit for a minute and finish these", she suggested.

Alex smiled and took a seat. "We'd like it if you would stay with us while you're here," Rachel offered, bouncing Dylan on her lap.

"Consider yourself one of the gang. If you agree, we can head out now to the party, and then get you settled in later. Is that ok?"

"That would be great," Alex said, "but I don't want to impose, you know, with the little guy and all. Are you sure I won't be in the way?"

"No trouble at all," Rachel assured her.

"Good, now that that's settled," Grey jumped in. If he hadn't, they might have been late to dinner. "Let's get out of here and have some fun," he insisted. Everyone agreed.

Rachel grabbed Dylan and headed for the car. Alex and Grey were right behind her. When she wasn't looking, Alex gave Grey a wink. Everything was going according to plan.

Grey was relieved. The party would be a lot more fun for him now, knowing that he wouldn't be dealing with this thing on his own. It was going to be much easier, knowing that someone was covering his back. For the first time since the accident, Grey knew that he wasn't alone. Having Alex around in the old days was one thing. Having her here now, available, and eager to openly participate, gave him a much stronger sense of security.

Today was the first day on the road to understanding. What had started earlier that morning in church was now set in full motion. Thanks to the help of a friend, they were now prepared to travel down a new and different path. Neither one of them knew what to expect, nor what they would find along the way. They would be doing it together. It would be just like the good old days, all for one and one for all. As they drove off to the party, Alex sat in the back seat playing with Dylan. From the sound of things, they were having a great time. Grey smiled. He finally had a chance to relax. In terms of his universe, all the pieces were slowly returning to their proper place.

* * * * *

He could feel the excitement building, as they drew closer to the house. He was anxious to see everyone again and to introduce Alex. When Rachel pulled up in front, there were other people arriving too.

Her brother Russ and his wife, Brianna, were unloading their kids. Grey took the opportunity to give Alex a little background on them.

"Russ is Dylan's godfather. He has two children, Jay 5, is from his first serious romance. Then there's Justine 3, from his marriage to Brianna. And who knows, there may be one on the way. Personally, as far as kids go, I think they may be done for awhile."

As the Thomas family got out of their car, Grey walked over and offered to help Russ. He looked like he had his hands full. Rachel looked a little perturbed that he got out so quickly, and left her, Alex, and Dylan waiting. They should have come first. Once things got organized, Grey came back to their car to help. Russ followed him. As they approached the car, Russ asked, "Wow, who's the redhead?"

Grey made a simple introduction. As they unloaded Rachel's van, Grey told Russ, "I'll give you the details later."

Much to her dismay, Rachel ended up introducing Brianna to Alex. With everything finally ready to go now, the whole group made their way into the house.

Alex couldn't help but take mental notes of the personalities and attitudes involved. There was a lot of interesting stuff going on here. In the back of her mind, she expected to see some friction in some places, but not this soon. She could sense a tension between Rachel and Brianna. Then again, that was probably no big deal. They were sister-in- laws. As they walked through the house, out onto the back patio, Alex got a surprise. There must have been thirty to forty people in front of her. This was all family?

Fortunately, Alex recognized a few people. Frank was in the pool with all the kids. Lyanna and Liz were in the Jacuzzi with a couple of young girls who she remembered seeing at the hospital. It turned out they were Liz's daughters, Maggie and Kelby. Until today, she hadn't known their names. Everywhere she looked, there were more people. Grey was right. Rachel had a big family. Rachel led them over to the Jacuzzi, and introduced Alex to her mother and aunt. They were both very polite. Everyone said their hellos and Lyanna offered them food and drink. After the introductions, Rachel excused herself for a minute and went inside. Grey and Alex were left alone in the crowd to fend for themselves.

"Let's get a drink and I'll give you the nickel tour," Grey offered. "Why not?" Alex exclaimed, so off they went.

After about twenty minutes, they had made the rounds. Grey found a spot where they could be comfortable, and where they could see everybody. Alex was impressed. It would take her awhile to get all the names and faces straight, but at least now she had some general idea.

"You ok?" Grey asked.

"Yeah, fine," Alex responded. "No Uncle Tony though. Is he going to be here?"

Grey was surprised. He couldn't believe he hadn't noticed that Tony was missing. It completely slipped his mind. He went over and asked Lyanna if Tony and Katherine were coming. She said they would be arriving shortly. Grey went back to tell Alex. Then he asked her, "Why the sudden interest in Tony?"

"I want to see if I can pick up on anything strange by meeting him," she answered. Grey contemplated the idea for a moment, and then understood her train of thought. He wanted to have a few words with Tony as well.

"Good idea, he told her. Let's see what you get. It certainly couldn't hurt."

They were on the same page. Grey finished his drink. Out of the corner of his eye, he noticed that Rachel was getting in the Jacuzzi. Grey knew if he wanted things to stay cool, he'd better offer her a drink as well. He would need to keep an eye on what was going on with her. He didn't want to take the chance that Rachel might think he was ignoring her. Alex found a lounge chair and stripped down to her suit. Grey smiled. The years had obviously been kind to his friend. She was still dangerously beautiful. He wasn't the only one who noticed. Russ and his cousin Lance had both been watching her every move. The guys looked up at Grey, and when it was safe, gave him the thumbs up. The three of them were like brothers. In the past, they always seemed to find either trouble or adventure together. Which one, depended entirely upon one's point of view. Grey laughed when he saw them signal, then turned and went to the bar for drinks.

Tony showed up a few minutes later. Grey and Alex were sitting on the far side of the patio. Grey saw Tony first. "Hey, Uncle Tony," he yelled in his best New York accent. Tony laughed. He was as happy to see Grey as Grey was to see him. After their last meeting, Tony felt kind of strange. He knew something was bothering him, but he couldn't put his finger on it. The two men cheerfully exchanged the traditional handshake and strong hug. Alex stayed in her chair and played the role of quiet observer.

After some mild chit-chat, Grey brought Tony over and introduced them. Alex managed to get a good firm handshake. It didn't take her long to size up Tony. She could see how a man with his personality could have gotten himself into the mess he was in. He was kind, gentle, and unassuming. She hoped that before all of this was over they could find a way to help Tony gain his freedom.

While Grey was getting drinks and being politely social, she'd been quietly listening to various conversations and taking more mental notes. Actually, this was a nice group. Grey was right on the money with this one. You were never a stranger around these people for more than five minutes.

Alex discovered that she was resenting the fact that she was an only child. She was alone now. Her parents had been killed in a small plane crash when she was seven. Grandma Boulier had taken her in, and kept her until the old woman had passed on in '79. Since then, she'd been on her own. It was Granny B. who first saw what was inside Alex, and taught her how to use it. Everyone thought the old woman was crazy. Maybe she was.

Or maybe she was just smarter than everybody else. Over the years, she had helped Alex learn to use her gifts. When her lessons were completed, she made young Alexandra promise to find another person to teach, someone to whom she could pass her knowledge on to when she was ready. At the time, Alex was sixteen, young and scared. Granny B. told Alex to just follow her heart. Grandma Boulier died a week later.

It was twelve long years before Alex met Grey. Now, that seemed like a lifetime ago.

* * * * *

The party was great. Alex was really enjoying every minute of it. Everywhere she looked, there was something going on. Everyone had come by to meet her, say “Hi” to Grey, and talk for a while. Grey got up a few times to get things for Rachel, and even she looked like she was having a good time. She was still in the Jacuzzi, only now half a dozen people had joined her. Rachel looked like she was having fun, so Grey just catered to her when she needed something.

As the party rolled on, Tony had worked his way over, and joined them about half an hour ago. He mentioned that he wanted to ask Grey a question when he first sat down. It took him awhile to get up the nerve. He told Grey that ever since the incident the other day at the pool, he’d had a funny feeling about something.

“You probably think I’m being crazy,” he said, “but I feel like I have no secrets from you. I figure that maybe one of your clients knows me, and has said something to you. I know that I can trust you, but the strangeness of it all still bugs me.

Grey saw the opportunity and took it. “Well, I have heard some things, but I wasn’t in a position to say anything. It’s not any of my business,” Grey told him. “If what I know is true however, I am sorry. I wish there were something I could do to help. No worries though, your secrets are safe with me.”

Tony looked relieved. Now he was certain Grey knew. It wasn’t just his secret anymore. It would be nice to have someone he trusted, know what was going on. At least now he had someone he could talk to. He knew he could trust Grey to keep silent.

Alex sat quietly through the entire conversation. When Tony got up, she leaned over to Grey.

“That was too easy,” she said. “You really got lucky with that one.”

“No shit!” Grey replied, “That was one in a million.” They both laughed.

Grey had dodged a bullet. If the rest of the party was this kicked back, they had it made. It would be easy to stay out of trouble. Other than a few hugs, he had been contact free. Actually he was feeling pretty good. The beer he was drinking had started to kick in. It was time to slow down with the booze. The doc had said he should not be drinking at all, but if he did, to stop immediately if he started getting a buzz. His head was going to be sensitive to alcohol for a long time. Besides, he really wanted to keep a clear head. He asked one of the kids to bring him a soda. Alex wanted one too.

Grey turned his attention to Rachel. Someone had handed Dylan to her in the Jacuzzi. He was having a ball just splashing around. She waved. Grey waved back. Things had really begun to lighten up. After his talk with Tony, he didn't feel like he was walking on pins and needles anymore. It was nice to have the thing with Tony under control.

Alex turned to Grey, "Think I'll go join the girls, and get the low down on things." Grey waved her on.

"Be my guest. It might be fun," he said.

As she passed him she winked. Grey knew she was up to something, but at this point he didn't care. He was sure he'd hear all about it later. For now there was nothing to say, why not let Alex have her fun.

Grey returned to his chair and popped open a soda. He watched as his friend flowed gracefully across the patio. When Alex got to the Jacuzzi, she paused. Then she said something to Lyanna. The woman nodded, and Alex stepped in. It was almost a tease watching her, as she slid gently into the bubbling water. Grey watched carefully, as each glorious piece of her disappeared below the surface. It was quite a sight, but for him it wasn't sexual. He was reminded of an old saying: A vampire can't come into your house unless they're invited. He wondered if the same rule applied to the kind of people he and Alex had become. Her wink said it all. She had decided to go fishing. For the moment, she was the predator. He wondered what she would catch. When it was over, with any luck, maybe she would let them off easy.

* * * * *

It was an hour later, when Alex lost interest in her game and she and Grey had a chance to hook up again. By this time, Grey had moved over to the other side of the patio and found a seat next to the fire pit. It was about ten feet from the Jacuzzi. The men liked to sit by the fire at night, drink Port or brandy, and enjoy a good cigar. Grey had brought Alex's duffel over with him, on the assumption that she would want to join them. She did not disappoint him. When she got out of the water, he politely tossed her a towel. She thanked him, and went into the house to change. He asked Rachel if she was getting out too, but she declined. She said she wanted to stay in for awhile. She did want another drink though, so Grey went to get her one.

While he was standing at the bar, Alex came out of the bathroom. She gave him a look. Apparently, her time in the Jacuzzi had been productive.

"If you're having a brandy, would you mind bringing me one?" she asked.

"Sure," he responded. "Do me a favor. Give this to Rachel on your way out."

Alex laughed. She'd just spent an hour in the spa with her. During that time, she had intentionally tried not to look Rachel straight in the face. She didn't want to make eye contact with her for too long. She didn't want Rachel to remember her from their run in at the hospital. So far, she hadn't remembered a thing. Alex wanted to keep it that way. She took the glass from Grey.

"No problem, got you covered," she said, and headed for the door.

Grey watched her through the window as she went outside. She was up to something. As she passed the Jacuzzi, she spotted Kelby and got her attention.

"Can you hand this to Rachel please?" she asked. "You got it Alex," Kelby replied.

As Alex turned to walk away, Rachel yelled over, "Thanks, Alex." Grey laughed. Alex was so smooth. He made a mental note to remind himself to ask her about that one.

When Grey came outside again, the fire pit was on and Frank was enjoying a cigar. Alex made herself comfortable in a chair next to Frank. She had saved a chair for Grey. He handed her a brandy and sat down.

"How are you feeling?" Frank asked.

"I'm going to try working tomorrow. Guess we'll see how it goes," Grey answered.

"That's great," Frank encouraged him, tipping his glass in a gesture. It's nice to have you back!" Grey tipped his glass back at him. Alex joined them to finish the toast.

"Nice to have you here as well," Frank motioned to Alex.

"The pleasure is mine," she assured him. "I can't thank you enough for your incredible hospitality." Frank nodded a thank you, and took a long pull on his cigar. Here was a man who was truly in his element. He had class and a style all his own.

Grey went back to his brandy, nurturing it like a newborn child. Alex sipped hers, and was lost somewhere, staring deep into the fire. From the look on her face, you could tell she had lots on her mind. Grey wondered how much of this was beyond even her understanding. They had survived the party. Things had gone well. Alex was now like one of the family. They had embraced her as one of their own. Later, when it came time to say goodnight, she was gracious and appreciative. Both Frank and Lyanna told her they had enjoyed her visit as well.

On the ride home, Alex was strangely quiet, even for her. She was almost too cool. Grey knew that she was still trying to get a grip on everything. She'd seen a lot for one day. Maybe after a good night's rest, they could both start fresh in the morning. He didn't have to be at the Kendall's until noon. If he could just keep everything light and easy, a couple of massages should be a breeze. Worst case scenario, he'd end up learning a few things about Katie and Blake that he might not want to know. It wouldn't be that bad. They were a friendly couple.

So what if something came to pass and a few things slipped out? He wasn't going to tell them he knew anything anyway. When they got back to the house, Grey took Dylan and put him to bed. Rachel followed them inside. Alex grabbed her suitcase from her car and collected her things. By the time she got in, Rachel had made up the bed in the guest room.

"If you need anything, please let us know, ok?" she told Alex. "We're glad to have you here. I'll see you in the morning." She left Alex alone, and closed the door behind her. Rachel was ok, but it was still a little strange for her, having this woman in her home. Alex got settled in. A few minutes later, there was a knock on her door. It was Grey.

"Goodnight, my friend. You have no idea how glad I am that you're here," he said.

"Where else would I be, silly?" she said with a smile. "Time doesn't change the rules, just plays with the heart a little. Get some sleep. When you finish with work tomorrow, we have some work of our own to do. You know me well enough to know that where I am is where I want to be."

Grey smiled. "See you tomorrow," he said, then smiled and left her to the night.

As he wandered down the hall, a strange sense of peace settled around him. The world was different now. Maybe tonight, he could sleep. The demons would be happy. He and Alex were together once again. As he put his head down on his pillow, he heard a familiar sound far off in the distance. It was like music to his ears. He closed his eyes and drifted away.

CHAPTER 8

It was still dark outside when Blake made his way out to the balcony. The view was spectacular. He could see for miles in every direction. The lights of the city were beautiful, but they always took second to the view of the sea. There was something about the strength and power of the ocean that excited him beyond belief. When they moved into the house, he insisted that the balcony off of the master bedroom be expanded to twice its original size. He wanted to be able to enjoy moments like this one. From here, he could sit and gaze out at the horizon. Staring at the imaginary line where the sky met the sea always gave him peace. This parapet gave him the perfect view. Somewhere, off in the eastern sky, the sun was rising, starting a new day.

From the sound of things, so was his daughter Christine. Blake heard a noise below him which diverted his attention. He watched as she stepped outside on the patio below him and headed toward the garage. The motion lights tripped on as she passed into each new area. He could see her clearly, as she made her way down the walkway that ran between the back patio and the garage. She moved quietly and effortlessly down the path. Wrapped ever so tightly in her spandex and sweats, Blake figured she was off to the gym. For Christine, the gym had become an early morning ritual. Same time, everyday, for the last eighteen months, she was up before the sun.

She was dedicated. At seventeen, it was nice to see that she was committed to something. She had really stuck with this, and it showed. Blake was impressed. She looked so much like her mother. Her long dark hair, the soft eyes, and the firm, slender body ran in the family.

Guys would definitely see her coming. She was still a kid, but the way she looked, he doubted that she'd ever been carded trying to buy a drink. At her age, she was what the boys called 'dangerous'.

Blake really loved her. She had her mother's looks, but most importantly, she had his brains. She was very smart. Next June, when she graduated from high school, she would be pretty well set. She had received scholarship offers from four big ten schools. Three were academic, one was athletic. Chris liked to play volleyball. She had all that beauty and brains too. Blake knew he was lucky. When the time came for her to settle down with someone, whoever he was, the lucky man would definitely have his hands full. Blake laughed quietly to himself. This was his baby, and unlike her mother, Chris could be trusted. As he saw the headlights of her white BMW convertible going down the hill, he had a good feeling. He knew he had done something right.

Over the years, because of his relentless schedule, he hadn't been much of a "hands on" father. He was forced to buy both her loyalty and her love. Even with that being the case, he knew she would still turn out ok. Aside from her looks, she was nothing like her mother. Christine had style and class. He would never find her like he'd found Katie, at the home of a friend, skirt off, legs in the air. Chris had plans for college. She knew what she wanted to do, and she knew how to get there. She would make it standing on her feet, not lying on her back. When he thought about it, he couldn't even remember the last guy he or Katie had seen her with. That fact alone kept his mind at ease. She was a good kid. He had a lot of faith in her. He had missed a great deal. He woke up one morning, and discovered that his little girl was almost all grown up. Maybe later, when she got back, he would take her aside and talk to her; see if he could find out what was going on in her life. He was feeling a little guilty.

Yeah right, like she'd tell him! Lately, they only seemed to talk when she wanted something. He had the credit card bills to prove it. Still, it was always sad, watching her drive away. He had one consolation. He was the gravy train. He knew she'd be back. She knew where the pot of gold was. As he watched her taillights disappear into the darkness, he was discouraged. There were some things that money couldn't buy. He had to learn that lesson the hard way. He could see it every time he looked in Christine's eyes. Blake gave himself a mental reprimand then went back to enjoying the view.

* * * * *

The paper boy always came early, so Blake trudged down the driveway in search of the morning paper. He was anxious to see if anything new had come up with the Casey thing. When he arrived at the bottom of the hill, what he found really pissed him off. The little bastard had landed the paper on the lawn instead of the asphalt. The morning sprinklers had already run a cycle, and totally ruined the morning news. He would have to call and order another one. Any news about Casey would have to wait. Frustrated, Blake bent down and picked up the wet newspaper. It felt cold and soggy in his hand.

The clammy feeling it gave him made him shudder. It reminded him of Casey's wet robe. In his mind, he could see her naked, on the rocks again. It was a vision that quickly aroused him. He remembered his last kill. How he would love to have caressed that incredible body. He longed to be able to salivate over it again and again. To toy with her, like a hungry cat teases a mouse. Part of him hated himself for not taking her when he had the chance. The other part of him thanked him for not stooping to Katie's level; for not giving into forbidden desires. He could have had each one of them: each glorious, young, vixen, to ride wildly into the night. He could have taken all they had to offer, but he chose to take the one thing they never thought they'd have to give. It wasn't about sex.

There were more important things. There was loyalty and trust. There was betrayal. When it came right down to it, it was really about revenge. Katie fucking Walter wasn't the problem. Doing it behind his back was.

When he first found out about the affair, he swore to himself he would kill her. You know the simple fantasy or sarcastic comment, spoken in a moment of extreme anger and pain. In his dreams, he had killed Katie many times. For awhile, the dreams had satisfied him. That, and the fact he almost never saw her. She was out of sight, out of mind. It was the only way he was able to deal with it. Then, one day, back in early January, he dropped by Walter's place unannounced. He saw Katie's car in the driveway. He originally planned to just remain in his car and drive away, but his curiosity got the best of him. He had to know what was going on.

Carefully, he worked his way up to the house and peeked through a window. There he found his beloved wife riding the wild pony. Unfortunately for Blake, Walter was the horse. Ever since then, he couldn't get that image out of his head. Every time he looked at Katie, the emotional knife plunged deeper into his back. Soon after that day at Walter's, he decided he wanted to show her what his knife could do. But there was a problem. She was still the mother of his child. For some strange reason, that still counted for something. Or did it? For now, it was the one thing that kept Katie alive.

After finding out about her and Walter, killing Katie became a fantasy. It remained that way, until the day he spotted Kelly Richfield. Until then, he was able to maintain his self control. At first glance, he thought Kelly was Katie. When he realized she wasn't, he knew what he had to do. Killing Kelly, in his mind's eye, would be just like killing Katie. Her suffering would satisfy his cold, hard, undying thirst for revenge.

He remembered how the idea of killing his wife had first come to him one morning while shaving. How totally evil it made him feel, and how totally satisfying it would be.

Until the night that he spotted Kelly, he never believed that his idea could become a reality. It simply remained a dream. He remembered watching Kelly for hours before making up his mind. She'd come into the restaurant alone one night for a drink, and then stayed to do some dancing. During her visit, she'd been drinking pretty heavily. She looked depressed. He kept a watchful eye, and a careful distance. He found her later that evening, puking her guts out in the parking lot behind her car. He went to her aid. Soon afterwards, she passed out.

It was easy from there. He helped her into his car, and took her out to the lake. When they arrived, he threw her over his shoulder, grabbed a duffel bag from his trunk, and carried her off into the darkness. When he found the right spot, he stripped her down, and sat her semiconscious, dazed and confused in front of him. They were sitting on some large rocks, near a deep point on the lake. She thought he wanted sex. She was too drunk to say no.

Blake could still remember the look in her eyes, when he made his move. With great precision, he opened her throat from ear to ear. One quick flick of the wrist was all it took. His advance took her totally by surprise. The light in her eyes slowly went out as the warm dark liquid ran from her body. Her last sound was a mixture of a whisper and a gurgled scream.

After the life drained out of her, he took out some duct tape from his duffel bag, and bound a few large rocks to her chest just below her breasts. He taped a few to her ankles as well. Even in death, she was beautiful. What a terrible waste he thought taking one last look at her delicate breasts. Those might have been fun to play with. The more he stared at her, the more he could feel the growing stiffness in his slacks. Then, without hesitation, he passed his hand over her face, closing her eyes. He rolled her body over the edge and watched it slip into the lake. For a moment, she floated out a ways and then sank quickly, disappearing into the darkness. Kelly was gone. Katie was dead.

He sat for awhile, watching the surface of the water. He half expected to see her body suddenly pop back up. Nothing happened. Then, amazed by the ease of his handy work, Blake concluded that it was in his best interest to clean up his mess. He had to finish the job. He wrapped her clothes around another rock, taped them up, and threw them in after her. He reached into the duffel again, and brought out an old, empty plastic container; the kind that once held a gallon of milk. He moved down to the water's edge and filled it up. He returned to where they'd been sitting, and used the water to rinse off the remaining blood. It took him only two trips with the milk container, to remove the last remains of Kelly Richfield. The blood hadn't dried, so it was easy to wash away.

The entire escapade took less than three quarters of an hour. He was quick and efficient. He was also lucky. There was no moon out. The darkness hid his evil. Blake gave himself a pat on the back. He'd actually done it. He had found an opportunity to vent his anger in a constructive way. It made him feel whole again. Best part was, he was smart enough to leave no trace. From years at work, he'd learned from other people's mistakes. He'd learned well. Completely satisfied with himself, and the clean up job he'd performed, Blake made his way back to the car. He was sad that he was leaving alone.

On the drive home he discovered he was on a natural high. By the time he got to the house, Katie was asleep. She was beautiful. Still, looking at her face while she lay there in bed was like seeing a ghost. In his dreams, he had killed her a thousand times. Now, it felt like he had killed her for real. The rush he had received from killing Kelly was still fresh in his mind. He had taken his revenge, and enjoyed it. It really was better than sex. Blake was happy. His dreams had become a reality. Once again, Katie was gone, at least for today.

* * * * *

The barking of a neighbor's dog, suddenly jarred Blake back to the present. As he began to re-focus, he noticed the sun had started its climb into the morning sky. He looked at his watch. About twenty minutes had passed while he was lost somewhere thinking about Kelly. Sitting on the planter wall at the bottom of the driveway, he decided it was time to go back to the house. Katie would be up soon, and wonder where he'd wandered off to. He wasn't planning on going to the office today. He was going to just hang around the house. Katie was getting her massage at noon, so Grey wouldn't be ready for him until about one-thirty. That suited him just fine.

After her massage, Katie would be in a better mood. Maybe they'd actually have a chance to be friendly to each other. He loved to toy with her for the sake of appearances. He would, of course, never let on that he knew all about her little secret. She could have her deceptions. He had his.

As he walked up the driveway, Blake reminded himself to call for a new paper. He'd love to know what the good old boys at the FBI were up to today.

"Growing some more gray hair," he said out loud to himself.

Then, a voice came out of nowhere.

"What did you say, dear?" Katie asked.

"Oh nothing, just talking to myself," Blake answered her.

She was positioned on the balcony directly above him. He wondered how long she'd been standing there.

"The sunrise is beautiful, don't you think?" she said.

"Yes, it is at that," he replied. "I'm getting a mimosa, you want one?" Katie nodded her head.

"I'll be right up with it. Hang on," he told her.

Blake went into the house. A few minutes later, he emerged on the balcony with a silver tray and two glasses. Katie looked good for a ghost. With the white terry cloth robe she was wearing, she reminded him of Casey.

At first glance, he swore her throat looked like it had been cut. The shadows were funny. His eyes were obviously playing tricks on him. It wasn't until the first bubble of champagne hit his tongue, that he knew he wasn't dreaming. It was so refreshing it brought him back to reality.

"Thanks, this is wonderful," Katie replied. "Listen Blake, what time is Grey coming today?" she inquired.

"I told him to be here around noon," he answered. "You still getting one too?" she asked.

"Yeah, I need one if you don't mind. You can go first if you want," he told her.

"That would be great," she said. "I want to go shopping later this afternoon, so that should work out fine. Maybe I'll see you for dinner."

Blake agreed, but in the back of his mind, he wondered if she was really going shopping. Was a massage in the morning just an appetizer for a riding lesson later that afternoon? What the hell! Why did he care anyway? He would get his massage and then head for the office. The odds of Christine coming home anytime soon were between slim and none. It was Monday, so after her workout she'd be at the beach for most of the day. Taking a Monday off had really screwed up his day somehow. He kept thinking it was still Sunday.

After some more deliberation, Blake arrived at the conclusion that going to the office would be useless. Maybe after the massage, he'd go for a drive, but first he needed a newspaper. His curiosity was killing him. Blake grabbed the phone on the table and called information. Then he called for a paper. The woman who answered the phone was pleasant. She assured him they would have another one out to him within the hour. Blake was pleased when he hung up. His plans were set. He would read the paper, get a massage, and then quietly relax and enjoy the rest of the day. With Katie gone, he would have some time to himself. He could sit and enjoy the rush that still lingered from the past week. He could still feel Casey's energy flowing through his veins. Then, he could figure out when the time would be right to go out and kill Katie again.

* * * * *

When Grey woke up, he could hear the sound of Dylan laughing. Not really a big deal if you thought about it. It was nice to hear his laughter echoing through the house. Funny thing was though, the clock on the nightstand said nine thirteen, and the laughter wasn't coming from Dylan's room. What was even stranger was that Rachel was still in bed next to him. What the hell was going on? Grey got out of bed, and followed the laughter into the family room. There in the middle of the floor, were Dylan and Alex. They were sitting Indian style across from each other. Strange thing was, they looked like they were having a conversation. Grey was a little surprised. Almost immediately, Alex saw him and the laughter ceased.

"What are you two up to?" Grey inquired. Then he caught himself. "Never mind," he said. "I should know better than to ask."

Alex just gave him a big smile. "He was up early, so I thought I'd entertain him for awhile. Give you guys a chance to sleep in."

That was a good answer. He had to admit she was quick.

"All right, I'll let you off the hook for now," he told her. "Just remember, Alex, I know you better than that. Whatever you're up to, it's obvious from all the laughter that Dylan is enjoying himself. Just promise me one thing," he pleaded.

"Nothing weird, ok?"

Alex knew she'd been caught. "Ok," she said, "I promise, nothing too weird."

Dylan started to laugh again. Grey couldn't help wondering if somehow the little guy understood what they were saying. Then again, he was dealing with Alex. Did he really want to know? He decided to let it go.

Grey opened the fridge, and got a glass of milk. He also got Dylan another drink. He told Alex that after Rachel got up, they'd all go out to breakfast. Later he had to go to work. The Kendall's were expecting him around noon. He would work on both Blake and Katie and then come home. Two, ninety minute massages were his limit. He didn't want to wear himself out. Alex agreed. It would be another week or two before he would be ready to go back to his regular schedule. Right now he would be ok, but he had to take it easy. No point in doing too much too soon. Besides, he and Alex were both very curious to see what would happen when he tried to give a massage.

When Rachel came out a few minutes later, she found Grey and Dylan wrestling on the floor. Alex was reading the paper. She heard all the laughing and came out to check on her 'boys'. After everyone exchanged a pleasant good morning, Grey let her in on the plans for breakfast. Alex had already showered and was ready to go. She offered to watch Dylan while Grey and Rachel got themselves ready. Dylan made his way over to Alex, and sat at her feet laughing.

"He sure does like you!" Rachel exclaimed.

"Yeah, I guess he does," Alex responded. "I've always been good with kids."

Rachel turned back to her husband. "Let's go, Grey," she announced.

She looked over at Alex. "We'll be right out, and thanks," she said.

Rachel grabbed Grey by the arm and playfully dragged him off. As they walked to the back of the house, she said, "I like Alex, Dylan's in good hands."

Grey was surprised. "I'm glad, honey, Dylan likes her too." Grey shook his head. Just leave it to Alex to get things done. It was no surprise that she had found a way to make Rachel comfortable.

As Rachel got into the shower, Grey couldn't help smiling. His wife looked "hot". That and the fact that things were going as planned. The way things were headed reminded him of the way things used to be when he and Alex first met. Back then, Alex had a way of making everything so simple and easy. That was just Alex. When they were working on something together, everything seemed to just fall into place. Watching her with Dylan and Rachel, Grey knew that she had only gotten better over time.

As he followed Rachel into the shower, he saw the bruises on his shoulder. They reflected back at him in the bathroom mirror. Rachel wondered how hard his body must have thrashed about during the accident. How could the doctors have missed the stress fractures? Why had the injury shown up later? Rachel realized that she would probably never know. Only Grey and Alex knew the truth. What happened took place both physically and mentally in the depths of their minds. The event was so powerful that it produced obvious physical changes. It had taken them years to understand these awesome powers and the forces behind them. These abilities were beyond the realm of simple understanding or explanation. Now, because of the accident, they had been thrown a new twist. A door in Grey's mind had opened. It was a new experience for both of them. It would be very enlightening to see what would happen after breakfast. What would Grey's hands see when he gave a massage? Grey was both excited and nervous. Was he ready to handle the ecstasy or the agony of the outside world? Was he ready to deal with the intimate details in the lives of others? In a few short hours, he would have the answers. For now, all he could do was wait.

* * * * *

It would take half an hour to drive from the restaurant in Anaheim Hills to Blake and Katie's place in Laguna Beach. Breakfast went well. It was quiet and uneventful. Grey was at peace with himself. He and Alex had agreed to meet later back at the house around four. Alex told Rachel that she had some shopping to do, so Rachel had directed her to the nearest mall. Rachel and Dylan had errands to run, so after breakfast, they all went their separate ways. On the drive down to Laguna, Grey thought about how pleasant breakfast really was. It was so nice to have Alex and Rachel getting along. He knew that Rachel would really do her best to try to make Alex feel welcome. As he drove through Laguna Canyon, his mind started to work overtime. He had not given a massage since the accident. Was he up to this? And now, with this startling new addition to his routine, being able to concentrate on his work was going to be interesting.

The closer he got to the Kendall house, the more Grey wished he'd thought of a reason for Alex to come along. It was like he was going for a solo flight without his instructor on board. Was he crazy for even trying this? Even the rental car didn't feel right. Grey started to prepare himself mentally. He had learned earlier that if he expected something to happen, and then it actually did, he was better equipped to handle it. That way, it would be very similar to his experience with Richard.

Being prepared for that encounter in advance had given him a greater sense of control. It was like going to the movies and waiting for the previews to start. You knew it was coming, you just didn't know what you were going to see. If you didn't like the show, you could always leave. Whatever came, at least he could face it head on.

With that in mind, things would be more tolerable. Katie Kendall would be easy to handle. This was a sweet woman, who appeared to have very little excitement in her life. She had long since fallen into the rich, non-working wife routine. She was lost in her weekly schedule. Monday massage, Tuesday hair, Wednesday lunch at the club routine. Then of course there was shopping. That was an almost an every other day affair. Katie apparently adapted to it with ease. She performed her job well. She looked good, always dressed in style, and made her husband look good as well. Even after all these years, she was amazing. She still managed to look like a trophy on Blake's arm.

Blake on the other hand seemed far more interesting. His personality, his public persona, and his job, gave him exposure to all kinds of different people. Blake was a very well known and respected individual. Grey was sure that if anything strange was going to happen, it would most likely come from Blake. As he drove through town and got closer to the beach, he got caught in some traffic. Sitting at a red light, his mind drifted back to yesterday, and his meeting with Richard. He wondered how his friend was doing. He was curious to see if he had slept last night.

Thanks to their recent visit, Grey was sure that Richard would be doing a lot of soul searching. They had given him a lot to think about. He felt bad about having to burden his friend that way. He wished there had been some other choice. Maybe, when he got home, he would give the good Father a call.

The light changed. As he made the turn south on Pacific Coast Highway, Grey could see the Kendall house. It sat comfortably on a bluff about a mile down the road. Even from a distance, it was truly magnificent. The house consisted of four levels, which had been carefully cut into the neighboring hillside. From a distance, it looked like a small hotel. It was white, very old world in appearance, and a classic. It was highlighted by a large number of windows that made up nearly the entire ocean side of the residence. Inside, everywhere you stood, there was a view overlooking the ocean. On the bottom level, the pool and Jacuzzi were designed so their outside edge ended against the side of the cliff. A sheet of clear Plexiglas, a couple of feet tall, kept swimmers from falling over the edge. Terraces of grass and flowers were cut in levels, giving the yard fascinating depth. At the top of the driveway, there was a four car garage with a guest house above.

The driveway itself ran down the hill about fifty yards, winding its way down to the street below. There, it ended in an electric wrought iron entry gate. The actual entrance to the driveway was about two hundred feet off the main highway. As he drove south, he made a left off P.C.H., drove up a little ways, and stopped at the gate. Then, the Kendall's would buzz him in. The whole estate was pretty impressive. Blake told him once that the place had been built by an old movie star from the fifties. Grey couldn't remember the guy's name, never the less it was still damn amazing. The place looked like it was built yesterday.

It was elegant and classy. He made the left and stopped at the gate. It was closed, so he pulled up to the security camera, found the intercom, and called up to the house. He was expected.

While he waited to be let in, Grey started to get himself together. Katie answered the intercom and buzzed him up. He waited patiently for the gate to open, giving him access to the driveway. As his car moved slowly up the hill toward the house, he remembered something that Alex had taught him years before. To be in control, you had to be willing to take control. If he spent all his time worrying about the "what ifs", he would forfeit any chance there was of staying calm.

When he reached the top of the hill, he could see Blake and Katie standing on the balcony above him. They waved to him as he pulled up and got out of his car. He yelled,

"Hello," and waved back.

As he walked around to the back of his car to get his equipment out, he noticed that one of the garage doors was open. Christine's BMW was missing. Then he remembered it was Monday. She'd be at the gym. He would miss having her around today. He always found her entertaining. Grey took out his table, and headed up the stairs to the house.

Katie met him at the front door: typical, Katie. There she was, standing in the doorway, with a glass of champagne in her hand. She was quite a sight. While the big terry cloth bathrobe did its best to hide her figure, Grey knew from experience what lay underneath. His hands had traveled down that road before. Then again, there was the one feature that even the robe couldn't hide; Katie's eyes. They were a deep, dark blue. They were the perfect highlight to her soft, exquisitely sculptured face. The masterpiece was completed by the framing of her face with her long, dark, flowing hair. She was simply breathtaking. She wore little or no make-up. She was perfect. When Blake had chosen, he had chosen well.

Katie stepped aside, as she waved Grey into the house. He knew that she usually had her session upstairs in her bedroom; it was more private that way. The layout of the house was quite unusual. Grey had come in on the third floor. The master bedroom was one flight up. He was now on the kitchen and dining level. Below him, were two additional levels:

these contained four additional bedrooms, two bathrooms, guest's quarters on one floor and a large entertainment level complete with indoor Jacuzzi on another.

The staircase was wide and drawn out, and wound its way up through the house. Even with the portable massage table, the climb was a fairly easy one. The staircase was user friendly. Katie told him that she wanted to go first. On the way up, she explained that she had plans for the rest of the afternoon. As usual, Grey was accommodating.

While he was setting up his table, he started to worry again. In the back of his head, he heard Alex's voice reminding him to take control. He looked for an answer. He found one. Katie liked to talk during her massage. If he could get her involved in a conversation, maybe he could keep his mind centered on other things. It was certainly worth a shot. Distracting himself might help keep the flashes away.

Katie came out of the bathroom in a very short towel: her way of getting extra attention. Grey tried not to stare. She had her hair up. She was beautiful, and damn it, he'd told her a thousand times to be more appropriate. Her behavior was nothing new, however, and he found it even more bizarre that it never seemed to bother Blake. Grey wondered many times if this was intentional. With some clients you could never tell.

When she got on the table, she moved the towel around a lot trying to get comfortable. It always seemed like she was trying to flash him a little. Maybe she was. After working on her for as long as he had, he figured it really didn't matter. He was almost blind to it anyway. The old rule was, if you ever got flashed, it was seen one, seen them all. What a crock! Bottom line was, some were a lot better than others. You just couldn't admit that, and still be professional.

Over the years, he'd seen more than his fair share. There must be something different about having a guy's hands all over you. Well, almost all over you. Keep it professional! There were rules. Lyanna had a line he liked to borrow on occasion. She'd used it repeatedly to tease Frank. "No touching in the swimsuit area." That said it all. The way he had it figured, that was about as good a rule as you were ever going to get. It kept things simple; simple and professional.

Katie was ready. Grey turned, took a deep breath, and walked to the foot of the table. He grabbed a bottle and squeezed. The lotion felt warm. It was like shaking the hand of an old friend. He put the bottle down and lifted one of Katie's feet. On contact, her foot seemed to melt into his hand. It was an incredible feeling. He noticed immediately that the sensitivity of his touch had greatly increased. There was a tremendous amount of energy. Carefully, he brought his other hand over, and had it join the first. Slowly and rhythmically, Grey's hands went to work.

He had actually completed one entire leg, before anything strange started. It probably took longer for anything to happen because his point of contact kept moving with his hands. The kaleidoscope of colors and light came on slowly this time, but there was really no stopping it. By now, nothing was a surprise. Question was, if he took both hands off Katie, would it stop? If it did, would it start again if he continued to work? It was decision time. Grey thought about Alex. He thought about Father Richard. He knew what he had to do. There was no time like the present. Grey continued the massage.

At first there were only colors. Then shadows and lights that seemed to clash or reflect back at each other. After a short time, the picture started to come into focus. She was in a shopping mall, walking with a man. They were headed into a women's lingerie shop, Victoria's Secret. Grey recognized the mall. It was The Main Place in Santa Ana. He and Rachel had been there many times before. Katie was going into the store to shop.

The man she was with accompanied her. He looked very familiar. Grey was sure that he had met him before. He recognized the face, but struggled to place the name. As it turned out, Katie was picking out some very provocative things. She took one particular bustier off a rack and turned to her gentleman escort.

"What do you think of this one, Walter?"

The gentleman nodded his approval. Katie kept the garment and laid it over her arm.

Grey was intrigued, Katie Kendall in a lingerie store shopping with another man? It didn't make sense. Or did it? Then it hit him. He remembered who Walter was. Walter Greenberg, Blake's law partner. He'd met him at the Kendall's Christmas party a few years back. So that's who he was seeing putting his hands all over Katie's ass. They were obviously involved. This was unbelievable!

Instantly, the questions began to pop into his head. Did Blake know? He seriously doubted it. How long had this been going on? God only knows. How had Walter and Katie been able to hide this? He wanted to know more. While he finished Katie's other leg, he watched and waited for answers. Sadly, all he saw was two lovers, engaged in the playful adventure of sensual shopping. He'd seen enough. Grey let go.

When he broke contact, the reaction he received was exactly what he expected. The moment his hands left her body, the tape stopped and things returned to normal. This was a great relief. A break in the action allowed him to get some more lotion, and give his mind a rest. Katie was so relaxed already she didn't even notice the pause. As he started working under her hips and low back, the flashes did not come back. This was strange. Even after five minutes, there was no reaction. Grey was puzzled. He watched his hands go back and forth, disappearing and then reappearing from underneath Katie's body. Then he noticed something.

The palms of his hands were against the surface of the table, the back of his hands were in contact with Katie's back. Although she was face up, he was working on her back from underneath. Could this be making a difference? Grey turned his hands over, palms up and continued to work. That was it! It didn't take long for the next episode to start.

Over the next forty-five minutes, Grey participated in more of Katie's private thoughts than he ever dreamed of. Every event that ran through her mind was brought to life in his head. There was even a surprising moment when he saw her completely naked, by seeing her reflection in a mirror while she was trying on some lingerie. If she had been looking at him from the table at the time, she would have seen him blush. It caught him off guard. He practiced turning off the tape for brief periods of time, by simply letting go. It was great to have a temporary escape, but he had to finish the massage.

By the time he was finished working on Katie, he was having serious doubts about how he was going to look her straight in the face. He was hoping he wouldn't have to. Over the last hour and a half, he'd been witness to some pretty amazing stuff. After the massage, she was totally relaxed. He left her floating somewhere between conscious and unconscious. He covered her in a warm towel, and told her she was finished. He suggested she go straight from the table and take a hot shower. She gratefully agreed.

"Don't forget to drink some water," he called in after her.

Grey watched as Katie rolled over, and headed for the bathroom. He found himself staring at her towel draped figure as she walked away. What crazy things were going on in this house? What would drive such a sweet woman away like that? What was happening between her and Blake that would put her in the bed of another man?

What a strange way to come back to work. In all the years of being a therapist, he never worried about giving a massage. Now, the thought of ever giving another one was very disconcerting. But what choice did he have? It was time to wipe down the table, and get ready for Blake.

He looked at the clock by the bed. It was one-thirty in the afternoon. Lunch hour had passed and he had never even noticed. He wanted a drink, anything cold would do, but a scotch right now might settle his nerves.

"Yeah, but for how long?" Grey chuckled.

He wondered what Alex would think of all this. He could use her help right about now. He was sure that working on Blake would be another wild adventure into the unknown. Then again, maybe Blake's behavior would help explain Katie's. Working on him might answer a few questions. Grey hoped that after Blake's massage things would make more sense. In the mean time, he had a few minutes to kill before starting him. He walked out on the balcony to get some air and enjoy the view. The fresh air would do him good; that, and a change of scenery. The balcony offered the perfect escape. Not wanting to miss this opportunity, Grey had made his way outside.

It was funny. Grey must have been day dreaming, staring out at the ocean. He didn't even acknowledge her the first time she spoke. It wasn't until the chill of the glass hit his hand, that he realized she was standing next to him.

"I was in the shower winding down and all of a sudden, I had the weird thought that maybe you could use this." Katie handed him a scotch. "Three fingers, two cubes. Isn't that the way you like it?"

"That's so strange," he replied, "I was just thinking the same thing."

"Well, great minds think alike," Katie joked. "Thanks for the attention."

"You're welcome Katie, it's always a pleasure. Thanks for the drink." Grey said and tipped his glass.

"You're welcome," came in a deep voice from behind both of them.

Blake had joined them on the balcony.

It was another twenty minutes before Grey got back to work. Blake kept both him and Katie engaged in some light, casual conversation, until finally Katie excused herself and left to get dressed. Once she was safely inside, Blake asked about Katie's session. Grey reminded him about the therapist-client confidentiality rules, and explained that it even applied to husband and wife.

Blake was not amused. "What kind of bullshit is that?" he blurted. "Well it's the same as lawyer-client, or doctor-patient rules, "Grey responded."I don't mean to sound evasive, but I am required to follow the same ethical code that you are." Grey paused then took a long pull on his drink. "I can tell you however, that she slept through most of it."

Blake looked frustrated. "Nothing good huh?" he asked. "Not that I'm aware of." Grey lied. "You ready to get started?"

"Why not," Blake answered as he rose from his chair. Grey followed his lead, and together they went back into the house.

While Blake got comfortable on the table, Grey quietly prepared to go at it again. This time, it would be easier. He had mastered a new trick. He knew from working on Katie that he could stop anytime that he wanted to, by just letting go. It helped him stay in control. Now all he had to do was get through the next ninety minutes. An hour after that, he'd be safely at home talking to Alex about all of this and probably having a good laugh. There was a light at the end of the tunnel. Grey smiled and walked to the end of the table. When Blake was ready, Grey picked up his lotion, and reached for a foot. In the back of his mind, he heard a voice say Lord, here we go again. He wasn't amused. He placed a hand on Blake and said a silent prayer. Then Grey headed off into the world of colors and lights.

* * * * *

Twenty minutes into Blake's massage, the adventure started. He couldn't avoid real contact. Grey was sure of one thing, something about his new gift was completely out of whack. Whatever was going on, everything he was seeing was so abstract that none of it made any sense. Working on Blake was like watching an old "B" movie, like the old 'slice and dice' movies where the special effects were lousy, and the acting was worse. In Blake's memories, the scenes always began with someone looking down at their hand. From the size and shape, you could tell, the hand belonged to a man. The hand alone wasn't that interesting, but what its owner held in it was.

Surrounded by a set of strong fingers, was an antique straight razor with the blade open. The instrument itself was beautiful. Ivory and gold handle, with exquisite workmanship. The blade appeared to be as deadly as it was magnificent. Every time Grey saw it, he got an uneasy feeling. He knew there was more than what his mind could see. Because of this, he was forced to break contact with Blake several times. This prevented the visual narrative from continuing any further. Problem was, each time he tried to proceed with the massage, the tape would run a little further. It was as if he were pressing the pause button on the remote. This continued until finally, Grey got to witness what the shadowy figure was up to.

After observing the first young woman having her throat cut, Grey pretty well decided, that some part of his new mental toy was broken. What he was seeing didn't make any sense. If this was indeed what Blake was thinking about, there had to be some logical explanation. He was probably dreaming. He must have watched a late night monster movie, or read a horror novel. Maybe he was thinking about an old case.

Grey wasn't particularly interested in which scenario it was, but this was ridiculous. Up until now, this exercise had been basically for fun. Now, this was getting disgusting. There was also something strange. In the tape, the killer had performed the task more than once. There were at least three victims. On each occasion, the intensity and detail of each mutilation was carefully orchestrated. What Grey was seeing was making him sick. With each new sequence of events, he was forced to let go before a feeling of nausea overtook him. Blake's taste in entertainment was obviously pretty outrageous. Grey had to admit though, that with all the nut cases Blake had defended over the years, he'd probably seen just about everything. Still, it was very surprising and all of this stuff was apparently still fresh in his head! The great Blake Kendall into "Ripper" films! Who would have thought? All in all, it was very traumatic. Grey found himself counting the minutes until he'd be finished. At one point, it felt like time was standing still. Finally, he was finished.

The most surprising thing about the whole experience was he saw nothing about Katie, just the "B" movie crap. During the entire session, Blake had not once given any thought to anything about Katie! Grey didn't know whether to be relieved, surprised, or disappointed. He settled on being relieved. He somehow managed to get through Blake's massage. So his client was into sick horror genre. Things could be worse.

As Blake got off the table, Grey wondered if he would ever find out what was really going on between him and Katie. After what had just happened, he wasn't sure he even wanted to know. As he was cleaning up, Grey shook his head, and laughed quietly to himself. All of this would make for a good story. If Alex thought what happened with Father Richard was interesting, wait until she got a load of this! As Grey started to pack his things, Blake came out of the bathroom in a robe. "Nice job my friend," he said. "Care for a refill?" he asked, pointing to Grey's glass.

"No thanks Blake; I've got a long ride home," Grey said, "Maybe next time."

Blake nodded and changed into some sweats. Grey gathered his things and headed down stairs. He would have a lot to tell Alex.

When he got to the car, a white B.M.W. was pulling up. Christine was driving. She waved at him as she passed by, and pulled into the garage. Grey waved back. Maybe she had some insight into the Kendall soap opera. When Christine got out of her car, she came over to say hello. Grey was just getting ready to leave.

"Hi, Grey," she said as she approached them.

She came up, gave him a quick hug. "We need to do lunch," she whispered in his ear. Then she backed away.

"Hi, Daddy," she said as she turned to Blake. She left both men standing there and walked into the house.

Blake laughed. "She must like you, my friend, and I have to admit, she has good taste. Give my best to your wife, and thanks for everything."

With that said, he handed Grey an envelope and said goodbye. Grey didn't bother to open it. He knew what was inside. A couple of old 'Ben Franklins' were always there. Grey laughed. Something about hundred dollar bills always made him smile. He'd get to them later. Grey turned the rental car around and headed down the driveway. His welcome back to work had been more than he'd bargained for. He and Alex had to find a way to get a handle on this thing. If not, he knew that sooner or later, he would drive himself crazy. He was fearfully aware now that having the ability to see into the intimate thoughts of his clients was something he definitely did not want. At times it might prove to be fun or entertaining, but it carried with it an enormous responsibility.

In the past few hours, he'd exposed himself to way too much information. Dealing with it all required too much thinking. This whole thing was beginning to stress him out. He needed to relax.

On the way out of Laguna, he stopped at a gas station and bought a candy bar and a coke. It was just what the doctor ordered. Now, it was time to go home. Rachel and Dylan would be waiting.

As he turned north on to Highway 133, he dug out an old Billy Joel CD out of his gym bag sitting on the seat next to him. He needed some tunes. He popped the CD into the player, turned up the volume, then he and Billy went singing together through the canyon. Billy's words just danced in Grey's head.

"In the middle of the night, I go walking in my sleep. From the mountains of faith, to the river so deep."

There was something there, something that hit home. If only Billy knew. Then again, maybe somehow he did. Grey just kept driving.

The more he thought about what had happened today with the Kendall's, the more his curiosity began to work overtime. Could some of what he was seeing just be dreams, or was it possible that everything he observed were in fact, real events? Only time would tell. It was another puzzle for him and Alex to solve. Billy started another verse. As Grey sang along with the music, his mind wandered.

There was something ominous out there; something dark and evil. He could feel it. Alex always said, everything happens for a reason. Maybe there was a purpose for all of this. Maybe, for some reason, there was something out there that only he was supposed to see. That would explain why all of this was happening. It was a lot to think about.

Suddenly, a car horn shattered his train of thought and grabbed his attention. It brought him back to reality.

In the background, Billy had just started a new song. Grey went back to singing and tried to catch up. He let the music take him away. The more he drove, the more he swore that he could really feel the road. His sensitivity was getting stronger. It made him uneasy. He wondered what would happen tonight, when he wanted to go to sleep. Would the sandman come or would he casually wave as he passed by again? Grey tried not to think about it. He had bigger worries.

What if he closed his eyes, and instead of sleeping, he started to walk through his own river of dreams?

CHAPTER 9

It was nearly four-thirty when Grey arrived home. He was a little surprised to find, that he had come home to an empty house. Everything was so quiet and still. It was ominously peaceful. Still, at first glance, everything seemed to be in its proper place. He decided to enjoy the silence while it lasted. Why look a gift horse in the mouth? He knew that he wouldn't be alone for very long. Making his way through the house, he stopped in the kitchen.

There on the fridge he found a note that Rachel left for him. It said that she and Dylan were at her parents' house swimming. Her timing could not have been better. Without knowing it, she'd done him another favor. Because of her absence, he and Alex would have a chance to talk in private. He had spoken with Alex earlier while he was on his way home. During their conversation, he outlined everything that had happened at the Kendall's. He kept it simple, giving her only general information. He said he would give her the details later. Alex told him that she was on her way back to the house as well. She'd be returning about five. Anxiously, Grey looked at his watch. She should be pulling up any time now.

While they were talking, Alex said that she had spent the better part of the afternoon doing some research. He wasn't exactly sure what she was investigating, but he trusted her instincts. One thing for sure, he knew if he'd gone out looking for her, he wouldn't have found her hanging out in the local library. If Alex was looking for something, you could bet she would find whatever she was after. Ever since they met, she always had the ability to get what she wanted and if she chose, manage to keep a low profile. Grey was anxious to hear what she had come up with. Heaven only knows what she was up to. He looked at his watch again. It was a quarter to five. He had just enough time to get cleaned up and change clothes.

He was pulling on a clean shirt when he heard the Mustang pull up in front of the house. By the time he got out to the front hallway, Alex was coming in the front door. She was dressed all in black with her hair in a pony tail.

"Hey, so how are you?" she asked.

"I wish you were there today," he replied. "I could have used your advice. It was all very interesting. I've got a few things I want to discuss with you."

"Sure," Alex said, "I'm all ears. Where's Rachel?" Grey filled her in about his wife's note.

"Great." Alex said, "For a change we can just sit here and talk." Grey nodded.

"I'm getting a beer, you want one?" he asked.

"Sure, give me a minute to freshen up," she said. "I'll be right back." Alex disappeared down the hall.

When she returned a few minutes later, she did look better. Her hair was down now. She'd brushed it out. Her make-up was touched up, and her jacket was gone. Now she was in a black T-shirt and jeans. Funny thing was, she was barefoot! He hadn't noticed when she first walked in, but now that he thought about it, she did seem shorter when she passed by him in the foyer. She had left her boots outside on the porch. He could see them outside through the screen door. Alex found a spot on the couch, kicked back and put her feet up. Grey handed her a beer. Her bare feet caught his attention. They were pretty as far as feet go and her toenails were painted. The polish looked wet but he seriously doubted that she'd just had a pedicure. It wasn't too long before she caught him staring. He thought to ask, but didn't. He knew better. Any explanation would soon be forthcoming. Grey took a seat in the chair next to her. Alex opened her beer. She took a swallow and then said with a smile, "So, how was your day?"

Grey gave her a funny look, and then started to laugh. He rolled his eyes. "Where would you like to start?"

* * * * *

The morning paper had been a big disappointment. It arrived at the front gate within the hour just as the lady on the phone promised. After an exhaustive search, Blake discovered there was no mention of Casey's murder within its pages. All of his anxiety was for nothing. His mind worked the problem. One of two things was possible. Either there were no new leads on the case, or the authorities were keeping any new information confidential and away from the public. Blake figured it was the latter. He'd just have to pay close attention, watch the news and follow the paper for the next couple of days. By then, the investigation would almost certainly have hit a dead end. He had really left nothing for them to follow. He was on top of his game. As usual, he had been careful and thorough. His mind was at ease.

Katie had left the house about half way through his massage. Blake wondered if she'd really gone shopping, or whether she was headed off for another pony ride. At this point, did it even really matter? He felt so alone. Even Christine ignored him. She had been more interested in talking to Grey than speaking to him. After Grey left, Blake went looking for her. He found her in her room. The conversation was short. She said she was going to take a shower and then go meet some friends for dinner. She wouldn't be home until late. Blake left her alone. From the looks of things, he was going to be on his own again. He resolved not to let any of it get to him. He had better things to think about. His evening with Casey was still fresh on his mind.

Over the past few hours, his outlook on the day had definitely improved. Once again, Grey had put Katie in a better mood. As long as Katie was happy, the atmosphere around the Kendall house seemed to stay calm and relaxed. After a massage, Katie would instantly go from bitch to bearable. That was a major accomplishment. Blake wondered if he was paying Grey enough. The guy had hands that somehow managed to change Katie's entire disposition. Something else was strange. Grey having his hands all over Katie didn't bother him in the least. Thinking about Walter's hands gave him the chills.

After giving the matter ample consideration, he wasn't even sure that his feelings about it had anything to do with sex. He was long past caring about that anyway. It was more about trust. Every time he thought about what he had seen that day at Walter's house, it reminded him about whom he could really trust. When Katie plunged her "knife", she had twisted it hard and deep. It was a wound that would never heal. It was late afternoon by the time he decided to leave the house.

The weather was still warm, and along with the temperature came the comfort of a nice summer breeze. Blake climbed behind the wheel of his Mercedes and headed off down the hill. With the top down, he could feel the wind in his face. The adrenaline rush came on quickly as he sped down the highway. It just added to the already incredible high that he was still enjoying from his latest adventure. As his mind began to wander, he could feel the power and thrill he had felt as he watched the life gently flow out of Casey. The large scalpel like cut he had inflicted allowed the skin on her neck to separate slowly. The natural inner pressure from within her body had gradually forced the wound open, turning a once fine incision into a large, gaping tear. The blood came. What started as a small trickle quickly opened like a flood gate. The end came quickly. For Blake, it was exhilarating. He could feel the energy flowing from her body. The life ran out of her like the sands of an hourglass.

As his mind returned to the present, Blake realized he was still heading down the Coast Highway. He wasn't exactly sure where he was going he just knew he had to keep moving. His adrenaline had reached the point where he thought if he stopped driving these incredible feelings he was having would stop too. He wasn't prepared to let them go yet.

Back in January, after the first adventure, the rush stayed with him for only three days. After the second, it lasted five. The results of the third were even more gratifying. He had gone almost a week. Now all he wanted was to never come down. He was like a junkie, willing to do anything to get more of the same high. Everything about it elevated his senses to new heights. He had become an addict. He had to have more!

Each time he took Katie down, he got a better fix. The raw power that came to him from watching her inner light go out somehow revitalized him. With each new execution, the euphoria lasted longer. Casey had been the best so far. She was so vibrant and energetic. She had served him well. Blake enjoyed the ride.

He went back to concentrating on the road. He discovered that somehow, even on an unconscious level, he had chosen to drive south. About two miles up on the right was the street that led to Walter's house. Was there some inner part of him that had to know? By the time he made the decision to swing by for a look, he was already past the turn off. Maybe that was a sign. Maybe he should just keep moving. Maybe some things were better left unknown. Truth was, he knew if he found Katie's car at Walter's again, all it would do was set him off. It would be another knife in his back, compliments of Katie. Strange, she was so civilized this morning back at the house. She was even pleasant and kind. She almost made him feel wanted. They even shared small talk together. He was impressed. He realized she had played him well. As the car shifted gears, Blake's mind shifted as well. He could feel the warmth of Casey's breast in his hand again. He could feel the warmth of her naked body against his. The feeling was incredible. His heart started to beat faster in his chest. He could actually feel the blood pumping through his veins. These feelings of euphoria began to take control of him again. Just thinking about Casey was enough. He turned the car around and headed back toward Walter's. He had to know. If Katie were there, it might just be a good thing. It would give him a reason to go hunting again. The 'Cat' smiled and stepped on the gas.

* * * * *

When the phone rang, it startled him. It seemed like they'd been sitting there talking for hours. His mind was somewhere else. Grey excused himself and went to the kitchen to answer the call. It was Rachel. She sounded in good spirits. Her mom wanted to know if they would like to join them for dinner. Grey politely agreed and immediately checked with Alex. After a quick nod, he informed Rachel that they were both in.

"Ok then, we'll be over in a few minutes," he assured her.

Then Rachel asked him about work. "How did it go today?" she inquired.

"No problems," he assured her. He wasn't really lying. Why should she worry? "Thanks for asking. We're on our way," he said. Grey hung up the phone and went back to the living room.

Alex looked puzzled. He noted the confused expression on her face, "Guess you caught most of that, huh?" he asked. "Sorry if I put you on the spot."

"That's ok," she responded. "We're done here anyway. Tell me something though. How much of this stuff with the Kendall's do you think is real? There's a big difference between day dreams and reality."

"I don't know yet," Grey offered, "but we have a week or so to find out. I work on Katie once a week, but I don't work on Blake as often. It was his massage that turned out to be the weird one. Think I should offer him another one?"

"Yeah, that might not be a bad idea," Alex agreed. "In the mean time, let's play with this thing a little and see what we can learn."

Grey nodded and said, "Ok, maybe later, but for now let's get the hell out of here. Rachel and her parents are waiting."

As they headed for the Mustang, Grey noticed her boots on the front porch. He was so involved in their conversation he forgot to ask her about them. Alex, on the other hand, neglected to offer any explanation. She stopped on the porch and slipped them on. Grey remained silent. It wasn't until they got into her car that Alex spoke up.

"You going to ask or what?" she said in a serious yet almost sarcastic voice. His silence to this point must have puzzled her.

"Why ask?" he replied. "You'd tell me if you wanted me to know." "I'm sorry," she said, "I figured you already did. I keep forgetting that you're still not one hundred percent. Sorry, my mistake. Anyway, during my research today, I walked through a lot of small shops. Each was owned by a practitioner with whom I was not personally familiar. I traveled through some pretty strange places. A few of them were as you say, a little out there, if you know what I mean. On the way home, I decided that I'd better play it safe. You know how some of these people operate. Most of them are just wannabes. Then again, there is no telling what I might have stepped in. I didn't want to take the chance of bringing anything strange into the house. It's better to be safe than sorry."

Grey was silent. She was right. It could have been dangerous. The thought of something like that had never even crossed his mind. It made him realize that he had to get his head together quickly, no matter what it took. He looked over at Alex.

"Thanks," he said. "I can't believe I didn't think of that."

Alex laughed, "Don't worry, I've always got your back, babe. Hey, we do need to make one quick stop though. I need to rub some red clay on these heels. You know, like at a baseball diamond. Is there a park around here?"

"There's one around the corner," he informed her. "At the next street, hook a right."

Alex smiled. "Good deal, that clay will fix these boots. Then we can go to dinner. By the way, I like your wife's family. They're great!"

"Yeah, they are great," Grey thought. Alex made the turn. "It's up there on the right," he directed. When the park came into view, Alex pulled to the curb and got out.

"Be right back," she said and gave him a wink. Then she was off.

Grey watched as she walked across the grass to the baseball diamond. She obviously knew what she was doing. Once she was standing on the clay surface, she moved like a batter digging in before a pitch shuffling her feet back and forth in the dirt. When she was finished, she turned and headed back to the car.

"Hand me that rag behind the seat, please?" she asked. Grey handed her the towel. She wiped the red dust off the side of her boots.

"That ought to do it," she said. "I hate amateurs. Now, let's go to dinner." Grey smiled, nodded and pointed her in the right direction.

* * * * *

Walter's neighborhood was unusually quiet for a late afternoon. Especially, since it was Monday. Blake assumed that people would be coming home from work at that hour. To anyone watching around the neighborhood, he'd be just another passing car. As it turned out, he was the only car moving on the street. It felt more like a Sunday afternoon. Walter's house was at the end of the block and slightly around the corner to the left.

From this distance, he couldn't see the driveway. It was impossible to tell if anyone was home. He had to wait until he drove around the bend. Blake slowed the car down to a crawl. He took his foot off the gas, and let the engine just idle, pulling the car along. The Mercedes' engine purred softly. As he rounded the corner, Walter's house came into view. Blake's heart sank. Much to his dismay, the driveway was empty.

There was no one in sight. He was relieved but disappointed at the same time. A part of him was genuinely hoping to find Katie's car in the driveway. Seeing it there would have added more fuel to the fire. It probably would have been enough to send him over the edge again. In the past few months, he had grown to love the excitement of the rush, the high that came to him every time he crossed over to his other self. He had learned to depend on the feeling to make him feel whole.

Over time, it had become easier to allow his inner being to be seduced by its power again and again. Not finding Katie there was like having the wind taken out of his sails. He had almost counted on her presence. He felt as though he'd been robbed. Katie's absence from Walter's had deprived him of another chance to go hunting, another chance to get high. She had ruined the moment. Now all he had left to entertain him were some memories from the past and fantasies of the future. The reality was, the high he was on would only last so long. It would be over soon. Then he would need another fix. He was always living on borrowed time.

On the inside of his slacks, he could feel something hard pressing against the inside of his thigh. For a change, the object wasn't made out of flesh and blood from the present, but rather a masterpiece of ivory and gold from the past. It was the instrument of his addiction, the symbol of his power. He was the maestro. This was his baton. He had to perform. Carefully, he reached down to touch his friend. He could feel the pure intensity of its power, as he ran his fingers back and forth down the length of its bulge.

To Blake, it felt like he was playing with a bolt of lightning. As long as he had his instrument, he could continue to conduct his symphony of death. With the completion of each new act, he was rewarded with a new and more intense level of pleasure. This added sensation, allowed him to completely enjoy his other side.

Now, thanks to Katie, there would be no chance for a new performance. Blake's mood became somber. All the way home, he was troubled. He worried about how long this present ride was going to last. He had been lucky so far. Lucky, in that each new interlude lasted longer than its predecessor. But there were no guarantees. It was inevitable that sooner or later, the energy would start to fade. He would feel the slow, steady withdrawal as it subsided and start to become anxious again. The degeneration process always began much sooner than he wanted. This time he needed to be prepared. There were plans to be made. He had to make certain that another Katie could be found when he needed her. Hunting, it seemed, would be the only way to insure his survival. He had to refuel the fire, before it died out. He had to find another toy to play with.

Tomorrow was Tuesday. He would be expected back at work. That meant he would be downtown. His office was close to the courthouse. His firm had chosen a building only a couple of blocks away. On many occasions, its ideal location allowed him the luxury of working right up to the wire before heading into court. It was both comfortable and elegant. From his view on the fourth floor he could almost window shop, as a constant flow of people moved around on the street below. Until today, he had never even considered the possibility of having to go out and actually find a victim. In the past, they had somehow, always, just fallen in his lap. On each previous occasion, he enjoyed the luxury of being in the right place at the right time. It wasn't until now, after Casey, that he felt the fear of coming down. He had to find another Katie before the euphoria went away. He needed time to think. Right now, he just wanted to get home.

On his left, the sun was beginning to hang its head for another night's rest. The view was simply breathtaking. Blake found it increasingly hard to keep his eyes on the road. As he got close to home, he discovered that he had been day dreaming. His brain must have been driving on auto pilot. When he turned into his driveway, he prayed that the sun would not vanish completely below the horizon until he could reach the comfort and safety of his balcony. The colors that God had chosen to end the day with, reminded him of what he saw every time he played his instrument. He didn't want to miss a chance at a free show. The light show would only pacify him for the short time that it lasted. It just wasn't the same. The reminder was a welcome gift, but the opportunity to be able to play again was what he really desired.

When the car stopped at the top of the hill, Blake jumped out and ran toward the house. He had to get upstairs quickly. Out of the corner of his eye, he caught a glimpse of Katie's car as he passed the garage. She was home. He didn't even care. His mind could only work on one thing at a time. Right now, he had to watch the final moments of the sunset. He had to let the majesty of its colors bleed into his soul. He was drawn to them. It would be like getting a quick fix. He needed the rush. He needed the moment. He needed the peace. Blake flew up the stairs.

His prayers were answered. When he reached the balcony, the sun was just slipping into the sea. He swore that he could see imaginary steam rise, as the hot, fiery ball hit the water. It was simply an illusion, but one that he'd loved and enjoyed since he was a child. The sky it left behind was a dazzling eruption of brilliant colors. Each one seemed to melt into the other. Blake relaxed and allowed the energy to over take him. He could feel his blood pumping through every inch of his body. The moment was his and his alone. He just sat there, staring at the sea, completely satisfied. He was in ecstasy. He was along for the ride.

* * * * *

When they arrived at the in-laws, Alex headed off to the kitchen to see if she could be of any help. Grey soon found himself behind the bar, shaking a pitcher of martinis for Frank and himself. The atmosphere was pleasant and the company was sociable and relaxing as usual. Alex, of course, blended right in. She sat and visited with Lyanna and Rachel, while Grey and Frank set the table and talked about wine. This would be a real family dinner. It had been a long time since Alex had a similar experience. Russ, Brianna, and their kids would be joining them soon. Grey had told her on the ride over, that Rachel's parents invited them all over for dinner once a week so they could see the grand kids.

All the talk about family made Alex think about Grandma Boulier again. She had been a grand old woman. She had always done for Alex the best that she could. During their time together, Alex never felt as though she'd been deprived of anything. One way or another, Granny B. had always come through. Truth was, until recently, she'd never even given a second thought to having a family. It had never been in the cards. For a long time, it was only her and Granny B. Now it felt strange. While she would always be grateful to Granny B. for her efforts, she was still envious of the family that Grey was now a part of. She was happy to be included even in a small way.

During the entire evening, Grey made little or no physical contact with anyone. He told Alex that he wasn't prepared to open anymore unwanted doors. In his mind, he could still picture some of the things that he saw at the Kendall house earlier that day. While some of Katie's thoughts were humorous, almost playful in nature. Blake's were quite the opposite.

When he thought about Blake, it worried him. All he kept seeing was the hand in the shadows, the hand with the blade. Every time he saw it, he couldn't help but wonder who it was attached to. With each replay, the anticipation of possibly seeing a face only added to the relentless suspense. The images that he received from both of their subconscious minds had somehow been put into the easy recall file in his head. He could conjure them up at will. He was curious to see if he could play them back in slow motion. Being able to do so would give him an opportunity to look for details or possible clues that would help establish whether they were fantasy or reality. So far, just simple concentration worked best. If he focused his attention, he discovered that he could recall in detail each of the events that he shared with Lisa, Tony and Father Richard.

Things around him were an influence as well. Earlier today, on the way home from the beach, he had seen a delivery truck that reminded him of Tony's. The recollection triggered something and an instant replay of the incident at the pool the other day went running through his head. The images were both sudden and intense. He was driving at the time and the display caught him completely off guard. It was a major distraction that, under the circumstances, put him in a dangerous situation. For a brief moment, he forgot he was in the car. Lucky for him, the tape ran at high speed. He saw everything within a few seconds. He'd only traveled about seventy-five feet before regaining his focus.

As the miles had rolled by, something else had come to mind. What if these re-runs continued to happen on a regular basis? The one he'd just had earlier in the car proved they could be dangerous. It came out of nowhere, and forced him into a potentially deadly situation. Because of the circumstances, he might have lost control of the car, injuring himself or someone else. It was as if he were driving blind. Things were becoming clouded. He had no way of knowing when or from where the flashes would come.

For now, he was completely helpless. If he had to walk on eggshells, how long could he realistically keep himself together? How long would he be able to maintain his objectivity or his sanity? Everything considered, things were going to get more and more difficult if he persisted in working on clients. He had to find a way to get back to normal. Right now, that seemed almost impossible. He just wasn't himself. Or was he? In the last few minutes, he'd caught Alex glancing over at him a few times. Her expression seemed to be one of concern more than anything else. What was she thinking? Was something wrong? Did he look distracted or distant somehow? He didn't think so. If he did, Rachel certainly hadn't said anything. She was usually very observant when it came to that kind of thing. Then again, this was something different. Maybe it was something only Alex could see. Once again, there were too many unanswered questions. Frustration started to weave its way through him again. He was too tired to fight it. He had to get some rest.

Cautiously, he stared carefully at his face in the hallway mirror. He did appear to be a little different. There wasn't anything specific that he could put his finger on, but it was different somehow. The longer he stared into the glass, the stranger it made him feel. Then he noticed something. Hiding behind his eyes was a bright light where there used to be darkness, and an eerie darkness where there had once been light. The new face in the mirror called out to him, drawing him in closer. He just stood there, staring in silence, mesmerized by his own reflection.

A hand on his shoulder brought him out of the trance. Alex noticed him starting to slip away. She came to his rescue again. "You ok?" she inquired.

"Yeah I think so," he responded. "I saw something in the mirror. There's something about my eyes. Honestly, I'm not sure if that's me I see in the glass."

"It's you," she assured him. "I see it, too. Don't let it worry you though. I've noticed a few subtle changes over the past few days. I think what we're seeing might just be the beginning of a new and improved version of the original. I think this is all related to whatever is happening to you. So far, I don't sense any danger in it. We should get you home. You need some rest."

He was too tired to argue. Grey nodded his approval. Alex was right. It had been a long day. His emotions were maxed out, and he was physically tired as well. Even holding his martini glass steady had become a chore. His hands were shaking. He had to work at keeping his composure. Grey analyzed the situation.

If Alex wasn't worried, he wouldn't be either. Over the years, her feel for things had proved to be astonishingly accurate. It was part of her gift. Still, something strange was happening to him, something that was beginning to make him question everything. Grey looked over at his friend again. Alex winked. He decided he had to keep the faith.

* * * * *

Dinner was a complete success. While Grey and Alex were occupied in the hallway, Rachel started to collect her things. During their absence, she had decided that it was time to get going as well. By the time he and Alex found her in the den, all of Dylan's toys and supplies were packed and ready to go. Alex mentioned that she wanted to stop at the store on the way home, so she was going to say her good-byes and head out. Rachel was tired. She asked Grey if he would drive home. He agreed. Quietly, he carried everything out to the van. Alex was just pulling away when he got to the street. She pulled up next to him, and rolled her window down.

"You going to be ok for a little while?" she asked.

"I'll be fine, don't worry. I'll wait up for you. I'll be out on the patio."

"All right," she said, "See you in a few." The Mustang roared away.

As he turned back toward the house, his mind raced. Things were getting more confusing by the moment. It was time to get down to business. Tomorrow, they would have to start experimenting with this thing. Maybe paying another visit to Father Richard would help. He was not one of them, but he was someone they could trust. Having him around would be to their advantage. If approached, Father Richard would not only be willing to observe as an innocent bystander, but if necessary, become an active participant. He was not only a good man, he was a good friend.

Alex had just turned the corner when Rachel and Dylan came out to the car. Rachel was tired. Grey could see it in her eyes. So far, she hadn't asked a lot of questions, and for that he was thankful. He wasn't prepared to lie to her, but he knew he couldn't tell her the truth either. Someday, maybe he could explain it all, but for now it was way too much for her to handle. Maybe one day he could tell her everything. Maybe one day she'd be able to believe him. For now, it was all a long road with no end in sight and nothing but darkness on either side. It was a journey into the unknown.

The ride home was a blur. He remembered turning the key and starting the engine, but everything between that and his own driveway just didn't exist. When he hit the button to open the garage, the remote activated not only the door, but apparently sent a signal to his subconscious as well. It brought him back to the present. Grey took mental inventory. Rachel had said nothing on the ride home. At least nothing he could remember.

Dylan had fallen asleep. Now they were home. Without really saying much of anything, they unloaded the van. Rachel went inside and put Dylan to bed. Then she headed off as well. Grey went straight for the den and flopped down on the couch. When Rachel came looking for him a few minutes later, he was fast asleep. She was almost relieved. He had been so pale earlier and looked totally burned out. He had tried his best to hide it but she saw right through his act. As she started to cover him with a blanket, Alex came in behind her. Rachel didn't even notice. Alex remained silent. She just stood in the shadows and waited patiently, as Rachel spread the blanket over her husband. Seeing her do this made Alex smile. Grey looked so peaceful. She knew he was wiped out. She hadn't really expected him to be awake when she returned.

For a couple of minutes, both women stood quietly and watched Grey sleep. When Rachel turned to leave the room, she saw Alex standing in the darkness. Rachel jumped.

"Sorry, didn't mean to scare you," Alex apologized.

"That's ok," Rachel responded, "I didn't know you were standing there. I didn't hear you come in." There was a brief silence. "Think he'll be ok out here?" she asked.

"I don't see why not," Alex reassured her.

Rachel smiled. Then she turned to face Alex. "Can I ask you something?" she said. Alex nodded.

"Think he'll ever be himself again? He seems so different right now."

Alex grinned. So Rachel had noticed something. She wasn't completely blind. That was good to know.

"Oh yes, Rachel, I'm sure he'll be just fine. Just give him some time. The dust is probably still settling in that thick head of his." Alex retreated. Would her attempt at humor work?

One look at Rachel's face, and she knew that she had said the right thing. Rachel laughed. "You do know him, don't you?" she said. "Thanks, I needed to hear that. I'm going to go to bed. I'll see you in the morning. Good night, Alex."

"Good night Rachel," Alex replied.

Rachel left Alex alone in the entry way. With the den lights off, all she could see was the moonlight shining in through the skylight. It gave a soft, iridescent glow to the room. Grey lay quietly on the couch, all but motionless. The only sign of life was the subtle rise and fall of the blanket on his chest. It assured her that he was still breathing. She knew better than to wake him. He needed his rest. Anything she had to say could wait until morning.

Tomorrow was going to be a long day. He was going to need all of his strength to get through it. Very soon they would be visiting the dragons, and this time they might not be going alone. Fate would dictate that this time they bring a friend. Alex acquiesced. She thought about Father Richard. She remembered something that Granny B. once said.

"It is difficult at times to test the limits of your own faith. You must remember that it is also much harder to expect a friend to be willing to do the same. This is especially true when the beliefs in question are not commonly shared by both parties. Always be careful what you ask for. You just might get it."

Alex could not help wondering just how far the priest would be willing to go. Then she laughed. Somehow after meeting the man, that seemed like a silly question. She remained for awhile and watched Grey sleep. She wondered whether he was at peace, or whether his dreams were being tormented by the events of the day. For the moment, he appeared to be enjoying the calm. He was ok. No need to worry, she'd be right down the hall. Even at a distance she could feel his heart beat. She could hear him breath. She would be available in an instant if something went wrong. She felt good. The night had always been her time. After observing him for a while, she decided it would be best to keep a watchful eye.

Now that she was close by, she knew that she could protect him. Even though her physical being would have to sleep down the hall, she could leave a part of her there beside him to guard him through the night. Her talisman would protect him from any and all things that tend to go bump in the night.

Carefully, she laid her ring on the end table next to his head. She concentrated and looked for a response. After a few moments, the creature's eyes came to life, shining through the darkness. Grey was being watched. Now he would be safe. Alex took one last look at her sleeping friend. He looked placid and serene. She was pleased. Then, satisfied that everything was in order, she allowed herself to leave him. As she turned away, the guardian hissed. Its watchful eyes acknowledged her presence and followed her path as she left the room. Lost in another world, Grey went on dreaming.

* * * * *

The couch felt like a coffin. Grey grew more and more restless. Hour after hour, all he could do was toss and turn, his mind wrestling with the grotesque images that kept floating in his head. It was as if his thoughts were trapped in some sort of a mental hurricane. Over and over, he had the same dream. It continued to haunt him until he was sure it wasn't a dream anymore. It was like he was actually living it.

Once, about two a.m., he woke up violently, in a cold sweat. He sat looking down at his hands, as if he were searching for something. He swore he could feel something in his hand, but his eyes told him it was empty. When he closed his eyes again and tried to relax, it got worse. He could still see things, but this time everything appeared to be from a totally different perspective.

In the beginning, the dream was a blur, but after viewing several repeat performances, things became clearer. He began to notice more detail. Now, when he looked down, he could clearly see an arm coming out of the shadows were his body should be. At the end of the arm was a muscular hand. It was closed with the palm side up. It seemed to be floating against a sea of darkness. Protruding from its grip was part of a handle and a shiny steel blade. The hand itself appeared to be about average size. The fingers were bare with no visible jewelry. The only markings of any kind were on the handle of the instrument itself. It was carved out of a single piece of ivory that was intricately detailed and trimmed in gold. The straight edge blade was made of finely polished steel and appeared to be razor sharp. Dark stains were smeared where the blade disappeared into the handle. The cuticles on three of the fingers were stained with the same color. There was something vaguely familiar about the whole scene. He was sure that he had seen something like this somewhere before. It gave him the creeps.

After the third or fourth re-run, Grey would have given almost anything to know who the hand belonged to. Each time he saw it, even though the picture became clearer, the visual depth and dimensions still stayed the same. In the shadows, all he could make out was a forearm, wrist and hand. There were no other points of reference. It was the knife, however, that frightened him the most. It looked used. He was sure that the dark stains on the handle were blood. It was unsettling. That, and the way the instrument seemed to fit into the stranger's hand. It looked comfortable, in an eerie sort of way. It was like it belonged there. Grey got the feeling that it had been there many times before. He could feel the danger.

Suddenly, it came to him. He was watching Blake's dream. The tale of terror was playing itself over and over again in his head. Grey started to panic. This was all he needed! It was more than his mind could take.

Desperate to escape, he wanted to wake up. His wish was granted. Something inside him forced him to roll over. When he opened his eyes, he was laying on his back on the floor, looking up at the moon through the skylight. It took him a moment to settle down. As he climbed back onto the couch, he saw the red eyes staring up at him from the table. He wasn't surprised.

"Thanks, I think," he said out loud to the entity on the table.

"You're welcome," her voice echoed from behind him. It was Alex.

"I thought you might be in for a rough night. What happened?"

Alex appeared as a mere shadow in the doorway. She seemed to materialize as she entered the room. In her long, black robe she could have easily been mistaken for something out of a bad dream. She looked sexy in an evil sort of way.

Grey just shook his head in disbelief.

"Over and over again it came, an arm, a hand, and a knife. Everything else stays hidden in the shadows. It's the same one Blake was having earlier today. But, I have no idea what it means. It's getting more coherent though. Last time through, I started looking for details. I ended up finding a few clues, but they don't help much. All I can see is just a big hand holding what looks like an antique knife. You know the kind guys used to shave with."

"A straight razor?" she asked. "Nice weapon."

"Yeah, I think that's it," he answered her. "But that's about all. The knife had what looks like blood on it and that worries me. What the hell is this all about?"

Alex looked puzzled. "Based on what you're telling me, I think it must be something out of the past. At this stage of the game, there's really no way of telling. Maybe in the morning, we can go over all of this in detail. You'll need to tell me a lot more about this Blake guy and everything you can remember. Right now, I want you to try to get back to sleep. Something tells me the show is over for tonight."

Grey was too tired to care. He'd have to take her word for it. There'd be no more couch tonight either. He picked up his blanket and headed off to bed. As he passed through the room, the eyes on the table followed his every move. When he was finally out of sight, Alex walked over to the end table and carefully returned the ring to her finger. It was warm and it felt good as it slid along her skin. When it was back in place, she smiled.

"Thanks," she said under her breath.

As if to answer her, the ring got warmer and she heard a small hiss. Alex smiled again. It was the sound of dragon's breath. Now, she knew that Grey could sleep. In his dreams he was being shown whatever it was that he was supposed to see. Whatever was going on here was changing something in him and it was doing so a little at a time. There was some reason he alone was allowed to see what was being offered. Sooner or later, all the pieces would have to fit. For now, all they could do was wait. They would just have to be patient.

Tomorrow, they were planning on seeing Father Richard again. Grey had not forgotten his promise to the priest. If Father Richard wanted to be involved in all of this, then by God he would be. It certainly couldn't hurt to have the church on their side. Strangely enough, even Alex approved.

As she approached her room at the end of the hallway, Alex could hear Rachel's voice. She was awake and asking Grey what was going on. She heard him explain to her that he'd had a nightmare while he was sleeping on the couch, so he decided to come to bed. Rachel conveyed her apologies. There were a few quick words, and then silence took over the house once more.

Alex sat on the foot of her bed, and drank her tea. As always, her tea helped her to escape to a place where she could think. The more she thought about the situation, the more things began to make sense. A few pieces of the puzzle were actually starting to fit. With the limited information she already had, she was able to start creating a possible scenario.

So far, it was pretty simple. Something bad was going on. There was an evil force at work. For some reason, Grey had tapped into it. Whatever happened to his mind during the accident had opened a door for him that allowed him to have insight into the situation. The dream he was having was providing him with bits and pieces of the puzzle. If they could gather enough of the pieces and put them together, maybe they could figure this thing out.

At the time, Alex had no way of knowing how close she was to the truth. It all sounded good in theory but she had to admit that at this point, any of her ideas were nothing more than speculation. But it was a start. So far, everything they had learned leaned toward an established pattern. If only she could figure out why. For now, she would have to rely on Grey to keep her informed about everything he was seeing. Her skills would be useless if she couldn't get closer to the source. If he could manage to put a face to the shadowy figure, they might have a chance of solving the puzzle. Whoever "he" was, he was going to great lengths to keep both his identity and covert behavior a secret. From the looks of things, there were violent, and perhaps deadly, consequences. The whole idea wasn't that impossible. So far, the individual's calling card appeared to be a straight razor.

There was one other thing that worried Alex. Up until now, she and Grey had both assumed that whatever he was seeing was a dream. Initially that made the most sense. As troubled as it might appear, the dream was simply part of someone's imagination. But what if it wasn't a dream at all? What if it turned out that it was a memory instead; a flashback of a past event? Something that had actually happened!

Just thinking about that possibility made Alex very uncomfortable. It opened a whole new world of ideas. It did however also fill in a few blanks. Had the puzzle started to take shape? In the morning, she'd run the idea past Grey. Now it was time to get some much needed rest. Alex pulled up her blankets and listened to the silence.

It didn't last very long. Down the hall, she heard Rachel sneeze. It sounded like she was getting a cold. Alex laughed. Maybe she'd have to make her some tea. Then Alex listened to see how Grey was doing. His breathing was shallow and even. He was in a deep sleep. Alex focused harder. In his other world there were no dreams now, just simple, quiet serenity. She was pleased. He was getting stronger. Alex got a feeling that somewhere deep inside Grey knew a lot more about what was going on. He already had some of the answers locked away in his head. All he had to do was find them. She was sure that he could. Fate had brought her here to help him through the maze. They would find their way together. It would be just like old times.

Outside, the wind blew the branches of a small tree against her window. The soft scraping sound they made against the glass reminded her of a cat scratching to get in. If she listened carefully she could hear the leaves rustling in the wind. They were talking up a storm. Their interaction with each other created a soft, musical sound. It was a song of the night. Ever since she was a little girl, the night had been her friend. It had invariably been her savior and her constant guide. The darkness always protected her and the moon and stars always showed her the way. Tonight would not be any different. She would be there listening, in case it had something to say. Grey was safe. She was content. Tomorrow was another day. Alex relaxed and finished her tea.

* * * * *

CHAPTER 10

The radio crackled, but it was hearing the sound of his call sign that got his attention. The voice repeated itself,

"Sixty-four Echo, what's your twenty?"

Slowly, he reached over and grabbed his mike. "Sixty-four Echo, code seven at Beach and Adams over."

"Sixty-four Echo clear."

"Thanks dispatch. Sixty-four Echo clear."

Galleon opened his eyes. For the next hour or so, his time was pretty much his own. Frankly, he was amazed that he'd made it until his break. For awhile there, he'd toyed with the possibility that wasn't going to happen. His stomach was in knots. For the past couple of hours he'd been feeling a little unsettled. He needed to get some space. After his last call, instead of heading for the station, he drove to his favorite parking lot. It was dark, empty and off the beaten track. There, he could sit and be alone for awhile. He was burned out. You see a lot of disturbing things on the job. Tonight, he had seen enough. He needed a few quiet minutes to himself. It was a just after midnight and the way things were working out, it was going to be a long night. After his break, he would be just starting to work his way into the second half of a twelve hour shift. At this rate, the night was going to last forever.

The last few hours had seemed endless. He and a fellow officer were stuck doing security detail at a crime scene. They were forced to wait patiently, while the coroner did his clean up job and started his investigation. Being that he was the first officer on the scene, he was required to hang around until the body was ready to transport. He had passed the time trying to figure out why, earlier in the evening, some guy had said goodbye to his wife, climbed into the front seat of his sixty-seven Corvette and blown his brains out. What a waste.

It turned out the guy was only twenty eight. After running his name through the system, they turned up nothing. He was squeaky clean, not even a parking ticket. His wife had no answers either. She was as clueless as they were. Galleon was disgusted. Situations like this were pathetic and just didn't make any sense. That and they were a lot of paperwork.

Even after a year on the job, there were still some things you never got used to. Fact was, a few of the more seasoned officers had told him that you never do get used to it. Cops have to learn to deal with the insanity and madness in their own way. Tonight's incident was just another senseless act of violence. Galleon shook his head. Why would somebody do something like that to themselves? The world wasn't that bad. Hell, if nothing else, the guy had a great car! It was a classic. It looked like it was one sweet ride, before its owner decided to redecorate its interior with his gray matter. Now, it would be a miracle if anyone could ever get it clean. It was a terrible scene. Then it got worse.

Somehow, the press got wind of the whole thing and turned it into a sideshow. Insensitive bastards! It was hard enough keeping the wife away from the car after they found the body. The whole area looked like something out of an Alfred Hitchcock movie. "Fucking 'Looky Lou's'"! As a cop, he'd seen a lot of this kind of things go down. Still, it was always difficult to get these kinds of images out of your head. Tonight would be no exception. This one had been especially gory. He could still see the victim's eyes staring up at him, even though the top of the poor guy's head was missing. This one was definitely going to take some time to adjust. He rolled down the window and took in some night air. The breeze felt good. Galleon sat alone in the dark and collected his thoughts. Who knows, maybe they'd find some answers when they finished the autopsy. The radio cut in, breaking the silence.

"Sixty-four Echo, do you read?" The voice was familiar. Galleon picked up the mike.

"Sixty-four Echo, go ahead," he responded.

"Sixty-four Echo; Sixty-five Charlie, go to white." "Wickmann here, I'd like a word."

"Sixty-five Charlie, sixty-four Echo, Ten-four, switching to white." Galleon switched over.

"Sixty-five Charlie, this is Galleon, go ahead, over."

"Tim, my man, how's it going? Are you all right? That suicide call was a bad one."

Wickmann's voice was deep, and slow. It sounded serious as it came out of the speaker.

"Yeah Sarg, No problem here." Tim assured him. "Everything's fine. I just wish sometimes these guys would pull this kind of shit on the other side of Bolsa Chica. Then they'd be a problem for the Seal Beach guys. Know what I mean?" There was a short silence, before Wickmann answered him.

"I hear ya Tim, I hear ya. Our bad luck, that's all. You're cool though, right?"

At this point, Tim knew Wickmann was trying to feel him out. "Yeah, I'm cool. Just going to take my lunch break, then I'll get back out on the streets. I'll be fine."

Wickmann was listening carefully. The last thing he needed tonight was one of his officers losing a few screws. Tim sounded ok. Wickmann was satisfied. He only had one more question.

"Want to roll Sugar's at zero one-hundred?" he asked.

Tim laughed. "Sure Sarge, sounds like a plan. Sixty-four Echo out." "Sixty-five Charlie, ten four." The radio went silent. Wickmann was gone. Tim was alone again.

Sugar's in an hour. That might be fun. There was nothing as amusing as doing a walk through at a lingerie bar. If nothing else, it would take his mind off things. Truth was it had been a rough couple of months. Between working the job, vying for Renee's affections and dealing with Grey's accident, the compilation of things left him pretty stressed out. The guy in the Corvette was just the icing on the cake. Watching strangers die was hard enough. He was glad he hadn't lost any friends.

He'd only known Grey and Rachel for a little over a year. They were good people.

Rachel was Renee's best friend. They'd known each other for many years. When the accident happened, it was hard on everyone. He'd seen pictures of the car. Grey was lucky he got out alive. Rachel didn't realize how close she'd come to becoming a widow. As it was, Grey had been in a coma. He was very fortunate to have survived at all.

Galleon kicked back and drank his coke. As he did, the radio continued to spit out new bursts of information. They were busy tonight. He heard a call come in that concerned him. Officers from his department were currently in pursuit of some yahoo who thought that driving a hundred miles an hour down Beach Blvd was the way to go.

It wasn't! When Wickmann's voice came over the radio, he wasn't amused. Galleon knew why. People like this end up killing innocent bystanders instead of themselves. That makes them extremely dangerous. What makes them think that they can out run a police radio anyway? Wickmann made it clear he wanted them stopped. The call originated about two miles south of his present location. Because of the speed involved, they were already too far south. Galleon was off the hook. They'd have to catch him at the other end. From the sounds of it, the individual chose to ignore the officer's request when he was asked to pull over. Tim figured that from what he heard so far, the suspect wasn't even going to make it make it to the beach. He didn't.

The driver came to his senses a few minutes later and pulled over. He heard Wickmann radio in the arrest. Tim smiled. Speeding a little was expected and common place. It was always a judgment call. Reckless driving and stupidity were another. The last idiot he could remember driving that way had almost killed Grey. He'd been caught too. That was all that mattered.

After the car chase, things slowed down again. There was little or no chat on the radio for awhile. Galleon played with his drink. His straw searched the bottom of the cup twice now and it still came up empty. It was almost time to get back to work. A quick trip into the 7- Eleven on the corner for a pit stop and a refill, and he'd be good for the rest of the night. A little more caffeine and he could just cruise around until the sun came up. It would probably stay quiet until then. In the mean time, he'd go meet Wickmann at Sugar's, do a walk through, and then hang out on his own until it was time to go home. It would be an easy way to finish a bad night. At sunrise he would be free.

Sitting alone in the dark, Galleon could see most of the surrounding area. In the early hours of the morning the city took on a completely different personality. The fast paced energy of the day was gone. This late at night all that was left was the bright, sterile glow of neon lights. Across the way in a nearby shopping center, he could see them shining in virtually every color of the rainbow. Parked where he was, he could hear the crackle of electricity as it made its way through the wires that were splitting the sky above him. They almost sounded alive. The city was sleeping, but its nerve center breathed on. In a few short hours it would come to life again and the show would start all over. Galleon grinned. By the time it got up to speed again he'd be safely tucked away at the marina. But for now, it was time to move.

Once he got himself motivated, he could go out looking for trouble. That would keep him busy for awhile and help him pass the time. What he really wanted was to be home in bed. He longed for the slow roll of the tide that would gently rock him to sleep. The rhythmic slapping of the waves against the hull was music to his ears. The air was always fresh and clean; so much so that he always left a hatch open, even in the winter months. There was nothing like the smell of sea air. Yes, living on a boat was a blessing. It gave him a place to hide; one that was far away from all of this, like his own private sanctuary. To him, the boat was forty-nine feet of pure heaven.

Grandpa Eddie left the boat to him when he died. The gift came as a great surprise. He was the only one in the family that ever liked the "29th Precinct" as much as Eddie did. Eddie had named her after an old Ed McBain novel. Tim spent a lot of time on her while he was growing up. Over the years, Eddie taught him how to handle every inch of her. At first, it wasn't easy. On a boat, you learn by doing. After a while he was an old pro. Together they'd made the Long Beach to Catalina run more times than he could remember. Day or night, any conditions, Eddie always had faith in him. They'd even made the run to Ensenada a few times. There, they would end up sitting in the Mexican sun, shooting tequila and eating fish tacos. They had shared a sacred trust.

He learned a lot from his grandfather. Eddie taught him a lot of things. Maybe that's why he became a cop. It was all about respect.

He was twenty-four when Eddie passed away. The last time the old girl was out of the harbor was to spread Eddie's ashes. Eddie would have approved. It was a gorgeous day for sailing. He'd gotten her up to full sail. When they returned to the dock, the lawyers informed him that the boat was now his. It was one of Eddie's final wishes. The family hoped that he would sell it and use the money to settle down, buy a house and get married. It didn't happen. Selling her never even crossed his mind. She was like an old friend. The lawyers had moved fast. As soon as the paperwork was settled, he moved on board. Everything was finished in about three weeks. That was two years ago in March. He'd been living on board ever since. Lately, he thought about Eddie a lot.

As he pulled his car into the parking lot at Sugar's, he thought about something that Eddie had once said one night during a storm out at sea. "If ya want to get through something, Timmy my boy, you've got to stay focused."

Tonight was a perfect example of what the old man meant. No matter how tough things got, you had to keep your head on straight. Eddie was right. He still had a job to do. He could see Sugar's just up ahead on the left. Over in the corner of the lot, he could see Wickmann, just getting out of his cruiser. Tim waved. He pulled next to him and parked.

"Are you ready for a little fun?" Wickmann asked.

"Yeah, what the hell," Tim responded. Both cops zipped up their jackets, and headed for the back door.

As they approached the bar, they were greeted at the door by a tall blonde, wearing nothing but a G-string and a black lace bra. It was chilly outside. She was cold. They could tell. She was pretty in her own way, but she still looked like she'd been ridden hard and put away wet. Tim had to laugh. There were some aspects of the job that just made you laugh. Even with all the anxiety that came with the territory, if you played your cards right, you could still end up having a few laughs. Right then Tim knew he was going to be all right. The blonde with no clothes was a reality check. The world could still be funny. He and Wickmann went inside.

Over the next few minutes, images of the guy in the Corvette slowly disappeared. As they walked through the bar, a smile made its way onto Galleon's face. Wickmann was right. There was nothing better to take your mind off things than a visit to Sugar's. He was starting to feel like his old self again. The old Tim Galleon was back. He was going to make it. Just a few more hours and he'd be home free.

* * * * *

It was still dark outside when the wind finally died down. Grey rolled over one last time and woke himself up. The room was quiet at first and then he heard a strange sound off in the distance. At first he thought he was dreaming, until he opened his eyes and realized that the sound was still there. It was a familiar sound but he couldn't seem to put his finger on it. He was sure that he had heard it before. It was then he realized he could smell coffee. Both the sound and the aroma must be coming from the kitchen. Funny, while it did smell like coffee, there was something about it that was different. Apparently his nose was working overtime as well. Everything else was quiet. The slow, even drip of the Mr. Coffee machine bubbling away echoed in his head. As it did the sound seemed to be getting louder. The steady increase in volume aroused his interest.

Rachel didn't drink coffee. They hadn't had the pot out in months. What was stranger still was the fact that he could hear it at all. As the crow flies, the kitchen was only a few feet away, but to get there from the bedroom, he had to go down one hall a ways, go right about ten feet, and then work his way back about half a dozen steps. The house was built in the early seventies and had very thick walls. Under normal circumstances, there was no way he could possibly hear the coffee pot doing its thing. Still, he could hear it chugging away, as if it were sitting on the dresser in front of him.

Logic told him it must be Alex. She must have gotten up early and found her way around the kitchen. If he remembered correctly, the last time he'd seen the coffee pot it was still in its box on the bottom shelf of the pantry. She must have found it and dusted off the cobwebs. He stared at the clock. It was five a.m. The sun would be coming up soon.

Ever since the accident, he had noticed that his senses were becoming more acute. They were sharpening themselves on almost a daily basis. Lying there in bed, he couldn't decide whether or not this growing level of sensitivity was a good thing or not. At the very least, it was certainly entertaining. He decided to try an experiment. He listened carefully to see just how sensitive his hearing had become. He found that he could hear a rustling sound as if Alex were turning the pages of a book, or perhaps the morning paper. As he expanded his interests, he discovered that he could hear Dylan's shallow breathing coming from his room down the hall. All in all, it gave him an eerie feeling. Somewhere in the background the coffee pot was headed for the finish line.

He looked over at Rachel. She was still asleep in bed next to him. All he could see of her was the back of her head. The rest of her was completely covered in a mountain of pillows and blankets. No wonder he was cold. She had commandeered all the covers. During the night, the temperature in the room had dropped considerably. It was time to find a shirt. He thought about moving and wondered why Alex was up and about. If the clock was right, he'd been asleep for only four hours. Then again, saying that he was sleeping was kind of stretching it a little. He had awakened twice during the night in a cold sweat. The whole endeavor seemed a useless attempt at getting some rest. It failed. He was still tired. Bewildered, he contemplated his next move.

Over the past few minutes the smell of the coffee had gotten stronger. He could almost taste it. At last his curiosity got the best of him. Carefully he slipped out of bed and found a sweatshirt. Rachel and Dylan would be asleep for awhile yet. He didn't want to wake them up. Quietly he made his way toward the kitchen.

He'd guessed right. As he turned the corner at the far end of the hall, he could see Alex at the opposite end, sitting in the family room. She had made herself comfortable in the easy chair. She was reading the paper and sipping coffee. She looked tired too. He wondered if she'd slept at all. She must have sensed his presence.

"Morning," she said, without looking up.

"Morning, I think," he responded. "What's up with the coffee?" "I'm not sure," she admitted. "Just a feeling, I guess. And besides,

Rachel drinks it right? You know me though. I had to add a little something for flavor. How come you're up?"

She motioned toward the coffee pot.

Grey found that he couldn't resist the temptation.

"Once the wind died down, things got too quiet," he said. "It made me feel lost again."

Coffee in hand, he headed for the couch.

"By the way, I think I'm starting to understand some of this," he continued. "If I'm not focusing on something, everything is normal, but if I concentrate, it's like I'm turning up the power. Everything works better; like hearing the coffee pot. That was wild. It really caught me off guard. After I discovered that I could hear the coffee brewing, I tested my hearing. It was incredible. I could hear you turning pages of the newspaper and I could hear Dylan breathing. It was so easy it was almost frightening. But if I stopped paying attention to any of the sounds, they all but went away. When I focused in on them again, they returned instantly. The whole experience was really strange, but it did help. I think I'm learning how to control some of this; a small part of it, anyway."

Alex was impressed. While Grey was looking at this as a small step, she knew how much of a major advance it really was. Here was the confirmation she was looking for: his ability to focus on specific things around him and be able to perceive them on a much higher level.

"That's very interesting," she told him. "If you can get a handle on controlling your senses with that kind of accuracy, you'll be one step closer to completing this puzzle. Next time you're stuck in the dream, see if you can manipulate your senses into helping you identify your surroundings. Knowing where you are, where everything is, and what's happening around you, would give you a big advantage."

Grey agreed. Establishing the environment would be a big step in the right direction. It was a lot to think about. For awhile, they sat quietly and let the coffee do its job.

"So what's your schedule like today?" Alex asked, breaking the silence.

"I have one client this afternoon at four," he answered. "Clyde Hobart, great old guy. You'd like him. He's a class act. I've seen him every other Thursday for the past five years. Today is not his regular day on my schedule."

"Sounds like you know him pretty well then?" she inquired.

"Yeah, he's really a nice guy. We've had a lot of interesting sessions together. I think I want to get there early so I can take things slow and prepare myself. You know, get a feel for it. I want to see if the same thing happens when I touch Clyde as it did when I was with Blake. I'm curious to learn if I get the same flashes or not. Anyway, that might provide us with a few answers."

Alex agreed. "We can compare what you see with Clyde to what happened when you were with Blake. If you see the same thing, then we know that we're dealing with just one repetitive situation. One we must consider might even be generating from inside you. However, if what you see turns out to be just regular, normal, everyday stuff, then we have a different problem. The person in Blake's dream appears to be very dangerous. We may have some kind of nut case running around loose. Do you understand where I'm coming from?"

Grey nodded. He definitely understood. "That's what's been bothering me" he responded. "It's the "what ifs?"

As he spoke, he could feel a chill go through him. He could feel the little hairs on the back of his neck standing up. His mind shifted gears and he slipped into deep thought.

As scary as it sounded, what Alex was saying made perfect sense. If the dream was revealing something that was inside of him, that was bad enough. But if it was all centered around something inside of Blake, that was a whole new talk show. They had to find out the truth! The decision was made. Without knowing it, Clyde was going to be part of the experiment. Nice thing about Clyde was, if the details of what they were doing ever got out, he probably wouldn't care. He would more than likely think it was cool. Grey turned back to Alex.

"There's one more thing. I want to see Father Richard this afternoon. I need to bring him up to date on everything."

Alex understood. "We can go see him after breakfast if you'd like. I would love to hear his perspective on all of this especially now that he's had some time to take it all in." "He might just surprise you," Grey assured her.

Alex laughed. "Believe it or not, I'm counting on it," she said. "I would never make the mistake of underestimating that man. He's quite obviously one of the good guys."

"After breakfast then?" Grey asked.

"After breakfast," she assured him.

Grey smiled. For as long as he could remember, they had always been on the same page. There was a bond between them that knew no bounds. Behind her, through the sliding glass door, he could see the first glimpses of a new day. There in the backyard the flowers were starting to take shape. One by one he could see them emerging from the darkness into the early morning light. Somewhere in the east, the sun had started its ascent into the sky. With it came the promise and hope of a new day. Grey sat staring out the window, watching the shadows fade, and quietly finished his coffee.

* * * * *

When Blake left the house that morning, it was still dark. Somehow, he managed to shower and dress without waking her. He felt alive and refreshed. Sleep had come easy. His dreams were both erotic and exciting. Memories of his night with Casey still danced in his head. Distracted by all the eroticism, he entirely forgot about his idea to go hunting.

As he got ready to leave, he took one last look at himself in the bathroom mirror. The face he saw was tired and ragged. The five-o-clock shadow left over from yesterday had thickened during the night. He couldn't believe he'd forgotten to shave. It too had totally slipped his mind. He opened the drawer in front of him and found his friend. Then he remembered his plan!

There it was, sitting so casually in front of him, staring up at him from the drawer below. The sheer beauty of it demanded his undivided attention. He was mesmerized. It was as if the instrument was sitting there, waiting to be played with. It all but begged for his attention. As he stared at it long and hard, he could feel the rush beginning to build. He started to reach for it but never completed the motion.

A sudden wave of sadness engulfed him and prevented him from picking it up. He knew that there would be no performance that day. There was no symphony to conduct. There was nothing to play. Today, his baton would be useless. He would have to wait for another time and place, when that special feeling would come to him again.

And it would come. For now he had other things to do. He had to prepare. First, he had to go shopping. He had to find his quarry. Only then, could he arrange to continue his symphony. In the meantime, he would have to be patient and hope that the ride he was still on would last. It was time to go. He had to get to the office. He was curious to see what he would find there. The window was calling out to him, pleading for his attention. He could almost hear its voice inside his head. It was time to go shopping and he was sure he knew the perfect place. Quietly he made his way downstairs and headed for the garage.

He made it to work, but for the life of him, he couldn't remember how he got there. His mind would only cater to one thought. The view from his window was better than he expected. Looking out at the world, Blake grinned and gave himself a good mental pat on the back. His assumption was correct. This was the perfect place from which to survey his prey. His office was no more than thirty feet above the sidewalk, giving him a bird's eye view of everything that passed beneath him. Even at six thirty in the morning, the street below was starting to come to life. In an hour or so it would become a virtual sea of people, moving about in every direction. It was always like this, an endless parade of human traffic. Like a hawk, Blake sat perched in his chair and carefully examined each female pedestrian as she passed.

He took an electric razor out of his desk and finally shaved while he passed the time. To his surprise he had a lot to choose from. At first it was all very exciting. He was aroused by all the new faces and shapes.

As time passed, his task became more tedious. The harder he worked the problem, the more challenging the search became. It was like looking for a needle in a haystack. Finding another Katie was not going to be easy. He had very specific needs. His "order" was apparently going to take some time to fill.

There was only one consolation. For a few minutes, he found that "people watching" was actually entertaining. Everyone seemed to have an attitude. At the present hour he figured that he was dealing with a world that was lost in an overdose of caffeine or in need of their own kind of fix. Everyone was moving in high gear. He needed to catch up.

After about twenty minutes without any success he was ready to give up. The entire exercise seemed futile. It reminded him of a trip he and Katie once took to the mall. Katie was looking for a new outfit. They must have been in twenty stores and she was still unable to find anything. By the end of the day she was so completely frustrated that he thought she was going to explode. Nothing she saw was the right size, the right shape, or the right color. The more she tried to find something she liked, the more discouraged she became. At the time he thought she was nuts. Shopping couldn't be that important. She was way too intense. Now, sitting here at the window, he began to understand. Shopping here was just like being at the mall. Occasionally, he saw something that bore a resemblance to what he wanted, but he would not allow himself to settle for anything less than a perfect fit. There was no room for second best. He had to have another Katie. He needed a fix!

When he thought back to shopping with her that day, he remembered laughing about the experience. He was more than amused at the sight of Katie work her "panties into a wad". Her behavior was almost amusing. He felt no sympathy for her at the time, just contempt. That was then. It was different now. The shoe was on the other foot. He understood her dilemma. It wasn't so amusing anymore. He could almost feel her frustration.

Down below him, the parade continued but he had a specific order to be filled. Age was partially a factor. Blondes and redheads were a bust. Who was he kidding? Had he expected this to be easy? It wasn't like buying a car, where they were just sitting there, waiting on the lot. You pick your color, your available options and drive away. This was work. Maybe it wasn't such a good idea after all. The office would be open in a little while and Sheila, his secretary would be in around eight. He was running out of time.

Then something strange happened. He had a craving for coffee. Strange, he wasn't even a big coffee fan. He remembered the small vendor cart in the lobby. It smelled good when he passed it on the way up. That was it! He needed a cup of coffee. Maybe even a cappuccino. The caffeine would wake him up and take his mind off of things. His brain was going to need a jump start anyway.

Walter had left a new case file on his desk and he would want a decision on the matter by lunch time. A quick trip downstairs was beginning to sound better by the minute. He took one last look out the window and shook his head in despair. It was like a needle in a haystack. There were so many pieces of straw; but no needle in sight. Blake looked out the window again. Yeah, it was a big haystack. He concluded then it was going to be an uphill battle. He grabbed his jacket of his chair and headed for the elevator. When he pushed the call button, it arrived faster than he expected. Then: on the way down, something strange happened. For a second, he caught himself thinking about Katie.

Not the new Katie toys he had been playing with over the past few months, but the real one, his wife. Dear, sweet Katie. He felt a deep pain in his chest, one that he had never felt before. What was happening to him? Was this a sign of guilt or remorse? Was he losing his grip? The elevator touching down brought him back to reality. The bell sounded and he knew he was safely on the ground floor. The doors opened and the smell of fresh coffee overwhelmed him. Any thoughts of Katie disappeared.

* * * * *

On the ride over to the church, Grey found himself distracted. He kept thinking about what Alex said earlier. Was this bad dream coming from deep in his own mind, or was there a nut case running around loose? Either way, it was a no win situation. It all meant the same thing, big trouble. There were only a few ways to find the truth. At this point, his vote was in favor of the nut case idea. It had to be an outsider. Any possibility that this could be a depiction of his own behavior seemed ludicrous.

He had posed a question to Alex. If the bad dream was manifesting itself from events in his head, why were there no violent episodes of any kind, during his contact with Father Richard or Tony? What about the girl at the hospital? His experience with Lisa was anything but violent. There was nothing abnormal or dangerous in any way. Only Blake's dream had given him the impression that something dangerous was going on. And God only knows what went on in Blake's mind. He spent most of his days defending degenerates anyway. Maybe he was remembering a bad experience. Grey figured that after seeing Clyde that afternoon, they might have some answers. Knowing that he would be indirectly testing himself as well as Clyde, didn't help the situation. Only time would tell.

When they arrived at the church, the place was basically deserted. After all, it was a Tuesday morning and most of the congregation was probably at work. As Grey drove to the far end of the parking lot, they could see that the back door to the sanctuary was open. A few of the pews had been carefully placed outside on the lawn. The door itself had been tied open with a bungee cord, insuring a much greater space for easy access inside. He parked the car, and he and Alex went to investigate.

As they approached the doorway, Grey could hear Father Richard's voice echoing through the building. It sounded as though it was coming from somewhere high above. Curiously, he and Alex entered the room.

Once inside, Grey was shocked to find his friend, high in the air, standing alone in a cherry picker. It was a big red portable crane with a basket on top. He was about thirty feet above the floor, near the ceiling. The priest was in the process of trying to communicate something to his assistant below. He didn't appear to be making a lot of progress. The good Father seemed agitated. Grey looked at Alex and motioned her away. He wanted them both to stay out of sight. Together they moved aside and stood against a nearby wall so they could enjoy the festivities.

Father Richard had a look on his face that reminded Grey of an enraged Shakespearean actor. His face was red and his words were quick. He was forceful when he spoke

"I would love to be able to get a hold of the son of a gun who designed this blooming lighting system," he bellowed. "He obviously didn't give a moment's thought to the poor lad who, sometime in the future, would find himself responsible for maintaining this arrangement. He undoubtedly assumed these bulbs would last forever."

There was a brief pause, and then Father Richard continued.

"This thought of, course must have been part of some agreement he thinks he made with the Almighty. Apparently, God never answered that prayer. Now, by the luck of the draw, it appears that I have been the one chosen to stand up here with his arse hanging out in order to change a few bulbs."

Grey laughed quietly as he listened. Alex was amused as well. This was definitely a different side of Richard. His speech had changed to a brash Irish drawl. Grey knew why. He understood his friend's aversion to heights. Father Richard's accent only came out when he was angry or frightened. In this instance it was probably a little bit of both. He and Alex moved into view. Father Richard must have caught the movement out of the corner of his eye. He turned in their direction.

"Good morning, Father," Grey yelled up at him, as soon as they made eye contact. "I see that you've decided to become closer to God!"

Grey was surprised when he saw the expression on his friend's face. He looked pale. Father Richard's words earlier conveyed one mood. Now his present face conveyed another. It betrayed him. There was no longer any anger. A smile had started to return. Grey remained silent. The priest stared down at him for a minute and then offered a typical Richard response.

"When I chose the road to the priesthood, my son, I don't remember any of this being in the travel brochure!"

For a moment there was nothing but silence. Then simultaneously, almost as if it were planned, they both broke into laughter. Alex and the poor guy who was standing at the foot of the crane just shook their heads in amazement. It appeared that Father Richard had decided to throw in the towel.

"If you would be kind enough to bring me down from here, lad, I think you might find my disposition to be a bit more hospitable." As he spoke, the priest's voice began returning to normal.

Grey nodded and went over and joined the gentleman standing at the controls.

Carefully, he began to lower his friend. Alex smiled. You just had to love Father Richard. Here was a man who, even while he was in the middle of dealing with his own fears, never seemed to lose his sense of humor. As the basket slowly made its way toward the ground, Alex went over and stood next to Grey. He had now completely relieved the good Father's assistant and taken control of the lift.

Grey looked like a kid with a new toy, playing with the large remote control panel. At one point, he actually stopped Richard's descent, sent him back up a couple of feet, and then went back to the task of bringing him down again. Father Richard had no choice but to be amused. With a little patience, the priest found his way back to solid ground. He smiled at Alex and playfully smacked Grey.

"Very funny", he said." Now let's go you two. I want to hear everything."

* * * * *

When the bell sounded, Blake got his wish. There, across the lobby in front of him was the portable vending cart. Standing behind it was a little old gentleman who was serving coffee. Out in front, a small group of people had gathered. The old man was eagerly attending to his customers, handing over both coffee and pastries with equal enthusiasm. He moved slowly and with great care. His actions were slower than one would have thought necessary to effectively manage the cart. Still, the small line of people who assembled was being catered to quickly and efficiently. From the sound of things, each customer was as desperate to get their hands on some coffee as he was.

In all the time that Blake had worked in the building, this was the first occasion he had stopped to take notice of the vendor. Sure, he had seen the cart before every morning on his way upstairs, but hearing people identify this man and call him by name somehow put the whole matter in a different perspective. The lady standing in line in front of him had just asked him about his children. She called the man Sylvester. It became obvious that some of these people did business with this guy on a regular basis.

When Blake finally found his way to the front of the line, he had his first contact with the coffee man. It was easy to see why he was so well liked. Sylvester greeted him with a pleasant "Good morning," and a big smile. The smile was genuine. Not one of those put on solely for the benefit of doing business. Blake could read people. It came with the territory. Here was a man who was genuinely happy with what he was doing and wanted to share his happiness with everyone around him. When you left with your coffee, you left with something else to: an attitude adjustment. Sylvester made you smile.

Blake ordered a large black coffee and dug for his wallet. The deep, rich smell hit him before he was even handed the cup.

Sylvester asked, "You're a first timer here aren't you, sir?"

"Yes, as a matter of fact I am," Blake answered.

"Well, I hope you like it," he offered. "It is one of my favorites, my own blend."

By the way, I'm Sylvester. Please come see me again." He offered his hand.

Blake shook it and said, "Blake Kendall, fourth floor and the pleasure is mine."

"You have a nice day, Mr. Kendall." he added.

The smile never left his face. Blake returned the smile, picked up his coffee and headed toward the elevator. The experience with Sylvester was worth the trip downstairs. He felt better already. If the coffee was half as enjoyable as its distributor, it would be worth it to come back for more.

Now, he had to get back to the office. He needed to review the new case file for Walter and then go hunting again after lunch. It was a simple plan. He took a sip from his cup. For a moment, Blake was dumbfounded. One taste was enough. He swore he'd almost died and gone to heaven. The coffee was fantastic! Blake turned and looked back at the cart. This Sylvester guy really knew his stuff. Quickly, he took another sip. It was even better the second time. He had never tasted coffee like this. If he had, he would certainly have become an avid coffee drinker. This was obviously not regular coffee. Something about it was quite different.

He was so impressed, he wanted to go back and say something to his new friend, but he heard the elevator bell ring as it arrived on the ground floor. His compliments would have to wait. He needed to stay focused. He had to get to work. After lunch, he would make the time to go out and play. He was so excited about the whole hunting thing that for a brief moment his mind wandered away. Dreams of feeling the rush again filled his head. Erotic visions of both Casey and Kelly called out to him from somewhere in the darkness. He could hear the sweet sounds of their voices. He could almost taste the sweetness of their flesh. When the elevator doors opened, his mind suddenly snapped back. At first he thought he was dreaming, but when things came into focus he saw her. It was like seeing a ghost. Blake dropped his coffee.

* * * * *

She was beautiful. He knew he was saved the moment her face came into full view. Her eyes were a deep blue. They were hypnotic and instantly commanded his full attention. In a matter of seconds, he visually worked his way around her body from one end to the other. She was flawless. From her well turned ankles to her soft, inviting lips, she was absolutely stunning. Her long dark hair fell gently off her shoulders as it traveled downward into the curve of her back. Her hips were slender and her legs just seemed to go on forever. She was tall.

Even without the heels he was sure that she measured around five-ten. She was wearing a short dark skirt with an electric blue silk blouse. She looked very professional. His mind went crazy. As she passed by him on the way out of the elevator all he could see was Katie! Quickly, he turned and allowed his eyes to follow her. He didn't even notice that the elevator was leaving without him. His mind was on other things. He had found another Katie! Once again she had somehow fallen into his lap. This was incredible. He could feel the rush and the anxiety building. The fire inside him was starting to burn. There was a stiffening feeling in the front of his slacks. He knew that he had to take a closer look.

As he got closer, he saw her move around behind the cart to the serving area. She looked like she had arranged to get her order herself. She took a large cup from one of the dispensers and began to fill it. All the while, she maintained her conversation with Sylvester. Blake approached slowly. He knew that he had to think fast. Then he remembered his coffee!

He turned and looked back toward the elevators. There on the floor he saw the remains of what Sylvester had given him just moments before. His coffee was splattered all over the floor just to right of the elevator doors. The bottom of his cup had imploded when it hit the tile floor. Napkins! He needed lots of napkins to clean up the mess. This gave him the excuse he needed to go back to the cart. That and he wanted another cup of Sylvester's magic formula. It would be a little embarrassing, but he decided that it was worth the risk. He stepped closer to the stand.

Sylvester saw him first and waved. "Problem, Mr. Kendall?" he inquired.

Blake nodded. "I could sure use a lot of napkins," he responded. "I had a bit of a mishap over there by the elevators."

The young woman looked up at him just as he was finishing his sentence. Their eyes met. He was close enough now that he could smell her perfume. She was truly unbelievable. Blake gave her his best smile. She returned the favor. Then her eyes wandered across the lobby. She grabbed a dish towel from under the cart and started for the elevators.

"I'll help the gentleman, Dad," she said. Her words caught Blake completely off guard.

Dad! She called Sylvester, dad! This beautiful woman was his daughter?

Sylvester reached out and tried to stop her.

"You shouldn't be doing things like that the way you're dressed," he said.

She just smiled back at him. "Don't worry, Dad, I've got it covered," she said as she took off across the lobby. Once again, Blake's eyes followed her every move. All he and Sylvester could do was watch as she moved away. Sylvester caught him looking.

"She's beautiful, isn't she?" he inquired.

Blake was a little flushed. "Yes sir, that she is," he answered, "Quite beautiful."

Sylvester smiled. Together they stood quietly and watched, as she made her way to the other side of the room.

Blake remained silent, and allowed his eyes to feast on the beauty that moved before him. Every subtle motion of her body made his heart race. She was perfect. Once again, another representation of his wife had somehow been delivered to him. His early morning arrival was not a waste of time after all. He had successfully accomplished his objective.

This acquisition, however, would present a few problems. While the fact remained she was a stranger, she also worked in the same building. Sacrificing her would bring things dangerously close to home. He was going to have to be careful. This effort would call for his best performance to date. It was not going to be easy. Setting her up would demand a lot of time and attention, but it would be well worth the effort. He would have to do his homework and then find a way to get close to her. She was a gift and he knew he couldn't afford to let her slip away.

As he continued to watch from a distance, he did notice a resemblance between her and Sylvester. Her hair, skin tone, and facial structure were remarkable, but it was the seductive innocence of her eyes that would not let him turn away. He felt sad. He really liked this Sylvester character. Taking his daughter away from him was not something he was going to enjoy doing.

The whole thing started to mess with Blake's head. He had never gotten to know any of his prey beforehand. The reasons were obvious and he wanted to keep it that way. Still, he knew what he had to do. There was really no choice in the matter. Even from a distance, one look at her and he could already feel the rush of her erotic energy. She alone would satisfy his needs. He knew he had to have her. When she returned a few minutes later, Blake took a closer look. This time he wasn't in a hurry.

* * * * *

CHAPTER 11

As always, Father Richard never ceased to amaze. Now, safely on the ground, he invited them to follow him to the comfort of his office. It was only a stone's throw away. There they would have some privacy. Once inside, the charismatic priest started to become his old self again. The single shot of Irish whiskey he took from his bottom desk drawer only seemed to help matters. It went a long way toward calming his nerves. When he discovered that his guests were watching him, he was a little embarrassed. His pride forced him to look away for a moment. The stained glass window on the far wall of his office became his temporary focus.

While Richard still conveyed a strong interest in what was going on, Grey could tell that his friend was not himself. He could sense it when they first shook hands. The Kelly Richfield murder had come back to haunt him. Richard was distant. It was like he wasn't all there. Grey remembered that even though members of the clergy deal with pain and death on a regular basis, it was a safe bet that his friend had never been able to put this one behind him. It was like an old wound that continued to fester.

As it turned out, his assumption was correct. Richard's initial inquiries were one dimensional. He insisted on revisiting a lot of what had taken place during their previous visit. Grey's knowledge of every intimate detail of the funeral had left Father Richard both dazed and confused. He was anxious to share his feelings. Until now, because of his position, he'd had no choice but to keep them in check on the back burner. Now he could finally share some of his most intimate thoughts with his two friends.

He began by explaining that when they had left him the last time, he had experienced some strange feelings of abandonment. He was having a hard time accepting everything that had happened between himself and Grey. The experience had forced him to relive the events that surrounded Kelly's death. It was still hard for him to believe that she was gone. The walk down memory lane had not been a pleasant one. It was a cold, hard, reminder of her loss.

What was even harder to accept was the fact that there were still no answers to any of the basic questions or even a list of possible suspects in the investigation relating to her death. After hours of deep thought, he discovered that he was no closer to understanding any of it; what had happened to Kelly, or Grey's newly acquired talent. Richard was shaken. Logic was failing him and faith was trying desperately to take its place. In the last twenty-four hours, he had found himself praying repeatedly for guidance. He had investigated many possibilities, but always arrived at the same conclusion. What did he really believe? The incident with Grey was real! Grey was able to watch Kelly's funeral through his eyes! Grey had the ability to see what he was thinking, and it was all possible through his delicate sense of touch. Try as he might, he could not find a reasonable explanation for any of it.

Richard was humbled before his Maker. There must be a reason why all of this was happening. Occasionally, the good Lord did work in mysterious ways. Maybe this was why God had decided not to take Grey after the accident. There was still a purpose for his continued presence. Grey hands were a gift, and God doesn't give people gifts he doesn't intend for them to use. Of that the old priest was certain.

Then there was something else. Obviously there was a lot more to this than what appeared on the surface. It was quite possible that what they were seeing was only the tip of the iceberg. Fortunately, they were all friends. Grey had a good head on his shoulders and trusted him. Apparently so did the Almighty. Father Richard decided to follow his heart and found comfort in his faith.

Grey and Alex listened with care, as Father Richard let it all go. It was obvious to them both how badly he needed to get everything off his chest. Grey could relate to that. So far, he had been lucky. Alex was his escape. Her strong presence proved to be a blessing. She continued to provide him with the outlet he needed. Without her counsel, walking the thin line between mental stability and insanity would have been impossible. As things stood, simply maintaining a balance was enough of a challenge. Grey knew how important it was to keep things in proper perspective.

The longer Father Richard spoke, the clearer things became. Grey began to understand the magnitude of the situation that he and Alex had created for his friend. While Richard's interest was genuine, he was motivated from both a personal standpoint and a religious one as well. By agreeing to participate in all of this, the priest had placed himself in a rather precarious position.

Here he was forced to not only examine a few of his own personal issues, but burdened himself with also having to maintain his vow of silence. Father Richard was a good man. He was also a good friend. Grey could see the frustration building in his eyes as he finished his dissertation. Grey felt for him. Richard would soon learn there was not always a sane or logical explanation for everything. At least not on the field they were playing on at the moment. Even if there were a method to the madness, the truth might not be within the realm of Father Richard's understanding.

Still, he had made a promise to his friend. He and Alex would have to decide quickly just how deep they would allow Richard to become involved. They didn't want to drag him in any further than necessary. For now anyway, he seemed to be holding his own. Richard's curiosity was just getting the best of him

"I'm going to be seeing my friend Clyde this afternoon," Grey blurted out.

"We're going to use him to run a few tests."

Richard looked surprised. At this point Grey decided it was safe to repeat the conversation he and Alex had shared earlier.

"I want to see what's going on in his head. If what I observe is anything like what I saw at Blake's, we may have an answer. If what I find, matches in any way, we can conclude that the material I'm viewing is originating from somewhere inside of me.

Grey grimaced "Frankly Father that scares the hell out of me!"

The priest lowered his head and made the sign of the cross.

"However," Grey continued, "if there is no similarity, I'm off the hook. If I am eliminated from the scenario, that will point our investigation in a different direction. Based on what we know so far we'll have a good idea where to look next."

Father Richard and Alex both nodded. They were all in agreement. Grey stood to take a breather. His explanation seemed to satisfy everyone. Father Richard felt included and Grey had carefully escaped, divulging little or no pertinent information.

Father Richard was relieved.

"You will let me know how it all works out, lad?" he asked.

"That's a promise, my friend. You'll be the first," Grey answered. "In the meantime, don't you be letting all this get you worked up in a lather," he continued doing his best impression of Father Richard's earlier "Irish" drawl.

Richard laughed. "It would be just like you, at a time like this, to be taking jabs at an old man. You best be moving yourself out of my church and be on the way to getting about your business. Can't you see I've still got work to do?" he chuckled as he motioned with his hand to the pile of papers that had accumulated on his desk.

Grey was pleased. Richard had obviously not lost his sense of humor. That was a good sign. Still, Grey hated to see his friend so overwhelmed. He took a quick glance around the room, hoping that something brilliant would come to him. Then he got an idea. Grey got up from his chair and headed over to one of the bookcases. He picked up an old book and began thumbing through the pages. He quickly found what he was looking for.

"Here, Richard, read this aloud if you'd like. It's a little food for thought."

Richard looked down at the open page. It was Webster's dictionary. There was a puzzled look on his face.

"Scan down about half way on the left hand side," Grey told him.

Richard did as instructed and immediately found what Grey had him searching for. He read the passage out loud.

"Faith, n, 1. confidence or trust in a person or thing, 2. A belief that is not based on proof."

Richard was surprised. He closed the book and looked up at Grey. There was a brief silence. "I guess the Bible isn't the only book that has something to tell us today," he said. "Thank you, my friend."

"No problem, Father, I just remembered something you told me once. It is always good to have faith in God, but it is also good to have faith in one's friends as well."

Richard smiled. "I forgot how well you listen, but I am happy that you do."

The priest's face seemed to relax now, but he still looked tired. Grey knew it was time to leave. Alex saw an opportunity and took it.

"All right, Father," she said, "But rest assured I'll keep him under a watchful eye. He won't be getting into anything too deep while I'm around."

Then she leaned over and gave Richard a hug.

"We'll be back to see you later," she whispered in his ear.

She kissed him on the cheek. The priest blushed as a smile took over his face.

"I like this one, Grey, I really do."

Grey nodded his approval. "I do too, Father, Believe me I do," he said. Then he turned to Alex. "Let's get out of here," he said. "I've got a couple of things I'd like to do before my appointment with Clyde."

Alex moved toward the door. Grey turned back for one last comment to Richard.

"God be with you my friend," he said, raising his hand to wave.

Richard smiled and waved back.

Grey turned to Alex. "God must have been rather pleased with Himself the day He created Richard," he said. "I'm sure that he continually provides the Almighty with a constant source of amusement."

Alex laughed. "Richard will be a great ally down the road," she said. "I can feel it. Trusting him was a smart thing to do."

Grey nodded. Once again, he and Alex were on the same page.

* * * * *

As they headed for the car, Grey relaxed a little. Richard was more comfortable now, and that would make things easier for all of them. Still, he couldn't help thinking about this appointment with Clyde. What would he see when he touched his friend? Would there be simple everyday thoughts and feelings, or would the carnage begin again? One way or another, when the session was over they would finally have some answers.

For now all he could do was shudder when he thought about what he had seen earlier at the Kendall house. It chilled him to the bone. The grotesque images he'd seen were both violent and disgusting. The executions were quick and evil. The actions deliberate. He was left with the impression that they were probably crimes of passion, brought to fulfillment in an erotic and perverse sort of way.

Still, there could be no excuse. The executioner in the shadows had left him with memories that were both gruesome and cold. Was the killer trying to send him a message? Grey thought for a second that he was finally beginning to understand. The acts of violence themselves were hideous, but by the same token they were self gratifying. In his own way, the executioner was submitting for display the extreme depths of his madness. Somewhere along the line, something inside the monster had snapped.

Grey was getting anxious. As he was presented with each new piece of the puzzle, he became more concerned. He prayed that his adventure at Clyde's house would be harmless and uneventful. The anxiety he was experiencing came with his still believing in the possibility that the images he was seeing were of his own creation. If that were true, it was more than he was presently prepared to handle. Also, if this 'gift' was a side effect of the accident, what was to say that his mind wasn't being influenced by the same new forces as well? There really was only one way to find out.

Unfortunately, his appointment with Clyde was still hours away. There was a lot to do between now and then and he found that he was growing steadily more impatient. Grey shook his head in frustration. At this rate it was going to be a long afternoon.

* * * * *

It was nearly noon when Blake finally finished looking over the case file that Walter was kind enough to leave for him. It turned out to be a complicated mess of sex, money, adultery and murder. It was right up his alley. He decided to tell Walter they should take it, but the truth of the matter was, he'd actually read very little, if any, of it. For the past few hours he couldn't seem to concentrate on anything but the girl downstairs. Every time he closed his eyes all he could see was her tight, erotic figure, kneeling down on the floor in front of him. The image was a memory of what he'd seen earlier, with a little of his own sexual appetite thrown in. He remembered looking at her like a wolf looks at a sheep. He could taste her already. Even hours later he was so wrapped up in the fantasy that when he heard Sheila's voice on the office intercom it startled him out of the trance.

"Mr. Kendall, there's a detective MacKensie here to see you. He doesn't have an appointment. Should I still send him in?" There was a brief silence.

"Mr. Kendall Mr. Kendall?" It took her a few tries to even get him to respond. His mind was in another place. Finally he answered her.

"Sure, send him in. Tell him I'm sorry to keep him waiting."

"Right away sir," she responded. Then Sheila's voice disappeared.

Blake stood and put on his jacket. This visit was not totally unexpected. Casey's face had been all over the news. He knew that several people had seen them together at dinner. It just came sooner than he'd hoped. As always, he was prepared for it just the same. Before MacKensie could get to the door, Blake, adjusted his pants, checked his fly, and buttoned his double-breasted suit coat. He looked sharp in a dark suit, especially the one he'd chosen that morning. It cost him more than the average house payment, and had taken longer to make than most new cars.

He had just finished straightening his tie when there was a knock on the door. With his permission, Sheila opened the door and allowed MacKensie to step through from the hallway and into his private office. As MacKensie walked in, Blake's mind shifted gears.

"Mr. Kendall, I presume?" MacKensie asked as the pudgy old cop offered his hand. Blake nodded. Reluctantly, he was forced to shake MacKensie's rough, un-manicured paw.

"I'm Detective MacKensie, Laguna Beach Police Department," MacKensie continued. "I saw you on TV last week after the Bolerno Trial. That was some pretty fancy stuff there, Kendall. You're some kind of lawyer!"

Blake smiled and then wiped his hand clean with a handkerchief. He found MacKensie's attitude amusing at best. After a short silence, Blake found his zone and immediately took control of the conversation.

"You may call me Blake, detective if you're so inclined, and thank you, I try," he assured him politely. His voice carried a definite hint of sarcasm.

MacKensie wasn't impressed. He held his ground.

"If that's the way you want it, Mr. Kendall excuse me, I mean Blake, then so be it, but I'm here on official business. I'd like to ask you a few questions." His tone became more serious as he spoke. Then MacKensie threw a curveball of his own.

"Any objections," or would you prefer to have counsel present?" His question carried with it an equal, yet irritating level of belittlement.

"Touche'," Blake responded, now making a mental note to watch his choice of words more carefully. "No, Detective, I hardly think additional counsel will be necessary. What exactly is it that you think I can help you with?"

MacKensie took a breath. This Kendall guy was smooth but he'd be damned if he was going to let him get the best of him.

"I'm working on a new case and you might be a material witness," he began.

"Ever heard of a girl named Casey Riddell?"

Then MacKensie paused. His eyes were glued to Blake's face looking for any kind of reaction. What he got was nothing like he expected. To his surprise, Blake answered him almost immediately.

"Yes, I've met her. Why do you ask?" he inquired carefully.

His quick admission caught MacKensie off guard. Blake could see it in his eyes.

He had decided earlier that things would go much easier if he told the detective the truth. Not necessarily the whole truth, but at least as much as he was comfortable with. He could safely admit to everything the authorities already knew. Now, appearing to be genuinely interested, he offered the aging cop a chair. MacKensie quickly accepted the invitation.

"So would you mind telling me what this is all about?" Blake asked candidly, already knowing what direction the entire conversation would go. It was almost too easy. To Blake, MacKensie was like a big canary. When the cop gathered himself and began to ask questions again, the 'Cat' was eager and waiting. It was lunch time in Cheshire.

* * * * *

As he anticipated, the cop wanted to know about his recent association with Casey. Blake played his role to perfection. He began by wanting to know why. When MacKensie told him she was dead, Blake didn't even blink. He had been waiting for this moment. The look he gave MacKensie was one of complete shock. Olivier would have been proud. It was because of that look that MacKensie decided to play his hand.

He told Blake everything he knew about the restaurant. He could describe the entire evening in such great detail it was as if he himself had been sitting at the table with them. He appeared to relish the fact that there were so many witnesses to Blake and Casey's dinner together. MacKensie was very proud of himself. "Let Kendall try to weasel his way out of this one", he thought.

Blake was quiet for a moment. He knew better than to react. MacKensie had just thrown everything the cops knew right in his lap. However, the bottom line was that was all they knew. Anything else after that would just be a fishing expedition. Other than him being seen with the girl at dinner, the cops had nothing to go on. They didn't even have a clue. For Blake, this was no surprise. He decided it was safe to play his own hand as well.

He told MacKensie everything. How he came across the broken down car on the highway and offered his assistance. How he gave her a ride into town and at the last minute invited her to dinner. Everything was totally innocent and out in the open. The staff at the restaurant could confirm this.

He left nothing out, including how the evening ended when he placed her in a cab and watched her drive away. He admitted to giving her cab fare and extra money for a hotel if it became necessary. He felt sorry for her. He gave her his business card so she could contact him later if she wanted to pay him back. His dissertation was very specific and completely thorough. After all, he had nothing to hide, even from Katie.

Through it all, MacKensie listened quietly and nodded a lot. He was in fact fishing. He had already spoken with the valet on duty that night, as well as several members of the restaurant staff. He knew that Kendall was telling the truth. Everything that he said was true. His story checked out perfectly. There were no discrepancies.

Everything was as it should be with only one exception. The body of Casey Riddell was lying on a table at the morgue. Her throat had been slashed. Something had certainly happened to her between dinner and when the sun came up.

There were other facts as well. According to witnesses, Kendall had stayed at the bar for several hours after the girl left. Then he'd gone home to bed. MacKensie suspected that Kendall's wife could place him there about midnight. She would remember him waking her, and then having a conversation with him around that time. The coroner said Miss Riddell was killed between twelve-thirty and one a.m. There just wasn't enough time for him to have driven down the coast to the hotel where the cabbie had left her.

The cabbie's alibi was solid too. He was seen returning his car to the dispatch garage in Santa Ana about twelve forty- five. He couldn't possibly be in two places at once.

MacKensie knew Kendall's reputation. He also knew that he was barking up the wrong tree. The lead was shaky at best, but it was still his job to follow up on it. At least now he could report back to the brass that he had gone through the motions. As far as he was concerned, they were back to square one. He thanked Blake for his time and headed back to the station.

* * * * *

When he was alone again, Blake sat quietly at his desk and closed his eyes. He reminisced about that night on the rocks with Casey. He immediately started to become aroused. He could still feel her warm naked flesh. There was no need to worry. His alibi would hold up. Sure, they would call Katie and what would she tell them? She would tell them the truth too. She did have a conversation with him in their bedroom around midnight on the night of the murder (at least she thought she did). He was home next to her in their bed. As for his "good Samaritan" dinner with the girl, who was Katie to judge him?

Blake laughed. Now he could focus his thoughts on better things. His mind zeroed in on the girl with the coffee. She was out there, waiting. So close that he could almost touch her. So erotic that he could still smell her perfume. He loved the way the lines in her stockings ran up the back of her legs. They were like a road map leading you home. In a way they reminded him of a wishbone.

"Mmm A tender little morsel," he laughed to himself. "How I'd love to break her in half. Maybe I could even make a wish!"

Blake stopped himself. He was starting to get worked up and began to sweat. There was a time and a place for everything. This was neither. When the opportunity presented itself, he would be ready. Now there was work to be done. Staring out the window, he looked hungrily at the women below.

Once again, he could feel the energy starting to course through his veins. Soon he could feed the fire that burned deep inside him. Revenge was so sweet. It had a flavor all its own. Soon he would be able to feast on another Katie.

Relieved now, he walked over to the wet-bar and made a drink. As usual, he poured himself a double and glanced at his reflection in the mirror. Staring back at him was that all too new familiar face. It was one that over the past few months he'd grown to love. The look in its eyes made him happy. The 'Cat' smiled, swallowed his bourbon, and went on about his business.

* * * * *

The meeting with Father Richard went well. Grey quickly discovered that he and Alex both were equally impressed by the priest's inner strength. Through it all, Father Richard had been able to maintain his composure. If nothing else, his faith was holding him together. The man was obviously dealing with many emotions. Grey wondered if privately Richard had ever allowed himself to shed a tear. Maybe he was waiting for God to provide him with some answers. From all indications it didn't appear that the spiritual phone had rung yet. Father Richard was still patiently waiting for the call.

As they stepped outside, they noticed that the sun had changed positions. The morning, it seemed, had come and gone. It was time for them to get moving. There were a few things that needed to be done before the afternoon appointment. Since Alex was still driving, Grey told her where he needed to go. His errands were simple.

First, he wanted to go to the office to pick up a few supplies. If he was going to work on Clyde later, he would need at least a few things. Clean linens, a handful of towels, and a bottle of lotion were a must. Second, he wanted to swing by his friend Cynthia's place, borrow a couple of special prop pillows, and introduce her to Alex. He and Cynthia were friends from way back. She was a retired therapist who still liked to stay involved in the business every once in awhile. After that, they could grab some lunch.

Since the accident, his appetite was greater than ever before. It took a lot of energy to keep his mental level up. Besides, he had a craving for Italian; real Italian. Not the phony restaurant chain stuff, but the real, authentic Mom and Pop hole-in-the-wall kind of action. Fortunately, he knew just the place. Alex could tell he was a little more than just interested when he made the suggestion.

"Nothing like a little pasta and vino to brighten you day, huh?" she responded with a chuckle!

Grey laughed. "You know me too well, my friend. Besides it'll be fun. A friend of mine owns the place. He's going to love you!"

Alex couldn't help smiling. Grey seemed rather pleased with himself. "It works for me," she agreed as she watched his smile grow.

"It's a date then," he announced as he pointed her toward the highway. "We'll head there after we make our stops."

Alex was happy to see him in such a good mood. Lunch at an old hang out with some friends might be just what he needed. Besides, it was a beautiful, sunny day. There they were, cruising down the highway, top down and wind in their hair. The road stretched out before them like a long black snake with white markings. All they needed to do for a little peace of mind was play connect-the-dots.

It was then Alex felt a warm sensation on her hand. It almost tickled. At first it was nothing more than a mere distraction. It was probably just the warmth of the sun. When she glanced down to assess the situation, she got a surprise. There on her finger, a set of eyes was looking back at her. Her guardian was awake. Her attention immediately turned to Grey. On his left hand, another creature had opened its eyes as well.

Suddenly, out of nowhere, a large tractor trailer blew by them in a hurry. The odor it left behind smelled rank and moldy. The smell, though, was familiar. At first Grey couldn't put his finger on it. Then it came to him. It was the essence of old, wet leather. Their dragons were nearby. This was just their subtle way of making their presence known. Through it all, his attention was somewhere else. When he finally noticed what was happening he stared curiously over at Alex. When their eyes met, they didn't say a word. They didn't have to. After all, what was there to say? Some things never change. When Grey looked down to check out his hand he saw nothing unusual. There was nothing but an old tarnished ring on his finger. The piece of silver showed no signs of life or personality. The eyes of his friend were closed. The dragon slept.

As expected, Alex met with the same result. The moment had come and gone. Grey looked up just in time to notice that they were getting close to their turnoff. Before he could say anything, Alex broke the silence.

"Nice day for a drive," she offered reluctantly.

"Yeah, I hear ya," Grey replied. "Funny thing though," he said in a 'matter of fact' tone, "you never know who might drop by for a visit."

Alex burst out laughing. "You never quit, do you?" she asked.

"No, not really," Grey was laughing too.

"It's what makes me an original," he threw back. "You wouldn't want me any other way. Hey, get off at the next exit will ya? I don't want to miss stopping at my office.

Alex nodded and started to pull back on the reins. Quickly, she changed lanes and let the Mustang slide diagonally over three lanes allowing them to get off the highway. Minutes later, they pulled up in front of the office.

"Let's make it quick, I'm getting hungry," she said.

"No problem," he answered her. "I was thinking the same thing".

* * * * *

Cynthia James sat on her patio dusting her rocks. Although the day was heating up, she'd decided earlier to keep at it for as long as she could. She'd been working steadily for some time now, trying to repair what the weather had done to her sanctuary over the past couple of days. After about a couple hours, the patio was finally starting to return to its former beauty. The Santa Ana winds had taken their toll. The leaves and dirt had covered everything, filling up the small enclosed area and even clogging the fountain. Things were definitely out of order and untidy. Chaos, no matter how small, was not Cynthia's way.

Fortunately, she had done most of the heavy work the previous morning before things heated up. She was now in the process of 'dusting things off'. She was monitoring the temperature closely, being careful not to stay outside too long. Heat and Cynthia did not agree with one another. The sun god tended to keep Cynthia indoors during the summer months. For as long as she could remember, it was always heat and heights. However, that changed recently when Grey found a way to help her with the heights problem. Her graduation to a higher state of acceptance came several weeks back when she was able to take a ride in a glass elevator. For seventy-two, Cynthia was a crazy old broad but she was smart, kind, and had a big heart. She was a true friend.

The sound of the water fountain, fresh again, continued to relax her as she worked. Things around here were almost back to normal. Her patio was her church, her tabernacle. It was a place that brought her peace. Soon, everything would be perfect again. There was only one thing missing now, the presence of her friend.

She was here when she first got the call. The accident was a bad one, but she never lost hope. She sat there on her patio after hearing about the accident, praying that he would wake up. God must have been listening. Grey's office called her the minute they heard he was awake. She wanted to go to the hospital, but had chosen to wait here in the sanctuary instead.

That was a week ago and he still hadn't checked in. His silence concerned her, but she knew he would call when he was ready. He was like a son to her and that would never change. It was just the waiting that was needling at her. She knew he was home now and she knew he was safe. That was all that was really important anyway. Still, it was driving her crazy waiting for the phone to ring.

Lately all the calls she seemed to get were those stupid telephone solicitors trying to get people to change their long distance phone company. When she heard the phone ringing once again, she hardly paid any attention to it. Her first thought was, why bother? At the last second, she changed her mind and ran for the receiver. When she picked up the phone the caller had already hung up.

"Lousy sales people," she grunted as she set the phone back on its cradle. Don't they have anything better to do than to bug me? Boy, that gripes my girdle!" she grumbled as she went over and closed the apartment door. Her Cat looked puzzled.

"That's enough for today, Dootle's," she said to the little fur ball who had now decided it was time to rub up against her leg. Let's get you some lunch."

The cat purred. Cynthia made her way into the kitchen and went about feeding her cat. She would kick herself later for missing that phone call. If she had gotten to it only one ring faster, it would have brightened up what was starting off to be a long, hot day.

* * * * *

It was around one thirty when the Mustang roared into the parking lot at Restaurante Genovesse. Their timing was good. The regular lunch crowd had already started to disband. Grey assumed that most of the lunch guests were in a hurry to get back to work. All the better for he and Alex. A quiet, relaxing lunch would do them both good. It would be like a little calm before the storm.

Alex laughed when she saw the small painted signs, which hung over each individual parking space. There was a personalized space for just about every type of guest. There were parking signs for Italians Only, Germans Only, Russians Only, etc. The list went on and on. Each sign had been carefully chosen and reflected an individual's charm and personality.

"I wonder what ours should say?" Alex said with an evil grin.

Grey just rolled his eyes.

The owner evidently had a great sense of humor. There was even a space marked Mafia Parking Only. Grey couldn't help laughing when he saw a Gold Lexus parked there. He immediately recognized the car. The personalized plates read SUH WHAT. The car belonged to his friend Charlie. He was probably inside grabbing a late lunch.

Charlie was a great guy. The fact that he chose to park where he did was kind of a joke anyway. Grey paused for a moment shaking his head.

"Hey, what's so funny?" Alex asked.

Grey knew he had to let her in on the joke.

"That car belongs to my friend, Charlie," he said. "Charlie's last name is Kim. His father is the head of the Korean Mafia here in southern California. Charlie himself doesn't think much of the family business, though. He runs his own construction firm across town. He handles everything himself, insisting on absolutely no ties to his dad. I met him one day working for one of the doctors I know. He came in one day with a frozen shoulder and I fixed it. We've been friends ever since.

"He always says, Hey, if you ever need a favor...... well, you know."

Alex snickered and patted Grey on the shoulder. "Not a bad guy to have around I would think," she said.

Grey nodded, "Yeah, Charlie's a good guy. I can trust him. Hope I never need to collect the favor, though. Anyway, I'm hungry. Let's go inside."

Alex took his hand and followed him inside.

* * * * *

Nice thing about Genovesse was, you always seemed to end up staying there longer than you originally planned. A simple lunch could easily turn into two hours or more.

Both the food and the atmosphere had a way of making visitors so incredibly comfortable, it was easy to lose track of time. It was a quiet little place where guests always felt at home.

It was a good thing that people liked to hang out, because with a few groups of people still eating, it wasn't too late to order lunch.

As they approached the bar, a gentleman came up to greet them. He immediately said hello and shook Grey's hand. Grey took the opportunity to introduce Alex.

"Al, this is my friend Alex. Alex, this is Al. He owns the place. Best food in town. It reminds me of that little place you and I used to hit near the lake house back home. In his place, you're only a stranger once."

Alex shook Al's hand. "I'm honored," she told him. "I've heard a lot about this place and you. To hear Grey tell it, it's his own personal Mecca. He speaks quite highly of you."

Al was flattered. He smiled and nodded. "He should have nice things to say after all of the food he's eaten in here. He's a good guy as well. He even likes my singing."

He and Grey both laughed.

"Let me get you two a table," he said and then quietly led them deeper into the restaurant. He made them comfortable at a table near the fireplace.

Once they were seated, Grey started checking out the room. Over in the opposite corner, he found what he was looking for: his friend. After a few minutes, Charlie noticed him as well. Grey waved and Charlie tipped his glass. There was that old, playful smile. Alex was right. He was probably good to have around.

During the exchange, Alex had been paying close attention. "So that's your friend, Charlie, huh?" she asked. "Nice eyes; Trustworthy, no fear."

Grey nodded. "Yeah, I like Charlie," he said. "With everything he's got going on, both personal and professional; he still manages to be one hell of a nice guy. His wife Candice is a sweetheart also. You'd really like her too!"

Alex was intrigued. This Charlie character sounded interesting. When she glanced over to take a better look, she was pleasantly surprised.

Charlie couldn't have been more than thirty-five. He appeared to be a tall, handsome, Korean businessman with long dark hair and a soft complexion. He looked sharp in the dark suit he was wearing; black pinstripes, a white shirt and red silk tie. From what she could tell, he and the gentleman he was sitting with were concluding whatever business they had been discussing. She also made the observation that both men would have to pass directly by their table in order to leave the building.

Charlie rose from his seat a few minutes later. Alex took note that her assumptions were correct. Charlie was at least six-one and extremely well built. The trench coat he had thrown over his arm did little to hide his physique. Everything about him looked neatly pressed. Even his shoes were special. They were probably handmade.

Charlie's guest would be passing them first. Alex could hear him thanking Charlie and telling him that he'd be in touch.

Alex thought "Touch; now there's an interesting choice of words."

She must have said it softly under her breath because Grey suddenly said, "What?"

It was right then that Grey saw Charlie wave, so he waved back. He motioned for Charlie to join them. Charlie nodded, got up, and made his way over to their table.

"Hello, my friend. Nice to see you," he said with a smile, offering his hand. Grey stood and offered his.

"How are you?" Charlie inquired. "I heard about the accident. Is everything all right?

"I think everything is good," Grey lied. "Would you like to join us?" Alex was pleased with Grey's invitation. She remained quiet,

patiently waiting for an introduction.

"Seriously, everything is great so far," Grey assured him. "Guess I have a hard head!"

Charlie smiled. "So I've heard," he replied. Suddenly Grey remembered his manners. "How totally rude of me," he said. "May I present to you my friend, Miss Alexandra Matthews. "Alexandra, this is Mr. Charles Kim."

"A pleasure I'm sure," the gentleman replied. "And hey, just call me Charlie."

"All right, then, you must call me Alex," she responded. She offered her hand, hoping he would take it. She wanted to get a good feel for Charlie.

"The pleasure is mine, Charlie," she told him.

Always the gentleman, Charlie graciously shook her hand. He had a firm grip. Alex didn't let the moment go to waste.

Once she touched him, she knew that he was trapped. He hadn't planned to stay for more than a graceful hello, but there was something about her smile that made him want to hang around for awhile. He reached eagerly for his cell phone.

"If you two would be kind enough to excuse me for a moment, I need to let my office know that I won't be back for awhile." He reached for his cell phone.

Alex smiled. She'd caught another fish. This one looked like he was going to be a whole lot of fun. Grey just shook his head.

"Another toy for your amusement?" he whispered sarcastically.

"Do you mind?" Alex asked playfully.

"No, actually not at all," he confessed.

"In fact, I find the idea rather entertaining. It's been forever since I've seen you in action. Please, be my guest, but try to remember to behave," he warned her. "I happen to like Charlie."

"As you wish," she conceded. "I think I like him too."

It was strange that neither one of them saw Charlie return to the table until he sat down.

"Ok, you two, what did I miss?" he inquired.

"Not much of anything," Alex answered, "but who knows," she said, "the fun might just be beginning!"

"All right!" Charlie said, "But first I want to know what happened to you, buddy.

All I've heard so far was gossip. Talk on the street says you had a really rough ride."

Alex grinned. "That's one way of putting it," she said.

Their attention shifted to Grey. He told them both what he could remember about the accident. At one point Alex was certain he was going to tell him everything, but he never did. As the conversation continued she understood why. Charlie was the kind of man who liked to fix things. It was in his blood. He was an honest and just man. He would be there to help in an instant, if he thought it was important. He really had a thing for good people. He would always be there to protect his friends.

Charlie stayed with them for the entire meal. He listened closely, sipping a brandy, as Grey recounted each of the events relating to the accident. True to his nature, Charlie listened intensely to every word.

"You're lucky to be alive," he said. "You really must have a hard head!"

Everyone laughed. Then Charlie looked at his watch. It was getting late. It was almost three o'clock. Another quick lunch at Al's! He couldn't afford to stay any longer. Once again, Charlie excused himself, but this time it was for good.

"It's been great seeing you guys, but I have to get back to the office. It was nice to meet you Alex. I hope the three of us can get together again before you head back east."

Alex smiled. "It was nice meeting you as well, Charlie. I'm sure that we'll all be doing just that in the not so distant future," she assured him.

Charlie smiled back. "Until then, my friends, stay safe; and Grey, if you need anything." Charlie offered.

Grey cut him off, "Yeah, yeah, I know; just pick up the phone."

"Until next time," he said as he got up.

Grey offered his hand and Charlie shook it. "Take care, my friend," Grey said.

Charlie nodded, then turned and walked away.

For a moment there was silence. Then Alex spoke. "You going to be ok this afternoon?" she asked.

"I'll let you know that when I'm finished," he said. "For now, I'd better get you back to the house."

Shortly afterwards, they said their thank you's and good-bye's to Al, who reminded them, as always not to be strangers. Alex promised him they would be back.

Neither of them said a word on the ride home, though they were both thinking about Clyde's appointment.

As they pulled up in front of the house, Grey asked, "Mind if I take the Mustang? I don't feel like taking my crappy rental car."

"Not at all," she said. "I have some reading I want to do anyway. Have a good time! We'll touch base when you get home."

Grey got out of the car and headed for the garage. He looked at his watch. He was pressed for time. The trip to Cynthia's was going to have to wait. A few minutes later, he returned with a portable therapy table and tossed it into the trunk.

"Thanks again," he said waving to Alex. "See you in awhile. I'll call when I'm on my way home."

As Grey drove out of the complex, a million things started rushing through his head. Some anxiety, some fear. In the back of his mind, he kept his mental fingers crossed. If he got lucky, everything would go well at Clyde's. With no problems and no surprises, he could move ahead and concentrate on more important things. If things went sour though, it would be just the beginning of a long and wild ride.

Behind the wheel, he liked the renewed sense of control. The accelerator felt good under his foot. He got back on the freeway again and headed south toward Clyde's. After about a mile, he noticed a faint smell in the air. It wasn't gas or exhaust fumes as one would expect. The distinct odor, like the smell of wet leather had returned. It got his attention for the second time.

Curiously, he looked down at his hand. Once again, there was no sign of life or animation. Still, his ring felt unusually warm. Grey relaxed a little. He knew he wasn't alone.

The demon from his past had not forgotten him. Even when he decided to walk away from everything, the creature had not abandoned him. Instead, it chose to remain dormant, in a state of hibernation. It would never leave him. Their connection was too strong. Grey was surprised to discover that over the past decade, he was never really alone. He had tried to deny it, but the guardian was always there.

Now, when he needed it most, he remembered the strength and power of the other world that was once his. With it, he found a certain inner peace. One that made him feel whole again. Things were beginning to make sense. His new talent was indeed a gift! It really was a blessing in disguise. Over time he would learn to control it. He would learn to use it well. Somehow the guardian would teach him.

For a brief moment, he felt like his old self. The wind blew through his hair as he flew down the highway. He felt good. He was ready to face his friend.

* * * * *

CHAPTER 12

The gates at the Hobart house stood open and waiting. They were always that way when guests were expected. The simple but elegant set of green wrought iron sculptures protected a single opening in the massive, white stone wall which surrounded the front of the house. As one passed between them, they entered a large courtyard that was so welcoming it greeted you like an old friend. Flowers of every color had found a home here. They added a sea of color to the deep green foliage which surrounded you at every turn. It was a peaceful place. It was here, in the garden, Grey found his friend lounging casually about in a white wicker chair and smoking a good cigar.

Clyde hardly noticed him when he first arrived. He barely looked up. His mind was somewhere else. Grey knew why. He was hopelessly lost, deep in the sounds of classic jazz. The music seemed to come from everywhere. Each plant appeared to be breathing it. The audio system was designed in such a way, that the music was filtered out onto the patio through a complex set of speakers; each one carefully hidden in the shadows of the garden. This arrangement allowed Clyde to create the illusion of a large botanical symphony.

Then, of course, there was the cigar. It smelled good. It had to be Cuban. Clyde always said there was a fine line between legality and luxury. Having Cuban cigars wasn't really breaking the rules; it was contributing to the world's economy. Besides, when you were finished, there was never anything left to incriminate you. The evidence generally vanished in a cloud of smoke. At the moment, Clyde's indiscretion was close to disappearing.

Grey made his way across the courtyard and leaned the therapy table against the wall by the front door. Then he turned to say hello. He'd taken only a few steps when Clyde's deep, burly voice came out from behind the cigar.

"Grey, my boy, how the heck are ya?" he bellowed.

"I still couldn't tell a joke if my life depended on it," Grey replied.

Clyde laughed. "You do realize that that statement alone is actually funny? That's strange coming from you!"

Clyde's sarcasm was refreshing as always. Grey smiled. "Sorry to disappoint you my friend, but I'm still a smart ass. Some things never change."

Clyde was amused. "I guess I should have expected as much. Glad to see you're all right then," he chuckled. "I didn't want to have to find a new therapist. They're so hard to break in!"

Both men laughed. Even though Clyde was nearly twice his age, there was still something 'kid-like' about him. Grey had great respect for the man. He had learned a lot from him.

Clyde stood and gave Grey a bear hug. It was a brief one, but definitely from the heart.

"I don't need this kind of stress, Kid," he said. "You better be more careful from now on. I don't have the time left to figure out which one of my friends is going to be in trouble next. You sure you're up to this?" he asked.

Grey nodded, "Yeah, what the hell," he lied. "I'm kind of looking forward to it. You know, getting things back to normal." Grey wanted to laugh. Normal? Was anything ever going to be normal again? Normal was just a word that described things that once were. "I'm going to go set up," he told Clyde. "You finish that thing and I'll see you inside whenever you're ready."

"O.K. Kid, I'll be right there," Clyde assured him. Grey grabbed his things and went inside.

Clyde joined him sooner than expected. He had finished the cigar rather quickly and then sauntered into the house. As usual, he found Grey setting up shop in the master bedroom. He grabbed the towel Grey extended to him and went straight to the bathroom to change.

As time passed, the minutes seemed more like hours. The longer it took for Clyde to come out, the more anxious Grey became. He really wanted to get this whole thing over with. There was no way he could relax until he got some answers. He was worried enough as it was. By the time Clyde finally got on the table, Grey's hands were shaking. It took him a few seconds to get himself under control. He took a few breaths, and was ready to start.

The session got off to a slow start. The first fifteen minutes of contact were completely uneventful. Clyde's feet and legs were basically silent. There was nothing to see that was of any real interest. The same thing happened with his arms and hands. No colors, no lights, there was nothing at all. This left Grey with a good feeling. Things were starting to look up. Maybe the whole carnage thing was over, but it was still too early to tell. It wasn't until he started to work on Clyde's neck and shoulders that things began to come to life. As it happened, everything started to go in a different direction.

When the total blackness began to fade, Grey was ready. This time, he had a plan. He would concentrate carefully on what he was seeing. He wanted to be able to give an accurate description of everything that happened, to Alex and Father Richard. Detail was important. Much to his surprise, when the colors came and the movie began, he saw no signs of violence. There was really nothing to see at all. Maybe this time, things were going to be different. Maybe, everything would be ok.

When the colors and lights began to fade, all Grey could see was a lot of heavy smoke. As it began to dissipate, he could vaguely make out something taking shape in front of him. There in the shadows, was an oil painting. It was one he'd seen before. He remembered having seen it before, hanging over the fireplace in the Hobart living room. Why was he seeing Clyde's living room? Grey slowly closed his eyes attempting to refocus his attention. When he opened them again, the picture was still there.

The painting was an impressionist work of three jazz musicians. They were hard to see at first, but someone could make them out if they looked closely at the right angle. The players themselves were all partially hidden by the elaborate 'colors of music' that came splashing out of their instruments onto the canvas. As Clyde's mind became one with his, Grey discovered Clyde's travel plans. They were going to a special place. Grey was amazed when he walked into the picture itself. Here, inside the portrait, he was now Clyde Hobart, jazz entrepreneur.

He entered the painting by stepping between the sax player and the drummer. His momentum carried him through the musicians and landed him on the sidewalk in front of a small nightclub behind them. Once he got his bearings, he quickly turned back to the trio, reached deep into his pocket and eagerly slipped 'Mr. Jackson' a twenty dollar bill into each one of their instrument cases. Now excited, he turned his attention back to the Club.

At the first good ear, Night Owls embodied a real jazz club. As Clyde went inside, he had to walk through a dark cloud. The Club seemed to suck the tobacco smoke back in with him, rather than letting it escape through the front door. This gave Grey a weird feeling, but he was still curious to go inside. After a few more steps, he was very glad he did.

Inside, there was a short hallway which soon opened into a large room. The lighting was poor and at first he had trouble making out the interior layout of the club. When things started to come into focus, Grey's jaw almost hit the floor. He could not believe what his eyes were seeing. The place was incredible. It was the kind of private heaven, Clyde Hobart would call home.

* * * * *

Everything there was as it should be, "in the world according to Clyde". As Grey began to take inventory, he noticed something shiny across the room that instantly jumped out at him. Over in the corner, on one of the private tables, Grey could see a soft, angelic glow, radiating off what appeared to be a finely polished trumpet. A dark hand lay next to it, stroking it softly, the way a gentle lover would caress a woman's breast. As Grey continued to observe, it became obvious that both hand and instrument were intimately connected. The contact between the two of them paralleled being erotic. For Grey, it was like watching a seduction. He wanted to see more.

Because of the gentleman's position at the table, the stranger's identity remained a secret. He was well hidden in the shadows. It wasn't until he leaned forward to reach for a drink that Grey could make out his face in the soft candlelight. What he saw made his heart skip a beat. There in the booth, less than thirty feet away, was the great Louie Armstrong.

There was no mistaking his face. His eyes were bright and his smile, all but made him glow in the dark. He was caressing his 'friend' with one hand, and a double with the other. "Satch" was taking a break.

Grey was in shock. He had to remind himself that this was a dream. Armstrong himself had passed on years ago. This Louie wasn't real. Or was he? At this moment in Clyde's mind, he appeared to be alive and well. Armstrong was one of the players in Clyde's escape. Here, his presence was as real as Clyde wanted it to be. In this sacred place, Louie was just hanging around, having a drink and passing time between sets.

Grey's curiosity ran wild. Rather than remaining content with just being along for the ride, he decided to see if he could control Clyde's attention enough to check out the rest of the room. It didn't take much. Perhaps Clyde had the same thing in mind. Grey understood why they were here.

Clyde loved music; jazz music in particular. This was his heaven. Night Owls was the one place where he could always go to let everything else disappear. Even though it was only a fantasy, in some ways it was still very real. Real enough in fact, that Grey could still watch the video. He could do this because Clyde had created everything in his head. When Clyde's mind saw the club as being real, it allowed Grey to access it as well. All of the guests were just part of the illusion.

Grey was completely overwhelmed. Working on Clyde was not at all what he expected. The fact that he was able to participate in any of this, was incredible. Not only was he able to see actual events but now, he realized that he could literally walk into someone's dreams. Reality on its own was frightening enough, but dreams were an entirely different adventure! It was simply amazing waiting to see what would happen next. He didn't have to wait long. Clyde caught him off guard when he turned his attention to the bar. Grey thought he was ready for anything. He soon discovered he was wrong.

"Good evening Mr. H.," the bartender greeted him with a smile. "Your usual?" he asked.

"I believe that will do me just fine, Rocky. Better make it a double," Clyde responded.

Grey paid close attention as the bartender reached below the counter and unlocked a special cabinet. Carefully, he removed a single bottle of well aged Armanjac that had been collecting dust for quite some time. Taking great care, he poured three fingers in a glass for Clyde.

"Here ya go, Boss," he said as he handed him the crystal snifter. "Just the way you like it."

Clyde swirled the liquor around in the glass, enjoying its gentle aroma. Then he took a long, sweet swallow. His lips touched the glass with the softness of a kiss. It was just what the doctor ordered. He tipped the glass toward Rocky.

"Thank you, my man. You are a gentleman and a saint," he told him. "How are things going around here tonight?"

"Oh there fine, Boss, just fine." Rocky repeated. "Bird played a few and Louie just finished a set, and I think Miss Ella's gonna be by later. You plan on hangin' round?"

Clyde grinned. "I'm planning on staying awhile, so please don't entertain any ideas you might have about putting that bottle away."

"No sir, Mr. H. The thought never crossed my mind," Rocky assured him. "I'll be leaving it right here for you to enjoy at your leisure."

Clyde smiled. He liked Rocky. Rocky was a good pour and knew his place. Respect was important. It was something the two of them shared. "Miss Ella's sure gonna be happy to see you, Boss," Rocky said. "She's missed seeing you the last couple of times. Darn shame you never stay for very long. It's a sad thing, man owning a club as fine as this one and never having the time to enjoy it."

Clyde was dejected. He knew Rocky was right. Every time he came to Night Owls, it was harder for him to leave.

"Better to be able to enjoy a small taste of something exceptional on a regular basis, than not to be able to indulge in it at all," Clyde responded.

Rocky wisely assumed that he meant both the liquor and the club. "I hear ya, Boss, I hear ya," he replied. Then he went back to polishing glasses. All through the conversation, Clyde's back had been facing the stage. He never saw Louie get up from the table. He was just finding the bottom of his glass, when he heard the long, sweet notes begin to come out of Satch's coronet. They floated around the room like birds on the wind. The great horned owl had started to fly.

As Louie was finishing "West End Blues", Clyde felt a hand on his shoulder.

"Hello there stranger, Come here often?" Her sweet voice was music to Clyde's ears.

Clyde swung his bar stool around to properly greet Miss Ella. This time, Grey was ready to savor every precious moment. Clyde took her hand and kissed it. Then he gave her a big hug.

"Always nice to see you, my dear," he said.

Ella smiled. "You got time to hum a few bars with me, baby?" she teased.

Clyde laughed, "Sure, why not?"

Ella smiled, "Hey Satch, would you mind playing "Jeepers, Creepers" for me and the Boss? We're going to sing one together!"

When Ella said this, Grey figured that it was a good thing he couldn't see his own face in the mirror. He didn't want to see his eyes bug straight out! Clyde was cool, but Grey wasn't sure that he could sing. This was going to be interesting.

With typical Clyde style, the old Jazzman surprised him once again. Once he got going, he really wasn't that bad. As they started the second verse, Louie made his way off the stage and sat down next to them on a bar stool. As he played, Ella and Clyde's voices echoed gracefully through the Club. Grey was so overwhelmed, he had to let go. The moment he did, all the images of Night Owls faded away.

Clyde Hobart shook his head in a hazy sort of fashion. He was back in the real world. Off in the distance, he could hear the sounds of someone humming "Jeepers, Creepers". The party would never end. He was happy. He loved going to the club. It always made him feel special. He was totally relaxed.

Then suddenly it hit him. He was awake and he could still hear the music! For a brief moment, Clyde panicked. Where was the song coming from? When he opened his eyes, he looked up and saw that Grey was humming Satch's tune. Grey was even on the same note and the same beat that he and Ella were on when he left the club. It was as if Grey was singing along with them. How could that be possible? How on earth could he know?

It took Clyde a minute before he got up the nerve to ask. Truth was, he wasn't really sure he wanted to know. He wrapped the towel around himself and sat up on the table.

"Hey, Kid, why the old Louie Armstrong tune?" he asked. "I didn't know you listened to any of the old stuff."

Grey was surprised. He hadn't realized that he'd been humming out loud.

"I'm just trying to keep up with you, my friend. I didn't think you'd mind," Grey answered. "Sorry, I didn't mean to embarrass you."

"It's no big deal," Clyde assured him. "No harm done. I just didn't realize I was singing out loud. I'm actually impressed that you know the tune. That kind of music is from a whole different generation."

"I'm just sorry that I wasn't around back then to see them," Grey replied.

Clyde understood. "I was lucky enough to see a few of them along the way," he said. "Those are moments in time that I will never forget. Part of me still sees them whenever I have a mind to. I just close my eyes and I'm back there once again."

Grey nodded. He knew just how Clyde felt. After all, he was just there.

"I know it's hard to believe, but I think I know what you mean," he confided.

Clyde patted him on the back. "You know something, Kid," he said, "There are times I believe you do."

Grey was relieved. If Clyde only knew! He was safe now. Clyde's suspicions were put aside. He had Clyde convinced that he had been singing out loud.

Clyde offered one final thought, "It's too bad you weren't around to enjoy them, Grey. You of all people would have loved it," he said.

"I do anyway," Grey told him. "Coming here and listening to them with you, has made me feel like I was part of it all. I just love Jazz. I have you to thank for that."

It was a lie of sorts, but only a little white one. He had in fact learned a lot about music during the time he spent with Clyde. Only difference was, up until today, he'd never actually been there. While he was grateful to his friend for sharing the experience, he wasn't about to let him in on what just happened. Not even Clyde would have been able to handle that!

Grey packed up his things and headed out to the car. As he passed through the living room, on his way to the front door, the painting seemed to stare back at him. It made him feel better. While his adventure with Clyde was entertaining, it was also violence free. That meant that whatever he saw at Kendall's was Blake's creation and not his. It was a relief knowing that the morbid fascinations were not coming from inside of him. Still, it was hard to believe that Blake could find it entertaining.

What was really going on inside Blake's head? Were they re-runs of old horror movies, or something based on reality? Next time he was at Kendall's he was going to have to pay very close attention to what he saw. He was going to have to get to the bottom of this and quickly. His mind raced as he started to load the car. He'd just put the table in the trunk, when Clyde came out to say good-bye.

"Thanks for the memories, Kid," Clyde said in an almost playful fashion.

"Thanks for the song, Mr. H.," Grey responded.

Clyde's face went blank. He tried to hide it, but Grey saw the brief, startled look in his eyes. He'd caught Clyde off guard. He knew that it was time for him to go, but he needed to let Clyde off the hook. As he backed out of the driveway, he called out to his friend.

"See ya in two, Mr. H.,"

Clyde waved, "See ya in two, my boy. Say 'Hello' to the wife and kid."

Grey nodded and waved back. Then he sped off down the street. It felt like a great weight had been lifted from his shoulders. The meeting with Clyde had gone smoother than expected. Not only did he share a new experience with his friend, he also learned that the horror clips would not be present on a regular basis. The content of the videos must depend entirely upon the thoughts of the person he was in contact with. His mind was not responsible. The violent scenes and images were created in someone else's fantasy.

Assuming that they were limited to whatever specific individual he was working on only made things more interesting. It was scary to think that Blake Kendall had this kind of weird imagination. He was a well respected legal professional. Then again, he had defended the slime of the system for quite some time. Who knows what he'd seen or done over the course of his career?

Clyde on the other hand, was harmless. The experience with him, all but confirmed that the images he was seeing were individualized. Night Owls had been a totally innocent adventure. It was Clyde's own private little world. It didn't appear to pose any threat. Blake's scenario could easily be a representation of the dark side of his profession, but even that was a reach. There was really only one way to find out. He would have to wait until he could work on Blake again to be sure. Without touching him, there was no way to tell.

The entire idea sent chills up Grey's spine. Blake was a friend that he'd known for years. In a sneaky, conniving sort of way, he was convincing himself to invade the man's privacy. Grey laughed. In reality, he would be putting the great Blake Kendall on trial! And so what if the man did have a few disturbed ideas about entertainment? Fantasies were generally harmless. It was fun to be able to see some of these things, but not at the cost of being forced to sit in judgment of his friends or family. Did any of this really matter? He wasn't scheduled to see Blake for a few more days. Maybe by then, he wouldn't care anyway.

Right now, all he wanted to do was call Alex and have her meet him back at the church. He had a lot to share. She and Father Richard were going to love what he had to say.

* * * * *

It was late in the day and Blake was restless. The afternoon had dragged on endlessly. For some time now, he'd been staring at the clock, slowly watching the minutes tick away. He was sure the battery in the little sucker was going bad. The second hand took forever to make a single sweep. When it finally did, it was almost a tease because it immediately sat motionless again, apparently waiting until it was damned good and ready to make its next move.

He would have to leave soon if he wanted to catch her. It was already four-thirty, and he had no idea what time she would be leaving. He wanted to be certain that he was ready and waiting in the lobby when she came downstairs. The first step would be to follow her to her car. As soon as he discovered the make and model, he could have one of his connections let him run the license plate for an address. Once he was able to secure that information, he could begin to formulate a plan.

Just thinking about her made him aroused. Her tight body in that short skirt did wonders for his libido. The way she smelled; the way her hair fell gently off her shoulders as it softly cascaded down her back. Coffee my ass! He wanted the cream! It wasn't caffeine that fed his addiction. It was something much more. Something so primitive he could almost taste it. He'd experienced it before and he wanted it again. The thought of her made his tail grow.

It all happened so fast, finding her the way he did. She became an instant obsession. He knew that he would have to calm himself down before he could casually leave the office. Otherwise, he'd run the risk of having to limp past Sheila's desk. Timing of course, was everything. He was drawn back to the clock again. Much to his dismay, the little bastard had only managed to grind out a few more clicks. It was now four thirty-five. But if he didn't hurry, he might miss her. He had to get downstairs.

Blake got up and started to adjust himself. He was a little surprised by the size of his problem. If his present condition continued, he was going to need a distraction. He tossed the new case file into his briefcase and grabbed his jacket. His first thought was to drape it casually over his left arm. He could use the jacket to run interference. That would look perfectly natural. Unfortunately, folded in half, it was too short to do him much good. Length was an issue here.

His mind quickly searched for a solution. As it did, he grabbed his briefcase with his other hand and headed for the door. He had to move fast. Suddenly, without even thinking, he shifted the briefcase into position, protecting his groin as he passed by Sheila's desk. Sheila smiled at him as he walked by.

"Goodnight, Mr. Kendall," Sheila remarked.

She'd caught him just as he got to the elevator. The Cat smiled. When he turned back to address her, the briefcase held its ground.

"Goodnight Sheila, see you in the morning," he said. "Have a pleasant evening."

"Thank you, you too sir," she replied.

Blake waved then turned back toward the elevator. As he did, he heard the sound of it arriving on his floor. His heart was pounding when he got on. He could feel the excitement building throughout his body. "Katie" might be somewhere close by. If he kept his cool and played his cards right, he would soon have the opportunity to get another fix. His mind went crazy with anticipation. Lucky for Blake, it was a quick ride down.

When the doors opened, the first thing to catch his eye was the coffee cart. It was shut down for the night. Curiously, he walked over to check it out. According to the sign, Sylvester closed up shop at three p.m. every afternoon. The notice on the sign read "back at" with the red paper clock hands set at six a.m. That made perfect sense. By mid-afternoon, the old guy had already put in a full honest day's work. Who could blame him? Blake couldn't help but wonder if Sylvester's daughter was the reason the old man chose to work in this building. He also wished that he had spent more time talking with him. That would have at least allowed him to ask a few important questions. Knowing where she worked would have made his present task much easier. He could have avoided his present "needle in a haystack" approach. For starters, just knowing her name would have been helpful.

Truth was, if he missed her leaving the building, he could always catch up with Sylvester in the morning. Then, he could strike up a new conversation. Actually, he was planning on doing that anyway. His sudden new interest in coffee gave him a great excuse to get friendly.

One by one, people from upstairs began to arrive in the lobby. At first there were just a few, but the closer it got to the five o'clock hour, the more frequently they appeared. Blake found a seat next to the fountain in the corner of the foyer and made himself comfortable. From there, he could take a good look at each person as they left the building. His choice of location was brilliant. His presence would not be obvious to anyone exiting the elevators. It strategically kept him just out of their direct line of sight, leaving him in a position where he was able to maintain an adequate vantage point.

Blake paid careful attention to each person as they ran the gauntlet between his position and the door. As he anticipated, they were all forced to pass through his territory. He didn't want to take a chance of her slipping past him. The entire exercise quickly became a game. To his surprise, there were a lot of interesting people. For a while, time stood still.

Blake glanced at his watch. It was ten past the hour and he was beginning to grow impatient. "Katie" was nowhere to be found. Maybe she was running late. He was becoming frustrated. He conceded the fact that the situation was probably his own fault. During his visit with Sylvester he should have pursued more information. Now, for all practical purposes, he was flying blind. That; and he couldn't escape the fact that his problem continued to persist. He was still relying on his briefcase for protection.

"Don't the majority of most corporate employees bolt for the door or head for a bar at the five o'clock hour?" he thought to himself. "Where the hell was she?" He was almost thinking out loud.

Blake started to panic. For a second he thought he'd actually missed her. He couldn't stand the thought of that. He just wasn't himself lately.

The energy surges from each fix were transforming him somehow. He was totally on edge. Anxiety was getting the best of him. Having these feelings at all was so completely out of character for him that it forced him to stop and re-evaluate his course of action. He concluded that in his present condition, he could not afford to indulge in any more obsessive behavior for the moment. His investigation would have to wait.

Blake stood, re-positioned his briefcase and headed for his car. He was a little discouraged, but hardly ready to throw in the towel. Tomorrow was a new day and a new opportunity. He would make it a point to come in early. He would be the first one in line when Sylvester opened for business. The coffee would be fresh and the conversation would be even more stimulating. In no time at all he could familiarize himself with the menu and decide when to make a reservation. Sylvester would make a great waiter. He would never know that he was serving up his own daughter on a silver platter.

The 'Cat' grinned. His mouth watered at the thought of her. Blake fumbled through his pants trying to find his keys. He found something else instead. The cold, hard ivory felt good in his hand. He knew it was time for another performance. It was time to go. After a little searching, he found his keys in his other pocket. By the time he finally got the car started, there was something else stiff in his pants. The engine wasn't the only thing purring.

* * * * *

The ride to the church seemed to take forever. Time always had a way of feeling that way when you're in a hurry. Everything runs in slow motion. Actually, in this case it was a blessing. It gave him a chance to think. Grey spent the entire drive carefully reviewing what had happened at Clyde's. He wanted to be sure that the story he was going to tell his friends would be as accurate and detailed as possible. He wondered how Father Richard would react to this one. Another log on the fire if you please! As he drove, the gears in his head turned, slowly keeping pace with the bumps in the road. By the time the church finally came into view, he had all his ducks in a row. He was ready to talk to his friend.

Much to his surprise, Father Richard was nowhere to be found. The church grounds keeper told him that the Father had left about an hour earlier. He had gone home to rest. It had been a long day. His morning battle in the rafters had worn him out. Between his problem with heights and all of the work that was involved moving things around, Grey figured that his friend was pretty burned out. Grey decided that he could catch up with him later.

Driving through the parking lot, Grey noticed that all of the pews had disappeared from the lawn. They were probably back safe inside returned to their normal places. The job of putting them back into the sanctuary would have taken some serious effort. He hoped that his friend had not attempted to replace them all by himself. For a minute, he considered calling Richard's house to check up on him, but decided against it. What he had to say could wait. It was more important to let his friend rest. In the meantime, he'd find Alex. Together, they could decide what their next move should be.

* * * * *

When he heard the phone in his pocket ring, he expected it to be Alex. She'd been missing in action most of the afternoon. There was really nothing to worry about. She could hold her own with anyone. Still, he was curious. He had so much to tell her. Anxiously, he answered the phone. The voice he heard on the other end was not who he expected. It was Rachel. She was worried. Her speech was fast and animated. Whatever it was she wanted it must be important! She immediately hit him with all the usual questions;

"Where are you? When are you coming home? Is everything ok?" she asked.

He never got a chance to answer. She went straight to the real issue. "Renee and Tim want to go to Mama Cozzas' for dinner," she continued. "Do you think there's a chance you could get Alex to baby-sit?"

Pizza, she wanted to go out for pizza? Grey laughed. Typical Rachel was a social butterfly at her best. If she only knew how simple the answer to her question really was. If he could find Alex, he was sure that getting her to baby-sit wouldn't be a problem. She would jump at the chance to spend more time alone with Dylan. Who knows what fun they might have together? What wonderful mischief would Alex come up with next? Then again, did he really want to know?

He brought his attention back to Rachel. He told her just what she wanted to hear. He assured her that he would be home shortly and would find Alex. This was just what the doctor ordered. Rachel was excited. He could tell by the sudden change in her voice. She was less stressed. He had succeeded in pacifying her for the moment.

As soon as she hung up, he dialed Alex's number. He was a little surprised when she didn't answer. Her voice mail clicked in on the second ring. What could she possibly be up to that would keep her from answering the phone?

Curious, he left a message, hoping that it wouldn't take long for her to call him back. He was pleased to discover that it didn't. Within minutes he got a response. When the phone rang, he knew exactly who it was. He could feel her. Strange as it was, he could really feel her presence. It was like old times.

Grey smiled. The old ways were coming back. He knew he was getting stronger. With any luck, soon he would be his own self again. Eagerly he picked up the phone. This time his instincts were right.

Their conversation went just the way he intended. Alex would baby- sit. She was genuinely amused by the fact that he even thought it necessary to ask. Of course she was willing to help. She even teased him about some ideas she had for the evening. She and Dylan would have a blast! She assured him that he had nothing to worry about. Grey was relieved. In a few short hours, Rachel was going to get exactly what she asked for.

* * * * *

When he caught the red light, he wasn't really surprised. It had been that kind of a day. Traffic at that hour was always ridiculous. At least he was the first car in line. Sitting at the corner where Highway 133 met Pacific Coast Highway, Blake discovered he was actually glad that he had stopped. There, on display in front of him was an awesome sight. He was facing west and staring directly toward the sun. Once your eyes got past the small section of beach on the other side of the intersection, there was nothing but clouds and ocean as far as the eye could see. The colors of twilight had started to gather near the edge of the horizon. It was going to be another beautiful sunset.

The colors were incredible. Blake wished he were home. The view from his balcony would have made this sight even more spectacular. The way the light played off the water, reminded him of a fix. When he left the office, he had been distracted. The drive home had done nothing but make matters worse. The traffic added to his tension. Now, gazing out across the waves, he took a moment to clear his head. He needed a break. It was worth it.

When the light changed, Blake allowed himself to relax. He had to forget about the girl for now. He had other things to do. He was concerned that his priorities were temporarily out of whack. The fact that he wanted to see her so badly was disturbing. Had he somehow lost control? His need was growing stronger than ever. With each new conquest, he grew hungrier for more. Today was definitely no exception. He could hardly wait for his next cup of coffee.

Now, time had become his enemy. He knew that he would be counting the hours until morning, hoping for a chance to see her again. He looked at his watch. It would be his nemesis for the next twelve hours. He knew that he would look at it again and again in anticipation, only to be greeted by its continuing torment. With each glance, he would have to convince himself that the hands were not moving slower and slower. It was going to be a long night.

Blake reminded himself that he had to be patient. He would be home in a few minutes and could settle in for the night. A brandy on the balcony would probably help. The 'Cat' smiled. Tomorrow was a new day. If he was good, really good, he might get something special for breakfast.

* * * * *

Dinner turned out to be very relaxing. Wine was flowing freely and Grey quickly discovered that mentally, he was just paddling along. Rachel and Renee who were both school teachers had been talking "shop" so his lack of interest wasn't noticed. He just sat, quietly amused and poured himself another glass of wine. Renee always asked him to pick the wine. His choices were usually right on the money. More often than not, it was a deep red, not too sweet and frequently not the cheap stuff. Grey did have good taste. Tim was always a good sport about it and never took offense. He kept himself busy by nursing his favorite beer.

Grey liked Tim. He was always fun to talk to. The fact that he was even free for dinner was unusual. His rotation schedule at the police department left him working a lot of night shifts. After the recent suicide/shooting, Wickmann insisted that he take a couple of nights off. Renee was thankful. She knew he needed some rest. It was she who suggested they come to Mama Cossa's. It was Tim's favorite place. When she called Rachel, the two of them decided that all of them having dinner together would do the guys some good. Pizza and beer was always a welcome break. So far the girls were right.

Grey enjoyed Tim's stories and if coaxed, Tim was usually willing to offer up one or two upon request. Tonight was no different. After listening to what happened on a couple of his calls, Grey asked him what his thoughts were about the series of recent murders that were being covered by the local news. He was fishing for information and hoped Tim would bite. He wasn't sure why having the information was such a big deal, but knowing the inside story had suddenly become very important. Even if it was just a gut feeling, it still felt right. Something inside him was telling him, he really had to know. He wondered how much Tim would be willing to cooperate.

"Is this guy they're talking about for real?" Grey blurted out, figuring it was ok to try to slip in a quick question or two.

Tim looked up from his beer. "You really want know?" he responded. His eyes were fixed hard on Grey.

Grey just nodded.

"Well, unfortunately we think so man," Tim answered. "This guy is a real sick mother!" He took another long drag on his beer. "Why the interest?" he asked.

Grey played it cool. "No real interest, just curiosity. I deal with so many different people all the time. I wondered if there was any way I would be able to tell if someone wasn't 'all there.'

"I honestly can't see how," Tim explained. He rubbed the beer bottle against his temple then gestured as if he were pointing inside his ear. "Not unless you have some way of getting inside someone's head, he continued. You know, like being able to tell what they're thinking."

Grey had to control his excitement. Tim's words hit home! There was a way he could tell what somebody else was thinking! Tim's observation struck a chord inside him. Maybe this was the answer he had been looking for. Could he really tell? This was a major piece of the puzzle. Now the big question was how much could he actually see?

Still, it was one hell of an idea. It really made him think. His conversation with Tim proved to be much more useful than he ever could have imagined. Grey wanted to pursue the subject further but he didn't get very far.

Tim played along, but just a little. The only other insight he was willing to offer was, from what he could tell, the killings were all being done by the same individual. Off the record, he would admit that the police did have a few ideas, but he wasn't at liberty to share. Whoever was doing this was extremely dangerous. The authorities wanted to keep a lid on things for awhile. Tim's voice was honest but evasive. It left Grey wondering if the cops knew anything at all.

The rest of dinner was uneventful. Grey had hoped to get more out of Tim, but it wasn't meant to be. While the girls planned a trip to Vegas, he and Tim made a lot of small talk. Grey was a little disappointed. His primary objective had been to get a profile of the killer. Sadly, Tim did not allow him to get that far. He had however, given him a totally new perspective. Rather than hassle his friend any longer, he decided to back off. Maybe later Tim would have more to offer. For now, he would simply respect his friend's space. Grey wondered how far he could trust him.

* * * * *

By the time they got home, Grey was completely wiped out. He had been tired to start with. The dinner and wine just added to his condition. It wasn't until he and Rachel pulled into the driveway that he wondered about Alex and Dylan. They had been together for almost three hours. For all he knew, that was time enough for Alex to teach Dylan a new language! He was relieved to find her in the living room reading and Dylan safely in bed fast asleep. She smiled when she saw them come in.

"How'd it go?" Grey asked.

"We had a nice, quiet evening," Alex answered.

"Did he go right down for you?" Rachel asked.

"Like an angel," Alex told her.

"Well, I want to thank you again," Rachel added. "You did us a big favor. I think Grey had a good time. I really think he needed to get out."

Alex nodded. "I'm sure you're right. I'm glad I could help."

Rachel tossed her coat over a chair and headed into the kitchen. Grey quickly shot Alex a glance. Neither one of them said a word in her absence. Rachel returned a few minutes later with a glass of water.

"Well, good night you two, I'm going to bed," she said. "Thanks again, Alex, I'll see you in the morning." Then Rachel turned and walked down the hallway.

Once she was gone, Grey gave Alex a look.

"Not to worry," she chuckled. "Nothing happened. You know you can trust me."

Grey remained silent and just nodded his head. There was nothing to say. He knew she was right. Whatever there was between her and Dylan would have to remain their secret. It was probably better that he didn't know. Grey got up and walked over to Alex. He bent down and kissed her on the cheek.

"Thanks," he said in a subdued voice.

Alex looked up at him and smiled. "Go get some sleep, silly. I might want you to try something for me tomorrow," she said. "I have an idea how you might be able to learn to control this thing."

Grey looked puzzled. "Don't worry about it tonight," she told him. "We can discuss it in the morning."

Grey scratched his head. "All right Alex, as you wish," he said. "I'll see you tomorrow. Besides, I was talking to my friend Tim at dinner and he said something that got me thinking. We'll discuss it tomorrow after I've had a chance to really give it some thought."

Alex smiled and nodded her approval. Then he said good night and followed Rachel's path down the hall.

An hour later he was still awake, lying in bed wondering what Alex had in mind for the following day. Whatever it was, he was sure it would prove to be interesting. She seldom failed in her efforts to please. That's probably why she suggested he get some sleep. He would most likely need it.

By now, the full darkness of night had taken over the Thomas house. With it, came an eerie silence that filled each room. Grey was surprised to discover that if he listened carefully, he could once again hear Dylan breathing in the next room. With minor effort, he could even hear the sound of his son's heart beat. The strange, yet beautiful rhythm of life was truly a miracle. Hearing it so clearly though, made him feel strange.

His senses were getting sharper with each passing day. He had noticed that if he concentrated, he could see clearly even in the pitch black. His night vision was nearly perfect. His eyesight was comparable to that of a bird of prey. It was simply amazing. His other senses were more acute as well. Even from this distance he could smell the wetness of Dylan's diaper. He also remembered that during dinner he could have sworn that he could taste each individual spice as it fermented in the spaghetti sauce. His taste buds were that alive! The entire experience was completely overwhelming. There were so many new things to see and do. He felt like Dylan at Christmas time. He had all of these new toys to play with. It was a lot to absorb. Carefully, he put his head back down on his pillow. Rachel was still asleep. Somehow, he had managed not to wake her. He closed his eyes and prayed for the sandman. His prayers were never answered.

When the first light of dawn appeared through the cracks in the window blinds he didn't even care. A strange calm had come over him. There was a quiet sense of peace. For some reason he wasn't even tired. He actually felt refreshed. Anxiously, he watched as the light grew brighter and brighter. A new day had begun. It was then he wondered if he would ever find sleep again.

* * * * *

CHAPTER 13

Alex had bad dreams. Not one or two mind you, but a series of illusions that systematically formed an ongoing pattern like chapters in a book. Each image was so vivid and realistic that by the time morning came, Alex wasn't sure whether they were actually dreams at all. For her, it was like she had actually traveled back to another place in time. All she could focus on was the most recent entry, one which seemingly brought the dead back to life. In it, a ghostly apparition appeared. The distorted skeletal face of an old woman was staring down at her as she hung helplessly over a great abyss. Fate had left her dangling by one arm, clinging desperately to the woman's outstretched hand. Alex could see herself as a young girl again. As the minutes passed, her strength slowly disappeared. Despite her best efforts, Alex could not maintain her grip. When their fingers finally separated, she fell terrified into the shadows below.

The maelstrom seemed to swallow her up as she plunged downward into its belly. Fear quickly engulfed her as she continued her descent into the whirling darkness. She never hit bottom. In the depths of her mind, the adult Alex screamed. Her body shuddered and she woke up violently in a cold sweat. She was visibly shaken, and needed a moment to regroup. Admittedly, her dreams had always been a little out of the ordinary. Ever since she was a small child, her nightmares had come to visit on a regular basis. As an adult she found them easier to deal with, but as a child they were hauntingly traumatic. She had spent many nights in her Granny's arms afraid to close her eyes, fearful of what she might see. On those occasions, she would force herself to stay awake and wait patiently for the comfort of the morning sun. Looking back at it all now, Alex realized that these dreams were just a part of the learning process. They were all directly related in some way to understanding her "gift". It was all about power. It was all about her destiny.

Through it all, Granny B. was always there to comfort her. When things got a little overbearing, she was especially kind. It was strange though, that no matter what happened, Granny B. never once said or insinuated that any of these incidences were abnormal or even unexpected. Everything was apparently just as it should be. She firmly insisted that everything was perfectly normal. Alex however, had other ideas. For many years, she kept them to herself and quietly maintained her suspicions. It wasn't until much later, when she finally learned the truth that she was very glad she did. It was an awful lot to handle.

* * * * *

The night was relentless. She thought it would never end. It had been a long time since the dreams had last come. They had not been missed. As the first light of day began to show though her window, Alex put the pieces of the nightmare together. She was surprised to discover how quickly she was able to understand the significance of her latest dream. It was an abstract representation of the day Granny had died. The old woman had been forced to let go of her. From that moment on, Alex was left completely on her own. Her fall into the abyss was her release from the past, and symbolized the beginning of her future. She had never hit bottom because her life was still in motion. At first, it was all pretty hard to swallow, but the more she thought about it, the more it made sense.

Just thinking about that day, and having to say goodbye to Granny B. left a dry taste in Alex's mouth. Once again, for a brief moment, she felt totally alone. She remembered wondering at the funeral, who would be there to hold her when the dreams came again? Who would be there to listen when she needed a kind ear? She had learned so much about their "ways", but she was still just a young girl with limited experience. Was she strong enough to make it on her own? Only time would tell.

Many years had passed before she found Grey. From the moment they met, she knew that she would never be alone again. He was special. She could see it in his eyes. They were the "same". But that was a long time ago. Now she wondered if he would ever be himself again. What really happened to him during the crash? What new part of him had been unleashed and set free? He was different somehow, but at the same time better. His abilities were much stronger now than she ever could have imagined. Would the student now outshine the teacher?

Alex anxiously ran her fingers through her hair. She was tired and uneasy. Her curiosity was getting the best of her. What was really going on here? She needed to talk to Grey. He was the only one who might have some answers. She took a moment and collected her thoughts. In a few hours, the rest of the house would be awake and the playful sounds of Dylan would fill the halls. Alex knew she had to keep herself together. Grey was counting on her. She had to be ready for whatever was going to happen next. Gingerly, she climbed out of bed and headed for the kitchen. She really needed some tea.

* * * * *

The clock on the nightstand glows an eerie shade of red. According to the numbers, it was seven minutes after five when Blake rolled over and got his first look at the time. He was very groggy. The just one more bourbon from last night refused to let go. It took a few seconds for his eyes to adjust. When things finally came into focus, what he saw made him nearly fall out of bed. The ominous little red digits were staring back at him. He had seriously overslept and was running dangerously late!

Still half asleep, he forced himself out of bed and made a B-line for the shower. He only had forty-five minutes to get himself together and still make it to the office in time. Each passing minute worked against him. He could have sworn that he'd set the alarm before going to bed. It was going to be close. Damn close. Then of course, there was the old man.

Sylvester struck him as the kind of person who was very organized. He was certain that he would arrive early to set up and be open for business on time. Blake scolded himself. He was usually punctual as well. Now, thanks to his extra "nightcap", his plan was in jeopardy. He had to move quickly and pull himself together.

A blast of cold water stung his chest. As it did, a million liquid talons clawed at his flesh. The sudden chill took him completely my surprise. His eyes blew open in a moment of total disbelief. Blake couldn't imagine why he was paying so little attention to what he was doing. He was in such a hurry to get going, he had forgotten to turn on the hot water.

It was a rude awakening when the icy water found his groin. He was instantly forced to jump back out of the way. Quickly, he reached for the hot water handle and spun the knob. Within a few seconds, the heat came on and he was able to step back into the stream of oncoming water. With it, the warm sensation brought an instant calming effect. Blake took a deep breath.

"That was a close one," he thought to himself. "I almost froze the 'boys' off!"

He reached down and turned up the heat. The results were immediate. All of his important parts gradually came back to life. Blake was relieved. He decided to stand there for awhile and let the water warm his inner core. As it did his mind searched for answers. Not being in complete control of his thoughts wasn't like him. He needed a moment to collect himself. After a couple minutes of steam, he was fully awake. He turned off the water and grabbed a towel. When his hand brushed the side of his face, he confirmed that he needed a shave.

The clock was friendly. His adventure in the shower had cost only ten minutes. He could squeeze out maybe another fifteen before he had to be on the road. He looked at his face in the mirror. His "five o'clock shadow" lingered and had grown darker since the previous day. He was getting down right scraggily. The stubble didn't bother him as much as his reflection in the mirror. It was still his face, but there was something different about it. The longer he stared into the glass, the more he saw a stranger.

The eyes staring back at him were distant and cold. His cheek bones were more shallow than normal. The smile in front of him appeared evil. The heavy whiskers gave him a different appearance. Blake wondered if he looked like something similar to this every time he got a fix. Looking at the face more closely made him think of Dr. Jekyll and Mr. Hyde. At first it scared him a little, but he decided that he liked it. He discovered he was amused by the fact that his dark side seemed to have its own personality. Once again, he ran his hand across his face. Was shaving before he left really worth the risk of being late? He could always catch a close one later at the office. He gave the clock another look. This time it wasn't so kind. Blake frowned. He was running out of time and he still had to get dressed.

Fortunately, all of his suits were aligned perfectly in his closet. Because of careful planning, it required little or no effort to decide which one to wear. There was even an appropriate set of matching shoes sitting on the closet floor under each one. Each ensemble had been carefully coordinated and arranged by color and cut, to satisfy his every mood. He could grab one on a whim and be out the door in ten minutes. At least he'd done something right!

Blake gave the row a quick once over. He'd stick with a favorite. The charcoal pinstripe would do nicely. He grabbed it quickly and headed for his dressing area. Being prepared ahead of time had saved his ass many times before. Today was no exception. By twenty of six, he was clean, pressed and safely in the car.

Driving down the highway, his mind worked overtime. Over the past few days, he'd noticed some definite changes in his personality. Lately he just wasn't himself.

Something was messing with his head. Each mental mistake he discovered, troubled him even more. Each one created within him an even greater level of anxiety. Like earlier in the shower; the stupidity of the whole thing made him even more agitated. He couldn't afford to be stupid! There was too much at stake. He had to stay cool.

Now, all he wanted was a cup of Sylvester's coffee. If the traffic continued to cooperate, he would be there just in time. Blake was excited. He couldn't wait for a chance to pick up her trail again. He loved the smell of her perfume. The way it had blended with the aroma of the coffee. He wondered what the flavor of the day would be. What erotic tastes would Sylvester tempt him with today?

Blake laughed. If the old man only knew! Just thinking about the girl made him start to stiffen up again. Blake just smiled and licked his lips. His mouth watered. Breakfast would soon be served. The Cat purred.

* * * * *

Alex was surprised to discover she wasn't the only one awake. As she turned the corner of the hallway which led into the kitchen, she saw Grey. He was sitting in the living room in his big leather chair, staring out the window. At first glance, he appeared to be almost catatonic. His eyes said nothing with their cold, blank stare. His mind was obviously somewhere far away. Alex was curious, but thought it best to keep her distance. She decided to maintain her present position for awhile by remaining silently in the shadows of the hallway.

It was a good five to ten minutes before Grey realized she was there. Even after he did, his behavior didn't change. He remained seated and didn't say a word. He acknowledged her presence with only a simple nod. Not wanting to press the situation, Alex cautiously nodded back. It was an all but effortless exchange. Once completed, Grey turned his attention back to the window again, allowing his mind to return to its previous endeavor. Alex was puzzled. There was something peculiar going on but she couldn't quite put a finger on it. She decided to relax and let her instincts take over. Carefully, she moved toward him, attempting to secure a better vantage point, one which would allow her to get a look outside. She was hoping to get a glimpse of whatever was holding his interest. She moved like a shadow clinging to the wall. Grey didn't even flinch when she entered the living room.

From her new position she could see everything. Much to her disappointment, the view out the window told her nothing. It had rained during the night and the street outside was covered with patches of water and light. The puddles glistened like shattered fragments of mirrored glass lying helplessly on the asphalt. Grey seem to be lost somewhere between them. She was standing much closer to him now, but he still made no attempt to acknowledge her. It wasn't until she focused her attention back on him again, that she finally got a really good look at his face.

His eyes told her everything. She could sense the inner conflict festering behind them. Grey was exhausted, but his mind was still hard at work. She could almost hear the gears turning in his head. Whatever was going on in there was demanding all of his attention. He looked like something the cat dragged in. His eye lids were heavy. His mind was apparently shuffling through the deck, trying to organize the onslaught of information and come up with the best hand. She couldn't help wondering if he'd ever gone to sleep.

Alex had to force herself to dial her curiosity level down a notch. She wanted to help him if she could, but under the present circumstances her hands were tied. All she could do was remain vigilant and wait to see what would happen next. In the meantime, she would not allow her eyes to leave him. She didn't want to miss a thing. She wanted to be ready. Her patience paid off. Grey finally broke the silence.

"Alex," he said, his voice softly echoing through the room. "This stuff is unbelievable. I wish you could see what I'm seeing. It would really blow your mind!"

Alex was relieved but took a breath before responding. He was still staring out the window. Nevertheless, she decided it was safe to play along.

"I bet it would," she responded. "Are you all right?"

Grey nodded slowly. "I've been wondering for the past few days if there was any way you know of, that would allow you to see any of this," he inquired. "Any brilliant ideas?"

"No, not that I'm presently aware of," she told him, "but that doesn't mean one doesn't exist."

"That's too bad," he said sadly, now turning to face her. "I'm not sure I'm strong enough yet to deal with this by myself."

"Well, maybe I can still find a way to help you," she said. "What exactly are you up to?"

Grey stood slowly and walked toward her. His color was much better now than when she had first come in. He offered her a hug. Alex gladly took it.

"Let's go in the other room and talk about this," he suggested motioning her toward the den.

He took Alex by the hand and led her into the other room.

"Sorry if I gave you a bit of a scare," he said.

"You didn't scare me," she conceded, "just set my curiosity on fire, that's all! I'm sure that it's got to be rough going for you right now."

Grey smiled, "You're kidding right?" he asked sarcastically as he took a seat on the couch.

Alex sat down beside him. She just rolled her eyes and shook her head. They both knew that she wasn't trying to be funny.

"You're beginning to make sense out of some of this aren't you?" she asked.

Grey nodded slowly. "Yeah, a little I guess but things are still pretty vague. There are too many missing pieces. If you'd like, I'll try to tell you what I've been doing." Alex nodded and Grey began.

"Last night, I had what I thought was a dream. In it, I traveled back to the beginning, just after the accident, when all of this craziness began. I discovered that I could play back each individual episode in my head; the hospital, Uncle Tony, the Kendall's, Father Richard, everyone. Everything was right there in full color. All I had to do was think about them. I could watch each incident in vivid detail. It was like I was actually there.

After a few tries, I found that I was also able to pick and choose which ones I wanted to see again. I could even slow them down or speed them up at will. It was absolutely amazing. It was like having a remote control in my head.

Also, if I left things alone, each sequence would run in its entirety. There was a brief pause between episodes and then a different one would start. After awhile, I began to see a few things that really rattled my cage. I started to get uncomfortable. I had to find a way to turn it off. As my mood began to change, I woke up."

Alex was fascinated. "And what time was that?" she asked.

"About four a.m. I guess," he answered. "Why?"

"I'm not sure yet," she admitted, "but the timing of certain things may prove to be important in the future. I'm just taking a few mental notes; that's all. Is there anything else?" Grey nodded. "Oh yeah, there's more," he said.

"At first, I wasn't sure that anything had actually happened. My mind was a complete blank. I lay in bed wondering what to do next. I tried to convince myself that it was all probably just a dream. Anyway, I couldn't get back to sleep. I was antsy and didn't want to wake up Rachel. That's when I decided to come out to the living room. As soon as I got comfortable again, my mind started to wander. When I stared out the window my thoughts began to drift. My mind started to go fuzzy and a tape started to roll. At that moment, I realized that I wasn't in control. I figured that the only way to make them stop was to focus my mind on something else. Coincidentally, that's was right when you walked in. Good timing, huh?"

Alex smiled. "It always seems to be that way between the two of us doesn't it?" she said as she settled back deeper into the sofa, once again playing with her hair.

"You've got that right," Grey agreed. "Things usually do end up going our way."

They were enjoying a quick laugh when the sound of another voice interrupted them. It was Rachel. She was standing in the hallway between the living room and the kitchen. They both wondered how long she'd been there and just how much of the conversation she had heard. When Grey saw her face, he doubted she'd been paying much attention. She looked tired.

"Good morning, you two. Up early I see. Did I miss something good?" she asked.

"No, not really," Grey said. "We were just remembering something funny from the old days, no big deal. You look beat. Are you ok?"

"I'm fine," she said as she wandered into the kitchen. "Just tired, that's all. I didn't sleep very well. How about you? What are you two up to today?"

Before either of them had a chance to answer, Rachel noticed that the light on the Mr. Coffee was on. Someone must have set it up the night before.

"By the way," she said, "I see someone made coffee. This morning even I'm game. Anybody want some?"

Grey and Alex just looked at each other. What harm could it do? By a show of hands, she instantly got two takers.

Even half asleep, Rachel was still willing to play hostess. She reached for some mugs and started to pour. She was almost awake now.

Looking at the two of them sitting together, something struck her as being odd. The way Alex was sitting was very provocative. Maybe she really hadn't really given it much thought before but as she handed Alex her coffee, she took note of it again. The robe Alex was wearing was certainly long enough, but for some reason, intentional or otherwise, a large section was folded back, off to one side. Alex was showing a lot of leg. Too much leg in fact, if the rules of good taste still applied. You could almost see your way clear to home plate! What made it even worse was that Alex had really nice legs.

Rachel couldn't help wondering over the years how many players had been allowed to steal home. Had Grey been one of them? What was Alex up to? She wanted to say something but decided to mind her manners. A quick look at Grey convinced her that even if he had noticed, he wasn't paying much attention. She decided it was best to curb her suspicions for now and move on to something else. She immediately began to inquire about Grey's plans for the day. That seemed like a safe enough approach.

"So you never answered me before," she said to him. "What are you up to today?"

"Nothing special," he said. "I'm spending the day at the chiropractic office. I have a lot of catching up to do." He shot Alex a quick glance.

Taking the cue, she instantly volunteered her plans as well. She said that she had a meeting to go to in L.A. She wouldn't be home until late that evening.

Rachel was happy. The conversation was both pleasant and honest. Any further suspicions she may have harbored quickly disappeared.

Knowing that the two of them would be miles apart gave her additional peace of mind. She felt better. In fact, she was almost lightheaded. She decided she wanted more coffee.

Watching her moods swing back and forth, Grey wondered what Alex had put in the coffee grounds the night before. Whatever it was, it seemed relatively harmless. Why did Rachel have to choose this morning to decide to start drinking coffee? Still, he assumed that she'd be ok. Alex had obviously chosen to let it slide. With a simple thought, Grey thanked her for doing so.

When Rachel returned, she brought the coffee pot with her. When she looked back at Alex, the robe had magically repositioned itself in a more ladylike fashion. How convenient. This aroused her curiosity again. The whole scene was just a little too calculated to ignore. Rachel was pissed. Still, she had nothing tangible to go on. She was probably overreacting. She was feeling a little strange anyway. For now, it was easier to forget about it and move on. No point in seeing things that weren't really there. She needed a break. Pacified for the time being, Rachel grabbed her mug and poured herself another cup of coffee.

* * * * *

Somewhere out over the pacific, the first light of morning was beginning to creep its way up from the horizon. As the highway gently wove its way in and out along the coastline, Blake was lucky enough to witness the dawning of a new day. The delicate shades of color that materialized during the transition were so intoxicating, that Blake had a difficult time keeping his eyes on the road.

Ever since he was a young boy, the heavenly transformation between darkness and light continued to fascinate him. The world had its own established game plan. Each sunrise brought with it a new opportunity; another chance to play. Every sunset was a festival of color and light; a glorified celebration of the accomplishments of the day. You had to love the system, and Blake did.

The whole idea of something beginning with such a soft, subtle approach and then building up its way up to such a dramatic presentation always seemed to put things in the proper perspective. Even before the change began, this philosophy was a big part of his inner self. With it, he found both power and solace. He had easily mastered its application and then practiced it on a daily basis. It quickly became the foundation of his emotional framework. This "system" had served him well. This morning was no exception.

During the past six months, he had acquired the habit of driving with the top down. It was a little chilly on occasion, especially in the wee hours of the morning, but the tingling sensation of wind in his face made him feel more alive. There were times he wasn't sure whether or not this change in his behavior was a product of his own initiative, or one conceived by his friend in the mirror. Either way a little discomfort was a small price to pay to get a quick rush. Sadly, it wasn't a fix by any stretch of the imagination, but it was a welcome distraction. These small diversions allowed him to relax and concentrate on more important things. As his mind wandered, Blake crossed over.

He remembered her perfume. In his mind he could still smell it; that and Sylvester's coffee. The sensation was very strong now. Things were so intense in fact that the salty sea air could do nothing to diminish it. In his heightened state of euphoria, he could taste them on the breeze.

Now, for the first time, the flavor was familiar: vanilla. You know, like the ice cream. As a scent on a woman, the effect would be seductively subtle, but when combined with the additional aroma of the designer coffee, it left a rather strong impression.

Blake was surprised. How could he have failed to notice something so obvious?

He prided himself on always paying attention to the little things. He was a slave to detail. His very survival was based on observation and perception. Without them, he would never have made it this far. This obvious oversight was a serious problem. Why wasn't he thinking straight? It didn't make any sense. He had no choice but to consider his lack of attention as another mistake. He became confused. This sudden brush with instability forced him back into reality.

The broken white lines in front of him slowly blended into one as the road continued to disappear beneath him. Blake looked at his watch.

He was making good time. The office was only a few miles away now. He could feel the energy starting to grow. He could see her kneeling down by the elevator. Every curve on her was a work of art. She was beautiful. She was sexy. She looked just the way he remembered her the day they first met. There was 'Katie', dear sweet 'Katie'; the shape of things to come.

He had to have her. And he did. For nineteen years she was everything. She appeared to be the perfect loving wife. But things change. An evil now possessed her as well. She wasn't just his anymore! He'd seen her in a different light. That whore! That lying, cheating whore! How could she do this to him? How could she betray him like this? How could she pretend? Blake's mind raced. He had no choice. He knew he had to kill her! It was only a matter of time.

As he turned the corner into the parking structure his eyes caught a glimpse of something off in the distance. He knew that he had to check it out. Rather than head for his assigned space, he decided to pull around in the opposite direction so that he could take a closer look. He was glad he did. What he saw brought the 'Cat' back out to play.

There, in the far corner of the entrance level, was an old man in a baseball hat getting out of a truck. Even with his back to him, the man's height, build and clothing, gave him away. Blake's smile grew. He knew he was watching Sylvester.

Once again, he could smell the scent of vanilla in the air. He could feel the fire and electricity starting to smolder deep inside him. This was the beginning of a new adventure, one which would directly lead him to another fix. He longed for the climax of pure energy and ecstasy. Very soon, he would have another reason to celebrate. Blake parked his car and headed for the lobby. He needed a cup of coffee. He wanted it now.

* * * * *

The family room at the Thomas house was quiet and still. Alex's concoction was apparently doing its thing. Each of its three occupants was lost somewhere, deep in their own little world. To an outside observer, the entire scene was a moment frozen in time. Everything seemed to be at a standstill within the immediate four walls. An eerie silence hung heavy in the air.

It wasn't until Alex sensed that Rachel was starting to get restless, that things began to show signs of coming back to life. Alex knew that she was considering making a move toward her third cup of coffee. She also knew that she could never allow that to happen. It was obvious that Rachel had already had more than enough.

After her first cup, the poor girl's eyes had taken on a new twinkle. Her movements had become over emphasized and her speech had slowed considerably. She was slightly lethargic, definitely entertaining, and certainly well on her way. The only reason that Alex had let her go for a second cup was strictly for her own personal amusement. Three would be taking it too far. Alex watched closely as Rachel's mind raced frantically, trying desperately to adapt to the sudden chemical manipulation. By now the coffee was a completely mutilated version of its original form. Because of this, the continuing modifications to Rachel's behavior were almost immediate.

For the average person, the strange elixir acted simply as a mild hallucinogenic. The more one consumed, the better the trip. Rachel had quickly reached her limit. Fortunately for everyone, she just looked stoned!

Through it all, Alex remained silent, choosing to behave and enjoy the show. After all, she had a front row seat.

"Nothing like a special 'wake-up-call' to corrupt the mind of the innocent," she giggled softly to herself.

Fact was Rachel was performing quite well. She was much more relaxed and uninhibited than usual. To tell the truth, Alex was very surprised that Grey had kept quiet and allowed her to play with her for this long. She wondered if he found her behavior amusing as well. It wasn't until Rachel actually voiced her intent on getting another cup that Alex new that it was time to step in. When she stood and made a move toward the kitchen, Alex quickly shifted into a position that blocked her path.

"Why don't you let me make us a fresh pot?" she asked politely, hoping that her suggestion would be accepted.

Rachel paused for a moment and considered the idea. As she did, a panicked look spread across her face. She realized that she had just lost the ability to think. It took her a few seconds to mentally re-lock and load. It was another minute or so before she could gather her thoughts.

When she finally spoke, Grey could hear the hesitation in her voice. "On second thought, I think I'll pass," she said. "I think maybe I've had enough! I'm going to take a shower. See you guys later.

A bit unnerved, she brushed past Alex and headed down the hall. When Alex glanced back at Grey, he was slowly shaking his head. His eyes told her everything. She carefully made her way back to the couch.

"Enjoying yourself?" he asked with a mild note of sarcasm. Alex didn't answer. Her smile betrayed her. Then suddenly, she could not contain herself and burst out laughing.

"And why not?" she answered him. "Don't you know I'm Rachel's biggest fan?"

There was a brief silence. She could almost hear him thinking. Grey was confused. "And why is that?" he asked with a puzzled look on his face.

"Well, she's got you, doesn't she?"

Alex said. Grey just smiled. He knew he'd been had.

"All right, you win," he said. "But let's not waste anymore time playing around like this. Don't we have more important things to do?"

Alex nodded. "All right," she said, in a pouting but in a funny sort of way. "There you go again ruining all my fun. So what's the real game plan, anyway?"

"I'm going to my 'office' for awhile," he answered. "It might actually be fun. Maybe I can practice using this thing on a few patients. No harm, no foul, right?"

"Sounds like a good idea to me," Alex agreed. "I'll be around if you need anything."

As she spoke, she made certain that she was looking directly at Grey. She wanted to make sure he was listening. When their eyes met, she knew there was something wrong. The blank stare had returned. She could tell that he'd missed the last part of their conversation. The lights were on but nobody was going to answer the door. Grey had crossed over. Alex took a deep breath. There was nothing she could do but wait.

* * * * *

Dylan woke up. Under ordinary circumstances this would have been a perfectly normal event. You know; baby makes noise, baby cries; baby wants attention. No big deal, right? The problem was, there were no sounds coming from Dylan's room. No crying, no screaming, no anything else for that matter. To the normal ear there was nothing but silence. Or was there?

Grey swore he could hear a strange sound coming from the back of the house. It echoed like a drum beating slowly in a nice, even tempo. Then suddenly, the sound got faster. The rhythm increased gradually to more than twice its original speed. It was Dylan's heartbeat; that magical little sound of life. Dylan was awake! He knew it! The little guy just wasn't saying anything yet.

It was so subtle, but Grey couldn't help but notice the difference. His level of sensitivity and instant awareness had surprised him enough to cause this sudden distraction. Confused, he turned to Alex. Her eyes begged him for information. The question at hand was obvious. He knew better, but decided to ask anyway.

"Can you hear that?" he inquired, simply out of curiosity.

All he got was a funny look. The question was pointless. It was Alex's turn to be confused.

"Hear what?" she answered him with a puzzled look on her face.

Grey's eyes were serious. She knew he wasn't fooling around.

"Dylan's awake," he said. "I just heard the sound of his heartbeat change."

Alex was overwhelmed. This was not an answer she was prepared for. "What? Are you serious?" she asked in a shouted whisper.

Grey just nodded and motioned toward the back of the house. For a few minutes, neither of them said a word. Alex strained to listen, but only Grey could hear the music. It was Dylan who finally broke the silence.

"Milk daddy, I want milk." The words were clear. Even Alex could hear them this time.

"Guess you were right," she admitted while still trying to hide her surprise, "He is awake!"

Grey spoke now with his hands. She got an 'I-told-you-so' gesture. "I've been trying to tell you, Alex, this thing is really bizarre, it's just like before, remember?" he said, "What really bothers me that I don't know how to completely control it as yet. It seems to just work on its own, independently, in order to show me things that it thinks I should know. That's why I think that going to work is such a good idea. I can practice on people quietly without attracting any unnecessary attention."

Alex was listening carefully. "I see your point," she agreed. "I think that makes sense. It's definitely the best idea I've heard so far. Try it, and we'll see what happens. I'll leave my phone on all day. Call me if you get into trouble or need my help."

As Alex finished speaking, they could both hear Dylan complaining in the distance. His requests were becoming more indignant by the minute. Grey got up and started for the hallway.

"I'm going to go get him," he said. "Then I'm going to go take a shower. I guess I'll catch up with you later."

"All right," she responded. "But please keep me informed. I know you think that you can handle this all by yourself, but I really believe we should try to see this thing through together."

"You know me too well," Grey conceded. "Don't worry though; I'll keep you up to date on my every move."

"Ok then. I suppose I'll get going too," Alex said. "I have some things I've got to check out. I'll probably be out of here before you're ready to leave, so we'll have to finish this later."

As Grey stood up, Alex got up with him. She reached over and gave him a hug.

"You be careful, my friend," she whispered in his ear. "I know you're good, but do me a favor and be careful anyway."

Grey tightened the embrace for a moment; then backed away. As he did, he made a point to be certain that their eyes met. "Tell me what you see." he requested softly.

"What do you mean?" she replied.

"C'mon, seriously, look close. Tell me what you see." Grey insisted.

Alex paused briefly, and took a long, hard look into the mysterious eyes of her friend. The lights were bright and scrambled, but behind them she sensed a powerful inner strength. Alex smiled.

"You're almost home aren't you?" she asked, her voice echoing a sigh of relief.

Grey just nodded. He was very close to being his old self again. Only this time, he came with a few added attractions.

"Life is too short, my friend," he said. "You have to enjoy the ride."

He leaned over, kissed her softly on the cheek, and ventured off to find his son.

By the time he wandered back to the front of the house again, Alex was long gone. He found Rachel sitting on the couch, holding a large bottle of water. She looked tired. Grey put Dylan on the floor next to her, to play.

"You ok?" he asked.

"I'll be fine," she said. "Now I know why I don't drink coffee."

Her voice was muffled

"That stuff was really strong. Too much caffeine I think. It made me light headed, and then gave me a headache. How about you?"

"Aaaah......I'm ok, "he assured her. "Hope you don't mind, I got Dylan showered and ready. If it's ok with you, I'm going to head over to the office. I need to check in. Need anything before I go?"

His voice echoed in her ears. The effects of Alex's coffee still lingered. Her movement was slow when she turned to answer him. The chemical adventure had worked her over hard. She looked like hell.

"No, but thanks for asking," she said, "and thanks for handling Dylan. My head is just starting to feel better. I think I'll be fine in a little bit."

"Drink lots of water," Grey reminded her as he headed for the door. "I'll call you later to see how you're doing."

Rachel lifted her water bottle to let him know she was listening. Grey gave her a quick wave. For a second he felt guilty. Maybe he and Alex were out of line playing with her like that, but what the hell. No real harm done. Her secrets were still safely hers. Still, he'd make it a point to remind Alex not to let it happen again. Rachel might be a pain in the ass on occasion, but mostly she deserved better. Sooner or later though, he'd have to get close to her again. It would be interesting to finally see what was going on inside her head. For now, deep in the shadows of his being, the thunder rolled.

* * * * *

Alone at last, the ride to the office gave him some time to think. The hours he'd spent back at the house staring out the window had opened a few doors, but they also presented him with a couple of new possibilities. There were a few moments when he actually felt like he had learned something. For instance, the ability to stop, play, fast forward, or rewind the tapes was probably just the beginning. He had the mental clicker. Now, all he had to do was figure out how to use it. Unlike the TV in the den, this one hadn't come with an instruction manual. It was all trial and error. It was going to take a lot of practice to get everything working the right way.

By the time he opened the office door, Grey was feeling better. Alex was right. Learning how to use his new gift was the key which would open the door to solving everything. He had to practice if he was ever going to get the hang of it.

He opened the appointment book and checked his schedule. Tara was smart. She hadn't booked him much of anything. He'd have to thank her for that later. Maybe when she got there he could have her call a few patients and see if they wanted to come in. Practicing would be much more comfortable on people he already knew. That and he wanted to get re-acclimated. In order to maintain his "independent massage" license he had to have an established relationship with a local chiropractor. Dr. John was a good man and Grey respected him a lot.

Grey took a look around. The office was like a morgue. Dead quiet, and a little on the chilly side. Tara or Dr. John must have forgotten to kill the a/c when they locked up the night before. He felt very unsettled. He decided that what he really needed was some tunes: something deep and powerful, something with a message.

It was still early, and the office wouldn't be open for another hour, so anything was fair game. He checked his CD rack and found one he thought might do the trick. He removed the special "prescription" from its plastic case and placed it carefully in the CD player. Moments later, it came to life. At its first breath, he locked the front door and turned up the volume. Grey waited for redemption.

The sound of church bells echoed through the hall. It was the deep, ominous ringing of AC / CD's "Hell's Bells".

"How appropriate," he thought. "Maybe somebody's trying to tell me something," he whispered out loud.

As he started to set up a massage table, the bells got louder. The lyrics began and the words dug deep.

"I'm rolling thunder; I'm power and rain.... I'm coming on like a hurricane."

Grey laughed. Hemingway once wrote "Ask not for whom the bell tolls; it tolls for thee." He couldn't help wondering if the guy was right. Grey closed his eyes and waited alone in the darkness. It was going to be an interesting day.

* * * * *

CHAPTER 14

A quick glance at his old friend "Mickey", and Willie Beaumont was happy. According to the tiny cartoon hands on his badly tarnished Timex, he only had an hour left before he could pack it in and go home. He'd been on duty since midnight, and this last eight hour shift was almost a memory. When he thought about it though, he had no complaints. The graveyard shift had always been his favorite. There was something comforting about the still of the night. It was quiet, and that's the way old Willie liked things; quiet and uneventful. This was his kind of gig now.

At Sixty-seven, he considered himself lucky. He'd survived segregation, two tours in Nam, prostate cancer, and most recently the south side of Chicago. In early June, he'd moved out to California to be closer to his son's family. They'd offered him a place to live but Willie was too proud. Between his Army pension and his Social Security checks, he made enough to survive. He'd only taken the job as a security guard to make a little extra cash. Just getting by wasn't his style. He'd always had a taste for the finer things in life when he could get them, and the extra three hundred a week allowed him to stay friendly with a few bad habits. He was rather fond of his relationship with Mr. Johnny Walker Black.

There was also Bessie, his 61 Cadillac convertible who from time to time required a little love and attention, and of course the fetish he'd acquired a few years back for the taste of a good cigar. (He and Clyde would have enjoyed each other's company). On most nights, these modest indulgences were enough motivation to keep him going.

Tonight however, for some reason he was dog tired. All he wanted to do now was sleep.

He'd taken lunch around three a.m. and the break had done him a world of good. The gumbo in his Thermos had given him the energy he needed to make it a few more hours. Esther's stew was good going down, but it always came back to haunt him. She was a nice old thing that lived down the hall and had decided to 'adopt' him about a week after he first moved in. While her regular acts of kindness were always welcome, she did seem to go overboard with her need for certain spices. Most of these tended to wreak havoc on poor Willie's delicate plumbing. But oh, it was worth it! Still, fact remained that soon after enjoying one of her fine culinary endeavors, he'd be forced to make a run to the head to clean out his pipes. This evening was no exception. Since then however, he hadn't moved from his seat at the guard station in the lobby. He'd spent the last few hours watching the monitors on his desk. So far, all he'd been treated to was an endless display of frozen pictures of lifeless spaces. There wasn't anything even remotely interesting to see. For all practical purposes, the night had simply come and gone.

Willie's eyes perked up when he saw Blake Kendall coming out of the parking structure under a full head of steam. He wasn't at a dead run, but he was sure moving fast. At that speed, Kendall would be at the front door before Willie could get there to unlock it. Willie knew that it would be in his best interest if he was there first, waiting to let Mr. Kendall in. Besides, a quick walk from his desk to the front door would probably do his sciatica a world of good. Doc Davis had told him time and time again that he needed to stretch things out on a regular basis. That was easy for him to say. Willie figured that the whole idea of exercise was political hype. At his age, pain was never a good thing. Whether or not something was worth the effort depended entirely on one's immediate priorities.

Today was a good day. Everything seemed to be working ok. A little activity was no problem. Besides, he liked the lawyer. Mr. Kendall was always friendly and treated him with respect. That meant something. Willie decided that he'd make the effort. The old bones didn't move like they used to, but his mind was still sharp as a tack. Without giving it another thought, Willie made a move for the door.

As it turned out he beat Kendall by four steps. There was just enough time for him to turn the key and open the door before he met Blake's eyes.

"Good morning, Mr. Kendall," Willie fired off quickly.

"Good morning, Willie," Blake gestured as he slipped past him into the building.

"Nice move there old man, I presume you saw me coming?"

Blake smiled as he said it. He appreciated the fact that Willie respected him enough to get off his ass and not make him wait.

"I did at that Mr. Kendall," Willie replied. "From the looks of things, I figured you to be in a bit of a hurry. I didn't want to be the one responsible for slowing you down."

Blake marveled at Willie's powers of perception. He knew how to play the game. Blake made a mental note to give Willie a few extras points for that one.

"No problem my friend," Blake assured him. "I'm just anxious to use the men's room," he chuckled. "That, and get a cup of coffee."

His response surprised Willie. "The bathroom," he said to himself. He was kidding right? The way Kendall was moving outside, he must have really had to go something bad. Why stop then to make idle conversation. Willie wondered but didn't ask. Not his business anyway. Blake turned to walk away.

"Hey, Mr. Kendall," Willie spoke up. "Sylvester's not here yet, "he said. "Strange though," he continued while scratching his head. "I ain't never seen him run late before." Willie looked at his watch again. As usual, Mickey was keeping time.

"He should be along any minute now," he assured Blake.

Blake wasn't worried. He'd already seen Sylvester. Breakfast was definitely on its way. Blake's body tingled. He could feel an aching in his groin. Come to think of it, he did have to pee. He headed for the corner of the lobby. As he opened the restroom door, he glanced back over his shoulder. He was just in time to see Willie letting Sylvester in the side door. The fun was about to begin. Blake hurried inside eager to mark his territory.

* * * * *

Later, as he was washing his hands, Blake trembled. The cold water in the sink reminded him of his earlier adventure in the shower. There was work to be done and he needed to find away to concentrate. He had to stay focused. Between the new girl and Walter's new case, he couldn't afford to make any more mistakes.

He splashed some water on his face and looked in the mirror. There were no surprises. The image he saw was not his own. Blake couldn't believe his eyes. The stranger was back. This time though, its features were more defined. The figure before him was trapped somewhere between the lawyer and the 'Cat'. Behind its eyes danced the faces of both frustration and fear. Two creatures were fighting for survival. Blake wondered how long he could keep them from becoming one.

Reluctantly, he turned away. For the moment, they would have to wait. Right now, there were more important things to think about. Bottom line....... he needed a fix. The energy he had received from Casey had all but disappeared. His time was running out. If he didn't do something quickly to stoke the fire, the flames might smolder and die. Silently, he prayed. He needed to relax. He took a deep breath. He needed a 'good cup of coffee'. That and a breakfast sandwich with dark hair and long legs. After all, the show must go on! It was act two, scene six and his talents would surely be required. Blake dried his hands, adjusted his tie, and then opened the bathroom door. As he did, he knew that Sylvester was at it again. The strong smell of vanilla slapped him hard in the face.

* * * * *

Grey was lying on a massage table staring at the ceiling when he heard the sound of bells again. This time though, they were different. The music had long since ended, so it took his brain a couple of seconds to register what was happening. As the dust settled, he realized that it was the waiting room door. Curious, he peaked out into the hallway. When he did he was greeted with a smile. As always, Tara was on time.

Grey liked his secretary. She was cool. She was young but tough and dedicated to her job. She could hold her own against the somewhat playful attitudes of the all male office staff. She gave great phone and even better face. In the rehab business, a smile went a long way, that and a sweet disposition. Tara was blessed with both. She was also a good friend. He and Dr. John were lucky to have her. She was very happy to see him. It only took a second before she started to ask questions. "Well hello stranger: You new in these parts?" she teased him.

Grey smiled. "It sure seemed that way when I first walked in," he said. "This place feels different somehow."

"Well, it's nice to have you back in one piece," she assured him. "Dr. John showed everyone pictures of your car. You're lucky to be alive!"

Grey nodded and smiled. "Hard head I guess," he said.

Tara smiled. "I'm walking the mile," she said, referring to her daily run to the bagel shop at the other end of the complex. "Can I get you anything?"

"No thanks, I'm cool," he said, "See ya in a few."

The bell rang again as she stepped out, and then immediately again as little Zac Gorman attempted to work his way in through the door. He was only two, but full of smiles and energy. He came in three days a week with his mom when she came in for adjustments. Grey was glad Joy brought him. He loved the kid. Zac reminded him of Dylan. He or Tara would always 'baby-sit' while mom was getting treated. Zac liked to play with the fountains in his office and the big therapy balls. He always had a blast.

Grey kept a careful eye on the door. After a brief struggle, Zac fought his way inside. His mom was not far behind. Joy was surprised to see him. She looked liked she'd seen a ghost.

"Hey! You're back," she said. "How are you?"

"I'm ok," he answered nodding his head. "Only the good die young," he chuckled. Joy smiled. "Well, I'm really glad to see that you're all right. We were worried about you!"

Grey walked over and picked up Zac. "Hey, little guy, how are you buddy?"

Joy looked concerned. "If he's too much for you.....," she started to say.

Grey cut her off. "Nah...No big deal," he said pointing to his head. "I'm as good as new," smiling and rolling his eyes.

Joy just shook her head. She knew he was ok.

The front bell rang again. Tara was back. She smiled again when she saw Zac.

"Well, I guess it's back to business as usual," she snickered.

Grey nodded, "I'll be in my office if you need me," he said. "And hey, would you do me a favor? Would you make a few calls for me? See if anybody is around. You know the usual gang. Tell them I'm back and see if anyone wants to come in. If not, no worries. I was just thinking I need the practice."

Tara looked surprised. "What? You that rusty after being gone for only a few days?" she teased.

"Yeah, maybe a little," he conceded. "I just want to get busy again."

He gave her the thumbs up and then headed back to the safety of his office. Once inside, he relaxed a bit. The group of people he had suggested to her was safe enough. He didn't really feel rusty but if he wanted to practice, he wanted a fairly easy go of it. He'd been very careful to only give her the names of patients that he thought would be easy to handle.

As much as he wanted to learn, he really wasn't up for any more of the Blake Kendall type of crap. Things were difficult enough as is. He needed to take it easy.

Grey took a long hard look at the pictures in his office. The ones of Dylan were especially reassuring. They made him smile. Being back at work again did make him feel better. It was good to be able to see his friends.

For the moment, the four walls of his office protected him from the outside world. They provided him with a temporary refuge from reality, a shelter from the storm. Here, he could sit alone in the flickering shadows of the fountains and let the bubbling sound of the water keep the madness at bay. Problem was the storm wasn't brewing outside. It was building inside his head. The only hope he had of keeping it under control was to not think; or so it seemed. Right then, not thinking didn't sound like such a bad idea. It was time to re-direct. He needed to escape. Maybe a little Jazz would help. Grey reached over and grabbed another C.D.

* * * * *

Sylvester's cart was open for business. Blake was surprised to discover that he wasn't the first in line. During the short time he'd spent in the men's room, more than half a dozen people had entered the building. Most of them had gathered around Sylvester's cart. When he turned to find Willie again, he saw that the guard was already on top of things. Willie had a fresh hot cup of coffee in his hand. The old rascal was sipping it slowly and appeared to be enjoying himself. Willie had taken full advantage of his position and had been first in line. Blake shook his head. It hadn't been that long of a piss! Now, he was forced to wait patiently with the rest of them. As much as he detested the thought of standing in line, he had no choice. He had to have his coffee.

Time became his enemy. He hoped to God he hadn't missed her. If he had, his mind couldn't deal with another mistake. If the circumstances had been any different, he would have just blown the whole thing off and gone upstairs. It would have been so easy to walk away.

But somehow, over time, the rules had changed. He didn't want to have to think anymore. He just wanted to act. This was the first time since the power and the need began that he had ever felt threatened. His options were limited. Casey was slowly becoming a memory. The idea of having regular contact with her immediate replacement was a dangerous proposition. Especially since him and the new 'Katie' in question worked together in the same building and had already met. The others had been strangers. To even add more pressure, he had never had the added misfortune of being acquainted with any of their family or friends. Blake wondered if he was losing control.

He couldn't help wondering if the conquest of Sylvester's daughter was in fact a bad idea. Certainly, if he applied himself, he could find a suitable replacement; one that would carry with her less 'identity issues' and a minimal amount of stress. So far, this girl was becoming more trouble than she was worth. He needed her but at what price? What was he thinking anyway? Or was he thinking at all?

Maybe the stranger in the mirror had his own ideas. Finding this 'Katie' had been quite challenging at first but things had still managed to come together. Who could say that with a little time and effort, another one might be found. He could walk away right now with a clear conscious and go back to the hunt. There were lots of bars and clubs in the area. Surely one would yield a foot that would fit the magic slipper.

Blake remained distant as his mind worked the problem. Then he heard a strange sound. For a moment, he swore that he could hear someone calling his name.

"That's odd," he thought, and then the voice came again. Fortunately this time, he was paying more attention. He recognized its owner.

"Good morning Mr. Kendall, it's nice to see you again," Sylvester greeted him.

"Back for more I see," the old man chuckled as he continued on with his work.

"I am at that," Blake admitted giving Sylvester one of his famous Cheshire smiles.

"So tell me my friend, what is it you have back there that you'll be trying to impress me with today?"

Blake chose a tone of voice specifically designed to immediately recaptured Sylvester's interest. The old man turned around and gave Blake his undivided attention.

"Is that a challenge Mr. Kendall?" he asked politely with an almost playful grin.

"No not really," Blake responded. "Just more of what one might call a healthy curiosity. I certainly hope that you don't find my inquiry offensive."

If anything, Sylvester looked amused. This of course confused Blake. He was always used to being in the position where he had the upper hand.

"Not at all Mr. Kendall," Sylvester assured him. "As a matter of fact sir, I kind of expected that you'd be back."

As he spoke, he handed Blake the cup he'd been preparing since the beginning of their conversation.

"What's this?" Blake asked trying hard not to sound ungracious.

"I believe it's what you came for, isn't it sir?" Sylvester replied.

He delivered his answer with a totally straight face.

Blake looked down at the coffee cup in his hand. Much as he hated to admit it, the old man now had him curious. He was smart too. He'd put a lid on the cup to prevent Blake from having any clue as to its contents. The challenge had not only been met, Sylvester had taken things to a new level. He'd put him in a position where he had no other choice but to taste the contents strictly on faith. Blake hesitated for a moment and stared at the cup in disbelief.

"Is there a problem sir?" Sylvester asked politely.

Blake couldn't help but notice the confident, almost cocky look in his new friend's eyes. It made him realize that he was being played. He'd been led to this point in conversation like a horse to water. The worst part was that he knew he had to drink. He had to concede that coffee or not, this guy was good.

"Guy thinks he's a smart ass," Blake thought to himself refusing whole heartedly any chance of the words escaping from his lips.

He had no choice but to keep on playing. His curiosity grew as he was reminded of the last time that he'd sampled Sylvester's wares. In all honesty, he didn't know what to expect. He hoped that this concoction would prove to be as exciting as the last. Carefully, he raised the cup to his lips and took a sip. As it turned out, he was pleasantly surprised.

The scent of vanilla was as strong as ever, but this time the taste carried with it the subtle flavor of something different. The problem however, was identifying the new ingredient. So far, his mind was at a stalemate. He didn't have a clue. For anyone else, this simple lack of information would have been nothing more than a minor inconvenience.

To Blake though, it was something different: another unsolved problem. Granted in the big scheme of things, it was rather insignificant, but, because of his present state of mind, it also irritated him to no end. He was a stickler for details and desperate for facts. He simply had to know.

To add insult to injury, he became even more discouraged when he tried to take the matter up with Sylvester. His attempt to inquire was belittled at best. When approached, Sylvester dismissed him with the casual wave of his hand. This of course did not sit well with Blake. He was not accustomed to being ignored. His first instinct was to fight back.

"*Who the hell did this guy think he was talking to anyway*?" he thought. When he opened his mouth to ask, he found that he couldn't speak. Something inside him was preventing him from saying anything. He immediately took it as a sign that he needed to keep his cool. Blake remained silent.

In the end, the only response he could generate was a rather unpleasant sigh. It wasn't very satisfying. About the same time, whatever it was that was controlling him suddenly gave him an idea. Feeling a little cocky himself, he decided to take a chance and go along for the ride. Blake cleared his throat.

"Why the cold shoulder?" he asked, trying to re-establish their original conversation."What's the big deal?"

Sylvester turned back to face him. He looked serious. Their eyes met. Not wanting to appear rude, he attempted to offer Blake an explanation.

"In my country, we never ask a magician to reveal his secrets," he began. "Isn't a cook or a bartender basically the same thing? Aren't they always up to something special, secret ingredients and all? It is not my wish to offend you sir, but sharing my recipes with you would take all the fun out of this don't you think?"

Blake was stunned. For a moment the 'Cat' had become road kill. Once again, he couldn't find anything to say. It was just as well. Sylvester didn't give him a chance to respond. He had already moved on to another customer. Blake was left there alone, with a cup of coffee in his hand and nothing to do but think.

There was a long silence while Blake mourned the fact that he had lost again. Then he chuckled softly to himself. He couldn't help wondering why the hell this guy was peddling coffee. Sylvester would have made a brilliant attorney. What really disturbed him though, was that the old man had out maneuvered him every step of the way. He was beginning to feel foolish.

Wait a minute! Suddenly it hit him! What if he wasn't himself? What if the stranger was slowly taking over! Up until now, the face in the mirror had always been just that, a simple reflection; an almost humorous look at the dark side of his personality. He had never taken its appearance seriously enough to appreciate it as anything more. Now, because of his recent erratic behavior, he had to acknowledge the fact that he was rapidly becoming the victim of some bizarre change.

For Blake, this discovery redefined the rules completely. He had never even considered the possibility that the transformation was affecting more than just his physical appearance. It was frightening to think that whatever forces were at work here might be taking over his mind as well. If that happened, there would be no way for him to maintain any part of what was once his former self. The lawyer in him would quietly disappear.

Blake was confused. He liked being in a position where he could play both sides. He cherished the ability to be able to slip out of his 'legal' persona and into something else. The 'Cat' was supposed to be simply a form of entertainment; like playing a live version of a video game. Exciting yes, but here the stakes were much higher. Over time, the challenges and rewards of the game had developed into an obsession. Now after many months of adaptation and compliance, his addiction to the kill had become stronger than ever. Even he had to admit that the battle between his two personalities had gotten dangerously out of control. Somewhere along the line, the lawyer had begun to fade, surrendering to the darkness of the 'Cat'.

Blake knew that he couldn't afford to take sides. He had to keep them both on a short leash. He liked the feelings of domination, strength and power that his two identities shared. They seemed to work better as a team. He wasn't prepared to give in to either one of them. It would just be nice to know which one of them he was operating as, at any given time. A look in the mirror didn't cut it anymore. It had come way too far for that. They were at odds, and he had to find a way that would allow them to co-exist.

In the meantime, he had other priorities. The best he could do for now was just attempt to maintain a peace. He would deal with them later, separately if necessary as things went along. He promised himself that he would learn to utilize and benefit from the power of them both. Together, they would be unstoppable. Blake grinned.

When he looked up again, attempting to locate Sylvester, he found his opponent looking off in another direction. Blake called out to him but the old man paid no attention. Blake started to feel like he was invisible. Had he done something wrong?

In the back of his mind, he could hear footsteps approaching across the marble floor. Suddenly, from behind him, he heard the sound of her voice once more. The cheerful sound of "Morning Dad" floated softly through the air. Blake's heart raced. When he turned to face her, their eyes met. It was then he knew exactly what he had to do. All the hopes he had previously entertained about forgetting her, vanished into thin air.

* * * * *

And the band played on. Safe within the walls of his private sanctuary, the piano danced, the sax set the mood, and the singer paid homage to "Miss New Orleans". Except for the music, the room was quiet and peaceful so Grey took a moment to relax. Somewhere during the second verse, his thoughts slowly drifted away. He wasn't really sure where his mind had gone, but Tara would swear later that she had knocked three times and gotten no response before concern forced her to open the door.

She found him sitting in his chair, feet up on the table, staring endlessly into space. He looked so lost, that for a moment, she had second thoughts about disturbing him at all. She had to ask herself if she really wanted to interrupt him. He'd been through a lot lately.

She decided that her best bet was to wait until he noticed her. She maintained her position in the doorway of his office and watched him, trying to see if she could figure out what he was up to. She quickly found his point of focus.

His eyes were fixed on a particular water fountain sitting in the far corner of the room. It was almost hypnotizing to watch the lights dancing on the water as it bubbled its way out over the rocks. If you paid very close attention, your mind could all but disappear into the spaces between the water and light. One close look at him, and it was safe to say that his mind was somewhere else. Tara paused for a moment before deciding that it was safe to speak. The words came slowly.

"You all right?" she asked softly, not having the slightest idea of what to expect.

At first he didn't respond at all. She got worried when he didn't answer right away. She waited. When he finally turned to face her, she didn't like what she saw. Even in the shadowy ambience of the room, she could still make out his face. The look in his eyes was cold and eerie. Maybe it was the lighting, but they almost seemed to glow in the dark. Tara froze. A chill came over her and all she could feel was a cold sensation against her chest where the silver cross she wore around her neck made contact with her skin. Her body tingled then the moment passed. His voice broke the silence.

"I'm fine," Grey assured her. "Just a little zoned out."

Tara looked uneasy. She wanted a closer look, so she stepped further into the room. This proved to be a mistake. A better view did little to help matters. He didn't look any friendlier. Her face betrayed her. Grey could sense her apprehension and offered a kind word.

"Sorry about that," he said. "I didn't mean to startle you. What can I do for you?"

The sound of his voice frightened her. Without thinking, her hand reached over and switched on the main overhead light. As the fresh neon illuminated the room, the appearance of his face changed. In the new bright light, he looked considerably more normal.

"Whew, that's better," she thought to herself. *"It was the lighting."* She let out a sigh of relief!

"Hey, what did you do that for?" Grey asked, obviously surprised by the sudden onslaught of light.

"I couldn't see you very well," she lied, knowing that at this point, she didn't want to go anywhere close to the truth.

"Could you turn it back off please?" he said softly "It's too damn bright."

Tara shuddered at the thought of the lights going back off again. His simple request was the last thing she wanted to hear. Reluctantly, she reached for the switch.

In an instant, the shadows returned. Silently she prayed that when she turned around, the face she had seen a few moments earlier would be gone. There was something about it that just wasn't right.

"So what can I do for you?" Grey asked, repeating his original question.

The strange tone in his voice startled her again.

Slowly, she turned to answer him. This time, when she looked up, he was staring straight at her. Luckily, even in the shadow play, she could make out the blue of his eyes. Wherever it was that he had gone before, he was back now. His eyes were warm and friendly. Tara smiled. Her prayers had been answered. It was ok to let down her guard.

"Guess what?" she said. "You've got a walk in. Angie's here. She saw you pull up outside and popped in to see how you were doing. Do you want to see her?"

"Yeah, what the hell, I've got to start somewhere," he replied. "Give me a minute then send her in."

"Ok, Boss," she laughed, as she headed for her desk. She felt better. So much better in fact, that she wondered whether or not it had all just been a figment of her imagination. Grey could feel her thoughts. Her mind had settled. The subject was closed. Her curiosity had moved on.

Once he was sure she was safely behind her desk, his attention went back to the fountain. The water and light continued their evil courtship. For a moment, he started to slip away again but this time, before he could crossover, he quickly looked away. Grey shook his head in frustration. This was ridiculous. He couldn't even concentrate for more than a few seconds. He really needed to find some answers:

anything that would help lead him in the right direction. The thoughts themselves came easily. It was the 'detours' that were the problem. He remembered sitting there earlier thinking about the tapes. His mind must have 'slipped' while he was trying to concentrate. But slipped where though?

Whatever it was that had taken over his perceptions had done so at will. His mind had not participated. Unfortunately, this time, he'd also had an audience. It was a mistake for him to have allowed Tara see him in that altered condition. He should have locked the door. Whatever she saw must have scared her a bit. When she first opened the door and caught sight of him, she turned pale. For a minute there, she was acting kind of strange herself. In the future, he would have to be more careful.

Until he had control of the situation, he would be at the mercy of the process. Right now, this 'thing' could play with him at will. He had to learn how to control it and fast. Grey reached over and turned off the fountain. It was time to move on, time to get back to living. Sooner or later he had to go back to work. He had to practice, but practice what? What a strange way of thinking about it. But what other choice did he have? He tried to remember a time before the accident and the freak show, but his mind wouldn't go there. Everything seemed to focus on the here and now. He opened the door and stepped out into the hallway. Nothing happened. Had he really expected anything to? The hallway was clear and Tara was systematically working away the morning behind her desk. It was just another normal day.

Grey looked back into his office. Things certainly looked safe enough. Still, he couldn't help wondering what demons might be unleashed when he started to touch his friends. In a very short time, the 'gift' might not be so amusing anymore.

He took a quick peak over the counter at his appointment book. The cold black lettering stared ominously back at him. Tara had been busy. She had easily found a few willing takers for his experiment. Grey looked up at the clock. He wasn't going to have to wait long. Angie was in the lobby.

* * * * *

Blake was happy. Speechless: but happy. One look in her eyes and he knew that somehow, everything was going to be all right. His first assessment was right on the money. She was beautiful; another perfect 'Katie'. So much so, that for the first few seconds, he was thinking primarily with his little head instead of his big one. For now, the way things were, even that was ok. Even if he had to pursue her using a little bit of both 'sides', he could live with that. She was all right there for the taking. The only requirements were that his timing be good and that he asked the right questions. He had to be careful.

Suddenly, his mind went blank. Luckily for Blake, he didn't panic. Things just happened to go his way. He got off easy. The girl spoke first.

"Well hello again," she said to him, her words catching him off guard.

The soft, almost whisper like sound was music to his ears. Blake didn't know what to say. His mind searched frantically for an intelligent response, but nothing of any substance clicked in. He couldn't believe it when the old mental slots came up empty. His entire train of thought derailed.

After a brief pause, a confident "Good morning" was all that he was able to muster. His simple response made him feel childish. Thank God it was enough. The girl smiled. In turn, Blake gave her one of his best. It was enough to break the ice. He started to say something, but Sylvester beat him to it.

"How silly of me," the old man said. "Mr. Kendall, this is my daughter Holly. Holly, this is Mr. Kendall. I forgot to introduce you two properly yesterday. Please forgive me." Holly smiled. "Thee Mr. Kendall?" she asked as she extended a hand. Blake eagerly stepped forward and offered his as well. Her small delicate hand pressed gently into his.

"Excuse me?" Blake replied.

"I'm sorry," she continued. "Aren't you the famous lawyer that works upstairs?" She was almost blushing. "I've been reading a lot about you in the paper lately. You really must be good!"

Holly gave her father a deprived look.

"We only met yesterday," Sylvester replied in his own defense. "I was hoping he would come back."

"And so I have," Blake interjected. "Your father makes one interesting cup of coffee. But he won't tell me what's in mine. Do you have any thoughts on the subject?"

Holly looked at her father, then back to Blake. "Sorry, Mr. Kendall," she said. "If I knew I'd probably tell you, but he won't even tell me! He's so stubborn when it comes to all of the old family recipes."

Blake decided to retreat. He'd already gotten what he came for.

"All right, Sylvester, you win for now," he conceded. "I have to go to work. Maybe we can continue our conversation later? Holly, it was pleasure meeting you. I hope that we will have the opportunity to see each other again."

Holly blushed, "The pleasure was all mine," she assured him. When she did, Blake began to feel a mild, stiffening in the front of his pants. She was so beautiful, so totally inviting. The 'Cat' was trying to get out. He had to get upstairs. "Until later then," he said politely. "And thank your dad for the coffee."

Sylvester heard him and gave him a parting wave. Blake turned and headed for the elevator. He had a lot of planning to do.

* * * * *

As the morning began, Grey got his first chance to experience contact with a regular person. He was a little apprehensive. Angie was going to be an interesting way to start. She was not exactly what he had in mind for a trial run. Tara had tried to reschedule her but she had insisted on seeing him. He'd been hoping to start with an easy one. Someone low key and uneventful. Angie spelled issues. No real trouble, but a deep inner conflict that could make for an emotional ride. Grey seriously wondered what the tape on this one was going to look like. It wasn't that there was anything unpleasant about her. She just seemed to be under a lot of stress. Between the custody battle over her grandchild, styling hair at the salon, the real estate business and her unfortunate fall down some stairs, she was still managing to hold up pretty well. She was one tough lady. Somewhere along the line, she had found strength though her faith. Angie was a survivor who hid her scars well. Grey knew that by working on her, he could be in for a rough go.

If the day was going to be structured like a prize fight, he'd have to come out strong. He could only guess where Angie's thoughts would take them. At least with her though, round one would be interesting. If there were problems, he'd have to find a way to work through them. Besides, he'd never been one for taking the easy way out. With her street smarts and candid sense of humor, working on Angie might actually be fun.

Grey took a deep breath. He thought about Tony and Clyde. Mostly he thought about Blake. He thought a lot about Blake. For a split second, all he wanted to do was put his head between his legs and kiss his ass goodbye. Instead, he settled for a few more minutes of peace and quiet and a chance to close his eyes. He sat alone, in the shadows of his office trying to prepare for what possibly lay ahead.

* * * * *

As expected, Angie was her usual enthusiastic self. She was changed and waiting in a matter of minutes. As far as Grey was concerned, everything was moving far too quickly. He tried to slow things down a bit by taking a little extra time to wash his hands before knocking on the treatment room door. It seemed to help. Once inside though, he found her anxious and ready to go. She was ready to unload.

The things that transpired during the next thirty minutes all but blew his mind. He hadn't really expected too much, and that was probably his first mistake. Hearing someone talk about their issues was one thing, getting the entire visual parade was another thing entirely. The video approach took things to a whole new level. It all began with her lousy first husband. Abusive piece of shit he was. Then came Tracy, the soon to be ex-daughter-in-law with the drug problem (who made the custody battle for little Michael so difficult). Now, it was just the everyday fight to stay one step ahead of the game. Truth was, she considered herself lucky. If she hadn't turned her life over to Jesus a few years back, she would have completely lost her mind.

With Angie, there was nothing but disillusion, sadness and pain. At times, the inner torment seemed to be overwhelming. While her feelings were strong, she generally managed to keep them under control. She quietly maintained a modest affection for most of the players involved. But she couldn't bring herself to excuse some of their behavior and attitudes. Most, if not all of the self serving holier-than though bullshit had to go.

Somehow, through it all, Angie had managed to hold on. She had done so by turning to prayer. She prayed a lot. Mostly, her words were for the good people to become even better and for the bad people to see the light. She was honest and fair. When it came to Angie, Grey was pretty sure that somehow, God was listening.

His time with her flew by. Not once, during the entire session, did he feel the need to let go. He did practice a few 'stops' and 'starts' but everything seemed to go smoothly. If the rest of his morning patients were like this, maybe he'd learn to get the hang of it. Grey focused on what he was doing and kept working.

* * * * *

The knock on the door was a welcome relief. He'd been paying so much attention to what he was doing, he'd lost track of time. The note under the door was Tara letting him know that there was someone else waiting to see him. Grey gave Angie a few long stretches then let her go. As soon as his hands left her body, the movie came to an end and the world of Angie faded away.

Grey let out a sigh of relief. He had done it. He had made it through his first real situation back at work where he felt in control! Everything was ok. Angie had even thanked him for his efforts before he left the room. He smiled as he stepped out into the hallway. He was excited by the fact that their time together had gone so well. Each section of Angie's tape had been interesting on its own, but the total experience had given him a much deeper insight into her life. He had been privy to a completely private and intimate side of her. He was amazed by the clarity and detail of the entire encounter. He was feeling pretty good about the whole thing.

Everything was going great until he heard a familiar voice coming from the corner of the waiting room. Her soft, seductive whisper was always a pleasant surprise. Tara blushed when she saw the look on Grey's face. She probably should have warned him. She knew that Jackie was one of his favorites. Jackie, sweet lovable Jackie, had come out to play.

Even before the accident, seeing her had always been a thrill. She reminded him a lot of Alex. Same fire and passion for life, Jackie was a handful and definitely eye candy. He had come to the conclusion long ago that working on her usually required two things; a stiff drink before he started and a cold shower afterwards. Unfortunately, at the moment, neither of these options was readily available. It didn't really matter though, Jackie was a handful. She was smart, sexy, and always made him laugh. He was lucky to know her. Besides, whatever she had on her mind would probably be a lot of fun. Grey got ready to go at it again. Funny thing was, this time he was the one who couldn't wait to get started.

* * * * *

Quite frankly, Blake was amazed that he'd made it upstairs in one piece. Emotionally, he was a wreck. His contact with Holly left him excited and aroused. To him the handshake was much more than just a simple touch. It border lined being erotic. The energy was so intense, he hadn't wanted to let go. Seeing her up close again confirmed any doubts he might have had about what he needed to do. She was incredible. Her smile alone had made him rise to the occasion. He was physically out of control. The 'Cat' was taking over.

A timely exit to the elevator was his only logical choice for escape. It was the perfect place to hide. The decision was already paying off. Once inside, he felt safe. Still, nothing but the set of shiny steel doors protected him from the judgment of the outside world. As he traveled upward, his anxiety grew with each passing level. It was only a short ride. His office was only a few feet away. Blake pulled his coat closer to his body as the elevator came to a stop. He tried to convince himself that he was ready for anything. A chill ran through him as the doors began to open. Blake closed his eyes and took a deep breath.

Truth was, if there had been anyone sitting in the reception area when the doors opened, his mind would have completely unraveled. His problem had become more pronounced during the ride upstairs. He knew that he had to keep a low profile at any cost. One look from an unsuspecting stranger and the humiliation alone would be more than he could handle. His nerves were hanging by a thread. He had grossly underestimated what effect seeing the girl again would have on him. With his feline friend in the driver's seat, things had quickly gotten out of hand.

He was relieved to find the outer office empty. It was a good thing Sheila was running late. The lack of her presence saved him from any immediate embarrassment. Even though he was alone, he still found himself in a rather awkward position. While his trench coat sufficiently disguised any visual identification of the problem, it did nothing to assist him in his need for normal body mechanics. His options; stay in the elevator until things calmed down, or try to struggle to the privacy of his office.; He hit the "open" button to let in some fresh air. After a few seconds, the doors closed again. He was beginning to feel trapped. He knew that he had to move fast. Suddenly, his feet froze. He could swear that he could hear people talking on the other side of the doors. Blake held his breath. Then the voices went away. He realized that he was running out of ideas. He pressed the button again and the doors opened.

His anxiety faded as the office came back into view. It was still empty. The coast was clear. Blake let out a sigh of relief. Hopefully, for a change, things were going to be easier from here on out. He gathered himself together and made his move. In a final act of desperation, he forced himself to limp comically from the elevator to his desk.

* * * * *

CHAPTER 15

As twilight fell on gods and men, the shadows stalked the fields. The headstones sat in quiet rows of silence, staring back at anyone who was brave enough to acknowledge their existence. A light rain fell gently from the sky as the large gathering of mourners looked on. There, in the garden of death, everything was colorless, an endless sea of shades of black and white. Everything: except for the body that is. Everything: except the girl.

To the naked eye, she was as soft and pretty as the day she had kissed this mortal world goodbye. Her essence glowed like a white rose that had been tossed into a dark sea. She was a light in a tunnel of darkness. The funeral artist had done his job, and done it well. The gathering would never see what existed beneath the bloated, rotting flesh that was once their friend or loved one. Together, they had come to say goodbye.

The casket had been left open during the graveside service at the request of her family. The stories surrounding her death and the recent discovery of her body had left so many concerned with foul images, that the family wanted her to be seen and remembered as she once was. While the weather had not been kind, the raindrops on her face simply looked like tears. In a better light, some of these were surely signs of sadness for the moment. Others perhaps were more of a grateful nature, a final token of appreciation if you will for the kind man at the funeral home. He alone possessed the skills necessary to restore her once angelic look for her impending trip to heaven. The truth of it all was only for her and God to know. It was His job to get her there. Father Richard was just the conductor on her one way train to heaven.

Richard bowed his head as each member of the assembly paid their last respects. Their words were few and far between. Many could only find tears themselves. Others, lay roses in Kelly's arms. As they did, each petal took back its own color of life. Whatever evil had taken her body, it had not taken her soul. The goodness of Kelly's spirit lived on. The vibrant change of color within the flowers proved that. Soon God would have another angel to entertain him. The thought made Richard smile as he began to close the lid. That was his first mistake.

When he looked down to her for one last goodbye, his eyes saw through the mirage. The blue, grotesque, decaying face of Kelly Richfield lay before him. The deep gash now visible across her throat was obviously not the coroner's handy work. It was a painful reminder of all that is evil. Richard had to look away. That was mistake number two. As he did, an icy hand reached out of the coffin and grabbed him, pulling his face down to hers. Her empty eyes penetrated his soul.

"Why Father, why?" the gargled voice whispered.

All Richard could do, was scream.

* * * * *

When he opened his eyes, he was surprised to discover that he was safe in his own bed. The hands on the front of his nightshirt belonged innocently enough to his wife Judy. She had reached over and shook him, attempting to snap him out of it. While her efforts paid off, she had no way of knowing that her actions actually contributed to the intensity of the nightmare. Richard on the other hand was more than elated after realizing that he was miles away from the cemetery. Even so, he couldn't stop shaking even after forcing himself to sit up.

"Do I even want to know?" Judy asked, as she carefully laid a hand on his shoulder. Her touch was warm and friendly.

"I thought I was over this," he said softly. "I honestly thought I had laid this one to rest."

Judy put her arms around him and held him close. "You've been a little preoccupied lately," she said. "Is there something you want to tell me?"

Richard just shrugged his shoulders. He knew that he had to say something.

"I was discussing the Richfield funeral with someone recently," he began. His voice was a bit shaky. "Talking about it again must have opened up some old wounds. I guess I should have left things well enough alone."

Judy nodded her understanding. "I remember what happened to that poor girl as if it were only yesterday," she said. "Her death was such a shock to everyone. What on earth made you travel down that road again?"

"I don't really know" he admitted. "Maybe it had something to do with Grey being in that accident. The possibility of losing another friend was terribly unsettling."

"I can understand that Dear," she replied, trying in some small way to comfort him.

"You're in an especially vulnerable position being "Father" Richard. You may feel for all of God's children, but I'm sure that on a more personal level, you probably have a few favorites. After all, you're only human."

Then she smiled and kissed him on the cheek. She always knew how to make things better.

"C'mon silly," she coaxed him a little." Let's try to get some sleep."

Richard agreed. He knew that it was in his best interest not to challenge her. He gave her a hug and reached for his pillow. As he closed his eyes, he prayed for a quiet, peaceful darkness. This time God gave him a break.

* * * * *

Grey was ready for anything. Truth was, he was actually hoping for a little excitement. Angie had left him with a dry taste in his mouth.

When the door opened into Jackie's world, he knew that he would not be disappointed.

He immediately found himself surrounded by a tropical paradise. She was alone, standing under a waterfall, letting the water run through her hair. The small white bikini did little to distract ones attention from what she had to offer. If anything, it was just another added attraction. He could see her reflection in the lagoon below. She was beautiful, wet, and glistening in the mid day sun.

It took him a minute to settle in, but then he remembered why this setting seemed so familiar. They had talked about this place a few weeks earlier. Now, once again, she had chosen it as a temporary escape from reality. She was back on vacation. Jamaica was a welcome break.

She had gone to the islands to "get away from it all" and relax. Apparently her plan worked. Saying that she looked relaxed was a gross understatement. From the looks of things, her holiday had played out well. So well in fact, that for the moment, she had decided to return. Grey smiled. Bikinis and waterfalls were much more his speed. He was thankful to be along for the ride.

Working on Jackie was a different experience all together. The only contact with her was on her face and neck. She didn't even want a 'back rub'. She would just lay face up on the table and make him concentrate his efforts on her neck and jaw for the entire hour. It was his job to get rid of her headaches. Sometimes, they would become so unbearable that she would have trouble even functioning. When they reached that level, she'd be forced to pick up the phone and call him.

Over the years they had become friends. In the past, they could always talk about anything, but today things were different. The rules had changed. It was sad. He couldn't tell her. There was nothing he could say. All he could do was go along for the ride. He had no choice but to keep working.

Every time things started to heat up, he had to force himself to let go. He really liked Jackie. He respected her so there were some things he couldn't bring himself to see. He tried to establish a rhythm that would allow him to break contact on a regular basis. After a little practice, he managed to choreograph his hand movements in such a way that the motions almost became a new "routine". Jackie never once complained. She was more interested in just getting the attention she deserved.

By the end of the hour, they were both in better shape. Jackie's headache was gone and Grey had learned something new. This time, the contrast of the videos was different. Everything was easy going. His laid back train of thought had allowed him to relax and concentrate on what he was seeing. He understood now that the more he practiced the better chance he would have of isolating any specific details. In the future, if he paid close attention, maybe he could figure out how to deal with Tony and Blake. Jackie had been a big help. There was a lot to tell Alex. Grey wondered where she was.

* * * * *

The rest of the morning went off without a hitch. After a brief conversation with Sheila outlining his schedule for the day, Blake buried himself in his work. At first, it was difficult to concentrate knowing that just a few floors above were the answer to his prayers. He could not stop thinking about her, and he liked it that way. There was nothing quite like a little self inflicted torture before lunch. Mental motivation if you will. The 'Cat' was apparently developing a sense of humor.

An empty Styrofoam cup sat proudly at the end of his desk. In a sadistic sort of way, it had become a talisman of sorts after his earlier run in with Holly. He could almost smell her perfume on the side of the cup. It was simple but compelling. Sheila had tried to dispose of it earlier but he had insisted that she leave it alone. Truth was, he liked looking at it. It made him smile. When she looked at him funny, he gave her some lame excuse about possibly going downstairs for more. This of course made little or no sense, but what the hell. He didn't owe her an explanation. She was just hired help. And besides, she wasn't exactly known for her ability to make coffee.

Blake smiled. He could still taste the flavor of Sylvester's last concoction. It still remained playfully on the back of his tongue. The desire was there. Come to think of it, he did want more.

'More, now there was a concept, more. More what? More coffee? More gratification? More Holly, perhaps?' "Yeah", he whispered out loud to himself. Why the hell not?" *'It was all part of the game.'*

Blake's mind started to wander. All he could see were those long legs again. They were absolutely incredible. He wanted to enjoy every inch of her. One free hand quickly made its way into his pants pocket in search of his friend and was immediately rewarded. The cold ivory handle felt good to the touch. So good in fact, that he could almost hear music. The rapture was starting to grow. He knew that he had to back off. His claws were beginning to show. He had no choice but to let go.

Controlling his emotions became his first priority. Giving the very thought of her too much attention would rekindle his excitement. He couldn't afford to be trapped again in the same position he had caught himself earlier. He no longer had the luxury of being alone. He needed to be careful. It had taken him a good while to calm himself down after Sheila arrived. Only then did he feel confident enough to venture out from behind the safety his desk and move freely about the office.

Blake glanced over at the clock. It was almost twelve. Walter would be checking in sometime within the next hour during the courts noon recess. He didn't know it yet but he would find his cool, southern genius missing in action. Blake would make sure that he was "unavailable for comment". The morning had passed quietly and without incident. He wanted to keep it that way. He buzzed Sheila and told her that he would be going out for awhile. He needed some fresh air, and maybe some fresh... well. She would never see him leave. He slipped out quietly through his private entrance. When he did, the cup went with him. Part of him was hoping that Sylvester was still open.

* * * * *

Over the next few hours, Grey started to get comfortable with his new routine. Working on more patients gave him the opportunity to concentrate on his own relaxation techniques. The short thirty minute sessions made it easy for him to just turn it on and off. He kept things simple and nobody was the wiser. To the outside world, nothing had changed. His first tour of duty had played out well. The only damage was superficial. He was tired and hungry. A break for lunch was a welcomed intermission.

Truth was, he discovered that he could actually go home if he wanted to. His afternoon schedule was clear. For whatever reason, Tara had been kind enough to not press him into service for the rest of the day. At first he was a bit suspicious, but he made a mental note to thank her for it later. The game was beginning to get interesting, but the past few hours had taken a lot out of him. He could use a little time on the sidelines. The big question for the moment was what to do next.

He couldn't decide who to call first. Finding Rachel would be easy, but if she had needed anything, she would have called him by now. Father Richard would be hanging around the church or out on the golf course. Alex of course was nowhere to be found. Problem was, she was the one that he really needed to talk to. Both Rachel and Richard could wait. He wished that Alex would at least call. He wanted to get going. He reached in and turned off the light in his office. Somehow everything looked safer in the dark. Maybe it would be better if he called Alex first. Then he would try getting Richard just to check in. Grey walked slowly to his car. When he heard the sound of his cell phone ringing, he got a feeling that the decision had already been made.

* * * * *

The hot dog from the clubhouse just didn't taste the same. Even the Gatorade he was trying to wash it down with seemed to have a funny after taste. In Richard's world, something was definitely out of whack. His first thought was that he might be coming down with something, a cold perhaps. Then he contemplated the relationship between the weather and his allergies. He even considered the possibility that his blood sugar was low. After taking a few minutes to consider his options, he realized that there was only one thing that made any sense. It was his inability to concentrate in general that was making his morning so difficult. For whatever reason, his mind was refusing to recognize even the most ordinary things; like the simple taste of food. It was as if, all it wanted him to do was focus his attention on one thing, Kelly.

The nightmare, it seemed just wouldn't go away. He became even more discouraged when he picked up his score card and checked his performance. The first nine holes were obviously an exercise in futility. He would have had more luck chopping wood for the past few hours than he'd had swinging a golf club. His mind just wasn't in the game. It had been two years since he remembered recording numbers like these which reflected such an emotional disaster. Thank God for Pastor Bob. So far, his playing partner had been kind enough not to say anything. Out playing Richard was not something he was accustomed to.

These moments were few and far between. He wasn't about to look a gift horse in the mouth. Truth was, Bob was concerned. There had to be something seriously wrong that would create such a distraction to his friend. As much as he wanted to help though, he didn't want to interfere. He decided to wait for the right opportunity before trying to approach him. It wasn't until they took a break for lunch that Bob saw the opening that he was looking for. After a quick run to the snack bar, he went over to check on him.

"Everything all right Richard?" Bob asked, sipping a coke while taking a seat next to him in the golf cart.

"Just tired I guess," Richard replied." I haven't been sleeping to well lately. Give me a minute and I'll be fine."

Bob smiled and said nothing. To Richard, his silence conveyed a message. It was one of both patience and respect. As curious as he might be, Bob would never push an issue. At the same time, Richard knew that his friend would always be available for counsel if needed. Over the next few minutes, both men kept their thoughts to themselves and moved on. Richard figured he was safe when the pastor got up and announced he was going back inside for another bottle of water. It was no surprise when Richard declined an invitation to join him. Bob patted him on the back and stepped out of the cart.

Richard was relieved. He had escaped an awkward moment without any further explanation. His brief response was only a little white lie if you measured it correctly. Besides, Bob would be the last person to suspect anything. They had been friends for far too long. Richard was glad for the moment alone. It gave him time to collect himself.

A little more mustard and the rest of the hotdog finally went down. Richard could only hope that his playing scores would follow as well. He really didn't expect much. His tension level had already gotten way out of hand. He was even having trouble just gripping a club. Every time he let his mind wander, he ended up back at the graveyard looking into Kelly's face. He couldn't break free from those eyes. They sliced though his soft outer shell like a knife through flesh. They had shackled the limbs of his subconscious mind and taken him prisoner. Deep in his own thoughts, he knew he was not alone. Even in the peaceful stillness of an empty fairway, he could still hear the sound of her desperate words echoing in his head. Her gurgled cry pleaded with him for answers and redemption. Richard's mind started to slip. Lucky for him, the sound of Bob's voice snapped him out of it.

"You ready to move on Dick?" he asked, this time being a bit more personal.

Richard nodded, and then chugged down the rest of his drink. After taking a deep breath, he smiled and reached for the steering wheel. "Hang on old man," he chuckled back," I feel my second wind coming on. Lord, have mercy on the people playing in front of us!"

With that, Father Richard put his foot on the accelerator and immediately tore out of the snack area. Only the course Marshall was close enough to observe poor Bob making the sign of the cross through the ensuing cloud of dust. He couldn't help but laugh as he watched the two men of God go forth, in search of the tenth tee.

* * * * *

Grey was lucky. He caught it on the fourth ring. One more and it would have transferred over to voice mail. He hated voice mail. Recorded messages were so impersonal. In his line of work, most of his clients required one on one attention. People expected that. That's why a lot of them had his cell phone number in the first place. Oddly enough though, this particular call was completely unexpected.

"Hello, Grey?" the stranger asked. The soft, gentle tone of her voice caught him off guard. At first, he wasn't sure if he should acknowledge her. He hesitated just long enough that she had to try again.

"Hello?" the voice asked again. This time, it was a little more insistent. She knew that he had picked up.

"Uh, yeah, this is Grey," he answered. "Who's this?"

A heavy silence hung in the dead air. There was a long pause before she spoke again. Part of him could almost hear the gears turning in her head.

"This is Grey, right?" the voice insisted. This time, she sounded desperate.

"Yes it is," he admitted. "How can I help you?"

"I've got to ask you something," she blurted out. "You might find it a little strange."

"Really?" he inquired, attempting to draw her out. "Not anymore bizarre than the beginning of the conversation."

He was almost playing with her now. "Who are you anyway?" Once again, silence, only this time it didn't last.

"That's not important right now," she hurried. "I just need to know something."

"All right, he said, calmly taking the bait. What is so important?" "I really need to know, she repeated. "You have to tell me! I haven't been able to sleep for days!" The fear in her voice was starting to show through.

"Tell you what?" he insisted.

He could sense her frustration now. She knew that it was now or never. She finally had his undivided attention.

"Ok listen, you're going to think I'm nuts," she conceded," but I don't know how else to say this. I think... I think you've been inside me!" "Excuse me?" Grey responded. He was more surprised than agitated.

"What the hell are you talking about?"

"Oh man, I'm sorry," she continued. "This is just all so crazy. I don't mean like sexually or anything. I mean like, you know, like inside my head. You know like reading my mind or something. It really freaked me out the other day when you teased me about the cigarette."

"I what?" he began to say and then suddenly he remembered. The hospital: the pizza, the wheelchair, everything. He remembered holding her hand. He had used her and somehow she had figured it out!" It was his turn to be silent.

"You still there?" she asked timidly.

"Yeah, I'm here," he mumbled. He was caught. She had him dead to rights. There was no point in hanging up on her or even attempting to blow her off. They had shared an experience so there was no use trying to deny it.

"I'm here, Lisa," he assured her. "I'm here." His voice reeked with sincerity. "I didn't mean to scare you. You ok?"

"I'm more confused than scared," she confessed. "I really don't know what to think. I don't understand any of this. It's just so weird. Is any of this for real?"

Grey paused for a moment to consider his options. He decided to take a chance. "I'm sorry to admit this, but yeah, it is," he told her. "Truth is, I'm not exactly sure what it is. The only thing I am sure of is that it allows me to see some really strange things; like you and that guy."

Then his voice got softer. "I am sorry about that."

Lisa paused for a minute to let his words sink in. She decided that she had to know. "So what did you see?" she asked.

"Enough that I offered you a cigarette," he said sarcastically. He was doing his best to appear unemotional. She'd had enough to deal with already.

Lisa giggled. "Guess you got a good look then huh," she said playfully. Her initial wave of embarrassment was now beginning to recede.

"More than you'll ever get me to admit," he assured her. "Sorry, I wish I could tell you more."

"Can't or won't?" she asked.

"Probably both," he admitted. "At least for right now anyway; I haven't been able to figure this out yet myself but when I do, I promise I'll call you."

"You still have my number?" she asked.

"You know I do," he said. "It's at house in my bathroom drawer on my hospital I.D. bracelet. By the way, that was pretty slick of you putting it there. Nice move, and speaking of nice moves; how did you get this number. It's unlisted?"

"I got it off your chart in the hospital, silly. They brought your cell phone in with you in the ambulance. It was in with your personal effects." Her voice was bubbly now. She wasn't some dumb blonde! He could almost see her smiling.

"See. And you thought I was just another pretty face," she added for good measure. Grey had to admit she was right. He was impressed. Up until now, he had totally underestimated her.

"Guess I'll know better next time," he said. "Once again, I commend your efforts. So where do we go from here?"

"Dinner, drinks?" she teased him. Sadly, she couldn't see him smile. "Well, I suppose that would be the next logical step," he replied. "After all, where else could we possibly go after the pizza, cokes, and the truly unique ambience and chemical sterility of a hospital room? Oh yeah, and let's not forget the... uh well you know, the movie!"

Lisa just giggled again. Thank God she did. For a second there he thought that he might have taken things a little too far. He had to admit he liked her. For a kid she was ok. "I really am sorry I bothered you," she conceded.

"No big deal," he replied. "I guess I should have expected something like this. How'd you figure it out anyway?"

"It was the crack about the cigarette," she began. "I couldn't figure out why you would say that, and the timing was too coincidental. In all honesty, I let it go at first but then it started to bug me after a few days. Then, it took me a couple more days before I could get up the nerve to call."

"Sorry about the peep show," he offered apologetically. tone was genuine and sincere.

"That's all right," she snickered. "As long as you enjoyed the show, the pleasure was mine. No harm done." Then the silence returned.

"Hey, will you call me when you can tell me more, ok?" she said.

"That's a promise," he assured her. "You take care."

"You too," she said. Then they both said their goodbyes.

As he hung up the phone, Grey couldn't help but wonder what she was really thinking. Maybe she would accept their experience as just a freak accident? That would make things simple. He liked simple. Actually, she had been very laid back about the whole thing; that is once both of their cards were safely on the table. She hadn't even pushed the issue after his confession. She was going to be all right.

In any case, Lisa was now more of an ally than a threat. She would keep his secrets, and keep them well. They had a bond. He could live with that. He knew this would not be the last time their paths would cross. She was now officially a new player. He had no choice but to deal her in.

* * * * *

Much to Blake's relief, Sylvester was still around and working his ass off. His entire trip downstairs had been a mental game of prayers and what ifs. He needed Sylvester to be there. He didn't know why, he just did. Still, he couldn't help feeling a bit foolish when he saw the line of people waiting to get coffee. It was only lunch time and still early in the day, so why had he assumed that he would be the only person in the building still interested in what the old man had to offer. He should have known better.

To the locals, Sylvester was like a portable 'Starbucks' at their personal beck and call. Apparently his wares were very popular even after breakfast. Blake could understand that. He had no choice but to get in line.

He must have appeared hurried because the old man gave him a funny look when he noticed him waiting. By the time he reached the counter, he had broken out into a sweat.

"Is everything all right, sir?" Sylvester asked? "You look pale."

Blake glanced over at his reflection in the glass. He did look washed out. The color had all but abandoned his cheeks.

"Rough morning, Mr. Kendall?" he asked again.

Blake heard the question but ignored him. He was too busy staring at his image in the glass again to answer. What he saw before him did nothing but confuse him even further. His mind was working the way he thought it should, but the face in the window lead him to believe otherwise. His eyes, there was something about the eyes. The 'Cat' was staring back at him.

Blake was worried. The 'Cat' had never surfaced before without adequate provocation. This time, there wasn't any. His dark friend had appeared strictly on its own volition. There was no invitation, no girl, no fix, no longing for his baton! Everything around him seemed to be perfectly normal; typical Blake, everything except the depth of his face. Was he seeing things? Were his eyes playing tricks on him? Apparently something was different about him or Sylvester wouldn't have made inquiries. Cautiously, he looked up at the coffee man. He could see the concern in Sylvester's eyes.

"I'm fine," he told him." I really am. I'm just overtired," he added. "I have a lot on my mind. Sorry if I wasn't paying attention. I wasn't trying to be rude."

"No problem, Mr. Kendall," Sylvester responded. "We all have bad days."

Blake nodded. "Maybe I'm just running low on whatever it was that you put in my coffee this morning," he said. It was almost an accusation, but not quite.

Sylvester grinned but refused to play along. "Well, if that's the case, would you like to try again?" he asked. Then he winked at Blake.

"You're a scintillating old thing aren't you?" Blake mumbled.

"I am at that, sir", Sylvester replied. "Makes things between us even more interesting, don't you think?"

"That it does my friend", Blake assured him. "That it does".

Actually, he was more impressed that Sylvester was educated enough to know what he meant in the first place. Lawyers like to use big words. That went with the territory. The fact that his mind had chosen the word scintillating was a good sign. It meant that he still thought like a lawyer, even if his reflection didn't support it. For a moment, just knowing this made him feel better.

"So about the coffee," Sylvester asked? Blake eagerly handed over the magic cup.

"This looks like the one from this morning," he told Blake after noticing the stains on the bottom inside edges.

Blake nodded. "As a matter of fact, it is," he said. "I was hoping to get a refill."

Sylvester looked down, disgusted with the used container. He was slightly offended "Nonsense," he said. "This simply won't due. Everyone deserves a new cup." His words were still warm as he crushed the fragile Styrofoam shell in his hand.

When he did, a whisper of her perfume brushed past Blake's nose. Instantly, Blake could feel a violent compression starting to engulf his chest. It felt as if the air was being squeezed out of him like a balloon. Blake thought he was going to die. Time as he knew it, stood still.

It seemed like an eternity before he was able to get the feeling of life back into his lungs. When he finally came to his senses, he saw Sylvester filling him a new cup. The aroma was magnificent. It smelled the same as the one he'd gotten earlier; heavy on the vanilla. To his surprise, the old man left the lid off.

Sylvester turned to face him. "I believe this is what you came for," he said as he handed the hot coffee to Blake. "This should certainly do the trick."

Blake gave him only a quick nod. He wasn't sure that he could breathe yet, let alone speak. He took a deep breath hoping to reset his balance. He immediately felt better.

"Thank you," he said as he took possession of the cup.

He reminded himself that he had to be careful. He was forced to pay especially close attention to the transaction by the simple omission of the lid. He couldn't help wondering if the intended distraction was deliberate.

"What, no surprises this time?" he inquired, attempting to catch Sylvester off balance.

"None needed," the old man answered. "You're in a different place now. I hope you feel better sir," he continued while he worked. "It worries me when my friends are under the weather."

Blake smiled. His own, I'd like to think. "Well, thanks for the coffee and the sentiment," he offered. "And please tell your daughter that I said hello."

"Why don't you tell her yourself," Sylvester suggested, taking a quick look at his watch.

"She should be down any minute."

As the old man's words lodged in his brain, Blake could feel his chest begin to tighten again. That and something else began to grow. A smile graduated across his face, and this time there was no doubt what was really behind it. Blake could feel the difference now. Looking back at the glass once more, he caught a glimpse of his reflection.

His face had changed. It was darker now, especially around the eyes, the nose, and the draw of his neck. The usual friendliness was gone. The shade of his jaw and the shadows of his cheeks had all melted together to complete the eerie transformation. Then there were his eyes; transparent liquid eyes, ones that radiated both the innocence of life, and the evil of death; the ones that spoke to him and kept him in focus in the maelstrom of his dreams. They were the windows which lead to the deepest dungeons of his soul.

Blake stood in silence, his mind lost in a world trapped between ecstasy and fear. His eyes told him everything. The longer he stared into them, the more intoxicating they became. In the kaleidoscope of never ending colors, he saw visions of things that once were, and a multitude of others that were yet to be. He tried desperately to maintain control, but his mind was slowly beginning to scramble. He couldn't decide whether to celebrate the voyage into insanity or cower at the feet of madness. All he could do was tag along for the ride. And then he heard her speak. He blinked and it was over. The instant his mind recognized her voice, it immediately shut down the existing program. The screen went blank and he was forced to go back to square one.

He had trouble catching up. For a moment, he thought that maybe the lights were on, but there was nobody home; a hard concept to consider when relating it to one's self. He was even more surprised when he discovered that his entire psychological adventure had taken place in a matter of seconds. It had felt like a much longer ride.

* * * * *

Once back in reality, the only thing that had saved him was that the girl wasn't talking to him. She was too heavily engaged in a conversation with her father to notice his mental absence. By the time she acknowledged his presence, he was completely back to normal. When she smiled at him, he eagerly smiled back. (His again, I think). When Sylvester smiled too, Blake took it as a sign that there must have been some noticeable improvement. Holly of course, looked like an angel.

"Hi Mr. Kendall," she said in a slightly flirtatious voice. "It's nice to see you again." Her sexy little inflection echoed through his head.

"Hello Holly", he replied. "It's nice to see you as well." He found that he had no trouble breathing for this one. Catching his breath maybe, but certainly not using it. She easily commanded his undivided attention. He did have another problem though. His reflection in the glass was changing again. He could also feel the beginnings of another "situation" down below. Guess his on /off switch was busted. That or the 'Cat' was starting to operate one step ahead.

"Holly," he said, trying to find an easy way out. "I'm sorry I can't stay and get better acquainted. I have a meeting across town that I can't afford to miss," he lied. "Maybe we can get together later and talk, he chuckled. Perhaps I might even be able to persuade you to tell me stories about your father."

Sylvester just grumbled. He wasn't quite sure that he was fond of the idea. Blake handed her a card, (a duplicate of the one he'd given Casey).

"Try the cell phone number later this evening if you're at all interested in continuing the conversation," he said. "Who knows, you might find it rather amusing."

"I'll call you later then, Mr. Kendall," Holly assured him as she gave him a parting wave. She was obviously excited by the invitation.

"And please, call me Blake," he insisted.

Holly nodded her approval and then they both said their goodbyes.

On the way to his car, Blake couldn't help but laugh. He knew that he had to make a decision about Holly and soon. Personal involvement or not, a choice had to be made. He searched his reservoir for any sign of Casey but it was hopeless. Her energy was gone. Now he had no choice. He had run out of both time and excuses. He had to have a fix! He worried about his lack of planning. Even if she called him later, he couldn't perform tonight. It would be far too risky. He was desperate but not stupid. At the very least, he now had a foot in the door. It would either kick his ass, or take him to the next level. God: how he hated to wait. All he could hope for now was getting that first call.

The Mercedes purred as he punched the gas pedal leaving the parking structure. Blake glanced up at the rear view mirror to check traffic, and discovered that 'those' eyes were back again. Maybe they'd never left. Apparently, he was losing control of the 'switch'. Funny thing was, at this point, he really didn't care. He had a job to do. It was of little consequence to him how he managed to get it done. He put his hand in his pocket and found his faithful companion.

"Patience my friend," he told the piece of cold steel, "Patience." Blake looked up at the sky. It was a glorious warm shade of blue with large puffy cotton balls for clouds. Life was good. It was a beautiful day.

"*To hell with work*," he thought," *To hell with Katie and Walter!*"

The 'Cat' grinned. He needed some fresh air. Blake headed for the beach.

* * * * *

CHAPTER 16

Galleon sat quietly in the corner of the boat's forward salon carefully nursing the remnants of a cold beer. Truth was, that even after a good night's rest, nothing seemed to help. He'd been staring for hours at the pile of photographs on the table, hoping to get one of the pictures of the "Ripper" girls he'd collected to talk to him. He thought that maybe, if he stared at them long enough, one of them might break their silence and give him a clue as to who was behind all of the recent murders. He'd tried to get a copy of the whole case file, but the lead detective on the case, some old cop named MacKensie, didn't want it released. Tim had been forced to start piecing one together of his own by relying on some of his old connections downtown. He'd been at it since dawn and so far, he'd been fighting a losing battle. When the sun began to shine brightly through the port side windows, he realized that it was getting close to noon. Fact was, the "Ripper" case wasn't even his. MacKensie was actually running the show out of Laguna Beach. He and a bunch of other detectives from south Orange County and the F.B.I. were working this one together. The task force had been set up after the body of the Riddell girl had washed ashore.

Tim was just fishing anyway. Laguna Beach wasn't part of his jurisdiction, but he figured that these guys could use all the help they could get. This psycho had been at it for the last six months and still nobody had any real clues. He'd only taken a personal interest after the latest girl had been found mangled on the rocks just south of the marina. Frankly, things were getting a little too close to home. That's when he started to investigate on his own. From what he could see, the entire case was one big mess. The only thing that anyone could agree on was that all of the killings had been done by the same individual. He had arrived at this conclusion as well after carefully evaluating the evidence. From where he stood, the key to this was the position, angle and depth of the wounds. They all had the same pattern. He was pleased when he read that the coroner's findings had suggested the same.

After studying all of the victim's remains, he determined that the odds were the killer was male. He based this on the size and strength the attacker would have needed to subdue the victims. He was also confident that the killer was left handed judging by the way each laceration dipped across the throat from the victims from right to left. The killer would have to be very strong in order to maintain the pressure needed to make such a vicious incision. Because of the close contact involved, there was even a possibility that the girls knew their assailant.

Tim looked harder into the pictures. What was he missing? There had to be something there. He wondered what the murder weapon would turn out to be; a blade yes, but what kind; a knife or possibly a military weapon. There was no telling without further forensic investigation. That's where it was going to be tough. This guy was smart. Smart enough to insure that the evidence was contaminated long before the bodies could be found. Floaters were difficult to trace.

Pictures didn't usually lie. Everyone agreed that the same weapon had been used to kill each of the women. What really concerned him though was the time frame. Based on the "Ripper's" previous behavior pattern, there was a strong possibility that he might be ready to attack again sometime in the immediate future. Tim shook his head. This nutcase had to be stopped. There was no telling when or where he might strike next. It was just a matter of time.

Tim counted his blessings. Wickmann had forced him to take a few days off. The sergeant had politely insisted upon it. Renee was at work, so he was in a hurry to go nowhere fast. He tossed the last of the now warm Bud into the trash can and cracked open a fresh one. Once again, he found a seat and made himself comfortable. After a few chugs on the bottle, he went back to staring at the table. An hour later, there was still nothing.

Tim was discouraged, but he wasn't about to quit. He still had time. Renee wouldn't be looking for him until after four. He could maintain his vigil over the coffee table until then. He grabbed another beer and went up on deck. The sun was warm on his face and a light breeze was blowing in from the east.

"The answers are down there," he said out loud to himself. "I know there's something there. I just have to be patient."

He took a big swallow, then a breath of fresh air and headed back below. That's when he decided to settle in for the rest of the afternoon.

"Dead people can talk," he'd heard his friend at the medical examiner's office say on more than one occasion. "You just have to know how to listen."

Maybe she was right. So Tim kicked back and waited. Sooner or later, someone was going to say something and damned if he wasn't going to be there when they did.

* * * * *

Grey hadn't been in the car for more than five minutes when the phone started to ring again. The caller I.D. was most informative but there was still no sign of Alex. He could have let the call go, but in the end decided to take it. Apparently the word was out. Toby was probably just calling to check up on him. Grey saw no point in avoiding the old man and making him worry.

Toby Foxworth was a good friend. Over the years, he and his wife had become like family. Their kindness and quick wit had seen him through many a crazy afternoon. Their good nature consistently made his job fun. Today would be no exception. After a short conversation, Grey decided to go see them.

Actually, he worked on them both. In the beginning, it was Jane's back that required attention and brought him to the house. As time passed though, Toby learned to take advantage of his visits as well.

There was always something a bit unsettling though about working in Toby's den. No matter where you ended up standing or sitting, you could not escape the feeling that you were being watched. Upon entering the study, you were greeted by the room's resident maître de, an antique cigar store Indian. Once one became accustomed to his sentry-like stare, you were then bombarded by the ever watchful eyes of the room's many other inhabitants. The faces on the walls seemed to stare down at you from above, always curious about the reason for your presence. For Grey, it was like repeatedly playing to a captive audience and always being center stage.

As he worked, hundreds of eyes would follow his every move. An hour in the den was (in a bizarre sort of way), a psychotic form of history lesson. All of the room's residents were characters out of the past. At first, the aura they commanded really bothered him. Over time, he had learned to adjust.

Toby collected mugs. These were not your average coffee or soup carrying kind mind you, but intricate works of art. Each one was individually cast and handcrafted to depict the head and face of a famous character out of history. They were imported from England by Royal Daulton and most bore price tags that one might choose to compare to their monthly mortgage payment. They were called "Toby's" and hence forth, that's how Charlie Foxworth had acquired his nickname.

On this field, Grey was completely outnumbered. The shelves above and around him were home to literally hundreds of pieces, each with its own personality and accompanying story. The collection was quite elaborate and over the years, Toby had accumulated enough of them to start his own little exhibit. He had been collecting them for over forty years. They had become like children to him.

Jane however had other ideas about the Foxworth collection. On more than one occasion, she had expressed her dislike for both their dominant appearance and financial commitment. Every time one arrived in the mail, her concern would grow stronger.

"Those damn silly mugs," she'd always say. "Those damn silly mugs." Unfortunately, Grey did little to help the situation. He loved the characters, (Once of course he got used to them staring at him all the time). On many of his visits, he would persuade Toby to tell him about a particular piece. This of course only fueled the fire by sparking the old man's interest. Jane would just sit back, roll her eyes and try to make the best of the situation. After a good attempt at exercising some patience, she would mumble some wise crack about the space, the time, or the money involved and Toby would snap back with some statistical reference to the size and holding capacity of her closet. Needless to say, the fun continued on from there.

All in all, it seemed like a fair trade. He had his mugs, and she had her closet. Together, they shared the dogs (her live-in version of children as it were and designed to help alleviate some of the 'empty nest' syndrome). They were good kind people and the time he spent there was certainly never boring. Grey couldn't help wondering what would happen when one of them got on the table. Oddly enough, on this particular afternoon, they both ended up being concerned about the same thing.

The argument was usually predictable, (With a little help from Grey that is). It was always the mugs. Grey had made a comment about the Henry the Eighth piece when he first came in. It apparently started some trouble. Go figure. By the time he was finished however, he was more impressed by what he learned, than by what he had seen. The mugs, as traumatic and antagonistic as they could be, were a major part of everything that Toby and Jane were. They helped to chronograph an enormous part of their lives. They had actively participated in helping to build over fifty years of marriage.

When Grey mentioned this to Jane however, she looked at him as though he had been smoking something. Being the 'mug man,' Toby at least was curious enough to inquire. Trapped somewhere between playing offense and defense, Grey was more than willing to offer an explanation.

"In all the years I've known you guys," he began, "these mugs have always managed to find away to waggle themselves into our conversations; be it through my developing interest or Toby's excitement or pride. Probably a little of both I would suspect. At first, I almost expected them to receive that kind of attention because of their dominate presence here in this room. However, as I watched and listened, I discovered that their very existence here was in fact a representation of something much greater. Jane, Toby is particularly fond of them for a variety of reasons, most of which I'm sure you find senseless. You on the other hand would have me believe that you allow them to reside here under an umbrella of simple tolerance. In either case, it's not my place to judge. I am however of the opinion, that you are both missing something here. A point in fact that is of much greater value than the financial investment involved."

There was a long pause and the room became silent. Toby mumbled something unintelligible from the face hole in the table. Jane just gave him a funny look. Grey wondered if maybe he had crossed the line.

"Should I bother to continue?" he asked.

Toby rolled over toward him which removed his face from the hole in the table and allowed him to speak.

"By all means," he said. "I'd love to see where you're going with this. That ok with you?" he asked motioning to Jane.

Jane just nodded her head and remained silent. Grey figured that he'd better be careful.

"All right," he said. "What the hell? Here goes! It's actually very simple if you think about it," he insisted. "Look at it this way. You both admit that you've been collecting these things for as long as you've been together, right?"

Toby and Jane nodded in response.

"Well every time I ask one of you about them, Grey continued, there is always this amazing story about how and where you bought it. Toby might start the story Jane, but by the time we get through it, you too have shared equally some of your fondest memories of the experience as well. Your travels in Europe, the Russian gold; the mug you found at Stratford on Avon. Maybe I'm crazy, but I see a definite pattern here."

Grey paused for a moment, and then chose to continue.

"Are either one of you following me on any of this?" he asked.

The Foxworths were too surprised to comment. Then suddenly, Jane began to smile. It was a big, glorious smile that reminded him of his own mother's face the day that Dylan was born. Jane had apparently seen things in a whole new light.

"Oh Grey," she exclaimed! "What an absolutely amazing observation. In a million years I never would have thought" Toby cut her off.

"The kid's right you know," he admitted as he got off the table. "It makes perfect sense. I can't imagine why neither one of us had thought of it before. There is a lot of history in this room. Not just about the great men and women here on the walls, but more importantly, us."

"Thanks, Grey," Toby added.

"No problem," Grey assured him. "I've been trying to figure this one out for a long time now, but there was always something missing. Maybe the accident knocked a few rocks loose, huh?"

Then Grey laughed. Toby and Jane laughed with him. The anxiety of the moment had passed. By the time he said goodbye, he was really feeling more like his old self again. And there was a new twist. He had used the gift to help someone and to be honest, it felt good. He didn't realize how tired he was until his butt hit the seat in the car. It was only four o'clock by his watch but it felt more like six or seven. To his surprise, there was still no word from Alex.

"Oh well, what the hell," he thought. "She'll show up sooner or later."

In the meantime, he'd stop by the church on the way home and try to 'catch up' with Richard. The good Father was probably still having trouble dealing with the whole thing anyway. Richard would never admit it, but Grey knew it would be a blessing if he swung by the church and gave the priest someone to talk to.

As he drove, he caught himself thinking. Was God enough for Richard to turn to now, or because of the circumstances, did his friend need someone more human? Only Richard could answer that. It was all Grey could think about as he made his way from Toby's to the church.

* * * * *

His 'lunch' meeting had gone well. Blake hadn't really lied to Holly about having one. He just didn't tell her that his date was with a computer at the Department of Motor Vehicles. An old client owed him a favor, and arranged for him to get access to one for a few minutes (no questions asked of course.) In a matter of seconds, he managed to run Holly's license plate and get her home address. Another connection had paid off.

Phase one was complete. Tonight, he could get down to business. He would go back to the office and work late making sure that he was seen going in by the right people. (Willie alone would make a great witness if his story was ever questioned.)Then he could slip away quietly and go stake out her condo. He had to learn her routine in order to find a weakness, one which would allow him to quietly make his move. He would perform like a well oiled machine.

To date, his record was untarnished. The execution of all of his previous escapades so far had been flawless. This one too would have to be perfect. He couldn't afford to get careless now. His heart raced like an avalanche out of control. Blake headed back to his car. It was time to get back to the safety of his office.

His hands were shaking slightly as he pulled out on to the highway. For the first time, since the beginning, time itself had become a factor. The 'Cat' inside him was growing impatient. Every hour that passed brought with it more anxiety and stress. He was tired and becoming more frustrated by the minute. Creating the perfect scenario with Holly was not going to be easy. The need was stronger now. Quite frankly, he wasn't sure how long he could wait. Blake lit a cigar and tried to calm himself down.

Control... If he did nothing else, he had to stay in control. The face in the rear view mirror was an ominous reminder of that. Not that he didn't like what he saw you understand, he just feared losing control of what was behind it. It was the only thing he feared more than not getting another fix.

As he made his way down the highway, he listened to the sound of the engine grinding away in the warm summer sun. Mile after mile of hot asphalt methodically disappeared beneath the comfort of his seat. In his mind, the ravenous V8 chattered like hundreds of sharp teeth gnawing into bone. It was an eerie carnivorous sound, an aria if you will, created by his subconscious as an inspirational form of motivation. The message was crystal clear. When the time came, the meal would be raw. Pure unbridled energy would once again flow through his veins. The 'Cat' was hungry. It was time to come out and play.

* * * * *

For Grey, the world was becoming a cold and distant place. The warmth of the summer sun beating down on him from above was nothing more than a temporary distraction. He could still feel a cold disturbance brewing in dark corners of his mind.

Over the past few days, he had seriously begun to wonder what was happening to him. Every one of his senses was now totally refined. Even simple things, (ones that he would have taken for granted just a week ago) were now whole new adventures in awareness. The sights, sounds, smells and tastes of everything around him were now overbearingly clear. His eyes had become binoculars by day and infra-red by night.

Even more amazing, was the fact that he could smell the food cooking at the In & Out Burger several miles ahead. All he'd had to do was think about it. It just came. And that was just the beginning. Grey looked at the car to his left. The woman driving was talking on the phone and he could hear the entire conversation as clearly as if she were sitting next to him.

His ability to focus on the situation was the key. With simple concentration, he could easily tune in to the things around him. So far, there seemed to be no limits. There was no way of telling where his capabilities might end.

As he got off the freeway, Grey shook his head and began laughing out loud.

Maybe he was becoming a side-show freak. If Richard thought they were having a good time before, wait until he got load of this. The Hail Mary's would be tossed around like confetti, especially if he decided to show the good Father exactly what he could do! If that happened, he was sure that by the time he was finished, Richard would probably have just cause to find his way back to the glass in his bottom drawer.

The parking lot at the church was empty except for a few cars which belonged to some of the "daycare center" parents. He noticed that there was an old blue truck parked way down at the far end by the chapel. The truck was a good sign. It meant that Richard was somewhere in the vicinity. As Grey got close to it, he shook his head again. "Pray for me on #17", a small sticker on the back window begged. The seventeenth hole at Riverview Golf Course was one of Richard's greatest adversaries.

For him, golf was both a blessing and a curse. While the game provided him with a well earned escape, it also taught him patience and humility. Unlike most people though, even on the worst of days, Richard maintained a sense of humor about it. After all, he had faith. You had to admire that. The man was for real. Grey parked next to him and then ventured inside.

There, in the front row of the chapel, a shadowy figure knelt quietly before God. Even from a distance, it was easy to recognize his friend. He took a seat in the last row of pews and waited patiently. Richard was whispering, but he could hear every word. After a few minutes, the priest finished his conversation with the All Mighty and addressed his new visitor.

"How are you my friend?" Richard said without turning around. His insight took Grey by surprise.

"How did you know it was me?" Grey inquired as he slowly walked up the aisle.

"You're not the only one around here who knows things," Richard answered. "But on a more serious note, if you must know, I could tell by the sound of your footsteps. You do have a rather heavy step."

When Richard turned to face him, Grey smiled.

"You don't miss much do you?" he said.

Richard was tired. Grey could see it the moment he got close. He looked like he hadn't slept in days.

"By the way, I'm glad that you came by to check up on me," he said.

"You been out partying all night or what?" Grey asked sarcastically. Richard rolled his eyes. "No, not hardly," he replied. "That's a taste I've long since outgrown. It's the sandman my friend. He and I aren't getting along so well lately. Last night, I had a dream about the Richfield funeral. It scared me half to death!"

Grey put his head down and turned away. There was no way that he couldn't help feeling responsible.

"Man I am so sorry that I brought you into this," he said. "You're supposed to be one of the good guys."

"It's not your fault," Richard assured him. "This started long before our little escapade the other day."

"Yeah, but us talking about it the way we did sure didn't help matters any," Grey responded.

"Eh... I'm a grown man," Richard countered. "I should be able to take care of myself. And speaking of that, why are you here? I know that it's not solely to check up on the emotional stability of some bewildered old man."

Grey laughed.

"All right, you got me," he said. "But after you telling me about your wonderful enchanted evening, I'm not so sure that I want to blow more sunshine up your collar."

Richard appeared unafraid of the possibility of being exposed to anything new. He was actually more interested now than ever before.

"I could use a good ray of sunshine right about now," he said. "It might give me something different to focus on for awhile (if you know what I mean)."

Grey nodded. "Well, all I can say is that whatever it is, it's getting better or worse by the minute; depending on your point of view, of course. I'll give you some examples."

Richard listened carefully as Grey explained about the hamburgers, the lady in the car and his praying in the front row.

"That's why I stayed and waited." Grey said. "I knew you were almost done."

Richard just shook his head. "I have to admit, it's a great little toy," he said. "But I can't help wondering what lies further down the road. I truly believe this is happening for a reason. I just can't imagine what it is."

Grey took a seat on the alter steps. "Well, I wish somebody had a clue," he said. "This is starting to get old fast."

"So what does Alex think?" Richard asked.

"I couldn't really tell you," Grey answered. "She's been missing in action since this morning."

"Is that a problem?" Richard inquired.

"No, not really," Grey replied. "It's pretty typical actually. She's the type that just does her own thing. I'm not worried though. I'm more curious about what she's doing if anything."

There was a brief silence as Grey caught himself staring up at one of the stained glass windows.

"You still care for her, don't you?" Richard asked quietly.

"Yeah, I guess so," Grey nodded. In his own way, he supposed he always would. "She's definitely one of a kind," he added.

"That she is," Richard agreed. "So where do we go from here?" he asked.

"I'm not sure," Grey admitted. "It seems to me that eventually, all of this might add up to something. I don't suppose you're willing to hang in there for awhile and enjoy the festivities?"

If Richard was amused, he certainly didn't show it. Grey wondered if maybe his lean toward sarcasm was taking things a bit too far. Truth of the matter was the priest looked worried.

"Sorry Father, you know how I am," Grey sulked. "Sometimes I just don't know what to believe. If God's trying to tell me something, I sure wish it would come in better focus."

"Maybe the perception of this from a different angle is coming from your end not his." Richard suggested.

The remark caught Grey off guard. If it had been anyone else, he would have found the comment offensive. Instead, because it was from Richard, he was more interested in getting an explanation. Grey got to his feet.

"So let me get this straight," Grey began, "I'm not paying enough attention? In case you've forgotten, this whole thing wasn't my idea in the first place! And as for my degree of perception, I'm not trying to point fingers, I was just hoping for a little help along the way."

Richard looked worried. Grey's sudden outburst made him think twice before he spoke again.

"You going to be all right?" he asked putting a hand on Grey's shoulder.

Grey sat back down on one of the alter steps and put his face in his hands. "Yeah, I suppose so" he answered. "It's just so damn frustrating sometimes. I know that I'm missing something and it's right here, inside my head. I can't seem to put it together."

Richard searched his heart looking for the right words. "Well I suppose then, he began, in time, everything will work itself out. It seems to me though, that you're the only one around here that's always been any good at puzzles. Maybe that's why whoever is running this show gave you the job."

Grey stood up. "Yeah, go figure that huh," he said. "But why me?" he joked.

"Well," Richard continued, "you do have this uncanny perception of people and things around you. Maybe that's why fate dragged you into this."

"Next time, I'm going kicking and screaming all the way," Grey chuckled.

Richard smiled then his face betrayed him. "Hopefully, there won't be a next time my son," he said. "Let's make this one for all the marbles."

Then he put his hand back on Grey's shoulder and began walking him to the door. Grey almost smiled. "Pray for me father?" he asked.

"You know I always do," Richard assured him.

"All right my friend," Grey responded. "I'll see you in a few days. Oh yeah, and if you don't mind, Grey winked, "I'll pray for you on #17."

Richard could do nothing except shake his head. "Don't you ever take anything seriously?" he inquired in a soft voice.

"Not unless you tell me I have to Father," Grey answered. "You will of course, let me know when the time comes," he insisted.

Richard rolled his eyes toward the heavens then looked back at Grey.

"I will at that," he promised. "Now get out of here. I have things to do," he said.

Grey bowed his head and headed for the door. At the last possible moment, he turned back to his friend.

"You ought to get out of here sometime today Father," he said. "It really is a beautiful day."

"Maybe you're right," Richard agreed and started to move toward him. "Maybe a little fresh air will do me some good."

When he got close enough, Grey put his hand on Richard's shoulder. "You know, you're all right," he told the priest as he patted him on the back. "Good thing I didn't have to seek counsel from the other side, huh?" Grey snickered.

Richard laughed. "Well lad, after some of our recent conversations, I wouldn't be too sure that you haven't."

The men laughed in unison as they headed outside. Once he was exposed to the fresh air, Richard smiled. Grey was right. It really was a glorious day. The warm sun pressed itself gently on his face. There was nothing above him but blue sky and billowy white clouds. It was as if God had laid out a beautiful map of heaven before him.

Grey wasn't so lucky. The colors had appeared right after he had first placed his hand on his friend.

* * * * *

When his voice mail picked up for the third time, Sheila thought she was going to scream. Truth was, if she could have gotten away with it, she damn well would have. The mayor's office had called twice in the past hour, and once again, she'd been forced to play stupid. The old "I'm sorry, but Mr. Kendall is unavailable at the moment," line was getting to be rather implausible. She was tired of having to cover his ass. Why wouldn't he answer the God damn phone?

To the rest of the civilized world, Blake Kendall might be one hell of a legal deity, but lately to her, he was just one big pain in the ass. God knows she'd been loyal. In the good old days, communication was never a problem. When she'd first came to work for him ten years ago, she could at least get him to answer his cell phone or return her calls with some moderate level of efficiency. For some reason though, over the past few months, he had become completely inaccessible once he left the office. While it wasn't her place to complain, she couldn't help feeling frustrated by the obvious lack of attention. It was very seldom that he'd left her hanging out to dry.

In the beginning, the job had almost been fun, playing organizational leader to one of the most successful lawyers in town. But lately, something about the way things worked around the office had changed. Things just felt different the past few months. A new strangeness lingered in the air that she couldn't help noticing. Sheila was at a loss. It wasn't even about his prolonged absences at inappropriate times. That was nothing new or unusual. She had long since gotten used to the sometimes bizarre hours they kept and Blake's tenacious approach to his work. It had simply come down to the fact that something didn't feel right every time he was in the room. An eerie chill came over her every time she was forced to make eye contact with him.

She wondered if he knew about Katie and Walter. If that was the case, at the very least it would explain a few things. She also wondered if he knew that she knew about the affair. She had suffered the misfortune of being in the wrong place at the wrong time (in a stall in the ladies the bathroom at last year's Christmas party). She had kept her silence over the past six months only to protect him from any further embarrassment. Now she was sorry that she had not gone to him with the truth. She had never meant to betray him. It had been twenty minutes since her last attempt to reach him. He was obviously avoiding her calls, but why? She decided to give him another ten before she'd begin trying to hunt him down.

* * * * *

Grey pulled into his driveway the same way that he always had for the past five years. For some odd reason though, today the garage door just seemed to reach out to grab him. For a second he became dizzy. His mind went blank and then began to erupt into an explosion of colors and lights. Suddenly all of his visions came back to him in the blink of an eye. Images of the people he'd touched since awakening from the coma flashed uncontrollably before his eyes. The pictures came to him now with astonishing clarity. Every sense and detail was amazingly clear. He could read the clock on the wall in his hospital room. Allow himself to once again be intoxicated by the smell of Lisa's perfume. He could feel the intense strength of Tony's grip. He could even hear the rain falling in the cemetery as Father Richard's words echoed through the heavy air.

But there was also something different: a repetitive flashback that he had neglected to take note of during the earlier episodes. It now reached out to him from the darkest corners of his mind. It was all about the hand, the hand with the blade. He knew now that it could not possibly belong to a stranger. It was one that he had seen before in the real world; one that existed outside of the cyclone that was trapped inside his head. The fingers were so familiar yet he couldn't seem to place them. His mind drifted in and out of consciousness. Grey thought he was going to blackout. A new strangeness lingered in the air.

All of a sudden, the blood must have rushed out of his head. He was lucky that his foot found the brake pedal when it did. He missed hitting the garage door by just a fraction of an inch.

It wasn't the near miss that bothered him it was his inability to shake the lack of concentration that had manifested itself within him over the past few days. The 'possession' or lack of control was so overwhelming, that at times 'simple reality' became a question. He almost panicked when his sanity returned and he saw the garage door going up. Only the smile on Dylan's face was convincing enough to save him.

Rachel had opened the door when she saw him pulling in. Grey immediately got out of the car and went over to greet his son. The look in Dylan's eyes was one of comfort and hope. Grey knew then, that for the moment he was safe.

"You ok?" Rachel asked after noticing the distracted look on his face.

"Yeah, I'm fine. Just another day at the office," he sarcastically assured her. It was easier to cut the conversation short than to explain the dizziness in the driveway.

"Any sign of Alex?" he asked.

"I haven't seen or heard from her all day," Rachel answered him. "Does she usually disappear like that?"

"It's been a long time," Grey tried to convince her, "but not that I remember anyway," he said. "I wouldn't worry though," he assured her, "Alex is more than capable of taking care of herself."

Rachel laughed. "Somehow that doesn't surprise me," she replied. "Your friends have always seemed to be a little on the strange side."

Grey smirked. "Do I detect a note of sarcasm or jealousy?" he inquired.

"I'm not sure," Rachel answered him. "Let's just say for now that it's probably a little of both."

Grey laughed, "Well, l get back to me if you ever figure it out ok!"

Rachel just shook her head. "C'mon you two, let's go inside," she said. "It's going to be a long afternoon."

Grey glanced back at the garage door and shook head. He couldn't help wondering what was going to happen next.

* * * * *

Blake blew past Sheila so quickly that she didn't even have a chance to stand up; much less get a word out. When she heard his door close behind him, she figured that she'd better give him a few minutes to get a handle on whatever was bugging him. The truth of the matter was, she was still reeling from having to run interference for him the past couple of hours so why risk adding any fuel to the fire. Yeah, she'd give him some time to collect himself and then venture in with his messages. He would surely take note of her body language and the rest could be left unsaid. She wanted a cigarette but that would have to wait. On the other side of the door, Blake was beginning to get his ducks in a row. Now more than ever he had to be on top of his game. He found comfort in this room. He could relax and think here. His office was truly his lair. He sat quietly for a moment and collected his thoughts. There, surrounded by the comfort and security of his big leather chair, he was starting to feel like he might just have a chance. And a chance was all he needed, another opportunity to seek his revenge. Blake got up and moved toward the bar in the far corner of the room. He poured a double and downed it quickly to steady his nerves. He looked in the mirror and found the face he expected. This time there was no fear, just a hunger that was vicious and undeniable. The 'Cat' purred.

* * * * *

CHAPTER 17

Now that he was finally home for the day, Rachel decided to put him to work. If they were going to continue to have a house guest, things were not going to get messy or out of hand. Not on her watch.

"No rest for wicked I guess," he joked as he headed for the kitchen. The pile of plates and glasses was no big deal. He rinsed and stacked everything in the dishwasher with ease. Even the crystal wine glasses from the previous night were not a problem. He was wiping down the counter in an attempt to finish things up when he caught a glimpse of something out of the corner of his eye. He turned and took notice of the coffee pot by the stove. The pot itself was empty but he realized that he had forgotten to rinse it out. Grey grabbed the pot and made quick work of it. As he was returning the pot to its place back on the machine, he remembered something else. When he decided to check

the filter basket, his curiosity ran wild.

Alex had made her 'tea' in this machine so whatever she had used to brew her concoction was probably still inside. Carefully, Grey opened the lid. Sure enough, the remains of Alex's last endeavor were still there. He took a good, long look and waited for something to 'click'. Surprisingly enough, he could immediately identify the contents even in their wet and almost moldy state. 'Alligator Teeth' and 'Devils Shoestring' filled the bottom of the filter basket.

In the wrong hands, these herbs if consumed together in the wrong dose could produce a lethal combination. He was little surprised to say the least but was sure that Alex would provide him with a perfectly reasonable explanation. He wasn't as worried as he was curious. After all, Alex had allowed Rachel to join them for a cup. He also remembered Alex cutting Rachel 'off' after her second round. Alex was obviously in control of the entire situation. This would also explain Rachel's strange behavior at the time. Alex's 'teas' were usually pretty serious stuff.

Engaging Rachel in the first place was probably not a good idea, but he figured Alex must have been up to something. She always had a plan. Did she create the situation with a particular goal in mind, or was she simply 'playing slightly to the crowd' for her own personal amusement? In either case, his opinion or position on the subject didn't seem to matter. He was merely allowed to be a spectator. He decided he'd better get rid of this stuff before Rachel discovered it. If she did, there would be too many questions.

Taking great care, he removed the basket from its holder and carefully dumped its contents down the sink. A quick flip of the 'disposal' switch and the evidence was gone. He rinsed out the basket and returned it to its proper place as well. Everything was back to normal. It was almost time for dinner and there was still no word from Alex. Grey wondered when she would make an appearance. He decided to go find Dylan.

"What the hell?" he muttered as he left the kitchen and headed down the hall. "Maybe he knows something." Truth was, maybe he did.

Sadly though, he would never make it to his son's bedroom. Rachel ambushed him on his way down the hall and insisted that he follow her back to the kitchen. His time with Dylan would have to wait.

* * * * *

Blake knew that today's little escapade with Sheila was going to cost him plenty. Occasionally, in the past, he'd pushed her too far. Today he shoved! When he brushed past her earlier, he could tell most assuredly by the look in her eyes that she was not happy about being left in the position that he put her in today. Yeah, he was the boss, but even he knew better that she of all people deserved to not be left hanging out to dry. She had saved his ass many times over the years and today was no exception. Even now, when he assumed that she was under a great deal of pressure, she had still managed to do her job of covering for him once again, all with what would have had to been astonishing precision.

But that was nearly two hours ago and she still had not tried to approach him, or for that matter, him approach her. Maybe if he just kept quiet, the anger and or awkwardness would go away.

There was a part of him that really liked Sheila. God knows how she found the strength to put up with him; especially when it seemed like no one else would. He did have quite an ego after all. He almost felt bad when he heard her yell, "Goodnight, Mr. Kendall" through the door as he cowardly snuck out the back of his office through his private exit. The door between them was thick, intended to maintain a certain level of privacy for his clients. She had either amazing ears or an acute sixth sense. Blake pondered the moment. She had let him off the hook for now but he wasn't sure if that was necessarily a good thing or not. Guess he'd find out in the morning.

He headed down the back stairs toward the parking lot and soon found safe refuge in his car. There was one more thing he needed to do before heading home. He reached into the breast pocket of his jacket and removed the print out he'd obtained earlier at the DMV. The GPS navigation system so thoughtfully provided by the folks at Mercedes would make quick work of the address. His future was now just a few short clicks away. A few buttons and a few flashes later, Blake was on the move.

* * * * *

Renee had gone home shortly after seven. After all, she had school in the morning and had to deal with dozens of rowdy kids. Dinner was pleasant enough and Tim was almost sorry to see her go. Still, he quickly dug out the "Ripper's" file as soon as he saw her Explorer leave the parking lot. The dishes in the sink would have to wait. This case was starting to get to him and he wasn't going to quit. Once again, he spread the photographs and their corresponding bio sheets out across the table in the galley.

The women all had similar characteristics. Each one had long dark hair and deep blue eyes. Their height and build were as they say 'close enough for who it's for'. They all shared a strikingly uncanny resemblance. Even to an untrained eye, some of the details would have been obvious. For Tim, a reaction was immediate. As his eyes scanned over the arrangement of pictures, he noticed that the faces seemed to reach out to him again. This time, one in particular caught his attention. The message he was getting from this one was not just a reminder of the apparent 'look alike factor', but actually suggested that her individual face was familiar. He 'knew her' it said.

"Think Tim, think," his inner voice commanded him! "You'll get there," it beckoned.

Tim looked hard into her picture again. He could not quite put a finger on it, but he was pretty confident that he had seen her somewhere before. Her face was hauntingly familiar. Maybe he'd seen her at the gym or the grocery store. Did she look like someone back at the station? Was the setting he was trying to place her in somewhere familiar? Had he been there before? Tim shook his head. He just couldn't seem to remember. He proceeded to read her bio sheet to see where her body was found in hopes that it might jog some of his memory.

This proved to be another dead end. He knew an answer would probably come to him though if he thought about it long enough. Frustrated, he decided to literally throw in the towel. (The dish towel flew silently across the galley and landed harmlessly on the pile of dinner debris in the sink.) He reached out and gathered the photos back into a pile making certain that the particular face with its new found message remained on top. For now, the beer was calling. With little hesitation, Tim answered.

The cold bottle met he lips again and he finished off the bottle with one big swallow. He stared at her for a few more minutes before closing the file again. It was getting late. He was going to need another beer.

* * * * *

As predicted, the GPS worked like a charm. All he had to do was listen to the woman's voice tell him where to go. Blake laughed. (It was much better than having to listen to Sheila tell him!) He was safe now. It was a relatively short ride up the 405 freeway to Holly's apartment in Huntington Beach. This was going to be a simple reconnaissance mission. All he intended to do was check out the neighborhood and get a feel for the area. Once he located the building, he did a drive-by and circled around the block. About a hundred feet from the entrance, he pulled over to the curb to do some mild surveillance. He put down his window, lit a cigar and waited.

After about fifteen minutes, he had visually gathered all of the information he needed. He now knew exactly where to find Holly when he needed her. It was a long drive back especially at this hour so he decided he wanted something to drink for the ride home. Anyway his mouth was dry from the cigar. To his good fortune, during his recon, he had spotted a convenience store across the street from the apartment complex. Blake got out of the car and headed in its direction.

The clerk was friendly enough but reluctant about the hundred dollar bill Blake handed him. Even the 'extra large' Dr. Pepper was still only a dollar eighty-nine. He grumbled about having to make change after Blake assured him that while he was sorry, in fact he had nothing smaller to offer. There was a quick "Thank you, sir" that surprisingly came from Blake when the lawyer took his drink and headed back to his car. Once he was safely tucked in behind the wheel, he took a long hard pull on his straw.

The syrupy based soda was not something he would normally ever consider drinking. He couldn't handle the sugary overkill of the flavor. Blake wondered why he had chosen it in the first place. When he took a good long look in the rear view mirror, his mind shifted gears. There was the Cat again. Now, that presented a whole new and different set of possibilities. He took another sip and this time, in a different state of mind, his taste buds exploded in ecstasy. Now the sugar acted more like an aphrodisiac. He shifted back, slid down a little in his seat and closed his eyes. A few more minutes wouldn't kill him. Then he took another sip.

He must have drifted off to another place because he missed the first knock on the window. The second round of contact only registered as a dull thumping sound in his ear. It wasn't until he could clearly make out the sound of knuckles wrapping on the glass for a third time that he turned his head and was startled out of a trance. There was now a woman standing next to him making a gesture with her hand indicating to him that she wanted him to roll down his window. Because of the uniform she was wearing, Blake immediately complied.

"Excuse me sir, but you're sitting in a loading zone," she informed him in a somewhat casual sort of tone. "Coincidently, you're also blocking the path of the street sweeper that's a couple of blocks behind you."

Blake rolled his eyes. "Oh great, parking enforcement," he thought, "A glorified meter maid." Fortunately he was smart enough to keep this comment to himself.

The young woman pulled out her ticket book and proceeded to ask him for his I.D. Blake reached for his wallet, and then for the glove compartment. He handed her his license and registration and was about to engage her when something unexpected happened.

Her poker face suddenly changed.

"Hey, don't I know you?" she said. "Aren't you that guy, that fancy hot shot lawyer guy from downtown? I saw you on the news the other night."

Blake saw the opening and pounced on it. Out came the Cheshire smile.

"Yeah, that's me," he chuckled while taking another 'hit' off his straw. "Smart enough I guess to do all of that but apparently too stupid to find a safe place to park!"

This admission instantly changed the atmosphere of the conversation.

The woman turned her head to her right focusing her attention now on the street sweeper that was steadily approaching but still a good three quarters of a block away.

"How fast can you move this thing?" she asked, as her hand patted the roof of his car.

Blake took a chance, reached for the dash console and pushed the ignition button. The engine started with a roar. During this entire exercise, his eyes never left hers. He sat for a moment waiting for her next instructions. He could hear the sweeper now closing the gap behind them.

"Would you mind pulling over into the parking lot across the street?" she asked (Ironically this is the same one he had just passed through when he returned with his drink). I'm not going to make you sign a ticket today, Mr. Kendall. I do however have one small request if you wouldn't mind indulging me." She gestured again, this time toward the parking lot.

Blake looked puzzled but nodded and pulled across the street. He missed meeting the sweeper by less than a couple of car lengths. As promised, for his compliance, he didn't get a ticket just another surprise. She offered him a clip board instead and asked him for his 'autograph'.

"Seriously" Blake inquired giving her a confused look?

She nodded and smiled. "My kid wants to be a lawyer someday," she responded. "He'll think this is so cool; that and that I met you of course. Beats getting a ticket, doesn't it?"

Blake smiled, accepted the clip board and asked for her son's name.

"Michael, Sir," she responded.

Blake reached into his shirt pocket and got out his favorite pen. This was going to be fun. Blake was suddenly 'Blake'. His ego had been caressed. The Cat would have to wait. In a matter of just a few seconds, he drafted a small note. He just couldn't resist. It was a formal and eloquent little draft that would surely impress and excite his young fan. It read....

> Dear Michael,
>
> Your mother tells me that you want to be a lawyer someday so I offer you this advice and support. Always be honest, always be fair, and always be tough. Knowledge

is power. Study hard. Always ask questions, and always be true to your heart

Good luck my friend,
Blake Kendall

He reviewed it twice to make sure it was what he wanted. "I think you will approve of this," he said as he handed the clipboard back to officer Rangel. "What do you think?" (He had noticed her name tag earlier but chose to not personally address her).

She scanned the page with great enthusiasm. It was the first time since their initial meeting that their eyes were not completely focused on each other. When she finished reading the note, she looked back up at him.

"This is amazing Mr. Kendall, I don't know how to thank you!" she exclaimed.

"No problem," Blake replied. "You just did, glancing down at the ticket book in her other hand as it made its way back into her pocket. If you're ever near the court house, bring your son by. Maybe, he could come in and watch me in action."

"I will," she said, (now happy as the day is long). "And thank you again."

Blake gave a quick wave as she turned and walked back to her patrol car. Another bullet dodged. He looked at his watch. All in all, the only damage the unfortunate mishap had caused was that he'd lost about fifteen minutes. His mission had still been successful. The fact that he had been recognized had done his self esteem some good. Even the extra time he took to write the note to the kid had made him even more appealing. She had 'known' the great Blake Kendall! He backed out the car and headed for the highway.

The sun would be going down soon so a drive home down Pacific Coast Highway seemed like just the right ticket. (Much better anyway than the one he just avoided). The drive down the coast would do him good. It would give him a chance to think.

"The great, Blake Kendall!" she said. Just repeating that to himself again bothered him a little. Then the gears turned a little more. Had he become that easily recognizable? If so, that could create a lot of problems. The 'Cat' would not be so 'incognito' anymore. Because of his recent appearance on television, he had become 'noticeable.' This changed everything! Killing Holly now was completely out of the question! He'd been seen with her on more than one occasion. The connection would be obvious: Blake meets Casey, Casey turns up dead: Coincidence? Blake knows Holly, Holly turns up dead; a little more suspicious. MacKensie wasn't that stupid. This scenario alone would bring the cavalry to his front door!

His mind raced, frantically searching for a way to justify his continued quest for Holly. All efforts were in vain. The 'Cat' fought hard, but Blake was strong enough to win out. Much to his chagrin, he would now have to divert his attention away from Holly and start from scratch.

From now on, there could be no mistakes. No miscalculations, definitely NO associations. Everything would have to remain random if he wanted to protect his secret. He spoke out loud as he drove, explaining and then repeating everything to 'himself' as he continued on down the road. His mind was made up. Holly would never know how close she came. He was going to need help. Dark: evil help. He hoped that the 'Cat' was listening.

* * * * *

Grey watched silently as the battle began. The darkness of night, now fully engaged in its descent from above, seeped slowly down from the heavens to devour what remained of the light of day. Armed with a glass of cabernet in his hand, the view from his patio gave him a front row seat for the performance. The length of each 'feast' was directly dependent on the immediate condition of the weather. Inevitably though, the day would always fall victim in the end and succumb to the powers that be as it had done so at every sunset since the beginning of time. This would always be the cycle.

Sometimes these meetings were nothing more than a small 'skirmish', highlighted by only a few subtle shades of faded blues and grays that floated helplessly in the sky after the sun had slipped below the horizon. But there were also times like this when the battle chose to rage on. The night appeared to 'bleed' as its deepening darkness melted into the colorful reflections of the day. Brilliant shades of color, reds, pinks, purples and blues tried their best to hold the night at bay but their fate had already been sealed. It was during these explosive episodes of color and light, that Grey was able to find an inner peace. Little did he know that across town, another set of eyes were watching.

Right now, the keys to Blake's kingdom were the keys to his shiny black car. Once again, he could step on the accelerator and hear the sound of carnivorous teeth grinding away. It fed him well. Without it, the moment in which he was now lost, would not have been possible. The combination of wind in his face and the magnificent sunset now displayed off to his right would not be his to enjoy. He gave himself a good mental pat on the back for remembering to put the top down before he left Officer Rangel in the parking lot. Her upgrade from 'meter maid' to officer had come after her 'recognition' of the finer things in life (his identity of course). It was with her reassurance of his stature that reaffirmed for him what he thought the 'Cat' was slowly stealing away.

As he drove on, the colors penetrated his soul. He could feel them giving him strength and a renewed level of energy he would need to start over. He felt better now than he had in days. Blake looked up in the rear view mirror. He liked what he saw. The hunt was on. There was no time like the present. Tonight, he would plan. Tomorrow he would find a new quarry.

They were miles apart, but the battle they had just witnessed had left a similar impression on each of them. It brought to the surface, a level of comfort to each of them that was desperately in need. Although neither man would ever be privy to what the other had 'seen', the relationship between them had already been set in motion. Yes, they knew each other fairly well, but this was something much more. It had manifested itself within them the last time Grey's hands were on Blake, and this was only the beginning.

In the aftermath, each man found solace in his own small way. Blake, in the roar of his engine and smoking the length of a good cigar; and Grey by simply enjoying his way down to the bottom of his glass and then pouring himself another.

But it wouldn't last. The struggle had gone dark for both men. Blake wondered about his next 'fix', and Grey wondered who's hand had just been laid gently on his shoulder. The world as they knew it was about to change.

* * * * *

It could only be hers. He didn't even flinch as she stepped out from the shadows and took a seat next to him in an empty chair. After a brief moment, their eyes met.

"Long day?" he asked while swirling the cabernet around in his glass.

Alex just nodded and smiled. She looked tired. Then her focus shifted to the glass in his hand.

"You wouldn't by any chance have another one of those lying around would you?" she inquired.

Grey motioned to the small table at the edge of the patio. On it were two more wine glasses and another bottle of cabernet. He got up and went to get her a glass. She continued.

"It's safe to assume that you were expecting company sooner or later," she observed. "Rachel perhaps, but I suspect that the third glass means you were also expecting me."

"Expecting you, no, anticipating your next move; yes." he smugly assured her. "I learned a long time ago never to underestimate you. Truth is, you'd be less than pleased with me if I did," he said. He handed her the glass he had just filled.

"Thanks," she said taking the glass from his outstretched hand. "Did I miss anything interesting?" she asked.

Grey turned to swirling his wine around in the glass again. "Well, the sunset was amazing!" he offered. "I'm sorry you missed it. Other than that I saw a few patients at the office today but that was pretty uneventful. Nothing I could see was out of the ordinary. There was a lot of personal stuff that was interesting but nothing like the side show at Blake's."

A long moment of silence fell between them. Grey could read the discouraged look on her face.

"Any luck placing the hand?" she asked. Grey was yawning now. It had been a long day.

"No, not really," he answered. "I can pull up the visual in my head, but I can't seem to keep things in focus long enough to finish the whole episode. I wish I had a way to keep things rolling."

"Well then, we'll just have to see what we can come up with won't we," she said placing her hand on his shoulder again.

"Oh really?" he inquired. "This should be good. What have you got up your sleeve this time; some kind of weed or root or something?"

Alex gave him a look. Her eyes looked right through him.

"Sorry, it's just the wine talking," he assured her.

"I know, my friend," she responded. "Sometimes I'm not sure what you actually remember. Anyway, you're not that far off. The American Indians are said to have used Peyote for thousands of years because they thought it brought them into or closer to the 'spirit world'. I happen to like Peyote myself but it's not my first choice for what we need to do. We need focus not hallucinations. Our 'talents' can wait. Right now, I'm more interested in you getting your hands on Blake again. He seems to be the key."

"That's what I was thinking," Grey agreed but I have to tell you that part of me is not looking forward to going through that haunted house again."

"The fact is, we both agree that the hand is the key then, right?" she concluded. "We identify the hand, we identify the killer."

The wine was good but Grey was beginning to miss his scotch. With one simple statement, Alex had brought it home; the missing piece of the puzzle. That brought on another moment of shared contemplation.

Then Grey broke the silence. "Call me crazy but I have a dumb question," he said. The weight of concern laid heavily on his voice. "What do we do if we figure this out?" he asked tipping his glass back to his lips until it was empty again. "And uh, how do we explain……?" That's where she held up a hand and cut him off.

"I guess we cross that bridge when we come to it," she replied. Her voice was calm and reassuring. "You're forgetting something important Grey. We may discover who the killer is because of you, but that doesn't mean that he'll know we have uncovered him. That would give us a tremendous advantage. As for us having to offer any explanations down the road, we can figure that out together as we go along. Nothing's fool proof but we make a pretty good team."

As usual, Alex was right. Grey got up and put his glass on the table. "If you don't mind, I'm going to go help Rachel put Dylan to bed,"

he said. "Save me a glass, I'll probably be back."

"All right," she replied tipping her glass in his direction. "Hey, why don't you persuade Rachel to join us when you're finished? That might be entertaining."

"I just might do that," he chuckled. Then he realized what he had just said. Grey shook his head. "Well, here we go again," he mumbled to himself as he made his way down the hall to Dylan's room.

Soon after Grey's departure, Alex finished her first glass of the deep red cabernet and started on her second. The night had completely taken over now and only a faint glow of light still lingered on the horizon. A light breeze came, carrying with it a soft whisper as it passed through the neighboring trees. Then, for a moment, the rancid scent of sweat and leather violated her nose. Alex looked up into the night sky but saw nothing. Still, she knew they were out there in the shadows, lying in wait until they were needed. They were always there. And they always would be.

Alex took another sip and smiled. Grey would be returning shortly. She found herself hoping that Rachel would be in tow.

* * * * *

The house was almost completely dark when Blake started to make his way up the driveway. The large angled structure stood quiet and eerie, a silhouette poised ominously in the foreground against the hills behind it. Only the remnants of a few distant street lights allowed it to be seen at all, only adding to its appearance of being 'dead on arrival'. In the deep darkness, the lagoon pool looked more like a castle moat than a luxurious place to swim. As the car approached the front entry way, the headlights ricocheted off random areas of the property which began activating the motion sensors and lights. With this simple engagement, the apparition before him slowly began to show signs of life.

Blake pulled around the pool to the north side of the house and parked the car in the garage on the lower level. He was sorry to have to extinguish the gnawing V8. When it stopped breathing, a cold silence descended upon him. All that remained was the slow 'heat tick' of cooling metal and an empty space where Katie's Porsche should have been. Blake turned and headed for the stairs.

He entered the house through an access door that connected to a small hallway between the laundry room and a downstairs bathroom. Having utilized this route many times before, he easily made his way through the dark and into the main living area.

At first, the only light that was available flowed in through some windows from the outside. Right now that was all he needed. The kitchen, dining room, and entertainment area were also all on the first floor. The west side of the house was composed almost entirely of large triple paned sheets of glass that allowed its inhabitants a complete panoramic view of the ocean below. The security lights took full advantage of this arrangement and did their best to provide adequate illumination.

As usual, the place was well kept so Blake ran little or no risk of moving about freely. As he approached the stairs which led to the upper floors, he thought he heard music. He hadn't noticed any signs of life when he pulled up, but Christine's room was one floor up and down at the south end of the house. Her room faced the ocean as well but the lights may have been off if she wasn't hanging out there. She was probably in Katie's little home gym riding her mother's exercise bike or something. Alone or not, it didn't really matter. He would know soon enough. Blake grabbed the banister and headed up the stairs.

From his vantage point at the top of the stairs, he could now see light around a door frame at the far end of the hall. It was, in fact coming from Katie's workout room. The door itself was not completely closed so it opened easily as he made contact with it with his hand. When he entered the room, his heart jumped.

There in the far corner of the room was 'Katie' on a treadmill? Her back was to him but that was of little or no consequence. He knew his wife, front or back. But wait a minute, no, he thought! It couldn't be Katie! Were his eyes playing tricks on him? He reminded himself that the Porsche was missing downstairs so it had to be Christine!

Blake was confused. He knew the difference between the two but apparently the 'Cat' didn't. It took him a few seconds to process this and the lawyer part of was him was then horrified when he discovered that his left hand was already in the pocket of his suit jacket firmly clutching his cold steel friend. The 'Cat' had subconsciously made the first move! Sickened by the just the thought of what might have happened next, Blake instantly let go of the weapon, turned around and made a quick move for the door. He'd only taken two steps when he heard a voice say:

"Hey Daddy, What's up?" Christine asked. Blake stopped dead in his tracks. He was speechless. He had no choice but to turn around.

"You ok?" she continued. "I didn't see you come in. You look tired."

"I'm fine," he assured her. "Why are all the lights off in the rest of the house?" he asked.

"I'm sorry Daddy. I've been in here working out for the past two hours. I didn't feel like driving to the gym. I called mom and she said she didn't mind if I used her stuff. The sun must have gone down while I was running and I didn't notice. I guess I lost track of time."

Blake gave her a sympathetic look. After all, this was his baby. "I didn't mean to scare you," she teased him.

"I just don't like the thought of you alone in a dark house," he confessed. "It makes you an easy target. There are a lot of bad people running around these days (and I would know from hands on experience, he thought). I just want you to remember to be careful."

She was hot and sweaty but still put her arms around him, and gave him a big hug.

"I will Daddy, I promise," she said. "I'm going to take a shower and then watch a movie. See you down stairs?"

"I'm headed for the showers myself," he informed her. "I'll think about the movie and let you know."

Blake grinned. His last remark was definitely his. Acknowledging this simple fact made him feel better. He was beginning to get some control back. The key to controlling the behavior lie solely in his ability to suppress the 'Cat.' The deeper he chose to bury his alter-ego the easier it was to be 'dad' again. This was his territory, and he would protect it as such. The 'Cat' had no authority here. He would only be allowed to exist in the outside world. Blake took a deep breath and realized that tonight was just a warning, an ominous reminder of how easy it was to take one step over the line. He had to remain vigilant.

Blake followed Christine out into the hall where they parted company. Then he headed upstairs to the third floor where he and Katie had established their personal, private retreat. When the French doors swung open, he felt an immediate sigh of relief. He moved effortlessly through the sitting room and into the master suite.

Once again, the view was breathtaking. All but a few feet of the one hundred and twenty foot ocean side exterior wall was composed of the triple paned glass. When they had remodeled the house before moving in, they had spared no expense. They had wanted the ultimate view of the ocean and that's exactly what they got. He had even installed remote control blinds to help manage the sunlight in the later part of the day. Properly used, they also helped to maintain an intimate level of privacy. They were open now, so all that was on display was a glorious view of endless miles of ocean. Blake started to throw his jacket over his dressing chair when he suddenly remembered that his 'friend' was still in the left pocket.

When his searching hand made contact with the instrument, a momentary flashback to the gym made him uneasy. It wasn't that he didn't like the 'Cat', on the contrary it was an active symbol of his ultimate power. But it was his power and his alone to control. He strongly objected to any outside interference. He would never allow his inner demon to assume a superior position of authority. Blake took the razor and tucked it safely away in his vanity drawer. It was as good a place as any. When he glanced up in mirror, he looked haggard but his eyes were clear. Christine was right. The shower beckoned.

The steaming water did its best to wash away the trials and tribulations of the day. What normally would have ended with a pair of black silk pajamas, turned into a more impoverished get up of 'holy' sweat pants and an oversized T-shirt. The shirt advertised a company called Bad Ass Coffee, with lots of little donkeys on the back doing 'ass' related things. Christine had thought it was pretty funny when she brought it back for him from Hawaii last year. He had smiled at the time to amuse her, but secretly rolled his eyes behind her back.

Right now though, he kind of liked it. It brought a temporary sense of humor to his always serious world. Maybe he would go downstairs and spend some time with his daughter. He knew it would be quite a shock to Katie if she walked in and found the two of them sitting in the dark watching a movie together. His present attire would only add to her confusion. It would be fun to mess with her head for a change. He reminded himself to check her clothes for the smell of Walter's cigars. She told Christine she was out shopping but he suspected otherwise. Anyway, the decision was already made. Blake walked over to the wet bar, poured himself a double and headed for the stairs.

* * * * *

The bottle was almost empty when she saw them coming down the hall through the front window. The wine was helping to mellow her out, but there were still a few mental bases to be covered. Alex laughed when she saw both Grey and Rachel step out the front door. Grey had a bottle of cabernet in each hand and a small towel was tucked into his back pocket. Rachel was carrying a bottle of something as well. After the other night, it was fair to assume it was chardonnay. When the two women saw each other, they spoke at the same time. Alex stood to greet Rachel (it was polite after all) and they exchanged a brief hug.

"How are you?" Rachel asked as she set her bottle down on the table.

Grey had already set both of his down and was in the process of opening one. When he was finished, he reach for Rachel's and opened it too. Then he reached for the towel, threw it over his arm and addressed the gathering.

"Might I pour the wine?' he inquired with a stuffy British accent. His behavior caught Rachel off guard. She was speechless.

"By all means," Alex teased him by responding with her version of an 'upper crust' impersonation. "But please, make sure you serve the lady first," she ordered gesturing toward Rachel.

Grey poured a glass of chardonnay and handed it to his wife. "This should do well I think," he snickered with the same accent.

Rachel just shook her head. "Seriously, you guys?" she asked.

Grey smiled and took a seat. Alex sat quietly and tried to contain her laughter. "Wine is a good thing," Grey offered, this time in his own voice. "What do you think honey?"

Rachel looked up and said "Well, I guess I have some catching up to do then, don't I?"

Alex immediately offered a toast. "To catching up then," she said as all three glasses met with a clink. "To catching up," they all spoke in unison.

As the wine went down, Rachel suddenly got a strange look on her face. "You guys smell that?" she asked.

"Smell what?" Grey replied. He actually did smell something. He had recognized the odor when they first came out of the house.

"Smells like a wet dog or something," Rachel answered. "Boy that's nasty," she continued, but as soon as she got the words out, the aroma faded away. She sat for a minute trying to focus on the scent again but it was gone. It was as if it had just flown away (in reality it just had). Confused but content, Rachel turned her attention back to her wine.

Grey looked up at the night sky hoping to catch a glimpse of his guardian. Above him, all that was visible were stars. Alex noticed he was distracted but remained silent. She knew what he was looking for but couldn't comment in front of Rachel. They both just had to let the moment pass.

Over the next few hours, the wine and the conversation flowed with equal enthusiasm. Everything remained low key, non-evasive and even humorous at times, but by the end of the last bottle, Grey was ready to pack it in.

"I think I'm going to call it a night," he said as he rose cautiously from his chair. "It's been a long day." Neither of his companions objected.

"Good night, Alex" he said making sure that they made eye contact. Then he turned to Rachel. "I'll see you inside?" he inquired. Rachel smiled. "I'm right behind you," she assured him.

Grey said good night again to both of them and then headed inside. Alex and Rachel were suddenly alone. For the next few minutes, neither of them said a word. Then somehow the awkwardness of the moment passed. Rachel stood up and turned to face Alex.

"Well that's enough for me too I guess. Sleep well, I'll see you in the morning," she said as she tried gracefully to acknowledge her nemesis.

Alex smiled. "You too," she responded sincerely. "And thanks again for everything."

Rachel made a move toward the door but paused right before going inside. She turned back and looked at Alex.

"I'm not stupid you know," Rachel said. "He's obviously not back to being his old self again and he doesn't want me to know," she said quietly almost under her breath. "I know you see it too, the difference I mean." Alex just nodded.

Rachel bowed her head, emotionally defeated. "Would you do me a favor then?" she begged. "Help him, protect him, do whatever it takes to get things back to normal again ok. I don't know why, but I think I can trust you." She was serious now. Alex could see it in her eyes. The fear and uncertainty showed on her face.

Alex was so surprised by Rachel's sudden plea for help she knew she had to say something. "For what it's worth, I promise I'll do whatever I can," she assured her. "I think he's already on his way to figuring things out, but I understand where you're coming from.

"After hearing this, Rachel showed signs of relief. "Thanks," she said. "I'll see you in the morning then."

Alex waved as Rachel turned and disappeared into the house. Alex couldn't help thinking that was a pretty impressive attempt on Rachel's part to get her and Alex on the same team. She would have to remember that in the future.

Now alone on the patio, Alex quickly found the bottom of her glass as well. Tomorrow was another day. Hopefully Grey would get some sleep and they could start fresh in the morning. The evening had been a pleasant distraction but they had to get back to business.

Alex got up and made her way inside. When the time came for her head to hit her pillow, she knew Grey was already asleep. Tonight he would dream. Her ring was warm.

"Oh, to be a fly on the wall for that one," she whispered. They were close now. So very close. Who knows where the journey might take them.

* * * * *

CHAPTER 18

The darkness swallowed him whole. Grey was helpless and could do nothing to control his fall as he descended deeper and deeper into the bowels of the abyss. As he traveled down, he could see faint glimmers of light floating in the air around him. Then, transparent images of people, places and events materialized before his eyes. Each manifested itself only long enough to make its existence known and then mysteriously evaporated back into the vortex around him. Each face was grotesquely mutilated from rot and decay. Some bloated flesh bubbled out of control. They all shared one common visible denominator, a gaping wound across the throat that stretched from ear to ear. His mind searched for answers in their muffled screams. The longer he listened, the more he understood. The meaning behind the presence of these desperate apparitions became clear. When he felt something cold and wet surround him, Grey screamed.

He immediately woke up or at least that's what he thought at first. It took only took a few seconds for him to realize that wasn't the case. He could hear the sound of the pounding surf behind him and feel water rushing past him toward the shore. As he tried to stand, a sudden surge of the tide knocked him back down on his knees. Grey fought through the current to get his bearings. He was now standing in knee deep water about ten yards off shore and staring at the beach in front of him. A Harvest moon bled in the sky, illuminating the sand and blending together the rock formations and cliffs behind it to the north. A tree line ran south along the shoreline about a hundred feet up from the high tide marks. The roar behind him was getting louder so Grey knew his first priority was to get himself out of the water. He focused his eyes on the top of the sandy slope in front of him and dragged himself up to safety.

Once he was on top of the embankment, he fell to his knees again to rest. While he spent a minute to catch his breath, he took inventory of what lay in front of him and then turned his attention back to the water. The sea was a dark shade of emerald green and a little unruly. The roar of the waves had increased in volume in just the past few minutes. The tide was coming in now and out there, just a short distance away, he could see the white caps of the waves churning away. He quickly glanced at the incoming tide level to gage it against the high tide line. The water was coming in fast.

Grey concluded that he would be safe as long as he stayed comfortably above the high water line. The most important thing now was to figure out where he was. Maybe then he could establish why he was here. His first objective was to find some higher ground. From there, he would be able to better assess his situation. A football field or two to his left, he saw a place where the rocks were in close proximity to the beach. If he could find a way to climb up them somehow, he could probably see for miles.

The clothes he had on were wet and cold so he had to get off the beach and out of the open. The walk to the rocks would warm him up a little and probably do him some good. It did strike him as being a little odd that he wasn't wearing any shoes. The shirt and pants he had on did belong to him, but he couldn't recall having worn them for many years. He was surprised they even fit. The last time he'd seen them, he was in his early twenties. If this was a dream, the wardrobe department for this one had really dropped the ball. Whatever the case, Grey knew he had to get moving.

* * * * *

The movie turned out to be good. Either that or the bottle of eighteen year old Scotch he was working on was playing well to his sensibilities. Spending time with Christine wasn't bad either. While they didn't speak much, their simultaneous laughter or ooh's and aah's at the appropriate times were almost conversational. Blake caught her on several occasions glancing over at him looking for his reaction. She seemed pleased to see him laugh or smile and he, her. However the big thrill for both of them came when Katie arrived home and entered the still dark house.

They had left the lights off intentionally to give the television room a more theatre-like atmosphere. When Katie came in through the 'garage' door there was very little light to guide her. She stopped dead in her tracks when she discovered the two of them, sitting together on one of the cozy leather couches. Christine appeared to be comfortable, relaxed in her pajamas and a blanket. It was the combination of both Blake's presence, and his attire, that almost sent her over the edge. His bare feet up on the coffee table were the final straw.

Anger wasn't the issue. Shock, surprise, confusion were a much more appropriate description. Katie was speechless. She couldn't help thinking "*What was the real message here?*" She made her way around the edge of the large sofa and stood between them and the television. With her thin physique, she didn't end up blocking much of their view. Blake reached over and grabbed the remote. A quick click on pause and she now had their undivided attention. She looked at them both again as if she were sizing them up. Then she spoke.

"What's up with the two of you?" she asked. She shifted nervously back and forth on her heels. The two of them hanging out together was more than she could fathom. "I'm not sure what to make of all this," she continued. "Is something wrong? Did something happen that you need to tell me?"

Christine looked up at her mother, "It's just a movie Mom, seriously?"

Blake nodded and swallowed a big gulp of Scotch. Then he stood up and approached his wife.

"How was your day, dear?" he inquired. "I like the skirt and heels."

Katie wasn't sure what rattled her more, his attitude or his clothes. She couldn't take her eyes of the "BAD ASS" donkey logo on his shirt. In her high heels, it was right at her eye level.

"Actually I had very nice day," she replied. "Thanks for asking. So I see you've decided to go for a different look," she observed. "It's interesting to say the least."

To Blake's surprise, Christine jumped in and defended him.

"Come on Mom, when was the last time you saw us hanging out like this? What was I, five? Dad's just trying to be a little more 'kick back' than usual. Give him a break!"

"Wow," Katie thought. Christine going to bat for her father, now she had seen everything! Things had been unraveling around there for a long time but this was quite an adjustment in the opposite direction. She honestly didn't know what to make of it. She turned to Blake and said, "Well, don't let me spoil your fun then, you two. You'll forgive me if I go upstairs and into something more comfortable myself. "Her eyes shifted down toward the assortment of shopping bags in her hand. She winked at Blake as she said it, but a part of him was confused about how to handle that kind of behavior. Yeah, she didn't smell like Walter's cigars but what message did that really convey anyway?

"I'll be up when it's over," he offered, trying to be positive.

"See you then," she replied.

Their hands brushed one another as he moved past her and found a seat back on the couch. It felt awkward, but ok. When they were alone again, he said to Christine "Dodged that bullet, didn't we?" Christine just pulled up her blanket.

"Oh Daddy, give it a rest," she giggled. "We got off easy. You know this is going to mess with her head for awhile. Just try to be nice, ok?"

Blake knew that the tension between him and Katie over the past year had been obvious to Christine. She had put up with a lot. Although they had never engaged in a conversation on the subject, Blake knew she wasn't stupid. She had already formulated some kind of opinion. He didn't think she knew about Walter though. That chapter was still a secret. Any kind of hint at discovery would have certainly been discussed and would have probably caused irreparable damage. For now, he was just going to enjoy the rest of the movie. He picked up the remote again and turned to his daughter.

"Ready honey?" he asked. Christine nodded and Blake's finger pressed the go button. It would be another hour before he made it upstairs.

* * * * *

The rocks were closer to the water than he originally estimated. By the time he reached them, the surf was beginning to claw at their base. He had to go back in the water to get up the first few feet. His initial impression was that it would be a fairly easy climb. There appeared to be levels that had been carved out by years of wind and rain. His assessment was correct. It was not very steep and there were large areas for foot holes. Even without shoes, he made quick work of the first few sections. He was now about thirty feet above the beach. The view from even such a small change in elevation gave him a completely different perspective of his present predicament. He realized that he would have to go higher if he wanted to see what was beyond the trees. The sea was no longer a threat as long as he kept his footing and didn't slip. He rested for a few minutes on a small step and then continued his assent up the formation.

As his eyes became level with the expanse of the next section, he could see that this area was like a large shelf that had been sliced out of the hillside. Here, there was plenty of room to move around. He made his way over to the opposite end and looked over the edge.

In the shadows, he could see a narrow trail that slithered its way back down the hill to the ground below. He could make out that it ended at what looked like a small clearing in the trees. There appeared to be something down there, a group of small objects that were arranged in some kind of row or pattern. Fortunately, the end of the path was a good hundred yards inland. It was safe there and would never be subjected to the tide. That was huge because he was going to have to make his way down there in order to find out exactly what he was dealing with.

He carefully followed the outline backwards with his eyes until he could locate the entrance. It turned out to be only a few yards away. He moved across the ledge and found the opening to the trail in a chasm between two large rocks. It was well hidden. He would in fact have missed it had he not visually 'back tracked' its direction first. Grey leaned up against one of the enormous slabs of rock to catch his breath and contemplate his next move. He turned his attention once again to the ocean, trying to get a 'feel' for the situation. Somehow, it wasn't reassuring. For just a split second, there was an eerie silence. Then the silence grew. He turned his attention back to the clearing in the trees.

"Oh, well, what the hell?" he mumbled to himself. His feet started moving and he found himself headed off down the trail.

* * * * *

Blake got a hug. It was a totally unexpected finish to a pleasant evening spent with his daughter. At first, he didn't know whether to be happy or frightened. It was so outside the box, his mind could not have even suspected it, yet, there it was, a big warm 'teddy bear' hug. He would not have seen it coming, even if it had been standing right in front of him. (Actually it was). He had just gotten to his feet and suddenly she was there. Her small arms simply wrapped around him and then there was a big squeeze.

"Thanks Daddy," she said. All he saw was the big smile that went with it. It reminded him of a better time; a time when things were simple and easy. It was good to know that after everything that had happened in the past year, she was still his little girl. Blake couldn't resist the temptation. He hugged her back. The 'Blake' part of him liked that. The 'Cat' was very confused. Still locked down deep in his inner cage, it struggled to make sense of the entire exchange. But it was useless. Blake won out in the end.

"That was fun," he conceded, conveying another strong admission that convinced him that he was in control. "Maybe next time we can get your mom involved," he proclaimed continuing his pursuit of total dominance. He could start to feel a pounding in his chest.

"That would be cool," she answered. "Good night, Daddy, see you in the morning."

Blake watched as she moved across the room and disappeared into the darkness.

At this point, the 'Cat' was helpless, but Blake liked it that way. Nobody controlled him, nobody. Tonight it was only about him, his family and his choices. If he survived, tomorrow would be a new day. He knew that the cage would not stay locked forever. Tonight had been a 'one time only' exception to the rule. He fought hard for it and won, but he knew the 'Cat' grew stronger every day. It was only a matter of time. Blake worried that someday, very soon, the cage that helped protect what was left of him might not exist at all. For now, he would just enjoy the moment. Christine was happy, Katie was happy, and might even be upstairs waiting for him. Unbelievable! Now there was a whole new set of problems; Katie and sex.

"And how does one put the thought of Walter and Katie playing jockey and horse out of one's mind?" he considered. He wondered if even his feline friend could do that.

His fantasy was killing her, not sleeping with her. There was no love anymore, just the underlying betrayal. Making love was out of the question, but raw, unbridled animalistic sex, now there were some possibilities. The big question now flashed in bold neon lights! Could he fuck her but NOT kill her? Would he or the 'Cat' allow that to happen? And just think, he had to consider all this and devise a plan of attack, all before he got to the top of the stairs!

If Katie were asleep, the answer was easy; no problem. But if she were waiting for his arrival, he would have to think fast. He knew he could control 'Blake' but in the heat of the moment, probably not the 'Cat'. His mind raced.

"Lock the razor in the bedroom safe," his mind told him. "If the 'Cat' makes an appearance, he won't have access to it, only you. Then it will just be you and Katie alone. That way, you're assured that the only thing out of control will be the two of you. She's probably going to be surprised either way."

Blake paused as he reached the top of the stairs. The anticipation was killing him. He could see a sliver of light coming from under the bedroom doors down the hall. It wasn't too bright but it meant Katie was probably still awake. If she were, he wondered what she was up to. More importantly though, he had already considered all of the possibilities of what his next move was going to be. Blake reached for the knobs and opened the French doors. He told himself he was ready for anything. He wasn't.

The lights were on but the room was empty. The sheets were folded back on the bed but Katie was nowhere to be found. This was both a blessing and a curse. Good because it allowed him to go into the vanity area and recover his straight razor. He immediately put it in the safe that resided behind the Troy Carney painting (an original mind you) that Katie had purchased in Hawaii on the same trip as Christine's now popular 'coffee' T shirt. While Katie's taste was much more expensive, he really liked the painting. So much in fact, that he had encouraged her to purchase two more of Carney's pieces after she got back. They added a relaxing charm to other walls in the bedroom. Now that the 'safety issue' was under control, Blake returned to his search for Katie.

* * * * *

After a few steps, Grey paused at the top of the ridge and considered the possibility of there being another way down. The path was fairly narrow and unlike the climb on the way up, the back side of the formation was covered in deep foliage. His first thought was a pair of shoes would have been nice. A flashlight would have even been better. The moon was a big help with open navigation but it didn't give him a great deal of assistance in the tight shadowy details of the trail. His decent down the hill was going to take much longer than he'd planned.

The harvest moon shone red in the dark night sky. It was a celestial symbol signifying the end of the 'growing season' and the 'harvesting' of the crops in the fields. Many a farmer has looked out over a field; be it large or small and seen the carefully plowed rows of his labor laid out before him. Each mound of soil is designed to feed and protect the seeds of life within it. The trenches on each side allow the flow of water to reach out and feed the growth designed by nature. It was a pretty efficient arrangement.

As he approached the clearing, it appeared at first that someone had decided to plant some kind of garden. The earthen mounds were meticulously arranged in a row facing north/south and appeared to have been recently excavated. Grey could only wonder what someone had planted beneath. The first five had some kind of identifying markers already in place but they were impossible to read at a distance in the limited light. The next few, oddly enough, seemed to be just large holes in the ground. It was the size of the holes that worried him. Grey knew he had to move closer and investigate.

The closer he got to the center of the ring, the more the anxiety and fear set in. Then he could smell a faint hint of wet leather in the air. He knew he was not alone. Grey made his way over to the first mound. This was not a garden from which seeds were meant to grow. This was a graveyard for the unfortunate and tortured dead. He thought he was going to keel over when the first headstone came into focus. The name on the headstone simply identified the owner as Kelly Richfield. Father Richard would have lost his mind. Grey forced himself to take a step back. This did little to change his perspective or his comfort level. It was then he realized the magnitude of the situation. Kelly wasn't alone.

If she wasn't the only one here, then who was buried next to her? Grey turned his head and looked over at the other four headstones that were lined up to his right. He had to know.

According to the next marker, Jessica Davis had also been laid to rest there. Unfortunately for Grey, the name meant nothing to him. He had to keep moving. The names on the third and fourth headstones were strangers too. Shelley Hendricks and Tiffany Freemont both lay quietly at his feet. They were gone, but he hoped they were not forgotten. When he got to the last stone, it was the final inscription that set the wheels in motion and brought everything home. The name was Casey Riddell.

Grey had read about her in the paper, the body, the murder, the ongoing case. Hell, he'd even talked to Tim about it! Now everything was starting to make some sense. He remembered the police believed that both Kelly and Casey were victims of the individual they called the "Ripper". He could only surmise that these other three girls were all victims as well. That would explain their presence here together. It also made him wonder if the cops knew about these other three casualties. Kelly and Casey's families were lucky. At least their bodies had been recovered. They had buried their daughters and this had allowed them to establish some kind of closure. The other families might not even know where their children were, worst of all that they were dead.

Grey promised himself that he would make sure he remembered their names. When the time came, he could have Tim check them out and see if they were on anybody's missing persons list. The danger was obviously much worse than anyone suspected. Now all he wanted to do was wake up. Instead, he just stood for a minute staring at the dark holes.

He figured this 'dream' was part of some elaborate representation to help him understand what was going on so he could bring all of this information together. This entire episode explained a lot. But there was still something evil going on here. There were still two freshly dug 'graves' to be concerned about. He would swear that the ground from them was still warm. There was something about the dark empty spaces that bothered him. He was about to discover why

* * * * *

Blake found Katie on the far end of the balcony staring out at the ocean. A soft, black, satin robe was all she was wearing other than a smile. She completed the ensemble by having a fully loaded crystal champagne flute in her hand. Blake could feel the danger beginning to creep forward. In his mind, just for a moment, it reminded him of his adventure with Casey. The cage door began to rattle, but he quickly got it under control. Quietly he moved in and came up behind her.

"I wasn't sure if you were still interested Counselor," she said in a soft, low voice. "You've been very distracted lately." (She thought he might have been seeing other women. He had, but she never could have imagined the 'real' end game.)

Blake stood next to her at the railing, trying to decide what to do next. Katie just giggled and consumed more champagne. *"Yes,"* he thought, *"I have been distracted Katie. But then again, so have you."*

"You see," she began. "I have been a very, very, very bad girl, Mr. Kendall," she continued while running her tongue around, over and in the mouth of her glass. She then took the top half of the entire glass slowly into her mouth and swallowed the remaining contents in one gulp. She deliberately left the whole top of the glass in her mouth for much longer than necessary, just for the effect. Then after a brief moment, she set the glass on the edge of the railing and slowly bowed her head. When she looked back up, their eyes met.

"I think I might need a good lawyer," she said with a serious but giggled tone. "Know anybody?"

Blake knew at that moment, he had to open the cage door. He was not stupid enough to give the 'Cat' more than a short chain, but nevertheless he had to make him available. He knew that he would be all but impotent without him. He'd never be able to get the idea of Walter out of his head. On the other hand, his dark malevolent friend wouldn't care. The predator always thought with its little head instead of its big one. Blake concluded that with his drive, and the 'Cat's' insatiable insanity, together they were the perfect combination. When Katie motioned for him to follow her in back into the bedroom, Blake eagerly obeyed.

What started as a simple taste soon became a ravenous sexual feast for both of them. For the most part, it was like two wolves fighting over a piece of meat. Battled and bruised, they went on for hours, neither of them willing to admit or concede defeat. Bottle after bottle of champagne disappeared down their throats in hopes of replenishing the massive loss of fluids. The alcohol burned off as fast as it was taken in and only the chilled bottles of Evian managed to keep them replenished. They finally passed out in the arms of exhaustion around three o'clock in the morning. Both Kendall's slept like the dead.

* * * * *

And the rains came. Grey had been so busy focusing his attention on the insane condition of his current environment, that the change in the weather had completely escaped him. He was aware of a delicate mist that had been forming since his arrival, but that humidity had already changed into a light but steady rain. To the southeast, the Harvest moon still hung low in the sky. To the northwest, the wind was picking up and he could see the 'real' storm clouds moving in. It would only be a matter of time before they were overhead.

His first thought went out to his wet leathery friend who was out there watching from the shadows. The creature had guided him safely through everything so far and had obviously been monitoring the situation from the very beginning. Because of its presence, Grey had allowed himself a much greater comfort zone. Now, with the conditions around him changing rapidly, all he wanted to do was 'wake up' before the weather moved in; but his curiosity about the two remaining 'graves' was still unsatisfied. He was glad they were empty, or at least they appeared to be. Ever so carefully, he inched his way over to the nearest one, hoping that he could get close enough to peek over the edge and get a look at what was inside. The ground was getting softer as the rainfall began to saturate it deeper. As he moved forward, he could feel the mud squishing between his toes.

His idea quickly died when it became clear that, with the dark clouds moving in, his light was even more limited. He was losing his ability to make out even the outline of the deep hole. In a matter of minutes, he would be standing in total darkness. With each small step, his feet continued to sink deeper into the muck. Grey shivered now as he approached the pit. The rain poured down on him from the heavens, and without warning, a lightning bolt sizzled down from the sky. A tree behind him exploded into flames. There was a large burst of energy and suddenly he got bumped from behind.

He immediately felt himself falling again into an abyss. From what he could see, he was back in the original vortex from which he had first come. There were no faces on the walls this time, lost in the swirling wind. Instead they had been replaced by a white apparition of a hand and a knife. Grey realized in an instant that it was the same scene from Blake's delusions. It was then he began to hear the sound of muffled voices calling out to him again. They all repeated just a single word over and over again; "Blaaaaame! Blaaaaame"! Then everything went black.

Grey woke up. He knew that he was really awake because something felt different. There was nothing but silence. For a moment, he was afraid to open his eyes. He reached out and felt something cold next to him. He shuddered to think he had fallen into one of the graves. He drew his hand back and then decided to try again. This time, he opened his eyes. When he did, he felt a light breeze in his face and saw what he thought was a group of big brown wings spinning over his head. He blinked his eyes a few times to readjust his focus and took a deep breath. Now the 'beast' above him was just a ceiling fan. He was awake all right and safely back in his own bed.

The cold body next to him was Rachel's, but she was alive and well lying in the bed next to him. She had kicked off the blankets during the night and the fan had cooled her bare skin down a little. Grey looked over at the clock. It was five-fifteen in the morning. He had maybe an hour before Alex would be up so he had time to get his ducks in a row. Boy was she in for an earful! He thought about waking her but decided against it. Right now it was more important for him to try to remember everything that had just happened. He considered writing it all down but for the first time since the accident, his memories were intact. All of the details of this dream were still very clear. It would be easy to discuss them at length.

What he was most concerned about now was the relationship between the escapades in Blake's mind and the combination of the hand and knife. Blake's mind had traveled down the same road involving the weapon on several occasions. Could it be possible that one of his clients was responsible for all of the killings? If so, was Blake privy to that information but forced to remain silent by the attorney/client privilege? And then there were the voices again, pleas from the dead girls, their tormented, gurgled voices that still lingered in his head.

"Blame," they had said. "What about blame?" The voices had continued to reiterate the single word, 'blame'.

Grey repeated the word several times to himself quietly before he slipped (Freudian or not) and said "Blake". What followed was a long, empty silence. His mind was trying to grab hold of what he had just said.

"Oh shit!" he finally said out loud. Not because he had slipped, but because for a second he knew that maybe his mistake was somehow intended from the start. Was that even a possibility? Rachel stirred and rolled over. Grey hardly took notice. His eyes were too busy watching the clock, counting the minutes until Alex would wake up.

* * * * *

Blake's alarm went off at six. If he were only acting as himself, a night like that would have damn near killed him, but because of the presence of the 'Cat' he didn't feel all that bad. A little run down maybe, but really not that bad. He snuck out of bed and headed for the shower. As he passed the mirror, he knew he was going to have to shave. He couldn't risk waking Katie and having to explain his razor being in the safe so he borrowed one of her disposables. Much to his disappointment the effect was not the same. He picked out a suit, dressed himself and headed downstairs. He needed to be at the courthouse by eight. As he passed through the kitchen, he saw that the coffee pot had never been set so he was out of luck. A bottle of Perrier would have to do. He grabbed one from the refrigerator and headed for the car.

The sound of the engine growling brought him back to reality. It erased his mind set of the past twelve hours. The 'Cat' was still purring at the cage door, happy but confused. Blake knew he would have to lock him down and suppress him again or he would never be able to concentrate for the preliminary hearing he was about to attend. This was a big case and he would really need to focus. Once again, all he could hear was the sound of the ravenous teeth chewing away under the hood. Blake backed out of the garage and headed down the hill. He had another date with destiny this morning, one he fully intended to win.

* * * * *

Katie Kendall woke to the warmth of sunlight on her face. In the erotic confusion of last night's escape, both she and Blake had neglected to drop the blinds. The morning sun streamed gloriously in through the window as it glimmered off the deep blue water of the ocean below. She didn't bother to roll over. She knew that he was already gone. He had to be in court early, so she forgave him his indiscretion of leaving her alone in bed. That is, at least what little was left of her. Last night had been a series of awkward moments, outrageous ideas, playful intentions and insatiable appetites. They had shared an unspoken yearning for a trip down memory lane hoping for once to recapture a feeling from the past, a time when things were good, when everything was about their love and nothing else mattered. Instead, it had all culminated into an all out, 'no holes bared' sex fest. There was no love there, just pure, raw unadulterated sex.

Part of her felt completely dilapidated. She was sure there was nothing left. What little she could recover, knew she needed a large 'Bloody Mary', (A little hair of the dog if you will.) She decided to get up and get herself a drink. As she walked around the far side of the bed, she caught a toe on some papers on the floor. When she bent down to check them out, she discovered they were one of Blake's files. Upon further examination, she knew he was going to be in serious trouble if he didn't get them right away. They were all or part of this morning's case. She could not imagine how he could have possibly forgotten them!

For a moment, she considered leaving him hanging out to dry. After all, the past twelve months or so had been what they were. Still, last night kind of spoke for itself and her thing with Walter was really nothing more than a pleasant distraction, a sideshow if you will that was solely brought on by a lack of attention. That was certainly not the case last night. It was obvious to her that something about him had changed. Even his bizarre attire and interaction with Christine was different. Suddenly, there was a lot to consider. Katie went to her purse and grabbed her phone. She hoped she could catch him before it was too late.

* * * * *

He was almost to the courthouse when his cell phone rang. It was Katie. At first he wasn't sure if he wanted to answer it, but after last night he almost felt an obligation. Turned out, it was a good thing he did. The news from Katie was devastating.

"Honey, it's me," she said. "Where are you?"

"I'm almost at the courthouse, why?" he asked.

"You mentioned something about the Carlyle case last night, remember? Isn't that the one you're handling this morning?"

"Yes, that's right. We go before the judge at nine o'clock. Why?"

"I have the case file here in my hand," she said in a panicked voice. "You must have knocked it off the night stand last night and missed it this morning when you left. I found it half covered by a pillow. What do you want to do?" There was a brief silence. "Oh, and about last night".

Blake cut her off. "Hang on a second ok?" he responded. He glanced at his briefcase on the passenger seat. He knew something was wrong. He quickly pulled over to the side of the road and opened it. Everything was in order with the exception of the one missing file. This was a disaster! He didn't have time to turn around and go back.

To his surprise, before he could even get a thought out, Katie offered a solution. He should just continue on to the courthouse and she would bring the file to him. That would cut the travel time in half. If she left soon, she would have no trouble making it in plenty of time. No one would ever know the difference.

They agreed that she would call him once she got inside the building. She could give him the file and no one would be the wiser. She was in fact saving both his ass and his reputation. (He hoped she wouldn't try to rub that in.) Blake had no choice but to go along with the idea. Truth was he was grateful. He was about to hang up when she decided to take the conversation back to where it started.

"Blake?" she asked in the soft toned voice again.

"I'm still here Katie," he answered.

"About last night....she began." He interrupted her again. Not because he wanted to but because he didn't have time to get sentimental.

"Sorry honey, but can we discuss this later?" he interjected. "I know you want to talk about last night but I have to focus on this case right now. I promise we can take this up later."

"Sure, I guess," she said. "I'm sorry. I know you've got a lot on your mind. I'll see you in half an hour, ok?"

"That's great," he assured her. Then he paused, "And Katie," he spoke in a soft monotone voice, "Thanks. I really appreciate you doing this."

"I'll see you in a little while then," she responded. "I better go."

The phone went dead. Blake sat for a minute trying to figure out what had just transpired. He had dropped the ball big time and low and behold it was Katie who was going to save his ass! She was actually trying to be nice. Did she harbor guilt about her affair with Walter? Odds were probably not. Was she just trying to play it cool with him after their adventure last night? There the odds were getting better. Whatever the reason, she was willing to get up, get dressed and drop everything to come downtown to help him. He knew that she hated the courthouse almost as much as he thought she hated him. But apparently, even after all the freedom and distance she had established over the past year, there was still something there, still something between them.

Blake started the car again and went back to the comforting sound of the engine grinding away. The courthouse was just a few blocks away now. All he had to do was keep a low profile until Katie arrived. It was only seven-thirty and Katie was still a good distance away. He figured he had time for a quick cup of coffee since his office was right around the corner.

If Sylvester were there, the coffee and the conversation would do his mind some good. Blake passed the courthouse driveway and headed up the block. As he turned the corner in front of his building, he could see the old man and his cart through the large glass windows. Blake smiled. With a little help from Sylvester, today was going to come together nicely.

* * * * *

CHAPTER 19

Tim watched the sunrise from the center cockpit of the 29th Precinct. He'd been sitting out on deck for almost an hour, when the first glimpse of natural light began to peek its head over the horizon. The new light of day glistened off the large captain's wheel a single spoke at a time as it climbed its way up unto the early morning sky. The bow was tied up facing west, so he had made sure he was sitting on one of the long bench style seats that ran either side of the cut out cockpit. The sun began to come up just over the edge of the stern. From his position near the top of the stairs, he could hear the coffee pot chugging away below while he took in the magnificent view to start the day.

He and Renee had spent many weekend mornings doing the exact same thing, watching the sunrise and the birth of a new day. The rigging and hardware rattled against the mast like wind chimes in the light breeze. In the early morning silence, he could hear the rhythmic sound of the tide slapping ever so gently against the hull. It had been a long night. Sleep had not been easy to find. The wheels in his mind had continued to grind on throughout the night and into the wee hours of the morning searching for answers that might help him find the missing piece of the puzzle. The photographs had something to say.

A few minutes earlier, the appointment calendar on his cell phone reminded him that he had to be in court this morning. He was needed to testify on a domestic violence case involving a drug dealer and his girlfriend. The guy had been under surveillance for months for drug trafficking, but they had no choice and were forced to intervene and make an early arrest when they saw him beating his girlfriend within an inch of her life. Now, Tim's observations and opinions would all but insure a conviction for the District Attorney's office. The massive array of illegal controlled substances that were found in his apartment: (Ecstasy, Oxycontin, and Vicodin) for personal use, sale and or distribution, would just be added on as additional charges. The guy would be off the street for a long time. Tim hated going to court. He'd much preferred being out on the street. Most of all, he hated having to wear a tie.

He understood the respect for the judge and the court thing, but he was a twice decorated, gold shield undercover detective. The suit and tie were just a façade. He was much more comfortable, and for that matter more recognizable to his friends and colleagues in blue jeans and a leather jacket. That was the real Tim. Renee had bought him a black pinstripe suit for such auspicious occasions, but he always felt like he was going to a wedding rather than to court dressed up in a 'monkey suit'. Now it hung ominously in the master cabin below waiting for his inspection. Tim conceded defeat and went below to begin the unpleasant task of assembling himself in it.

He was already running late when the 'tie issue' finally surfaced. He could tie one fast enough, but that wasn't the problem. Truth was, he just didn't see the point. He'd seen one too many bizarre things on the job that involved ties to last him a lifetime. Dead lovers left tied to bed posts, a guy who hung himself in his office downtown, and oh yeah, his favorite by far, the beautiful blonde stripper from across town who apparently pissed off the wrong people and ended up with a "Columbian neck tie", (a vicious form of torture and trade mark of many Columbian drug cartels in which a victim's throat is cut open and their tongue is pulled out through the hole). No matter how hard he tried to get clear of it, that little episode just wouldn't go away.

But Hey! It comes with the job. Just like having to put on the occasional suit and tie. Once again, he'd learn to live with it for a couple of hours. He walked back to his bedroom and grabbed the royal blue neckwear off the hanger that his jacket was hanging on and draped it around his neck. There was something funny to him about a tie and a shoulder holster. Then he made it a point to grab a fresh pair of jeans and a black 'Van Halen' T-shirt. He threw them in his gym bag so he could change into them later. He tossed the bag up the ladder and onto the deck. A quick stop at the mirror next to the steps, and the tie was on him in one seemingly fluid motion. He grabbed the stair rail and turned back to look at his image in the mirror again. "*Well, Renee would have approved,*" he thought. Then he headed up himself into early morning sun.

* * * * *

Blake could smell the intoxicating aroma the second he passed through the doors. Sylvester was quite obviously doing what he did best. He could almost smell the magic in the air. Over at the far end of the lobby, Willie was just finishing up his shift. He raised his hand, coffee included, to acknowledge Blake and then shook his coffee cup a little as if to tease him. Blake simply nodded his head and waved back. Blake liked it when things were consistent. Seeing Willie and Sylvester did wonders to help him settle down and get focused. Blake looked at his watch. Katie would be meeting him at the courthouse in less than half an hour. It seemed like forever.

Truth was, he really didn't want this case in the first place. He despised all of the overly ambitious corrupt politicians of the world. Walter had asked him to take it as a favor. Ever since he had first got his hands on the case file, he had begun to question Walter's motives. What 'big wig' was pulling Walter's strings? If they had their teeth into Walter, how long would it be before they tried getting their claws into him? Blake was certain that somewhere at the top of the ladder sat another, bigger politician. For the moment, that idiot and his troubles would have to wait. Sylvester's coffee was more important.

The old man was currently being detained by a feisty blue hair with a 'story' as Blake approached the cart. Sylvester nodded and smiled as it never seemed to end. Blake admired his new friend's patience as much as anything else, but he didn't have time for this. Finally, he saw a chance to cut into the conversation and took it.

"Excuse me, Mr. Rodriguez," he began.

Sylvester's eyes suddenly got really big. The words caught him off guard. The woman immediately stopped speaking and moved away. When Blake felt she was out of earshot, he looked back at Sylvester.

"Sorry about that," he almost chuckled. "You looked like you'd had enough," Blake observed.

Sylvester nodded again. "Mr. Rodriguez?" he asked. "I wasn't aware that you knew that."

Blake smiled and pointed to a small brass plaque that was mounted on the side of the cart. It read

Coffee Express
Sylvester Rodriguez: Proprietor

Sylvester shook his head. "You don't miss much do you?" he said. "By the way, thank you for intervening. Most of the time, I love to listen to what people have to say, but occasionally they wear me out. That lady needed more attention than I was ready to give today. Let me get you a cup of coffee to express my appreciation."

Blake watched as Sylvester reached down behind the cart and started to work his magic. His hand only disappeared for a moment and then emerged again with a large Styrofoam cup. With the other hand, he brought up a pot of coffee and proceeded to fill the cup. As the hot liquid flowed in and the steam began to rise, Blake realized that it had to be one of the old man's special blends. Everything appeared to be innocent and proper but Blake knew to expect more.

"No surprises today?" he inquired.

"I wouldn't say that my friend," Sylvester replied as he carefully slipped the new concoction into a heat sleeve and handed it to Blake.

"This should help get you through court this morning," he continued.

Blake looked puzzled. "How did you know that I wasn't going up to my office today?" he asked.

"You didn't come in with your briefcase sir," Sylvester pointed out. "You only came in for my coffee."

You could feel the hammer fall. Blake stood there in silence for a moment trying to assimilate what the old man had just said. He knew the guy was perceptive but seriously? Blake thought carefully before offering a response. "Your observations and insights never cease to amaze me," he began. "And besides, while we both know I could get my coffee anywhere, I would be hard pressed to find any nearly as good or some that was accompanied by such interesting repartee." (An observation, a compliment, and a concession all in the same response), Blake was pleased with his comment. He looked at his watch again. He was running out of time. He had to meet Katie on schedule. He turned his attention back to Sylvester.

"You'll forgive me my friend but I must go," Blake apologized. "As usual, your observation was correct. I do need to be in court this morning, but I need to speak to someone there before going in. Thank you again for the coffee and the conversation. I'm sure we can continue this later."

He offered his free hand to Sylvester. When they shook hands, Blake noticed the strong and confident grip. Both men seemed to be satisfied with their encounter. Blake turned and headed back toward the door.

"Good luck today Sir," Sylvester called out from behind him.

Blake paused at door and turned his head.

"Thank you," he responded. "I'll try to remember to let you know how things worked out." Then he waved and was out the door. He had fifteen minutes before he had to meet Katie. He was right on schedule.

When Blake pulled into the parking lot at the court house, he let out an immediate sigh of relief. In the first row of visitor parking was Katie's little red Porsche. There was no mistaking her car for another. The vanity plates gave it away. 'DIVINE 1' was kind of obvious. Blake had done it initially as a joke. Katie of course considered it a compliment. Fact was, she was there and that was all that mattered. He reminded himself to say something nice and to sound grateful when he saw her. That would be easy. He was. He knew she didn't have to do this, least of all for him. He figured her motivation was a kind response to their encounter last night. Either way, if she had the file, his ass was out of danger. For this completely unselfish favor, he might have to offer to play with her again. Blake parked the car and headed inside. The 'Cat' was safely tucked away back in his cage.

* * * * *

Katie Carson Kendall had legs. There was certainly no denying that. Long, endlessly tan works of art that seemed to flow gracefully upward from her obsidian perfectly polished Prada heels. A few heads turned as she made her way up the courthouse steps and entered the building, but it wasn't until she came to a stop at the security screening area that she really gave the 'early morning boys club' a front row seat. Even a few females that were within range turned to take notice. She knew that she was probably dressed a little too provocative for the courthouse, but what the hell, after her rendezvous with Blake last night she was feeling pretty good about herself. Truth was, she hadn't been this self confident in ages.

The guard with the metal detector wand took one look at her, a good long look, and simply waved her through. It was quite obvious that the fit of her short black dress left little or nothing to the imagination. It was treading a fine line of being professional and certainly left no room for any possible concealment. She flashed the guard a sexy little smile to reward his decision. Her outfit was one of Blake's favorites. It flattered her all too well. Apparently, it was quickly becoming appreciated by more than a few other gentlemen. Katie glowed with confidence. Her parents might have created this impressive genetic arrangement, but it was her hard work and effort that had allowed her to maintain this figure into her late thirties. Her looks made men hungry and women jealous and frankly, part of her liked it that way. And the best part was, everything was real. No trips to Mattel for spare parts or Hoover for quick cleanups. What you saw with Katie was the real thing and she was damn proud of it. It was abundantly clear that all of her time had been well spent. Yes, people were focused on her appearance, but probably not the least bit curious as to her intent. She retrieved her purse and satchel off the x-ray conveyor table and headed down the hall. Her trip through the security check point had been easy. She was already almost half way to their agreed rendezvous point.

In order to maintain a low profile, Blake had instructed her to meet him down the hall across from the information desk. This was conveniently away from the elevators he would be using to get upstairs. There were bench seats that ran in sections down the length of the hallway allowing both visitors and participants who had business with the court to have a place to sit. Katie would find a comfortable spot and wait for him to arrive. The low key part was already a bust. The dress had blown away any subtlety that might have been part of the original plan. This obvious oversight had little effect on Katie. Even though in recent months she was not a frequent visitor to the courthouse, many of the deputies on duty in the building would recognize her anyway. They would assume that she was simply there visiting her husband not knowing that secretly, she was actually participating in a mission of mercy.

Katie looked at her watch. If Blake was on time, everything would go as planned. Katie took a quick glance around to get a feel for her surroundings. People were starting to fill the hall and she knew that she would attract far less attention if she was sitting down. Once she had established her position, she would take out the file and be ready to make the hand off. She decided on a bench that was just south of her but still across from the information desk. It was safe and easily accessible so she turned and headed directly for it.

* * * * *

Blake could feel his heart pounding as he made his way up to the top of the courthouse steps. Now that he knew Katie was somewhere in the vicinity, the immense pressure he'd been feeling about the situation had started to subside. It was going to be a close one, but thanks to Katie and her quick thinking, he was confident that his reputation would remain unscathed. His ability to focus now on the task at hand was all that really mattered. He could not afford to let anything, even the 'Cat', interfere with his plan. Things had to play out smoothly.

The line at the security check point was a bit crowded, but he had already considered that and had factored in the extra time for any reasonable delay. Because of his attention to detail, he would have the necessary time to run the gauntlet. As he waited in line, Blake's eyes began to survey the lobby. He smiled when he saw Katie sitting on a bench down the hall. She seemed to be focusing her attention on the deputies sitting behind the information desk. Even at a distance, he could still make out the gentle beauty that made up her silhouette. Blake breathed easier, her mere presence acted like a sedative. The file that was now visible in her left hand helped to slow his heart rate and bring it back to normal. In the next few minutes, everything would be as it should.

Then suddenly, he felt the 'Cat' stir. He could feel an uncontrollable hunger beginning to creep up inside him. His eyes were no longer his own. Her legs, her skirt, her profiled silhouette began to stimulate his senses in violent and evil ways. Blake knew that if he didn't act fast, things would quickly get out of control. He glanced up at Katie and this time their eyes met. When they did, his mind screamed "it's Katie". The simple acknowledgement that it was her, Katie, mother of his child, seemed to make all the difference. The painful clawing sensation in his gut started to diminish. Seeing Katie's face confirmed her identity as far as his mind was concerned and she was no longer the appetizing form of entertainment she had been a moment ago. Blake discovered that as long as he could concentrate on her face and persona, the 'Cat' in him would be forced to leave her alone. Blake didn't look back at her again until he was safely through the security line and could focus his attention on her image the way he wanted. He smiled when she stood to greet him. Then he laughed and shook his head,

"Low profile huh?" he teased her.

"What, you don't approve?" she asked in a soft, sexy tone.

"I didn't say that, did I?" he replied. "But we'll have to discuss this later. I've got to get upstairs." He leaned over and kissed her gently on the lips. "Thanks Katie," he said softly. "I do appreciate this" he continued as Katie slipped the file into his hand. "It really means a lot." Then he turned and started toward the elevator.

He'd only taken a few steps when he turned back to her again. "When I said thank you a moment ago I meant thank you for everything," he insisted. He spoke in the same soft tone in an effort to assure her of his sincerity while sizing her up with his eyes. Katie was stunned. There was nothing she could say. Behind him, the elevator bell rang and Blake quietly disappeared.

As soon as he was out of sight, Katie smiled, blushed and giggled like she was back in high school. The outfit had worked. He really liked the dress. Maybe last night was the start of something new. The feeling stayed with her the entire ride home.

* * * * *

Tim was just catching a ride up from the lower level garage when a light flashed indicating that someone had made a request for a stop on the first floor. When the elevator doors opened, there, standing in front of him was a beautiful woman with long dark hair. Her face and physical make up were a dead on match to the photographs on the table back at the boat. The likeness was so stunning, it was almost uncanny. For a moment, Tim felt like he was seeing a ghost. In the back of his mind, the photographs started to whisper.

A large man brushed by him entering the elevator. "Excuse me," he thought he heard the man say but his mind was in a fog. He paid little or no attention to the contact between them because he could not draw his eyes away from the woman in the hall. He remained standing there frozen with a silent stare. As the doors began to close in front of him, the woman slowly disappeared. Blake caught him looking but didn't say a word. The two men were now alone in the elevator.

Blake noticed that the fifth floor light, his stop, was already illuminated so apparently he and this guy were going to the same floor. As the elevator started to rise, Blake decided to have a little fun.

"Pretty lady, don't you think?" he threw out as a quick opener in a soft but firm voice.

Blake noticed him stiffen up a little. As he intended, his comment caught Tim off guard. Maybe it was the suit. The guy didn't look to comfortable in it.

Tim remained facing forward, eyes on the door and simply replied, "You could definitely say that," in a calm and pleasant voice. It was an awkward moment, like two guys talking while standing at the urinals. Then Tim turned to look at the man standing next to him.

"You'll have to excuse me," he began, "but you look and sound very familiar to me. Have we met somewhere before?"

"My name is Kendall," Blake replied offering an outstretched hand. "Blake Kendall, and yes, I believe we met last year at my firm's Christmas party; Greenburg, Weisman and Davis." The two men shook hands. "You're a police Detective, I believe," Blake continued. "I'm sorry, but your name escapes me for the moment, some kind of boat if I recall?"

He was politely toying with Tim now, entertainment for the ride up. In reality, Blake actually remembered their meeting quite well. The guy's girlfriend from the Christmas party is what originally caught his eye. She had pretty blue eyes. Blake wondered if they were still together. Truth was, he didn't miss much and it was his exceptional memory that helped get him through law school.

"That's very good, Mr. Kendall. I'm flattered you'd remember me. The name is Galleon. Tim Galleon and as a matter of fact, I am a Detective. I work homicide, out of Westminster. Now that I think of it, I'm a little embarrassed. The woman back there looked very familiar to me, which is why you probably noticed me staring. While she is unquestionably beautiful, she bears a striking resemblance to the victims in a case I've been working on. Add that to the mix and now I'm even more humiliated to recall that the lady in the lobby is your wife."

The elevator bell sounded signaling their arrival to the fifth floor. Tim waved Blake on through when the doors opened and then followed him out into the hall. Blake stopped to address Tim.

"Detective Galleon, it was nice to see you again and thank you for the compliment about my wife. As for this case you're involved in, I would love to hear more about it, especially the information you referred to regarding my wife." He reached into the breast pocket of his jacket and produced a card and handed it to Tim.

"Please call me if you'd like and we can continue this conversation at a later time." Once again Blake offered his hand. "Have a good day sir," Blake said as the men exchanged a second handshake.

"Thank you sir and you do the same," Tim responded. Then the two men went their separate ways.

For some odd reason, Blake's head was finally clear. He knew exactly what he was going to say to the judge as he made his way down the hall toward this morning's preliminary hearing. The 'Cat' was under control and for the next thirty minutes (Blake figured he'd clean house quickly) he would be on top of his game. When he walked into court and headed for the defense table, he cradled the file in his hand like a gunslinger handles his firearm. It was show time in Cheshire.

Tim's attention was a million miles away; or at the very least, back on the galley table on the boat. Seeing Mrs. Kendall had shifted his mind into overdrive. He took a note pad out of his jacket and jotted down a few thoughts and ideas that he wanted to remember later. Right now, he had to focus on his impending testimony. He had already planned for a long, boring morning on the witness stand. Now, knowing that he had more exciting things to do would simply make it last longer.

As he made his way down the hall, Tim noticed his reflection in one of the buildings large glass windows. He stopped for a minute outside the courtroom and straightened his jacket. Then almost humorously, he took a moment to adjust his tie. Renee's influence had gotten the best of him. A bailiff opened the door and got his attention.

"Detective Galleon?" he asked.

"Yes sir," Tim nodded.

"They're ready for you inside sir," he informed Tim.

The bailiff opened the door and Tim stepped through. Almost immediately, his eyes went to the defense table. Part of him was relieved to not see Blake Kendall sitting there. That would have ruined his day. He did make eye contact with the defendant though and from the smug look on the guy's face, he realized that his initial assessment was probably right. He was going to be there for awhile.

* * * * *

As daylight began to peek its way through the bedroom curtains, Grey was laying in bed staring up at the ceiling fan. Subconsciously, he was thankful that it really was there. At the moment, any confirmation of his sanity was a welcome gift. His eyes shifted over to Rachel again, confirming that it was her presence on the bed next to him and not that of the cold, wet corpse he had imagined just a few short minutes ago. Unlike the random pieces of the previous episodes he'd been able to remember, the events of this latest dream were fresh, alive, and crystal clear in his head. Grey closed his eyes for a second and ran a few tests. He was relieved when he discovered that every detail of the ordeal was easily retrievable and immediately at his disposal. He would have no trouble giving Alex a complete account of everything he had seen and experienced. Right now though, he was thirsty. There was a strange, almost salty taste in his mouth that he needed to get rid of. He climbed out of bed and headed off in search of a glass of water.

Alex was waiting for him in the kitchen. At first, he was a little surprised to find her there but what the hell, he was dealing with Alex. Still, he couldn't help wondering how she made it down the hallway without him hearing her. The coffee pot was on again but had just finished bubbling. She couldn't have been there very long. He could tell by the smell that this time there was nothing brewing that old 'Juan Valdez' himself wouldn't have approved of. That alone was a great relief. Grey looked haggard as he entered the room. His hair was matted on one side and his cheeks were a bit pale. Alex knew something was up.

"Good morning, I think?" she offered. "Would it be safe to assume that you had a bad night?" Grey offered no response.

He reached for an empty cup and started to pour. Then he had second thoughts. He hesitated for a moment and leaned down to smell what he was putting in his cup. Alex let out a small sigh.

"I know what you're thinking but seriously, it's just coffee silly, I promise," she insisted.

Grey looked up and gave her one of those "do you blame me?" kind of looks. Then he went back to filling his cup. When he finished, he made his way over to the couch and sat down. It took a few sips before he was ready to engage her in conversation.

"I don't think it was necessarily bad," he injected softly into the silence that had taken over the room. "Just more than a little overwhelming," he suggested, nodding as he spoke. "It was definitely a wild ride." Then his lips went back to the coffee cup for another swallow.

Alex wondered if he was trying to convince her or himself. After a brief pause, he continued. She was completely focused on him now but his eyes told that her they were not on the same page yet.

"Don't look so confused my friend," he suggested. "Don't you remember I always look this good in the morning?" he teased, raising his cup to toast her in jest. Alex let out another sigh and smiled. She knew that he was just warming her up. Grey continued to sip at his coffee and gather his thoughts. All she could do was wait.

"You've got some new information don't you?" she finally whispered under her breath.

Grey nodded and then looked down into his coffee. He knew that he had to start someplace.

"I'm having a hard time with the 'what I know' as opposed to the 'what I suspect,' he replied. "Remember, our goal is trying to get to the bottom of this and figure out what the hell is really going on. After last night, I have an idea that we can check out but I'm still having a hard time getting my head around it." Then he turned to her and made eye contact.

"Seriously, I had the most intense dream last night but I have to tell you, it felt so real," he continued. "When I finally woke up and realized what was going on, it started to help me put some of the pieces of this thing together. It's just that some of the details seem so farfetched that I'm not sure what to make of them. I think that's where you come in."

Before Alex could respond, Grey got up and headed back into the kitchen. He reached for the coffee pot again and started to pour himself another cup. He motioned to Alex but she declined. He wasn't sure if he really wanted or needed the coffee; or whether it was just the steady flow of heat generating from the cup into his hand that made him feel better.

"Maybe if I lay it all out for you, we can come up with a plan together," he proposed. "I know we said we'd bring everything straight to Father Richard but I think I'd like to run this stuff by you first."

Alex was still silent. Grey could all but hear the thoughts formulating in her head. It was his turn to be patient. While he waited, Alex decided that she did in fact, want another cup of coffee. They both liked it strong and black, none of that foam or whip designer crap. There was a certain level of comfort and simplicity to it that way. When she returned to the couch, he finally began. At the time, neither one of them realized that the walls had ears.

* * * * *

Maybe it was Rachel's 'footie' socks that silenced her pilgrimage down the hall. It was even possible that he was tired and distracted by his brief conversation with Alex, but the simple fact remained that neither he nor Alex ever heard her coming. As Rachel approached the kitchen, she could hear them talking in the family room. Almost immediately, she realized that she was privy to a private conversation but couldn't resist stopping at the end of the hallway to listen. She leaned up against a wall out of their field of vision and focused her attention intently on their discussion. After ten minutes of eavesdropping, she discovered that she was trapped in a world somewhere between fear and shock. It took everything she had to not come flying around the corner and demand an explanation. Instead, she made a bee line back to the bedroom and grabbed a pen. She wanted to get whatever she could down on paper before she forgot anything. Even the simplest notes would do. Her hand was shaking as she started to write. She didn't get very far.

Grey was already standing behind her before she noticed. She jumped when she felt his hand come to rest on her shoulder.

"Whoa," he said calmly as he quickly pulled his hand away. "I didn't mean to startle you."

Rachel popped up out of the chair and quickly moved a few steps away, establishing some distance between them. She appeared to be more scared than upset, especially when she realized that in her panic, she had left the paper with her notes behind her on the desk. Grey noticed them immediately but decided not to let on. He would just be verifying what he already suspected.

"I'm sorry," he continued. "I guess I kind of snuck up on you there."

He wasn't being entirely honest with her. His move was intentional, but this seemed to be the most calm and logical approach. He had in fact, heard something as she made the turn and, at the very last second, realized that she was nearby and moving back down the hallway. That's why he got up and followed her. He knew by the shuffling sound of her feet, instead of the rhythm of her regular steps, that she didn't want to take the chance of being heard. She had to have been listening to the conversation but he had no way of knowing for how long. Even if she had heard everything, what sense could it have possibly made? Still, Rachel was now visibly shaken. He had no way of knowing whether it was from his hand on her shoulder or from what she had overheard. It was probably a combination of both. She had moved now, across the room and found refuge on the bed. He wondered if she was waiting for something, an explanation perhaps. He was wide awake now and alert thanks to the caffeine so he decided to go fishing with a big net.

"Well, my first thought is, are you ok?" he said trying to get a foot in the door. "That had to be a rather bizarre conversation to be listening to, huh?" he asked. He kept his voice low in a calm and curious tone. Rachel just sat there with her arms crossed in front of her and a terrified look on her face.

"It was a dream honey," he tried to assure her. "Just a stupid, silly dream," He didn't stand a chance. His words took a moment to set in.

"That's bullshit," she mumbled in quiet, trembling voice. "Nobody gets that serious or intense over some stupid fucking dream."

Rachel swearing was not a good sign. Grey had to think fast. By this time, he knew Alex had quietly moved to the end of the hall and was listening in. He decided to take up a position in a chair next to Rachel's nightstand. He crossed the room slowly, attempting to not set her off again. The casual act of kicking his feet up on the bed seemed to calm her down a little. He seized the moment and ran.

"So what do you want to know?" he asked nonchalantly, shifting his body around in the chair and moving his feet a bit like he was trying to settle in. As he intended, his manner and body language were now very confusing to her. This put Rachel back on her emotional heels. Even so, she still had nothing to say. He hoped that was a good thing because if she wasn't talking, it meant she was thinking and Rachel was an intelligent and logical woman. It was definitely to his advantage to let her think for awhile, so they just sat for a minute staring at the wall.

Grey finally broke the silence. "C'mon honey, it's really ok," he said. "Everything is all right," he assured her again. "I meant what I said before. If there's something you want to know, just ask." He regretted having to leave the door open like that but it was a delicate situation. To his surprise, nothing changed. Then quite suddenly, Rachel didn't look scared anymore. The color slowly returned to her face. Now she was just pissed. One look in her eyes, and Grey knew exactly where this was going. "You just don't get it, do you?" she snapped. "I'm not even going to pretend that I could begin to understand what the two of you were talking about, and at this point, I really don't care. What pisses me off is that if it is, or was, something you considered important or serious, why the hell were you talking to her about it instead of me?"

It all came down to this. He had successfully navigated her attention away from the original issue and now Grey knew that everything rested on the strength of his response. He stood and looked her straight in the eye.

"You're right Rachel, and I'm sorry," he confessed. "I should have come to you first." His tone was genuine, even if it was just for the purpose of trying to put closure on the issue.

"I was just afraid that after the accident, you might overreact to some of this weird stuff and think something was wrong with me. Alex is an old friend who thinks I'm kind of nut job anyway so I thought she might be a more objective listener. If it makes you feel any better, before I had a chance to talk to her, I was feeling a little worried myself."

As Rachel processed what he was saying, the tension in the room began to evaporate. His explanation was reasonable and far more pliable than what she had expected. Within a few minutes, things were almost back to normal.

"I'm going to go check on Alex," he announced, "If that's all right with you? We should probably look in on Dylan too. He's usually up by now."

"Ok," Rachel nodded, "I can handle that. I'll get Dylan and meet you inside." Grey turned and headed back down the hall.

"Hey you," Rachel called out after him. "No more creepy conversations without me ok?" Grey stopped, turned slightly, and lifted a 'thumbs up' over his head acknowledging her request. The 'thank you' from her that followed was a welcome sound. Her voice was much calmer now. Grey smiled and kept on moving.

Alex was waiting for him as he made the turn toward the kitchen. He could tell by the look on her face that she was having trouble containing herself. His ability to be calm and cool under pressure never ceased to amaze her. They didn't speak until they were safely, back in the kitchen and Grey could hear Rachel talking to Dylan in the back room. Alex had this 'stupid' look on her face. He tried to ignore it but couldn't.

"What?" he asked sarcastically. Whatever it was, it needed to be addressed quickly. Rachel and Dylan would be joining them any minute. "I swear, I have no idea how you managed to pull that off," Alex whispered.

Grey let out a little laugh. "Me either," he confessed. "We got lucky. If you had overheard our conversation, what would you think?" he asked. "I'm being rhetorical of course," he snickered.

"I guess you're right, but let's make it a point to not let that happen again," she suggested.

Before he could answer, Rachel and Dylan appeared. She was all smiles now and so was Dylan. Grey was relieved. It was if their last exchange and his apology had laid the matter to rest. He greeted them both with open arms.

When Alex said, "Coffee Rachel?" and Rachel nodded, they knew they had dodged another bullet. Now all they had to do was figure out the meaning of Grey's dream.

* * * * *

CHAPTER 20

It was around 4:30 in the morning when Father Richard concluded that there was no way he was ever going to go back to sleep. A recent string of nightmares had once again, left him dazed and confused. He looked over at his wife quietly sleeping next to him and knew that he was destined to work through the anxiety alone. He didn't have the heart to wake her, so he decided that he would take a shower down the hall in the guest bathroom. He would take his clothes with him, get dressed in the spare bedroom and then head over to the church. Once there, he could always find something to do. Ever so carefully, he slipped out of bed, put on his slippers and quietly snuck down the hall.

Standing there in a hot stream of water, he thought he could wash away the evil that had permeated his dreams. He revisited the latest one in his head, hoping that something in his memory would trigger an answer to their cause. One thing he knew for certain was that while the first installment had come soon after the murder of Kelly Richfield, the nightmares had become drastically more frequent after Grey's experiment with him; that and his subsequent involvement in the investigation. Now the bad dreams were coming on with a vengeance. It was only a matter of time before he figured out that he wouldn't be able to sleep at all. He'd kept this issue private for the time being but maybe now, after last night's episode, he needed to share this with Grey. His mind drifted away.

Richard lost track of time under the spell of the rhythmic spray. He only noticed the distraction when the water began to run cold. He shut off the water and hurried to get dressed. When he was ready to leave, he peeked in on Judy who was still fast asleep.

"I love you," he whispered, standing in the doorway. "I'll see you again very soon." Then he closed the door and headed for his truck in the driveway.

It was half past five now, and the sun was just beginning to hint that it might be coming up. It was still dark enough though to need his headlights, so he was rather startled when he turned them on and saw the shadow that was reflected on the garage door. They only appeared for a moment, but there was no denying their existence. Somewhere, out there, was something with a pair of large, dark wings. Richard shut off his lights and waited. When he turned them back on, everything about the door seemed normal. Just a little peeling paint on the rafter and a black rubber line where he'd accidently backed into it a few weeks earlier. He looked over his shoulder and saw nothing behind him. Richard shook his head.

"Well, that's one hell of a way to start the day," he mumbled. He almost never swore, but under the circumstances, he'd say a few 'Hail Mary's' and forgive himself. He was pretty sure the Lord would too. Not wanting to deal with any more surprises, Richard turned the key, threw the stick into reverse, and headed off to the church.

As he drove down the street, he found himself looking for a sign, any kind of sign mind you, that the good Lord might have to offer. The only response he received was a growling in his stomach, an obvious reminder that he was hungry. Suddenly they appeared; the golden arches of McDonalds. He looked inside as he passed by and realized they were open. He quickly made a U-turn and headed back for the drive-thru entrance. "Carpe' Diem," he said out loud remembering his Latin. Judy would never have to know that he was eating something greasy and bad. After what he'd been through lately, he could write off this small indiscretion as just a simple reward for all his recent trouble. Richard rolled down the window as he pulled into the drive-thru and could smell the heavenly aroma of sausage cooking. By the time he got to the window, he decided to make it "two." If he was going to bad, he was going to be really bad. His work at the church would have to wait.

* * * * *

Richard sat alone in his office eating a Sausage and Egg Mc Muffin. It came with the little hash brown thing that bore a striking resemblance to a little potato tombstone, but that part of his breakfast really didn't interest him. He slowly nibbled away at the fried meat and cheese as he read through some of the correspondence that was scattered across his desk. A voice in his head kept distracting him as he went.

"Are you starting to think you got the devil in you, Richard?" the voice drawled away in a soft whisper.

This was followed by a minute or so of silence, probably designed to give him time to think.

"Well, I've got the devil in me, Richard!" the young voice taunted him.

It was kind of spooky at first, seeing that directly overhead, hanging on the wall in front of the desk was a large crucifix staring down at him. They say the Lord works in mysterious ways, but this was not the priest's idea of a typical breakfast meeting. He was much more accustomed to mortal conversation. Truth was it might have been easier to play along if the statue had in fact been speaking. At least that would have made some sense, spiritually anyway. Richard decided to ignore the voice for now and went back to eating his muffin. The silence didn't last long.

"I understand your confusion Father, I feel your pain," the voice returned. "Come on Father, take a chance. Dance with me."

This time, the insinuation rattled the priest a bit. Suddenly, he was afraid to look up. He kept both his eyes and attention focused on his desk. He held his ground until he couldn't resist the temptation any longer. He raised his eyes to the crucifix above and was aghast. Now, staring down on him from above was the image of Kelly Richfield nailed ceremoniously to the cross.

"Really Father, I carry a rather large purse," she informed him. "Just sell your soul to me and all of your most intimate questions will be answered," she whispered.

Now Richard was visually shaken. His hand, still clutching his muffin, was trembling in the air. There were only a few bites left. He set it down and reached for his coffee. A shot of the steaming hot liquid might snap him back to reality. By the time he looked back at the crucifix, the body of Jesus had returned. He sat for a few minutes with his face in his hands trying to get his sanity back. An occasional glimpse at the statue reaffirmed his place back in the real world. Jesus was in trouble, but at least the Savior was still there. Richard returned to his labors.

He was in the middle of a reviewing a report from one of the church benefactors when he heard something ringing. It was his cell phone. When he answered it, he was pleasantly relieved.

"Good morning Father," Grey announced. He and Alex had set up shop on the back patio after Rachel went to give Dylan a bath. After a brief conversation, they had both agreed that it was time to give Richard a call. "Sorry to call you so early," Grey said, but I figured that you'd be up. Hope I didn't wake the wife."

"No chance of that," Richard responded. "I'm at the church. I couldn't sleep so I snuck out and came over here early. I didn't want to wake her either. So, anyway, how are you my friend, any news?"

When Grey began to answer, "I'm good Father, very good," his words were all but drowned out at Richard's end, by another interjection from his ominous new opponent.

"Remember the funeral Father?" she asked. "Do you remember the colors? No one can ever see your tears Richard, when you're crying in the rain."

That was the last straw. If he didn't get out of there fast, his mind was going to snap. He had to get out of his office. Richard immediately rose from his chair and moved quickly toward the door. He kept moving until he got to the sanctuary. In the heat of the moment, Grey had been forgotten.

"Are you still there Richard?" Grey asked after a long silence had passed.

"Yes, Grey, I'm still here," he answered as he was taking a seat on the stairs in front of the altar. "I had to get out of my office," he continued.

"Anything I can do?" Grey inquired.

"As a matter of fact, there is," Richard said. "Any chance you and Alex could come by this morning? I'll be in the sanctuary. There's something I'd like to discuss with you."

"Sure, no problem, my friend," Grey began. "That would work out great for us because I was actually calling to find out when we could come over."

"Very well then," Richard agreed. "Shall we say around ten-o clock?"

"Ten it is then," Grey confirmed. Then he paused for a moment and said, "Will you be all right until then?"

"It will keep," he assured Grey. Under his breath he mumbled, "That is if I stay far away from my office." Grey said goodbye and hung up the phone.

"Is something wrong with Father Richard?" Alex asked. "You've got a funny look on your face."

"I'm not sure," Grey admitted, "I'm really curious about what's going on with him. He didn't sound like himself."

"Well, I guess we'll learn more when we see him," Alex offered. "In the mean time, what do you say to the idea of me taking everyone out to breakfast. We can drop off Rachel and Dylan when we're done. We'll swing back by here on our way to see Richard."

"That's a great idea," Grey responded. "I'll go run this by Rachel. I'm sure she'll be on board." Grey made his way across the back patio until he found the bedroom slider and then disappeared inside. Alex was left alone with her thoughts. She returned to the comfort of the futon and put her feet up on the table.

"I wonder what we're going to do if it does turn out that he's right about this lawyer friend of his," she said out loud, talking to the little blue jay that had landed on the back wall. The bird shook his head as if he was listening (he probably was) and looked at her like he was paying attention. Alex got up and walked over to the wall. The bird never flinched. When she got right up next to him, he jumped up and landed on her outstretched hand. They chatted for a minute and then he was gone, probably because he saw Grey coming out the slider. Grey saw just enough to register that the bird had been sitting on Alex's hand.

“Seeking some counsel?” he inquired in a calm but surprisingly serious tone.

“I guess you could say that,” she replied. His eyes were a bit concerned. “This friend of yours, do you really think?” Grey held up his hand as more of a pause, not intending to completely cut her off. She knew what he meant.

“I don’t know what to think,” he said, “but I know that I can’t just sit around and wait for something else to happen.”

“So where do we start?” she said. He never had a chance to answer her. Rachel and Dylan appeared at the patio door. “All set, everybody?” Rachel asked.

Grey glanced over at Alex, then back at his wife. “Good to go here, honey,” he said.

With Rachel and Dylan in the lead, they made their way for the front door. Alex said, “Hey, can we put Dylan’s car seat in the back seat of the Mustang? It’s a beautiful day and we can put the top down. He might just like it.”

Grey looked over at Rachel. “I can sit in back with him if you want honey, no problem,” he volunteered. Rachel thought about it for a minute and nodded her head.

“All right, as long as he doesn’t get cold,” she admonished.

When everyone was safely aboard, and Dylan’s seat was properly facing to the rear, (which was not only legally correct but also kept the wind out of his face) off to breakfast they went.

As the wind whipped through his hair, Grey paid no attention to the conversation in the front seat. He’d put a pair of sunglasses on Dylan so he couldn’t see his eyes but the smile on the little guy’s face spoke volumes. As Grey pushed back into his seat, he let the sun beat down on his face. He found himself drawn to thoughts about Richard. His friend seemed very distant on the phone. Something was definitely wrong. Then there was Blake. Was it really possible that the “Almighty” Blake Kendall was part of this somehow? There were still missing pieces to the puzzle and without them, he and his friends were still in the dark. They had a couple of hours before they had to meet Richard, so for now he was going to enjoy the ride and spending time with his family. Alex was right. It was a beautiful summer's day.

* * * * *

Right before it was time to break for lunch, Tim learned that the prosecution had won the day. His testimony at the hearing had in fact been the reason that the judge ruled to hold the case over for trial. Tim counted his blessing that the defense team had not included Blake Kendall. That would have been a disaster. The opposing counsel turned out to be a couple of shysters, who were known mainly for defending the well connected on the criminal side of the population. Because of this, the prosecution had no trouble utilizing the term 'probable cause' when laying out a very reasonable case.

The morning had gone by much faster than Tim initially anticipated. Now, he was free to grab some lunch and head on back to the harbor. His run in with the Kendall's, Katie specifically, was still fresh in his mind, bubbling away on the back burner and he wanted to give the matter his full attention. The resemblance between her and the other women was probably just a coincidence but he wanted to take a closer look. He figured that he could get some recent pictures of her off his computer. She and Blake were always attending local social events, so he could probably 'Google' everything he needed. The idea of her becoming a possible target for the "Ripper" was probably just a long shot, but right now it was all he really had to go on.

"What the hell," he thought. *"Sometimes you just have to play a hunch."*

On his way to the car, Tim took out his phone to check his messages. Sure enough, the call light was flashing. Renee had called earlier while he was in court. He remembered overhearing her on the phone the night before talking to Rachel about hair, nails or some such thing. They were probably up to something, the usual girl stuff. He'd call her back when he got in the car. He almost made it. He was about three steps away when suddenly a picture of the open elevator door flashed through his head. There she was again, Katie Kendall, long dark hair, deep blue eyes and long legs; just like the other victims. And then it was gone. He took a few steps and reached out for something to hold on to. He leaned against the trunk of the car and stood there for a moment trying to clear his head. When he was satisfied, he moved over to the door and climbed in.

The entire incident only reaffirmed what he was already thinking. There was something here, if only he could make the connection. Mrs. Kendall was the very 'public' wife of a rather well known and powerful attorney. This made her vulnerable. Her husband had most likely accumulated a large list of enemies during his illustrious career. If the killer was truly 'serial' in nature, then maybe these other girls were just a rehearsal for his ultimate act of revenge. He knew the answers had to be somewhere in the file back on the boat. Now that he had a possible motive, he could start to really do some digging.

Tim flipped open his phone and pressed Renee's number. Once he got this call out of the way, he could spend the rest of the afternoon focusing on the case. She picked up immediately and after a few pleasantries, things got down to business. She and Rachel wanted them all to get together for dinner again. She hadn't mentioned it yet to Rachel, but she thought maybe they could all come down to the marina and have dinner on the boat. There was a long pause as Tim considered his options. He really wanted to focus on the file but figured he'd have at least the better part of the afternoon to do so before anyone would arrive.

"Tim? Are you still there?" Renee asked.

"That's fine," Tim assured her. "I've got a lot of work to do this afternoon so can we try to figure out the food and details early?"

"Really? That's great honey. I'll call Rachel right away. And don't worry babe, I'll handle everything. If we show up around five, will that give you enough time to do what you need to do?" she inquired.

"Five is fine," Tim said. "I'll get some gas and fire up the stern barbeque. We can throw on a few steaks or whatever you guys come up with. See you then."

Tim hung up the phone and started the car. He wanted to get back to the boat and get on the computer. If any part of his new theory was even close to being part of the puzzle, he wanted to start connecting the pieces as soon as possible. Tim looked at his watch. He had a little over five hours before he would have to play host to their friends. There was plenty of time to start solving the case by himself.

* * * * *

Tim Galleon had ruined his morning. Not the preliminary hearing mind you; that had lasted all of about fifteen minutes. The judge had dismissed the case on the grounds of a general lack of evidence. The D.A. was furious, but the law was the law and open to interpretation. Blake had carefully persuaded the judge to be in favor of his client's argument. The charges had been dropped for now, but he was certain that this idiot client of his would be back in court expeditiously. As for Detective Galleon, his comments or suggestions about Katie being a target for the "Ripper" had hit a little too close to home. His short ride back to his office had been consumed with nothing but curiosity about the possibilities the direction the cop's mind could be taking. He was so concerned about Galleon's implications that he didn't even bother to stop to see Sylvester. He just gave him a quick, acknowledging wave as he headed for the elevator. He had to get upstairs.

About half way up, he reconsidered and realized that a visit with Sylvester would have done him some good. It might have at least calmed him down a bit. When the doors opened, he hesitated for a second before stepping out of the elevator. Truth was, if Sheila hadn't seen him, he probably would have just gone back downstairs. She smiled at him as he approached her desk.

"Well, you certainly made quick work of the Carlyle case this morning," she began, "The phone's been ringing off the hook since I figure, oh, about ten minutes after you stepped out of court. Carlyle's people think you're a god but the D.A. is ready to explode. Should I get him on the phone?" she asked sarcastically.

Then something strange happened. Blake took a seat in one of the reception area chairs. If it had been anybody else, it wouldn't have raised an eyebrow, but in all the time she had been working for him, she had never seen him sit casually out front. He always carried himself above the idea of having a casual persona at work. He commanded the respect that came from sitting behind his massive mahogany desk in a black leather chair that was set at a specifically designated height that allowed him to always be looking down at his clients.

"No," Blake snickered. "Let him stew for a while. He's just pissed off that I found a loophole in his attack strategy and exploited it. He would have done the same thing if the roles had been reversed."

Sheila was speechless. Not only was Blake sitting slouched in a chair in the front office, but he had just used the word 'pissed'. She didn't think that word was part of his notably advanced vocabulary. The whole exchange was fascinating and she couldn't wait to see where the conversation was going to go next. Much to her dismay, it stopped there. Blake got up slowly and excused himself.

"I'll be in my office if you need me," he said and then disappeared into the next room.

Sheila sat for a minute processing their exchange. Then the phone rang and interrupted her train of thought. "Mr. Kendall's office, can I help you," she said. It was the D.A's office again.

"I'm sorry, but he's still not in," she lied. She didn't know that Blake had come out of his office to get a file and was listening to the conversation. "I'll tell him immediately," she continued, "and thank you for calling," she said. Then she pushed the button to disconnect and he was gone. Under her breath, the word "asshole" slipped out.

"I agree," his voice echoed from behind her. "I don't pay you enough, do I?" he asked.

Sheila smiled but didn't turn around. "Sometimes I wonder," she insinuated. "I guess I should see about negotiating a raise then?" she teased.

"Leave your terms on my desk and I'll review them before the end of the day," he assured her. He was actually serious. Then he turned to go back to his office. He stopped at his door and finished his thought. "Oh, and Sheila, if I don't say it enough, thank you."

"Let's see if you still feel that way after you get my terms," she joked with him again.

"I'm not worried," he said as he put a foot inside his office, "and neither should you."

Then he closed his door behind him. He needed a 'fix' but more importantly, he needed to get a hold of this thing with Galleon. He sat back in his chair and started to review every detail of his previous actions. Right now, the cop didn't pose a threat, but Blake wanted to make sure that things stayed that way. It was several hours before Sheila stuck her head in and asked him what he wanted for lunch, but he had slipped out the back again. She also left an envelope on his desk. The only clue to its contents was a question mark on the outside.

* * * * *

Father Richard looked pale. The ever expanding formation of dark circles under his eyes was only the first indication to both Grey and Alex that their friend hadn't been sleeping. From his first words, they could tell that he was emotionally tired as well. After escorting them into his office, he figured there was safety in numbers, Richard moved slowly back to his desk. As he returned to his seat, he tried to shove the remnants of his breakfast into his top desk drawer. Grey noticed the wrappers but decided not to comment. Richard didn't bother trying to hide the coffee cup. That was easily explainable. He simply poured what was left into an empty mug that was sitting on his desk and then tossed the cup in the wastebasket. Now that everything was in order, he was ready to engage his friends.

"Thank you for coming," he commented. "Before we get started, if you don't mind, I'd like to share with you both, something that has been troubling me for the past week or so. It all started initially with me having a bad dream. I understand that this phenomenon is a relatively normal experience on occasion for a lot of people so at first I really wasn't concerned. Especially when one takes into account all the parameters of the issues we have been addressing lately and what they entail." Richard took a breath. "Murder, violence and death have a way of leaving their mark on people and I don't think that any of us would argue that. These incidents however, have since escalated into a lot of horrific nightmares. The thing they have in common is that they are related somehow to the Kelly Richfield murder. The reenactment of the funeral, the body, her voice crying out to me for help, has certainly robbed me of many a good night's sleep. Now, while I consider myself a very strong minded individual and definitely a man of faith, most of what took place in theses dreams felt very, very real. I'm confident that the two of you can understand my concern."

Grey was now completely at a loss for words. He glanced over at Alex who wasn't in any better condition and then motioned for the priest to continue. Alex nodded. Richard was relieved because he knew they were taking him seriously. He took a big gulp from his mug and then continued.

"What's really bothering me isn't the issue with Kelly," he began. "It's the others, the other voices that seem to coexist with her. There are at least four or five other women who are trying to communicate with me. This has been happening to me all week. The last straw finally broke for me this morning. I was sitting here, alone at my desk a little after five-thirty. I was reading over some paperwork when a strange voice started to talk to me. It came to me from above, so it immediately got my attention.

I don't know if you remember but behind you, overhead on the wall is a rather life size crucifix. Imagine at that hour of the morning where my mind raced. It took me a minute but I soon realized that the voice was Kelly's. It was deeper and more gurgled but most definitely hers. She was taunting me, trying to get me to acknowledge her. She said she has the devil in her. Maybe she thinks that because of the way she died," he mumbled under his breath almost as an afterthought. "She told me she understood me, my confusion and pain about her death, but she said she had the devil in her now and wanted to buy my soul. I tried not to look up, but after a few attempts to ignore her, the temptation was too great. When I looked up, it was no longer the body of Christ staring down at me. It was Kelly hanging there crucified to the wall."

"That's unbelievable!" Alex suddenly blurted out. This outburst of course was completely out of character for her but Grey knew that she only beat him to it.

"Sorry Father, I didn't mean it like that." she said apologetically.

"Don't worry Alex, I completely understand. I want to emphasize that this all took place while I was under the impression that I was awake! Then Richard took a deep breath. His shoulders dropped noticeably as he slumped back slightly in his chair. "Thank you both for hearing me out. I know it was a lot to swallow," he said. "If you will excuse me for a minute, I'll be right back." Then he quietly stepped out of the room. His two friends stared at each other in total disbelief.

"Well, that certainly puts an interesting spin on things doesn't it?" Grey quietly admitted.

Alex got up and walked slowly over to the window. She stared at the colors in the stained glass and then turned back to Grey. "Are you going to tell him?" she asked. There was a long pause.

"You mean about my dream?" Grey responded.

"Considering that you're his friend, it might help him to know he's not crazy," she said.

"You're probably right," Grey agreed, "but do you think he can handle that right now? The poor man is more than likely, in the sanctuary as we speak, down on his knees praying for something to give. I only hope he gets some answers before he decides that he's losing his mind."

"That hasn't happened quite yet," Richard said as he came back into the room. "I only manage to catch the last bit of that but, yes I did need a moment alone in prayer. If we're going to discuss the stability of my mind however, at the present time I believe that my level of sanity or for that matter, insanity, is entirely up to the two of you."

Grey looked over at Alex who remained silent. He turned back to Richard, put his hand on his friends shoulder and said, "Well, thanks Father, that's a comfort, good to know. No pressure right?"

His sarcastic tone instantly broke the tension that had taken over the room. The three of them started to relax. "You're not alone my friend and you're definitely not crazy," Grey continued. "I recently had a very similar dream. One of the reasons we came over here this morning was to discuss it with you. You see, I think I've started to figure this whole ordeal out, but some of the pieces of the puzzle are so outrageous that I have to be a hundred percent sure before we say or do anything. There is far too much at stake.

"All right," Richard said as he returned to his chair. "I guess it's your turn."

Grey began by reminding Richard about the discussion that the three of them had a few days earlier about the massages he'd done on Blake. It was during these sessions that he had his first visual of a hand and a knife. At the time, he had written the incidents off as just being a little weird. Now, he wasn't so sure. He spoke firmly about the information that he now knew he had been exposed to during those sessions. He and Alex had compared that information with what he had seen while experimenting on Richard. After working on Richard, and then discussing the matter with him, there was no way to discount the accuracy and features of what Grey was seeing. Everything he recounted about the experience was exactly correct. He also discovered that as time passed, every time he touched someone, the detail was always getting clearer. It all came down to one inescapable conclusion. If the information exchange he had experienced with Richard was beyond reproach, then what did that say about his encounters with Blake?

It was here that Richard decided to jump back in. "So where do you suggest we start?" he asked. He was now sitting upright in his chair at full attention. He reached over and chugged the last of his coffee. When his face went sour, Grey knew that it had turned cold. Grey and Alex shifted their chairs closer to his desk.

"Is there any way you can possibly confirm any of this?" Richard inquired. "Otherwise we are just flatuating in the wind."

Grey and Alex just looked at each other. That was funny. Father Richard was actually trying to be funny? Ok, he was under a lot of stress. Neither one laughed but he did have a point. Grey was first to speak up.

"If all of these things I see happen when my hands are on Blake, then why don't I try to get him back on my massage table? He would never know what I was really up to, and maybe I can find something that will help us. I don't think it will be difficult at all to get him back in that position.

"That sounds like a good idea," Richard agreed. "What do you think Alex?"

"I think that at this point, there's no danger in Grey trying to get more information," she said. "It would be different if Blake suspected something. As long as he remains oblivious to the thought that anyone is on to him, there shouldn't be a problem."

"I guess that settles it then," Grey concluded. "I'll find a way to set up another session with Blake. I'll work on him with my only intention being that I try to find something in his memories that will confirm or negate our suspicions. If I come across anything even the least bit substantial, then we'll reconvene afterward and try to decide what to do next. Does this sound good to everyone?"

Both Richard and Alex expressed their approval. They all agreed that the next step now was in Grey's hands, literally. He assured them both that he would try to set something up with Blake before the end of the day. Time had become a factor now because who knew when or where the "Ripper" would strike next. In order to eliminate Blake as a suspect, Grey had to get his hands on him as soon as possible. It was time for Grey and Alex to get on with their day.

Grey got up and went over to give Richard a hug. "Hang in there, my friend," he said. He was getting ready to leave. Alex leaned in for one too.

"We'll keep in touch Father," she said softly. "And thanks for listening."

"Go with God," Richard blessed them as they made their way out the office door. Then he had a second thought. "Hey, would you mind leaving it open?" he requested as Grey began to close the door behind them. Grey waved as he headed off through the sanctuary. Once again, Richard was alone in his office. He decided to risk it and looked up at the crucifix on the wall. Jesus was still there.

"You know, I'm going to need your help with this," he informed the statue, the one that represented everything that held his world together. The room remained quiet. He really didn't expect a response. After a few more minutes, his Savior had still resigned from turning back into

Kelly and that was good enough for Richard. Some signs, he figured, are better left unseen.

* * * * *

The computer search revealed an abundance of information. Apparently the Kendall's were a lot more popular on the invitation circuit then Tim had originally anticipated. Their well documented appearances at charity functions alone, filled page after page of local magazines and gossip 'rags'. He started with the old stuff and worked his way up to the new. He was not surprised to discover that his initial assessment was correct. The resemblance between Katie Kendall and the other victims was astonishing. She was almost a dead ringer for several of them. Almost all of her physical characteristics were an easy match with all of the "Ripper" victims. Now the big question was: coincidence or potential target? Tim decided that his best bet was start back at the beginning.

With this new idea in mind, it would be like reading the file again with a fresh pair of eyes. If the only connection between all of these women was their physical appearance, then the killer must have some kind of vendetta against a woman who fit their description. The victims were simply reminders of her.

This is what triggered the idea when he saw Katie Kendall. She could very easily be a target. With her husband's track record and known associates, it wasn't a big stretch to say that maybe someone out there could be trying to send Mr. Kendall a message. That, or get even with him for some other issue. Either way, it was worth checking out. Tim glanced at the time. Renee and company would be there in a couple of hours and that would pretty much kill the rest of the day. Tim knew he had work to do, so he figured he better get started.

* * * * *

CHAPTER 21

Katie Kendall was lying on her bed wearing nothing but a smile. The sheets were freshly changed and she hoped that her champion was on his way. Christine wouldn't be home until late so she had the house to herself. Katie rolled around in the bed playfully splashing herself with champagne; mostly because on various parts of her body, it tickled. After the nasty little text message and accompanying picture had been received, it probably didn't take long for him to get the idea. She wanted to play. Her outfit for court was her idea of foreplay. Fortunately for Katie, Blake didn't get the message, the 'Cat' did. The dress had done exactly what she had intended it to do: played to his dark side. It had disturbed his libido enough that he had even baited the conversation with Tim in the elevator just to exploit his opinion.

To Blake's credit, he had made it back to the office still in control until he received Katie's text. After that, he had to give in to the 'Cat'. At this point, anything that Katie was up to was most certainly bad but he liked it that way, bad. Bad Katie, Bad Katie. As long as his alter ego was in charge, Katie was in no danger. He had never removed his razor from the safe and his friend had no way to get to it. Even Katie didn't know the combination. It was designed that way as another form of protection. Right now, Blake was still able to keep the majority of the mental aspects of himself and his counterpart separate. Eventually though, one would attempt to transcend the other and that would be a disaster.

In the beginning, his decision to cross over had never been about sex. He had deplored the idea because it made him think about Katie and Walter. He couldn't hurt Katie the way he wanted to, so he had found an alternate way to take out his anger on suitable replacements. The other women had all been young and desirable, but he couldn't bring himself to engage them in any kind of illicit behavior because of the hatred and betrayal that he carried around in his head. It was easy to ignore the obvious sexual implications of each situation because at the time, he was still in charge. Last night however, things changed. It wasn't that he felt any different about the sex, but the 'Cat' did. For the first time, Blake was beginning to understand the depth of its dark influence and how it had changed him over time. It was now sharing control of that part of his personality too. Blake knew that he still had some authority, but for the moment, he was going to take full advantage of the delicious invitation from his wife, and his friend was going to help. He stepped on the gas and the Mercedes gnawed at the asphalt. He hoped he would get there in time.

* * * * *

Grey and Alex headed back to the house after leaving Father Richard. Grey was quiet on the ride home and had a worried look on his face. Alex didn't question him right away just in case he was trying to work something out in his head. As they were getting off the freeway, Grey finally had something to say.

"You think Richard's all right?" he asked. He was staring off in the other direction. There was a brief pause. "I'm still not sure that he's up for all this," he continued, his focus still off somewhere in the distance. Alex was going to engage him, but he didn't give her a chance. "And what about these dreams of his? This whole thing is getting stranger by the minute, even by our definition. I'm really at loss here."

"You want me to pull over?" she responded. "Give you a chance to get your head on straight?"

"Yeah, I guess," he answered now turning his head to look at her. "Why don't you pull into the parking lot over there? Maybe if I call Katie right now, I'll feel better about getting this thing started."

"That might be a good idea," Alex agreed. "If you can get this set up, then we'll have an initial time frame to work with," she observed as she pulled into the liquor store parking lot. "You make the call and I'll get us a couple of sodas, ok?" Alex turned into the parking lot and parked near the front door. "I'll be back in few," she said as she got out and headed inside. Grey grabbed his phone and pulled up the Kendall's number. He sat for a minute before hitting the call button. He had to convince himself he was just booking a massage. Katie answered on the second ring.

"Hey baby, is that you?" she answered. She sounded a little buzzed.

"Sorry Katie, it's Grey. I'm sorry to bother you. Hope I didn't catch you at a bad time." He didn't get to see Katie blush. At first she was embarrassed but then it occurred to her that he had no idea that she was butt naked and fairly well covered in champagne. Naked, alone and a nice looking guy on the other end of the phone, well the possibilities were just endless weren't they? She guessed she had about twenty minutes before Blake would arrive.

"No, everything's fine," she assured him. "It's just me and my morning mimosa. Well it's not actually a mimosa. I wanted it to be, but we were completely out of orange juice. Of all the luck," she giggled. Then her voice changed and she tried to get serious. "I'm sorry Grey, what can I do for you?"

"After I left last time, I forgot to set your next appointment. We talked about it, but I forgot to put it in my book. Should we talk about this later?"

"Oh no, God, this is wonderful!" she exclaimed. "Your timing is perfect. I had a really rough time last night and today's not going to be any less brutal. I'm kind-a beat up. I think I put myself through too strenuous of a workout." (It was more like a major overload of hardcore sexual insatiability and masochism, completely consensual of course.)

"Sounds like you could use some help," he offered. Katie smiled with pleasure and rolled back across the bed. Grey couldn't see her erotic smile or any of the aroused body parts their conversation was creating. He also couldn't see what she was doing with her free hand.

"I definitely could," she flirted. Grey considered this a mild tease or at the very least, the champagne was kicking in.

"Why don't you take it easy this afternoon after your workout and I'll see you in the morning?" he suggested.

Katie laughed. She wondered what if anything would be left for him to fix. "All right," she said. "Can you come about nine?" She giggled as the words came out.

"Nine will work, no problem," he assured her, "and as always, even at that hour of the morning," he snickered, "service with a smile."

"You have no idea," Katie thought out loud.

Grey only heard a mumble so he didn't respond. "See you in the morning," he said. He was about to hang up when he remembered why he had called in the first place. Katie had him so distracted that he almost forgot. "Hey Katie," he tried to catch her, "Is Blake going to be around?"

There was long silence. Katie sounded like she was running on a treadmill. Suddenly she was back. "What? Oh yeah, you better plan on him too," she requested. "He's not doing much better than I am."

"See you tomorrow, Katie" he confirmed. "Bye Grey," she said and then she was gone. Her voice was almost a whisper. Grey flipped his phone closed.

Alex had returned a few minutes earlier and managed to catch the tail end of the conversation. "Wow, she sounds like a live one," she commented.

Grey could only shake his head. "Yeah, you could say that," he responded. "Anyway, I'm sure you heard enough to know that we're on for tomorrow morning at nine. All I have to do is get through tomorrow morning and we should have all the evidence we need. Right now, all I want to do is go home and relax. Maybe later, we can all take Dylan to the park for an hour or so." Grey sighed. He slid down in the seat and ran his fingers through his hair. "The next twenty four hours are going feel like eternity," he muttered.

Alex laughed and started the car. "No one ever said this was going to be easy," she reminded him. "At least now, maybe we're on the right track." She revved the engine a little as she slid the car into gear and she and Grey shot back out on to the highway. She didn't want to admit it, but he was right. It was going to be a very long wait.

* * * * *

The Mercedes flew up the driveway like a fighter jet landing on a carrier deck. Good thing that the cable on the E-brake worked. Luckily, he came to a stop, just inches from the garage. Blake didn't bother to open the car door, he simply vaulted over it and landed on his feet, his kind always do. His next few decisions were going to be important ones, so he hesitated for a moment to think.

"Hey, I stopped to think," he thought. *"Blake 1, Cat 0."* Then he felt a push. Well that didn't last long. The little head always wins out. Now they were even. By the time he got to the top of the stairs he only had one thing on his mind, a replay of last night. When he opened the bedroom door, he knew why. There was the divine one in all her glory. The sun pouring through the window glistened off her wet champagne coated body. There was a bottle of Moet' et Chandon on her nightstand and a second waiting glass. There was also a bowl of fresh strawberries. If that wasn't temptation enough, one lucky piece of fruit was doing an erotic tongue dance in her mouth. It all looked like a truly delectable feast ready to enjoy.

Katie was sitting in the middle of the bed sitting on her heels. She didn't have to say a word. She tipped her glass just enough to let the slightest of drops dribble down the middle of her chest and then disappear between her legs. Her performance was unbelievable! At least for the moment, it appeared that his friend did seem to have his best interests at heart. There was nothing like an afternoon snack. Blake looked over at the Carney painting hanging on the wall. Part of him really wanted to open the safe. His dark side quickly reminded him that eventually he'd have to kill her, but for right now, he had more appetizing things in mind. Blake smiled. For now, only the champagne would run cold.

When he took a step forward, everything inside him seemed to ignite. He slid slowly out of his Armani suit the way a snake sheds its skin. With absolutely no account for care or dapper, the elegant ensemble in which he had arrived was tossed nonchalantly on the floor. When he gazed over at the bed, he saw the hunger in Katie's eyes. It crossed his mind for a second that now he might have suddenly become the prey. He moved in for a closer look. When he did, he was met by a set of soft, wet lips on his with the familiar taste of strawberry. Their tongues became formal appendages as the luscious fruit passed between them. There was a brief moment of silence and satisfaction, and then it began.

Like an earthquake that happens thousands of miles off shore and sends a small wave traveling across the ocean at increasingly high speed, the Kendall tsunami was born. In its own right, it manifested itself as another dangerous but exhilarating act. Like the many movements and rituals of courtship in the animal kingdom, the thrill was in the danger and the excitement is the lust. That being said, the only thing in the Kendall's bedroom that afternoon that was left unscathed, unappreciated or not manipulated was the painting which hung on the far wall so auspiciously over the safe. While the one combination of Kendall and Kendall had once again erupted in a fiery glow, the lack of the other amalgamation is what undoubtedly saved Katie's life.

When Blake eventually woke up and looked around the room, it finally hit him as to how far out of control things had actually become. He had passed out under the wet bar with an empty bottle of Moet. Katie was laying in a crumpled mass off in the far corner of the room. If he hadn't been able to make out the movement of the sheets she was wrapped in, he would have thought she was dead. To his relief, she was breathing slowly and probably just sleeping it off. The room around him was tossed about like a robbery had taken place. Blake sat up at tried to get his bearings. The nightstand clock said it was four thirty in the afternoon. That couldn't be right. He had first arrived around one. Even worse, he really didn't remember much after that first kiss. "Strawberries?" he thought, "Strawberries." That was the last time Blake remembered he as himself was there. He quickly surveyed the damage his friend had inflicted and hoped that Katie was still in one piece. He could only hope for the best.

Blake pulled himself up off the floor, wrapped himself up in a sheet, and made his way over to his wife. He couldn't help but stop and stare at her for a minute as she just lay there battered on the floor. She was definitely breathing, but he could tell she was pretty worn out. He knelt down, scooped her up and carried her over to the bed. For the moment, his anger was nowhere to be found. There was also no sign of the 'Cat'. He covered her gently with another sheet and headed off to the shower. As he walked into the bathroom, he saw his reflection in the mirror. He was Blake. He looked tired and beat down but he was still Blake. A huge weight was suddenly lifted from of his shoulders. It was almost five o'clock now but he still needed to shower and clean up. He would try to do damage control in the bedroom after he was finished.

He decided to let Katie sleep while he did his thing. Blake ran his hand across his face. His five o'clock shadow felt more like the two day kind. He really needed to shave. He opened the vanity drawer in search of his razor before remembering that it was still taking up residence in the safe. He started to make a move in that direction but then had second thoughts. Right now, the timing, the location, and the 'Cat' were all too close for comfort. It wasn't worth the risk. One more night wouldn't kill him, or him Katie. Blake reached over, turned on the shower and gingerly stepped inside. The steaming water would soon erase all evidence of the day. There was a trickle of blood it the water but this time it was his own. Katie's nails had dug deep and the hot, pulsing water was there to remind him exactly where she had left her marks. It took longer than he expected, but eventually he started to feel better.

Katie slept through his shower and more. He had completely reassembled the bedroom and she had only rolled over once. He was surprised to find his favorite suit crumpled up in a pile on the floor. Knowing his flair for perfection, his friend at the dry cleaners would certainly be full of questions. Whatever had happened between them earlier had been obviously out of control. It was almost seven now and Christine would be home soon. Blake decided he was hungry. He would go down to the kitchen and make up a plate, maybe some cheese and crackers and bring them back upstairs. Then he would check on Katie.

By the time he returned it was close to eight and Katie was still asleep. It would be several more hours before they spoke again.

* * * * *

As he had promised, the barbeque was hot and ready when Renee pulled up at five. Tim tipped back and swallowed the last mouthful of a Heineken as he saw her car approaching. Rachel and company wouldn't be far behind. Renee got out with a couple of bags but declined his offer for help. She had more stuff in the back but had already utilized an empty boat dolly so she could wheel the stuff down by herself. From the looks of things, she'd gone a little overboard but hey, that was Renee. Tim saw Rachel's van pulling up behind her so he went below deck and collected all of the materials he'd been reviewing earlier. He stuck them in a briefcase and shoved them under one of the salon seats.

Out the window, he could see Grey and Rachel getting out of the van. When they opened the back door, he expected to see them get Dylan out. Instead, someone in the back seat handed Dylan to Rachel. Apparently they had brought another friend along. When Alex stepped out of the van, Tim was a little surprised. Renee had mentioned that Grey had a friend visiting from Florida but this was not what he had imagined. He wondered if Rachel was having a hard time with this. Tim went back up on deck and gave everyone a comforting hello wave.

Rachel had Dylan under control so Grey offered to wheel the dolly down to the boat. Before he took over for Renee, he made sure he introduced Alex. He'd dropped the ball the last time at her parent's house and didn't want to disappoint Rachel again. The girls took off for the dock, leaving him alone with the dolly. There was still some room left to pile a few things on, so he took all of Dylan's stuff and threw it on top. Now he could catch up with the girls. The plan was to keep Dylan below deck for safety reasons but good old 'Uncle Tim' had planned for any contingency. He had modified a small toddler size life vest for Dylan to wear on deck so even if he fell in the water, there was no way he could drown. Grey was impressed to say least.

While the girls were doing prep work down below, Grey hung out on the stern by the barbeque with Tim. Chicken, ribs and baked potatoes were already cooking away. Dylan was down below exploring. Tim had left a few toys and stuffed animals in the guest cabin for his special little deckhand to play with. It didn't take long for Dylan to find them. Tim offered Grey a beer and the two men sat and talked while dinner was cooking. They talked sports and music for a while and then Grey decided that he needed to take a chance and see if he could get Tim to talk about work.

"So how's work treating you?" he asked, hoping to open up a topic of conversation.

"It's getting better, I guess," Tim responded. At first he sounded a bit animated but that quickly tapered off.

"Sorry man, bad subject?" Grey suggested. "I didn't mean to pry. I guess you guys, the whole department anyway, are under a lot of pressure with that "Ripper" thing going on. You guys getting anywhere?"

Tim reached for another beer and gestured, offering one to Grey. He politely declined. Tim twisted his top off and flicked it into the trash bag hanging on the railing. "Off the record?" he asked, giving Grey the impression that he wanted somebody to talk to.

Grey changed his mind and grabbed a beer. "As far as I'm concerned, it always has been Tim, ever since you first took me on that first ride-along."

Tim laughed offered Grey a seat. "I think you've already guessed that I'm not officially working this case right?" Tim asked. Grey just nodded. "Well you know me; I've kind of taken it upon myself to look at it on my own with a different set of eyes, if you will. I've managed to collect some pictures and information on the victims through some of my connections. I felt like I was just beginning to get somewhere when something strange happened to me at the courthouse this morning."

He then proceeded to tell Grey about his run in with Blake Kendall in the elevator and the head game they played regarding his wife. At the first mention of Blake's name, Grey wanted to speak up but he could that tell Tim was on a roll and he didn't want to break his momentum.

This Kendall lady was such a perfect match with these other women that I went home and downloaded pictures of her off the internet to compare with the ones in my case file. The resemblance is unbelievable!" Tim was getting louder and more animated as he spoke. This was a bit unusual for him considering his normally calm demeanor.

"Everything ok up there honey?" Renee called up from below. That got Tim's attention and he slowed things down again.

"It's just a long shot, but maybe this "Ripper" guy is an old client of her husband's out for revenge. He's trying to get Blake's attention or get even with him for something. I'm starting to think that Katie Kendall is a possible target, or at least is in some way, motivating all of this."

Grey was surprised to hear this coming out of Tim. The way he was laying it all out did make sense, but Grey knew there was more, much more. He wondered if he should continue with his plan of talking to him but knew that he had really no choice. There was too much at stake. Down in the galley, Alex was starting to sense Grey's apprehension. She asked Renee if she minded her checking out the rest of the boat. It was really an excuse to go out on deck. Renee told her to have fun exploring and off she went. As soon as she was out of earshot, Renee quickly cornered Rachel.

"Some friend, huh," she teased Rachel. "What's up with that?" She was surprised when Rachel didn't even flinch. She just kept on cutting tomatoes for the salad. She didn't want to indulge Renee but then she realized that she had to say something.

"You know, I had my reservations about her in the beginning," she answered reaching for her glass of wine. "But now, for some strange reason, I think that she's actually helping Grey. She's good with Dylan too. I think I can trust her, at least I hope I can."

Renee grabbed the salad bowl and headed for the stairs. She was just starting up when Rachel persuaded her to come back down. "Hey Renee, keep an eye on them tonight and tell me what you think, ok?"

Renee was already on top of things. "Sure, no problem, I'll let you know," she said. Neither of them saw Alex slide by the salon window during their exchange. She made it to the back of the boat just in time to hear Grey start his response.

"Well Tim, I don't know how to start, so I'm just going to put this out there and see what you think," Grey began. Just like he did with Richard, he opened the conversation with, "You may think I'm crazy, but I'm hoping that you can keep an open mind." Tim nodded and worked harder on his second beer but assured Grey that he would try. He kept flipping things on the grill as he went.

"I know you're a cop so that makes this even more weird so bare with me ok?" Grey continued.

Tim's face turned serious. "All right then, what's up?" he asked.

Alex was just a few steps away so at least he didn't feel like he was alone. "Let's start with an awkward coincidence. This guy you're talking about, Blake Kendall. He and his wife are both clients of mine. Truth is we've been friends for over ten years." Tim looked surprised but decided to let Grey continue. "Small world, huh," Grey pointed out. "Everything you said earlier makes perfect sense to me, however, I have some additional information about the Kendall's that you might not know. This is going to have to be a two step process because telling you what I know, and how I know it, are going to test your ability to keep an open mind to the limit."

Grey had baited the hook. Now all he could do was hope that he hadn't pushed the conversation too fast or too far and that Tim was still interested. "Are you still with me?" Grey asked.

Tim nodded and set down his beer. "Are you telling me that you're withholding information from a formal police investigation?" Tim inquired. He was now pulling everything off the fire and transferring it to a tray.

"Not really," Grey responded. "Just shooting off some ideas with a friend about a few things, like you were a few minutes ago. See, that's where the confusion is going to set in. The 'what and how' are going to be a big rock thrown into the pool and you might be very concerned about the ripples." Now, Tim looked more interested than ever. They were about to continue when Renee came up on deck.

"Everything ready to go up there?" she inquired. "We want to start bringing stuff up."

"We're good," Tim replied. "Everybody up on deck," he commanded. The girls all passed him going up the steps, when he spotted Dylan down in the hallway. "Hey buddy, no slackers on my ship," he said trying to sound like a pirate. Dylan just laughed so Tim picked him up and carried him up the stairs. "I found a stowaway below deck, I say we keep him," he insisted, continuing the pirate drawl. Then he handed the lad to Rachel. "If we keep him here in the center cockpit area he should be fine. Besides in that thing, he could float from here to Hawaii."

Rachel laughed when she realized he was right. Dylan looked like a little fishing buoy in his big red vest. She thanked Tim again and then he went back to the stern for another beer. Luckily, Grey was sitting close by. "We need to get back to our conversation after dinner," Tim firmly insisted as he bent down to open the cooler.

Grey nodded. "Find me later," he said. Tim gave him a 'thumbs up' gesture indicating that he was on board and then went off to help Renee.

Alex kept her distance until Grey walked past her. He'd gone only a few feet when he heard her say, "So far, so good, I take it?"

"Yeah, Tim seems pretty responsive so far," he responded. "He wants to pick up the conversation where we left off after dinner. I think he's genuinely interested in what I have to say. Otherwise he would have blown me off or changed the subject by now."

"Well I guess we're off to a good start then," Alex commented. "You mind if just I just hang out with the girls after dinner? It might be easier and a lot less awkward if I chill out with them."

"You're probably right," Grey admitted. "But do me favor, try to stay close. Remember, you're the only backup I've got."

They both heard the boat's bell ring. "Dinner everybody," Renee announced. And what a nice dinner it was. Tim had set up a table in the center cockpit so everyone could sit together. The conversation was both light and pleasant. The guys ate like they were in a hurry and got more than their fill. The girls, always polite ate like ladies but indulged like the men. Even Dylan got in on the act. At one point he gave up on the idea of using his hands and stuck his whole face into the middle of a baked potato. He'd been playing with it for a while and finally decided to just dive in. He looked pretty funny with sour cream coming out of his nose, so everybody got a good laugh.

After dinner, the girls picked up and took everything back down below. Rachel washed, Alex dried and Renee scrambled around to make sure everything made it back to its original place. She knew she could have left it all for Tim, he really wouldn't have minded. It was one of the reasons she loved him, but she'd promised him that she'd handle everything and so she did. Rachel and Alex were in good spirits and didn't seem to mind at all. Grey and Tim had returned to the cooler on the stern hoping to pick things up again. Tim opened another beer but Grey chose to decline again. For what it was worth, he needed a clear head.

"So, are we going to do this, or what?" Tim asked. Then he saw the reaction on Grey's face and tried again. "Sorry man, I'm not sure what to say."

"That's understandable considering I'm not sure what to say either," Grey responded. "So here's what I figure we do. I'm going to tell you the what and the how, you're going to look at me like I've lost my mind, and then I'm going show you something to back up what I'm saying. Everything will work out ok as long as you're willing to be patient and listen."

"Now you're sounding serious," Tim assessed. "Am I going to need another beer for this?" he asked.

Grey had that look on his face again and said, "Am I wasting my time here? Just tell me and we're done. Seriously man, I could really use your help."

"All right, all right, I'm sorry," Tim conceded. "This entire case is frustrating the hell out of me. You can talk to me man. I'm listening. Let's see what you've got."

Nothing could have prepared Tim for what Grey had to say, and Grey had a lot. He didn't tell him the details about his and Alex's former adventures. It wasn't really relevant, but he did say that he would explain their relationship later. Right now, they had to focus on all of the strange events that had taken place since the accident. Tim was all ears and as Grey explained everything from after he woke up, his first encounter with the nurse, his contact with the Connors girl, and even the incident with the candy striper. Tim sat quietly and listened as Grey labored through all of the details. All in all, it was a pretty amazing story. Tim was amazed by the even the possibility of what Grey was saying being true.

When they took a short break, Tim's curiosity was on fire. "So what does this have to do with the Kendall's?" he inquired. Grey was obviously trying to set things up so that Tim would understand.

"Everything or nothing," Grey responded. "That all depends on what I'm about to tell you and you're personal and professional opinion on the subject," Grey insisted. He had come this far with the conversation and Tim had not tried to shut him down. It was time to lay it all on the line.

"All right, here we go," Grey started. "Based on what I've told you about my interaction with the people at the hospital, you know that after whatever happened to me in the accident, I can see what people are thinking when I'm in more than just momentary contact with them. Can we say for the sake of argument that you're willing to accept this from me as being true?"

"I think its wild but for the sake of argument, sure, why not." Tim replied. "But this is way off the scope my friend."

"I'll give you that," Grey admitted. "So, you know that Blake Kendall is a regular client of mine, right?"

"I do now," Tim answered.

"Well, what if I told you that I've seen the Kendall's since the accident for massages, and when I worked on Katie the first time, I found out she was having an affair with Walter Greenberg. I'm sure that you've heard of the firm, Greenberg, Weisman and Davis. They originally offered Blake a partnership, but he turned them down. He didn't want to have to answer to anyone. Anyway, when I put my hands on her, I got a video feed in my head of what she was thinking about. Turned out she was remembering a shopping trip to Victoria's Secret that she took with Walter recently. They spent a lot of money; enough that I'll bet if you checked it out, the sales girl would remember them."

"So Kendall's wife is cheating on him huh?" Tim asked

"You could say that," Grey admitted. "I wasn't sure until I flipped her and I worked on her back, but after that, it was a no brainer."

"Does Blake know?" Tim continued. "I mean, that would be huge."

"I really don't know the answer to that one," Grey conceded. "But that brings us back to Blake. This is the time where the 'You'll think I'm crazy' part comes in." Grey paused for a second, deep cleansing breath, and then proceeded to just lay it all out on the table.

"My first experience with Blake after the accident was strange to say the least. When I started to work on him, all he was thinking about was B horror movie type stuff. You know, girls screaming, blood and guts kind of stuff. I do admit though that I didn't give it to much thought at the time, I just wrote it off as a little bizarre. I mean, after all, he is a defense lawyer and has probably represented some pretty outrageous clients over the years. But then it happened. When I flipped him over on my table, I got an almost identical replay of the front side but with some additional information. A new face was added and now, there was a detailed close-up of a hand and a knife; a straight razor to be more accurate. Again, it didn't mean much at the time but now it's starting to make some sense. The hand, the razor, the girls, you follow me right? It's the perfect scenario for describing the "Ripper" case. To me, it all fits." "And you're seeing this all in your head like some kind of video feed?" Tim asked. There was only a slight hint of sarcasm this time but Grey figured there would be until he could provide him with some actual evidence. Cops liked proof. It made their jobs easier. "So let me get this straight, you are strongly suggesting to me that you think Blake Kendall could be involved in the "Ripper" case?"

"Yeah," Grey answered in a soft monotone voice. "The worst part is that if what I suspect is true, then the guy I've known and respected for many years is really a sadistic psychopath. How could someone get away with doing this for so long? More importantly though, if we can confirm any of this, how do we stop him? I can't just walk into the police station and say, "Hi, I'm Grey Thomas. I'm a massage therapist and I was in this car accident, and when I woke up I could see things in people's minds when I'm in contact with them during a massage. You know, when I put my hands on them. I think I know who the "Ripper" is because he's one of my clients and I saw girls getting killed with a straight razor, in his head, while I was working on him. I can even describe everything to you in detail."

Grey paused for a minute to catch his breath. Then he finished his thought, "Do you really think that's going to fly, Tim?" he asked. "All I can see is them locking me up in a small padded room."

Tim took another swallow. "Well, granted this is a lot to process. Especially because of whom you're talking about. For God's sake Grey, I was just talking to the man at the court house this morning. I even road upstairs in the elevator with him."

Tim just sat there shaking his head. "Funny thing is, even though I think it sounds completely insane, I know you wouldn't bring this to me if you weren't serious about what you're saying. The good part is, it also makes me wonder if it's possible. I'm not saying that I understand this getting into someone's head stuff, but you sure are serious, so for now I'll give you the benefit of the doubt."

"Thanks. At least that's a step in the right direction," Grey conceded. Then everything got quiet. The two men sat in silence, nursing their beers and listening to the sounds of the surrounding harbor. A good ten minutes passed before Grey spoke up. During the hiatus, he had come up with an idea.

"Hey Tim, do me a favor, will ya? Think about something. Just let your mind go. Something at work maybe, you and Renee, something only you would know, ok."

Tim gave Grey a peculiar look. "Why?" he asked.

"I want to show you something," Grey responded. "What have you got to lose?" Tim nodded and stood up. "One more thing, I need you to play along with what I do. I promise you, it's nothing weird, ok? Just ride it out for a few minutes. It might help us settle a few things."

Tim set his beer down and walked over to the rail. The lights on the shoreline cast a beautiful glow across the water. Grey left him alone with his thoughts for awhile and then approached him. Tim's right hand was on the railing. Grey simply put his hand on Tim's.

"Just stay focused," he told him. Surprisingly enough, Tim didn't pull away.

He heard Grey speak, but his mind was still at the ballpark watching the Angel game with Grandpa Eddie. It was the last game they'd seen together. The beer flowed. The peanut shells were scattered and there was a mustard stain on the front of Eddie's jersey from a hotdog he'd had back in the top of the second inning. When Salmon hit a leadoff home run to start the bottom of the eighth, Grey figured he'd seen enough. He let go of Tim's hand.

The entire episode had passed in a matter of minutes. As Grey stepped away, Tim asked, "So what was that all about?"

Grey stopped at the cooler and grabbed his friend a fresh beer. He opened it and handed it to Tim. "You might want to sit down for this," he warned. "It's time to go all in."

Tim looked up. "Maybe you are crazy man," he said. Grey knew he was starting to lose him, but he still had the upper hand.

"Really?" he responded casually. Grey shook his head a little and said, "So tell me buddy; how was the game?"

"What ga.....?" Tim started to reply. It was right there that Tim Galleon caught himself and his mind immediately hit the brakes. He knew that he hadn't been talking, even mumbling a sound for the past ten minutes. There was absolutely no way that Grey could have known what he was thinking about. He, himself hadn't thought about that game in years and he had certainly never discussed it with Grey. But Grey knew; but how? Then he remembered his hand, the hand on the rail. Grey had put his hand on top of his for a fairly uncomfortable length of time! Grey had set him up! The contact that Grey had mentioned earlier had definitely taken place. Tim's mind raced. When he looked up at Grey again, all he saw was a cautious grin.

"Interesting huh?" Grey commented. His voice was just above a whisper. Tim just sat there speechless trying to get a grip.

"Do you want me to go into the details, or is that enough to convince you?" Grey inquired.

Now, Tim was back to shaking his head again. Grey wasn't at all surprised by his reaction.

"This is only your first experience with this," Grey continued. "Imagine my confusion after a half a dozen times, give or take a few."

Then there was another awkward silence. Tim sat quietly with his face in his hands.

"That's just fucking amazing," he said quietly but firmly. "I'm real close to being on board with you now," Tim admitted, "But just for the sake of conversation, can you give me something else man, something you know, to push me over the top?"

Down below, the girls were finishing off the last of the chardonnay. Grey could see Dylan crashed out on bunk. For a moment, he managed to make eye contact with Alex. One look said it all.

Grey smiled. "You mean like the mustard on Eddie's shirt from the hotdog in the second inning?" he offered. It was all he needed to say.

* * * * *

CHAPTER 22

January 1984

Katie Franklin was hopelessly in love. About half way through her junior year in college, a tall, handsome young man had drifted into her life and swept her off her feet. He was young, strong, ambitious and devilishly good looking. He was on the A track for law school at Cambridge University and had a bright and promising future. He was kind, gentle and attentive. The only downside was that Blake was a senior and set to graduate with honors in June. Her studies would leave her a year behind, but neither one of them considered that to be a problem. Together, they would find a way to work it out.

During the week, he spent most of his free time studying while she waited tables at an off campus pub. On the weekends though, everything switched gears. From the wee hours of the morning on Saturdays when she got off work, until Monday morning at six a.m., they were inseparable. They almost never left her apartment. The Chinese food and pizza delivery guys knew them on a first name basis. Roommates came and went, but the two of them were always together.

And then one night in early March, things changed. Blake's obsession with the law began. He came home late from class and informed Katie that he had received a letter indicating that because of his exemplary academic performance, the powers that be at Cambridge wanted him to start law school early over the coming summer. They wanted him to matriculate in as soon as possible. This acknowledgement of his talents not only played heavily into his already inflated ego, but quickly put a stop to his and Katie's plans for an after graduation vacation in Miami. Katie did not take the news well but understood the importance of the opportunity and how it would affect their future. She quietly let the issue slide and she and Blake moved on.

Everything was right on track until about a week later when one morning Katie discovered that she was pregnant. Not the kind of news one wants to share with a significant other who is seldom available during the week, and about ready to start fast tracking his first year of law school. It was bad timing all around. They still had three months until Blake graduated so she decided to buy some time and keep the situation a secret for a while. She feared that under the circumstances, he might want her to terminate the pregnancy. That was something she could never do. Katie didn't know it at the time, but her silence was her first mistake.

It was the last week of May when Blake finally learned about the pregnancy. Katie had been good about leaving out her monthly supplies in a timely fashion which helped provided a great deception, but she was sure that with Blake's schedule, he hardly noticed much of anything. She knew she would start showing soon and that's where the problem began. Afraid of coming clean and risking their relationship she figured if she timed things right; work schedules, classes, study group time, after all, she had her own classes and G.P.A. to worry about, she could almost 'physically' avoid him for five days of the week. He was so lost in his own cloud of ambition, that maybe she could even pull the occasional 'girl's night out' thing on the weekends. It was a good idea at the time, but it all turned out to be wishful thinking.

Blake discovered the news completely by accident. He was studying one night over at the campus library when he overheard two of Katie's girlfriends talking. He was standing behind a row of books and they thought they were alone. He only caught the tail end of the conversation, but that was more than enough to light the betrayal fire. Katie had a secret and had gone out of her way to deceive him to keep it. He spent the walk across campus to her place, trying to decide how to handle the situation. Parenthood at the moment was certainly not an option and Katie would just have to see that. He was on the track, picking up speed and no one; absolutely no one, was going to derail him. He had no way of knowing that Katie had spent the last four months preparing to defend to the death, the rights of their unborn child. One way or another, she was going to keep the baby. She knew she was in for a fight. Her apartment was about to become a tinder box of emotions with Blake holding a match.

When it was over, Blake found himself in a hotel room in Queens, New York. Not a glamorous one by any means, but it satisfied his immediate needs. He was sitting on the bed, watching TV and dry shaving his face with a straight razor that his father had given him when he was a teenager. He had just turned thirteen and by the laws of Judaism, the religion his ancestors had practiced, become a man. It was a rite of passage for the men in the family. Someday soon, he would use it with pride. It was a beautiful thing and he enjoyed the feel of it in his hand. When he held it correctly, he and the blade became one.

He had driven south all night, trying to put as much distance between him and her evil deception as possible. At the time, the two hundred plus miles had seemed like enough. When he drew back the curtains in the morning and saw the light of day, it definitely wasn't. When he opened the door to let in some fresh air, he swore that he could still smell her hair on the breeze. Katie had loved him, motivated him and continued to feed his hunger for success. But now, to think she had the nerve to try to trap him with a baby! She called his phone several times during the night but he just let it ring. There was nothing left to say. She was trying to kill him. She was trying to destroy everything he had worked so hard to achieve. In a few years, all of his secrets and sins from the past would be forgotten. No one would ever know about what he did to the cat. He would soon become… Blake Kendall, Esquire: protector, champion of the law. He could not allow a baby to interfere with his plans for redemption.

Then his mind jumped back to Katie. He wanted to kill her. He knew he couldn't really kill her, open her up the same way he had killed the cat, but it would sure be fun to think about it. In his mind, blood flowed. The Jack Daniels ate away at his brain, the same way she had devoured his heart. Tomorrow, if he was lucky, he would sober up and go home.

It was two weeks before the first body showed up. It was found floating in a storm drain near Cambridge, Massachusetts. She was a young college kid, nice figure, long dark hair and blue eyes. She kind of looked like Katie. Her time in the water however, was not the cause of death. The coroner paid close attention to her throat which had been slashed from ear to ear with an extremely sharp object. The cause of death was obvious. He estimated that there were only a few seconds between point of impact and when she bled out.

In mid June, Blake graduated at the top of his class. After the cap and gown parade including what he considered to be a below average arrangement of pomp and circumstance, as valedictorian he was asked to deliver a few words of encouragement. He did so with a style all his own, shook a few hands and then carefully slipped away into the crowd. He headed directly for the quiet refuge of his apartment. For the next few hours, Blake sat alone staring out the window across the street. He was going to miss this view of the campus. Seeing it always motivated him to go out and accomplish something. He looked for Katie at the graduation ceremony but she couldn't bring herself to attend. She was showing now and the risk of infuriating Blake again was much more than she was willing to bear.

He had made several inquiries about her over the past few weeks through friends and even seen Katie pass through the courtyard below, the bounty of his seed was visible now, but he had never actually tried to make contact with her. Part of him missed her, but the darkest side of him hated her for what she had done. Katie's indiscretions had brought out another element of him that had been buried away for years. This sinister persona had remained dormant since early adolescence; back in the summer of nineteen seventy-six, when he'd taken his feline friend out to the shed. The cat had betrayed his love for her by spending most of its time now with the new little girl that had moved in down the street. He'd petted her for hours before turning on her.

For years, his dreams were haunted by her frightened and vengeful eyes. He could still hear her cries, feel her fur and smell her blood. It sent shivers down his spine and warmed the crotch of his jeans. For a moment, he even thought about the little girl. How he'd let her escape. Now, almost a decade later, that side of him was awake again, alive and well in the mirror. Blake took another shot of Jack Daniels and sharpened the cold steel in his hand. The 'Cat' had returned.

* * * * *

Three weeks after graduation, Blake Kendall started law school. He was smart, creative and unyielding with his research and arguments. His professors were astounded by his ability to think fast on his feet and then apply his newly developing skills in any and all situations. By the end of the summer, he was already beginning to surpass all of his professor's expectations. He had left all of his fellow classmates behind, that, and a few more ceremonial bodies. He had sought them out only when his anger and hunger for revenge was too great. He couldn't get the thought of Katie and his child out of his head. Blake was confused.

Maybe because of the child, and only because of the child, he could allow himself to try to trust Katie again. After all, shortly following his thing with the Casper, the urges had faded away. Well, not completely, but he had managed to suppress them and control of them for years. Perhaps now, under these unique circumstances he could do it again. It would all depend on his initial contact with Katie. If she was the least bit responsive to any possible reconciliation, then he would be motivated to try. The thought of her having their child, and then raising it without him was simply unacceptable. If he could re-animate his relationship with Katie, and they could find away to move ahead, then the evil hunger within him would recede and there would be no more blood. Blake knew what he had to do. He had to find Katie. A few hours later, he did.

When Katie opened the door, she was expecting to see Ethan the pizza delivery guy. She had no way of knowing that Blake had cornered him downstairs, paid him off including a generous tip, and then sent him on his way. When Blake rang the bell, he made sure to hold the pizza box high and dropped his head to shorten his appearance. He was hoping she wouldn't scream.

She did drop the twenty she had in her hand. Hell, if it had been October, the baby would have dropped too! For a minute or so; both of them couldn't come up with anything to say. Then Katie reached down to pick up the twenty dollar bill off the floor.

"What do I owe you?" she asked, not knowing what else to say. Blake decided to play along.

"It's more like what I owe you," he responded in a calm deep voice. "And right now, the answer is everything." His eyes shifted to Katie's tummy.

For the first time in his life, his attention was divided. He didn't know whether to focus on her or on the baby. Part of him couldn't escape the fact of how good it felt to see her face, but the subtle, bulging roundness of her was evident under her royal blue football jersey. She wore #7, Elway, the former starting quarterback for the Denver Broncos. Elway was her favorite player. Blake had bought it for her back in January to wear to a Super Bowl party they attended. He thought she would have thrown it away by now but apparently it still represented some kind of connection. Katie noticed he was distracted and let him stew for awhile. It amused her to see him so taken back and unprepared. He was almost nervous. So was she.

"How are you holding up?" he asked. Katie was surprised to hear the sincerity in his voice. It almost sounded like he cared.

"I'll be ok I guess, as long as you don't try to leave with the pizza." She teased. "And by the way, what happened to Ethan?"

"He's fine, and a little richer for the experience," he answered. "I took the initiative and intercepted him downstairs on the street and confiscated a larger pizza, Pepperoni. I hope you don't mind. I was getting hungry and thought that maybe I could talk you into sharing."

Katie was at a crossroad and she knew it. She could just shut the door and make him go away, or indulge him for a minute and try to feel him out. "You do know that this thing is way too complicated to work out over a pizza," she said. Blake nodded and lowered the pizza box.

"Of course," he said. "But this one is getting cold and at least it's a place to start. I upgraded us to a large because I figured you were eating for two."

Katie smiled. *"That was funny,"* she thought. It was enough to break the ice.

After a few weeks of careful planning, heated debate, and a lot of concessions on both sides, they managed to work things out. Katie announced that she wanted a wedding and surprisingly enough, Blake agreed. If he was going to be a respectable, upstanding individual, he might as well start now. They baby was due in October so they had to get busy. Katie volunteered to handle everything as long as Blake promised to focus his attention his career. She would put in the extra time now and he would take over when he graduated. It was a contract made in heaven, and sealed in everything but blood.

A few nights later, Katie overheard Blake talking to himself in the bathroom. He sometimes did this when he was rehearsing an oral argument so she didn't pay much attention. Truth was; he was burying the 'Cat'. The battle was fierce, but in the end Blake won. Blake smiled; a 'Cheshire Cat' smile, as the 'Cat' crawled off into the darkness to lick its wounds. It would be more than a quarter of a century before Blake would have to meet with him again.

* * * * *

July 2011

Grey could not get a word in edge wise so he settled for a little Rod Stewart music on the ride home. He wondered how Dylan could sleep through all that chatter. For the moment, the wine appeared to have equalized the playing field as far as the girls were concerned. Grey knew better than to think Alex was drunk but enjoyed her communing with Rachel just the same. Tim was still a bit anxious when he came out to say goodnight. The thank you handshake was definitely a little awkward, but Grey understood his friend's momentary hesitation. The second half of their evening had been much more than Tim bargained for. Grey told him to sleep on it and that he would call him as soon as he was finished with Blake. If necessary, they would get together tomorrow afternoon to discuss the results. Right now, he had to center his attention on details. If things went smoothly, he'd have Blake on a table sometime before lunch.

The girls were still swapping stories when Grey pulled into the driveway. He was amazed that Dylan was still asleep. "All right ladies, everybody out," he ordered.

Rachel stumbled as she got out, but Alex had her back. She winked at Grey as they passed him. Grey saw Alex roll her eyes to let him know that she, herself, was still in control. Grey pulled into the garage and removed Dylan from his car seat. He took his son into the house and put him to bed. As he made his way back out to the living room, he could hear the girl's still chatting away. He paused and said, "Anyone for a night cap?"

Even though they were home safe, Alex wasn't sure that having another round was a good idea. She was all right, but getting very close to her limit. She politely begged off. "No thank you, I think I'm done," she said. "It's been a long day."

Grey was suddenly relieved when Rachel agreed. "Yeah, I'm going to bed," she announced. "What about Dylan?"

"He's already in bed," Grey informed her. "He got tired of listening to the two of you and crashed out early," he laughed. "I took him straight to bed. I'm going to lock up. I'll be back in a few minutes."

He hugged Rachel and watched her walk away. When he was sure she was well out of ear shot, he turned to Alex, "Well, I think tonight went better than expected," he said. "Now I'm just worried about tomorrow. When my massages are over, it should be interesting to see where we stand."

Alex just nodded. Then she reached over and put a hand on his shoulder. "You sure you're up to this?" she asked. Grey moved quietly across the room and opened the front door. He walked outside and took in the beauty of the night sky. It was a clear evening with lots of stars.

"No, probably not," he answered, "but what other choice do we have? Frankly, I'll admit that part of me doesn't want to know. If it ends up working out the way we all think, then all hell is going to break loose. We can't just sit on this and look the other way. The four of us are going to have our hands full."

Alex agreed. "So I take it, Tim's on board?" she inquired doing the math.

"Yeah, I think so, but let me tell you, that was one hell of a weird conversation."

Alex grinned. "I'll bet," she snickered. "Nice move with the hand thing."

"Thanks," Grey responded. "I had to come up with a way to get through to Tim so he would take me seriously. It was the easiest and quickest way I could think of, so he would realize that I couldn't possibly have influenced the outcome. Then I told Tim about the baseball game. You should have seen the look on his face when I mentioned the mustard stain."

Alex smiled. "Actually, I did catch part of it. I was watching you guys from down below. You guys were up in the cockpit so you were sitting at eye level."

"Wow, you really do have my back." Grey observed. "Then you know Tim won't be able to sleep much tonight with all of this floating around in his head. The poor guy wants to catch this "Ripper" guy so bad. I hope we know what we're doing, or for that matter, what we're up against."

"Just like the old days huh?" she commented. "Guess we find ourselves once again with our asses hanging out in the wind."

"Guess you're right," he admitted. "So what else is new? The shit will undoubtedly hit the fan tomorrow and when it does, we better be ready. We can't go after this guy through the front door. We'd never get anywhere. Right now, it would be my word, (he laughs), as it were, against his. Now there's something for the five o-clock funnies."

"You sound like you're already convinced it's him," Alex pushed.

I didn't want to believe it I guess, but if you could see what I've seen, it's pretty undeniable," Grey confessed. "All the pieces fit. The question is now, what can we do about it?"

Alex was surprised. She hadn't expected Grey to disengage himself so easily from his relationship with Blake. She understood his reluctance to accept his friend's involvement in the entire morbid scenario in the beginning, but now that it seemed to be realistic, he had no choice but to try to protect other women from becoming victims. The fact that Grey; was still willing to go back to the Kendall house at all, and even put Blake on a table again, was simply amazing.

"Sleep on it," she suggested. "Focus and sleep."

"That's easy for you to say," he responded. "You got any of that tea left?"

Alex rolled her eyes and then gave it a second thought. "You know, that might not be such a bad idea, she said reconsidering her position. "I'll be back in a minute."

When Alex returned, she was carrying a small satin pouch about the size of an egg. She took a coffee cup out of the cupboard, filled it with water and stuck it in the microwave. Grey closely watched every move. "I don't want to end up like Rachel the other day," he said.

"Don't worry, you won't. I promise," she mumbled as she worked, carefully measuring out exactly what she wanted. "You trust me don't you?" Grey nodded. That was a bit obvious. Then he just sat quietly at the kitchen counter and waited for the buzzer to ring. He knew that he desperately needed sleep and in a couple of minutes, he'd be well on his way.

* * * * *

The tea did its job. There were no dreams, no nightmares, not even a glimpse of a mild hallucination. He slept like a rock until the alarm went off at seven. He figured that would leave him plenty of time to get his act together and make it to the Kendall's house by nine. He decided that working on Katie was the perfect opportunity to start honing his skills for Blake. After her adventure with Walter, he wondered what could possibly come next. She would really be a great warm-up for what he knew he had to do with Blake. His stuff was already loaded in the Mustang so all he really had to do was get showered and go. Rachel rolled over and mumbled something as he crawled out of bed. As he headed for the bathroom, he could hear Dylan laughing in his room and decided to check on him. Grey was surprised to find Alex sitting on the floor in a bean bag chair watching a kids T.V. show called 'Blue's Clue's' with Dylan. The little guy was having a blast. Alex was too.

"Well, good morning you guys," Grey announced. Then he looked down at Alex. "How long has he been up?" Grey asked.

"I heard him messing around in here about six, so I thought I'd let you sleep. The DVD was already in the player so I figured it was a safe bet. Get any sleep?" Alex inquired. She tried not to giggle when she said this.

"Oh yeah, you should patent that stuff for like, like a cure for insomnia or something," he suggested, playing right along. "It was the first good night of uninterrupted sleep I've had in months."

"We aim to please," she insisted. "Oh, and speaking of pleasing, How are you doing this morning? Is there anything we can do to make things easier for you today?" Grey smiled and picked up Dylan.

"I think you both just did," he answered hugging his son. Alex slid out of the bean bag and got to her feet. "The car is loaded I assume, table, linens, lotion, handgun?" she inferred. Grey gave her a startled look. "I was kidding about the gun, silly," she assured him.

"You are positively glowing with a distinct air of confidence, aren't you?" he implied.

"Just be careful," she insisted. "It took me a long time to train you, my friend. I don't want to have to start over with a replacement."

"That's funny," Grey recalled. "Clyde said the same thing about my massages. And all this time I thought I was more important to you all than that. What do you say, Dylan?"

Dylan just laughed and hugged his dad. If Grey was concerned or fearful about the rest of the morning, holding his son was the perfect counter-balance. After a few more minutes, he handed Dylan back to Alex. "I'm going to take a shower so I'll see you all later," he said. "I'll talk to you before I leave." Then Grey went off down the hall and back into the bedroom.

"You ok?" he asked Rachel.

"Yeah, I'll get up in a minute," she said. "You're going to Blake's house, right?"

"Yeah, I'm doing a double header," he confessed. "I won't be back until around one, one thirty."

"Where's Dylan?" she asked.

"He's just fine," Grey assured her. "He's in his room watching 'Blue's Clue's' with Alex."

"Oh my God!" Rachel said as she quickly maneuvered into position to get out of bed and put a robe on. "That poor woman must be bored to death."

"I doubt that very much," Grey responded. "Dylan can be both charming and extremely entertaining," he reminded her. "Anyway, I have to get ready. I'll see you in a little bit." He kissed Rachel on the forehead and went to take a shower.

When Rachel peeked in, Alex was back on the floor having reclaimed the bean bag chair only this time she had a friend sitting on her lap. Dylan had decided that the view of 'Blue' was much better down at his eye level than up in his crib. Rachel had barely cracked the door but Alex knew she was there watching. She let Rachel observe for awhile before saying anything to her. When the episode ended she saw an opening to end Rachel's recon.

"Good morning, Rachel" Alex said as she rolled out of the chair toward the door. They hadn't made eye contact so her move startled Rachel at first. Rachel jumped a little when she opened the door.

"I'm sorry, I didn't mean to disturb you," she said.

"Not at all," Alex responded. "Dylan and I were just killing some time waiting for you and Grey to wake up. You'll probably think I'm crazy, but the cartoon dog is pretty cool. The show is actually interesting."

"On the contrary, Alex, I happen to agree with you," Rachel admitted. "I'm not sure how much Dylan understands yet, but it has a good story line and some very simple lessons."

"Sure would be nice if everything was that simple," Alex suggested.

"Don't I wish!" Rachel exclaimed. "Speaking of simple," she continued. "Want to see if we can scrounge something up for breakfast?

Grey has to leave early but we can grab some coffee and see what's lying around?"

"Sounds good to me," Alex agreed. Then she handed Dylan to Rachel and said "Say Hi to your mom, little buddy." Dylan tried his best "Hi," but sounded less than enthusiastic. That was as far as he was willing to go so off to the kitchen they went.

By the time Grey was ready to leave, the kitchen was now fully under siege. "Wow," he exclaimed. "Am I glad I'm out of here?"

"Have a good time honey," Rachel encouraged.

It was Alex though who walked him out to the car. "Anything I can do?" she asked.

"Circle the wagons and be ready when I get back," he teased her. "Seriously no, not really, I just want to go down there and get this over with. The more I think about it, I'm more concerned now with how we're going to stop him. That, and the Oscar winning performance for "Best Hands in a Terrifying Role" that I'm about to give." His sense of humor had always been his best defense.

"You telling me you're scared right?" Alex interjected. "Would you think less of me if I said yes?" he asked.

Alex reached down and asked for his hand. "Give me your ring," she requested.

Grey hesitated for a second, but then took off his dragon. Then he placed it in her outstretched hand. Alex reached up and removed a silver necklace she was discretely wearing. Already hanging on it was her identical piece. She took Grey's ring and slipped it on the chain next to hers. Then she placed the necklace over his head. As the rings slid down and came to rest on his breast bone, a warm feeling came over him. The smell of wet leather passed through the air. Suddenly, it was ok to relax. Alex could see the change in him immediately.

"Just a little idea I concocted last night to get you through the day," she offered proudly.

"Very nice, very nice indeed," he conceded. "So you're sending me off on a wing and a prayer?" he mocked her.

Alex punched him in the arm. "You're such a pain in the ass!" she exclaimed. "Just get your butt in the car." Grey got in. As he backed out of the driveway, he stopped and waved her over to the window. "Everything all right?" she asked.

"I forgot to say thank you," he responded. Then he reached up his hand and held the dragons, together in his hand. If he was going in, at least he wasn't going in alone. "Save me some tea," he shouted as he drove away.

Alex watched the car speed away until it turned at the end of the street. She wasn't worried even if he was. Yes, he was rusty, really rusty. She'd only had a short time to give him a refresher course, but all in all they shared the same concerns. Safety wasn't a factor yet but if it turned out that Blake was the "Ripper", then everything in their world was about to change. They had to figure out a way to stop him and that was not going to be easy. There wasn't even a 'plan' yet but they'd have to come up with one in a hurry. They all knew that they couldn't afford to waste any time. He might already have another girl in mind, a girl that looked like Katie.

If Grey's suspicions were correct, Tim was going to be on fire when Grey received final confirmation. Then they were going to have a frustrated cop on their hands with detailed, indisputable evidence at his disposal, but no way of explaining or substantiating any of it. If they told the truth, the authorities would probably just write the whole thing off as some fanatic dream. After all, they would say that Grey had just recently come out of a coma. No, they were on their own with this one and would have to rely solely on the talents and abilities of themselves and their friends. Alex turned and headed back into the house. She wanted a cup of tea, her tea and a big comfy chair. It was going to be a very long morning, but for now, all she could do was wait.

* * * * *

Blake stood on the balcony enjoying the morning surf. He hadn't planned on going in late, but Katie was right, he was tired, worn out, and needed a massage. He wasn't repulsed by Katie right now and that in itself was strange. Maybe it was because as Blake, he was at the top of his game. He'd won his last couple of big case with little or no real effort. This convinced him that as long as he maintained control of both sides of his mental coin he would remain invincible. The last few days had been good, but the dark hunger inside him told him it wouldn't last. Sins of the father didn't apply here, in his world, only the sins of the mother.

The last forty-eight hours were amazing, granted, but they didn't even begin to erase the hideous wound that still festered away in his heart. The power of the crashing waves reminded him of the ultimate supremacy he had achieved over the past several months when he had permitted the 'Cat' to resurface. He allowed his wife to remain alive only because he was able to temporarily satisfy his need for revenge by engaging others and forcing them to pay the price for her indiscretions. The sex with Katie had only amounted to being a pleasant distraction, a rather stimulating one at that, but it was time to get back to business. He needed to play. His insatiable encounters had only just begun to feed his appetite for destruction.

The waves pounded against the shore. Then gradually he heard the sound of a different kind of rumble. He looked down at the end of the driveway and saw Grey heading up the road to the house. Out of the corner of his eye, he saw Christine's B.M.W. parked at the far end of the turn-around. She must have come in late. She only parked there when she wanted to make a quiet entrance. Good timing. That was a guarantee that she missed the show. Grey was almost at the top of the hill.

Calling him was a great idea. The last few days had be rough on both of them. Blake wondered if even Grey, with all of his abilities, could make Katie feel like her old self again. At least it was worth a try. As Grey pulled up in front of the house, he heard Katie calling again for champagne. Blake figured that he'd let Grey in first and then head down to the wine cellar for more of Katie's favorite potion. At this rate, his stock of Moet wouldn't last the day.

* * * * *

CHAPTER 23

It was still dark outside when Tim started digging. Not by a lot, but the night was only hanging on by a thread. Trying to sleep had been futile. Not with all the bodies residing in the file in the next room calling out to him for help. He had given the bed a real shot, even gone as far as the Tylenol P.M. on the nightstand, but it quickly became a losing battle. The events of the past few days just wouldn't go away. He climbed out of bed and set off to find his computer. He fired up the old laptop and started clicking away. Grey wouldn't be checking in until after lunch so he had all morning to shovel away. When the Google search came back, Tim just shook his head. More than thirty years of history had settled on the good old Kendall family crest and there was a lot of information to sift through. This was definitely going to take some time. For a brief moment, he actually considered getting some help.

The thought of calling the station, or even contacting that guy, Mackensie occurred to him, but Grey was right. Who would believe him? Their explanation of the events and evidence would be impossible to substantiate. He could just hear his opening statement, "So, my friend the massage therapist was rubbing this guy's back and, he started seeing, well, you know." In a matter of minutes it would be padded room time.

No, they were going to have to handle this one on their own. At least until they had something more irrefutable they could take to the D.A. to prove that this guy Kendall was also a serial killer. Grey had opened the door to the real possibility, so now Tim knew it was his job to help see what he could come up with. Granted, he was still having trouble with the whole baseball thing on the boat, but that would have to be settled later. Fortunately, Renee and Rachel were completely in the dark and they were going to have to keep it that way.

Grey's friend Alex however, seemed to know everything. That was a bit suspicious. Tim decided he would pursue an explanation for that one at the first opportunity. It wasn't a trust issue by any means. Grey obviously confided in her. Anyway, after what happened last night, Tim knew that almost nothing that came along now was going to surprise him. That's why he got on board and joined the cause. If Grey was this sure about Kendall, then they couldn't take any chances. Right now, he just wanted to do whatever it took to find out everything he could about the Kendall's. His instincts told him that the best thing to do was to go back and start from the beginning. There had to be something there, somewhere, and he was going to find it. He had to find it; they had to find it, before anyone else got hurt. As the keyboard clicked away, Tim thought about Eddie again. He thought about the game. Mostly, he thought about the mustard.

* * * * *

When the bell rang, Blake went to answer the door. As he made his way down the stairs, his heart jumped, enough that the 'Cat' began to stir. At the bottom of the staircase, standing in the foyer was a young woman dressed in a pair of tight black shorts. She had beautifully tanned legs and long dark hair cascaded down her back over a white spandex crop top. At first, he thought his eyes were playing tricks on him. There was no way Katie could have beat him downstairs. He was surprised when he realized that it was Christine who was greeting Grey at the door. He'd never noticed it before but from behind she looked just like her mother. They could probably share clothes. When Blake realized that the 'Cat' had shifted, he started to panic and immediately changed his focus. He said, "Hi" to Grey as he entered the foyer and thanked Christine for answering the door.

"I'll be back in a minute," he said addressing them both. "I have to get more champagne for your mother," he explained now speaking directly to Christine.

Christine took advantage of the opportunity. "I'll entertain Grey while you're gone daddy," she offered. She grabbed his bag and headed up the stairs. As she passed him, it was hard not to notice the shape of her ass. Grey didn't mind. He figured that out of the three Kendall's, she was probably the safest. Having a free hand always made things easier by allowing him to use the banister. They ascended the staircase and found Katie, wrapped in her puffy white bathrobe eagerly waiting at the top. Christine carried his bag into the master bedroom and then announced she was grabbing some breakfast and then going to the gym.

She winked at Grey, "I'll see you later," she said, and then slipped quietly out of the room.

He was alone in the room with Katie now. As he started to set up his table, Katie twirled her champagne around in her glass. "You have to try some of this," she insisted. "It's absolutely amazing. Blake turned me on to it when we went to France back in ninety-two and I've been a big fan ever since. I'm like the girl in the 'Queen' song," she said and then she began to sing,

"She keeps her Moet et Chandon, in a pretty cabinet. Let them eat cake, she says, just like Marie Antoinette." She was really starting to get into it when Blake entered the room carrying a new bottle of bubbly. "My hero!" she exclaimed.

Grey laughed. He knew Katie well enough to know she wasn't drunk. She was just having a good time. Blake couldn't help but smile, almost chuckling and shook his head. "You think you can fix that?" he inquired glancing over at Katie.

"I'm not sure I'd want to," Grey conceded. "She doesn't look broken to me."

Grey's right honey," Katie interjected. "I'm not broken. I just needed a little T.L.C. and judging by the bottle in your hand and the table in his, I think my two favorite men have everything covered."

Blake and Grey looked at each other and acknowledged Katie's observation with a ceremonious nod. Grey had thought about the possibility of going with a high five, but figured that might be considerably below Blake's normal operating standards.

Blake made his way over to the mini bar and opened the bottle of Moet. "Well let's get down to business then," he said as he walked over to Katie and filled her glass.

"I will leave you to your work Grey," he said. "I'm looking forward to seeing the results." Then he made his way over to the far wall and removed something from the safe.

Grey nodded as he finished setting up his table. "I'm looking forward to seeing them as well," he answered. "Guess we'll just have to give it our best shot," he suggested. Truth was, the end results he expected, were far different from what Blake and Katie were eluding to.

"That's why I retained you in the first place, Grey," Blake declared. "Attitude my friend, attitude is everything."

He patted Grey on the shoulder as he headed for the bathroom door. "If it won't bother you, I'm going to take a shower, get a shave, and then go down for breakfast." he announced. "Let me know if you need anything, ok?"

Just thought of Blake's hand on his shoulder sent shivers down Grey's spine. It took everything he had not to flinch. A single thought reverberated over and over again in his head, "Was that the hand he used to hold the razor?"

Grey glanced down at his watch before taking it off and setting it on the vanity table. It was almost time to start Katie. Once again, she would serve as a warm up for the main attraction. Part of him wondered if she and Walter still had something going on. At the very least, her last massage had been more than entertaining. He couldn't imagine what she'd come up with this time. As it was, he didn't have to wait long to find out. When Grey's hands went to work, so did Katie's recollections. Katie had made the first call to Walter from her car the previous morning on her way to meet Blake at the court house. She left the ominous message every guy hates about how "they needed to talk." Walter had tried his best to ignore her message, but over the last twenty- four hours, he had left her several crowd pleasers of his own. His communications were initially sad in nature, but became more desperate and even threatening over time as the reality of the situation set in.

At first, she actually felt sorry for Walter, but the truth was hard to deny. Walter had been nothing more than a distraction, a 'play toy' of sorts. He could never have truly imagined that he could replace Blake. His petty threats of exposure were just that, petty. If Blake ever discovered the affair, he would leave the firm loudly and publically, and that would devastate their reputation. No, Walter could threaten her all he wanted, but in the end his silence was all but guaranteed. Grey looked at the clock. He was only half way through the session. It was time to flip Katie.

Act two, scene one, started off with a bang. Deliciously and literally, and in slang terms, 'a bang'. Grey used to joke with Rachel that in his business, he'd seen just about everything. After his session with Katie was over, for the first time in his career he actually felt like he had. No amount of limiting or breaking contact could save him from getting most of her recent rendezvous' with Blake. He wondered if, had Blake or Christine been standing in the room while he was watching, his facial expressions would have betrayed him. This was the kind of thing only adult films were made of. Grey tried his best to keep his attention on his hands and eventually he was able to finish. He found he had no trouble saying yes when Katie offered him a drink.

Blake appeared shortly afterward with a large breakfast tray of fresh fruit, croissant, and a platter of bacon and scrambled eggs. "Don't thank me," he insisted. "This was Christine's handy work. I don't know what she's up to this morning but I don't see any reason to not play along." He carefully set the tray on the edge of the bar. "Maybe she wants something. With this kind of service, I can't wait to hear what she has in mind."

Katie was up and robed again. Grey could tell she was distracted by her hunt for the champagne bottle. She spotted it on the end of the bar and quickly refilled her glass. "You don't need to be so cynical Blake," she suggested. "Christine is probably, well, the more she considered his statement, the more she realized that he was probably right, I don't know, just trying to be nice. After all, when was the last time she saw us together in such a good mood?"

For a moment, Blake couldn't breathe. All of the air had instantly disappeared from his lungs. The 'Cat' shifted hard in its cage, enough so that he could feel a sharp pain in his gut stabbing away at him from the inside, a claw perhaps. Her statement was like a knife plunging deep into his side. "There was no nice here, only revenge and death!" a voice whispered in his ear. The 'Cat' hissed. The last time there was peace between them, Blake had forced him to recede; banished to that cold, dark place that each of us has inside. This time, he would not be so easily dismissed. He would fight to survive. Blake's eyes looked vacant.

"Blake?" "Blake?" "Are you ok, honey?" Katie inquired.

The sound of his name snapped him back to reality. "Yeah, I'm fine," he assured her. "I was just thinking about something at work, that's all. Are you ready for me, Grey?" he asked.

"Yes sir," Grey answered waving his hand in an inviting gesture, motioning for Blake to get on the table. "Are you ready for me?" Blake had asked. Grey wondered how he was going to answer that question. He carefully watched every subtle movement Blake made as he climbed on the table. He wondered about his friend's secrets. Not just Blake, but all of them. This thing in his head was becoming a curse.

All these years, he'd never really cared about his client's private lives. Why would he? Granted, he knew more about most of them than necessary but hey, that's just part of the job. Now, over the next ninety minutes, he was pressed with the task of gathering enough evidence about Blake to prove that he was in fact, guilty of a multitude of heinous crimes. Then he and Tim could use the information and work together to find a way to stop him. Grey looked at his friend lying comfortably on the table. He looked perfectly normal, towel draped over him and head on a pillow. But maybe that innocence was part of the facade.

"Why do I always get the creepy ones?" he said quietly under his breath. His stab at humor helped him relax a little. He was sure that this wasn't a joke, but his mind still couldn't register the possibility that the man in front of him, the guy in a towel, his friend, was a serial killer.

"Everything ok, Grey?" Blake asked, not realizing he was the opening of the second act.

"Let's get this party started," Grey responded, as he slowly approached the table.

* * * * *

"Blood: a small trickle escaping from a fresh wound."

"Time: the split second it takes for the brain to realize that there is a tear in the body's outer shell allowing pressure to escape."

"Expansion: the rapid acceleration of skin separating under stress causing the flow of blood to now stream. The warm, sticky liquid runs rampant down her chest."

"Look at her. Look at Katie," the voice said. "Her eyes say everything. They ask and answer every question. They open wide as the panic sets in, eager to swallow her whole. The energy they once contained begins to evaporate. They beg for forgiveness as the light behind them fades away and everything slowly turns to black."

If Grey wasn't already suspicious, his reaction might have been different. The brief soliloquy caught him completely off guard. The voice addition was definitely a new twist and its owner was directing its venom at Blake. Grey was just along for the ride. Grey knew he had crossed over into Blake's mind, but the voice he was listening to was not familiar. The tone was much deeper and the inflection was far more disturbing to be that of his friend. Blake would quote by definition, but only in a courtroom arena, and only then as an act of eloquence. This dark incantation was designed merely to solicit elevated anxiety and fear. The voice here belonged to someone else, and it had just outlined a murder; not just any murder mind you, but the premeditated, finely orchestrated death of Katie Kendall. Someone had it in for Blake's wife and wanted the counselor to watch her die.

Grey glanced over at the clock on the nightstand. "So much for the first seven minutes," he mumbled. He was off to a great start.

In the true spirit of the old R.K.O News Reels, Grey's adventure continued. He returned to secretly viewing the world through Blake's eyes. Small clips of memories flashed by like a slide show on a computer. The more time passed, the more pieces of the puzzle fell into place. He now knew that Blake had spotted the Richfield girl while attending a Baptism at Father Richard's church. He sat in the a back pew and listened to the Father give a sermon about the joys of life, all the while thinking about how he was going to kill the dark haired girl in the third row of the choir. He wondered what Father Richard would have said, if he had known what evil was being planned back in the cheap seats of his sanctuary.

The hunt for the girl had taken minimal effort. He had followed her for weeks after obtaining her address, (courtesy of his friend at the D.M.V.) using the plate number on her little blue Honda. It was easy to set her up after that. The Riddell girl was just luck, an opportunity that just fell in his lap. He was at the right place, at the right time, and his encounter with Casey satisfied the need.

Then, there was Holly Rodriguez who apparently, still remained a conflict. He had let her escape his wrath. She was the daughter of the coffee vendor in the lobby at Blake's office and had been a prime target for some time. Something however had changed Blake's mind about her. He suddenly called off the hunt because she was too close to the world he called 'home'. He had to let her go. At the time, he was visually frustrated, but he was forced to listen to the voice inside his head. It was the first time that he'd ever been ordered to retreat.

"A voice," Grey thought! "But what voice, who's voice?" he whispered to himself. And then he saw the hand again. This time, he recognized the ring, Blake's ring! The gold on his finger was only overshadowed by the glorious display of gold and silver evil clutched gently in his hand. The straight razor was magnificent. For a brief moment, Grey could feel the power it represented, the fear of its blade, the anxiety of the danger, and the consideration of its many possible uses. He was more surprised when the hand started to mutate. When the transformation was complete, the hand was still fully there but appeared to be much younger. The ring was gone and only the straight razor remained.

In the next frame, Grey could see Katie, a very young, youthful Katie passing by on the sidewalk below. She looked fat, not really fat, no wait, pregnant? Grey mind raced.

"Christine?" he thought. "This is when Blake was finishing college. They had to get married because Katie got pregnant! What would that do to Blake's future?" Grey discovered he was now hooked on the storyline. Then things went south.

The next slide was of a body floating face down in a river. This was followed by a newspaper headline two weeks later that read:

Second Body Discovered!
Girl found mutilated on garbage barge

A pattern seemed to be developing.

Then everything seemed to mellow, returning to a calm, peaceful view out a window into a large, park-like area surrounded by trees. The razor was now sitting on a small end table in the room because a glass of wine had replaced it in his hand. A few days later, he showed up at her door with a pizza.

Suddenly Grey realized that Blake probably wasn't thinking about all of this. He had found away to tap further into Blake's memories. He had no conscious idea of how he'd done it, but he wasn't going to quit now. Grey looked over at the nightstand again. The neon numbers took on an eerie bloodlike glow. At first he thought they were bleeding, but when he blinked the digits were back to normal. Grey shook his head. He'd been at it for almost an hour. It was time to flip Blake over. Face down, Blake was far less intimidating. He looked like just another guy in a towel. Grey took a little extra time, almost stalling for a minute before starting up again. It didn't take long for the slideshow to kick back into gear.

Bodies and blood, it's not as though he expected anything less. Now that he knew the truth, it was just a matter of getting through the rest of the massage. Any sane person would probably have just stopped and found an excuse to leave, but Grey knew better. He fully understood that he was in control of the situation at the moment. Blake was still oblivious to the fact that he knew anything. If he gave Blake any reason to suspect something iniquitous, that would jeopardize everything. It would also put him, Katie, Christine and God knows who else in possible danger. Right now, the most important thing he could do was to finish and get out. He had seen more than enough to satisfy his friends. Hell, he'd seen enough for anyone. Tim was going to have a field day with all of this. He could only hope that together, they would find a way to use it to bring Blake down. Grey hung in there. The longer he worked, the more the answers kept coming.

As the time ran out, he focused on details, anything that he could relate later in conversation. He wished he could stop and write it all down. In the end, it was kind of ironic. Blake was thinking about coffee. He was amused by the verbal fencing he did with the coffee cart owner. Grey looked up at the clock again. It was finally time to go. When he lifted his hands for the last time, the show stopped.

"And there you have it!" Grey proclaimed. This was followed by a long silence as he moved across the room and over to the bar.

"A point well made," Blake mumbled through the face hole in the table. Then he turned his head and his voice became clear. "You could raise the dead with those hands of yours," he offered as he shifted around on the table. Grey's back was to him so Blake didn't hear him mutter, "I think I just did," under his breath. Katie was sitting in the vanity area on a chaise lounge, nibbling on some bacon. When she heard the men talking, she came back in to the bedroom.

"Well boys, how are we doing?" she asked.

"I feel fantastic!" Blake announced smiling as he rolled over and sat up on the table.

Grey turned to Katie. "Everything's good," he said.

"Well, you boys need to grab some of this," she continued motioning to the tray Blake had brought up earlier. She made a mental note to thank Christine later. (Katie suspected that secretly, Christine had a crush on Grey). "Oh yeah, and don't forget to get some more of this," she insisted filling her champagne glass again.

Blake shook his head. He knew that later that afternoon he would be calling Carlos at 'High Times' and ordering a couple more cases.

"I'm going to go rinse off," he informed them. "I'll be back in a few minutes." Then Blake disappeared behind the door leading to the inner part of the master bathroom.

"Eat something," Katie suggested as Grey sipped at a bottle of Evian he found behind the bar. He discovered after the massage that he was really dehydrated.

"All right," he agreed reluctantly, "But let me go wash my hands first." Katie stopped him when he started to move toward the bedroom door.

"You don't have to go down the hall, silly," she giggled. "You can use the sink in the vanity area over there." Katie gestured toward the master bath.

"Thank you," Grey acknowledged as he made his way back across the room. At this point, Katie all but took over.

"When you're done, I'm going to make you a plate," she decreed as Grey was beginning to wash his hands. "Oh and I think there's a finger brush in the top left drawer," she continued. "Blake is meticulous about his fingernails."

Katie was now watching his every move. Not wanting to appear rude, he dried his left hand briefly on the leg of his jeans. Then he reached over and opened the top left drawer as instructed. At that very moment, everything in the world he once new changed. (Alex, Richard and Tim would all later question him about how in the name of the Father he managed to not react to what was on display before him.) It was quite simply, there.

For a moment, time stood still. While there were no words as well, his eyes must have betrayed him. Katie noticed his blank stare and knew immediately what he was looking at. To her, it was no big deal. She'd seen the damn thing a thousand times but to Grey the thing was probably pretty amazing. The gold and silver shined bright under the florescent lighting. Grey was so taken back that he forgot what he was looking for in the first place. Katie gave him a minute.

"It sure is a pretty thing, isn't it?" she whispered. There was a long pause before Grey answered.

"That, I believe is an understatement," he replied. "It's incredible!"

It belonged to Blake's grandfather's father's father," she tried to get out stumbling freely over the words. "It's been around his family forever it seems but honestly, Blake would have to explain it to you. To me, it's just some silly, fancy thing that he shaves with in the morning. If Christine had been a boy, our son would probably have it by now, family tradition and all, but no I only gave Blake a girl, a pretty one at that you must agree, but still a girl. Hell, I suppose he'll give it to her anyway."

Katie was rambling now. Grey smiled and nodded his head, acknowledging her comment about Christine. He still couldn't believe that it was actually, physically there. It was a startling confirmation of everything that he'd seen since he first woke up in the hospital.

"Anyway," Katie continued, "What's Christine going to do with that silly thing, shave her legs?" This last question made Katie stop for a minute and consider the possibility of what she just said. Christine could probably do just that. That concession seemed to make Katie happy. It meant Blake could pass the torch. The frustration in her voice during her earlier comments instantly disappeared. All Grey wanted to do was shut the damn drawer.

Grey took one long, last look and closed the drawer. He tried to take a picture of it with his mind and could only hope that it would last. He had considered the camera on his cell phone but that would have been way too obvious. The risk was too high with Blake on the other side of the door.

Katie had turned her attention back to the plate. "Come eat," she said. "Blake should be right out."

That's where Grey's sense of humor saved him. There was going to be a third act. *"Therapist Dines with Serial Killer and his Wife,"* he thought, *"Oh, the irony."*

The entire situation was not funny by any means but what the hell, legally anyway things were still nothing more than circumstantial. Even if the prints on the straight razor in the vanity drawer were Blake's; even if the cutting edge of the blade did match the incisions on the bodies of at least seven women; and even if all of the victims discovered so far all bore an extremely close resemblance to one Katie Carson Kendall. He could go into a sarcastically toned accounting of the details for hours.

Right now, it all meant nothing. All he and his friends had to go on were visions and dreams of a straight razor that lived in a friend's bathroom drawer. It was going to take a lot more hard evidence to make a case.

Grey found it strange that he had no trouble sitting with Katie at a small antique writing table in the corner of the bedroom and not only eating, but enjoying a small brunch. Blake did come out to join them and the three of them passed the time with light conversation. It was as if nothing was different or had changed in any way. Blake even carried Grey's gym bag out to the car.

"Thank you for coming and taking such good care of Katie," he said, extending his hand.

When their hands touched, there was a quick flash causing Grey to blink. For a split second, he remembered the photos of the girl's Tim had shown him on the boat.

"Thanks for breakfast", he replied. "Tell Christine I owe her one. That was a nice thing to do."

"I agree, and I'll pass that along," Blake assured him. "Until next time then, my friend," he said as he slipped Grey a small white envelope. Grey tossed it on the passenger seat. "Please drive safely," Blake requested. He patted Grey on the back as he was getting into the car.

"I always do," Grey responded.

Then, the car door shut and Blake turned away. Grey took a deep breath. All he wanted to do now was get the hell out of there. He had carefully managed to get what he came for and more. His friends would be happy but probably more relieved. The time of uncertainty was over. All he had to do now was get home.

* * * * *

Grey was long gone by the time Blake made it back upstairs to the bedroom. Katie had found her way into the shower so she didn't notice him take his razor out of the drawer. He stared at it lovingly for a minute before returning it to its resting place. He had decided it was safe to rescue his friend from the cold, dark, empty vault earlier that morning. He realized that for the time being, the urge to kill Katie was almost non-existent. Things actually seemed to be going well. Strange, he hadn't felt this way since before the Christmas party last year. Before that, it had been almost twenty years since being able to embrace that feeling. Having Christine had turned out all right. Together, they had survived, and Katie had learned to behave.

Now she had betrayed him for a second time, but as he expected, she found her way back to her place by his side. She would never know that her secrets were not her own. The fire that had fueled his anger again was now, just a smoldering ember. The calm would remain now that Katie had returned to the safety of his protection, (of this, Blake would try hard to convince himself). As eminent, the view from the balcony remained his constant friend and life would move on. It was time to enjoy the day. Blake watched the waves and waited for Katie to get out of the shower.

Everything was good, that is until Katie's phone vibrated off the nightstand and landed on the floor. He didn't even bother to look at it as he picked up the phone and returned it to the table. Then his curiosity got the best of him. The name "Walter" glowed ominously on the screen. Blake could feel a heat being turned up inside as the light continued to glow:

WALTER
3 MISSED CALLS

After everything that had happened between them over the past few days, this was more than Blake was prepared to handle. The ember was now a flame, a small one mind you but he would give it a chance to grow. And grow it would. This time, when he 'crossed over', he would have no control. The darkness within him would take over and there would be no mercy. The blood would flow and the casualties would rise. Blake could only be along for the ride. The 'Cat' stirred. Then one eye opened as the sleeping evil started to awaken. Just to be safe, Blake went to back to the vanity drawer, retrieved his friend and returned him to his prison vault. The game was on.

CHAPTER 24

All was not right in the universe. Either Jesus or Kelly was unhappy. The way Richard had it figured, it was probably both. The crucifix over the door in his office was acting up again. Richard tried to console himself to the fact that it was all some glorified illusion and that he wasn't losing his mind. His Savior wanted him to pray. Kelly just wanted him to listen.

"Hello again, Father," she said sweetly trying to engage him. "You don't look happy to see me," she observed.

As he had attempted to do during their previous encounter, Richard chose to focus his attention on the large pile of papers that had taken up residence on his desk.

"I just want you to know Father, that your friend is very close to setting me free," she announced. "Very close indeed. My time in limbo may soon be over."

Now, she had his undivided attention but he still wouldn't look up.

"You mean Grey?" he asked calmly. "How do you know about Grey?" His voice remained soft but inquisitive.

"Yes Father, Grey," she answered. "He's the one who sees. He's the one who sees everything. He can see me and all of the others," she insisted. "He knows the truth. He feels our pain. You must help him Father," she begged. "You must help him set us free!"

There were tears in Richard's eyes now. He was captivated by her every word. He knew now what he had to do. He finally looked up at the crucifix and stared into eyes of the image before him. They suddenly became the soft blue eyes of a dear, departed friend.

"I will try to help you Kelly," he whispered. "I swear to you on the love for my Savior Jesus Christ, I will try." Then Richard bowed his head and put his face in his hands. By the time he looked up again, Kelly Richfield was gone.

* * * * *

They needed a plan! Grey hadn't even made it to the bottom of the driveway before the thought started echoing through his head. Right now, all he wanted to do was make it to the Chevron station at the corner of Pacific Coast Highway and Highway 133 (a couple of miles up the road) so he could pull over and get his phone. His Bluetooth was on the dashboard in front of him but during his exit from the Kendall's, he forgot to get his phone out of his gym bag. He also needed to get something to drink and maybe even a candy bar to help calm him down. His left hand, the dragon ring hand, had started shaking about halfway down the driveway. He was almost too anxious to be behind the wheel anyway. The battle between the overall shock of the 'slideshow' and the relief of actually managing to finish the massage was intense. He didn't know whether to laugh or scream. All he could do was focus on getting to the gas station. He had to call Alex. He only had a few blocks to go.

On the way to Blake's that morning, he had come up with a strategy for after he was finished. If everything went as planned at the Kendall's, he would try to get everyone together over at the church. It would be quiet, empty and quite frankly, he wanted to give Richard the luxury of home field advantage. Grey wanted to cut him some slack. Getting Tim and Alex to rendezvous there wouldn't be a problem. They were probably going crazy about now waiting for his call. Katie had him running about forty-five minutes late. At the moment, he was in desperate need of a cold 'Snapple' and a 'Butterfinger'. As he pulled into the station, he looked at the gas gauge and got a friendly response. *"One less thing to worry about,"* he thought. He parked, got his phone and headed inside.

"Comfort food first," he mumbled as he grabbed a candy bar. The 'Snapple' immediately followed. He paid the cashier and headed back to the car. As he got in he chastised himself for leaving Blake's envelope on the front seat. Someone could have just walked off with it. When he got back in, he reached over and picked it up. It felt heavier than usual. He opened it and discovered four 'Ben Franklin's' inside. Blake was apparently very pleased with his efforts. He laughed for a second knowing Rachel would be too.

"All right," he said to himself, "Time to take a hit of 'Snapple' and start calling in the Calvary." He put his Bluetooth in his ear and hit #13 on his speed dial. Alex was his first call. He owed her that. The number thirteen represented a little superstitious joke they used to have. He put the car in gear and backed out. She answered as he pulled out of the driveway.

"Alex, it's me," he said the moment she picked up. "Everything's fine. I'm ok, but I'm sorry to say that things went almost exactly as we expected. Worse in fact, but we can talk about it later."

"You sure you're ok?" she asked. "You sound a little out of it."

"Yeah, I guess," he lied. "Can we talk about it when I see you?"

"Sure, what's your plan?" she inquired.

"I think we should all meet at the church; you, me, Tim, and Father Richard," he began. "It's safe there and it's private." Then he explained to her his concerns about Richard. "Tim won't mind coming up, he's been waiting for my call so I think we're good to go. How much time do you need?" he asked.

"I'm at your house, but I can be out of here in ten minutes," she assured him.

"Great, then I'll call Richard and Tim and let them know what's going on. It's one-thirty by my watch so can we say two, two fifteen at the church?" he asked.

"Sounds like a plan to me, she agreed. "See you in half an hour."

Before he could hang up, Alex slipped in one last question. "Grey?" she asked. "What happened today, it's not good is it?" There was a long pause.

"No Alex," he responded. "It's a lot worse than we thought. I'll see you in a few." The phone went dead and he left Alex alone with her thoughts. He knew she'd understand. He had other calls to make.

* * * * *

Father Richard was on a quest. He needed to avenge Kelly. He needed to fulfill his promise. First thing he needed to do was make a call. He knew that Grey was doing those crazy massages at the Kendall's that morning but it was after one o-clock already and he figured it was safe to call. As he was reaching for the receiver, the phone rang. He knew it had to be Grey.

"Father, it's me," Grey revealed. "I'm on my way to see you."

"I was just reaching for the phone to call you," Richard replied. "I was hoping that I would see you today. I knew you were going to have a rough morning, seeing the Kendall's and all. Is everything all right?"

"I'm ok, my friend, but I thought that I better let you know. In about thirty minutes, Alex, Tim and I are going to meet at the church. I'm already on the road. I'm coming straight from the Kendall's. We have a lot to discuss after my encounter with Blake this morning and we thought you might be more comfortable meeting on your home turf. I still have to call Tim, but I'm sure he's already waiting and available."

Richard was pleasantly surprised. "I was hoping you would all come over here. You see I'm still having problems with that crucifix in my office," he said in an almost embarrassed tone. "Maybe it will talk to you," he chuckled.

Grey shook his head and laughed. "Sure, why not?" he responded. What else could he say? "I don't mean to dump all this in your lap Father, but the church seemed like a good neutral meeting place," Grey explained.

"Don't worry my son, it's just fine," Richard began. "You're instinct was correct. It's quiet today so we can have all the privacy we'll need. I'll be in the sanctuary when you arrive."

* * * * *

"Hey man, you had me worried," Tim admitted. "I still can't believe that you'd put yourself in harm's way like that today. Man that took balls! Anyway, what the hell happened?" he asked with an elevated sense of urgency.

Grey reached down and took another hit of his 'Snapple'. "It's a long story man, but it played out pretty much the way we thought it would. Listen, I'm on my way to the church to meet Richard and Alex. I'm hoping you can get over there too. It's time we all sat down and figured out what we're going to do next."

"I'm on my way," Tim assured him. "It might take me a few. I'm down at the marina but I'm headed for the car as we speak."

"All right man, I'll see you when you get there," Grey conceded. "Drive safe," he added. "I'm still out on the 133."

"Will do, I'll see you there," Then Tim was gone. He set his phone on the passenger seat.

Grey breathed a little easier. Things were starting to come together. He let his mind wander a bit taking a mental inventory of everything that was happening. He didn't want to miss anything. Then something clicked in the back of his head. Back in May, he had attended a seminar for massage therapists in San Diego. He had recorded some of the lectures with an old micro cassette tape recorder. Unless he was mistaken, the little machine was still in the side pocket of his gym bag. It was worth a try.

Grey pulled over to the shoulder and went to the trunk to look. Jackpot! Now all he had to do was dictate everything he remembered from the entire morning all the way to the church. Even if he repeated some things, they could sort through them later. This was definitely his best chance to get as much as he could on record. They could chart the stuff out later if they had to, like those cops on T.V. Now he just had to get to the church. If traffic didn't clear soon, he was going to be late. He reached over and grabbed his phone again to call Alex. He didn't want her to worry. Rachel was off shopping and having a late lunch with Renee so he was in the clear. Grey grabbed the recorder. He hoped the batteries were still good. He had a lot to say.

* * * * *

Alex arrived first. Richard could hear her coming. He thought he recognized the sound of her boot heels on the tile floor. The sound only got louder as she turned from the outer lobby and made her way down the center aisle of the sanctuary. Her long red hair was out and flowing gracefully about as it moved with the rhythm of her steps. She nodded at him from a distance acknowledging his presence, but she didn't actually speak until they were only a few feet apart. There was only about ten feet now between where she remained, still standing on the floor of the sanctuary and Richard's chair that was sitting on the back of the dais. She smiled at him knowing that he could now see her face. Richard returned one as well.

"Nice place you've got here Father," she said quietly. "I really didn't pay much attention to all of this the last time I was here. I particularly like the stained glass windows." As she spoke, she opened her arms gesturing to the size and beauty of the room that she now appreciated.

"Thank you, Alex. I'm glad you like it," he responded. "And, thank you for coming." He started to rise, but she motioned to him and insisted he sit.

"It's not usually my kind of place," she kidded. "But I guess you already know that." "Strange thing is though I think I feel good in here. Maybe it's you Richard. Maybe it's just that we're working together," she said now stepping back and taking a seat in the first row of pews. She leaned back slightly, casually stretching her legs out and crossing her feet near the front step of the dais.

Richard found this almost entertaining. He decided to push her a bit further.

"Have you ever considered the possibility that maybe it's you Alex?" he asked. "This may not be a place of worship for you under the premise of your beliefs, but it still represents a place to gather and worship a higher power whatever that higher power might be. Maybe it feels good to you because it represents faith, and faith is something we all share, even if sometimes it wears different hats and manifests itself under different points of view."

Alex was surprised by Richard's candor, but impressed by his insightful position. His words left her with the impression that he felt God was willing to help you solve things as opposed to always solving them for you. Alex liked that. It made things more palatable.

"I think that's one we can agree on Father," she conceded. "Tell me, have you been giving any thought on how to proceed with our current situation? Of the four of us that are about to gather here, you will probably be the most calm and level headed. I tend to be a bit devilish, (if you'll pardon the pun) Tim's a cop, (strong but fair) and Grey is of course presently just a basket of emotional insanity. Does this sound about right to you?"

"Sounds like a very accurate description to me," a different male voice replied.

Tim had come in the same way Alex had through the front of the church. He was leaning up against the doorway of the left aisle and had been quietly listening to their last few comments. As soon as he announced his presence, he moved laterally across the back row pew and entered the center aisle. Then he made his way down the aisle toward the dais.

"Hello Alex," he said, smiling as he got closer. His manner was tall and confident. "And you must be Father Richard?" he asked as he stopped at the foot of the steps.

This time, when Richard started to stand, Alex acquiesced. Richard walked over to Tim and shook his hand. "A pleasure to meet you sir," he greeted him. "Welcome to my church and thank you for coming."

"Thank you Father, it's a pleasure to finally meet you," he began. "Grey has always spoken very highly of you. I'm sorry that we had to meet under these circumstances."

Richard was impressed. "I am sorry as well Tim, but not to worry my son," he assured him. "You are amongst friends here."

"And so I've been told," Tim said, turning to acknowledge Alex. She stepped forward and smiled.

"Thanks for coming," she said softly. "It means a lot to all of us."

Tim took a seat on the pew directly across the aisle from Alex. "No problem," he said. "I have to know." Alex gave him a funny look and returned to her seat.

"All right," Tim said, addressing them both. "Look at it this way. You see, when I was a kid, I loved to watch the Wizard of Oz. Not because I particularly thought it was cool or scary, but because I had to know what was really at the end of the yellow brick road, and I had to help people get there. I had to see it for myself, not just go on what other people assumed. That's really why I became a cop. I had to know the answers and solve the mysteries. This thing with Grey is a lot like that. I have to know if this guy Kendall is the "Ripper", and if so, I have to help you all stop him."

"That's an interesting analogy," Richard observed. "My question is now, following your line of reason, which character am I?"

Tim took a moment to consider his response. "I think that each one of us has a small piece of those characters in us. That's why we'll do well together," Tim commented trying to avoid having to answer Richard's question.

"Well said," Richard agreed. "But do I need to point out the obvious? We're still one man short."

"Your short anyway, Father," a voice echoed in from the back of the sanctuary. Richard looked up as Alex and Tim turned around. Grey made his way down the main aisle and joined the group.

"You just love to make an entrance, don't you?" Alex asked sarcastically as she stood to give him a hug.

"Sorry guys," Grey lamented, turning to the men. "Would you believe me if I said I've got a lot on my mind?"

"You almost sound serious," Richard observed. "That concerns me," he teased.

"Try spending a day in my head Father, then we'll talk," Grey chuckled. He walked over and hugged his friend. "You sure you're up for all this Richard?" Grey asked.

"I'm old, not dead," Richard insisted.

"Now, now, boys," Alex protested. She turned and noticed that Tim had disappeared.

"Hey Tim, you still with us?" she called out as her eyes explored the interior of the sanctuary.

"Yes Ma'am, I'm still here," his voice echoed back. They could hear the sound of doors closing at a distance. "I just thought I'd lock things up so we wouldn't be interrupted," he said. "Call it a hunch, but I think we might be here for awhile," he suggested. "If it's just those four sets of doors Father," he said motioning with his hands; "I think we're good to go."

"That should do it," Richard confirmed. "So what's next?"

Before anyone could speak, Tim remembered something he'd neglected to check out.

"Hey Grey, what's that in your hand?" he inquired. In all of the verbal foreplay, Grey had completely forgotten about the mini tape recorder in his hand. He had almost left it back in the car.

"Oh this?" he said now holding up the little machine. "This is my mini tape recorder. I still use it to tape lectures and stuff only today I thought why not use it to help me remember what I saw at the Kendall's. Once I realized that I actually had it with me, I pulled over and started talking into it in hopes that this way I wouldn't forget anything. It probably has thirty minutes or so of me rambling on about Blake."

"Wow, that was quick thinking," Tim admitted. "Do you want to play it for us now or would you rather just talk about it first?"

"I'd rather have a beer," he joked.

"I think I have some sacramental wine in the back," Richard offered always wanting to please. "If not, there's always the bottle I keep in my bottom right desk drawer, for medicinal purposes of course you understand."

"No, thank you Father, we're going to all need clear heads for this," he said. If everybody's ready, I think I'd rather just tell you guys what happened and move on from there."

Alex remained in her seat as Richard came down and took a seat on the top step. Tim returned to his seat as well. Only Grey remained standing and paced anxiously for a minute or so up and down the aisle.

"Well let's get right to it then, shall we?" he decided. "After today's visit at the Kendall's, I have no doubt in my mind that my friend Blake is the "Ripper". His voice was heavy and full of conviction.

"I didn't want to believe any of this, I really didn't. I guess that's why I was even willing to go there today and as Tim implied, put myself at risk. I was seriously hoping I was wrong, but after only a few minutes of contact, I knew that I couldn't deny the truth. Without going into too much detail, which isn't really necessary, I saw the murders of at least six women."

Grey paused for a moment and then took a seat next to Richard. The look on Tim's face had turned sour after hearing the updated number of possible victims.

"Here's another twist we didn't know," he continued. "Unless I'm crazy, this isn't the first time that Blake has done this. I saw things that I think went back to his and his wife's college days. Tim, this is definitely something you'll want to look into. Unfortunately, Kelly Richfield and Casey Riddell were the only two victims we previously knew about. I'm sadly afraid there are many more."

"Jesus, man," Tim exclaimed. Then suddenly, he remembered where he was. "Sorry Father," he said apologetically. Under the circumstances, Richard just waved him off. "This thing is turning out to be a lot bigger than we thought."

"I think the key to nailing this guy is gathering as much information as we can," Grey interjected. "I don't think he's dangerous unless you've been targeted, and we already have a good idea of what the next victim's going to look like."

Tim instantly reached for the file he'd been carrying with him. He opened the folder and started to lay out the photographs he'd brought on the step of the dais. He hesitated for a moment when he pulled out the one of Kelly Richfield. Still in his hand, he turned to Father Richard. "Grey told me that one of these women was a friend of yours," Tim acknowledged. "I'm very sorry for your loss. I can leave this one in the folder if you'd like."

Richard considered the idea, but then waved him on. "We're here to get justice for Kelly, not bury her face in a file," he replied disgusted but amicable. "But thank you for asking."

Tim finished laying out the pictures. The faces looked different somehow, sitting on a church step. Their eyes were more innocent, more alive. One could almost expect to look out into the congregation and see their smiling faces.

"That's quite a display," Alex said as she moved in to take a closer look. "This is such a waste. It makes me sad having to see this. I don't know whether I'm more frustrated or pissed off."

Grey was a little taken back by her show of emotion. She was mad and that meant trouble for whoever her anger was directed at. The faces had gotten to her.

"We'll get him Alex," Tim assured her. "We won't stop until we do." His confidence filled the room.

"I don't mean to be a pessimistic old clergyman, but have any of you given any thought to how we're going to stop him?" Richard inquired. The question hung heavy in the air for sometime before Alex finally spoke. "Blake," she said in a 'matter of fact' tone. "The answer is going to come from Blake himself."

No one said a word. An eerie quiet set in over the sanctuary as each member of the group tried to make sense of what she said. Tim was the first one to catch on.

"May I?" he asked, looking to provide a possible explanation for the others.

"By all means," Alex advocated. "By the look on your face, we might just be on the same page. I mean, it is logical don't you think?" she posed. Tim was smart and the facts were all in front of him. He didn't miss much.

"Well Grey, I think our friend Alex here is a genius," he declared. "Guess you're going to have to share your title. If nothing else, she's definitely got the right idea."

Richard still appeared to be a bit lost, but Tim could tell by the smile that now appeared on Grey's face, that he was already coming to a similar conclusion. Knowing Grey, he was probably quietly working out a plan of attack in his head. Tim gave him a minute to finish his analysis.

"Tim's right, Father," Grey agreed. "Alex is a genius. The answer has been right here in front of us all along. Alex, would like to take 'point' on this?"

"Sure, I'd be glad to," she said now confident of her assessment. "I think it's like this guys, we need to know who Blake's next target is going to be, right? So who knows that other than Blake? What Blake doesn't know is that we're on to him and that we have a 'magic eight ball' of sorts into what he's doing."

Grey and Tim both nodded their heads. Alex turned to Richard, "Are you with me so far, Father?" she inquired.

Richard nodded. "I think I see where you're going with this," he concluded. "So what you're saying is, there's a good chance that Grey here can figure out what Blake's plans are simply by doing what he did today correct; Contact?"

From the reaction around the room, Richard felt like he was now, back in the game.

"But how do we get you and Blake together again so soon?" he asked. "We can't exactly afford to wait around."

"There's the challenge," Alex conceded. "But I'm sure between the four of us we can figure something out. In the mean time Grey, you've got to think. Did you see anything this morning that would indicate that he's planning to kill again?"

"Sorry guys," Grey said. "Everything seemed to come from a 'memory file', if you can call it that," he continued. Alex could hear the frustration in his voice. "It was all kind of overwhelming."

"Ah, don't worry about it," Tim said, trying to tone down the conversation. "Right now, we need to find a way to narrow down possible targets. Maybe start with a D.M.V. computer search for of all local women who resemble Katie. It's not much to go on, but it's a start." Just then, Richard posed a question. "Why do you think she's still alive, Tim?" he asked. "His wife, I mean. Mrs. Kendall. What's the point of all the copycat killings?"

"That one had me going for awhile too father but I've got an educated guess," Tim answered. "It may be a moral dilemma. Revenge, most likely. Blake wants to kill his wife, but part of him can't bring himself to actually do it. The other women are merely stunt doubles, substitutes if you will, for the real thing. Whatever she did to him was traumatic enough to set this dark side of him loose."

Tim now had everyone's undivided attention. "From what Grey suggested earlier, this isn't the first time there has been a serious conflict with the Kendall's. If what he saw was them back in college, then maybe there were more killings we don't know about. I'm going to focus my initial investigation on tracking down whatever information I possibly can from that time in their lives. Somebody's has to know something, right?"

"So what can I do to help?" Richard volunteered. "Maybe I should I listen to the tape and see if we missed anything," he suggested.

Tim could tell the man needed to do 'something'. "That's a good idea," he responded making eye contact with Grey. Grey offered no objection. "Maybe you can organize the information on the tape so we can compare it with the notes I've been taking here," Tim suggested.

Richard quickly rose to his feet. "I'll get right on it," he insisted. Grey handed him the recorder.

"Let me know when you're ready and we'll all take a look, ok?" Grey requested. "And Father," he acknowledged, "Thanks."

"I'll be in my office if anyone needs me," he asserted. "I'm glad we all had this time together, he professed. "Thank you all, again for including me." Then he turned to Grey, "I'll be calling you later," Richard promised.

Grey nodded. "Oh, and don't worry about your problem in your office," Grey added. "Aren't you now doing what was asked of you?"

"I hate it when you know more about something that's going on in my church than I do," Richard scowled. "But this time I'm praying you're right." Then Richard took leave. He walked across the dais and disappeared through a partially hidden door.

"That looked almost like a magic trick," Alex chimed in, referring to Richard's disappearing act at the door. She was shaking her head. "I really like his style," she applauded.

"What a great old cleric, Grey," Tim conveyed. "Definitely a class act in my book,"

"Let's just get him through this with his mind and faith still intact and I'll be happy," Grey pleaded. "Now we can get down to the hard stuff," Grey pointed out. "Either of you have any brilliant ideas?"

"I'm going to get out of here and start working on this 'target' idea," Tim decided. "Why don't you and Alex work on the 'contact with Blake thing' and see what you can up with? You can reach me on my cell twenty-four seven if you come up with anything, ok?"

Grey looked at Alex. "I can live with that," he acknowledged, "How about you?"

Alex nodded. "Sounds like a plan," she said. "Like Tim said, we can all stay in touch as things come up."

Tim turned and started heading up the aisle. His friends could hear him quietly laughing as he walked.

"Hey Tim," Grey called after him. "What's so funny?"

He was almost at the top of the incline near the door when he turned around to answer him.

"Nothing really, I guess," he began. "I was just thinking about how the heck I'm going to write my report when this is all over. The whole idea of having to do it just struck me as being funny, that's all," he responded.

"I was an English major in college if that helps," Alex harassed him. Tim refused to be outdone. "I majored in Smith and Wesson," he replied, patting his side, the one that discretely held his custom 9mm Beretta. Grey just laughed.

Tim took a few more steps and then turned back to his friends. "Seriously guy's, don't go too far. When the time comes, I'm going to need all the help I can get. "As Ricky Ricardo used to say, Lucy, you got some splayning to do."

Then Tim, just like Richard, quietly disappeared. Alex went back to her seat on the pew and Grey watched her for awhile as she took in every square inch of the sanctuary.

"I really do like this place," she said.

"It does have something special about it, doesn't it?" he proposed.

Alex looked back at him. "Richard's going to be just fine," she assured him.

"I'm not worried," Grey replied. Richard is a good man and we gave him a simple but important task. He will answer the challenge like a true champion."

"Odds are, he's looking for guidance in his top right desk drawer about now," she teased him.

"More power to him then," Grey maintained. "I wish I had the luxury."

The two friends spent a few more minutes taking in their surroundings. The warm and comforting silence allowed Grey to take the conversation down a notch. "Seriously, Alex, how are we going to nail this guy?" he asked.

Alex just smiled. It was a kind of sinister smile that Grey hadn't seen in twenty years. The gears were turning in her head.

"Together," she said softly. "We're going to nail this son of a bitch, together." And then the moment between them passed.

"You ready to get out of here?" he asked.

"It's about that time," she answered, as they rose in unison.

Grey looked back at the dais. There, on the wall above, was a large cross. Grey stared at it for brief moment. "Take care of Richard please," he said. He hoped someone was listening.

"That was nice," Alex said as they made their way out of the church. She'd decided to take the lead. Grey didn't mind. He'd followed her into hell before and by all rights, he was about to do it again.

"It couldn't hurt," my mother always used to say, he offered, as they got in the car.

"Your mother was right," Alex agreed.

Behind them, down a hall, and through a heavy oak door, Father Richard had found some peace. The crucifix on the wall was silent. There were no voices or apparitions to be found. All that existed now was a tired old priest, sitting behind a large oak desk, diligently deciphering the voice of his friend on a tape recorder. The desk had been cleared of everything non essential. All that was left were Tim's notes and the charts that he was in the process of creating to help organize Grey's material. At his present rate of analysis, he was humbly confident that he would be finished and ready to present his findings to the team by the end of the day. Richard took off his glasses and rubbed his eyes. He was tired, but at least he was back in the game.

* * * * *

CHAPTER 25

Walter wouldn't leave her alone. The endless calls, the texts, the emails simply wouldn't stop. Her phone said there were three calls and four text messages just while she was getting her massage and having brunch with the boys. At first, Katie was more surprised than overwhelmed. It was kind of flattering in the beginning, the whole chivalrous 'fight for the woman thing' but now it just plain annoying. She had to find a way to get Walter to stop. Their secret was still that, a secret, a clandestine endeavor that would have to quietly disappear. She was certain Walter would be cavalier and walk a very thin line before falling back, retreating to his side of the field. Right now he was just trying to rattle her cage. The problem was, with all of this data exchange, Blake might eventually become suspicious. She finally had Blake back where she wanted him and she couldn't take that risk. Walter kept asking for a meeting and she figured that before the week was over, she might have to agree to one (with a few important stipulations of course). Hotels were definitely out of the question. Just agreeing to show up at one sent the wrong message. So were any local restaurants or clubs where they could be seen together. They weren't a couple. Right now they weren't even friends. It had to be low key but public.

In the beginning, it hadn't really mattered. Blake was always too busy to notice her absence. Lately though, they were working well together as a team. The incident at the courthouse was a testament to that. All she had to do was dispose of this last piece of unfinished business, and things would finally be back to normal. The water started to run cold.

Katie got out of the shower and threw on a robe. She could see Blake standing out on the balcony, so she sat down on the side of the bed to decide on the day's attire. She jumped at the sound when her cell phone started vibrating on the night stand. It brought her back into focus. "Oh, shit!" she whispered, knowing that Blake was within normal ear shot. She'd forgotten to put her phone back in her purse. The buzzing stopped as it went to voicemail. She immediately grabbed the phone in a panic.

"C'mon, c'mon." she continued saying in a soft voice. Then the screen lit up. It was Walter, again! The screen read: Walter: 4 MISSED CALLS. Now she started to tremble. Her phone had been out in the open the whole time! What possessed her to leave it out on the nightstand instead of the safety of her purse? In there, she could barely even hear it. As she looked back at the screen, a million thoughts raced through her head. Had Blake heard it buzzing while she was in the shower? She quickly checked for a time stamp. All four calls had registered in the last fifteen minutes. That was huge! It meant Blake was probably still downstairs talking to Grey. Katie immediately erased the calls and took a deep breath. She was lucky. The champagne escapade had distracted her and could have cost her everything! She adjusted her phone to 'silent mode' and stuck it back in her purse. When she looked up again, Blake was still out on the balcony enjoying the view. He was oblivious to the entire incident. Katie tied her robe and ran her fingers back through her hair. When she was ready, she decided it was safe to join him.

* * * * *

The plan as always was simple, track and kill. It was the precise specifications of the quarry that made things difficult. It was never just an easy 'search and destroy mission', but a rather well planned and orchestrated act of revenge. As Blake continued to gaze out at the blue of the Pacific, the flashing message on the cell phone kept running through his head.

"Walter!" he thought. "Really?" he presumed she was over that. "Apparently not," he concluded. Four missed calls was a good piece of evidence to the contrary. So much for a stay of execution! He didn't even notice that Katie was standing next to him until he heard her voice.

"So what are your plans for the rest day?" she asked playfully as she placed her arms around him.

"I'm going to swing by the office," he lied. "I've got some new stuff I have to look over for Walter."

Katie did her best not to react, but her body tensed up immediately at the mere sound of Walter's name. She had no way of knowing that Blake's comment was a set up and that he was looking for her reaction. She hoped he didn't notice, but her body had already betrayed her. He waited a customary second or two and then moved away. It felt like something was scratching his gut from the inside.

"I'll be back in a couple of hours," he said. "If Christine is around, maybe we can all go out for an early dinner."

Katie wanted to hug him again, but he was already on the move. Having dinner together as a family was basically unheard of at the Kendall house. It was almost taboo. Whatever was going on with Blake lately, he sure was more connected. Katie wasn't about to complain. Maybe the past few days were just what they needed to re-establish their relationship again.

"That sounds good honey," she said. "Why don't you call me when you're on your way home?"

"Sure," Blake responded. "I'll see you later." He grabbed his keys off the dresser and headed for the garage.

He wasn't stupid. He knew that the minute Katie thought it was safe, she'd be returning Walter's calls. She'd be watching carefully from the balcony until he was safely out and away. Blake fired up the Mercedes and backed out onto the driveway. Katie's silhouette was now visible in the window upstairs. Blake headed out. As he drove, he could feel Katie's eyes monitoring his every move all the way down the hill.

"When will you ever learn?" he said softly to himself, shaking his head as he pulled out onto the highway. "You have no idea who you're dealing with," he whispered under his breath. Once again, he could hear the sound of gnawing teeth, grinding away under the hood. In the excitement, Blake slammed his foot on the floor and sped off down the road.

He was immediately aroused by the smell of internal combustion and wind in the face. This was short lived because he was taken over by a dark emptiness inside. It didn't take long for him to realize it was there. The darkness was back. In it, was a small flame slowly flickering, searching desperately for more anger to help fuel its retribution. He felt the slow burn, the hunger; the insatiable appetite for revenge. He knew he needed a fix. This time however, he understood that his task was going to be much more difficult. After the Bolerno trial, the media had plastered his face across every major local T.V. station. He was far more recognizable to the public now. The notoriety was great, (his ego ran on high relentlessly for days) from the stand point of being the center of all that 'politically advantageous attention'; but it was also a dangerous drawback by creating obstacles for the kind of deception and co-version that he really needed to engage in. He had even considered the possibility of expanding his hunting arena and modifying his attire from the suit and tie environment, to more of a beach front casual format. The wardrobe change alone would alter his appearance enough to distract most curiosity, and give him a better chance to blend in. If he could blend, he could hunt. This new approach would allow him to keep a much lower profile.

The best part of his new plan was that down by the beach, the opportunities were endless. There were a lot of local beach bars to the south that would be good locations for reconnaissance. They would provide crowd cover as well and give him an opportunity for a quick acquisition. He had decided earlier, after his meeting with MacKensie, to start moving his clandestine operation further south in the interest of safety. He could not afford to be associated again with one of the victims. While the Riddell girl had brought him pleasure, being seen with her had been an unnecessary risk and ultimately a mistake. His identity had to change. The sport polo and khakis he was wearing were still too formal of a look. He wanted something far more beach oriented. The strip of Pacific Coast Highway he was on boasted a large variety of small shops and businesses. He decided to keep an eye open and see what he could find.

Board shorts to Blake were culture shock. Maybe not so much culture, but definitely body shock to his Armani slacked, silk shirted torso. When he discovered that he was going to have to dismiss his Ferragamo's for a pair of either flip flops or Vans, he cautiously chose the latter. The young girl helping him had no idea who he was, so that made the initial transformation process easier. It took him and his young assistant about thirty minutes to as she said, "set him up with some new stuff." When Blake saw himself in the mirror, the world was a new and bizarre place.

"Guess I won't be smoking a cigar wearing these," he laughed.

"No, more likely something else," the girl giggled. She was certainly pretty enough, and even built like Katie, but the blonde hair just….well.

"Think I can pull off this look?" he asked, hoping for a brief moment to be able to start over from scratch.

The girl, 'Sam,' the tag read, looked puzzled but confident. "It makes you look younger sir," she said, "and definitely more relaxed." He could tell she was serious. "You looked a little stressed out when you first came in," she continued, "but you look much better now."

"That's very observant," he acknowledged. "Can I wear these out?"

"Sure, no problem," she assured him. "Are you seriously going to take all this stuff?" she asked, gesturing to the rather inflated pile that had accumulated on the counter.

"I'm trusting you here, right?" he inquired. He gave her one of his best 'closing statement to the jury' looks.

Sam didn't flinch. ""Well, honestly?'" she said. "I'm not a big fan of the orange or purple tanks. You might do better with a blue or black."

Blake applauded her honesty with a smile. "Thank you," he said. "On second look, the blue and the black would be better. What about theses?" He held up one of the four pairs of board shorts he'd selected. "Too much?" he inquired.

"As long as you get a little color on those legs first sir, they should be fine," she suggested.

"Very well then, let's wrap all this up," he said, making reference to the pile. "I'm sure that you have better things to do than entertain the likes of me." So things got down to business.

She rang up his 'stuff' and he paid her in cash. "Thank you again, Sam," he said as he was leaving. "I'd like to come back and do this again."

"Then I'll see you next time," she said.

She waved as he left and headed for his car. He seemed familiar to her somehow but she couldn't put her finger on it. Oh well, she'd just made a big chunk of change for her mom's little store and the guy had actually been really cool. When he said he'd be back, she got the feeling that he meant it. It would be several months before Sam would put all the pieces together and realize that she had just met the "Ripper". She would lose many hours of sleep knowing that her favorite thing she ever got from her mother actually saved her life; her beautiful long blonde hair.

* * * * *

Grey and Alex were in a bit of a quandary. They knew their only real chance of stopping Blake, was getting him back on a massage table so that Grey could do his thing. Knowing Blake's plans in advance was the only practical way of trying to catch him; even if it meant running the risk of having to wait a few days. Having him followed or monitored would be useless. He could lay low indefinitely. Grey also understood now that the Katie betrayal factor was the trigger. All of Blake's memories regarding her indiscretions had been the catalyst for his killing streaks.

Because of this, Tim had suggested that short term surveillance might be necessary. It was a reasonable precautionary measure in case Blake already had something in the works. Getting Blake back on a table for another massage might take a week or two, so it paid to be careful. While Grey had not seen any evidence of a new target, a simple 'tail' might save someone's life.

"As long as Blake can maintain control of his dark side, there is still a chance for us to gather more information," he said confidently. "I want to discuss something else, ok?" Grey suggested. Alex was all ears.

"The affair with Walter had happened simply because Blake had continually showed a lack interest in his family," he began. "The other night, the wave of darkness inside him receded and he was suddenly reminded of his initial passion for Katie. The first night was strictly on impulse for both of them. The following day, after court, was completely planned by Katie. She hadn't had enough. It was easy for her to instigate, because she thinks Blake is interested in her again. The truth was, without Walter around, he probably is."

Alex shook her head. "She had no idea that there were other forces at work." she said. "She was just enjoying the moment."

Grey nodded. "Yeah, something like that," he agreed. "The two rendezvous' with his wife were completely confusing for Blake though, because they both played out in a positive way. This was a complete contradiction of their behavior the past six months. The last few days have redefined his options. As long as he makes Katie happy, her relationship with Walter will cease. Blake only kills to avenge Katie's betrayal. The problem now is, the dark side of him has a taste for blood again, and it wants to convince him to keep on killing. That's why we have to do everything we can to find out who his next victim will be."

"Any ideas about how you're going to set this up?" Alex asked.

Grey had been considering the matter the entire ride home. "You're going to ask me that question now that we're only a hundred feet from the house?" he inquired sarcastically.

"A little pressure never hurts," Alex snickered. "Seriously, pull over," he requested.

Alex pulled the Mustang over to the curb. "You can leave it running," he said. "This won't take long," he promised. "Katie is the key to getting Blake back on the table. She is a lot easier to approach and never turns down the opportunity for a massage. I can call her tomorrow and tell her I'm setting my schedule for next week. I'll convince her that she needs to be on it. She can handle the Blake part."

"If it's anything like the last phone call you two had, it should be interesting," Alex teased.

"Very funny," Grey chuckled. "Let's just get to the house and make nice for awhile. With all the coming and going we'll be forced to do, I've got to keep the peace at home. Normally, I would say something to Rachel, but I can't take the chance of putting her in danger."

"Your silence isn't good for the trust factor, but I think under the circumstances you're making the right decision," Alex acknowledged.

"Home, James," Grey ordered pointing at the house.

"Yes, Master," Alex answered. She let her foot off the brake and the car coasted along about hundred feet until she stopped again at the curb in front of the house.

"Here we are," she said as they both started to get out of the car. "Why don't you go grab a late lunch with Rachel. I'll keep an eye on Dylan."

"That's not a bad idea," Grey admitted. "That's a nice offer. I'll see if I can get her to agree to that."

"Rachel is going to be very confused about what's going on over the next couple of weeks," Alex conveyed," so making time for her when you can along the way is going to be huge. Do you see my point?"

Grey nodded and Alex continued. "You can explain your time away is with Father Richard. It's not really even a lie if you think about it. She even told you that talking to him about the accident was a good idea. We're just pushing her idea to the limit." Grey started subtle laugh.

"What's so funny?" Alex said.

"Just the irony of us pushing something to the limit," he remarked. "It just struck me as funny, that's all," he said shaking his head.

Alex didn't get a chance to comment. Rachel had heard voices and opened the front door.

"What's up with the two of you?" she asked.

"I think Grey here is about to ask you to lunch," Alex responded. "I've been ordered to Dylan patrol."

Rachel had this perplexed look on her face. "Are you serious?" she asked.

Grey fielded this one. "Is there a problem?" he inquired. "Can't a man take his wife to lunch anymore?" he proposed. "Father Richard thought it would be a good idea," he lied.

"I'll get my purse then," Rachel replied without any hesitation. Then she disappeared back into the house.

When she came back, she was all smiles. Alex winked at Grey as she was walking to the car.

Grey opened the door and let Rachel in.

"Don't forget these," Alex said, as tossed him the keys.

"Thanks," he said smiling as he got in himself. "We'll see you in an hour or so, ok?"

"Just relax and have fun you guys. Dylan and I will be fine," she assured them.

Grey turned the key and off they went. "Where to?" he inquired. "Let's go have some fun."

"Just drive," she said. "It's such a beautiful day."

The clouds played many tricks that day creating some beautiful shadows. The sun would shine and then suddenly disappear. Only Grey knew what was really blocking out the sun. He could smell the wet leather in the air.

* * * * *

As Blake's tires hit the highway, Katie's fingers hit the phone. It wasn't rocket science anymore. She knew she was going to have to consent to a meeting. She thought about texting Walter, but that would take too long. Besides, that left a trail. Anything she said now would become a permanent fixture in Walter's text file. No, she had to actually speak to him. But she did have a clever idea. Their house phone had an unlisted number. If Walter answered, it would show up as 'unlisted' and leave no trace. Katie wasted no time. She made the call from out on the balcony so she could monitor the road. She didn't need any unwanted interruptions. Walter answered on the third ring.

"Walter Greenberg," a strong male voice answered.

"You arrogant, self serving bastard." she whispered softly into the receiver. "You are one cold hearted son of a bitch." There was a long pause before she received a response.

"Is that the best you can do, baby?" Walter countered. His tone was monotone and smug.

"Don't baby me, you worthless prick." she continued. "You are a spineless excuse for a man. It was nothing more than a fantasy to think you could ever fill Blake's shoes. Walk away now Walter, walk away, or I'm going to tell him. I'm going to tell him everything and your life and career will be over." Her volume and tone never wavered.

Katie was on a roll now and Walter was starting to worry. The tone of her voice is what concerned him the most.

Her voice remained calm and ominous. "He will explode but when the dust settles, he will leave the firm; and he will do it loudly and publicly," she persisted. "The partners will dismiss you for ruining the firm's reputation and I will be disgraced."

"You really expect me to believe that you can live with that?" he protested. His tone was now obviously agitated.

"I won't tell you why Walter, but I can survive this," she insisted. "I already have him right where I want him."

Walter knew the Kendall's had survived some trouble in the past. He and Blake had been friends for years. If Katie was serious, it might be safer to just walk away. "I still want a meeting," he demanded.

"Maybe," she agreed, in the same and softy but condescending tone. "But it's going to be on my terms and with my rules."

"You're such a bitch, Katie. Name the time and place!" He was trying to play the hard and forceful tone now.

"I'll call you, Walter," she said. "You better pick up." Then there was a click.

She figured she'd make him squirm for a half an hour or so before calling him back. It was his turn to sweat things out for awhile. Besides, it would buy her some time to come up with a meeting place. Katie stayed out on the balcony and watched the waves. As she looked north, her mind shuffled through all of their usual spots. It was no surprise that nothing clicked as being right or acceptable. Then Katie's eyes wandered south. Maybe, they could meet somewhere new for a change. They had always headed up the coast or inland before. Walter would be more unsettled in a new environment. He wasn't big on change. He liked his comfort zones. That was it! Katie grabbed a magazine off the table that she'd been reading earlier and started flipping through the pages. It was a local rag with a great entertainment section which reviewed all of the best clubs and restaurants in the area. It turned out that south Laguna Beach had some great little places.

A restaurant called 'The Deck' sounded like the perfect spot. It had outdoor dining, a bar looking out at the ocean and sat just off the highway. She would get there early and scope the place out so she would have the upper hand when Walter arrived. A quick drink out on the 'deck', a few well delivered contemptuous words, and she could make a graceful exit. Katie smiled and headed back into the house.

"Now, first things first," she giggled. "What to wear?"

She had nothing but 'torture the bastard' on her mind. "Definitely heels," she said out loud as she started from the floor and worked her way up. The black dress from court was winner but it was on special reserve for Blake. Then out of the corner of her eye, she spotted a blue Ann Taylor mini dress. It was also dangerous, but it had to have just the right shoes. Fortunately for Katie, foot wear was never a problem. When fully assembled, the ensemble would display a look that was a little to 'young' for a women her age, but she had the body to pull it off, and the sensuously innocent face of a young sorority girl. In the outfit she was now planning, she should have attached a warning label.

Katie looked at the clock. It was pushing two o'clock. She was running out of time. 'The Deck' was a good ten minute drive. If Walter was at the office, it would take him at least twenty. If he was at home, it was only fifteen. Katie reached for the phone. He must have been waiting.

"Walter Greenburg," the voice said again. This time she could she could sense the frustration in his voice.

"The place is called 'The Deck' Walter," she whispered again. "South Laguna Beach. And you need to be there at three," she added.

"I don't know if....he began before she cut him off. She could tell that the tone of her voice alone had Walter back on his heels.

"If you're not there," she threatened, "I'm going to Blake." Then there was a long silence.

"Good-bye, Walter?" she inquired sarcastically. She could hear him breathing on the other end of the phone. Her voice never raised above a whisper.

"I'll see you at three!" he conceded, the anger now boldly apparent in his voice.

"Be a good boy, Walter, and don't be late," she toyed with him. Then she hung up the phone again before he could respond. He knew better than to call back. Now all she had to do was get dressed.

Nipples through the dress would be overkill, so she found a pretty strapless lace bra. As she started to wiggle into the dress she decided that panties weren't going to be part of the act. The mini was just long enough that if she sat like a lady, there wouldn't be a problem. Then again, if needed, she could change her seating position and simply have another weapon at her disposal. A fresh Brazilian wax never failed to do the trick. Katie sat on the edge of the bed and stroked the leather of each heel like she would a man as she slid each shoe on. Then she got up, checked what little makeup she ever had to wear, and sized herself up in the mirror.

"Fuck you, Walter" she said, as she ran her fingers back through her hair. "Fuck you."

Then she grabbed her keys and headed downstairs. She was surprised to see Christina coming up the driveway as she backed out. She rolled down her window as they passed.

"Your dad wants to take us out for dinner tonight," Katie told her. "Are you going to be around?"

"Dad wants to have dinner?" Christine responded, "Seriously?"

"That's what he said," Katie continued. "If you're willing to go, I promise to make him take us somewhere you like," she offered.

"Ok, Mom," Christina consented. "But let's go somewhere fun, not snobby ok? It will be better for everybody and we can all just chill."

"All right honey, I'll see what I can do," Katie responded. "I've got a quick errand to run, but I'll be back in an hour or so. Your dad's doing something for work so he should be back by then too."

Katie waved and then headed down the driveway. Christine went inside to take a shower. Her time at the gym had left her a bit on the sweaty side. As the warm water rinsed away the residuals of her workout, Christine tried to figure out what her father could possibly be up too. First, there was the night in front of the T.V. in sweats watching a movie together, and now his wanting to go out to dinner as a family. Something was different about her dad lately. She wasn't complaining, but she was sure that something was up. Maybe having dinner with him would provide some answers. Christine looked at herself naked in the mirror. She was hot! Just like her mother, the workouts paid off. Now all she needed was a boyfriend, someone who was worthy of all of her assets. Christine laughed and started to get dressed. "And someone brave enough to handle dad" she mumbled under her breath.

* * * * *

When the valet took her keys, Katie could feel the confidence building inside her. Within the hour, this thing with Walter would be quietly put to rest. If everything went according to plan she'd be home and getting ready for dinner by the time Blake got back. His 'two hours' were almost always closer to four. 'The Deck' was the perfect spot to kiss Walter's ass good-bye. It was dimly lit inside to create a relaxing ambience, and then opened up onto a patio deck that was built out onto the sand. Katie checked out the entrances and exits and of course the ladies room. She was comfortable now so anything that Walter might try, she felt confident she could contain. She had about fifteen minutes before he'd arrive so she took a seat at the bar and ordered a chardonnay.

As she sipped away at the first glass, her mind thought of another way to make Walter uncomfortable. She reached inside her purse and took out her wedding ring. She'd worn it on and off over the past several months but never in front of Walter. Its size and sparkle screamed "Blake". Today, she wanted it to be heard loud and clear. Trying to sit like a lady on the oversized barstool was a challenge, but Katie managed to find a way. Now, all she had to do was be patient and wait.

At two minutes to three, Walter made an entrance. He tried to play it cool, but she could tell that he was angry and distracted. When he tried to hug her, Katie simply moved away. She asked the bartender about taking her drink outside and he graciously waved her on. Walter ordered a drink and then followed her like a lost dog.

"So what do you want, Walter?" she asked bluntly as she took up a position leaning against the patio rail. She made a point of not making eye contact. He didn't deserve it. Instead, she focused her eyes out to sea. Her voice was still just above a whisper.

"Don't you know that it's time to graciously accept defeat?" she mocked him before he could respond.

Walter wasn't ready for the question. His long pause gave him away.

Now he was furious. He controlled women, not the other way around. There was only one unanswered question left now, and they both knew it. Would he call her bluff?

Katie raised her glass and set it on the railing making sure to flash her ring. When Walter saw it, he knew the battle was over.

"So that's how it is," he said forcefully under his breath. "The Christmas whore is going home." For Katie, that was game, set and match.

She had promised herself to be quiet and dignified at all costs. Somehow her hand just slipped and the remaining two thirds of her chardonnay ended up in Walters face. It was an accident, an involuntary muscle reaction, but a beautiful shot in that they were standing so close to each other that the rim of her glass lightly brushed the end of Walter's nose. His face took the full impact of around six ounces of good chardonnay.

"The defense rests counselor," she smirked. "Relationship is adjourned."

There was nothing more to say. Walter just stood there with the wine dripping off of his face and down his shirt. Katie approached the bartender on her way out.

"Sorry about the mess," she apologized. "Some guys are just assholes," she said calmly.

She had the, softest, sexiest voice he'd ever heard. Then she handed the bartender a hundred dollar bill.

"This should cover things," she said. "But make sure that you make that son of a bitch pay for his own drink."

"Yes ma'am," the bartender complied. He was trying hard not to laugh.

Katie let him off the hook. "It's ok to laugh," she said. "Just don't give him a towel, Jimmy." She was reading the name off his tag.

"Anything you say, ma'am," Jimmy said, as he moved down the length of the bar toward the cash register.

"And Jimmy," she called after him.

"Yes, ma'am," he answered for the third time.

"Keep the change!" she whispered. Then Katie turned and walked out of the restaurant.

She was standing waiting for the valet when she almost had a heart attack. Sitting at a red light in front of the restaurant was a black 500SL Mercedes convertible. Her panic only lasted a moment when she noticed that the driver was in a tank top, straw hat, and Ray Bans. She couldn't read the plate but she knew from the outfit that it couldn't possibly be Blake. She breathed a quick sigh of relief as the valet pulled up in her car. She thanked him, slipped him a five spot, and got out of there as quickly as she could. She had no way of knowing that the valet who had parked her car had done so on the street side of the parking lot with the rear end facing the street. "Divine 1." Her little red Porsche was hard to miss.

Blake hadn't actually seen her, but he did know now that she was at the restaurant. He suspected she was meeting Walter, but he kept on driving. She could never know that he knew about her secret, and she would never know about his.

He even decided to make and extra accommodation on her behalf, a small detour that would allow her the time to get home first. The bar at Las Brisas' overlooked the beach and would at least be an attempt to keep his promise to the creature that resided inside him. It wasn't much of a hunt, but it was certainly a start. Blake smiled as he passed his regular turn and kept on going.

"Happy hunting," a deep voice echoed in the back of his head. "Happy hunting indeed," Blake replied.

Blake looked at his watch. It was going to have to be a short trip. He'd give Katie an hour or so and then call her to say he was coming home. Even if she was still at the restaurant, she would have enough time to make a quick exit and easily beat him to the house. Their dinner plans could commence from there. Blake looked at his reflection in the rear view mirror. His eyes were hungry. The hunt was on.

* * * * *

CHAPTER 26

Father Richard was quite pleased with himself. It was almost four-thirty in the afternoon and he was ahead of schedule. As he looked around his office, he couldn't decide what made him happier, completing the task of organizing all of the materials he had been left with some three hours earlier, or the state of silence that the Jesus statue had graciously maintained ever since he began focusing on his work. There had been no more visits from any ghostly apparitions to hinder his progress. Apparently, Kelly had decided that he was, in fact paying, attention to her requests and was therefore; willing to leave him alone. Because he was able to concentrate now, he had done some good work. He had managed to collate all of the information he was given and it was carefully displayed, mounted on half a dozen easels that he had quietly 'borrowed' from the art room. Richard took a seat behind his desk and surveyed his work. He had created quite a nice visual presentation in the privacy his office and was fully prepared to offer an assessment of his findings to his friends. Once he was satisfied, he looked at the clock. He told Grey that he would call him around five, so he still had about a half an hour to kill. Then he looked up at Jesus. His Savior was still friendly. That was a good sign.

It was only then Richard realized he was hungry. All that work had given him an appetite. There was a small mom and pop sandwich shop across the street from the church so Richard decided to get a snack, (a six inch Italian with everything on it would probably do the trick,) while he waited to make the call. The walk and the fresh air would also do him good. He made sure to lock the door to his office so that no one could wander in and see what they were working on. Tim was going to have a hard enough time explaining all of this to the authorities when the time came. Richard chuckled at the thought of a future headline:

"Covert Operation Planned in Local Priest's Office"

"Well, they say the Lord works in mysterious ways," he announced to himself as he walked out of the sanctuary. He'd only taken a few steps into the parking lot when he saw the sign on the little shop across the street.

Any 6" sandwich, chips and a coke, $3.99 Richard smiled.

"Apparently, the good Lord will provide as well," he observed as he made his way closer to the sidewalk. Cutting across the street, there in front of the church would save him a few minutes. There was no oncoming traffic in either direction when Richard stepped off the curb. It was sort of a leap of faith. He had no idea that now, his trip would last a bit longer than he expected. Good thing he remembered to bring his cell.

* * * * *

The Mustang rolled up back in front of the house just before five. Alex had set up Dylan with some toys on the family room floor and they were busy playing together when Grey and Rachel walked in.

"Hey, you two, How'd it go?" she asked.

They both responded in unison, "Great!" This drew a laugh from each of them.

Alex winked at Rachel. "So it was nice to just be the two of you for awhile, huh?" she inquired.

"Yeah, thanks for the suggestion," Grey complimented.

"No worries," Alex assured them. "Hey Grey," she continued. "Father Richard called while you were gone. He wanted to know if you could come by and see him this evening. He wants to see how you're doing. Tomorrow being Sunday and all, tonight is the only chance that he'll have open for the next few days."

Grey looked tired, but Rachel seemed to be gung ho. "You should call him back honey," she said. "It would probably do you some good to go see him for awhile."

Grey had to hold back his laughter. Rachel had no idea how right she really was. Now came the tricky part. He decided to just take a shot and put everything out there on the table.

"Hey Alex," he said. "Want to go for a ride? You've never met Father Richard and I'm tired. I wouldn't mind the company."

To his surprise, Rachel answered first. "That's not a bad idea," she agreed. Then she turned to Alex. "I know it's asking a lot after you've been watching Dylan and all, but would you mind going with him? I'd feel better if he didn't go alone. I know you'll like Father Richard. The man is an amazing character."

Grey and Alex just started at each other. "Sure, I guess I could do that if you really don't mind," Alex offered. "You don't think your friend will mind me being there?" she asked continuing to play along.

"Nah, I'm sure Richard would enjoy the introduction," Grey parlayed. "I'll go give him a call and see what time he has in mind." Grey took out his cell and headed off into the living room. Alex took the opportunity to excuse herself and went to freshen up. After a brief conversation with Richard, Grey shot Tim a text message informing him of the meet. He also let Tim know that Richard was emphatic about making certain he was there. He said he'd explain why later.

Alex returned a few minutes later to find Grey and Rachel playing on the floor with Dylan.

"Did you get a hold of Father Richard?" she asked. She played a little excitement into her voice for effect.

Grey rolled his eyes. *"Damn the woman was good,"* he thought before he answered. "He asked if I could come by around six," he responded. "I told him that wouldn't be a problem but that I was going to bring a friend. When I told him who you were, he actually sounded excited. He said that I had mentioned you to him once before and that he would be delighted to meet you."

"I guess it's settled then," Rachel interjected as she returned to her feet. "You guys have about half an hour before you have to get out of here." Grey wondered where the conversation was going. Rachel went over and opened the refrigerator. "Alex," she continued, "Can I interest you in a glass of wine?" Rachel offered.

Alex looked at Grey but it was a customary gesture. She knew she didn't need his approval. Grey smiled and nodded. "I'll get two glasses," he said reaching for the rack that hung invitingly over the far end of the bar. "But Alex, let's not get crazy, ok? You'll want a clear head when you meet Father Richard," he conveyed.

"We'll be careful honey," Rachel promised as she grabbed a bottle of chardonnay out of the fridge. Grey handed her the glasses. "We'll be out on the back patio, if you need us," she informed him.

Grey looked at Dylan. "Well that was easy," he said to his son. Dylan just giggled.

Thirty minutes of down time with Dylan was just what Grey needed; silly giggles, and cartoons. What a seriously cool reality check. By the time he and Alex got back in the car, the weight on his shoulders had become more manageable. Rachel had kept her promise and Alex was more than ready to go. Neither he nor Alex had much to say on the ride over to the church. Grey figured that everything would be put on the table when the four of them were back together. As they pulled into the parking lot, Grey remembered something.

"Thanks for suggesting my spending time with Rachel today," he acknowledged. "It seemed to ease a lot of tension between the two of us that was apparently eluding me."

"I guess I just assumed that it was my job to have your back," she sarcastically reminded him as they got out of the car. Grey noticed Tim's car was already in the parking lot.

"I wonder why Richard was so adamant about Tim being here," Grey asked as they approached the building. He held the door for Alex as they entered the sanctuary again, only to be greeted by the sound of Richard's voice. He was unusually animated, but Tim was exercising a great deal of patients. Tim was sticking to a simple nod and smile approach. Richard's verbal rant didn't break stride, even when he noticed their arrival. Grey and Alex moved in closer and quietly took seats about half way back. Richard was on a roll.

When there was finally a break in the action, Tim took a chance and cut in.

"I'll fix it Father," he assured him in a calm and quite confident tone of voice. "I'll make a few calls in the morning and make it go away," he said walking over and patting the old man on the back.

"Thank you, my friend," Richard conceded. "I'm sorry I was so worked up about this. I've just been under a lot of pressure lately. If you will excuse me for a moment," he said, addressing the three of them now, "I think I'll go get some water." Then he took a few steps and disappeared behind the hidden door again.

"I've got to get me one of those doors," Tim insisted as he turned to greet his friends.

"Well, that was interesting," Grey observed. "Do we really want to know?" he joked looking over at Alex.

"If you must know," Richard's voice carried out as he returned from behind the dais, "Who in their right mind writes a priest a ticket for jaywalking?"

Grey realized that he couldn't keep a straight face. He started to turn away but noticed Alex had already made a similar move. He was going to have to face Richard.

"Seriously?" Grey asked as he made eye contact with his friend.

Richard looked over at Tim hoping for a little support.

"Apparently so," Tim said, coming to the old man's defense. "Don't worry; I'll take care of it in the morning."

"On a Sunday?" Richard inquired. He was almost anxious now.

"Cops never get a break, Father," Tim replied. "Besides I'm going to have some fun harassing the guy who wrote this," Tim confessed. "I hope that doesn't bother you, ya know like mess with your spiritual conscious or something."

"I think the Lord and I will be good on this one," Richard stated and with that, the matter was closed.

Alex had remained quiet throughout the entire 'boys club' exchange. "So who wants to go first?" she asked.

"Well, I'm going to call Katie in the morning and set up the Kendall's massages. Probably going to be the end of the week though, so I'm thinking Tim's idea of a little low key surveillance is going to be in order."

"That's good," Richard said because when I show you how things fit together using the display in my office, I think we'll all agree that it is a necessity to keep an eye on this guy."

"Father Richard is right," Tim whole heartedly agreed. "I've spent most of the afternoon digging into the Kendall's past and I think there may be a connection between Blake and some other murders. Grey was on target with the college days thing. Katie Kendall got pregnant her junior year as Blake was about to graduate. Their daughter Christine was born the following January. Strange thing was though, during the summer before, in the beginning of the pregnancy, five girls were found within a two hundred mile radius of the campus, throats slashed and floating in some form of water; everything from a busy river to the serenity of a backyard pool."

"That is a bit coincidental, don't you think, Tim?" Richard replied.

"Want to hear the kicker, Father?" Tim inquired. Richard just nodded. "All the victims then bore a strange resemblance to one; you guessed it, Katie Kendall! I'm trying to get a hold of some pictures of all five victims so we can compare them to the ones we have now."

Alex was at a loss. Grey could tell by the look in her eyes this was starting to more than simply anger her.

"We don't have to wait," she said suddenly. "For the massages, I mean."

All three men turned their attention directly at her. By the tone of her voice, Grey knew she was very serious. From the look in her eyes, he knew she also had a plan.

"We don't have to wait," she repeated her thought calmly. "And here's why."

* * * * *

As Blake casually indulged in his second late afternoon martini; the 'Cat' playfully bathed in a cascade of vermouth and gin. Katie, however, was in a rush to get home. She had to get there before Blake did. Hopefully, she would leave herself enough time to change out of her current outfit and into something more appropriate for a casual dinner. Time was working against her now. The traffic wasn't bad for most of the ride home, but she still managed to catch almost every red light. She breathed a huge sigh of relief when she crested the top of the driveway and discovered that Blake's car was nowhere to be seen. She grabbed her purse and quickly headed inside.

Blake was just finishing his drink when his cell phone rang. Katie's number appeared on the screen. "This should be interesting," he mumbled under his breath. "Hello," he said being more than pleasant. "Is everything all right?"

Katie had carefully rehearsed her response. "Hi honey," she began. "I was just calling to see how much longer you were going to be? Christine and I are starting to get ready."

Blake grinned. He wondered if she was really calling from the house. He glanced at the clock on the wall behind the bar and decided that she probably was. It was time for him to go.

"I'll be home in about twenty minutes," he informed her. "Will that work for you?" The truth was that he was actually only five minutes up the road, but he needed time to change. He couldn't afford to let Katie see him in his present attire. The gym bag at his feet had his shirt and slacks from earlier, neatly rolled up inside. The stalls in the men's bathroom were large enough to accommodate a quick change.

"That's great honey," Katie responded. "We'll be ready when you get here."

Blake had already tipped the bartender and was halfway to the bathroom before they hung up. Timing was everything. He was in and out in and back to his normal self in only a few minutes. Everything would work out great now if the girls just picked somewhere simple for dinner. Christine liked this place called 'BJ's' on the Coast Highway. Blake was hoping she had that in mind. Blake dialed his cell.

"Daddy?" Christine answered a little surprised.

"Christine?" he replied. "Yeah, it's me," Blake continued. When he said "yeah," he realized he sounded funny. There could be no 'Cat' tonight. "Sorry to bother you, but could you tell me where you and your mother decided on for dinner? I'm trying to gauge whether or not I'm going to have to change before we go." There, that sounded better, his Blake voice echoed in his head. "I was thinking about that place you like down the road, 'TJ's' I think you said. Then I wouldn't have to change. We could just take off when I get there."

"It's called 'BJ's' Daddy and actually, I thought about that, but Mom said it wasn't really your kind of place."

"I know this is going to come as shock to you honey, but it doesn't always have to be about me," Blake presented. "Let's go to 'BJ's'. If nothing else, it will confuse your mother and that might be fun. Remember her surprise when she saw us watching that movie together the other night?"

"Yeah, those sweats you had on kind of got to her huh?" Christine laughed.

"All right then," Blake ordered. "I'm coming up the driveway. Tell your mother the bus leaves in ten minutes." *Down Cat, down!,* Blake thought to himself. "*Really, the bus leaves?*" Then he hung up the phone. For a second, he thought maybe it was the martinis talking but that was easy to dismiss. Even at his most liquidated state, Blake still spoke correctly; slowly and slurred maybe, but still grammatically correct. The 'Cat' of course did not.

Katie had beaten him home by at least a half an hour. He knew this because the engine cover on the Porsche was almost cool to the touch when he laid his hand on it as he passed her car in the garage. Christine's B.M.W. was parked down in the turn around, so the Queen and the Princess were both present and accounted for. The castle was now full. As he requested, they were ready to go the instant he walked in the door.

Blake decided to ask Christine if she would drive. His excuse would be that he wanted to drink at dinner and that her mother would most likely join him. In reality, he wanted to be able to keep a close eye on the 'Cat' and that would require a great deal more focus. He could also keep him more 'medicated' that way. The 'Cat' was dormant now. Blake had discovered at the bar that the alcohol helped to suppress his counterpart's yearning for aggression. After the Porsche sighting earlier, the only bargaining chip that Blake had, was to promise to start hunting again. The simple trip to Las Brisas' had pacified that need and allowed him to ward off any further advances.

The big surprise came when Blake not only insisted that they take his Mercedes, but he also chose to sit in the back seat. "Do you think you can handle this for a short drive?" he asked a startled Christine. "The restaurant is only a few miles from here."

Christine was shocked. Nobody ever drove her dad's car, not even valets. "You sure it's ok Dad?" she inquired.

"It's a win-win situation," Blake responded. "I get two pretty chauffeurs, and I don't have to squeeze myself into the back seat of your car," he countered. "Case closed?" he asked.

"As usual, you win Daddy," Christine conceded. "I promise I'll be careful."

There was only one brief squealing of tires as the Kendall's went off to dinner. The first launch from their little side street out onto Pacific Coast Highway included a slight, momentary loss of traction. Christine turned white, Katie's eyes got really big, but the guy in the back seat never said a word. He did however smile. It was a Cheshire smile. It came and went as fast as the sound of the rubber on the road but Blake still knew it was there. He wondered how much longer he was going to be able to maintain control. Blake longed for another martini. Lucky for him, 'BJ's' was only a few blocks away.

The glass of Grey Goose helped. The bartender was obviously user friendly. The vodka to vermouth ratio was probably five to one. This was good because Blake suddenly found himself in a very awkward position. He was stuck in a booth sitting between the two special women in his life. This was fine for him, but a horrible distraction for the 'Cat'. With both of them having chosen to wear their hair down, and also deciding on similar outfits, Blake couldn't help noticing that Christine was a dead ringer for her mother. She looked like Katie did back in their college days. He tried to ignore the obvious resemblance, but the persistent growling in his stomach wasn't because he was hungry.

"Duck, duck, goose... Grey Goose" his brain formulated as he reached for his depleting martini. He had to be careful. He couldn't afford to get drunk. The plan was to stay just close enough to the line to suppress his

nemesis but still maintain his own persona. The idea of him drinking didn't seem to bother either of his dates. They seemed to enjoy the fact he was actually out with them. Everything was going well until Blake decided that he needed to use the bathroom.

She caught his eye as she passed him in the hallway near the kitchen. She had the usual layout but her eyes were an absolutely breathtaking shade of blue. Blake almost didn't continue into the men's room. He wanted to take a second look but she turned and went behind the bar. Blake went into the bathroom and did his thing. He hesitated when saw his reflection in the mirror when he stopped to wash his hands. The 'Cat' was awake now. The familiar smile and ravenous eyes stared back at him. There was no forgetting what they had both seen. When Blake left the bathroom, he made a point to make a detour in front of the bar. He wanted another look.

His disappointment was instantaneous. The only person behind the bar was a tall, lanky blonde guy washing glasses. Blake's 'Cat' face must have betrayed him. The young man looked up and said, "Can I help you sir?" he asked. "The bartender will be back in a minute."

Blake held his ground. "I'd like to compliment him on, and order another martini, Vince," he responded. Blake always made it a point to notice names. The guys name tag read Vince.

"Well, your bartender is a she," Vince began. "And from what I've heard, Melissa does make a damn good martini. She should be back any second. I'm sorry about the wait."

When Blake noticed Vince's eyes shift, he knew the girl had to be coming up from behind him. *Funny, he liked to kill them from behind.* In a matter of seconds, their eyes met and Blake knew that the hunt was on.

* * * * *

"So what do you boys think about me dying my hair dark, you know, this being a special occasion and all?" Alex said as she ran her fingers playfully through her hair. "I mean after all, I do meet the height and weight requirements for this little suare." She continued to toss her hair about as she took a few steps into the center aisle.

Grey smiled because he realized there was more to come. As always, Alex delivered.

"Are any of you gentlemen going to tell me that you figure I can't pull this off?" Alex asked as she turned a certain way to properly advertise her assets.

Richard began to blush. He was speechless. Grey remained silent, hoping that Tim would shut her down. It wasn't that he didn't think she could handle it; he just didn't like the idea of her being in the line of fire. He wasn't disappointed.

"That's a pretty neck you have there, Alex," Tim observed. "Along with everything else for that matter, but that might not be enough. So you won't take offense to the fact that I'd like to keep it that way?" Tim inquired. "But I do see your point. Why don't we bait the hook, right?"
"Something, like that," she responded. "Back home when we wanted to catch the big one, we always found the right bait."

"It's actually not a bad idea," Grey chimed in. "It's a good idea in fact, just the wrong bait."

"It would be an extremely dangerous situation for even a well trained professional," Tim added.

"Well, it all sounds very dangerous to me," Richard commented. "Does this mean we're backing off on the massage angle?"

"Not at all," Tim assured him. "Alex's idea is a good one, but we don't know if Blake has already chosen a new target."

Richard looked at his watch. "It's been just over five hours or so since Grey was at the Kendall's," he observed. "Should we really be concerned so quickly?"

"I honestly don't know what to think," Tim answered. "I do know from past experience, and all of the evidence we've obtained so far, that if we go with our current theory about his being unhappy with Katie, it won't be long before he needs to kill again."

"So that means I'm still calling Katie in the morning," Grey said. "We have to be sure that nothing new is happening between now and whenever we put together a 'set up'. Tim, do you have any thoughts on surveillance?"

"I thought I'd take a few days off and handle it myself," he responded. "My boss has been trying to get me to take some time lately so it's the perfect time to ask." He turned his attention to Richard. "All right Father, are you ready to show us what you've got?"

Richard stood and motioned toward the hidden door. "Gentlemen, and lady, right this way," he said, as he directed the group into the privacy of his office.

It was a toss-up when it came to deciding who was more impressed. Both Tim and Grey were silent as their eyes followed the path Richard had designed for them to travel. The priest had arranged a chronological display of events for everyone to examine. He had incorporated all of the notes, pictures and information from Tim's file as well as their group notes regarding the conversations about the information that Grey had provided. His personal comments and observations that he had formulated as he went along, were attached to the bottom of each poster board on three by five cards.

Alex broke the silence. "Wow, Father, this is impressive," she said. "It certainly explains a lot."

Tim walked over to the first display board. The first category was:

Pre-Kelley Richfield:

"I left that space blank for you Tim," Richard said. "I figured that we could add whatever you come up with later."

Tim walked by each easel carefully paying attention to each display. "Nice work, Father," Tim admitted. "This storyline will be very useful when the time comes and we have to explain ourselves."

"How did you manage to assemble this all so quickly?" Alex asked. "This is a lot of information."

"It was actually easy," Richard chuckled. "It was no problem, after Grey here helped me get rid of my audience." Richard cast a look up at the statue of Jesus again. Everyone understood his reference immediately.

Then Grey took over the conversation. "So Tim, tomorrow you're going to start setting up some kind of surveillance on Blake and I'm going to call Katie and make the massage appointments. Does that sound about right?" he asked. Everyone nodded. "Father, you take a break tomorrow and focus on church business. It will help you relax and keep a clear head. Alex and I will continue doing research on any possible earlier victims and help Tim out if or when necessary. Is everybody on board with that?"

Everyone nodded again. They we're all in agreement. "Hey, guys," Grey said, "If I haven't said it often enough, thanks."

Richard acknowledged this by stepping forward and giving him a hug. "Go with God," he said softly in his friend's ear.

Tim put four fingers to one of his temples and gave Grey a small salute, "We'll get him," he said confidently. "I'll call you in the morning." Then he held up his cell phone. "Twenty-four–seven, my friends, twenty-four-seven," he reminded them. Then he quietly slipped away through Richard's special door.

Alex was also ready to take leave. "Goodnight, Father," she said. "Go with God," Richard said hugging her as well.

Alex smiled. "You know something Father," she said, "If it's all right with you, tonight, I think I will," she replied.

Then she took Grey's hand and led him to the door. "Good night, Father, "she said softly as she and Grey departed.

As they made their way back through the sanctuary, Grey stopped and took a seat about half way up the aisle. "You ok?" Alex asked.

"Just a little overwhelmed," Grey admitted. "I always thought I was a pretty good judge of character," he said. "I used to swear that I could read people so well. I just can't believe I was so wrong about this guy." "Come with me," she said, as she pulled him back on to his feet.

"It's been a long day and you really need to get some sleep."

Maybe you're right," he admitted as they stepped out in to the warm night air. "I just wish there was something more that we could do. I don't want to take a chance here and then find out that I missed something."

"I know it's tough, but I'm sure Tim will find a way to have eyes on Blake in the morning," Alex assured him.

"You're right, of course," Grey acknowledged. "But that's still twelve hours away."

"Something tells me that Tim is not going to wait that long," Alex considered. "I wouldn't be surprised if he wasn't already headed down to the boat to pack a bag for a stake out. I think the time off he was talking about taking, started the minute he left the church."

"Yeah, no time like the present," Grey said. "I got that feeling too. He's not the kind of guy to sit around and wait for something to happen."

"Should we call him and make ourselves available?" Alex asked.

"No," Grey answered. "It's not necessary. He knows we're around. We'll just let him do his thing. I'll call him first thing in the morning and see what's happening."

"You driving, or am I?" Grey asked as they approached the car.

Alex just gave him a look. "From the looks of things my friend," she replied, "You are definitely the one in the driver's seat."

Grey got in and started the car. "Very funny," he said. "You want to trade places?" he asked hoping for a least a good laugh.

"Everything is as it should be," Alex reminded him. "That's why we're here, involved in this thing in the first place."

"It's going to get interesting from here on out, isn't it?" Grey conceded.

"I don't know how we can possibly assume anything less." Alex agreed. "Shall we?" she asked, motioning for Grey to get them going.

There was a quick nod exchanged between them. Then Grey threw the Mustang in gear and headed off into the night. The wind felt good in his face. For now, it appeared that the darkness was his friend. He would remain in its favor until late in the evening when the dreams came and the shadows grew. But the blade...the blade was a constant. It always remained the same.

* * * * *

CHAPTER 27

While Blake enjoyed his dinner, the 'Cat' contemplated his next kill. Blake didn't need the martinis now; his adversary would leave his women alone. His dark friend had found a new target. A little time, a little planning and poof, things would be back to normal. Right now, the bartender was just fun to watch. Katie and Christine were also having a good time. The wine and the dinner as a family, (combined with the earlier exorcism of Walter) allowed Katie to return to a state of emotional freedom she had abandoned long ago. Christine was simply enjoying being out with her dad; (the recently almost famous dad who was now, just learning to enjoy again, the art of sharing a pizza with his wife and daughter).

Christine wasn't even bothered by the fact that for brief periods of time, her father's eyes seemed to be focused on the T.V. over the bar. During these mental exits, his face appeared hard and cold as if something on the screen was engulfing him. She let these distractions pass, because his attention always found its way back to her. When it did, the intensity melted away and he returned to the warm, friendly, fatherly type that suggested they go out in the first place. She would never understand that during his absence, her father's dark side was devouring something else behind the bar instead. Now that a new target had been acquired, every move was being studied, looking for a possible weakness. When the opportunity finally presented itself, everything would come down to timing. Every nuance already learned, would work to his advantage. The set-up, the kill, and the escape all shared roles of equal importance. There could be no success if even one of these elements failed.

It would probably take several return trips to make contact again. Then, he could set up a tail, and track down any and all necessary information on the girl. From the dramatic change in the anxiety level he now felt, Blake could tell that the 'Cat' was starting to feel more at ease. There was a plan. The hunger would soon be satisfied. The needs were no longer being neglected. This sudden release of pressure allowed Blake to relax and completely enjoy his evening. At one point, he even allowed Katie to leave her hand on the resting place it had found on his leg under the table. The 'Cat' continued to watch, but from a much more passive perspective. Blake quickly discovered that he enjoyed finding ways to keep the evening going; another round for him and Katie, several fancy desserts that were shared by all. The 'Cat' watched quietly and got his fill. It would be several hours before the Kendall's would finally make it home.

* * * * *

Las Vegas, Nevada

Patti Garrison was about to call it a night. Her gold detective shield and weapon were as always, safely tucked away in the nightstand drawer. It was the middle of July and things there in the desert were really starting to heat up. The air conditioner in her mid-town condo was constantly working overtime. For that matter, so was she; at least until a few hours ago when her captain had sent her home. Now, she was just sitting in bed in a camisole and panties, messing around on her lap top, and trying to cool off. The glass of cabernet on the nightstand was more than an analgesic, it was a welcome friend. Her email consisted mostly of spam and re-fi ads and her Facebook page was all but empty. It wasn't her fault as much as the departments. She never had the free time for things like social media. The job kept her far too busy but lately, it just wasn't enough. She had to get out and meet somebody. She hadn't had a real date in months. She was certainly attractive enough, pretty blue eyes, long blonde hair, and the body and legs to match. Her only self proclaimed liability was that she also had a brain. She needed the great mental stimulation as much if not more than the physical and that made 'guy' shopping tough. Frustrated and tired, she decided to check out the news. That's when her eye caught the story on her homepage. The headline read:

"Ripper Case" remains a mystery

Detectives in Orange County, California are baffled by a recent string of murders. Several local women have been killed by who police and local authorities are now referring to as the "Ripper," nicknamed after the notorious murderer 'Jack the Ripper' of nineteenth century London who slaughtered a group of female prostitutes by slitting their throats. The new assailant has claimed the lives of a least three local young women so far, and the police fear that they may discover many more. Detectives from several cities as well as a team from the Federal Bureau of Investigation have formed a task force to handle the case. While the public has been made aware of the situation, few actual facts regarding the case have been released so far."

There were other comments and opinions but Patti moved on.

"Orange County," she whispered under her breath. Hearing the sound of her saying it out loud made her smile. The O.C. was Galleon's territory. She hadn't seen Tim in almost ten years but had thought about him on more than one occasion. They had dated for awhile back then, but at the time, he had ambitions of joining S.W.A.T. and she was trying to climb the sexist ladder to become a detective. Tim made the S.W.A.T. team in record time. A few months later, she was offered a chance at a homicide assignment by the Las Vegas Police Department. Tim was so distracted by the job that Patti jumped at the chance. She headed east the following day.

That was a long time ago. She wondered if he had anything to do with the high profile case. Tim was good friend and a good cop. Just remembering her time with him made her feel like she wasn't alone for a moment. Patti closed her lap top and turned off the light. She decided that if she was still thinking about the "Ripper" case or Tim in the morning, maybe she'd make a call down to So Cal and see if she could track him down. When she closed her eyes, she had a funny feeling that if Tim were anywhere close, he wouldn't be hard to find.

* * * * *

Alex and Rachel retired to the front patio. As Grey suspected, there was more wine involved. Rachel was trying to be polite and pick up the conversation where they had left off earlier. Alex was exploring the possibility that the wine might act as a sleeping aid for what she and Grey figured was going to be a long night. After checking on Dylan, who was already fast asleep, Grey headed out to join the girls.

"Father Richard is a very interesting man," he heard Alex saying as he stepped out the front door. "He seems to be rather fond of Grey."

"They've been friends a long time," Rachel confided. "It was a little strange for me at first," she continued, "them being friends and all. I'm sure you know that Grey here is not all that religious, if you know what I mean."

"Grey befriending a priest did strike me as odd," Alex confessed as she took a small sip from her glass. There was a brief pause; and suddenly Grey was all ears. "But after meeting Richard, and seeing the two of them together, I think I get it," she admitted. "They play off each other quite well."

"That they do," Rachel agreed. "That's why I was hoping that Richard could help Grey get a handle on things and start talking about the accident."

"You should know honey that Richard and I have been talking rather extensively about just that," Grey volunteered. "Alex just learned about this tonight because she was there when Richard pressed me on a few things."

Rachel glanced over at Alex. Much to Alex's surprise, her eyes were more friendly than confrontational.

"Well, what do you think?" Rachel asked. "Is Richard making any progress getting through that thick skull of his?" She said this while glancing back over at Grey.

Alex was ready. "While the details escape me, Rachel," she offered, "I did get the impression that the battle between the two of them was definite."

Alex went for broke. "Actually Rachel, I think there's a very good chance that Father Richard is going to play a big part in Grey working through all of this," she asserted confidently. (It was the well, and carefully manipulated truth.)

Grey knew that Alex's kind words of reassurance carried a lot of weight. Rachel thought he had been doing better, and in her own way, Alex had just confirmed it.

"It makes me feel better, knowing that Richard is helping you," she said. "Thank you, Alex for going with him tonight. You at least had a chance to hear them talking. If things weren't right, you'd know. I know Grey could never put one over on you," Rachel added with confidence. "It's taking some time," Alex responded, trying to assure Rachel, "but I'm sure everything is going to work out just fine. More wine, anyone?" she continued, as she grabbed a bottle off the table and offered to pour. It was a simple but effective distraction which allowed an

opening to change the conversation.

"So what do you guys want to do tomorrow?" Rachel asked. "Maybe we can all take a drive down to the beach in the Mustang. I'll bet Dylan would love it with the top down."

"That's not a bad idea honey," Grey responded. "Are you thinking Newport or Laguna with all the little shops?"

When Alex heard the name Laguna, she knew instantly where Grey was trying to go with the conversation. If she remembered correctly, Blake's house was on a hill above Laguna Beach. She wondered if Tim was already down there in the area trying to get set up.

"It doesn't really matter to me," Rachel replied. "I just thought it would be fun to show Alex the beach. It's has to be somewhat different than the Gulf of Mexico back home."

"It would be nice to go down and check it out," Alex commented. "Newport, I've heard of, but what's Laguna like?"

Grey knew by her response that she had figured out his angle. He waited for a moment to see if Rachel would play along.

"It's a small beach community a few miles south of Newport," Rachel replied. "Newport tends to be a little bit more 'trendy'. I personally prefer the small town, laid back attitude of Laguna Beach. It's more of an 'artsy' community."

Alex made a point to focus on every word and nodded her approval.

Her opinion now validated, Rachel smiled. "I'm just saying," she added.

"Well then, that's settled," Grey decided. "Laguna Beach it is. We'll get up in the morning and get going."

Rachel could not have been more excited. "We can check out the beach, have lunch in town and maybe even do some shopping," she proposed.

Grey figured that as they were driving around, they could cruise by the Kendall's house and show both women where he spent several hours every couple of weeks. (Looking for Tim was just an added bonus.) Grey knew he was already there. He just couldn't figure out where Tim could set up and not be noticed. The house was cut dramatically into the hillside and didn't possess a lot of area that was open to observation. The entire length of the driveway was visible from the master balcony and several upstairs windows as well. But that was only from looking down from the house. The entire estate was designed for privacy and offered very little viewing space, even if you were trying to observe from below. From a reasonable distance outside walls, there was little or no line of sight.

Alex reached for the surviving bottle, and took the liberty of topping off her and Rachel's glasses. She discarded the empty bottle and raised her glass.

"To tomorrow," she said, inviting Rachel to join her.

"To shopping," Rachel responded with a small, subtle giggle.

Grey just shook his head. "On that note, I'm going to bed," he informed them. "I'll see you two in the morning."

He looked in on Dylan before heading for the bedroom. The little guy was sound asleep.

"It's going to be another interesting day tomorrow, buddy,'" he told him as he pulled Dylan's blanket up a bit. "I hope your Uncle Tim is doing his thing about now."

Grey didn't know that Rachel had seen the light on and come up quietly behind him.

"Is Tim up to something tonight?" she asked placing a hand on his shoulder.

Without out even flinching, Grey kept his eyes forward and didn't turn around. He had to hold his ground.

"He said he had some new stakeout he was needed on," Grey answered. "I think it started tonight."

"Well, I'm sure Renee is going to be thrilled about that," Rachel observed. "Did he say how long he was going to be doing it? I mean being out all night and everything?"

"All I know is that he seemed pretty intent on catching the guy he's after," Grey volunteered. "I think he's going to be working long hours at night for maybe a week or two."

This was not what Rachel wanted to hear. "That's great," she said. "Does Renee know?"

"I don't know if he's had a chance to tell her yet," Grey replied. "I talked to him about an hour ago about the possibility of taking Alex out on the boat and he didn't mention Renee," he lied.

"Well, I'm sure that either way, I'm going to hear about it first thing in the morning," Rachel complained. "She hates the night shift stuff. It really puts a strain on things with them."

"I got the impression that it's a pretty big case," Grey offered as a concession. "I'm sure Tim will get a handle on it as quickly as possible. Tell Renee she has nothing to worry about."

"All right, I will," Rachel conceded. "I'm going to bed. Are you coming?" she asked.

Grey noticed a shadow lingering at the end of the hall. "I'll be there in a minute," he answered. I'm going to get some water." He turned and made his way down the hallway toward the kitchen. Alex was waiting as he made the second turn.

"Nice work," she commended him as they stepped into the kitchen. "So we're now in a position where we can check out the beach and Tim at the same time; brilliant. I also like the added touch about taking me for a boat ride. That was quick thinking. It occurred to me earlier that Blake's going to be pretty safe during the daylight hours. At night, the darkness seems to give him an added advantage he likes. He has too many responsibilities during the day to be out hunting. No, I think it's the cover of night we have to worry about. He may hunt by day, but he won't kill until after nightfall. We just need to find his target."

"That, or give him one," Grey reminded her as he filled a glass of water. "But for that, Tim would probably have to pull a rabbit out of a hat." Alex looked at him funny. "I know it's a cliché but I'm serious," Grey admitted.

"Something tells me that our friend Tim is full of surprises," Alex noted as they moved back into the hallway. "I'll see you in the morning," she said.

Grey nodded. "I just got finished telling Dylan that I thought that tomorrow was going to be an interesting day," he said.

"Then I guess you didn't lie," she teased him. "Goodnight," she whispered as she disappeared in to the guest room leaving Grey all alone with his thoughts. It turned out that his mind refused to shut down even after his head hit the pillow.

* * * * *

It was a clear night on the water and Blake was enjoying the view. He had trouble sleeping, so threw on a robe and headed out on the deck. The luscious bartender at 'B.J.'s' had gotten the best of the 'Cat', and therefore the best of him. It was Saturday night, and Blake had come to realize that none of his usual connections, like the one at the D.M.V. and his contacts at city hall were accessible. He was dead in the water until Monday morning. This presented a problem because his alter ego was not known for being patient. As an act of conciliation, he decided that tomorrow he would go back to the restaurant and see what he could find out about the girl on his own. This simple idea seemed to help keep the growling in his stomach at bay. It was proof he was paying attention.

As Blake looked out at the horizon, he could see the lights on an oil rig some five miles off the coast. He had set up shop on the balcony about an hour after they got home. A comfortable chair, a nice bottle of scotch, a small ice bucket, and a glass were all he needed to properly end the day. He had thirty-six hours before he could formally make a move on the girl, but an initial recon in the morning would temporarily pacify the insatiable hunger that was building in his inner sanctum. For the moment, his show of sustained interest in the hunt was going a long way. Now, in the wee hours of the morning, he found solace in the serenity of the ocean before him and a cold glass of twenty year old courage in his hand. He had come a long way since that first night in Queen's, when the memory of his encounter with the 'Cat' was first resurrected. It had been a long haul and although many had fallen, he had still been able to retain the prize. Blake turned his attention to his wife who was sleeping soundly in their bed. The trophy was still his to covet. He just had to find away to move on. Blake poured himself another drink and returned to his chair. He and Katie were at peace again, but this time, the hunger that remained in the aftermath was too great. It needed to be satisfied. Blake was hoping that it would only take one more.

* * * * *

At first, the house was a surveillance nightmare. There was limited visual access from nearly every feasible direction. The simple 'park and observe' thing was never going to work. The hillside streets were narrow and unyielding when it came to parking places. Down at the bottom of the hill, where Blake's driveway met a short access road to the highway, the property gate and perimeter wall were too tall to see over, (Basic fortress, 101.) Tim however, did not discourage easily. After twenty minutes or so of surveying the area on foot, he discovered that he could set up camp across the street on the opposite side of the highway. There, in a small parking lot armed with a pair of high-tech binoculars, he could at least have a decent view of the master bedroom balcony and part of the turn-around at the top of the driveway. The small flower shop was closed for the day so he wouldn't attract a lot of attention. The lighting was poor, so if he parked in the shadows, he would be virtually invisible to anyone up on the hill.

Tim decided early that his best chance at making things easy was to monitor the house, what little he could actually see, and then keep an eye on the three vehicles registered to Blake's address. The white B.M.W. and the red Porsche would be easy to spot, but if he was forced to tail it, the Black Mercedes 500SL that was registered to Blake himself, would be a bit more difficult. He could make out what appeared to be the red Porsche in the corner of the turn-around, but the Mercedes and the B.M.W. were either garaged or missing. Truth was; it was Blake's Mercedes that he was most concerned about. Being black, and especially from that distance, it was going to be hard to spot up there in the dark. Tim sipped at his Gatorade, (coffee just wasn't his thing and Renee said it made him jittery,) and surveyed the house again, hoping he would catch a break. About an hour went by before he saw the tall, broad shadow of a man suddenly appear to come out on the balcony. He could make out the strike of the match and the lighting of a cigar. Tim knew his quarry was safely at home. Now, the only question was, how long would he stay put?

Tim looked over at the pile of C.D.'s on the passenger seat. His truck was equipped with a dual battery hook up system so playing the disk changer all night was no big deal. On the floor was a cooler full of Gatorade and granola bars. The little sign on the edge of the dashboard still made him laugh; "NO DONUTS HERE". It was a playful reminder that Renee' had given him in his Christmas stocking last year. He had the "Ripper" case file on the floor next to him, but that was probably unnecessary. He had already committed most of it to memory. Right now, he just wanted to make sure that it didn't get any bigger. If Blake decided to stay put, it would be an easy night. Part of Tim wished he would. He was hoping Grey would have a chance to do his thing again and get some reliable information before Blake had another opportunity to strike.

Based on the timing patterns so far, there was a good chance that something was going to escalate in the next several days. Blake liked to plan. If he already had a target, they were screwed. If Grey's observations were correct, then they still had a chance to interfere. That's why the surveillance was so important; discover the target, and/or prevent the kill. It was the only feasible, and more importantly, legal way to catch him.

Tim cracked open another Gatorade. Then he eased the seat back, got comfortable and popped in the "Eagles Greatest Hits, 1971-1975". After all, a little good music was never a bad thing. He aimed his binoculars back up at the balcony. There was nothing to see. Then he hit a switch that converted his field of view to infra-red and he began to see the light.

"Well, hello there," he said, addressing the image out loud. He could now make out a large shape sitting on a patio chair behind the railing. The heat off a cigar ember glowed bright in the lens.

"A cigar and a nightcap, how quaint of you, Mr. Kendall," Tim continued, with his one-sided conversation. "But how rude of you not to offer me one," he said sarcastically.

The sad part was that under different circumstances, he might actually have found himself invited to share a drink on that very balcony with Blake. As it was, just the thought of being in the elevator with him the other day was overwhelmingly bizarre. Their conversation about Blake's wife was even more unsettling. Tim could not even begin to imagine the evil that was at play inside Blake's head. The active cross over between what appeared to be two completely different personalities is what he found to be the most frightening of all. It left him with a single immediate thought, *"We've got to nail this guy,"* slipped quietly through his lips. He reached down, grabbed a granola bar and settled in for the night.

Around one thirty, a white B.M.W. fitting the description of Blake's daughter's car went up the hill through the gate. The remote laser sensors he had placed at the foot of the gate during his walk earlier paid off. The car had triggered them exactly as planned setting off the remote speaker inside the truck. Tim could see it was a young woman driving, but couldn't make out any details. His eyes followed the headlights as they wound their way up the driveway to the top of the hill. At the crest, the car disappeared into the darkness, probably a garage and was completely hidden from view other than a heat signature that it had stopped. It looked like all of the Kendalls were present and accounted for. As long as it stayed that way, Tim knew there wouldn't be a problem. He tossed his now empty Gatorade bottle behind the seat and reached for another one. Sunrise was only five hours away. From the looks of things on the balcony, Blake wasn't going anywhere. Tim shook his head. The first night was always the easiest, but he knew that there were many more to come. Steve Miller was next on the play list. Tim wasted no time in firing him up. This time, the Gatorade went down slow.

* * * * *

Blake slept deeply and dreamed of the kill. It was all displayed before him in only shadows and light, but it was still his friend, happily engaged in some of his finest work. The blade cut, and cut deep, as it had many times before. When the blood flowed, the life in her eyes slowly faded away. In the end, there was a staggered moment of emptiness and then suddenly, the hunger, the gnawing, painful, insatiable hunger was gone. The inescapable rage he felt for Katie no longer existed. He sat quietly for a moment and collected his thoughts. It was almost melancholy. He remembered the feeling. He had experienced it before. It had first manifested itself back in the dark times after he had committed his final sacrifice before he and Katie were re-united. It told him it was time to stop. Blake rolled over and mumbled something in his sleep. If Katie had been awake, his words would have scared her to death.

Blake stayed trapped in the 'Cat's' dream until the early morning sun came shining through the window and he realized that the flashes of light in his eyes were real. At first, he was confused. He thought he was still dreaming. As he woke, he expected to see the blood and carnage of his friend's handy work laid out before him. He opened one eye and as soon as his vision adjusted, he could thankfully confirm that he was awake. Katie was already up and sitting out on the balcony with what he assumed to be a mimosa in her hand. She was safe.

Blake was seriously relieved. The dream he had just experienced was so vivid and real, that he honestly expected to wake up and find Katie playfully slaughtered on the floor. If the 'Cat' had really been loose, she never would have stood a chance. Blake knew that he needed to find out more about the bartender and quickly. As long as his friend was distracted, Katie would remain alive and well. Blake climbed out of bed and headed for the bathroom.

"First things first," he mumbled. "I've got to get rid of this scotch." Blake was so tired that he decided to pee sitting down. When he was finished, he went to join Katie on the patio. He still had trouble processing the fact that she was still all in one piece. The dream had left its mark.

Katie was already enjoying the day. She had taken up residence on a chaise lounge and was happily engulfed in a Patricia Cornwell novel. Her glass on the table was almost empty. He startled Katie when he suddenly appeared.

"Good morning, Honey," she said as she took her eyes off the book in her hands.

"Good morning," he replied. Blake looked down at the table. "Would you care for another?" he asked mischievously, eyeballing her glass.

"I'd love another one," she replied, "and when you return, I'd like some lotion on my back as well." Katie was having fun.

Blake took several steps back to the ice bucket, grabbed the bottle of properly chilled Moet, and proceeded to refill her glass. When he stopped at half way, assuming the rest would be orange juice, he met with some discontent.

"Silly man," she giggled. "I have no need for the orange juice anymore. Please just pour and smile."

Blake said nothing. He just continued to fill the rest of her glass. When he finished, he turned and started to move away.

"Oh sir," Katie beckoned causing him to pause. "I think you forgot about the lotion." For a split second, she considered the possibility that she was pushing her luck. When she saw his hand reaching for her lotion, she knew he would continue playing along. Katie rolled over and Blake's hands did their thing.

"Thank you," she said. "I'll have to come here more often," she teased.

"It would be my pleasure," Blake professed in just a bit more than a whisper. Then he wiped his hands on a towel and sat down in a chair at the table next to her.

The Sunday morning paper was already on the table. Katie informed him that Christine had brought it up earlier. This made him smile. It was a kind gesture on her part if nothing else. He would make it a point to thank her later. Then he sat down to read.

Blake was disappointed. After several minutes of flipping through the front section, he could not find a single reference to the "Ripper" case. Apparently his popularity had gone down. He couldn't imagine the public not wanting to know if there was any progress being made in the case. Maybe he was frustrating the cops so badly that they didn't want to admit they had nothing to go on. It was also possible that they didn't want to glorify his actions by putting them in print. Blake folded up the paper and set it back on the table. Then he started to grin. The hunt would begin soon and this time, he would really give them something to write about. This was going to be the most glorious kill yet. Blake reached for the bottle Katie had started and chugged it down in three gulps. Katie heard him swallowing but never looked up until she heard the now upside down bottle being returned to the bucket.

"That was certainly different," she commented, curious as to what he would do next.

Blake just smiled. "Don't worry, honey," he assured her. "I'll get you some more."

As he got out of his chair, the plan started to formulate. He had several hours before 'B.J.'s' would be open. He could spend the rest of the morning entertaining Katie with champagne and then slip away after lunch. Blake could think of nothing else as he headed inside to fetch his wife another bottle of joy. He was surprised to find a new rhythm in his step. He stopped when he saw his reflection in the hallway mirror. For a moment, he contemplated some concern. The look in his eyes was not his own. Blake kept moving. He was on a quest.

"More champagne for the lady," he announced as headed downstairs. The morning was going to be quiet and tasteful. The afternoon, on the other hand was going to be downright delicious. The hunger was good. The satisfaction would be better.

* * * * *

CHAPTER 28

During the night, everything remained quiet at the Kendall house. Shortly after sunrise, Tim heard the sensors go off as the white B.M.W. pulled out of the gate. (He'd have to thank his friend Garrett down in the surveillance division for recommending them.) The sensors worked like a charm. No one could move between them without him knowing it. If something crossed their path, they would set off a small clicker Tim kept in his hand. Garrett had even given him one to put on the Mercedes if he could ever get close enough. Tim really liked Garrett. The 'G-Man' was the king when it came to 'covert ops' toys.

The sun was up now so this time, he could really see. That only allowed for a bigger surprise. At first glance, he would have sworn it was Katie Kendall behind the wheel of the B.M.W., but as the car passed closer in front on him, he realized that it was her daughter Christine. The photos he had come across earlier while doing research on the family had indicated a similarity, but apparently, the older that Christine became, the more the family genes had taken over. There was no denying the resemblance.

Tim was afforded a good look at her while she waited to pull out onto the highway. She was stunning. The tank-top and pony tail suggested she was going to work out. That was simple enough to assume. According to her bio she liked to go to the gym. Tim studied her closely before she pulled away. That was several hours ago. It was close to nine now, and she still hadn't returned. Mom and Dad were still safely tucked away up on the hill. Who knew if or when they would decide to go out? There was a small café next to the flower shop and it was open for Sunday breakfast. The granola bars had worn thin so Tim decided to get something to eat.

He needed to check in with Wickmann and tell him that he had decided to take some time off. Calling Renee was also a priority. He'd left a voicemail for her late last night, but he wanted a chance to talk to her himself. He would be hard to recognize from a distance, but he put on a ball cap and sun glasses anyway. He'd only be exposed on the sidewalk for a few seconds so he figured it was safe. Tim locked the truck and walked the twenty or so yards to the café. He took the sensor clicker with him. He ordered a nice breakfast and continued to watch the house. Then he picked up his phone.

His first call was Renee. She wasn't particularly happy, but she said she understood. Tim knew it was going to cost him big. He was definitely going to hear about it later. This thing with Blake was probably going to interfere with some plans that they had made later in the week. He promised himself that he would try his best to not let that happen. He really loved Renee. The very thought of her would sometimes get him through the night.

Wickmann was much more supportive. (He had been there when Tim had to deal with the guy in the Corvette.) Tim had cautiously neglected to share that one with Renee.

"Take a week or two and come back fresh," he said, encouraging Tim to get clear.

The two men talked for a few minutes before the conversation ended with Tim saying, "Thanks, Sarg, I'll keep in touch."

He had just set down the phone when the waitress brought him his eggs. After a night in the truck, he was hungry. The eggs didn't last long. Neither did the pancakes that followed. He was tired, but thanks to Garrett's sensors he'd managed to get a couple of hours sleep. Without a partner to talk to, it was just him, his cooler and his C.D. player. That made for a long night. He'd been on the go now for nearly thirty-six hours. He paid his check and headed back to the truck. When he opened the door and climbed back in, his body told him that it was going to be a long day. It also reminded him that fairly quickly, he was going to need some help.

* * * * *

Little Dylan Thomas was all smiles. Even though he couldn't see where he was going, (his car seat was facing backwards), he was really enjoying the ride. Grey had asked Alex to drive so he could sit in the back seat with his son. That way the girls could talk. Rachel played co- pilot as Alex guided them safely along. For Grey, having the top down made all the difference. Dylan was just like his dad and loved the wind in his face. And he looked cool, even if his sunglasses were a few sizes too big. Besides, the warmth of the sun felt good. Grey just leaned back in the seat and closed his eyes. For a short time, it allowed him to step away and relax. His mind started to drift and he wondered what Richard had prepared for his evening sermon.

The ever popular, "Thou shalt not kill," perhaps, or the updated version "Thou shalt not covet or kill women that look like my wife."

Poor man was doing the best he could. No one more than Richard deserved to find peace when this was over. Somewhere close, a horn sounded and Grey opened his eyes. He could see the blue Pacific. They were almost there. He decided to text Tim.

"Good morning, Captain?" he inquired, hoping that his friend was out there somewhere and still in one piece. "Anything new?" It didn't take long for Tim to respond.

"The girl left at the crack of dawn, but Blake and Katie have stayed put." the first message said. It was immediately followed by "What's up at your end?" He and Alex's first assessment was correct. Tim had immediately started to keep an eye on Blake.

"Alex and I are in the area," Grey replied. "Have Dylan and Rachel too. Need anything?"

"Only for this bastard to go out and do something," Tim suggested. "Are you checking up on me?" he added.

"Just watching your back," Grey offered. "We'll be around if you need us."

"Thanks no worries," Tim responded. "I'll call you if I move." He was still sitting in the back of the flower shop parking lot. He had spoken to the owner earlier when the lady pulled in to open up. A quick flash of his badge, and she agreed to cooperate in any way. Tim assured her that her silence on the matter and the temporary use of the space were all he required. She was more than compliant. It would be lunch time soon and there was still no sign of any Kendall. Christine had still not returned and neither one of her parents had come down off the hill. According to Google maps, there was only one way in or out of the estate. He did notice however, a small access road in the back, but it was chained off. It was more than likely a fire access road. The satellite map provided a good aerial view of the property. Tim took some comfort in knowing that, at least in an emergency, he had some idea how the area was laid out.

Grey ended their exchange with a simple text, "Check in with you later."

When he looked up again, Alex had already made the turn south and they were on the coast highway headed through town. Alex and Rachel were busy taking in the sights. Dylan looked way too cool in his shades. Grey couldn't help but glance up at the elegant houses on the scenic ridge to his left. A mile or so down, he could see the outline of the Kendall house neatly tucked into the hillside. It reminded him that he had to get a hold of Katie. He had considered calling her earlier but, it being a Sunday morning; had decided to wait. It was late enough now that he felt comfortable making the call. He'd wait until the girls were out of the car. That way, he wouldn't have to watch his words in front of Rachel.

"Hey Honey," he called out trying to get Rachel's attention. As she turned, He pointed up to the house on the hill. "That big white one up there in the middle of all those trees is the Kendall's house. I thought you might want to see it."

Traffic had slowed, so they all got a pretty good look. Even at distance you could tell it was pretty palatial.

"The entrance is through the gates over there," Grey continued, pointing to the brick pilasters and hand-made wrought iron as they passed.

"That's really something," Rachel remarked. "So how do you get in?" "I just call when I get here and they buzz me in," Grey answered.

He didn't notice Tim as they passed by, but that was the general idea. The conversation had already turned.

The girls wanted to drive down a few miles to the Ritz Carlton Hotel so Alex could check out the view and then turn around and work their way back up through town. He was informed that there would be several shopping stops and probably lunch along the way. Grey looked at Dylan.

"At least you won't have to carry the bags little buddy," he laughed as he handed his son a ball that had fallen on the seat.

There was no way that Alex was going to let that pass. "Poor little Grey-Grey," she teased him. "We're big girls now. I think we can carry our own bags."

Rachel burst out laughing. "Well, I guess she told you," she taunted her husband.

"All right ladies, do you feel better now?" Grey responded sarcastically. "Make all the stops you want. Dylan and I are just going to stay put right here and catch some rays. At least until it's time for lunch," he snickered.

Alex just laughed and shook her head. "Still the same old Grey," she said, directing her comment to Rachel.

Rachel smiled. "Nice to know that someone else understands," she replied. Then Grey interrupted them.

"That's the Ritz Carlton Hotel on the bluff to the right," Grey announced. "Do you two want to stop and check it out, or is a drive-by enough?" he asked.

"I'm ok just pulling over for a minute to look," Alex answered. Rachel agreed.

Alex found a place to pull over so they could take a quick look. The girls got out, but he and Dylan stayed in the car. When they got back in, Alex turned to Grey. "The ocean is definitely different here than back home," she said. "It feels much calmer to me."

"I know what you mean," Grey acknowledged. "The gulf feels more violent because it is so prone to tropical storms and hurricanes. We get bad weather, but I don't recall ever hearing about us having those in this part of the Pacific."

Rachel looked at Alex. "I'm ready for some shopping if you are," she announced. "Let's whip this baby around."

Alex glanced over at Grey. He just nodded and smiled, so she pulled out back on to the highway and made a quick u-turn. As requested, they were now headed north back toward downtown. Grey was quiet, anxiously waiting to see if the girls were going to make a stop. He was just about to say something when Rachel asked Alex to pull over and park.

"I saw this place on the way down and thought we could check it out," she said.

Alex was immediately on board. As she got out of the car, she turned to Grey. "You sure you don't want to come," she teased.

Grey just smiled. "No, thank you," he replied. "Dylan and I will be just fine right here," he assured her, his hand patting the seat. "You two go have fun. Just don't leave us out here cooking too long."

The girls grabbed their purses and headed for the store. As soon as Grey was in the clear, he picked up his phone and called Katie. She was known for screening her calls but she picked up immediately.

"Good morning Grey," she answered. "Miss me already? What can I do for you?" she giggled.

Grey wondered sometimes if her playful flirtations were serious or not. He never had the nerve to pursue it.

"I was about to put my schedule together for next week and considering the amount of time we've all been spending together lately, I thought I would give you and Blake first choice at appointments."

"Well, I'm always game," she confessed, "But I'll have to check with Blake regarding his availability. He just went out for a few hours so I'll have to call you when he gets back."

All Grey heard was the words 'he just went out for a few hours.' It meant that Tim was now on the move. He knew that he would be getting a report soon, so he decided that he had to conclude their conversation.

"I won't book anyone else until after I hear back from you, ok?" he told Katie.

"I promise it won't be too long," she offered. "I can try to get him on his cell if you want."

Grey shook his head. "Seriously Katie, it's no big deal," he assured her. "He's probably busy and you certainly don't need to interrupt him." (Blake was out all right, on the move with Tim hot on his tail) "Just call me later when you know what you want to do," he suggested.

"I'll call you in a couple of hours then," she promised. "And Grey," she said, and then paused for a moment, "Thanks for the call." Then she hung up. Grey set his phone down on the seat. Katie was interested. Now, all he had to do was wait.

Dylan stared up at him with big blue eyes. His sunglasses were now on his lap. Grey wanted to reach out and take his son's hand just to see what the little guy was thinking about. He decided to unbuckle him and pick him up instead. It turned out to be exactly what they both needed. When the girls appeared a few minutes later, the two boys in the back seat were just laughing and playing.

Rachel looked at Alex. "Wish I could make him laugh like that again," she said quietly as they approached the car.

"You will," Alex assured her. "I promise you, you will. Just give it a little more time. I have a good feeling that very soon, things are going to change."

The girls put their bags in the trunk and then got back in the car. Rachel mouthed the words "Thank you" to Alex as they were putting on their seatbelts. Alex took note and simply nodded. Then Alex looked in the rear view mirror at Grey.

"So, where to next boss?" she inquired.

Before Grey could respond, Rachel interjected. "They're a few more shops I'd like to check out a couple of blocks up," she suggested.

Without saying a word, Alex looked back in the mirror. Grey waved his hand in a 'proceed' gesture and said, "Why not?" Rachel was happy, but surprised. Grey hated shopping and was either trying to make her happy by being compliant or putting on a show for Alex. Either way, she'd take it. Grey looked over at Dylan again for some comic relief. He had managed to get his sunglasses back on all by himself.

Grey leaned over and said, "When we stop again, I'll call Uncle Tim and see how he's doing." That seemed to make Dylan happy.

He and Alex were both surprised when they heard Rachel say, "If you talk to him, tell him to be careful."

Grey tapped her on the shoulder and gave her a curious look.

"I got an earful from Renee this morning about this new stakeout thing he's on," she informed them. "She's not very happy and he was not very forthcoming."

"He can't discuss the case with her or any of us for that matter," Grey defended. "You know the rules."

"It doesn't mean she has to like it, does it?" Rachel fired back. "Guys," Alex intervened. "Tim strikes me as the kind of guy who knows exactly what he's doing. Personally, I don't think you have anything to worry about." Then, a heavy silence fell between them. It was just as Alex had intended. Their minds were forced to analyze what she had just said. The next thing anyone heard was Rachel pointing out the location of another shop. The moment of concern had passed. In a matter of seconds, Rachel motioned Alex to the curb again.

Grey played his cards just as he had earlier. As soon as they were out of sight, he tried texting Tim. Tim saw the message coming in, but right now, under the circumstances, even Grey would have to wait.

* * * * *

Tim was counting the bricks in the Kendall's security wall when he heard his phone start playing the theme song from the movie S.W.A.T. It meant there was a text message from Wickmann. As he leaned over to grab his phone off the passenger seat, the gates at the Kendall's started to open. This time, the nose of the black Mercedes appeared between the columns. As it breached the gap and penetrated the sensor field, he could see Blake Kendall behind the wheel. His target was on the move. The message from Wickmann would have to wait.

Tim returned to his cheap disguise of the baseball hat and sunglasses as he started the truck and pulled out after Blake's Mercedes. It was not going to be hard to follow him because the seat in the truck sat up much higher than the seats in most cars. This was a major advantage because it allowed him to keep watch from a greater distance. Blake was headed north up the highway and did not appear to be in any particular hurry. He wasn't on the move for long.

Tim watched as the black Mercedes pulled into the parking lot at 'B.J.'s' restaurant. He waited on the street until he saw Blake exit the car and head inside. Then Tim raced across the street and into the lot on foot. As he passed the Mercedes, he remembered that the device Garrett had given him for the car was still in his pocket so he took a minute to 'tie his shoe' and slipped it under the car. As he stood up, he saw his reflection in the Mercedes tinted glass. He hoped that his hat and sunglasses would still offer him some kind of assistance.

It was going to be close quarters inside. He told the hostess that he was meeting a friend and offered Blake's description. She pointed him in the direction of the bar. When Tim turned the corner, he could see Blake talking to someone behind the bar. Whoever was behind the counter must have been kneeling down, so Tim kept his distance and waited. Blake's back was to him so he could afford to be a little less discreet. The whole event seemed harmless until the person stood up. When they did, Tim's eyes all but came out of his head. Even though he was a good forty feet from the bar, there was no mistaking the resemblance. The girl behind the bar was a dead ringer for Katie. Blake being here suddenly made perfect sense. The coincidence was too great. Somehow, he had found a new target.

Tim's thoughts were in a different place. He neglected to hear the hostess ask him the first time, "Is everything ok, sir?" so she repeated her request. Tim shook his head momentarily and then answered her.

"Yes," he responded. "Everything's fine," he assured her. "I'm sorry," he said. "Would you mind if I sat at that table right there?" he asked, pointing to a table that was slightly out of the way but still had a good view of the bar. Strategically, it could not have been better. Blake could actually leave the building without having to pass him.

"No problem," she agreed, motioning him to a seat. "Can I get you something to drink?"

"An ice tea to start with and maybe a menu," he requested. The girl nodded and told him she would be right back. Tim took a seat at the table and continued to keep an eye on Blake. There was no way to tell how long Blake would be staying. Tim could only assume that he was trying to gather as much information about the girl as possible. Blake was wearing his beach attire again so he was apparently trying to keep a low profile. That fit the pattern. With his mannerisms and ability to slip into his other personality, he came across as being quiet, low key, and very kicked back. He appeared charming and harmless. The girl didn't have a clue.

Tim was half way through his iced tea when he saw Blake reach for his wallet and close out his tab. By Tim's count, he'd only put away two Bloody Mary's. The waitress appeared as Blake was getting up and Tim used her to help block Blake's line of sight.

"Sorry," he said as he stood up. "Police business," he offered, flashing his badge in hopes of gaining her cooperation. He laid a twenty on the table. "This should cover the tea and the tip," he suggested. "And if you don't mind," he continued, "can we keep this conversation just between us?"

Tim couldn't wait for her to respond. Blake had gotten up and was headed for the door. With the tracker in place, he wasn't worried about finding him again. Garrett's 'toys' were far too reliable. As far as they knew, Blake only killed at night, so he was more concerned at the moment with being able to talk to the girl. He remained by the table until he was sure Blake had left. Then he went to the door himself to verify that he had in fact, left the parking lot. Only after he saw the Mercedes pull away did he go back to find the girl.

She was washing glasses as Tim approached the bar. Because of the way he and his friends were handling the situation, he wasn't exactly sure how he was going to handle the conversation. He started off by taking a seat and ordered a beer. *"What the hell,"* he thought, *"I'm not on duty."* Then he got serious. The first thing he looked for when she handed him the beer was her name. The tag said "Mellissa." He thanked her for the beer, introduced himself, and then identified himself as a police officer. The conversation went on from there. He explained what he could without causing a panic and emphasized the importance of her cooperation and discretion.

"It's probably nothing," he admitted, but your resemblance to the others is too coincidental for me to discount. A few days out of town with a friend might even be a good idea. Most importantly, we have to ask you to keep quiet about this. Our only advantage right now, is that he has no idea that we're interested in him. We can't afford to let him find out. That would be a disaster."

Mellissa nodded and agreed to keep quiet. "He's been in here before," she told him. "I saw him in here the other night with two women." Then she paused for a second. "Oh my God," she exclaimed, "You're going to think this is freaky, but from a distance, like from here to that table (she pointed about twenty feet across the room) they both looked a lot like me."

At that point Tim's "probably nothing" turned into "definitely something." He had to push getting her out of town.

"My friends and I will make sure that you can get out of town safely," he assured her. "Once that's happened, we can make a move on him. I just don't want you to be a target."

In her mind, Mellissa was already at home packing a bag. Her friends were all local, and her parents lived back east, but this guy Tim obviously knew what he was doing. He'd figure something out.

"When do you get off work?" Tim asked.

"Can you help me talk to my manager?" she asked. Tim was anxious and ready.

As it turned out, her boss was supportive and kind. When they were finished, he asked her to follow him to the station. It was an attempt to keep her calm and get things moving. He'd have Alex take Mellissa home to pack and then get her on the road. Meanwhile, he would keep an eye on Blake. Mellissa grabbed her things and they headed for the parking lot. Tim made a mental note of her car. She was driving a white late eighties series Firebird. He wrote down the license plate for future reference. He pointed to his truck and she agreed to follow him.

When he got back to the truck, Tim checked to see if the monitoring unit Garrett had given him was functioning. He turned the device on and it started to flash. Garrett had told him that if he plugged it into his G.P.S. unit in the truck, the screen would show the car's position on the satellite map for a range of up to ten miles. Tim took the time to make all of the necessary connections and as always, the equipment worked perfectly. A small red light now appeared on the truck's G.P.S. navigation screen. It was an overlay on the Google map of the surrounding area. Tim would have no trouble following Blake's car as he moved about.

Watching the screen reminded him that he had to check his cell phone. Wickmann's message was still waiting. But now, so was the girl. Tim waved to her to hold on for a second and she gave him a 'thumbs up'. Tim's finger hit the button for 'new text'. Wickmann's message was far from what he expected.

A Detective Garrison from Las Vegas P.D. is trying to get a hold of you. Should I give her your number?

Tim paused for a second. "Garrison," he thought out loud, "Detective Patti Garrison."

He hadn't heard that name in a long time. Tim smiled. He knew that she'd taken the job out in Vegas after his appointment to S.W.A.T. Time had passed after that and they had slowly drifted apart. If Patti was trying to find him now, after all this time, something must be up. He wondered what she would have to say. There was another text waiting on his phone and part of him hoped that it was her. He hit the 'new text' button on his phone and discovered that it was only a follow up from Wickmann.

I left the contact information for Detective Garrison on your desk. You can pick it up whenever you'd like.

Tim looked up at Mellissa again and gave her a sign that he was ready to go. He was taking Mellissa to the station and Patti's info was there waiting for him. Tim started to get his second wind. With any luck, he could get everything handled at once.

They had about a twenty minute drive to the station in Westminster, but he had already explained that earlier. He wanted to get her out of the area. Tim looked at the tracker unit. Blake was a couple of miles south of them so it was the perfect time to go.

As he pulled out on to the highway, Mellissa's car cut safely in behind him. They headed north to Beach Boulevard and then turned right and headed inland. Tim looked at the small black box on the seat next to him. The red dot hadn't moved. Blake was still stopped. Excited now, Tim made a fist gesture with his free hand. "Yes," he said to himself out loud. As soon as they got to the station, he'd figure out the safest destination for the girl and then call Alex and Grey. Eventually, he'd get up the nerve to call Patti too, but right now, Mellissa's safety came first. He glanced in the rearview mirror. The white Firebird was right where it was supposed to be. Tim took a deep breath and reached for another Gatorade. He kidded himself that he should have had a second beer.

* * * * *

It was almost two before Grey got the call. Tim asked to speak to Alex but she was driving. Instead, he gave Grey a 'cliff note' version of what was going on. Grey told him that they would be home in about twenty minutes. He played the whole conversation off as if he was talking to a client.

"I need to borrow Alex for a couple of hours later," he said. "Do you think she'd mind? I need her to make a delivery for me."

"Not a problem," Grey answered. "I think I can handle that. I'll call you when I get home and have my appointment book in front of me," he continued.

"It's important Grey, so try not to keep me hanging too long, ok?"

"Ok, I call you in a few," he said. Then he hung up.

"Doc, want you back at work?" Rachel asked.

"No, just trying to detour my clients for me for awhile," Grey lied.

That seemed to satisfy Rachel. Alex had been eavesdropping on the phone call and even she couldn't figure out what Tim could possibly want. They'd be home in a few minutes and once Rachel and Dylan got settled, she'd hit up Grey to solve the mystery. It was only mid-afternoon so she wasn't worried about Blake. She did know that Tim needed some sleep. Maybe he needed her help to relieve him for a few hours?

When Alex pulled into the driveway, Rachel immediately jumped out.

"Sorry guys; I got to pee," she exclaimed, as she went flying off into the house.

Alex and Grey just looked at each other. "All righty then!" he announced almost laughing at what had just happened. Alex shook her head and then got serious.

"Is Tim ok?" she asked.

Grey looked to make sure the front door to the house was shut. Then he briefly explained that Tim's 'tail' on Blake had already paid off. He told her about the bartender Mellissa, and why Tim needed Alex to be part of the solution.

"Tell Tim that I'll meet him at the station whenever he wants," Alex offered. "As long as you guys keep track of the Mercedes, Mellissa and I will be home free. We can go by her place and then head out immediately to wherever Tim thinks she should go."

"If it were me," Grey began, "I'd send her out to my Uncle Max's outside of Miami. We need to put some serious distance between her and Blake. He's got a nice place out there and she could spend a few days hanging out with his girls. At least that way I'd know she was in good hands."

"Assuming that you're going to make this suggestion to Tim, how would we get her out there?" Alex inquired.

"A last minute plane ticket via 'police business' is a possibility. That, or there's always my Visa," Grey joked. "Under the circumstances, a train ticket wouldn't be fair."

"I hate to remind you, but there's also the small matter of asking Max," Alex pointed out.

"If you knew Max, you'd know that isn't a problem. Moments in time, shifts in the universal plain, a good bottle of Chianti, that's what the man lives for. The man has a big heart. You live, you learn. The future is now."

"So when am I supposed to call Tim?" Alex asked.

Grey handed her his phone. "No time like the present," he said.

"He'll see the number and think I'm you," she reminded him.

"And in many ways, you are," Grey responded. "Just get him on the line. He'll make his sales pitch to you and then I'll simplify it by telling him that you should take the girl to the airport and put her on a plane to Max's. He'll either think I'm crazy or brilliant. I'm voting for the latter."

"All right, Alex said, "You win. What's the number?"

"Just hit # 12 on my speed dial," Grey responded. "And before you ask, "why the number 12? It's a joke about the old cop show Adam 12. I just thought it was funny at the time."

"Kind of like me and # 13," Alex snickered.

"Yeah," Grey chuckled. "Just like you and 13."

Alex pushed the button designated for speed dial # 12. Tim answered on the first ring.

"It's Alex," she offered immediately to avoid any useless confusion. "Grey gave me a run down and I'm at your disposal whenever you're ready."

"That's great Alex," Tim responded. "I knew I could count on you. How soon can you be here?" he asked.

"I can leave here pretty quickly," she assured him, "but Grey wants to talk to you first. He has an idea about where to send the girl."

"That doesn't surprise me," Tim admitted. "Ok, put him on."

Alex reached out and handed Grey the phone. "Talk to me man," Tim requested. "What's on your mind?"

"Uncle Max's," Grey proposed without any hesitation. "You know, Miami Max. Can you honestly think of a better place given the circumstances and short notice? That way, we don't need to worry about any surveillance or protection. We just need to stick the girl on a plane and Max's people grab her at the other end. She stays under his kind of 'protection' until things are safe."

There was a long pause before Tim answered. "Hold on a second," he said. "I think your right, but let me throw it past Mellissa first, all right?"

"Sure, no problem," Grey agreed. "Just give me the green light and I'll make the call."

While they waited for Tim to come back on the line, Alex offered to take Dylan inside. Grey stayed outside near the car to finish the call.

Grey couldn't help wondering what had to be going on in Mellissa's head. In the last several hours, her life had been turned completely upside down. She was politely being coerced by several strangers, granted one was a cop, into dropping everything and getting out of town so she would relieve herself of being a potential target of a serial killer. She was having a bad day. Taking her down to the station was good idea. It gave Tim and the rest of them a lot more credibility. Now, with any luck, Tim would be setting up a plan for Alex to take her home to pack a few things and then take her to the airport. In a couple of hours she'd be safely tucked away at Uncle Max's.

Alex returned to the driveway with a couple of Cokes in her hands. "Thought you could use one," she said. "Rachel's putting Dylan down for a nap so you've still got a few minutes. How's it going with Tim?"

"I'm still on hold," Grey answered. "With Tim, longer is better. I'm not anticipating a problem." Just then, Tim came back on the line. "Mellissa had some serious reservations at first," he said. "Can't say I blame her, but when I told her that Alex was coming down here to get her, that eased things up a lot. You know, having another woman involved. She probably thinks Alex is another cop, and I'm not going to volunteer otherwise. Let's work with what we've got."

"I agree," Grey acknowledged. "Once she's on the plane, we can get serious about finding the right 'bait' and nail this son of a bitch. So I have the green light on Max?"

"Yeah, get him onboard A.S.A.P. and don't worry; I'll work on getting her on a flight later out of John Wayne. You get Alex down here so they can get her packed and ready to go. The girl's place is in Costa Mesa. We're lucky it's within range of Garrett's little 'toy'. If Blake already has an address on her, we can see him coming long before he gets close.

"Sounds good," Grey said. "Talk to you later," and hung up the phone. Tim sat at his desk playing with the pink "While You Were Out"

message slip in his hand.

"I'm already on that my friend," he whispered to himself, twirling the paper some more. "I'm already on it.

* * * * *

CHAPTER 29

Blake was running late. He had nobody to blame but himself. The alarm went off on time, his shower was brisk, and he looked like a million bucks. The folks at Armani had always treated him right. It was just one of those mornings. Katie was still out cold, so he seized the opportunity to rescue his friend from the safe. Having the blade back in his hand again revitalized his confidence and put him in a better mood. The hearing was going to be the easy part of his agenda. It was the silent agreement he had made with the 'Cat' to go hunting after court that troubled him.

Last night at the house, Walter had the nerve to question his judgment and approach on the case. This morning, with great certainty, he knew that his performance would shove Walter's insinuations straight up his collogues ass. What he really wanted was for Walter to be in the court room during the hearing. The man needed a refresher course in how good he really was. Blake needed that, and a cup of Sylvester's coffee. Ever since the idea of recruiting Holly had been taken off the table, he didn't see the old man as often as he liked. This morning, he would have liked some of Sylvester's 'help'. Once again, his coffee was out of reach.

* * * * *

She didn't call first. That would ruin the surprise. She'd seen him moving around below deck earlier, but decided to stay put and just watch him for awhile. She didn't even ask permission to come on board.

When she eventually came over the railing, she just sat patiently on the bench in the center cockpit watching Tim cook down below. He'd been at it for about twenty minutes and seemed to be enjoying himself. The galley table was set, and a glass of orange juice was sitting neatly on her side of the table. Next to it was a small bowl of freshly made Pico de Gallo. She was touched that he remembered the Pico and how she liked her O.J. She liked the rhythm of watching him work. He was just about ready to crack an egg when she couldn't resist saying something.

"Still can't do that with one hand?" she observed.

Tim smiled but didn't turn his head. He kept his focus on the eggs. "Some things never change," he replied as several eggs made their way into the skillet. "Welcome aboard."

"Thank you," she said as she moved closer to the open hatch at the top of the stairs. "Is breakfast ready yet?"

"I'm working on it," he assured her.

He could feel her presence as she came down the stairs. They still hadn't made eye contact. When she passed behind him, he could smell her perfume even over the bacon. It reminded him of a time when he was young and crazy. He smiled when he realized that part of him still was. Patti took her seat at the table. It didn't take long before he heard her open the file. The eggs were done now and he was ready to serve. He set a plate on the counter and opened the small oven. He pulled out four, fresh croissant and put them in a basket. Now he was ready to face Patti.

The first thing he caught was her eyes. There was always something intoxicating about blue eyes. "Breakfast is served," he announced. The smile on her face was worth the wait.

"You look great Patti," he said. "It's really nice to see you again."

"You too Tim," she replied. "It's nice to be back on the 29th."

Tim nodded. "I talked to the chef," he informed her as he set a plate down in front of her. "I think he got everything right."

"Remind me to say something to the manager before I leave," she insisted.

"I'll do that," he acknowledged as he grabbed his own plate and sat down next to her.

There were a few minutes of silence as they both prioritized their plates. The food was the great silencer.

"Same perfume?" Tim asked between bites.

Patti smiled and nodded. "I'm impressed."

"Same Tim?" she asked.

Tim laughed and made a raised opened handed gesture. "What you see is what you get," he conceded. Patti made quick work of the contents of her plate and politely reached for another croissant. Even while they were eating, she was flipping through the file on the seat next to her.

"You've been busy," she said. "Now I'm really curious about what you're not telling me. You obviously wanted me to read this, but knowing you, you wouldn't have gotten me to come down here unless you were up to something. My guess is you need my help. I'm actually flattered that you would still be thinking about me. So spill it Galleon, What's going on?"

It didn't take long for Tim to bring her up to speed. If it had been anyone other than him, she would have called for a padded truck. The magnitude of what he was saying was almost incomprehensible. As it was, she was more than impressed by what he and his friends had managed to put together so far.

"You know you're going to have to catch this guy in the act, don't you?" she insisted.

"I'm sorry to admit, that seems to be our only option," he agreed. "As you can see," he said handing her the pictures; "the girl's appearances are mind bogglingly similar. Our theory is that this guy is killing 'replacements' for his wife." Tim took out a large photo of Katie and tossed it on the table.

"She's beautiful," Patti observed. Then she took a good, long look at Katie. "The rest is just to satisfy a need to kill her for her indiscretions and betrayal."

Tim loved it that she finished his thought. "That's what we think," he answered. "This other bizarre thing with my friend Grey just opened the case up by accident, literally. It was so unsettling, the way he chose to convince me. The truth is; Grey did what he had to do. I never would have believed him if he hadn't mentioned Eddie."

"If I had to deal with being able to do something like that, I think I'd lose my mind," Patti confessed. "How's your friend doing?"

"You can ask him yourself later today," Tim suggested. "We're all supposed to meet at Father Richard's this afternoon."

Tim grabbed the last croissant out of the basket as he got up and started to clear the table. He bit off a big chunk as he started to clean up. Patti waited until he took a second bite and his mouth was full before asking her final question.

"So why m..?" Patti started to ask. She caught herself in mid-sentence. The way she was standing, she could see her reflection in the full length mirror on the back of the master cabin door. Tim had hooked it open to let the breeze come through the salon. Her smile, her face, especially her body, her image was right there in the glass. Only the hair was different. She was perfect, right down to her big round, baby blue eyes.

Tim kept right on cleaning up. He didn't notice anything except her pause. He saw her pause and raised her one. Then he answered her question. His tone was honest and sincere.

"Really?" he asked. "Because A, you are one amazing cop, and B, quite frankly, you're the only one I know I can trust."

Maybe it was the way he said it, that calm serious tone. Maybe she was just happy that he recognized her talent. Maybe it was just the thrill of being part of a team that was going to catch the "Ripper". Patti looked in the mirror again, only this time, Tim was watching. She ran her hands over her ass that was protected by her tight jeans. Then she did the 'adjust the girls' move that women do for re-alignment purposes. She caught Tim watching in the mirror.

"I think this might actually work," she teased him. "All I need now is a quick change of hair color." As she turned around, Tim set the box on the table.

Patti shook her head and smiled. "Am I that easy?" she inquired. "No Patti," Tim answered softly, "you're just that good."

That was enough. Patti walked over and threw her arms around him and gave him a big hug. "Thanks Tim," she said. "Thanks for always believing in me."

There was an awkward moment because their faces were so close together. Then Patti pulled away. She moved over to the table and took a seat again.

"I'm sorry, I know things have changed," she said quietly, gesturing to a picture that was hanging over the boat's navigation station. It was a picture of Tim and Renee at an Angel's baseball game.

"I'm sorry too," Tim consoled her. "We have different lives now. You'd like Renee. She keeps me grounded."

"Not too grounded if you're involved in this," Patti responded.

"This is different and you know it," Tim reminded her. Patti immediately acquiesced.

"So where do we go from here?" Tim asked. "What do you think our next move should be?"

Patti thought about it for a minute and then smiled. "Got any old towels lying around?" she inquired.

"Patti, you're on a boat," Tim replied. "Of course I do. What a silly question."

"Then grab me a couple please," she requested. "I've got work to do." Being willing to follow orders, Tim went up on deck to get some towels. When he returned Patti had already stripped down on top, to a sports bra.

"Whoa! Tim exclaimed as he came back down the stairs. What am I missing?"

"Just hand me the box silly and turn around if you have to. It's time for me to become 'Katie' Garrison.

Tim handed her the box but didn't turn around. He was amazed at how quickly she took charge of the situation.

"I haven't done anything like this since high school." "Maybe we should cover the counter and floor with something," she suggested.

"On second thought, maybe you should go do it in the shower," Tim suggested. Then he blushed. "Sorry about that," he said.

Patti giggled. "You're probably right," she admitted. "If you don't mind, I am going to do this in the bathroom. It has to set for twenty minutes or so before I can shower it out so I'll see you in a few."

"You're amazing Patti," he called after her. "Absolutely amazing!"

It didn't take long for her to get things going. She came out of the bathroom a short time later with her hair in a towel and smears of black stuff all over her face.

"Now we wait," she announced proudly, as she climbed the stairs to go up on deck.

Tim didn't follow her. "I wonder if Blake is in court this morning," Tim blurted out.

"Can't you call down to Central Court and find out?" Patti yelled back.

It was after seven thirty so there was a good chance that someone would be in the clerk's office. Once the clerk verified his identity, Tim got the information he wanted. As he was finishing his call, Patti came back down below. She had a duffle in her hand.

"Kendall's got a case before Judge Sutton at nine," he informed her.

"That old guy's still around?" Patti asked.

"Yeah, I guess I should have remembered," Tim admitted. "That big money laundering case against Congressman Garcia starts today. Guess who's playing lead defense lawyer?"

"Think we can make it in time?" Patti asked.

"What? You want to see this guy in action?" Tim asked.

"No, not really Baby, I want him to see me," she said.

It took Tim a minute to process what she was saying, but less time to respond.

"You're serious," he said hoping to ease things back a bit.

"I'm going to go wash this stuff out," she announced. "I'll be ready to go in thirty minutes."

"You're crazy," Tim called after her as she headed aft toward the shower.

"Maybe," she admitted. "But if I have my way, this asshole is going to get an eyeful when he comes out of court." Then Patti disappeared.

Tim just shook his head. He knew better than to argue with her, especially when she had already made up her mind. It was time to make up his. Where could they make contact or an introduction? Outside the courtroom would be too crowded. Maybe, she could catch Blake downstairs on the way to his car. Tim figured that he could be the eyes in the hallway outside the courtroom and then call her when he saw Blake getting into the elevator. Patti would be waiting near his car at the other end.

"So Galleon, you got a plan yet?" he heard her say.

"As a matter of ..." he started to say. His mind scrambled when he looked up and there was Patti wearing nothing but a towel.

"Come on Tim, seriously?" she said, "It's nothing you haven't seen before."

Tim laughed. "All right, go get dressed," he said. "We can leave when you're ready. I'll explain everything to you in the car."

Patti winked and then disappeared again. Tim decided to go up on deck and wait. It was going to be a long morning. He'd bought a ticket on the Patti Garrison Express.

* * * * *

Somewhere along the line Blake must have made up some time. As he pulled into the court house parking lot, he noticed it was almost empty. Blake looked at his watch. He was in fact, a good half an hour ahead of what he'd planned. Now, he was really annoyed. He could have seen Sylvester after all! Walter and his fucking games! That asshole of a Congressman had better be on time! After Walter's unsolicited assault at the house last night, he just wanted his moment with the judge and then be done with it. He really didn't care at the moment who knew who, when or where, or what they all had to hide. It wasn't his concern. He would handle this one last fiasco for Walter and then sit the poor bastard down and dictate some new policies of his own. What could the firm possibly do, fire him? Garcia was a worm and deserved everything that was coming to him.

Blake felt trapped. As long as he was engaged in the hearing, he couldn't focus on the more important issue at hand. He had to hunt again. Blake tried to lay things out in his head in hopes that if he had plan in motion, it would satisfy the hunger for awhile. The hearing would begin promptly at nine. Both sides would present their arguments and then wait to see if the judge would bind the case over for trial. Depending on the length of the prosecution's argument, Blake estimated that he could be out of the courtroom, and on the move, within a couple of hours.

Then something strange happened. As soon as he finished his thought, he could feel something inside him change as a sense of calm took over. Blake functioned better in his world when he was relaxed and he could tell now, that the 'Cat' evidently understood that. It was clear to him that his dark side was cutting him some slack.

All Blake wanted to do now was find a quiet place inside so he could review his notes. As he grabbed his jacket off a hanger behind the passenger seat, the blade fell out of his pocket and landed on the floor. It was a good thing it did. Security at the courthouse was so tight lately, that it would have been interesting trying to explain its presence when he walked through the metal detectors. It was a hard fact, but he knew he couldn't take the weapon inside. Instead, he locked it the glove compartment, promising to return.

* * * * *

When Patti had first come back up on deck, Tim couldn't believe her transformation. The simple change in her hair alone had completely changed the air of her appearance. Not only did she easily resemble one of the girls in the file, but the change of color completely brought out and fully enhanced the depth of her deep blue eyes. Tim was speechless. He stared at her as if she were naked.

"So what do you think?" she asked. "Not bad?"

Tim didn't know what to say. She was perfect. Like the real Katie Kendall, she had the kind of figure that could pull off anything. The dress she had on certainly proved that. The dark blue fabric clung tightly to her body in all the right places. It was sexy, yes, but also classy and appropriate.

"I brought this thing with me in case I got a chance to go out, or hook up with some of the old gang. I haven't had a chance to get back here in a long time," she informed him. "Do you think he'll like it?" she teased as she ran her hands over several of her well displayed curves. "I never could have imagined that I'd be using this as bait."

"I don't think that's going to be a problem Patti," Tim joked. "Give me five minutes to change and we're out of here," he requested. Then Tim disappeared below.

When he reappeared, he was wearing nice jeans, a collared shirt and a sport coat. The shirt was unbuttoned and opened slightly at the top.

"That was fast," Patti joked with him. "I see you're still afraid of the tie," she giggled.

"Cute," Tim replied. "I don't have to see the judge, so why bother?" he pointed out.

"Nice to see some things never change," she admitted. "You ready to go?"

"Oh yeah," Tim said anxiously. "You have no idea how bad I want to nail this guy. Let's get out of here."

As they stepped down onto the dock, Tim shook his head. Just watching Patti move in that dress, he knew she was going to attract some attention.

"Which courthouse is this guy performing in this morning?" she asked.

Tim grinned. He like the way she had worded the question. "He's at Central Court in Santa Ana. It should take us about thirty minutes," he informed her.

"Good," she replied. "That means we've got some time. We'll take the rental car. I figure I'll hide my piece in the trunk so when I'm supposedly unloading my suitcase, if anything goes sour, it's hidden but handy."

"That's a good idea," Tim had to admit. "I don't see there being a conflict in the parking lot, but better safe than sorry."

Patti loaded her bag back into the trunk of her car. She took her 9mm Beretta and placed it under a towel next to the emergency kit. She gave it a second look and then closed the trunk.

"You ready?" she asked.

"I'm good to go," Tim assured her.

Patti made a move for the driver's side of the vehicle. Tim knew better than to argue with her. As they pulled away from the marina, Patti started to whistle. It took Tim a minute but then he recognized the tune.

"What's up with you and the seven dwarfs?" he asked.

Patti turned to him and smiled. Then she started to sing. "Hi Ho, Hi ho, it's off to court we go, whistle, whistle, whistle, whistle, whistle, whistle, whistle, whistle, Hi ho, Hi ho."

There a brief silence before Tim spoke. "You know what Patti?" he said. "I'm a seriously glad that some things never change."

Patti nodded gently and then broke into laughter. She didn't say a word. She just kept on driving.

* * * * *

Blake found the solace he desired sitting in a chair at the defendant's table in courtroom #14. The docket said he wasn't officially supposed to be there for another forty-five minutes, but he was comfortable in his surroundings and it was almost completely quiet. Only two other people had made appearances in the room. The bailiff was over at his desk doing paperwork and the court reporter came in and out several times while setting up her station. For Blake, the walls in the room were alive and breathing. Here, he was a gladiator and the courtroom was his coliseum. This was the one arena where Blake knew the 'Cat' couldn't touch him. This was his territory. Maybe he was protected by his unbridled focus or passion, but in the actual courtroom, he was a free man.

The bailiff looked up and acknowledged his presence so Blake nodded in return. The two men were already familiar with each other having done business previously in other parts of the building. The case was a simple one. Garcia was accused of taking bribes from two local big businessmen in exchange for assistance in helping to push through a freeway modification contract. The money had never actually touched his hands, but appeared to have been laundered through the Congressman's family owned restaurant. According to the prosecution, there was no possible way that during the time frame in question, business could have been good enough at the restaurant to substantiate the financial surplus.

His first hurdle was that the excess money did exist. It was there. Even Blake couldn't deny that. It was his task however, to offer a reasonable explanation regarding its presence. Then, he would propose a scenario that would distance the Congressman from any knowledge of its existence in the first place. Blake laughed as he reviewed the file. If Walter were handling the case, Garcia would be in jail, or out on bail before the end of the day. Blake rolled his eyes and tossed the file on the table. The irony of him being there to save Walter's ass as well, was almost too comical to bear.

Blake picked up the file and threw it back in his briefcase. Late last night, he had discovered a mistake; one that would cost the prosecution their case. They were probably not even aware of the error. Their star witness' testimony was about to be thrown out. The arresting officers had been so excited to finally nail Garcia, that on the day of the sting operation, they offered a deal to the restaurant's accountant Roberto Garcia, a nephew, while they were taking him into custody. Roberto was arrested as an accessory but then suspiciously released. He was told, "You talk; you walk." After careful inspection, Blake noticed that there was something missing in the arrest report. Roberto Garcia was never read "Miranda". When the judge got wind of this, the deal he had struck with the D.A.'s office would become null and void because of the civil rights violation. That would change everything. Faced with a possibility of an indictment of his own, Roberto would be forced to remain silent rather than implicate himself. Without his testimony, the charges against Congressman Garcia would be thrown out. No star witness, no case. It was all outlined in Blake's brief.

Saving the Congressman would be his last great act for the firm. When the 'Cat' was finally out of the picture, he and Katie would take a long, needed vacation. When they returned, he would hang out his own shingle and use the now 'eternally grateful' Garcia and his people to keep himself busy. Garcia would more than oblige him for keeping his sorry ass out of jail. Blake felt better. He had a plan, his plan, and it didn't involve the 'Cat'. Blake looked up at the clock. It was almost show time.

He wondered if the Congressman would want a review of his strategy, or just nod, smile, and shake Blake's hand before taking a seat. Blake hoped he would stay quiet. That way, his simple but brilliant observation would go unrecognized until the best possible moment. The judge's clerk had been given a copy of the brief when Blake first arrived. By now, he had had ample time to digest its contents. If there was anything inappropriate in it, he would have sent the clerk looking for Blake. Judges frowned on lawyers who attempted to waste the court's time.

There was a mild disturbance, as the Congressman entered the court room. A few reporters had evidently managed to get by the security that had been set up downstairs. The bailiff stood up for a moment, establishing a commanding presence and called everyone to order before he sat down. Garcia approached Blake with an outstretched hand. Blake hesitated for a second before he shook it.

"Congressmen," Blake acknowledged.

"Mr. Kendall," Garcia responded. "How are we doing?"

Blake looked down and away before answering the question. This bothered Garcia as he knew it would. "You'd laugh if I told you," Blake assured him, not speaking in his direction. "I can promise you however, that once I have a chance to speak on the matter, you won't be here very long." Then he turned back to Garcia. "If the judge read my brief, then I probably won't even need to address the court. You'll be able to just sit here and watch him rip the D.A. over there, a new one."

Blake wasn't surprised to see the Congressman's eyes get real big. His theatrical explanation had only been performed in such a manner because during their initial handshake, Walter had entered the courtroom. He had deliberately taken a seat within earshot. Soon after, the D.A.'s office made their appearance along with Roberto Garcia, who they neatly tucked away in the back row. Walter looked worried. When he got up and started to approach, Blake politely motioned for him to sit down. Walter did.

Suddenly, the bailiff said, "All rise. The Superior Court of the State of California is now in session. All those who wish to be heard, shall be heard. The Honorable Judge William L. Sutton presiding."

Everyone in the courtroom stood as the judge entered and took his seat on the bench. Blake noticed that the judge didn't look happy. Sutton glanced down at the file in front of him and then looked at the prosecution's table shaking his head. Then he looked back at Blake. Finally, he addressed the courtroom.

"In the matter of The People of the State of California vs. Jorge Garcia, are all parties present?"

"Susan Childs and Arthur Lampson for the people, your Honor."

"Blake Kendall for the defense, your Honor."

The judge's attention immediately went back to the file. He removed a document and asked the bailiff to hand it to the prosecution for review.

"Is this the arrest form submitted in this case by your office?" Sutton asked.

"Yes, your Honor," Lampson agreed after reviewing it with Childs. As he went to offer it back to the judge, the judge declined.

"You keep it," the judge suggested in slightly patronizing but irritated tone. "You might want to go over that again later."

Then he turned to Blake. "Interesting brief, Mr. Kendall," Sutton began. "I'm used to reading long winded summaries that are usually a waste of my time. Yours however, was clear and concise, not to mention 'brief'."

Sutton held up a single piece of paper with about three quarters of the page covered in single spaced typing. "Honestly sir, I thought this was some kind of joke or a mistake until I read it," he confessed. "But you and your client will be very glad I did."

Walter was speechless and the Congressmen, visibly confused. Blake remained standing and never broke eye contact with Sutton.

"Would you like to explain this to the court, Mr. Kendall?" Sutton asked, "Or should I?"

Still standing, Blake leaned back against the railing. "It would be my pleasure to hear your Honor's interpretation of my brief," he replied, motioning with his hand, as if he were granting permission for the judge to proceed.

The Prosecution's table was stunned. Lampson was outraged. "Any new evidence that your Honor has received was not given to us during Discovery," he began. "We strongly object and request the evidence in question be deemed inadmissible on those grounds."

Now, Sutton was offended. Blake could see the change in his demeanor. The judge was getting more irritated by the minute.

"Your objection is overruled, Mr. Lampson," Sutton began, "as I find that you have been privy to this evidence since day one," he said. "I would like to call your attention to the document that I had handed you earlier for review," he continued. "I find it rather fascinating that you and your colleagues are still missing the point."

Now, Sutton had Lampson back on his heels. He waited for a moment while the D.A. read through the paper again. Then the judge directed his attention to the back of the room.

"Mr. Roberto Garcia?" he inquired, his eyes scanning the room until he found the witness.

"Yes sir," the accountant said, getting to his feet and showing his respect.

"Do you have any idea what Mr. Kendall here is talking about?" Sutton asked.

"No sir," he responded. Judge Sutton slowly shook his head.

"Well sir, do you remember the day you were arrested at the restaurant?" Sutton asked.

"I do sir, very well," Garcia acknowledged. "It was on a Friday."

Lampson stood and objected again. "I don't see the relevance in all of this," he stated emphatically.

"Objection overruled," Sutton said. "I'm getting to the heart of the matter."

Lampson was angry but returned to his seat. Blake just grinned. The accountant remained standing in the back of the courtroom.

"Mr. Garcia," the judge continued. "When you were arrested, did anyone read you your rights or tell you that you could ask for a lawyer? I'm trying to establish whether or not you know what 'Miranda' is?"

Suddenly, Lampson and Childs were in a panic; so much so in fact, that when Lampson looked down at the judge's document again, his eyes betrayed him. He slammed the file down on the table in disgust.

"No sir," the accountant whispered bowing his head, until he was asked to speak up. Then he repeated what he said. "No sir, your Honor. When they arrested me, they took me down to a room at the police station and told me that if I cooperated with them, they would let me go. All I needed to do was tell them everything I knew about my uncle."

You could almost see smoke coming out of Lampson's ears.

"Is everything all right, Counselor?" Blake asked quietly. He didn't get a response.

"Well, Mr. Garcia," Sutton began again. "You may sit down now. I don't think the District Attorney will be in need of your services anymore."

Then he turned back to the prosecutor. "I think you know we have a problem here Mr. Lampson," he advised. "I'm starting to see this entire case as a waste of the court's time."

Lampson was now foaming at the mouth. "But your Honor," he started to say before Sutton waved his hand to cut him off.

"The fact remains, Mr. Garcia was never informed of his rights," the judge continued. "We all know that because of this, you have given me no choice but to declare Roberto Garcia's statement inadmissible as evidence. Furthermore, seeing as your case against Congressman Garcia is based solely on his accountant's testimony, I have no choice but to dismiss the matter at this time. You may choose to re-file charges at a later date, if or when you are able to obtain new evidence. Court is adjourned."

At the sound of the gavel, the courtroom went crazy. Blake smiled. It was just a few minutes before ten.

* * * * *

When the doors opened, Tim was in position. Patti's cell number was already up on speed dial. Now, it was just a waiting game. If he'd shown the officer at the door his badge, he probably could have gotten inside, but he decided it was better to keep a low profile. As it was, it took awhile before Blake came out of the courtroom and worked his way through the small group of reporters that had managed to get upstairs. Walter tried to get close enough to have a word with him, but Blake just blew him off. The thought of Walter kissing his ass at the moment was nothing less than vulgar. The bastard would have to wait. Blake had moved so strategically when he left the room that even the Congressman, who had turned to offer a congratulatory hand, did so to an empty space. Blake wasn't worried. He knew they would settle up later.

Once he was out in the hallway, he stopped to answer a few questions, but he did seem to be in somewhat of a hurry. Blake moved quickly to the elevator. The 'Cat' was calling. When the bell sounded, Blake stepped inside. He had to get moving. He had made a promise that he had to keep. It was time to hunt. Tim watched carefully as the doors closed and Blake disappeared. Tim's finger hit the send button telling Patti that Blake was on the way down. Tim snickered. The thought of seeing Blake slam on the brakes when he got an eyeful of Patti, was something he was sorry he was going to miss. Blake didn't know it, but he was in for the surprise of his life.

Downstairs in the parking garage, Patti got out of her car and walked to the back to open the trunk. The lid was just going up when she heard the ring of the elevator's bell. She reached inside and took out a fairly large piece of luggage. Then she turned her attention to the elevator doors.

As Blake stepped out of the elevator, she recognized him immediately. There was no doubt about it; he was a man on a mission. His body language told her everything. If she could time it just right, she'd make him swallow the bait whole. She didn't even have to look up. The sound of his shoes; echoing on the concrete, were easy to follow.

Patti started to struggle with her suitcase. She listened to his footsteps and counted out in her head *"one, two, three,"* she said. "Damn it!" she suddenly blurted out finally looking up and fighting with the suitcase. "You lousy piece of …."

And then he was there. Standing next to her, he seemed to be a much larger a presence than she had first anticipated. Her first thought was her gun, but that quickly passed.

"Need a hand?" Blake offered as a random act of kindness. He really didn't pay much attention to her until she stood up. The moment they made eye contact, his world exploded! Patti could see it in his eyes. All Blake could see was 'Katie'.

For Blake, the hunger erupted, as fragments of his sanity disbursed into thin air. Before she could even answer the question, the 'Cat' chimed in. "You could kill her right now and just flip her body into the trunk," his darker side advised in the most deep and sinister tone yet.

Blake did a double-take; shook his head, and then reached for the suitcase. It was heavy by female standards but not much of a challenge for him. He picked it up gently and placed it in the trunk of her car. As he passed close to her, he was intoxicated by the smell of her perfume.

"That ought to do it," he said. "That seemed a bit heavy, don't you think?"

Patti faked a good blush. "Information is power," she replied. "I like to be thorough," she said trying to draw him in a little. "And I like to be prepared."

"I do as well," Blake responded, doing his best to keep control of both the situation and the 'Cat'. "Do you work here in the building or are you just visiting?" he inquired.

"I'm here on a temporary assignment to the D.A.'s office," she informed him. "If they like me, maybe I'll get to stay."

Blake's mind raced. This was it. She was the one. Maybe the 'Cat' was right. "Just do it. Take a chance. Just do it now, and then throw her in the trunk," he heard the dark inner voice say.

For a slit second, Blake was on board until he realized that it just wasn't possible. He patted the pockets of his jacket and came up empty. For starters, his friend was still sitting in the glove compartment of his car. That would be an awkward pause if he excused himself and left her to go get it. Also, the parking lot had over a dozen surveillance cameras in operation. He wasn't stupid enough to throw it all away now. No, he had to calm the 'Cat' down and wait. This woman wasn't going far. It would be easy to find her again. For now, he just had to make nice.

Blake reached up and grabbed the lid of the trunk. "Is that everything?" he asked. His knew he had to get out of there. At least for now, he needed a distraction. The 'Cat's' influence was getting stronger. "That's it," she answered. "Thank you for coming to my rescue.

Maybe I'll see you around."

"Good luck with your assignment," he said. Then he reached into his breast pocket and pulled out his card. "If I can ever be of assistance," he offered, "Please feel free to give me a call."

Patti took his card and gave it a quick glance. "Oh my God," she exclaimed, "You're Blake Kendall?"

"I'm afraid so," he said softly "It was nice meeting you." He extended his hand. His level of animation had inwardly faded because of the painful clawing he could feel going on in his gut. Still, he maintained his composure at all costs.

"Patti," she responded reaching out with her own hand and firmly shaking his. "Patti Wheeler," she played.

"Well then Miss Wheeler, you have a nice day," he offered as parting words. Then Blake turned and headed for his car. The 'Cat' wanted him to run. He wanted to get to his friend before the girl had a chance to get back in her car. But that wasn't going to happen. Blake could feel his heart pounding in his chest. He needed to calm down. The sudden adrenaline rush of Patti was almost more than he could handle. Blake was high. A natural endorphin based high. He had literally stumbled across the final piece of the puzzle. In a day or two, the journey would be over, the 'Cat' would disappear and he and Katie could move on. He needed to think. He needed to relax. He needed coffee, Sylvester's coffee.

There were still media people outside the front of the courthouse as he left the parking lot. They had their needs, he had his. The old man's brew would work its magic and bring his mind back to a better place. Blake laughed. *"Today,"* he thought, *"I' ll even ask for a second cup to go."* He made sure to squeal the tires a bit as he pulled away from the courthouse. A little "media irritation if you will," he liked to say. All he wanted now was a hot cup from Sylvester and a few quiet minutes alone by himself in his office. Blake looked in the rear view mirror. His eyes were not his own. He tried to blink the images away, but was unsuccessful.

When he arrived at the office, he parked his car and tried to close his eyes for a minute, but the image of the new girl, Patti just danced in his head. He was on the verge of panic when out of the corner of his eye he could see Sylvester through the glass, inside serving coffee. Blake focused the attention of all five senses on the coffee cart and headed inside. The clawing however, continued on.

* * * * *

CHAPTER 30

Patti was leaning up against the side of her car when Tim stepped out from behind a pillar. He had immediately taken the stairs down after Blake left the third floor, but waited to show himself until he saw the Mercedes pull away. He was concerned about Patti, but as he approached, he could tell by her expression that she was somewhat relieved. She hadn't been alone with Blake for more than a few minutes, but seemed visibly affected. Patti smiled when he came up next to her.

"Are you all right?" Tim asked, "You look a little pale."

"I'm ok," she assured him. "I guess he just wasn't what I expected," she confessed. "If I didn't have all the facts on this one, it would be hard to believe that this guy is our "Ripper" suspect. He is quite a formidable presence."

"That he is," Tim agreed. He could almost feel Patti start to relax. "Do you think he took the bait?" he continued.

"Hook, line, and sinker," she said confidently. "He lifted my suitcase with his hand and my hemline with his eyes," she replied, smiling in a cute but silly sort of way. "Jealous?" she teased.

"If necessary," Tim returned fire, "But what did you say?"

"I stuck to our story about being assigned to the D.A.'s office," she answered. "So he knows I'll be around."

Tim leaned up against the car door next to her. "Good. If he tries to check it out, my friend Gretchen upstairs in personnel will be his first point of contact. She knows enough to keep any inquiring minds happy," he assured her. "I would plan though that sometime, before the end of the day, Blake's going to try to start keeping an eye on you. You might even have a tail before dinner. What Blake doesn't know, is that very shortly, he's going to have someone following him."

They both took a minute. Then Patti looked over at Tim. "So partner, where do we go from here?" she asked.

"Church," Tim answered without hesitation.

"Church?" Patti asked, giving him a look like she thought he had been smoking something and not sharing.

"I think it's time that you met the rest of my group and they got an eyeful of you," he suggested, his eyes wandering back to her many dangerous curves. "We need to bring everybody up to speed. What we just did is going to shake a few people up, but I know they'll approve."

"Well, let's get out of here then," Patti agreed. "While you're making your calls, I'll find us some coffee."

"Better make mine a Gatorade," Tim conceded looking away.

"Gatorade?" she asked, "Seriously?"

Before he could respond, Patti shook her head and started to laugh. "Renee!" she said.

"Just let it go, ok?" Tim pleaded.

Patti just kept laughing. "I'm still getting my coffee, Timmy," she teased in a 'little girl' voice as they pulled out of the parking lot.

She had no idea that several blocks down in the opposite direction, Blake was already enjoying his first cup of the best coffee in town.

* * * * *

"I was starting to wonder what happened to you." Grey said when he answered the phone. He was sitting in the family room talking with Alex. "You get any sleep?"

"Oh yeah, I got plenty of sleep," Tim answered," But I had an interesting surprise at breakfast this morning. I was wondering if you could call Father Richard and ask him if we could all meet at the church in say, an hour or two. There's something new going on that we need to talk about."

"Sure man, I'm on it," Grey acknowledged, "but what's up?"

"I'll give you the whole run down when I see you," Tim promised. "And tell Alex to come with you instead of heading down to relieve me."

"You think it's ok to leave Blake alone?" Grey asked.

"I'm not worried," Tim assured him. "Just meet me at the church in an hour or two," he said. "I'll explain everything."

"I'll call Richard right now and set something up." Grey said. "I'll let you know."

"Talk to you in a few then," Tim said. Then he hung up. He turned to Patti. "Give Grey a few minutes and we'll be set," he said.

"I really want to meet this guy," Patti professed. "It'll be fun to put faces to these people you've joined forces with. I feel like I know them already."

"I think it's safe to say that each one of them is very unique in their own way," Tim confided. As he was speaking, his phone rang. It was Grey.

"Richard said to be at that church at noon," Grey said. "Will that work for you?"

"See you then," Tim answered, and then he was gone.

Grey closed his phone and looked over at Alex who was patiently waiting for some answers. "Tim wants a meeting with all of us to discuss something new. Richard said we could all meet there at noon," he informed her. "He also said that you don't have to relieve him. Something has come up that is much more important."

"Did Tim give you any kind of clue as to what was going on?" Alex asked.

"He implied that it was better if we all heard about it together at the church," Grey continued. "If Tim's willing to drop the tail, it's got to be something important."

"You'd better let Rachel know we won't be here for lunch," Alex advised.

"It won't be a problem," Grey responded. "She likes it when I go talk to Father Richard," he reminded her.

"Well I'm just saying you ought to try to keep her involved somehow," Alex suggested. "She seems to like it much better that way."

"You've got a point," he admitted as he got up. "I'll be right back."

Grey got up and went to find Rachel. She was somewhere in the back of the house with Dylan. While she was waiting, Alex wondered how Mellissa had adjusted to the strange new world of Uncle Max. Grey had described her new environment like a scene out of a 'Godfather' movie. They had heard earlier that she had arrived without incident and figured that by now, she was probably sitting poolside at Uncle Max's estate. All the effort to get her there would be worth it, if they could draw Kendall out and nail him. As far as their meeting at the church was concerned, maybe Tim had come up with a plan of how to do just that.

When Grey returned, he confirmed what he and Alex had already suspected. As long as Father Richard was involved, Rachel was all for it. Besides, she and Dylan had already made plans to meet Renee for lunch.

"I wonder what's so important, that Tim is willing to leave Blake unmonitored?" Alex asked.

"Maybe, he figured that Blake would be in court this morning? He could have called downtown to see if he was on a docket anywhere," Grey suggested. "If I know Tim, he's got a plan. Come to think of it, I didn't hear from Richard yesterday, which leads me to believe that a day at church with his congregation was good for him."

"I definitely think he's better since Kelly's been leaving him alone," Alex observed. "I'm glad you got a handle on that."

"Handle on what?" Rachel asked. She had come in quietly just in time to catch Alex's last comment. She was holding Dylan in her left arm. He was dressed and ready to go.

"Richard's been helping me with my nightmares, Honey," Grey responded. He's also trying to help me get my head back on straight."

Rachel looked at Alex. "Poor Father Richard," she said with a mild giggle, "I don't envy the man that task," she snickered. "I've been trying to do that for years."

Alex's face started to break into a smile. Before she could start laughing however, Grey had something to say.

He tried to be serious but couldn't contain himself. The laughter just slipped out. "Very funny," he was forced to admit. "Aren't you late for lunch or something?" he said through broken breaths.

"I am at that," Rachel declared and slung her purse over her shoulder. "C'mon Dylan, let's go," she said as she started walking toward the door.

"Have fun," Grey yelled down the hall after her. "Maybe, you should let Dylan drive," he added for good measure.

Rachel didn't respond. She had shut the front door behind her as she left. Grey and Alex were alone again. It wasn't hard to tell that they both had the same thing on their minds.

"Tim's got to be up to something," Grey said, breaking the moment of silence.

"I think the party's about to get started," Alex agreed as she patted him on the shoulder.

"Well, let's get out of here then," Grey suggested. "Let's head over to the church. When we get there, we'll see if Father Richard knows something he hasn't already told us."

"I don't think he'd keep secrets from you," Alex observed.

"You're probably right," Grey admitted, "But I want to get there early. That way, we're all together and ready when Tim walks in. If I know Tim, whatever it is, it's going to be good."

Alex grabbed her keys. "Guess we're off and running then," she said as they headed for the car.

As they went down the road, Grey closed his eyes and tried to remember a time when his hands and mind were still his alone; when no one relied on what he could see by just a simple touch. He made himself a promise that when it was all over, if his current state of mental 'possession' still existed, he would try to bury it away; banishing it to the darkest corner of his mind, in order to protect the secrets of the ones he loved.

Grey hung his head out the car window for a moment so he could enjoy the wind in his face. He noticed immediately that there was a pungent scent on the breeze. Was it the familiar smell of burnt oil? Or perhaps, then again, it was wet leather. Grey smiled. The ring on his hand was warm. He was headed in the right direction

* * * * *

After Grey called, Father Richard found himself sitting on the top of the steps in the center of the church's alter. His eyes scanned the empty room, taking in the colors and light that shined through its magnificent stained glass windows. A light scent of Murphy's oil soap lingered in the air. After their late afternoon service, he had led a group of kids from the congregation's youth group on a great quest. Their mission was to wipe down all of the wood benches and pews as they did every season during 'ordinary time'. In exchange for their valiant efforts, he had pizza delivered to the youth hall when they were finished along with a variety of candy, soda and snacks. He would not allow their good work to go unrewarded.

It had been a time of both fun and reflection for Richard, being able to reach out and enjoy the energy that was contagious around young people. He had lost touch with that part of himself after what happened to Kelly. Now, he sat alone, staring out at an imaginary congregation and contemplating the possible insanity of what might be taking place next. Grey and his friends were on their way.

Ironically, he had his own confessions. There were times over the past week that he thought about taking a step back and letting these crazy young people handle things on their own. His hand had reached for the phone on more than one occasion, but his promise to Kelly led him on into the light. The evil would fall, and he'd be damned if he wasn't going to be part of aiding in its destruction. Both the crucifix on the wall behind him, and the one in his office were friendly now. Grey had managed to help him work through that. All that remained was making sure they found a way to catch this monster and put him behind bars. Once that was accomplished, he would go to Kelly's grave and tell her it was ok to move on. He would remind himself to bring red roses. The silence was broken as Grey and Alex entered the sanctuary.

They were early, but Richard was glad. It would give them time to visit before Tim arrived and the conversation had to turn serious. He wondered if either one of them had any idea about why Tim called for a meeting.

"Good morning, Father Richard," Alex said as they made their way down the aisle. Her voice echoed a bit in the empty sanctuary. Richard smiled and nodded his head.

He got to his feet as his friends approached. "How are you my friend?" Grey said, shaking his hand and giving him a hug.

Then Richard turned to Alex. It was her turn to share a warm embrace. He motioned for them to have a seat on one of the benches in the front row. The conversation stayed light. Grey asked about the services over the past weekend, and Alex inquired about how he was doing personally.

"Things have been going well over the past few days," he informed them. "I had a good time with some kids from the youth group last night, and I am pleased to report that there have been no more strange 'spiritual' incidents," as he turned his attention to the crucifix above. "I think I have Grey to thank for that."

As he was finishing his thought, they all heard the doors to the sanctuary open. Tim had arrived, but Alex could sense something was different. She was even more surprised when he entered the sanctuary alone.

"Hello, everybody," he said as he moved down the aisle. Then he was silent until his path brought him within a few feet of Father Richard. "Thanks for letting me call this meeting Father," he said. "I hope you all don't mind, but an opportunity presented itself and I really didn't have time to bring everyone in on it. You'll understand why, in a minute or so and I promise to explain everything."

Richard and Grey were curious, but Alex was forthcoming. "So, who did you leave waiting out in the foyer?" she asked.

Grey's eyes got real big. How had he missed that? In a matter of seconds, Patti entered the sanctuary and started to make her way down to the group. The moment they laid eyes on her, the three of them were speechless. It looked as though Tim had brought Katie Kendall to church. As she approached the group, it was Alex who broke the silence.

"That's amazing Tim," she said, "scary, but amazing."

Father Richard had a look on his face like he thought he'd seen a ghost. Grey, on the other hand, smiled and shook his head. "Bait?" he asked the lady in the dark blue dress.

"Bait," she nodded politely. "I hope you don't mind," she continued, "but we thought that introducing me this way would have a much more dramatic effect."

Before Grey could respond, Father Richard jumped in. "And so by God it has," he replied. "If you don't mind me asking Miss, who in God's name are ya?" Richard's Irish was starting to creep back.

Tim answered before she could. "My friend's, I'd like you to meet Detective Patti Garrison of the Las Vegas Police Department. She is an old friend who, through a bizarre set of circumstances, ended up having breakfast with me on my boat this morning. Our conversation and previous relationship led us into, not only changing her hair color, but also to her volunteering to help us. She started off by introducing herself to Blake this morning after he came out of court. Needless to say, he took the bait."

"Unbelievable," was all that Richard could manage to say.

"Thank you, Father," she said. "I'm Patti," she said introducing herself. "I've heard a lot about you." Richard almost blushed.

Then she turned to Alex. "So you're Alex," she said. "Tim said you'd make an amazing cop. He said your instincts are undeniable."

Alex was impressed. She could tell immediately that Patti was sincere. For her, that was huge because it helped her establish an almost instantaneous level of trust. Maybe not total, that would come with time, but certainly enough to not worry about her actions or motives where all of them were concerned.

Grey was quiet and just sat staring for a minute at Patti. Her resemblance to Katie was remarkable. "Do I pass the test?" She asked him quietly.

"I'm sorry," he said. "I don't mean to be rude." he apologized. "I've seen pictures of you as a blonde and I must say you are equally as beautiful with the dark hair.

Alex smiled and glanced over at Tim.

"As Father Richard said, this is really unbelievable," Grey continued. "I truly believed for a minute that it was Katie Kendall coming down the aisle." Then Grey stopped to size her up again. "But where are my manners?" he asked. "I'm Grey," he offered, extending his hand to her; "Friend, massage therapist, and for the moment, temporary nut job. I'm not sure how Tim managed to talk you into joining us, but so far, and I think I can speak for all of us, I'm really impressed."

Patti shook his hand and then found a seat on one of the front benches.

"Ok Tim, you're up!" Grey said. "I really want to hear what you two have been up to."

Richard and Alex both moved in as Tim took a seat on one of the altar steps. They didn't want to miss a thing. It took awhile, but Tim explained everything. He not only brought them all up to speed on the last few days, but he backtracked to the beginning of how he and Patti first met and the extent of their relationship. He and Patti had agreed on the ride over, that to establish a trust for her on such short notice, everything had to be out on the table.

"So the 'bait's' been set," Alex said. "I guess all we do now is watch and wait."

"If I know Blake," Grey replied, "he's already trying to gather as much information on Patti as he can. Once he realized what he'd found, he probably got the plate number off the rental car while they were talking. That's going to be a dead end, so he'll have to try something else. The D.A.'s office is covered. They only have limited information as well. The way we've set things up, he's going to have to come out of the shadows and follow her to find out anything. The irony of it all is that while he's following Patti, we'll be tailing him."

"Once you know that he's following you, you can lead him to where ever you want him to go right?" Father Richard asked.

"That's the general idea, Father," Patti answered. "I'm going to rent a house down by the beach. I like to run at night so maybe we can get him to follow me. I can set up a pattern by running at the same time every night. That way, he can get accustomed to my routine."

"The beach is pretty empty at night," Tim added, "It makes keeping an eye on Patti easier and also allows us to keep any possible outside interference to a minimum."

"There are a lot of details to work out, but I'm sure the five of us can handle it," Patti continued. "We just have to keep our eyes and ears open. It is imperative that we keep in close contact with one another."

This drew a quick nod from everyone.

"So what did you think of Blake this morning?" Alex asked. "It had to be weird, having to jump right in like that."

"He's has quite a commanding presence," Patti answered. "He was kind, gentle and eloquent. It scared me to think that had I not been aware of the history here," I would have been more apt to be drawn in by him. He's apparently very good at playing whatever character he chooses."

Alex noticed that Patti didn't even pause to consider her thoughts. She had already formulated a sound opinion.

Grey looked over at Alex. She seemed content with Patti's answer. Evidently, she'd passed the test. "So what's our next move?" Grey asked.

"One last piece of unfinished business before we get started," Tim replied.

He took a piece of paper out of his pocket and handed it to Father Richard. "A gift for the church Father, or at least for you," he said. Richard unfolded the paper, glanced at it, and then put it in his shirt pocket. Everyone knew what it was.

"In the future," Tim suggested. "You might want to try having your sandwiches delivered," he teased.

"Thank you for taking care of this, my son," Richard said thankfully.

Tim just nodded. He took a few steps back up the center aisle and then turned to face the group.

"It's time to get serious," he began. "The truth is, this could all be very dangerous and I'm not exactly sure how we can even begin to explain any of this when we're done. At this point though, Patti is right. It's an eyes and ears game. "Guys," he said, directing his attention to Father Richard and Grey, "we are just 'back up and cover' now. Alex and I are going to be following Blake on and off as often as Patti and I deem necessary. Patti, of course, is obviously the bait. If we get lucky, sometime in the next few days, Blake will make his move. Any questions so far?" he asked.

"All right, we're going to keep the times that Patti is completely alone, isolated to the beach," he continued. "Like I said before, we can limit the outside interference that way. He can't get into the beach house without us knowing it because of the tail, so she should be safe there. Tomorrow, we make sure that Blake gets a chance to see her again, even if it's only from a distance. We've got to keep him hungry and focused. The object is to draw him out and get him to make a mistake."

"So do we keep following him today?" Alex inquired.

"I'm pretty sure that won't be necessary," Tim answered. "I think we're safe until tomorrow morning. I'd be willing to bet he'll be waiting somewhere close if not in the courthouse parking structure for Patti to show up for work. He probably won't even approach her if he sees her. He'll just start trying to keep tabs on her from that point on."

"And where will we be in the morning?" Alex continued. "I'm guessing you have a plan? Surveillance might be difficult in an all but empty parking lot."

"That's one of the details we have to work out today. I figured that you and I could take a trip down to the courthouse and do some reconnaissance. We can pick observation points that will give us the best advantage."

"And what would you like Grey and me to do?" Richard asked. "For now, I just need you to lay low." Tim said. Richard looked

dejected. "But believe me Father; your time will come. I know how important this is to you."

Grey said nothing. He figured that if Tim had anything he wanted to say to him, he would bring it to his attention later.

"All right," Tim continued, now addressing the group, "Patti and I are going to go rent a beach house that I found yesterday. That will be her home base. Judging from its location, it looks easy to keep an eye on. Alex, I'll call you later and we can take run down to the courthouse. We can check things out and then decide who's going to be covering Blake tomorrow. In the mean time, everyone, take a small bit of pleasure in knowing the fact that Blake is probably going crazy right now trying to get a file together on Patti Wheeler." That seemed to make everyone happy.

Grey glanced around the room. "We're all good with this then, right?" he asked. Everyone nodded.

"Are there any other questions?" Tim asked. He got only silence in return.

"Good," Tim said. "Now don't forget to keep your phones on you so we can all stay in touch. I'll let you know what happens with the beach house or any new developments as soon as we know. Ok?"

Everyone followed, as Richard led them out of the sanctuary. He shook everyone's hand as they said their good-byes. He made a special point of addressing Patti as they exchanged words.

"Bless you my child for all that you have, and all that you are about to do," Richard prayed. It was typical Father Richard, but Patti was sincerely moved. He had no way of knowing that she had grown up with the church.

"Thank you Father," she replied. "That means a lot to me."

Alex looked over at Grey. "That man almost makes me believe in God," she said.

Grey smiled. "That's huge," he said softly, "coming from you. Let's make sure we don't let him down."

"You've got that right," she responded. "Now let's get out of here and go home. I think Richard could use some time to process all of this."

Richard stood in the doorway and waved as his friends departed. He was still amazed by the uncanny resemblance that Patti had to Katie Kendall. While his friends might not understand, he considered her timely arrival to be nothing short of divine intervention. In his world, all of the pieces were coming together. As the last car headed off, Richard crossed himself and prayed for his friends. In his heart, he knew someone was listening.

* * * * *

Sheila was right. He didn't pay her enough. He'd been watching the lights on his desk phone glow like lights in a casino for little more than an hour. The calls had started to taper off a bit, but reporters were like pit bulls, it was hard to get them to let go. Sheila had to be running on empty by now. Blake took a second to consider the past hour. He couldn't decide which of her assets was more valuable, her ability to control the front office the way she did, or her personal level of loyalty to him and his privacy. She had made a career out of both running interference and protecting him, and for that he would always be in her debt.

Blake looked at the large painting hanging on the far wall of the rural Pennsylvania barn that hid the office safe. He was sure there was enough cash in it to give Sheila a healthy bonus. His accountant had told him once, "A personal gift of less than ten thousand dollars does not have to be reported as income." He wondered what Sheila would say if she found an envelope containing a dollar short of that amount as a bonus in her center desk drawer. His curiosity got the best of him, so he went to go check out the safe.

As he expected, there was plenty of available cash. The hardest part; was having to break the last hundred dollar bill out of what he had in his wallet. Blake laughed as he counted out the last four ones, "ninety six, ninety seven, ninety eight, ninety nine. *"There,"* he thought. *"It's all there."* His humor on the subject stemmed from not only visualizing Sheila's reaction, but from the fact that this was his move. He was in control of the situation, not the 'Cat'. Blake opened a drawer and got out a large, yellow envelope. He'd send her to lunch and plant it in her desk while she was gone. The phones were still playing casino but then she could just turn on the answering machine. Blake smiled. That would piss a few people off. He reached for the intercom button and called Sheila. She thanked him for giving her a reason to get away from her desk. Within minutes, she was gone. Blake continued to draw strength as he sipped on the remnants of his second cup of Sylvester's. Things were peaceful until the voice came.

“Patti Wheeler,” the ‘Cat’ said almost nonchalantly, reminding him of his unfinished business. There was a momentary pause, and then the tone changed.

“Finish your damn coffee so we can get going,” the voice ordered. Blake’s face turned sour. He wasn’t accustomed to taking orders or being told what to do. Still, he knew he had to move.

Blake got out of his chair and walked over to the wet bar. The mirror behind the bar was the closest one he could find. When he saw his reflection, he was disappointed. The fire and passion he would normally see there after a victory like the one he’d had this morning was nowhere to be found. Instead, he could barely find traces of the man who had been in court just a few hours earlier. Blake turned away.

He considered the possibility that it was just his perception. Maybe the outside world was privy to a different presentation, but through these eyes, only an eerie, dark evil reflected back at him. The prize was waiting and the hunger would only continue to grow until his retaliation was complete. Blake headed back to his desk.

An hour later, he had little to show for all his efforts. Patti Wheeler was new at the D.A.’s office. She was so new in fact, that their first meeting had been a stroke of luck. She must have just come downstairs from checking in on her first day when he had the good fortune of running into her in the parking lot. Blake figured that she had made an appearance upstairs, said her ‘hello’s’ and then decided to go check out her new place and get settled in; hence the suitcase. If he had not been so pleased with himself after his morning performance, he probably would have been less distracted. Blake chastised himself for not immediately trying to follow her home.

The phones kept ringing. He thought about answering one, but then he came to his senses. A short time later, the idea still festered. It might be funny to pick up the line and say *‘Good afternoon, Blake Kendall’s office.’* After the inquiry, he could say, *“This is Mr. Kendall. How can I help you? ‘Talk about playing head games,”* he thought. *‘Hell, it would be fun to mess with some reporter’s ego. If the ‘Cat’ could play games, why couldn’t he?* As he started to reach for the receiver, his hand passed over the envelope on the way. He decided that he better put the damn thing in Sheila's desk soon or risk the chance of her coming back.

Blake focused on the money. The 'Cat' stayed focused on Patti. Mentally, it was a draw. Blake reached for his keys. Either way, he had to get out of the office. It would just be a matter of time before the people who couldn't get through on the phone would start showing up at the door. He found his key to Sheila's desk and stepped out into the front office. No one had invaded the outer office yet. *"So far, so good,"* he thought. Then he took a seat in Sheila's chair. This proved to be nothing less than an interesting change of perspective. He unlocked the drawer and put the envelope safely inside. Her name, in his handwriting stared back at him. He closed the drawer and locked it again.

Blake felt better now. He had made a choice and he had followed through. Blake got up and slipped quietly back into his office. Once he was safely, back in his chair, he let his mind drift away. He would wait until Sheila returned, before making his escape. The 'Cat' would just have to wait. The phone continued to flash.

The second hand on the grandfather clock spoke to him in loud ticks. The gentle rhythm it established, acted like the spinning sensation of a hypnotist's watch. Blake closed his eyes and soon he could visualize everything. Her hair, her eyes, the very scent of her perfume allowed him to create the fantasy of killing her in his head. He could almost feel the warmth of her blood oozing through his fingers. The only thing that tainted the reality was the emptiness he felt when he closed his hand. His talisman of redemption was still in the glove compartment of the car. Without it, he was helpless and alone. Blake opened his eyes and concentrated on the phone. When one light went solid, he knew that she was back. He didn't wait for her to get a chance to come in. He headed straight out the back door.

As soon as he reached his car, his phone rang. It was Sheila. Blake wanted to take the call, but his friend had other ideas. There was no hesitation as a finger redirected the call to voice mail.

"No interruptions," a dark voice echoed through his head. Blake acquiesced.

The truth was, he was motivated now, with or without the 'Cat' to just get the damn thing over with. Over the years, there were times that he had tried ever so diligently to convince himself he had a choice. The razor didn't have to continually be re-animated every time he thought there was a conflict or betrayal. It was the dark shadow in his mind that showed him the way; the dark, lifeless shadow that had been around the cat's eyes that eerie night in the barn as the blood flowed out of its neck. Blake had done no evil, but the shadow inside him had. The feline's eyes swore its revenge as the mask of death slowly swallowed it whole.

And so the spell was cast, and it followed him, manipulating his behavior whenever it could throughout the years. The carnage left in its path was reprehensible. The 'Cat' had carried out its vengeance through Blake; and had managed to do so with Blake simply along for the ride. He had turned a blind eye because of the strength and pleasure the experiences gave him. There had been several episodes of need for 'one last kill' to satisfy before. Blake wondered if this time would really be the last.

Blake turned the key and fired up the engine. The gnawing sound of grinding teeth was back. He knew he had to find Patti Wheeler. His dead ends could be rectified if she just showed up for work tomorrow. He would cut out early and wait. She had to be staying somewhere close and he would find it. He reached over and opened the glove compartment. His friend was still there. He grabbed the weapon and set it on the seat next to him. Just being able to see it again made him feel better. Tiny sensations of pleasure and strength started to creep up on him. Little by little, they nibbled away at his negativity. Thoughts of engaging Patti Wheeler again danced in his head. He was starting to become aroused. Not by the dress mind you, but by the thought of the kill. The Cheshire smile grew.

The afternoon was his. Even Walter knew better, and was smart enough to leave him alone. He was a free man. Blake pushed a button, and the top to the Mercedes pulled open, drew back and then safety tucked itself away. The sunlight on his face just added to the sensation. Both his body and mind rode the wave. It was almost a tickle, but the nibbling continued. After a few minutes, he noticed that it was slowly becoming more sexual in nature, but that was ok. Blake snickered and shook his head. He reached over and put his friend back in the glove compartment. It would be safe there for now. He wondered what Katie was up to this afternoon. After all, it was a beautiful day. He wondered if she might be interested in another round of miniature golf.

* * * * *

For the first mile or so, all Grey could focus on was the sensation of the wind in his face. Neither he nor Alex had said a word since they left the church. Grey looked over at Alex's hair blowing radically in the warm afternoon air. It would have been nice to be able to see her eyes, but they were hidden by her sunglasses. It really didn't matter though; he already knew what she was thinking.

"Am I crazy, or was the whole atmosphere at the church was a little weird?" he said calmly.

"You're not crazy," she replied, attempting to reassure him.

She let another mile pass before continuing. "Awkward," she observed, nodding her head as if she approved of her own opinion. "Patti and Tim were too comfortable with each other for this being planned in such a short period of time. There has to be a history between them, an underlying, unspoken confidence that they were both on the same page. Were they ever partners?"

"As cops, no," Grey answered. "I would have heard about that. I don't know about the rest though. It's funny; I was thinking the same thing."

"Well, if it is personal, it could play out for us either way. They'll either be overprotective or completely at ease. Being cops, they probably be a little of both."

"Is that going to be a problem?" Grey asked.

"I'm hoping it's going to be an advantage," she responded. Another mile whipped by.

Grey tried to plan ahead. "So, I guess I'm hanging out at home this afternoon," he conceded. "You've got to wait for Tim's call and then go check out the parking lot. It should be interesting tomorrow watching Blake's reaction to Patti."

"I know. It's scary how much she looks like Katie, isn't it?" Alex observed.

"Yeah, let's just hope Tim's right and Blake's waiting like we think," Grey said. "If he starts to follow her, then we're in business."

"Oh, if he sees her, he'll follow her!" Alex assured him. They were at their exit now, so Alex pulled off the highway.

"I don't like the fact that I'm going to be sitting at home while you're all out doing this," Grey stated.

Alex stopped for a red light. She tipped down her sunglasses so he could see her eyes. They were still warm and friendly, but radiated a seriousness he knew all too well.

"As far as I'm concerned," she said, "You're the one who's been doing all of the hard stuff. Going back in to work on this guy over and over again was way beyond the call of duty. For God sakes, Grey, you had to play inside that man's head! You alone had to deal with all of the images of the killings themselves."

Alex paused for a minute as the light turned green. Once she had made the turn, she pushed her sunglasses back up and finished her thought. "You know, you ought to give yourself some credit, Grey. You can be damn sure the rest of us do," she said. "That's all I'm saying."

Grey nodded but said nothing. The silence remained until Alex pulled up in front of the house. As Grey got out, she kept the motor running.

"Go spend some time with your family," she suggested. "I'm going to go drive around for awhile and wait for Tim's call. Tell Rachel I'm running errands or something. I'm sure she'll appreciate the time alone."

"You've always got my back, don't you?" he admitted thankfully as he shut the door.

Alex smiled. "I'll call you later," she said, as she backed out of the driveway. Then she waved as she sped off down the street.

Grey looked out the sea of white clouds that had gathered in the sky above him. It was an absolutely gorgeous day. He knew it was best to enjoy it while he could. Somewhere, out there in the distance, an evil darkness was beginning to stir. In twenty four hours, it would be tempted and teased until it snapped. When it did, it would rise up and try to extinguish another ray of light. But then, things were going to be a whole lot different. This time, they'd be waiting.

* * * * *

CHAPTER 31

The rest of the day went off like clockwork. Tim and Patti pretended to be newlyweds to make renting the house easier. When Tim flashed his badge at an appropriate time, it didn't take much more persuasion to get the old couple who owned the place to give them a key. The cash deposit Tim brought with him only helped to sweeten the deal. Once everything was settled, he called Alex to arrange to meet up. The plan was to have Patti take him back to the marina so he could get his truck. It would only take a short time for them to make the switch. At the last minute, he decided to take Patti with him because her experience with stake outs might come in handy.

"We'll see you in half an hour at the courthouse," he told Alex. "Between the three of us, we should be able to cover every angle of the parking structure and figure something out."

"I'm already in the area," she told him. "I think this is going to be easier than we thought. No sign of Blake's Mercedes though. Do you think we ought to go try and find him?" she asked.

"I think we're ok until tomorrow morning," Tim responded. "From what I've seen or read about this guy, or for that matter this case, he's going to do whatever it takes to find Patti again. It's all about ego. He just won another big case this morning so his mind is still feeding on that. We took away all of his usual options, so I'm betting that he'll be waiting for her when she comes out of the building tomorrow."

"You don't think he'll look elsewhere to get a quick fix?" Alex asked.

"Nah," Tim assured her. "His face is too high profile to be taking a chance on any spontaneous action. Every move he makes from now on has to be carefully planned."

"That makes sense," she agreed. "I guess I'll see you all in a bit then," she added.

"Ok," Tim acknowledged. Then there was a brief pause. "By the way, what did you do with Grey?" he asked.

"I took him home and then ditched him for awhile," she answered. "I thought he could use a break. You know, give him a chance to spend a little time with Rachel and Dylan."

"Good idea," he agreed. "Hey, seriously, is that thing that he can do getting any better or worse? I mean, that's got to really fuck with your head."

"He seems to be all right at the moment," Alex informed him. "But I'm keeping a very close eye on him. Under the circumstances, I think he's holding up pretty well."

"Good to know," Tim said. "All right then, we'll see you in a few." The phone clicked and Alex was left alone with the silence.

She could tell by Tim's tone that his inquiry was both sincere and thankful. For a cop, he was all right. She was now only a block or two from the courthouse. While she waited at a red light, she noticed a coffee vendor in the lobby of the building across the street. She wasn't a big fan, but something suddenly drew her in. She had some time to kill and now the coffee sounded good. Alex pulled through the intersection and then into the parking lot. It took only a second to grab her purse and head inside.

As Alex approached the cart, she got a funny feeling that she was in for something more than just coffee. The old Hispanic gentleman behind the cart certainly looked friendly enough. If nothing else, she'd get her coffee, sip it in the car and wait until the troops arrived. Oddly enough, Sylvester got the same feeling when he saw her approaching. There was a man waiting in line in front of her, so it was several minutes before they had a chance to speak. When the man moved on, they were left alone.

Their initial exchange was anticipated. "Good afternoon Miss, how can I help you?" he asked. His voice was both pleasant and inviting.

"I'm not sure what I want," she said politely making it a point to make direct eye contact. It was almost a stare as she tried to look right through him.

Sylvester was not the least bit shaken. His smile never dimmed. "Perhaps you'd allow me to make a suggestion?" he replied.

Alex simply nodded, giving him her permission to continue. As he shifted to one side of the service bar, he offered his submission. "If you'll give me a moment, I might be able to provide you with a variation of something similar to your favorite tea."

His statement caught Alex off guard. How did this stranger know anything about her or her tea? She decided to play along and nodded her approval again. He now had her full attention. She carefully watched every subtle move the old man's hands made, even as he continued to disrupt her concentration by asking, "So how is your friend?"

Alex wanted to look into his eyes but wasn't willing to take her eyes off his hands.

"You seem to know a lot," she conceded.

"More than I care to, actually," he admitted. "But the dreams come, and even as a young boy, I learned that it was better not to ignore them. They made me watch everything. I had little choice but to listen and learn. I guess that's why I'm here," he confessed.

"Where exactly is here?" she asked.

"For me, it has two parts," he began as he worked on preparing her a drink. "First, I mean here, as in being part of the greater everything. I utilize my ability to make a person's day better by providing them with something as simple as a good cup of coffee. I watch and I listen to their troubles and joys and help with a kind word if I can. You understand that, don't you?" he asked.

Alex nodded but didn't want to interrupt. His words spoke volumes about his intentions so his hands didn't concern her as much now. She lifted her eyes to meet his. She could tell immediately, that Sylvester took this as a sign of respect. He smiled and continued on.

"Second, it is important you know that originally, I was set up in business and doing well at the building across the street. On the night after the accident, I had a dream that told me that I needed to move my operation over here. It was important that I make contact with the people in this building. After a few days, I could really sense the moods of most of my customers. One in particular frankly scared me death. I think you have a good idea who I'm talking about."

"A lawyer from upstairs," she acknowledged.

"Yes," Sylvester agreed heartily. "He has recently developed a fascination for my coffee. There is something evil there that I cannot even begin to describe. The brew I make him, while good; is only strong enough to help confuse his demons for awhile. He is too smart and too cocky for his own good. He was friendly with my daughter for awhile, but he seems to have moved on."

Sylvester took a breath and then went about finishing her order. He reached under the counter and produced two small silver shakers. "I would venture to guess that you are well acquainted with the contents of these," he insinuated.

"You have no doubt seen me add them to my tea," she replied. She couldn't help wondering where and an old man like him would have access to alligator teeth and devils shoestring.

Sylvester nodded. "Well then, you know that I have had these here for some time hoping that you would come by," he said as he held a shaker in each hand over her cup. "With your permission, of course?" he inquired.

"I do, and you may," Alex granted.

Sylvester sprinkled a small amount from each shaker into the cup. Then he took a cinnamon stick and gave it a loving stir.

"So how did the dream end?" she asked.

"I'll let you know when it does," he promised as he handed her the cup.

Alex reached into her purse, but Sylvester waved her off. "Thank you," she said.

"No, Thank You," the old man said. "It has been a pleasure."

Alex looked at the time. "I have to go," she said. "I have to meet some friends that are helping me."

"I know," he acknowledged. "Good luck."

Alex started to turn and then paused for a moment. She realized that she had never answered his original question. "He's fine," she said. "Grey is doing ok." There was another pause. "By the way," she continued, "how did you come to know about any of this?"

"The dreams," Sylvester repeated. "They started happening again after your friend's accident."

"So you know about the accident?" she inquired.

"Everything," he said. "As fate may have it, my grandson was the one driving the truck."

Alex smiled and shook her head. "Does he know about your dreams?" she asked.

"Some things are better kept to oneself," he offered.

"I definitely understand that," she agreed. "I hope he's ok as well," she added. Alex took a few steps. "I will come back to see you," she promised. "And bring Grey," she added.

"I'd like that," he said. "I'll be looking forward to it." He waved to Alex as she moved away. He wondered when their next meeting would be.

* * * * *

Tim's truck was already in the parking lot when Alex pulled up. "Sorry I'm late," she said. "I just needed some coffee." (Grey would have thought that was funny or at the very least, suspicious.)

"We just got here ourselves," Patti volunteered. "Honestly, I don't see this as being a problem. You can see most of the ground floor from the second level. It would be easy to spot him unless he's seriously trying to hide." Her eyes scanned the area again.

"I'm thinking that it's all in where you park, Patti," Tim said. "If the lot is pretty full like on a normal day around here, then he's going to need a spot where he can see your car clearly. Unfortunately for him, it won't be there, at least as far as tomorrow goes. I figure we string him along for a while and don't offer you up until the end of the day. Between now and then, we start to keep regular surveillance on him. I think we're in good position to start pulling the strings now."

Tim took a few more steps and then re-directed his attention to Alex. "We'll set up another chance opportunity for him to see her," he motioned, "but give him no way to establish real contact. We'll make sure it's a good look. That ought to keep him hungry. He'll have to continue to use the parking lot because there will be less chance of being seen with her there than inside the building."

Tim walked around a bit and then shared an observation. "The second level of this structure might work as an observation point, assuming you park down here in the D.A.'s assigned parking, but he can't take the risk of being delayed coming down the ramp to stay with you. I think he'll come mid afternoon to look for your car. The lot is less crowded after lunch. Once he locates it, he'll find a spot he likes and then even leave his car if necessary in order to establish position. Then he'll come back around four and wait."

Alex remained quiet. She was amazed by the confident level of Tim's intuition.

"Not bad, Galleon," Patti said. "Not bad at all." "So where do we set up?" Alex asked.

"Anywhere that allows the best visual advantage and is not easy to obstruct," Patti responded. "Even though you'll be aware of my final destination, it is important that you stay close and keep an eye on things. After all, you'll be the one who's covering my back."

Alex's face got serious for a moment. "You can count on me, Patti," she assured her. "I promise you that."

"I know I can," Patti replied. "According to Tim here, you've got great credentials," she said, smiling.

"Anybody know where Blake is now?" Alex asked.

"No, but we can find out if he's anywhere around," Tim said, grabbing Garrett's little tracker off the front seat.

Tim hit a few buttons and magically, there he was. The flashing light was faint indicating that Blake was stationary but almost out of range. "It's a good thing that this contraption seems to work 'as the crow flies' rather than driving distance," Tim commended. "It looks like he's heading home."

"It's too bad we don't have somebody who works or hangs out in that area all day," Alex commented. "It would free the two of you up for other things."

"Good point," Patti answered, "Fortunately for us, Garrett designed this thing with a pretty good range. It seems to be even better than even he expected."

"So I guess that's it," Alex said, turning her attention to Tim. "We park Patti's car where it's easy to find in assigned parking. I'm assuming one of your friends upstairs can get you a tag or something?" she asked. Tim nodded. "Blake will have to hang out somewhere close so he won't risk losing her. That will allow me to watch both of them from a safe distance."

"Exactly," Patti responded. "As long as you can keep a constant visual on both of us, you'll be fine."

"Is everyone on the same page?" Tim asked. Both women confidently agreed.

"I'm going to head back to the house then," Alex announced. "I'll bring Grey up to speed. What do I tell him about Blake?" she inquired. "Tell him to relax. He's got nothing to worry about," Tim began. "He can call Richard and tell him the same thing. Patti found out that Blake has to be back here in the morning to finalize a few things from this morning's hearing. He's home now and I think he'll be staying put

for the rest of the day. We won't see him move until morning." "So, we're all on stand-by until tomorrow?" Alex asked.

"Yeah," Tim answered, but I'm going to stay close enough to keep him in range. He won't be out tonight. He'll be too excited about what he has planned for tomorrow."

"All right then, I'm out of here," Alex said. "Call me if you need me." "You're already on my speed dial," Tim informed her. "You're #13."

Alex shook her head. Tim could tell something about the #13 hit home. "Grey put you up to that; didn't he?" she solicited.

"No, not at all," he defended. "I know that's the number you are on his phone," Tim continued. "I figured it was easy to remember that way."

"I did the same thing," Patti offered. "Is there a problem?"

Alex took a minute to consider her options. These people were friends now and if Grey trusted them, then so could she. "Well, there was," she began. "Back when we were in school together, something happened, and there were thirteen minutes between us that changed our lives. I'll tell you what, when this is all over, we can all have drink together on the boat and Grey can tell you the story."

Patti and Tim watched as Alex turned and got into her car. Tim reached out a hand.

"Seriously guys; No harm, no foul," Alex assured them. "I just hadn't thought about it for a long time, that's all." When Alex pulled away, she waved again as a parting gesture. Once she was out on the road, she decided to call Grey. "I'm on my way back," she told him. "I should be there in about twenty minutes." Her voice was less animated than usual. Grey picked up on it right away.

"You ok?" he asked casually. "You sound a little distant." "Everything's fine," she answered. "Everything's ready to go for tomorrow," she assured him. Then she told him about the conversation she'd just had with Patti and Tim.

"So what did you tell them?" Grey asked.

"Only that the number meant something to us, and that when this was all over, you would tell them the story over a beer on the boat."

"And you're ok with that?' he inquired.

"I think there has to come a time when we can both forgive ourselves and move on," she said.

"We tried save them both," he reminded her. "The mother had just been face down in the water too long. Even the paramedic said we gave her thirteen minutes she never would have had."

"Tell that to her daughter," Alex replied. Grey could hear her voice starting to break. It reminded him she was mortal. Before he could continue, Alex regained her composure and moved on."So if we're free until tomorrow, what's the plan?" she redirected.

"Get home and we'll talk?" he proposed.

There was a long silence before she answered him. "I'll see you when I see you," she said, "And Grey, Thanks."

When he was gone, Alex tossed the phone on the seat next to her and turned up the radio. Something was bothering her about Blake. She decided to try to find a library and check it out. The Mustang ran like the wind.

* * * * *

When the phone rang, Katie was eager, but not surprised. She did wonder why it had taken him this long to call, but she also knew Blake had his own 'release phase' after every legal engagement. This usually involved a ride in his car with a good cigar and the top down. Still, it had been close to three hours since the hearing ended and he was just getting around to calling her. The local news had covered the story, but had reported that Blake was presently unavailable for comment. Walter was probably going crazy about the loss of free publicity, but Katie knew that sucking up to the press was the last thing on her husband's mind. As far as the firm was concerned, Blake knew he had put himself in a position where he held all the cards.

"Hi Honey, I'm just checking in," he said when he heard her pick up. "I wanted to see if you already had plans for the day?" he inquired.

"I take it, from the noise in the background, that you're out in the car somewhere," she said.

"Just taking a drive after my hearing," he said. "You know it relaxes me." "I know," she acknowledged. "But then you always come home

smelling like silly cigars."

"We'll my dear, I haven't lit one yet," he informed her. "And if you prefer, one this trip I won't. I'm actually on my way home to see you." (Blake knew this was the perfect thing to say.)

"Really, that's sweet," she said. "What do you have in mind?" "Lunch somewhere down on the beach," he suggested, "and then,

maybe we could go shopping though Fashion Island."

It took Katie a moment to process what Blake had just suggested. *"The lunch date was a great idea, but Blake wasn't much of a shopper. He'd been acting strange lately, but this...... well maybe he was simply in a good mood'*. "Are you sure about the shopping part?" she asked. "I know it's really not your thing."

"Nonsense," he proclaimed. *"If I'm going to spoil one of the women in my life,"* he thought, *"I might as well spoil the others."* He made mental note to call Sheila back as soon as possible. That would avoid any awkwardness on Monday morning.

"I'm going to spend time with you," he insisted. "I'm yours for the rest of the day," he added.

There was a long silence that followed. Katie was speechless. Blake figured she would be. The combination of his two personalities definitely gave interacting with him a new twist. There was a new level of excitement and unpredictability. Today he would relax and enjoy the fruits of his labors. Tomorrow, he would take the steps needed to close the final chapter of his vengeance so that his world could move on.

"Are you sure you're feeling ok, Honey?" she asked. Her tone was soft and playful.

Blake knew he had her right where he wanted her. "Never been better," he asserted. "So, are you going to help me spend some of this asshole Garcia's money, or what?" he inquired.

"I can be ready in fifteen minutes," she assured him.

"I'll pick you up then." Blake said. He was surprised by the speed at which Katie hung up.

'A little food, a little shopping, maybe later, a little golf?' the 'Cat' chimed in.

The idea went down smooth. "That's not bad," Blake agreed, mumbling to himself. "It will give me the down time I need to review the plan."

He was almost to the driveway now. The conversation had to end. By the time he got to the top of the hill, Blake was totally in control. As a reminder of his unfinished task, the clawing began again. It was subtle, but definitely there. He decided he wasn't going to let it bother him. The afternoon with Katie was all he wanted to focus on. When he saw her waiting by the front door, he was reminded why.

The blue sundress she had chosen did everything in its power to bring out the color of her eyes. Her heels were modest, but just enough to highlight the shape of her legs. There was an ample supply of cleavage, tactfully available and on display. Blake couldn't stop staring, as he got out of the car and moved into position to assist her. Katie was all smiles. She knew instantly that even under the time constraint, her efforts had not been wasted.

"Allow me," Blake said as he opened her door. Her dress hiked up a little as she got in, exposing a considerable amount of leg. While Katie had not consciously planned the move, the extra exposed flesh definitely added to the heat of the moment. Katie smiled when she caught him looking. Blake closed her door and then moved around the car and got in.

"Where to?" he asked firmly. His tone was now quite cavalier.

"I was thinking about us going to Las Brisas for a nice lunch, and then heading up to Fashion Island," she proposed. "How does that sound to you?"

Blake was just getting to the bottom of the driveway and waiting for the gate to open. "It's your afternoon," he proclaimed. "That sounds good to me."

Blake pulled out onto the highway. The restaurant was only a mile or so up the road.

"So I only get the afternoon?" she teased.

"Well," he replied, "I am available until tomorrow morning when I have to be back at the courthouse. I have a few loose ends to tie up."

Katie placed his free hand on her thigh. "I guess we'll have to set an alarm then, won't we?" she insinuated. "Tied up," she mumbled softly, "interesting."

Blake discovered that there was suddenly a direct correlation between the position of her hand and the depression of his foot on the gas pedal. Both objects seemed to accelerate quickly.

As Blake watched the valet help Katie out of the car, he became aware of something else. When he looked at Katie, his gaze was one of great love and admiration. The 'Cat' in him however, salivated as though she was an entrée on the menu. Blake tried to suppress his friend deeper. He began to understand that sooner or later, he wouldn't have any control. Blake came around to take her hand, and escorted his wife inside. The valet smiled and nodded his approval. Today would be about chivalry and charm. Tomorrow, the final step of his journey would commence. His vengeance and redemption were now only a few short days away. Blake looked at his wife. The 'Cat' was right. She did look good enough to eat. The claws cut deeper.

* * * * *

"Blake moved," Patti observed. "Not more than a mile or so, but he has left the house." she continued. "It appears he went about a mile or so north before stopping again. Do you know what's down there?" she asked.

"Mostly just shops and restaurants," Tim answered. "Do you want to check it out?"

"No, not really," she replied. "If you're not worried about his daytime activities to the point where we don't have to eyeball him; then let's just keep watch on this tracking thing. Maybe he just went out to grab some lunch."

"Speaking of food," Tim said, "Are you hungry?"

Patti nodded. "I could eat," she responded. "What do you have in mind?"

"If we jump on the freeway over there," Tim explained, "it will take us down to the coast highway. That will put us pretty close to the middle between where Blake is and the boat. We can keep an eye on him for awhile from there. After we eat, we can decide which direction we want to pursue. We won't be that far from the beach house."

"Do you mind if I drive?" she asked. "I want to try to familiarize myself with the area a bit," she added.

Tim got out and tossed her the keys. "Try not to hit anything, will ya?" he teased.

Patti just rolled her eyes as she climbed behind the wheel. "You should leave the tracking device with me tonight," she suggested. "I'll take you back to the boat later so you can get some sleep. I'll also pick up my car and then head for the beach house. I should be safe there tonight because Blake doesn't know it exists. I can monitor the tracking device and keep an eye on things. It'll keep one of us within range. If the son of a bitch moves, I'll just pick up the phone."

"That actually makes a lot of sense," Tim agreed. "Now that we have the house set up, you could stay there tonight. You sure you don't mind?"

"I'll be fine," she insisted, patting his leg. "You're just going to miss me, right?" she teased.

"Maybe I'll call Alex and get her to come down and stay with you?" he suggested.

Patti gave him funny look.

"C'mon Patti," Tim said. "Once a gunslinger, always a gunslinger," he teased.

"You're forgetting something," she replied, "I'm not the one who made me watch all of those 'Dirty Harry' movies."

Tim laughed. "Or the one who thought you were a natural with that Glock 9mm of yours and made you go to the practice range every day," he added.

"Yeah, that guy," she said. "Let's blame him."

"Seriously, Patti," he continued, "Having Alex stay with you was more about keeping you company. I wasn't looking for a babysitter."

Patti's face was almost pouty now. "I know me being at the beach house is going to be to our advantage," she conceded, "I know this is your baby, but I hate just having to sit around."

"Believe me, I get it, I get where you're coming from," he responded. "We're not going to sit on this any longer than absolutely necessary."

Patti gave him a look. "You don't fool me Patti," he said. "You're not just going to sit around and do nothing. By the time I check in later tonight, you'll know every square inch of the area within walking distance like the back of your hand. You've always been about preparation and attention to detail. I know you too well. Heck, you'll probably even find a way to even make it fun."

"You know you're an asshole, don't you?" she said playfully. "That's detective asshole to you, ma'am," he responded. "Relax, my friend. It's only going to be for a couple of hours."

"Well, you said you were willing to feed me first, so I guess that's a start," she giggled.

"You'll like where we're going," Tim assured her. "Cappy's is a popular place. It's low key and beach casual."

"Sounds like a plan then," Patti confirmed. "Just tell me where to go." Tim watched the miles pass and tried his best to stay alert.

As they got off the freeway, Tim got a text from Renee. Before he could respond, the tracker beeped and Blake was on the move again. Patti pulled over so they could wait to see what Blake was going to do next. He was headed their way. They didn't have to wait long. According to the map, Blake's car was now in the parking lot at Fashion Island.

"I'd love to know why Blake is at Fashion Island," Tim thought out loud. "I can't see the guy in a mall, high end or not."

"What's worse?" Patti asked, "Your hunger or your curiosity?" "Head for Cappy's," Tim said. "I'll watch the screen. If he's shopping,

he's going to be there for awhile. If he moves again in the next few minutes, then we'll go follow him."

"Maybe he took Katie shopping," Patty offered. "He just won a big case and can spread the wealth. Isn't that what a guy like him would do? Go home to brag and then spoil the wife?"

"You may have a point," Tim agreed. "If Blake thinks Walter's out of the picture, he can just continue to establish his own dominance and control by showering his wife with gifts."

"As far as Katie is concerned, a good day in court for Blake means a good day of shopping for her." Patti added sarcastically.

"I'm betting we have time to eat before he moves again," Tim considered.

"If he's still there when we're finished, maybe we can go check out the car?" Patti asked.

"Yeah, I guess it would be helpful to know if in fact he's got Katie with him." Tim admitted. "If we get lucky, he'll stay in tonight with her and the real fun won't start until tomorrow afternoon."

"Fun?" she asked.

Tim smiled. "It's always fun to catch the bad guys," he professed. "This time, it's just more personal."

"Oh, do I understand that," she agreed. Tim pointed out ahead. They were almost at the restaurant. Then he looked down at the device on his lap. "Blake still hasn't moved," he said. He didn't sound surprised.

Patti laughed. "From what I've been exposed to about Katie Kendall, if he decided to take her shopping, we're going to be able to have one very long lunch. I'd hate to be the one carrying the bags."

"Turn in here," Tim said as they arrived at the restaurant. He glanced down at the screen again. "Knock yourself out, Katie," he said chuckling. "We're getting something to eat."

Patti laughed. "I guess we better feed ya huh?" she said as she followed Tim inside. An hour later, nothing had changed.

* * * * *

He managed to get out of Nordstrom fairly cheap. Katie had racked up less than four figures and it all fit in just three bags. Neiman Marcus was even less. All he had to do was make it to one of the exit doors and he'd be home free. He actually managed to get close until Katie saw a mannequin in the Victoria Secret window that was something she apparently had to have.

"I think that would look even better on me," she said gesturing toward the store window.

Blake looked up and formulated an opinion. *"When you already have the best trophy, it's hard to be interested in anything else,"* he thought. The claws dug in, but Blake ignored them.

"That's nice, Honey," he remarked, trying ever so subtly to play along. "Why don't you go in and pick out what you like. I'll wait out here so I won't ruin the surprise."

Katie leaned over and kissed him on the cheek. "Can I?" she asked. "I promise, I won't be long," she said and then disappeared inside.

Finally, Blake got a break. He took her bags and found a place to sit. His phone had been vibrating in his pocket for several minutes, but he had no interest in answering it. At the moment, he just wanted to get home. As an afterthought, he looked at it anyway. It was Sheila. He knew he couldn't avoid her forever. When it vibrated again, he decided that he better answer it.

"Yes," he said, in very casual matter of fact voice.

"You left something in my desk," she replied. "Do I need to go make a deposit?" she asked.

"Please do," he responded. "I don't think you want to leave that kind of money lying around."

"Which account would you like it in?" she asked.

"Why yours, of course," he insisted. This provoked a long period of silence.

"Excuse me?" she said.

"Consider it a bonus," he replied. "Or an addition to your raise."
"When did I get a raise?" she continued.

Blake looked at his watch. "A couple of hours ago," he confirmed. "I hope it's enough," he added. "Listen, can we talk about this in the morning? I'm stuck in shopping hell. I'm at Fashion Island with Katie. If this keeps up, I'm going to have to hire a valet to help me carry all of these fucking bags."

Sheila laughed. "Reminded me to take you with me when I go," she said. "This is a lot of money," she observed. "You sure about this, Boss?"

"Do I ever do anything I don't want to do?" he inquired.

Then Sheila's voice got serious. "Thanks, Blake," she said. "It's nice to know that you really do appreciate me. I'll see you in the morning."

"No problem," he confirmed. "I'll see you then."

The timing was perfect. Just as Sheila was hanging up, Katie was on her way out of the store. Blake rolled his eyes, but then put on a smile. The 'Cat' was actually amused.

"Get anything good?" he asked.

Katie giggled like a school girl. "Only the most perfect things ever," she answered.

"I'm glad," he replied. "Anything else?" he asked gesturing to the rest of the mall.

"No, I think we're good," she said. "Are you ready to go home?"
"Sure," Blake offered. "We'll go home, have a couple of drinks and relax,"

Katie took his free hand and held it all the way to the car. Blake put her bags in the trunk and then opened her door. Katie was all smiles. It was nice to feel good about Blake and her family again. Once she was safely belted in, Blake went around and got in. He nodded to her as he started the car and off they went. Katie was all smiles. Blake had the top down, but she really didn't care what the wind did to her hair. She could fix that later. Right now, all she wanted to do was enjoy the day. The warmth of the sun felt good on her face. Blake had returned to his rightful place as her champion. For his undying devotion and forgiveness, she would always be his queen. Katie was all smiles. It wouldn't be long before a glass of champagne in her hand would guide her through the rest of the day. It was just the two of them, alone in the mid-day sun. She had no idea how closely they were being watched.

* * * * *

At Patti's request, they turned left out of Cappy's and headed south down the coast highway.

"We're in the area anyway," she said, "Let's see if we can spot the car."

"All right," he conceded. "If it will make you feel better. The street is a couple of miles down. I'll let you know when to turn," he said.

Patti tapped her hands on the on the steering wheel as she drove. I took Tim a minute before he recognized the rhythm.

"Crazy Train," he said. "No kidding," he laughed.

"You're going to need to turn soon," he said pointing to distant street light. "You really want to do his?" he asked.

"Your hunger won earlier, mine didn't," she said. "My curiosity is still there."

"Fair enough," he admitted. "You…

Before he could finish his sentence, the tracker started beeping. "Blake's moving," Tim announced.

"So what do you want to do?" she asked.

"Don't make the turn," Tim answered. "If this thing is right, he's headed back toward us. Pull over down here where we can see the corner and give us a little distance. If he's going back to Laguna, he'll make a left and head south. We'll see him make the turn."

Patti did as instructed as Tim kept an eye on Blake's signal.

"He should be coming up right about now," Tim said.

All eyes turned to the intersection. There was a short pause, but then Tim smiled and said, "There he is. And he's got Katie with him!"

When the light changed, Blake made the turn south toward home. "Do you want to follow him?" Patti asked.

"No," he answered. "They're probably just going home. Speaking of home, why don't you take me back to the boat?" he suggested. "I can get a nap, and you can get your car."

"Sure," she said, "Then I'll go get set up at the beach house and do my thing," she added as she pulled back into traffic.

"As long as he goes home and stays in tonight, we should have nothing to worry about," Tim granted. "I'll bet that after that shopping spree Katie will want to keep him close."

"Yeah, that's probably a safe bet," Patti said. "Is he still moving south?"

"Right on the money," Tim replied. "At this rate he should be home in fifteen, maybe twenty minutes. We may have to stop soon. He's starting to get out of range."

"Just let me know when," she said.

The signal was still visible when the Mercedes finally came to a stop. According to the satellite image, it was back in front of Blake's house. Tim could tell that it wasn't going to last all the way to the boat, but the system was still pretty damn impressive.

"We're going to be blind for about twenty minutes until you get back to around this spot," he said, "but I guessing that we'll be ok. He's with Katie, and knowing her, she's more than likely got him opening some of her fancy champagne about now." Patti laughed.

"Just promise me that if he starts to move strangely or you think something weird is going on you won't go off by yourself," Tim requested.

"Scouts honor," she replied, holding up two fingers.

"Very funny," Tim said shaking his head. "Otherwise, I'll be down at the beach house after dinner."

"Good, Then maybe we can have a beer or something," she proposed.

"That might be an idea," Tim agreed. "Still a Heineken woman?" he asked.

"You actually remember that?" she asked.

"I don't forget much," he replied. "Sometimes it's a blessing, Sometimes it's not."

"We'll see," Patti implied.

Tim just shook his head again. They were almost to the boat. When they pulled up to the dock, Patti was feeling more content.

Tim really did need some rest and she could put the free time to their advantage.

"Get some sleep," she told him as she got out of the truck. "I'll be down around seven," he assured her.

Tim watched thankfully as Patti pulled away. He was glad she was there. Her presence didn't change the way he felt about Renee, it just made him feel better about everything he and his friends were up against. He was too into the task at hand to sleep now, but he didn't want to tell Patti that. He went below deck and cracked open a beer. Then he sent Renee a text of his own.

El Faralito's at 5   Miss you,   We'll have to make it quick

It only took seconds for her to respond. She was in. Tim was happy. A quick trip back to reality was what he needed to get his mind straight. He grabbed his beer and headed for the shower. If he was going to pull off this little side trip, he had to be on the road in twenty minutes.

* * * * *

Grey and Rachel were sitting on the patio when Alex finally pulled up in front of the house. It was late. Grey knew she was exhausted. Had she not sent him a text earlier, he would have been worried. Rachel was kind enough to make up a tray for her after dinner. After a quick pop into the microwave, Alex took her plate, and took a seat on a barstool at the kitchen counter. From where she was seated, she could see the two of them sitting on the porch through the front window.

A bottle of wine was in temporary residence on the table between them. Alex noticed immediately that only one of the three visible glasses had been called into service. After a few bites, she decided she wasn't in the mood to eat alone. She grabbed her plate and headed out to claim one of the empty glasses. As she approached, Rachel called out, "Come join us." Alex smiled gladly, as she pulled out a chair and took a seat.

"You'll have a glass of wine with me, won't you?" she directed at Alex. "My husband has politely refused to share this bottle with me. He seems to have a bit of a headache."

Alex turned her eyes to Grey. "You all right?" she inquired.

"I'm fine," he responded. "I just haven't had a lot of sleep lately, that's all."

"Did you get your errands done?" Grey asked.

"Yes," she answered politely. "I accomplished everything I needed to do."

"No problems?" Grey wondered.

"No," she assured him. "I think everything is working out just fine."

Rachel had topped off her own glass during the exchange and was now forced to ask Grey to open another bottle. He reached behind her into the cooler and produced a new challenger.

"At the sound of the pop, you two need to come out drinking," he kidded.

Rachel gave him a look. Not because she was mad, but she hated him being a smart ass in front of company. Alex laughed. If Rachel only knew what was going on in her husband's head. At least he was able to maintain his sense of humor. A small headache was the least of his worries.

"I don't know how you guys can drink the white stuff," he suddenly blurted out. "It's so damn sweet."

"We're all too sweet for you tonight, Grey," Rachel replied. "Why don't you go get some sleep?"

Grey looked over at Alex. "Is this some kind of conspiracy?" he inquired.

"I wouldn't call it that," Alex responded. "You just look like you could use a good night sleep." Her back was even with Rachel's so she didn't see her wink. Grey decided that she was probably right.

"All right, you two, you win." he conceded. "I'll see you both in the morning."

He kissed Rachel on the forehead and headed inside. He was tired and didn't last long once his head hit the pillow. Sleep came, and for a moment, his mind was wiped totally blank. Grey knew it wouldn't last. If there is truly no rest for the wicked, then there is also very little for those who choose to keep them under a watchful eye. He was ready when Kelly Richfield came to pay him a visit. It was going to be a long night.

* * * * *

CHAPTER 32

When Grey opened his eyes, he realized that he had fallen back into the abyss. He found himself sitting on a rock at the edge of the clearing. Once again, the row of shallow graves lay ominously before him. He had heard a young girl's voice addressing him as he drifted off to sleep, but coming here again was not what he expected.

After careful inspection, he noticed that something was different. One of the tombstones was lying on its back and there was no long mound of freshly turned earth in front of it. The one to its right was also strange. The stone was standing up, but it was too far away to make out the name clearly. There was a shadowed outline of where the earth would be moved, but the ground had yet to be broken. Grey was about to move in closer when he could swear he heard giggling coming from behind one of the headstones.

Almost immediately, a young girl's face appeared. Even from a distance, he recognized her immediately from the photographs he'd seen at Father Richard's. Strangely enough, she appeared unharmed. As he worked his way toward her, he noticed she had a bottle of beer in her hand as she emerged from behind a head stone. After a quick attempt to size him up, she nonchalantly sat down, leaning up against the rock. Grey watched with great interest as she made herself comfortable. Their eyes made contact several times, but neither of them said a word. Finally, Kelly spoke.

"So tell me," she began, "How it is that you can see into my world?" she questioned in a slightly drunken tone. Her voice was calm and almost comical. Grey remained silent as she lifted the bottle to her soft, red lips and took a long, seductive swallow.

"You can see me, can't you?" she asked again, curious about the lack of any initial response.

This time Grey nodded ever so slightly. His simple reaction seemed to please her.

"Then I assume you can hear me too, huh?" she continued. Grey nodded again.

Kelly shifted around in her sitting position trying to get comfortable. "Do you know why you're here?" she asked. Her tone was now becoming more animated.

This time, Grey decided to engage her. "I'm under the impression that you want to show me something, Kelly," he responded softly. This seemed to do the trick.

"Yeah, that's pretty much it." Kelly said, laughing as she stood up.

Grey made a mental note that her balance was a bit off even after she got to her feet.

"I figured that if you've stuck with us this far, you might as well go all the way," she said gesturing toward the fallen head stone. You've already done more good than you know. The bastard would have killed her too if you and your friends hadn't intervened."

At his present angle, Grey could just make out the name on the toppled piece of granite. Mellissa would never know how close she had really come to dying. According to the date of the inscription, if he and his friends had not convinced her to leave town, she would have been dead by morning. This was a secret he would never share. Grey's face betrayed him.

"Anger or fear?" Kelly asked.

"Regret," he answered. "I'm sorry that none of this madness came to the surface until it was too late to save you," he offered.

Kelly contemplated his response as she lifted the bottle and took another swallow. She knew he was being sincere, so she decided to continue.

"Nice thought," she said; "Me too, now that you mention it. But what's done is done. My only concern now is that it ends here," she said, glancing over at the last shadowed grave. Her eyes grew sad as she turned and surveyed the row of tombstones. "We all just want to be able to find our own peace," she added.

Grey nodded, but she could tell his undivided attention had now become a stare.

"I look pretty good, don't I?" she kidded. Grey caught the beginnings of a smile. "What you're seeing now is definitely much better than what's buried over there."

Grey wondered how strange it must be for someone to have to make reference to their own grave.

"You're absolutely right," he agreed. "I saw you once the other way in a dream of Father Richard's. I must say that I definitely prefer you like this."

Kelly finished her beer and threw the bottle across the graveyard into the trees. Then she walked over and stood next to the one with her own name. "I never should have had that last beer that night," she confessed. "If I'd said no, I'd be at home tonight."

Even in this place of shadows, Grey could see the tears forming in her eyes.

"My poor mom," she added.

Grey gave her a moment to herself before he spoke. "We'll get him Kelly," he said. "I promise you, we'll get him."

Kelly turned to him with teary eyes. "I know you will," she whispered confidently. "That's why you're here. Father Richard prayed for help. I guess you're the one who got the call."

Grey shook his head. "Wow, that's a little heavy Kelly," he conceded.

"I'm sorry," she said. "I'm sorry for everything." Then she turned her back to him.

Grey could see by the wrinkling of her clothes and some subtle changes in her posture that some strange metamorphosis was taking place

"You'd better go," she said. "You'd better go quickly."

Grey turned and started walking back toward the trees. He knew what was happening. Whatever force was running the show would only let her keep her friendly appearance for so long. Grey paused as he put a foot into the tree line. He spoke again without turning around.

"I'll tell Father Richard you said 'Hi'," he assured her. "And if you let me Kelly," he added, "When it's over, I'll be back."

The 'thank you' that followed was gurgled.

Grey moved into the trees. Once inside, he could hear the whisper of a light breeze. When he opened his eyes, he discovered that it was his ceiling fan again. He was awake and Rachel was asleep next to him on the bed. It was only 5:00 a.m. He had another hour before the alarm would go off. Grey looked at his phone and then headed for the shower. He wondered if Tim and Patti were already on the move. When he was finished, he went looking for Alex.

* * * * *

For Blake, the morning came far too soon. This was probably not completely unexpected because golf wasn't the only game they played. At the end, neither one of them had much of anything left. Their erotic adventure had drawn all but the very breath from them. Granted, there were times when the encounter was sensual, but for the most part, it was just downright graphic. It was still dark outside when a familiar, but irritating sound erupted, shattering the early morning silence.

Blake's alarm clock became his worst enemy. It reminded him that it was time to step back into reality. He wasn't sure he could move. It took several tries before he managed to silence the ringer. He spent the next few minutes taking inventory of all his body parts and verifying their continued existence. Once he was satisfied, he carefully crawled out of bed. It was an unusually long walk to the shower.

An hour later, when he was finally able to climb into the comfort of his car, he was painfully aware that there were parts of him that actually ached. Then, something in his mind clicked that made him laugh. He wasn't sure, but there was a pretty good chance that one of Katie's ankles was still tied to the bed post with a pair of her silk scarves. Her legs had been covered with a sheet when he passed her earlier, and he didn't have the heart now to go back upstairs and wake her to find out. He had to get moving. Right now, he had a promise to keep. At the moment, he was lucky. The claws were at rest.

He arrived at the courthouse early with hopes of locating Patti. It didn't take long for him to realize that he was going to be in vain. His inability to control the situation only fueled the fire. He could have sworn that he remembered the make and model of her car, but it also was nowhere to be found. (Tim and Patti had kept it away deliberately to confuse him.) That worked like a charm. Blake figured that his failure was probably some kind of punishment, a payback for his earlier lie. His 'loose ends' story was a ruse. The only unfinished business he had left on his plate was with the Wheeler girl.

He tried again to contact his source at the D.M.V., but discovered that the license plate number he had submitted was registered to a car rental agency. He was discouraged but wouldn't quit. He tried patiently to utilize other resources, but even after exhausting the heart of his network, he was left with the simple fact that there was no local information to be had on a Patricia 'Wheeler'. Blake needed answers. He hadn't noticed a ring, but maybe Wheeler was her married name. If that was the case, he was screwed. Patti and Tim had covered her tracks well. This only added insult to injury. There was nothing he could do but wait. He was so distracted, that he remained completely unaware that he was being watched.

* * * * *

Alex and Grey had left the house around six. Alex tried to talk Grey into staying home, but he would not relent.

"At least you'll have someone to talk to," he said.

Alex insisted on driving. The Mustang was probably more conspicuous than any of Grey's vehicles, but not familiar to Blake. Besides, with the top up, they didn't have to worry about Grey being spotted. They were set up at the parking structure in a safe position before Blake even left his driveway. He was easy to spot when he finally pulled in.

It turned out to be a long morning. Shortly after noon, Blake was still hanging around the courthouse. After several more hours of uneventful boredom, Patti decided that she wanted to have some reckless fun and decided to toy with Blake. With some well executed timing, she put herself on display going down an escalator as Blake was coming up. Blake did a double take, but he had no choice to do anything more than smile and wave as she passed. By the time he reached the top and had the chance to turn around, she was already gone. Blake was furious. His inability to keep track of her was driving him mad. He was frustrated and running out of options. Patti watched playfully from a distance, but continued to lay low.

By the end of the day, the decision was made to start reeling Blake in. Alex saw him sitting in his car waiting and gave Patti a 'heads up'. Patti came out of hiding and got in position. This time, she made sure that he not only saw her, but that his eyes followed every wiggle of her ass all the way from the elevator to her car. Patti almost laughed. While he was notably a great attorney, he was almost childish with his attempt at covert tactics.

When she left the parking structure, she had no trouble keeping him close in her rear view mirror. He 'tracked' her for about half an hour to a beach house on 28th St. in Newport Beach. She had allowed him to follow her easily without arousing any suspicion. Blake had swallowed the hook.

Blake watched as she grabbed a gym bag out of the trunk of her car, and headed inside. He immediately noticed the rental sign in the upstairs window. She was obviously a new tenant. He hung out for most of the evening, and observed that she liked to run at night on the beach. That information alone was worth the wait. It created possibilities. Blake's mind raced as the two voices did battle inside his head. He decided that he would formulate his plan of attack from there. A dark, empty beach sounded appetizing. He had killed by the water before. He was certain he could do it again. The darkness was his friend. Now, planning the final stages of his vengeance could really begin. The 'Cat' in him wanted her now! He never noticed the dark outline of a man in the door way several houses down. Ever vigilant, Galleon remained in the shadows.

* * * * *

After making sure that Patti was safely tucked in, Alex suggested that she take Grey home. He argued with her a bit, but conceded it was better for him to keep out of sight. He and Father Richard would just have to stay put, and let the rest of them handle things for awhile. Alex was anxious. She was ready for anything.

Tim was actually impressed at how quickly she seemed to adapt to her new task. So far, she was handling herself like an old pro. She would have made a good cop. While comparing notes earlier, they had both noticed that something about Blake's behavior was changing. He was suddenly becoming predictable. Ever since he had made contact with Patti in the courthouse parking lot, he had immediately redirected his attention. As Tim had hoped, Blake instantly recognized that there was something different about Patti. Especially since Grey had coached her with a few of Katie's mannerisms. Since the bartender at 'B.J.'s' was no longer an option, Patti became his new focus. He was in tracking mode, and settled into a structured routine. It was all just a waiting game.

Over the next several days, both Alex and Tim observed that during the day, when Blake wasn't in court, he chose to seek sanctuary in his office. After dark, he would drive past the beach house on his way home. One night, he parked and went for a walk on the beach to work on his plan. Most of the time, he just spent waiting. He liked to watch her run. He kept enough distance to make sure that he wasn't recognized. Their next meeting had to be by accident. All he needed was an opportunity. If he was patient, it would come.

On Friday night, about an hour after her run, Patti reappeared on the steps in front of the beach house. Her run had been uneventful, but tonight, she wanted to do something different. A cold beer in a crowded room sounded good. With all of her friends keeping eyes on her, there was little or no risk involved if she decided to go out and show herself.

"If he's really keeping tabs on me," she thought, "it will be really interesting to see how close *he's willing to get."* She locked the door and secured her purse. Not even Tim was aware that she was carrying her favorite bag, a black Coach clutch that afforded her just enough room inside for everything a smart girl needed: touch up, lipstick, foundation, a purse size pack of Kleenex and of course her 9 mm Glock. Patti patted her bag as she moved down the side walk. Her destination was only a few blocks away.

Blake had hung around only because he could see her dressing through the upstairs window. When she returned to the ground level, she had apparently decided to go out again for awhile. She was now dressed in a skirt and sandals with low heels. She had her hair down and it moved slightly in the wind. It was only a couple of blocks or so to the pier and two of the local bars. An opportunity presented itself.

Blake watched carefully as she moved down the boardwalk. When he saw her walk into a place called Sharkeez near the end of the pier, he decided to make his move. If she was going to be the last of his sacrificial lambs, (and he hoped she was), he wanted to make it count. The Cheshire smile appeared. Tonight, for one last time, he would crossover and give in to the passions of his dark side.

Blake got out of his car and headed for the bar. He would have no trouble blending in to its casual low key environment. His new beach bum look would serve him well. His board shorts even had big baggy pockets so he would have no trouble concealing his 'friend' until he was ready. He stopped at the entrance to the pier for one final look. He was seeing the world through different eyes now.

The surf was mesmerizing. Ample waves of billowing white water broke and then rushed toward the shore. Blake looked out over the dark sea and felt the hunger starting to grow. Tonight, she would be his for the taking. When it was over, the 'Cat' could sleep again. He would marinate her with alcohol, put on his best charm, and then get her to take walk on the beach with him. Then, while Blake made her feel safe and secure, the 'Cat' would linger in the shadows. When the moment was right, he would strike. There would be no mercy. Without any reservations, he would finish her off by the jetty. His work would be done and his vengeance would be over. He had no qualms about simply leaving her body as a gift to the surf. There would be no need for any further co-version. Once his journey was completed, he could simply slip away, back into the night. The blood would flow and the world would move on.

* * * * *

Alex saw everything. She'd been on watch for the past several hours. She immediately called Patti's cell and gave her a heads up. It could be nothing, but Blake was going into Sharkeez's after her. Patti also called Tim and brought him up to speed. He and Grey were standing by. They were docked a mile or so away at a nearby Yacht Club. (Tim had managed to secure an empty slip a day earlier from one his contacts at the Harbor Patrol. Even by water, they were only a couple of miles away.)

"Game on?" Tim asked.

"Maybe," she replied. "We'll see how it goes."

"Any chance we can follow the plan?" he continued.

"I'll give it my best shot," she assured him.

Then there was a short silence. Tim was nervous, but for all the wrong reasons. He was starting to think personal, harm's way kind of thing, and that just wasn't going to work. Patti was a good cop, and he wouldn't have involved her in the first place if he didn't think she could handle herself. He had to stay on track.

"All right," he said finally, "You win. But please keep me updated as the evening goes along. Grey and I are ready to head your way. Our E.T.A. is about twenty minutes. We're sitting just south east of you on the other side of the peninsula. If we time it right, we should be set up and in position by the time he buys you another round."

Patti laughed. "Kind of like old times, hey Tim?" she said.

"Just be careful," he insisted, "and let me know when you go 'live'," he continued. Then he paused. "For the record Patti, all of a sudden, I really don't like this whole 'bait' thing idea."

"I've got to go," she suddenly blurted out. "I'm about to have company. I'll call you later." The phone went dead.

Tim turned to Grey who was already untying the boat. He was calm and cool like they were only heading out on a day sail. The boat was already floating free against the dock.

"Ready when you are, Captain," Grey offered and confirmed.

Tim turned the key and started the engine. They would have to motor out into the channel before heading north to the rendezvous point. Grey sat on the starboard deck and pushed the bow away from the dock with his feet. They were moving. The low rumble of the 29th's engine hummed like Willie Beaumont's old Cadillac. As soon as they were clear of the dock, Grey pulled the large rubber bumpers up on deck and stowed them away. Now, they were completely underway.

As soon as they passed by the Pavilion, Grey took Tim's place at the helm of the 29th Precinct and guided her gently south along the shoreline. The water was calm as the boat glided effortlessly with a slow moving tide. On the forward bow, Tim took some time to set up his equipment. The pressure was on now and everything had to be perfect. He knew that he would probably only get one chance to get a shot off, so he had to get it right. That's why he chose his .308 S.W.A.T. issued sniper rifle. He had clocked over forty hours of range time with it and his confidence level was high. Grey looked at his watch. It was close to eleven.

Even so, they wanted to get down to the agreed position early and establish their cover. Tim calculated that a thirty minute window after they were ready and in position would be enough. A little night fishing wouldn't attract any unwanted attention. A couple of lines in the water would look innocent enough. Grey watched the mainsail to make sure it stayed full. Hoisting the jib wasn't necessary and would only impair Tim's efforts.

Grey's eyes followed Tim's hands for a minute as his friend meticulously fit each piece of his high tech weapon together. Grey shook his head. It was kind of a bizarre sight. Leaning along the port rail now, was a row of fishing poles, a high tech sniper rifle with night scope and suppressor, and then another fishing pole. After all they were after a big fish. Grey looked up and noticed that the sail was flapping lightly in the wind. He turned the boat slightly until the wind caught and it was full again.

Using the boat was actually plan B. They had originally thought about taking over the end of the pier, it being a much more stable platform, but out there, a man with a military grade sniper rifle would stand out much more than a man with a fishing pole. Besides, a public set up would attract too much attention and require too many explanations. Protection coming from out on the water would also eliminate the possibility of someone accidently wandering into the line of fire. Tim had made the final decision and Grey was confident that his friend knew what he was doing. On a public pier, if anything went wrong, things could spin out of control fast. This way, there were only a limited number of players. The four of them were going to be operating completely on their own.

Tim had turned to Garrett again for some high tech 'toys' to help minimize the risks. Each of the three 'observers' had been fitted with the latest in communication hardware. They were each issued Comtech II military style headgear communicators to stay in constant contact. Tim wanted Patti to be in light body armor, but she would have nothing to do with it. It would ruin the look and be obvious to someone like Blake. Tim tossed it into Patti's trunk anyway. In addition, each team member had been trained how to quickly assemble and operate their communication equipment when the time came.

Tim had calculated that if he had to shoot, it was going to be from somewhere around a hundred yards. On land, this was considered a 'school yard shot', but out on the water, it was much more difficult. Tim figured he could limit the boats movement by setting an anchor at each end. A bow and stern line would help steady the shot. He would also have to compensate for the wind and hope for a calm sea.

Their preparations had been intense. There was lot to consider. Against his wishes, Patti would not be wearing a vest. If he chose the wrong caliber round, it might pass through Blake and hit Patti. The only way Blake would go for the kill was if he could get her totally alone. Alex and Patti would have to stall or expedite the situation in order to keep things in motion. He and Grey would have to watch from a distance and hope for the best. Together, the two men had their hands full. As Grey continued to watch the mainsail and keep the boat steady, he wondered how Alex was holding up. He wished he could be there to watch Patti in action. He wouldn't find out until later, but Alex had managed to finagle her way into a front row seat.

* * * * *

As he approached the entrance to Sharkeez, Blake was feeling pretty confident. For the moment, it wasn't difficult for him to recognize that he was emotionally being controlled by the 'Cat'. The place was packed, so the guy at the door hesitated for a minute before letting him in. The fifty spot Blake slipped him only helped to inspire his decision. Once inside, Blake realized that it was going to be difficult to find Patti in the endless sea of people. He decided that his best bet was to start by checking out the bar. Much to Blake's surprise, the 'Cat' in him moved gracefully through the crowd. Sharkeez was a virtual feast of exposed flesh and alcohol. Blake would have been out of place, but the 'Cat' was right at home. Alex actually saw him coming before Patti did and motioned to her. Patti played distracted and let him come up on her from behind.

Blake moved in to the right of her and ordered a drink. He waited until his drink came before playing his hand.

"My, my, my," Blake opened with, "Is that you, Miss Wheeler?" he inquired as he started to sip at his drink.

Patti looked up from the bar and played her surprise. "Mr. Kendall!" she exclaimed. Blake looked much different now in his beach comber attire. She was quite certain that his deceptive appearance was all part of a plan. "What are you doing in a place like this?' she inquired.

Her voice was elevated to almost a yell as she tried to compensate for the volume of the music.

"I was down here visiting a client," he lied without so much as a blink, "and decided to go for a walk on the beach."

"And you ended up in here?" she asked.

"You're giving me the impression that you think that this place is not my kind of establishment?" he replied.

"It's just a very unexpected look for you," she said, eye balling his wardrobe. "I've seen a lot of pictures of you recently, and you never looked anything like this."

Blake didn't miss a beat. She would have been disappointed if he had. "I'm kind of trying to be a little incognito," he confessed. "After my last few cases became so public, I received a lot of media exposure. Now people approach me like I'm some kind of celebrity. Frankly, it's a pain in the ass. I started dressing like this away from work so I could do exactly what I'm doing now, walk in somewhere and have a drink." Patti was impressed. Blake's logic and ego certainly matched his short dissertation. Problem was, she knew that he was a serial killer and the clothes and mannerisms were just part of the set up. He wanted to blend in to the crowd to help cover his tracks. Blake finished his drink and ordered a second.

"Can I get you another?" he inquired, shaking his empty glass at the bartender to communicate his intention. He motioned to her glass as well in case his verbal request was being drowned out. Patti nodded and smiled. It was going to be hard to 'play' drunk around this guy. He was far from stupid. She could easily handle a few, but knew she couldn't take any chances. The bartender arrived with fresh drinks and their encounter continued. When Patti excused herself to go to the ladies room, she wasn't surprised when Alex followed.

In a matter of minutes, they were both standing in front of the mirrors touching up their makeup.

"So how are you holding up?" Alex asked.

Patti wasn't one to be shy. "Honestly," she said and then paused for a moment as she began to check out the surrounding stalls. Once she confirmed they were empty, she continued her thought. "This guy is some piece of work. I mean he's married to Katie but hitting on me because I look like her, right?"

Alex nodded so Patti continued.

"He wants to kill her because she's been cheating on him, but for some reason, he can't so he finds a 'look alike' like me to take her place instead to satisfy his needs. All in all I would say that he is one sick bastard! That, and the fact that he's so fucking smug, I just want to take out my gun and shoot him now!"

Alex capped her lipstick and returned it to her purse. "Let's just hope he takes the bait and makes a mistake," she offered.

Patti smiled. "Yeah," she said, as she put on her headset. "Let's hope. My trigger finger is getting itchy. I'd better get back," she added as she headed for the door. At the last second, she stopped and turned around. "Thanks again, Alex for having my back."

Alex acquiesced. "I know it wasn't in the plan for me to be in here with you," she admitted, "But what the hell," she smirked. "We girls have to stick together." Then she put on her headset and disguised it by covering it with her hair.

Patti smiled. "Then I'll see you back inside then, won't I?" she said.

"I'll give you a minute or so and find my way back to my seat," she assured her. "Be careful," she added. Patti nodded and then disappeared. She was half way into another martini when Alex saw her again.

* * * * *

Grey watched carefully as the mainsail held firm in the wind. It was a warm night, so the breeze that greeted them as they passed beyond the jetty and headed north was a pleasant addition to a slowly rolling sea. It was late, and other than a few large tankers anchored several miles out, they were alone on the stretch of water at least as far as the eye could see. Off to the right, the beach itself was deserted, only because the local curfew was 10 o'clock when it came to having gatherings on the sand. Tim remained focused, diligently trying to prepare for the coming task at hand.

At first Grey paid little attention to what Tm was doing. He had enough on his own mind to worry about. Several minutes passed before he realized that his friend was actually talking to him and had been trying to get his attention. Tim moved to the back of the boat to where Grey was standing.

"You all right?" he asked. "I think I lost you there for a few."

Grey looked puzzled. When the flashes had come, he wasn't quite sure they were real. Now, with Tim's obvious observation and inquiry, he had no choice but to take them seriously.

"Sorry man," he replied. "Listen Tim, you're going to think I'm crazy, but I need you to drop me off on the end of the pier." Grey pointed to the floating dock at the far end of the structure.

"You suddenly know something I don't?" Tim inquired.

"Not necessarily," Grey answered. "I had this weird thought a minute ago when you say I was 'out of it' and I need to check it out."

"Sounds crazy to me," Tim responded. "But what the hell, so does all of the rest of this anyway. Let me finish what I'm doing and I'll swing you by."

Grey looked up at the sail again as he made a course adjustment. They were now headed directly toward the end of the pier. It was not more than ten minutes away. Then he reached down and grabbed his headset off the seat. He wanted to get comfortable using it before he stepped off the boat. Communication between them for the next few hours was going to be crucial. He asked Tim to turn his on as well and talk to him for awhile. There was only the length of the boat between them, but it made him feel better.

The lights on the pier got brighter, the closer they moved in. Tim spent the rest of their time double checking his equipment. Grey realized that once he was on the pier, he was going to be very exposed. He looked at Tim's rifle and laughed, but dismissed the idea. They were now only several feet away. As Tim eased the boat up against the dock, Grey stepped off onto the landing.

"You on?" Tim asked, pointing a finger to his ear.

Grey nodded. "Thanks man, I'll see you later," he said. He gave Tim a 'thumbs up' and headed for the stairs.

"Be careful and keep your mic on," Tim ordered.

"Will do," Grey responded. He was all alone now on the pier.

The stairs were dark and creaky as he made his way up. He was amused by his accent from the darkness into the light. Alex would have loved the irony. It was a slow and steady climb.

"I should have mentioned the lights," he mumbled to himself. Before he could even continue the thought, Grey heard a small pop. The light at the top of the stairs vaporized into thin air.

"Damn!" he exclaimed quietly as he could hear the sound of low laughter in his ear.

"That ought to make things a little more comfortable," Tim's voice said. "It will be dark now when you step out on to the pier deck," he assured him.

"A little warning next time would be nice," Grey requested as he reached to top of the stairs.

The loss of just that one light made a bigger difference than he thought. There was a huge patch of shadow on the left side of the end deck platform. It would be much easier to start his walk down the length of the pier. Grey got moving. He ran out of shadow sooner than he would have liked. All he wanted to do now was make it the rest of the way without attracting any unwanted attention.

After walking about half way, he turned and saw that Tim had stopped the boat about fifty yards south of the pier.

"Hey Tim, you there?" he asked reluctantly in his microphone. "Watching you through my scope," Tim replied. Grey wasn't sure he liked the idea of being in someone's cross hairs. "You're doing fine," Tim added.

"I'm going to be easier to see from shore here in a few minutes," Grey observed. "I might need you to darken things up for me again," he chuckled.

Tim scanned the length of the pier and the surrounding shoreline.

He saw only a few people.

"That shouldn't be a problem," he said. "Just let me know."

If everything went according to plan, Patti would be able to keep Blake on the south side of the beach. Grey kept moving, but started to have second thoughts about the whole boat idea. His mind was racing and he was now fully exposed in the light. He started to pick up his pace.

"Not liking this," he mumbled under his breath. He forgot he was wearing his headset.

As he took another step, another light bulb exploded. He didn't hear a shot and there wasn't much of a pop this time, just instant shadow. The light just suddenly disappeared.

"Son of a bitch!" Grey said now startled a bit. The light pole was only a few feet away. Grey could hear laughter on the other end of his receiver.

"Very funny," Grey responded. He took and few more steps and realized that he was home free. "By the way my friend, nice shot," he added as he stepped off into the sand. Tim watched as Grey disappeared into the shadows under the pier.

There was a short break before Tim was back on the air. "Not bad," he conceded. "I can barely make you out under there, even with my night vision scope."

"Let's hope you don't have to use it," Grey replied.

There was a long silence before Tim spoke again. "Patti's good Grey," he said trying to assure him. "I'm just back up. There's not much she can't handle."

Tim paused again to think about what he had just said. For a moment, he wasn't sure if he was trying to convince Grey or himself.

"She's damn good," he reminded himself under his breath. Grey heard him but let the moment pass. Grey knew he was lucky having Tim around. His cockiness was good. His humanity was better.

* * * * *

CHAPTER 33

Blake had to take a piss. He didn't want to leave Patti alone at the bar, but he didn't have much of a choice. When nature called, it called. The third martini he was working on was ready to hit bottom. She'd had her turn, now it was his. Now wasn't the time to start getting paranoid. For the first time, he wasn't afraid of losing contact with her. She seemed be having a good time. As far as the 'Cat' was concerned, her prior illusiveness was no longer an issue. There was an established level of comfort between them now. Blake figured he was on a roll. All he needed to do now was get a few more drinks in her and he'd be on his way.

"Let's go down on the beach and walk it off," he would say when the time came. It would be a totally plausible idea. With all of the vodka swimming around in her head by then, he would meet with little resistance.

The south side of the pier was his target. It was much darker there than going north because the houses were so set back off the boardwalk. Their light barely trickled out onto the sand. If they went north, a parking lot and a collection of restaurants ran for a good several blocks. The heavy onslaught of illumination carried almost all the way down to the water, increasing their exposure to a much higher level. No, south was definitely the answer and the later it got, the more desolate it became. Before he could get too excited, Blake got up.

"If you will excuse me for a moment, I'll be right back," he said tipping his glass again in the direction of the bartender.

Patti nodded and watched him disappear into the crowd. She turned just in time to see Alex get up to follow him. Patti took a deep breath. Having Alex there was already starting to pay off. Patti watched as she disappeared into the crowd. Once Alex confirmed where he was going, she stepped back into Patti's line of sight and gave her a signal.

Once inside the men's room, Blake discovered chaos. The wall units were completely occupied, so he quickly ducked into a stall to do his thing. When he emerged, the room was crowded, but he said nothing to anyone. He only stopped for a moment when he caught a glimpse of himself in the mirror.

The first thing he noticed was that his eyes were now yellow instead of their usual brilliant shade of blue. His million dollar smile was now filled with teeth that were more threatening than kind. He knew that the 'Cat' was taking over. He was so close now, so very close to the culmination of his quest, that all he could do was simply try to hang on. There was no point in fighting back. Blake washed his hands, grinned in the mirror, and then headed back into the main room. Alex remained vigilant, but waited until Blake had returned to the bar before moving back to her seat.

"Well, so where were we?" Blake asked as slithered back into position.

Patti laughed. "Somewhere between here," she said in a drunken giggle while pointing to the top of her glass, "and there," she finished now pointing to the bottom. "There's nothing better than a 'fresh' martini," she added. Then, she licked her index finger and ran it around the rim of her glass just to make sure he was paying attention.

Inside him, the 'Cat' was going crazy. This was exactly the situation his darker side had hoped for. Patti didn't know it, but suddenly, Blake could feel the claws begin to penetrate again.

Patti gave him a moment to consider her behavior and formulate his next move. Then she followed up with, "What do you think?" she inquired playfully. This time, she dipped her finger into her glass, swirled it around a bit, and then returned to licking her finger.

Blake looked at his watch. There was still a half hour before last call. Unless he wanted to have to carry her out, this was going to have to be her last martini. The 'Cat' grinned but Blake took a moment to consider what the word 'last' really meant. If the rest of his evening was successful, he could lock away the darkness in him forever. The 'Cat' would go clawing and screaming, but in the end he would be contained again. This time however, the last brick would be set and the mortar would dry.

"For the love of God, Blake," he heard the voice say. Blake laughed.

"Is something funny?" Patti asked. Blake snapped back in.

"No," he said. "I was just thinking that maybe we should take a break and go get some air. Martini's go down way too easy."

Patti looked at her watch. "It's almost closing time," she said. "They're going to throw us out of here soon anyway." In the back of her head, she knew the boys were listening.

Blake pounced on the opportunity. "Maybe we should go down to the beach and walk some of this off," he suggested. "*There! He'd said it, and it sounded well played,*" he thought.

Patti played the 'drunk' for a second by holding on to the bar and then slowly nodded her head. "Game on, Mr. Kendall," she heartily insisted.

Blake smiled. So did two men who were patiently waiting outside for her under the cover of night. When Patti turned, Alex had already left her barstool.

"Game on," Grey heard Tim reply. That was all that needed to be said.

Patti grabbed her purse off the side of her chair and started to find her feet. She knew where they were, but it was more important than ever now to keep up the charade. She knew that Blake was aware of her new residence down the street and wondered if he would say something about taking her home. He didn't. That all but assured her that once they were outside, they would be headed in the opposite direction. She was surprised that when they stepped out into the now cool night air, Blake made no move in any direction. Instead, he got her to take a seat on a large round concrete bench that was sitting in the middle of the foyer in front of the entrance to the pier. Alex could see them clearly and waited for Blake to make his next move.

"We can still take that walk if you want to," he offered, "but first let's clear your head a little."

Patti lit a cigarette. This was more to play the part than anything else. Blake was surprised.

"Give me a minute," she said, "and then we can go," she assured him. It had been ten years since her last one, but it went down smooth. Her eyes scanned the area but couldn't spot Alex. It didn't matter though. Alex was like a shadow. Patti knew she was close. The beach was deserted. Only the sound of the waves was there to break the silence of the night. Patti took one last drag on her cigarette and was ready to move. It was now or never.

* * * * *

Grey sat quietly under the pier waiting for the hammer to fall. The tide was coming in but there was still an hour or so before it might start to become a problem. He could see the 29th, anchored about fifty yards south of the pier. There was no one on deck, but he assumed that Tim was trying to stay out of sight so as not to arouse any suspicion. He could hear Patti engaging Blake as she stumbled along down the beach trying to sober up. He had to admit, she was good. Blake seemed to be salivating over her every word. When he looked down at his hand, his ring glowed. There was the distinct smell of wet leather behind him that conflicted with the fresh ocean breeze. Grey knew he wasn't alone. It was only a matter of time now before Blake and Patti would come wandering back this way. Blake would try to kill her near the pier. He knew it. He had seen it in his dreams. That's why he had made Tim drop him on the end of the pier. He needed to be here. He needed to finish what he started.

Alex was ready. She followed Patti almost step for step as she and Blake had left the bar. Their steps on the sand had been matched by hers on the boardwalk as she maintained her surveillance in the darken shadows of the houses as she moved along the waterfront. Through her headset, she had been able to follow every word of their conversation. She monitored Tim and Grey's exchanges as well. Patti had played the perfect drunk. Heading down the beach, she wasn't too awkward, but she definitely appeared to be losing steam on the way back. Alex advanced as close as she could without being seen. When they got close to the pier, there was nothing more she could do. She hoped the boys were waiting.

* * * * *

It was pushing three a.m. when Grey saw their silhouettes coming closer in the distance. They'd be on top of him in a matter of minutes. Grey eased his way back under the decking as far as he thought he could go. The light stopped a few feet in front of him so he was confident that the darkness would shield him. He had just worked himself into a safe position when he heard Blake's voice. This time it wasn't in the headset. They would be under the pier in a matter of seconds.

Blake could feel the adrenaline starting to build. The lawyer in him wanted to be more patient, but the 'Cat' knew he was ready. Blake guided Patti a few more steps into the darkness under the pier. He was ready to make his move.

With his left side to the water, only Tim could see what was happening with his hand. Grey had to rely on instincts and body language.

"I can't see his left hand," Grey whispered into his headset.

"It's in his pocket," Tim responded. Grey slumped down, further back into the shadows.

Patti was doing her part. She was trying to make it so that Blake would need both of his hands to steady her. This intoxicated dance went on for several minutes and eventually forced Blake to bring out an empty left hand to assist her. She was moving too much for him to get a clean attempt at her throat. Grey flinched when he saw her head shake and her headset fall gently to the sand. Blake was too busy trying to hang on to her to notice, so Grey breathed a little easier when she managed to drag her foot and cover it up. Blake finally had no choice but to lean her up and steady her against one of the outside pylons. The moment she was stable, his hand went back into his pocket.

Once again, Blake was facing north so Tim could see his left profile. Even through the darkness, Grey could see the vengeance in Blake's eyes. They were dark and cold. Grey was sure that at any moment, Blake was going to reach out, even though he and Patti were face to face now, and cut her throat just so he could watch her die.

Grey lost his breath when he saw Blake's shoulder slowly starting to move. Then, he heard Tim say, "I see something shiny." Ever so slowly, Blake's hand continued to rise. The 'Cat' was ready to strike.

"I got a blade," Tim said, describing to Grey what he could now see in his scope. Blake had been proficient enough to open it with one hand.

Suddenly, a voice came out of the shadows.

"Blake," Grey heard his own voice say sternly. He hadn't planned it. It just sort of happened.

For a split second, Blake thought he was dreaming. There was just enough of a pause that it allowed Tim to shoot.

No one heard the shot. What little sound it actually made was drowned out by the surf. Tim only kept the rifle in his hands long enough to watch Blake fall. In a matter of seconds, he was already on the move. As the bullet ripped through Blake's flesh, the blade fell helplessly down to the wet sand. Blake, himself wasn't far behind. The impact to his shoulder was so great, that it knocked him off his feet sending him flailing to the ground as well. Patti was forced down and away simply by the weight of Blake's body. Within seconds, she was back on her feet, gun drawn and on target. Blake was down and bleeding badly. Part of his upper shoulder was now splattered across her chest. She could feel small pieces of flesh and blood on her cheek. The bullet had done its job. His left shoulder was opened. The gaping wound looked like it had been formed by a small explosion. The fresh carnage was exposed and vulnerable to the elements. Each kiss from the incoming surf seemed to draw more blood.

Patti's eyes moved slightly away from Blake, trying to locate the razor in the sand. She had to move fast. At first, it was hard to spot, but then she saw something sparkle in the water. She was lucky. The receding tide had already started to bury it. She moved quickly and plucked it from the sand. Then her eyes went immediately back to

Blake. She could tell he was no longer a threat. Suddenly, she heard Grey's voice behind her.

"You ok?" he asked, as he stepped out from under the pier. "That was pretty close."

Both Patti and her gun stayed focused on Blake.

Before she could answer, Grey closed the gap between them. He looked out and saw the boat moving toward the end of the pier. Tim would be here in a matter of minutes.

"Don't let her take her attention off him until I get there," Tim said in his ear.

"That's not going to be a problem," Grey assured him. "What?" Patti asked, knowing she had missed something.

"Tim said to give him two minutes," Grey lied. He just wanted to keep her focused until Tim arrived.

Patti was breathing hard now. "Guess that 'Son of a bitch' can still shoot," she said almost laughing. She took a few slow deep breaths to help her get control of the moment. Then Alex appeared.

"You all right, Patti?" she asked. Patti's eyes never left Blake or her gun.

"I think we all are now," she answered.

Grey just nodded and smiled as the water kept nibbling at Blake. Then, they waited together, just staring at the body bleeding on the beach.

* * * * *

"Is he alive?" Grey finally asked. No one had bothered to go check him since he went down. Blake hadn't moved in several minutes.

"Not if we're lucky," Tim said as he came around the corner and ducked under the pier. "Is everybody all right?"

Everyone relaxed a little as Tim made his way over to Patti and relieved her of her weapon.

"Grey?" a voice said. It was almost imagined because it was so soft that it was nearly inaudible and drowned out by the surf. "Is that you?" it continued.

Grey looked down at the body on the sand. When he tried to take a step toward it, Patti stopped him. "No," she ordered him. "He could still be dangerous." Grey kept his distance.

"I called for an ambulance," Tim informed them. "It'll be here any minute. Nice work, you guys," he said.

"Grey, I know it's you," a voice came again. It was louder now and carried a deeper, more desperate type of firmness. "Did I get her?" it inquired.

Now, speaking in sentences, its delivery confused Grey. The tone, the depth and the even more chilling under tone were definitely not Blake's. Grey wasn't sure how to respond.

"Get who?" he said after a long pause.

Blake's good arm and hand moved slightly, but he couldn't seem to manage anything more than a few inches as he spoke. "The girl," he continued. "Is she dead?"

Blake's eyes remained closed during his inquiry. Grey was almost afraid to see what was behind them if they opened. He thought twice before answering Blake's question.

"No," he finally volunteered. "Detective Garrison is just fine. Not even a scratch," he assured him.

Grey watched as Blake's body wrenched a little and then stiffen in the sand as the words permeated their way in. His right hand became a clenched fist. He tried to move, but the loss of blood and impending shock from the bullet's damage kept him firmly on his back.

"Then all is lost," the strange voice conceded. "I have failed." Blake's face began to take on a demeanor of defeat. Grey could sense an evil behind his words.

Grey turned to move away, but then made one last attempt. "Blake," he began.

The body beneath him stirred. "Blake only exists when I want him to," the eerie voice responded. The 'Cat' was now center stage. "I am in command!" it added. "I am the reason he kills!"

Grey's face went blank. Alex moved in when she saw the color draining from his cheeks.

What the.....?" she began to ask when the voice continued from below.

"The little girl may have enticed me to stay with her, but I betrayed him by never trying to find my way home. I knew he loved me, but I didn't care. When he found me, he took his revenge by slitting my throat and hung me up on display in the garage. As I was dying, I looked in his eyes and swore I would make him kill again, only this time it would be the one he loved the most."

Alex and Grey just stood there in shock. Was this some kind of confession? Blake was obviously delirious now and Grey was relieved to hear the sounds of the sirens approaching and then pulling into the parking lot. Then, Grey heard something even more disconcerting.

"Am I going to die?" a voice asked. It was a bit softer, but this time it was definitely Blake's.

Grey looked out at the ocean. The 29th was still bobbing along, safely tied up at the end of the pier. "I don't know," he answered. Then he turned and moved away. He joined Patti and Alex at the entrance to the pier.

The paramedics came and tended to Blake, finally having to settle on placing him on a backboard in order to carry him off the sand. They transferred him to a gurney when they got him back on the boardwalk. As they passed their small group, Blake reached out his good hand and grabbed Grey's arm. Grey nearly froze when he saw his friend's eyes. Whatever creature was driving Blake now had completely taken over again.

"This isn't over," it assured him, its eyes cutting deep into Grey's soul. Grey started to pull back but then suddenly changed his mind.

"Can I have a second with him?" he asked Tim, making a point to hold out his own open hand. When Grey wiggled his hand, Tim understood. Grey stepped forward and grabbed Blake's hand. It was a long, strong grip. For a few brief seconds, he could see both personalities battling inside of Blake. It was horrific. Grey let go.

"Thanks, Tim," he offered. Tim just nodded.

"Just explain it to me later, ok?" Tim requested.

The four friends watched as they loaded Blake into an ambulance and off he went. Tim insisted on police protection for Mr. Kendall until further notice. The attending officer looked puzzled by the request, but complied and assured him it would be taken care of.

Tim grimaced when he saw Wickmann's cruiser pull up. The sergeant looked more concerned than angry. He took one look at their motley crew and said, "How did I know that I was going to find you in the middle of this, Galleon? I told you to take a few days off."

Tim offered an outstretched hand. Wickmann shook it. Then Tim turned to Patti.

"Sergeant Art Wickmann, This is Detective Patti Garrison, Las Vegas P.D. We worked together down here years ago when we were first starting out." Patti shook Art's hand.

"Sergeant," she said, subtly trying to be official. "Detective," he responded.

"As for these other two," Tim began, "Civilians, but more importantly, friends."

"Grey Thomas, Sergeant," Grey offered his hand. Wickmann took it and nodded.

"Alex Matthews," she said and offered her hand as well.

Now void of the pleasantries, Wickmann immediately took over. "I don't suppose that one of you can explain this to me?" he inquired.

This drew a blank response from everyone. "Know where we can get coffee?" Tim teased.

"Are you suggesting that we take this back to the station?" Wickmann asked.

"I am at that," Tim replied. "It will save us a lot of time and hassle in the long run. I figure, after this, we're all going to end up down there sooner or later anyway," he pointed out.

"You're probably right," Wickmann agreed.

"What about the 29th?" Grey reminded everyone. He was looking out at the water for a moment and suddenly remembered she was still there.

"I'll get the Coast Guard to keep an eye on her," Wickmann offered. "Or, if you prefer, I can even have someone move her back to the marina for you if you want."

"That'd be great, man, Thanks," Tim said gratefully.

Patti took a look around. There were a lot of cops working the scene and she knew from experience that they were going to be there for awhile. "So, are we ready to go then?" she asked. Everyone nodded.

"Tim, you ride with me," Wickmann insisted.

Alex grabbed her keys. "I'm close," she said to Grey and Patti. "Why don't you guys ride with me?"

"I'm in," Patti agreed.

"You'll probably want to call 'shot-gun' too then," Grey teased.

Patti smiled. "I'm probably safer in the back anyway," Grey conceded.

The two girls just laughed. Alex was only a block away, but no one said anything more on the way to the car. Each of them was lost in their own train of thought. The silence remained until they arrived at the station.

* * * * *

Things were quickly going from bad to worse. The chief wasn't buying their story. As much as Tim hated to admit it, he understood why. Even Wickmann was looking at him like he thought he was still shaken up from the Corvette incident. The four friends sat together in a large interview room waiting to see what the District Attorney's office was going to say. Their story had been the truth; and nothing but the truth; at least the part about following through on their suspicions was concerned, but they couldn't answer the 'how' or 'where' they had obtained their information from. No one would believe them.

Tim's explanation for shooting Blake was at least legitimate. He was taking appropriate action to protect a fellow police officer. Patti, of course concurred. They both insisted that it was a 'clean shoot'. The problem was that none of them could justify why they were out there in the first place. The entire incident was obviously a premeditated action. Tim couldn't prove that Blake intended to kill Patti with the straight razor. To someone outside of their circle, it was merely an assumption. Even if his prints were still on it, (doubtful after its time in the surf,) it could not be positively identified as the murder weapon in the "Ripper' case. If Kendall died, the four of them were looking at some serious charges. Grey considered showing the D.A. what he could do, but decided not to open another can of worms.

The press was already having a field day. The vans started to show up almost as fast as the ambulance. Reporting that someone had shot the legendary Blake Kendall was news. Fortunately, the department had managed to keep a tight lid on the situation. No one outside of the conference room knew the real truth. The A.D.A. had unloaded on the chief almost immediately, screaming something about off duty cops playing vigilantes, and how if anyone found out, Kendall's lawyers, if not the man himself (Blake was listed in critical but stable condition) were going to sue the living hell out of everyone especially the department. Walter Greenburg was already hounding them for a statement.

Grey felt his phone buzz and saw it was a text from Father Richard. It wouldn't hurt to look.

CAN'T SLEEP IS EVERTHING OK ?

Grey laughed and then showed it to Alex. "Guess I should have called him, huh?" he said.

"And say what?" Tim interrupted. "It's better if we leave the old man out of this, don't you think?"

Grey nodded, and then answered his friend. He knew Richard would worry.

IT'S ALL OVER WE'RE All DOWN AT
THE POLICE
STATION I'LL CALL YOU IN THE MORNING

"Think he'll be all right? Alex asked.

"I'm hoping he's tired," Grey offered. "It's after four," he observed. "Tim's right," he added. "Better if he sits this one out."

An hour later, they were all still waiting. Grey looked at the mirror on the wall. "That's one of those two way mirrors, isn't it?" he said directing his question to Tim.

Tim rolled his eyes. "Yeah, now that you mention it, it is," he chuckled. "We better not make any quick moves or obscene gestures," he joked. "We wouldn't want to antagonize Mr. District Attorney!"

That seemed to do the trick. Within seconds, the door opened and in walked the D.A., Elliot Callahan himself. He was furious.

"I guess you don't realize Detective Galleon how much trouble you and Detective Garrison are really in, here," he began. "Not to mention the two civilians you managed to drag into this nightmare."

This guy was a pompous ass. Grey had had enough. "Well you certainly had nothing going for you on this case before Tim and Patti stepped in, did you?" he smirked. This really pissed off Callahan.

"You think that's funny?" the D.A. exploded. "How about an accessory to murder charge if Kendall dies?" he bellowed.

Grey wouldn't back down. "Kendall won't die," he countered. "You'd never let that happen. Not from a shoulder wound anyway. You're lucky Tim is a damn good shot. If he wanted Kendall dead, he'd be dead. Tim was just preventing an attack on Detective Garrison. No, you'll get Blake back alive so you can have your high profile media trial, get your name in the paper, your face on T.V. and get even with Kendall for all the times he's humiliated you in court by kicking your ass. Hell, after the trial, you might even want to run for Governor."

Tim was speechless. Grey's outburst had caught everyone in the room completely off guard. "And by the way, sir," (the sir could not have been anymore condescending or sarcastic) Grey added, "They didn't drag us 'civilians' into anything. I went to them!"

Tim leaned back in his chair and put his feet up on the desk. Patti tried desperately to contain her laughter.

"You all think you're so God damn funny, don't you?" the D.A. shouted. He was poised to continue his verbal assault when suddenly he was interrupted by a knock on the door and in popped Father Richard. The D.A. was caught completely by surprise. He paused for a moment as he took note of Richard's white clerical collar, and then immediately began offering his apologies.

"I had no idea you were there Father," Callahan started to retreat.

Richard politely ignored him and directed his attention to the group. He held out his left hand which contained his Ipad and began to speak.

"While you all have been out playing "21 Jump Street," I decided to follow up on something that we discussed previously in my office." Then Richard looked at Patti. "Do you think I'm going to need a lawyer before I continue?" he asked.

Patti smiled. "I don't think so," she said. "Do you Mr. D.A.?" Callahan shook his head, embarrassed now and motioned for Father Richard to continue.

"Do you really think you can shed some light on this matter for us, Father?" he inquired.

"Yes sir, I do," Richard responded. "I have spent the past twenty-four hours on my computer trying to match any similar "Ripper" type murders over the past three decades to where Blake Kendall was known to be in the vicinity at the time. I have come up with at least a dozen matches putting him near the victims at the time of the killings. There were five back in his college days when he lived on the east coast. That's where he met his wife. The rest are the most recent ones that we know about now. They include Casey Riddell and Kelly Richfield whose names I am sure you are familiar with."

Richard was all smiles. "I can show you if you wish," he offered extending his hand that held the Ipad. "I also find it very interesting that all of the victims, both then and now bear a striking resemblance to Blake's wife, Katie," he added.

"Are you serious?" Callahan inquired. "Show me what you have, Father," he requested.

All eyes were now on Richard. Grey wasn't worried. His friend had lots of experience with being the center of attention. Pleasing his congregation was a much greater challenge to him, than having to impress some trigger happy D.A. Grey could tell by Richard's expressions that he was ready and able to step forward.

Richard took a seat at the conference table and fired up his laptop. He was ready to put on a show. "I tried to set this up like a power point presentation," he said. "I'm a little rusty, I'm afraid, so please understand."

Callahan watched as screen after screen went by with all of the information Richard had spoken of. He had even highlighted most of the major details in red. Richard also did his best to narrate as they went along. When they came to the last page, there was a picture of what appeared to be an investigation room setup, complete with write ups, and several display boards with names and ideas.

"What's this?" Callahan asked with sincere curiosity.

Richard almost blushed as he chuckled. "Oh, I'm sorry," he said. "That's my office at the church," he continued. "I've been trying to do my best to help out, sir."

Callahan looked at the group around him. "Did you know about any of this?" he inquired.

"We knew he was up to something," Grey answered. "I guess you'd just have to know Father Richard," he added.

Callahan looked back at Richard. "Well, Father," he began, "At first glance, I must say it looks rather impressive. When do think I could see it?"

"God is open twenty-four hours a day, sir," he offered. "We can go there immediately if you wish."

His response seemed to please Callahan. The District Attorney's tone was suddenly much friendlier now. The D.A looked over at Galleon and Wickmann. "You do realize that we're going to have to check all of this out right?" he insisted.

Wickmann nodded. "Of course," he said. "How would you like us to proceed?"

Before Callahan could answer, Tim interrupted. "You'd better plan to be there a while," he said. "Knowing Father Richard, I think you'll find that a trip to his office will be not only interesting, but that his research will be thorough an accurate as well."

"You seem to have quite a fan club," Callahan commended. Then he looked back at Tim. "I'm going to go clear this little excursion," he said. "I'll be right back." The door shut and the four friends were alone again.

For a moment, no one said a word. They all just stared at Richard. The priest was busy packing up his things. He caught Grey staring at him. "What?" he inquired.

Grey just shook his head. "What do you mean, what?" he responded.

"Well, you didn't expect me to sit around and do nothing, did you?" Richard replied.

Patti and Alex giggled.

"Actually Father, I'm glad you didn't," Tim interjected. "You may have just paid for our ticket out of here."

The girls were both smiling. "That's some really nice work, Father," Patti volunteered. On that, they all agreed.

"Let's just pray it's enough," Richard opted. Callahan is going to need all of the ammunition he can get. Blake has been at this for a long time."

Alex nodded and then made an observation. "If he was killing back then, what made him stop and go into remission for all this time? That, of course, and what triggered him to go off again?"

Grey figured he knew the answer. "He is manipulated by his other personality that he calls the 'Cat'. It comes from something horrific he did to one as a child. He slit a cat's throat because it ran away to live with someone else. It betrayed him so in his mind, the 'Cat' has haunted him ever since. When Katie Kendall got pregnant in college and it threatened his future, he took that as a sign of betrayal. He couldn't kill her or his unborn child, so the 'Cat' allowed him to substitute 'look- alikes' to satisfy the need. The killing started and didn't end until he found a way to reconcile with Katie. Life moved on."

Father Richard was completely enthralled by every word. "That makes perfect sense and helps explain everything I've found," he concluded.

"Now we skip forward to present day," Grey continued. The killings started again right after Christmas. This is about the time that Blake found out that was wife was having an affair with Walter Greenberg."

"Walter Greenberg?" Tim asked, slightly puzzled. "The one who's presently screaming downtown for answers from Callahan?"

"That's him," Grey assured him. "Blake finds out about the affair and, bam! Katie had betrayed him again, so the 'Cat' came back to the surface seeking his revenge."

Richard was clapping softly. It was a strange reaction, but he didn't know what else to do.

"It's as if you were looking over my shoulder the entire time I was working," he said. "If we can tie this all together with all of these factual examples, we should be able to avoid the 'how and where' we obtained our initial information issue."

"Of course Callahan will have to be the final judge as to how he makes the case," Tim added.

"Speaking of Callahan," Patti observed, "I wonder where he disappeared to."

As if he'd been listening just outside the door, Callahan suddenly re-appeared.

"Are you guys ready to move?" he asked. He didn't have to ask twice. "You're all officially in my custody for now," he informed them as they quickly filed out of the room. "At least until we're finished at the church."

Wickmann was the last one out. "Good call, Elliott," he said as he passed Callahan who was holding the door.

"The brass will have both our asses if this doesn't pan out," the D.A. said as they moved down the hall. "I hope you're right about this one." "I know Galleon wouldn't be doing this if he had any doubts,"

Wickmann replied. "If that crazy old priest is right, then you've got your killer and we're home free."

"Just remember to memorize the phrase, 'reliable source', Callahan joked. "We're going to be using it a lot."

When they reached the parking lot, the rest of the group was waiting outside. "How do you want to ride over 'Sarge'?" Tim inquired.

Callahan fielded the question instead. "Take your own vehicles," he ordered. "I have a feeling that after our little visit to the church, things are going to work out in your favor." Then he gave Richard a nod. "Father," he said. Richard just smiled.

Galleon and Wickmann headed for Wickmann's car. "I think I'll ride over with you," Callahan insisted. "It will look more professional that way." Tim opened the rear door and got in leaving the passenger seat available for the D.A.

"That's not necessary, Detective," Callahan observed.

"I know," Tim assured him and shut the door. (*"A little respect never hurt, now did it?"),* he thought.

Once they were safely in the car, Callahan shared some of his thoughts. "We're going to have to be very careful about this one," he began. "Blake Kendall is a major player around here and very well connected. When the press gets wind of this thing"

"They'll only get what we choose to give them," Tim interrupted. "We won't have to explain the investigation, just the end results."

"We can hope," Callahan offered as he shifted in his seat. "And about the details, if everything is what you say it is, then I don't think I want to know."

Tim looked out the window of the cruiser and watched the street lights go by. They gave off a weird glow in the early hours of the morning that made one think that something about them wasn't even real.

"You're right, mister D.A.," Tim mumbled softly to himself. "You really don't want to know."

* * * * *

CHAPTER 34

Everyone reconvened in the sanctuary of the church before being led into Father Richard's office. The early morning sunlight was just beginning to slip through the stained glass windows to start a new day. The brilliant colors cast an indoor rainbow over the entire room. Only Callahan was unaffected by their beauty. His mind was completely overwhelmed by the magnitude of the display Richard had created. Wickmann was impressed as well. For the first few minutes, no one spoke as the District Attorney and the Sergeant moved curiously from display to display. By the time they finally addressed the group, Callahan's mind was made up.

"Can I borrow these?" he said as he smiled gratefully to the old priest.

Richard nodded. "I've always enjoyed puzzles," he said. "Consider this one a gift," he offered.

Wickmann smiled and patted Callahan on the back. "I think we've got him Elliott," he said motioning to the display boards. "I'll be a 'son of a bitch,' but I think we've got him."

Grey walked over and offered his hand to his friend. Richard wanted no part of it. He grabbed Grey by the shoulders and proceeded to give him a big bear hug. "You're a crazy old man," Grey said.

"So where do we go from here?" Alex asked.

"I'm going to send over a team to photograph all of this and then have it transferred down town," Callahan answered. "Then we wait and see what happens with Kendall at the hospital."

"His status just changed from being a protected victim to a guarded suspect?" Patti gloated.

"That's right," Callahan assured them. "I'll make the call myself. You guys should all go home and get some rest," he suggested.

"So we're all free to go?" Tim inquired.

"Yes, Detective," Callahan insisted. "You're all free to go,"

A quiet calm slowly engulfed the room. For the first time since the accident, Grey's mind was suddenly at ease. Richard went to his chair and sat for moment, carefully admiring his work. Grey knew his friend was just making sure that he hadn't missed anything. Alex and Patti were talking in the corner and the three law enforcement officials were discussing their next plan of action. Grey found a spot in a far corner where all of the colors seemed to melt into one. He closed his eyes and stood in the light as it beamed gloriously in through the window. He hadn't been there long before he felt a hand on his shoulder.

"Wild ride, huh?" she said. He didn't have to turn around.

"I could not have done this without you," he said. "You made it all come together."

Alex patted him again. "No my friend, it was you and only you, that had the power to pull this off. You gathered us all together. There is no 'I' in team."

"Are you two about ready?" Tim asked. "You should take Grey home and get some rest. We can catch up with you later."

"I want to be there when Callahan confronts Blake," Grey insisted.

"You think he's going to live?" Richard chimed in.

"I know he is," Grey responded. "And I want to see the look in his eyes when they tell him. I promised someone I would," he said glancing over at Richard.

"So I guess we're off to the hospital then?" Tim inquired.

"After everything you've been through, I'm not arguing," Tim replied.

Someone will be here shortly to start handling this stuff, Father," Callahan said, "If that's ok with you?"

"That's fine with me," Richard answered. "I must say that I'll be glad to get rid of all of this. The subject matter has been very unsettling."

"You've done one hell of a job Father," Callahan began. Then he blushed a bit. "Sorry Father," he apologized. "It's just a bad habit. I can't seem to get it right with you can I?" he acknowledged.

"Nonsense," Richard said. "You've done a good thing here today.

Thank you for helping my friends."

"If you ever want a job as an investigator," Callahan teased.

"I'll stick to investigating scripture," Richard replied. "I find it to be a lot less stressful."

The two men shook hands and then Callahan left the room.

Everyone else was standing by the door.

"I'll call you when it's over," Grey offered.

"All of you need to go home and get some sleep," Richard ordered. "We will, my friend, we will. As soon as I see Callahan tell Blake he's finished," Grey said.

Everyone waved as they made their way out of the sanctuary. Once they were in the parking lot, Tim spoke up. "You sure you want to go to the hospital?" he asked.

"Blake just woke up," Grey replied. Even Alex looked at him funny. "Do I even want to know how you knew that?" Tim inquired. "Probably not," Grey responded. "Can we go now?" he insisted. "I really don't want to miss this."

"I'll get the car," Alex said, and quickly disappeared.

"I wonder what he'll have to say," Patti inquired. "I mean Blake that is." There was a brief pause.

"I just hope that there aren't any more victims than we don't know about," she added.

"Let's go put this to rest," Grey said. "I'm tired and I want to see my wife and kid."

Alex pulled up and Grey got in. "See you guys at the hospital?" he said. Patti and Tim waved.

"Nice job, Patti," Tim acknowledged. "You had me worried for a minute."

Patti leaned over and kissed him on the cheek. "Does Renee know how lucky she is?" she said softly.

"I'd like to think so," Tim responded. "Anyway, let's get going," he said. "I hate to admit it, but I want to be there too." It was a short walk to the car.

* * * * *

When Blake opened he eyes, he knew immediately that something was wrong. His head hurt, but that didn't even begin to compare to the pain he felt in his left shoulder. When he tried to turn his head to look over, all he could see was white bandages, and a tray of bloody medical instruments partially obscured by a drawn bedside curtain. It only took a second for anxiety to set in. Where was his arm? His brain told him to move his hand, but his mind was so numb that he couldn't tell if he was wiggling his fingers or not. When he tried to reach over with his right hand, he was shocked to discover that it had been tied down. Now the panic really began to grow. He started to move around in bed, only to find that his legs had been strapped down as well. The hospital staff had restrained him immediately after Callahan's call.

"He's waking up," he heard a strange voice say "Go get somebody." It didn't take more than a minute before a tall man entered the room. Blake tried to focus on the man's face, but it wasn't until he spoke that Blake could identify him.

"Blake," the man asked. "Can you hear me?"

"Callahan, Elliott Callahan. Is that you?" he inquired. The volume of his voice was almost non-existent.

"Yes Blake, it's me," Callahan responded.

"What the hell happened to me?" Blake inquired.

"You've been shot," Callahan answered. "By an off duty cop," he added.

It was quite obvious to Callahan by simply judging the change in Blake's body language, that the information he had just given was not being received well. "Did you get him?" Blake asked. This time, his voice was different, deeper.

"I think so," Callahan offered. "He should be here any minute."

"Why here?" the deeper voice continued. It was getting less groggy by the minute.

"I want him to tell you why," Callahan confessed.

The body in the hospital bed started to stiffen. Callahan knew he had struck a nerve. His phone buzzed so he looked at it. Galleon and his friends were in the building.

When Callahan looked back at the man lying on the bed, a chill ran down his spine. Blake's eyes were open now and the look in them was more terrifying than anything Callahan had ever seen before. He was about to take a step back, when suddenly, Blake spoke. This time, there was no doubt in his mind that whoever he was talking to now; it wasn't Blake.

"Restraining me was a good idea," the creature began. "How did you know it was me?"

Callahan was about to offer a response when another voice cut in. "He didn't," Grey said. "I did," he continued firmly. "I told them everything about you."

The 'Cat' was angry now and started trying to break free. He shook his body violently on the bed enough to start tearing out some of the stitches in his arm.

"Can't I just shoot him again?" a new voice inquired

"Galleon!" the voice screamed. "You lousy Son of a Bitch. I should have killed you when I had the chance."

Tim wasn't even remotely entertained. He grabbed a chair, sat down, and put his feet up on the end of the bed. "I should have aimed a little higher," he said. His comment and position of his feet just further irritated the situation.

"I want him arrested," the creature screamed. He was now fully agitated and out of control.

The officer assigned to guard the door stuck his head in for a moment, but Callahan sent him away. During the outburst, both Tim and Alex had joined them in the room.

"On what grounds?" Callahan asked.

"He tried to kill me!" the creature screamed again.

"How ironic is that?" Callahan said sarcastically, "You just tried to kill someone yourself. That's why Galleon over there shot you." He motioned to Tim who was still sitting in the chair with his feet up. The door opened and Patti came into the room.

"She's not dead!" the creature bellowed echoing great surprise. His body tensed up so much this time that it looked like it was going to explode.

"You lose," Callahan said as he motioned to clear the room. Grey was the last one out.

"This isn't over," Blake, (or whatever was left of him) reminded him again.

"It's over enough for me," Grey responded.

"You can't prove anything," the voice insisted. "There is no physical evidence that connects me to the crimes. Everything is pure speculation." There was a little breath of Blake but then it disappeared.

"We have a weapon," Grey volunteered. "We can place you near every one of the murders both now and twenty years ago."

The creature laughed; a little because Blake was now so submerged inside him that he couldn't dig him out in time to argue the point, or maybe because he thought Grey was just completely full of shit.

"Tell Blake I know what he going through," Grey said, deciding to fight back. "I get where he's coming from."

"You know nothing of my ways," the 'Cat' lashed back in fury. For a moment, Grey wondered if his being tied to the bed was going to be enough.

"You know the other voice Blake, the one you call the 'Cat'?" The creature's eyes glowed now in horror. "Well, I've got something too," Grey said. As his words left his lips, Grey put his hand on what was left of the mutilated arm of the 'thing' that was tossing in the bed. When he did, the door between them opened and the flashes began. The world turned to blood. Grotesque carnage was everywhere, a dead feline hanging from a rope in the garage. It didn't stop there. The mutilated faces of victims flashed by, crying out for help. Grey focused hard. He wanted it all. Suddenly, there was a large flash of bright light, and Grey knew instantly that anything that was left of the great Blake Kendall had just died.

The heart monitor flat lined and remained steady. Within seconds, a barrage of nurses and cops came flooding into the room. His friends weren't far behind.

"What happened?" Tim inquired after dragging Grey out into the hallway.

"I don't know," Grey lied. And then, Tim saw the blood on Grey's hand.

"You grabbed him, didn't you?" he asked softly.

Grey looked at the blood on his hand and nodded. "I needed to touch him," he whispered.

Tim grabbed a towel off a triage cart and made Grey wipe his hands.

"Heart attack," a nurse said as she passed them in the hallway. "It must have been a big one."

Tim looked at Grey. "You'll tell me about this later, right?" Tim asked.

"When we're all having that beer on the 29th," Grey promised.

"I've got to call Rachel," Grey said. "I'll tell her to throw on a pot of coffee. We've got a lot of explaining to do."

"This should be good," Tim said. "I'll have Renee meet us there too."

Patti and Alex weren't far behind. They caught up with the boys before they got to the end of the hall.

"What the hell happened back there?" Patti asked.

"I was just trying to give him a hand," Grey volunteered. Patti appeared confused for a second, but then she understood. Alex never said a word.

"I guess my intervention was more than he could handle," Grey conceded.

"That's some scary stuff, Grey," Patti admitted. "Hope you're always on my side," she added.

Grey was careful, but gave her a hug. "Let's take this back to my place and kick back for awhile," he proposed. "Tim and I have some fences to mend on the home front." Everyone agreed.

Callahan just nodded as they passed him on the way out of the building. He was talking to some guy named MacKensie who was in his face and demanding lots of answers. It was going to be a long day.

Back in the hospital room, the line on the monitor started to jump.

* * * * *

Walter Greenberg never saw it coming. He stood quietly in Blake's hospital room staring down at Blake's body. He'd slipped past Callahan at the end of the hall because he just had to see the corpse for himself. Katie would be upstairs in a few minutes and was going to be a basket case. She wouldn't know he was dead until she got out of the elevator. Boy, were they going to sue the hell out of this cop and the department. Professionally speaking, losing Blake Kendall was going to be a nightmare. Especially with his new found fame and what it did for bringing in new clientele. On the other hand, he could be the white knight again, coming in to comfort and rescue Katie in her time of need. Walter looked at the body for a minute before he realized that his friend had died in restraints. There was something very odd about the whole situation. He had been told earlier that Blake was in stable condition in ICU.

He was so distracted by the moment that he failed to notice the heart monitor beeping. Walter chose his words carefully as he addressed his friend.

"I'm sorry about Katie," he began. "I never meant for it to happen," he lied. "You were just so damn busy all the time. What kind of man leaves something like that alone?"

He took a few steps and moved around to the opposite side of the bed. "I mean Jesus, Blake, you had it all. How could you not know?" Walter continued. "Why would you sacrifice your queen?"

He was now standing right next to the heart monitor but the steady beeping sound didn't register in his brain. "I had to take a taste," Walter boasted smugly as he moved cautiously around all of the cables. "Now," he added, "she's all mine." The beeping got faster.

Ready to add insult to injury, Walter wanted one last word. He moved a crash cart that had been abandoned near the head of the bed and leaned down over Blake's still restrained right arm to whisper something to him. He thought nothing of it, because most of the emergency equipment was still surrounding the body. Walter moved in close for his one final jab. He spoke softly and with malicious intent.

"I'll be thinking of you every time I fuck her," he whispered.

Walter was now only inches from his friends face. Suddenly, Blake's eyes sprang open. The 'Cat's' eyes said everything. The smile grinned. The last thing Walter Greenberg would ever see was those evil yellow eyes and a row of razor sharp teeth. Blake's left arm, or what was left of it, came crashing in out of nowhere. Stitches tore, blood flowed, but the weapon found its way home. The scalpel he'd managed to acquire off the crash cart before Grey arrived had been well hidden. The arm was more functional than he'd originally assessed. He had deliberately disguised this fact while engaging Callahan. Now, in what appeared to be one last great act of defiance, he dragged the surgical tool across the side of Walter's neck opening him up like a ripe melon.

As Walter's eyes filled with horror, Blake's arm fell to the bed. The beeping stopped and the long, low tone returned. Everything from Walter was now a low mumbled gurgle. Katie entered the room just in time to see Walter's body fall to the floor. She screamed. The staff came running, but the damage had already been done. Walter's light flickered and was gone.

* * * * *

Rachel was tired. She hadn't slept well for the past few days. Grey staying out all night with Tim was probably not a good idea, but he was so lost lately, she hoped that maybe it would do him some good. His call and request for a big pot of coffee though, was completely out of character. Whatever was up with him and Tim, she was hoping to finally get some answers. As Rachel made her way down the hall to the kitchen, her cell phone rang. She dug it out of her bathrobe pocket and saw it was Renee.

"What are you doing up so early?" Rachel asked.

"Tim just called me and asked me to meet him at your house," Renee replied. "I thought it was kind of strange. Any idea what the boys are up to?"

"Your guess is as good as mine," Rachel confessed. "Grey told me to fire up the big coffee pot so maybe they're not coming alone." Rachel stopped and paused for a moment. "Come to think of it, I don't know where Alex is either."

"Well I guess we'll find out soon then," Renee offered. "We should all be arriving there in a few minutes."

No sooner had Renee finished her thought, Rachel saw the Mustang pulling up in front of the house. Grey and Alex got out of the car and moved over to the driveway. They were now out of her view. When she opened the door to greet them, she discovered that they weren't alone. Tim and another cop had pulled up behind them.

Rachel waved and said, "I'm going to go put on the coffee."

Grey walked over to her and gave her a big hug. This drew a big smile. "Hi Honey," he said. "We'll be in, in a minute," he added, giving her a big squeeze. "How's Dylan?"

"Still sleeping," she responded, "although with this crowd, I'm not so sure how long that's going to last. What's going on?"

"Tim will explain everything to you and Renee in a few minutes," he answered.

"All right," she said. "I'll go start the coffee. You all come inside when you're ready."

Renee came up to join them and then the two women went inside. Tim and Alex approached Grey. "So I take it, you want me to handle this?" he inquired.

"If you don't mind," Grey responded. "I think you can deliver this with minimal facts and lots of flash. That way we don't have to get too detailed."

"Yeah, no kidding," Tim agreed.

Now that the group was fully assembled, they made their way into the house.

It took less than an hour for Tim to explain the entire situation. Rachel sat speechless as she listened to Tim explain Grey's observations and instincts (most of which Tim was forced to fabricate on the spot). They had all agreed earlier that the real facts had to remain a secret.

"So let me get this straight," Rachel inquired. "Tim was on a stakeout. He discovered that this Kendall guy was one of Grey's clients and Grey was able to give you enough insight into him that you decided to do a full scale quiet investigation on your own that ended up with you catching this guy?"

"In a nut shell, yes," Tim responded. He knew both Rachel and Renee were much smarter than that so he fed them another cookie. "You guys know that I can't talk about an open case, so if you think I'm being a little evasive, you're probably right. Grey and Alex just ended up in the middle of it."

Tim's phone rang so he excused himself for a minute. It was Callahan. "Are you fucking kidding me?" Tim said out loud. Everyone's attention quickly turned to his conversation.

"I understand," he said. "I'll be available if you need me," he added. Then he said "thank you," and hung up the phone. He looked at Wickmann first and then at Grey, all the while shaking his head.

"You guys are never going to believe this one," he announced. "Walter Greenberg was just killed in Blake's hospital room." There was a brief silence and then he continued.

"Apparently someone stabbed him the neck with a left over scalpel." Grey's face went blank. "They're looking into a report that someone at the I.C.U. nurses station noticed a spike on the heart monitor in his room. It must have malfunctioned and when the staff came in to check on the problem, they found Greenberg on the floor dead with a scalpel in his neck. They're going over the video monitoring system as we speak to see if it caught anything on tape."

"You know Blake did it, right?" Grey inquired. His voice was calm and relaxed.

"Are you sure?" Tim pursued. "The guy died in his bed while we were there."

"I don't know what to tell you," Grey admitted, "but I'd love to see the tape on this."

"Well, he's dead now," Tim assured everyone. "They double checked the body this time. Callahan said Blake is now on his way to the morgue."

"So what do we do now?" Rachel asked.

"I for one am going home to get some sleep," Wickmann said. "You all should consider doing the same. By the way, Tim, the 29th is safely back in her slip. I'll call you later and tell you who to send the case of beer to."

Tim smiled. "Thanks Art," he said. Then he turned back to address the group. "Hey guys," he began. "Why don't we take the rest of the day to relax and take it easy? Then later, maybe around six, (his eyes were now focused on Renee) we can all get together at the marina and have a barbeque on the 29th."

"That's a great idea," Rachel agreed. The party planner in her was about to explode. "You need to come to Sergeant Wickmann and invite that D.A. guy too. Renee and I will handle everything."

Renee nodded and the plan was set. By the time everyone was out and gone, Grey was ready to admit he was exhausted. He stopped by Dylan's room on the way down the hall. Surprisingly enough the little guy had slept through it all. He closed the door and headed for his own bed. He was fast asleep the second his head hit the pillow. Rachel had stopped in the kitchen before coming back to the bedroom and found him fast asleep. She didn't have the heart to wake him. She would never know it, but Kelly Richfield didn't mind.

* * * * *

CHAPTER 35

When Grey closed his eyes, it wasn't long before he ended up back in the graveyard. There she stood, pretty as ever, waiting for him to return. Truth was, he actually expected as much. He knew that eventually he was going to see Kelly, but this time, she wasn't alone. Grey watched as one by one, other girls began to emerge from the shadows behind the gravestones.

"You came back," she said. He could tell by the tone of her voice that she was a little surprised. This time, he noticed immediately that there was no attempt to maintain distance. Grey watched as she carefully started to close the gap between them.

"I told you I would," he replied as she moved in. She was now almost close enough to touch. Grey paused for a second. He already knew the answer to his next question, but he had to ask anyway. "Who are your friends?" he inquired.

The other girls all started to approach, and then gathered in a small group in front of him. They were all beautiful as well.

"Remember their names," Kelly requested. "I know that you'll use them to help their families find some peace." Then, she waved her hand and each one in turn, had a chance to speak.

There were sixteen in all. Grey didn't worry about having to write down the names. He knew they would stick in his head the way one remembers a biblical prayer. When they were finished introducing themselves, they joined hands and stepped back into the shadows behind the graves. Now, only Kelly remained. Grey could not help but stare. She was now stroking a large fluffy white cat.

"Don't worry," Kelly assured him. "I'm not going to turn into that awful thing anymore," she said. "You and your friends have managed to free our souls. Her's too," she added as she stroked the cat's long white fur. "This time, when you and I leave this place, it will no longer exist." The power of her words seemed to comfort her.

Then, as she moved closer to the shadows, Kelly waved goodbye. Grey couldn't help but wonder what was waiting for her on the other side. She paused when she got to the edge of the darkness.

"Tell Father Richard I said thank you and goodbye," she requested. "Give him a big bear hug and lift him up a little when you do. That way he'll know it was from me."

When she saw Grey nod, she smiled. Then she too, crossed over into the shadows.

As soon as she was gone, the graveyard and the forest began to fade. In a matter of minutes they had completely disappeared. Everything turned white. Then little by little, colors started to seep through. They collected themselves until Grey could make out that he was back in his own bedroom.

Rachel saw him open his eyes.

"Hey stranger," she said playfully. "That was a good nap." "How long was I out for?" he asked.

"About six hours," she replied.

"What?" he said, now startled and jumped out of bed. "Is everything ok?" he asked. "How's Dylan?"

"Everything's fine," she assured him calmly. "Are you feeling up to going to the barbeque?"

Grey sat for a moment trying to clear his head. "I'd like to," he answered. "I think it would be good for all of us. Is it just us now?" he asked.

"We've been alone all day," she replied. "Alex went with Patti back to her hotel and Tim and Renee went to the marina. Everyone agreed that you needed to rest and we would all hook up later. I didn't bother to wake you because this is the first time since the accident that I think you actually got some sleep."

"I do feel better today," Grey admitted. "I'm going to take ashower and then I think I'll call Father Richard. I'll bet he'd like to come."

"That's a great idea," Rachel agreed. "It will be nice to be around a lot of our friends tonight," she added.

Grey gave his wife a quick hug and then headed for the shower. After his conversation with Kelly, he was excited by the prospect of being able to bring Richard some good news.

* * * * *

There is something undeniably peaceful about a sailboat on the water. Even tied up in its slip, the gentle motion of the tide helps to settle one's soul. The subtle rise and fall of the keel, even in calm water, is only out done by the occasional splashing sound of water against the sides of the hull. Anyone who ventures aboard will inevitably enjoy a calming sense of peace. The 29th Precinct was a prime example.

Tonight, the beer was cold, the food was amazing, and everyone was enjoying the company of good friends. C.N.N. was carrying the story with Wolf Blitzer on point. Callahan had spent the better part of the day weaving their story so that it was above reproach. At the moment, he was doing one hell of a fine job. Tim walked over to the T.V. and turned off the set.

"I think that's enough for now," he said. The girls, who we're talking in the salon agreed.

Tim looked at Renee. "I'll be up on deck," he said. He kissed her on the cheek and then disappeared up the steps.

He found Father Richard, Callahan and Wickmann on the stern talking about detective work. Callahan was still on a roll about Richard's work on the case. Tim put his hand on Wickmann's shoulder and gestured toward Grey who was standing alone on the bow some fifty feet away.

"Hey, guys," he said. "Can we just let this go for tonight?" he asked.

His three friends eagerly agreed. Then Tim left them to go find Grey.

He found him on the bow staring out into the darkness. Grey knew he was there, but for a minute, neither man said anything. It was Tim who eventually broke the silence.

"You all right, man?" he asked.

"I'll be ok," Grey responded. "I guess I just thought that when this was over, I could let go of this stuff in my head."

"Your mind's still going a mile a minute, huh?" Tim inquired. "Yeah," Grey admitted. "I can't seem to shut any of this off."

"I wouldn't worry," Tim assured him. "I'm sure that with everything that's gone down this past week, your brain is just trying to catch up. It sounds to me like this is a project for you and Alex," he offered.

"No matter what happens," Grey replied, "we keep this thing quiet," he insisted. "Rachel and Renee can never know the truth."

"You've got my vote on that one," Tim responded. "I think Patti and Alex would vote that way too."

"I'll let you know if anything changes," Grey promised.

"You do that," Tim acknowledged. "Now, let's go back and have a beer," he ordered.

"Aye aye, Captain Sir," Grey responded, saluting his friend and then choosing to lead the way.

They joined the others and for now, everything was forgotten. Grey wouldn't think about it for weeks until one night, the thought started to consume him again.

* * * * *

He couldn't explain why he'd built it. It wasn't particularly cold outside; something inside him had just said it was right thing to do. Dylan was asleep and Rachel was out to dinner and a movie with Renee, so he all but had the house to himself. When he started to smell the wet leather, he built a fire in the fireplace and grabbed a bottle of scotch. His mind raced. He'd been struggling with it a lot more over the past few days, trying to find a way to shut it down.

Alex had left him some of her special tea, but even that only worked for so long. His twelve year old scotch only seemed to help temporarily pacify the situation, but his frustration level remained high. To make matters worse, his ring was still warm. It was like it was trying to tell him something, that there was still something left unfinished. He'd searched every corner of his mind, or what was left of it, but his investigation came up empty. Grey looked at his watch. It was almost midnight. Rachel would be home soon. Maybe he could talk to her. She'd been acting really strange lately, but after all of the recent events, who could blame her. Grey got up and threw another log on the fire. When the flames erupted again, his mind went with them.

She'd been sitting next to him for almost five minutes before he even noticed she was there. The dancing tendrils of flame had taken him somewhere else. If she hadn't placed her hand on his, he would never have had any conscious recognition of her presence. As it was, for the moment anyway, she was still almost an apparition. When she closed her fingers around his, everything began to clear.

"Sorry, I didn't hear you come in," he said. "How did it go with Renee?"

"It was nice," she admitted, "but I wanted to get home to you."

She squeezed his hand and nothing happened. Then he realized it was the back of his hand.

"I don't know how you managed to put up with all of this," he informed her. "I wish I could tell you more."

"Well, you're here now, and we're all still together, so I guess it doesn't matter," she said. "You just have to learn to turn down the music," she teased.

"I'll get right on that," he said sarcastically.

"No, seriously honey," she insisted, "You need to be more careful. Dylan and I both need you."

Grey laughed. "Yeah, who else would do the laundry?"

Rachel punched him in the arm.

"Why the fire?" she asked.

"I really don't know," he admitted. "It just seemed the thing to do at the time. I can take all of my mental trash and toss it in. The flames will take care of the rest."

Grey took a long pull on his glass and then set it down on the table. "Can I have this dance?" he said affectionately.

Rachel smiled. Then she stood and took her husband's hand. This time, Grey decided to let it ride and didn't pull away. He knew it wouldn't take long for the colors to start.

* * * * *

In memory of Shannon Carl
You touched us all